Eugene McCarthy

Eugene McCarthy

The Rise and Fall of Postwar American Liberalism

Dominic Sandbrook

Alfred A. Knopf New York 2004

This Is a Borzoi Book Published by Alfred A. Knopf

Grateful acknowledgment is made to Lone Oak Press and Eugene J. McCarthy for
permission to reprint "Ending," "Lament of an Aging Politician," and "The Aardvark" by
Eugene McCarthy. Copyright © 1997. Reprinted by permission of Lone Oak Press and
Eugene J. McCarthy.

Library of Congress Cataloging-in-Publication Data
Sandbrook, Dominic.
Eugene McCarthy : the rise and fall of postwar American liberalism /
by Dominic Sandbrook.— 1st ed.
p.   cm.
Includes bibliographical references.
ISBN 1-4000-4105-8
1. McCarthy, Eugene J., 1916–   2. Legislators—United States—
Biography.   3. United States. Congress. Senate—Biography.   4. United
States —Politics and government—1945–1989.   5. Liberalism —United
States—History—20th century.   I. Title.
E840.8.M3S25   2004
973.924'092—dc22   2003026097

Printed in the United States of America

First Edition

You are one helluva great guy.
HUBERT HUMPHREY TO EUGENE MCCARTHY, 1960

He fooled me for a long time. As I've said many times, the only tender a politician has to offer is his word and Gene's currency is devalued even in Washington. He's a strange man.
HUBERT HUMPHREY TO EDGAR BERMAN, 1968

Gene just isn't a nice person.
ROBERT KENNEDY

I'd certainly like to be like McCarthy. But I'm not sure I am.
LEONARD NIMOY

Personally amiable, often hilariously witty, [and] easy to work with . . . He was not only an ideal candidate, but the most original mind I have ever known in politics.
RICHARD GOODWIN

Eugene McCarthy spent a good deal of his time trying to prove that he was too good for politics. What use was that? Most of us are too good for politics; but we do not make a career of demonstrating it.
GARRY WILLS

Every hero becomes a bore at last.
RALPH WALDO EMERSON

*In New York about five months ago I was crossing the street and a man said to me, "You are Senator McCarthy, aren't you?"
I said yes.
Then just as the light changed he turned to me and said, "But you aren't as much against the Communists as you used to be."
"Well," I said, "everybody has eased up a bit."*
EUGENE MCCARTHY, 1987

CONTENTS

Just after nine on the evening of 12 March 1968, Senator Eugene McCarthy stepped into the ballroom of the Sheraton Wayfarer Inn, just outside Manchester, New Hampshire, to a roar of acclamation from the waiting crowd. Outside, in the bitterly cold New England night, a thick blanket of snow had fallen over the city. But as McCarthy stood at the podium gazing coolly into the glare of the television lights, no one cared about the weather. Half an hour earlier, NBC projections had estimated that he stood to win around 40 percent of the vote in that day's Democratic presidential primary; what was more, he appeared likely to win the majority of the state's convention delegates. A tall man, graying but handsome in his dark, conservative suit, he looked the very model of a successful American politician. The results, he said calmly, were "encouraging." He smiled at his exuberant volunteers. "We can now go on to the nomination in Chicago." As a watching *Newsweek* reporter later put it, at McCarthy's words "bedlam broke loose." The volunteers, many of whom were in their late teens or early twenties, began chanting: "Vic-to-ry, vic-to-ry, vic-to-ry!" and "Chi-ca-go, Chi-ca-go, Chi-ca-go!," thrusting their arms into the air with each syllable to give the V sign of peace with their fingers. On the podium, their candidate grinned awkwardly and raised his own fingers in a tentative V to answer them. "If we come to Chicago with this strength," he told them through the cheers, "there'll be no riots or demonstrations, but a great victory celebration." At that, the applause doubled in strength. Small groups of volunteers broke into singing and chanting, or danced around with joy, or merely clapped and whistled with delight. Down at the front, press photographers jostled to capture the senator's image as he stepped down from the podium, exchanged a few remarks with aides and journalists, and then slipped quietly away into the night.[1]

That night in New Hampshire, Eugene McCarthy had pulled off a stunning political coup. In a straight fight, he had come within 230 votes of beating the incumbent president of the United States, Lyndon Baines Johnson. It was a sensational upset, perhaps the most dramatic in modern political history. And not only had McCarthy humiliated the leader of his own party, he had also propelled himself to the forefront of national attention and captured the hearts of a generation of idealistic young activists. For his youthful volunteers, McCarthy was a brave and dashing champion who would unseat the brutal Johnson and bring a swift and just end to the carnage of the Vietnam War. When Robert Kennedy entered the presidential race with apparently opportunistic haste, just a few days after New Hampshire, the luster of McCarthy's courage gleamed all the more brightly. Two weeks later, Johnson spoke to the nation on network television, offering to suspend the bombing of North Vietnam and announcing that he was withdrawing his bid for renomination as the Democratic candidate for president in November. The quiet man from Minnesota, the gray man with a professorial manner and a taste for obscure historical allusions, had beaten the most experienced and formidable political operator in the nation.

Eugene McCarthy's unexpected showing in the New Hampshire primary, his public opposition to the Vietnam War and his quixotic but ultimately unsuccessful quest for the Democratic presidential nomination established his place in history. His campaign began in the snows of New Hampshire as the romantic story of the unheralded underdog whose plucky student volunteers helped him to knock out the president of the United States. It ended in the claustrophobia and chaos of the Democratic convention that August, as tear gas wafted into his hotel suite and demonstrators fought pitched battles with policemen in the streets of Chicago. Few political campaigns in modern American history have been so dramatic; nor have many reached such peaks of tragedy or sunk to such depths of farce.

For most American political commentators, therefore, the 1968 election campaign marks a high point of spectacle and excitement. Not only does it serve as a watershed, bringing an end to a long period of liberal consensus, but it also offers ample scope for narrative flourishes: the romance of New Hampshire, the appalling murders of King and Kennedy, the blood and tears of Chicago, the tragic downfall of Lyndon Johnson and Hubert Humphrey, and the astonishing political comeback of Richard Nixon. Eugene McCarthy's own story forms part of this mosaic. McCarthy's career has largely been forgotten or neglected by historians, not least because he himself willfully courted the reputation of a frivolous maverick. Nevertheless, every four years, as the presidential campaign circus cranks into gear in New Hampshire, the old stories surface once again; and McCarthy's place in political legend, as the thoughtful underdog who championed the cause of peace and toppled his own president, remains ensured.

But the myth of McCarthy as the professorial crusader for peace does little justice either to the man or to his career. He was more than merely the standard-bearer for the cause of peace in Vietnam. Born in a small rural town of German Catholics on the flat plains of Minnesota in 1916, Eugene McCarthy was educated by Benedictine monks and then worked as a schoolteacher before becoming a Benedictine novice himself. For the young McCarthy, deeply impressed by the radical European Catholicism of his teachers, religious faith alone provided the answers to the problems of American life in the Depression. When he was expelled from the novitiate after a personality clash with his master, he and his new bride even tried to establish a Catholic rural commune where they could defend themselves against the evils of secular American modernity. He then moved to St. Paul, where he taught sociology at a small Catholic college and fell into politics as a way of realizing his religious ambitions. In 1948, McCarthy led a right-wing campaign within the Democratic-Farmer-Labor Party against the Communist-inspired Popular Front and then emerged as the party's candidate for the Fourth Congressional District. He won the election and moved to Washington, where he soon established a reputation as a bright, ambitious, accommodating young liberal, a rising star popular with the southern party barons. Ten years after his first victory, he was elected to the Senate. In 1960 he delivered a famous speech to nominate Adlai Stevenson for the Democratic presidential nomination, and in 1964 he narrowly missed out on a place alongside Johnson as the Democratic candidate for vice president.

To his colleagues and constituents in the early 1960s, Eugene McCarthy was not a maverick, an eccentric, a peacenik or a rebel; he was a cool, competent and determined political operator, a committed liberal who supported the Cold War, and a potential leader of the future who had worked hard to impress his senior colleagues in the Democratic Party. The McCarthy of these years was a very different man from the reluctant rebel who ran against Lyndon Johnson, Robert Kennedy and Hubert Humphrey in 1968;

and he was very different indeed from the embittered, misunderstood figure who retired from senatorial politics in 1970 and then spent the next thirty years defiantly planning abortive comebacks and hopeless independent campaigns for the presidency. Not only does this biography aim to dispel the myth of McCarthy as the antiwar martyr, it also uses his career to illuminate the politics of his time. So it traces his development as a public figure over the course of the twentieth century against the background of wider political and social change.

Above all, McCarthy's political experience reflected the rise and fall of the liberal consensus between the 1940s and the 1960s. His commitment to liberalism drew on the religious convictions of his youth; as a deeply pious Catholic inspired by European social thought, McCarthy was committed to welfare spending, union rights and racial desegregation. Like his liberal colleagues, and like his fellow Catholics, McCarthy was also a passionate anti-Communist, and it was this combination of vigorous anti-Communism abroad with limited reform at home that characterized the liberalism of the mid–twentieth century. During the 1950s, while McCarthy promoted himself within the Democratic Party as a pragmatic activist liberal, he also reaffirmed his commitment to fighting Communists at home and abroad.

By the middle of the following decade, however, this commitment was wavering. McCarthy, like other senatorial critics of the Vietnam War such as William Fulbright and George McGovern, began to criticize the commitment of American troops to Southeast Asia and even, very gradually, to re-examine the premises of the Cold War itself. McCarthy's moderate opposition to the war built on his own friendships with members of the Foreign Relations Committee and his increasing estrangement from the Johnson White House; like many of the other critics in the Senate, he felt that he had little to lose by attacking presidential policy. When he stepped forward to challenge President Johnson at the end of 1967, he was in effect challenging the very premises of the liberalism that he had himself championed for so long, from the commitment to the Cold War to the values of the Great Society. His presidential challenge is, as this biography suggests, frequently misunderstood: rather than the doomed odyssey of a gallant martyr, it was instead the resurgence of an old tradition of progressive reform and middle-class activism based on issues of conscience rather than class, a new episode in a long factional struggle within the liberal coalition itself.

By the mid-1970s, however, that struggle had left the coalition in deep disarray, and the liberal commitments that McCarthy had embraced after the Second World War no longer seemed relevant either to him or to millions of American voters. So McCarthy's own years of exile after he left the

Senate in 1970 were also wilderness years for American liberals, and by the time that George W. Bush took the oath of office in January 2001, the eighty-four-year-old McCarthy had little expectation of ever again seeing a genuine liberal as president of the United States.

Eugene McCarthy was an intensely private man. He was little given to public emotion, self-revelation or self-analysis, and neither was he a great diarist or letter writer. This book therefore focuses above all on his record as a public figure; it is a political biography, written to illuminate the development of American politics and society after the Second World War, rather than a personal biography written to investigate the most intimate corners of its subject's life. At the same time, however, it also presents a close account of McCarthy's early years, personal beliefs and life outside politics, based on a thorough examination of his private and political papers, as well as other archival, interview and secondary materials. It is not an authorized biography; although Senator McCarthy kindly gave interviews for the project and was never less than cooperative, his official stamp of approval was neither sought nor given.

Several dozen other interviewees, many in their seventies and eighties, also contributed to the project, from his late wife, Abigail, to the Benedictine monks who studied in the novitiate alongside McCarthy in the early 1940s. No doubt many of them will disagree with the conclusions reached here, just as they disagreed with one another's accounts of McCarthy and his career. For some of his contemporaries, Eugene McCarthy was witty and generous, a man of cool intelligence and unimpeachable integrity, whose thoughtful demeanor belied his intense passion for peace and justice. For others, he was selfish and willful, a waspish and arrogant man who cared little for his party, sneered at his colleagues and betrayed his friends.

To reduce one man's life to a short list of attributes probably does him little justice; after all, McCarthy was a complicated and contradictory man, and few of his own colleagues felt that they really understood him. This is no hagiography; the portrait of McCarthy that emerges is one of a talented and proud man, capable of great vision and compassion as well as considerable pettiness and spite: a flawed character, then, but also a very human one, whose life both reflects the politics and the passions of his times and also, I hope, stands as an intriguing story in its own right.

Eugene McCarthy

CHAPTER ONE

The Watkins Wonder

Eugene Joseph McCarthy was born in the small town of Watkins, Minnesota, on 29 March 1916. Although he was half German by blood, McCarthy always presented himself as an Irishman, relishing his frequent trips to Ireland and long conversations about Irish literature over a glass of whisky. His mother's parents were in fact German Catholics, while his father's family was Irish. His paternal grandparents, Michael McCarthy and Mary Harbinson, hailed from County Cork and County Antrim respectively; they had met in Quebec and moved to Minnesota in the 1870s. There was said to be much of the elder Michael McCarthy in his grandson. "He was always real interested in politics, and in reading the newspapers and finding out what was going on," recalled Eugene's elder sister Mildred. Eugene noted that his grandfather was said to have been "especially learned about and agitated by the British treatment of the Irish over the centuries." Eugene's father, also named Michael, was born in 1875, one of eleven children. Eugene's mother, Anna Baden, was the daughter of a Bavarian miller and blacksmith who had moved to Minnesota during the great surge of German Catholic immigration after the revolutions of 1848.[1]

Eugene was Anna's third child. He had two older sisters, Mildred and Marian, and when he was two his mother gave birth to another son, Austin. Anna was forty when Eugene was born, and took responsibility for the four

McCarthy children, since their father, a cattle buyer, was often away for months at a time. "Mother was the one who really raised us," explained her second son, Austin. She rarely raised her voice to her family, and was devoutly religious, walking every day to Mass whatever the weather and also leading the children in prayers at home. Eugene's mother, like her elder son, rarely showed anger or open emotion. He later wrote a poem entitled "Mother," celebrating her qualities "of tolerance, of strength, of gentleness / Of quiet voice, certainty, security." Not only did Eugene inherit Anna's reserve and patience, he also absorbed her religious passion. His mother dearly hoped that he would become a priest, and his wife, Abigail, later wrote that Anna had viewed the appearance of a girlfriend as a threat to her cherished dream. He may even have been his mother's favorite; his sister Marian remembered that "if she was sick or there was a crisis, she always wanted Gene to be with her."[2]

Eugene's father, Michael, was a very different character. He had been born in central Minnesota in 1875, into "a wilderness of meager hopes," and had endured an austere childhood. A staunch Republican, he had been the Watkins postmaster until displaced by Woodrow Wilson and the Democrats in 1913, and by the time Eugene was born he was a cattle trader, buying cattle in Minnesota and the Dakotas and shipping them to the stockyards in South St. Paul. Michael always regretted his son's choice of a political career; on one occasion, he complained, "Gene is a good boy, but he's in the wrong party." Eugene was evidently in awe of his father, and he recorded his precepts in a series of poems with titles like "Wisdom" and "Integrity." Michael was hot-tempered, gruff and caustic, "a strong Irishman and quite domineering," in the words of one Watkins neighbor. "Dad would flare up and shake you by the back of the neck when he got mad," recalled his second son, Austin. If Eugene did not inherit his father's temper, he certainly inherited his sense of humor. Michael McCarthy's wit was famous in the family: it was dry, bitter, unsentimental and even cruel. He was, his son later wrote, "doubtful of politicians," "suspicious of doctors" and "slow to take pride in sons or daughters." While the children admired him, Eugene's wife, Abigail, wrote that Michael "seemed to look on any show of tenderness and emotional dependence as weakness . . . his appraisal of his fellow men was almost universally sour and he had the habit of limning them unforgettably with biting, homely witticisms." He belonged, she concluded, "to that generation of men for whom the Depression was the last defeat." As later events were to demonstrate, Eugene's own personality owed as much to his father's hard-bitten cynicism as it did to his mother's gentle reserve.[3]

In 1968 a reporter visited Watkins and noted that it had changed little since McCarthy's childhood. It lay seventy miles west of the Twin Cities, across a flat, sullen landscape "deserted except for silos, cylindrical wire corncribs, fishing huts scattered across a frozen lake, black-and-white cows brooding or loping over a glassy coat of snow." Then, suddenly, he saw "a little huddle of buildings dominated by the spire of a redstone church." It was a railroad village, established during the building of the Soo Line across Meeker County in the 1880s, and had been named after a Soo railroad official. By 1930 its population had grown to 512 people, most of them connected with the railroad or dairy farming. "Its stability and growth," Eugene wrote in 1939, "is due to the character of its citizenship which is largely of German extraction with the exception of a scattering of Americans of Swedish and Irish descent. These citizens are thrifty, strongly attached to the soil and progressive in thought and action." All but a tiny minority were Catholics. Watkins and the surrounding area actually contained the highest concentration of German speakers in the state, many of whom had moved to the area even before the building of the railroad. Social life was based on the church and the local beer taverns, and the children studied German for several years at the parochial school. Visiting baseball teams from villages to the north often spoke German, and as Abigail McCarthy reported, "at church the people prayed in German and the sermons were often in German." Watkins, she thought, "seemed almost transplanted from rural Germany to rural Meeker County, Minnesota."[4]

The German Catholics of Watkins attracted little attention from other groups in the state. They were middle-class farmers who kept to themselves and provoked no great nativist animosity. "I don't have to recall how my grandmother was maid to the Saltonstalls as Kennedy did," McCarthy remarked decades afterward. In the early 1930s, however, the Depression hit the farmers of central Minnesota very hard. Farmers rushed to form cooperatives and sometimes violently resisted attempts by businessmen to close down the creameries on which they depended. By convention, the Watkins Germans were mostly Democrats, partly because they disliked the nativism of the Republican Party, and partly because they opposed Prohibition, which they cheerfully ignored after it was enacted in the county in 1915.[5]

While Eugene was growing up, however, the county was gripped by an atmosphere of increasing fear, agitation and class consciousness, exemplified by the popularity in the county of agricultural cooperatives and of A. C. Townley's Non-Partisan League, which paved the way for the success of the radical Minnesota Farmer-Labor Party in the 1930s. The sense of despair and hardship had a powerful impact on the young McCarthy. In 1961 he recalled watching Minnesota farm auctions with his father: "hard-working and honest" neighbors forced to sell all they had for shatteringly low returns. "The experience helped to teach me that we must look first to the needs of the people, and that when these needs are great, we should sur-vey our private and public resources and then determine a policy and work out a program of action," he explained. "Our society cannot operate well if each person and each family is left alone against the world." Michael McCarthy gave up handmade shoes and tailored suits and spent eight weeks at a time on the road, making only $150 a month. His son later wrote of "the spring of no hope . . . the winter of despair," and

> . . . the cries of women
> gone mad on the prairie
> being taken away in spring wagons
> because, they said, the grass
> did not turn green in May.[6]

The Depression notwithstanding, Eugene McCarthy had a happy child-hood. Watkins was a quiet town of small, neat stucco houses, proud of its church, its school, its baseball field and its hockey rink. He later wrote fondly about its rituals and seasons, attributing its contented character to four factors: nature, the church, baseball, and the railroad, the Great Soo Line, which sliced through the town and passed right next to Watkins' principal landmark, a bustling grain elevator. Growing up, Eugene and Austin fought and played together, and Eugene, who was older, taller and more aggressive, usually won. He played at emulating his father, selling toy horses to imaginary farms; he wrestled with his little brother and the other local boys; he flew kites and competed hard at baseball and hockey. He adored sport, not least because he was an excellent athlete. Indeed, while he was playing baseball in the Great Soo League, rumor had it that "Mac," as the locals called him, was even scouted by the Chicago White Sox, though an offer never materialized. Eugene thought his childhood was "disconcertingly normal" for a politician who later came to pride himself on defying common conventions. His poems about life in Watkins are gen-tle, nostalgic celebrations of spring days fishing, running and playing. He was, however, slightly unusual in two respects: he was extremely bright, and he was very well behaved, a "very clean-cut boy, didn't drink, didn't smoke," according to one neighbor. Unlike many of his peers, he loved reading: his favorite books were conventional children's classics such as

Tom Sawyer, The Last of the Mohicans, Ivanhoe and *Kim.* His maternal aunt Mary, who lived next door, owned a collection of Dr. Eliot's Harvard Classics, and the young Eugene worked his way through them one by one. According to Austin, he would "sit there reading them for three or four hours without saying a word." Not surprisingly, he was the academic star of the local parochial school, a staunchly Catholic institution teaching the children of Watkins until the age of about fifteen. McCarthy wryly recalled the fierce Benedictine nuns who administered both education and discipline. But Eugene had little to fear from them: he was an excellent student and the sharpest boy in town.[7]

At fifteen Eugene left Watkins and moved twenty-five miles north to the little town of Collegeville, where he enrolled in St. John's Preparatory School. Tuition and board cost less than $400, not an enormous amount, but even so his father had to rely on contributions from Eugene's sister Marian and a generous uncle to send his son north. The school was administered by the Benedictine monks of St. John's Abbey, and was attached to a university, which McCarthy entered the following year. It was rare for boys from Watkins to go off to college, but if they did, it was either to St. John's or to the College of St. Thomas in St. Paul. St. John's had an enormous impact on McCarthy, and it irrevocably molded his character and opinions. The university had been founded in 1857 by Benedictine monks from the Bavarian monastery of Metten, who petitioned the territorial legislature for a charter in order to fight off Methodist inroads into the hearts of German Catholic immigrants. The abbey and university enjoyed splendid isolation, lost in the middle of 2,480 acres of central Minnesota woods and lakes. Benedictinism remained the guiding spirit of the institution, which was renowned for its moderation, reasonableness and sense of community. Its ethic, wrote one member of the order in 1930, was "a kind of spiritual tolerance and ease, a spiritual elasticity and receptivity." The monks also prided themselves on their German traditions of scholarship; indeed, only a handful of monks were Irish rather than German Catholics.[8]

The university was in a period of transition when McCarthy arrived, transforming itself from a school for German pioneers to a haven for Catholic intellectuals. As one alumnus put it, its atmosphere in many ways epitomized "the rough camaraderie of an all-male universe," including the revelation that "Benedictine monks are human and can curse as imaginatively, drink as ruinously and laugh as uproariously as their secular counterparts." But the monks took their spiritual devotions extremely seriously, and the same writer also remembered "the medieval rhythms of Benedictine monasticism" and "the haunting, other-worldly sound of Gregorian chant and the awe-inspiring procession of black-robed figures filing two by two into the Abbey Church." For the 460 students who filled the classrooms of the school and the university, the Catholic influence remained extremely strong. Attendance at daily Mass was not obligatory, but most still came, and many groups of students also recited Compline in their own residences. Moral standards were still rigorous: fifty years after the event, Eugene still recalled the outraged reaction of the monks to a singer who appeared with her shoulders uncovered at a concert by the St. Paul Post Office Symphony.[9]

McCarthy studied at St. John's from 1932 to 1935. He was, said one of his teachers, "an outstanding student." English was Eugene's favorite subject, and he remembered with particular fondness his courses on English grammar, the *Canterbury Tales* and *Piers Plowman,* and the development of the novel. McCarthy's brother recalled mournfully that classes consisted of "a discussion between Father Dunstan Tucker, the teacher, and Gene." Eugene graduated cum laude with a major in English and an A in every course except Plane Trigonometry (C) and The Modern Novel (B). In 1933 the "Watkins Wonder," as his classmates called him, broke the university record by amassing eight consecutive As in his year's coursework. When he graduated in June 1935, the college newspaper reported that his professors were "mourning the loss of one of their chief joys in life"—a student who had finished the BA course with over three times the credits needed for a degree. Father Dunstan Tucker, his English teacher, wrote in 1970 that the "brilliant" McCarthy had set a standard that was "still one of our all-time records." He also noted that the young man had a sardonic streak: "He enjoyed it when someone made a fool of himself in class."[10]

McCarthy was equally renowned for his competitiveness on the sporting field. Sport was central to American Catholic life in the 1930s, and McCarthy excelled at it. In baseball, he was an excellent first baseman; in hockey, he made the first team at center for three successive years and was the top scorer in the conference championship team in 1935. Everyone remembered Gene McCarthy as a mean, rough opponent. "He was an expert needler," remarked his coach. McCarthy himself wrote proudly that if an opponent dropped his mask, he would kick it away: sportsmanship was "a sign of weakness." Abigail McCarthy observed that her husband "played with ferocity and a passion to win and would advance threateningly and vocally upon the umpire at the slightest provocation." At an alumni gathering in the late 1980s another old student accosted him. "He said that he had hated me for 30 years or so," McCarthy explained. "I asked him why, and he replied, 'You never played fair on face-offs.'" Indeed, McCarthy was no shrinking violet. He was a tough and passionate competitor, with a burning desire to win and no great regard for the finer points of the game.[11]

Although the young McCarthy was a busy student, working, for instance, on the college newspaper and yearbook, he was not a natural leader. His yearbook entry noted that though "genial and universally popular . . . the Watkins Wonder leans towards the serious side of life." One friend recalled that on Saturday nights, when the students would visit the girls of St. Benedict's or go into the town of St. Cloud, McCarthy's light would still be burning in his room. His wife, Abigail, later found that classmates thought of him as "a loner and an observer," who stayed silent during dormitory discussions and "did not date and did not drink." Indeed, the young McCarthy appeared indifferent to sex or romance. When he entered the novitiate in 1942, he wrote that he had been "disinterested rather than uninterested" in girls, and that the "indefinite or random associations" of his friends were "not in right order." Yet as his passion for winning in sport suggests, McCarthy was not a colorless individual. Contemporaries often remarked that he had an acerbic streak that could be both amusing and hurtful. Dunstan Tucker, who taught and liked McCarthy, reflected that he enjoyed observing the campus characters and eccentrics and "made them the object of shrewd, witty observations." Another monk commented simply that McCarthy "had little regard for people not as talented or as sophisticated."[12]

McCarthy's Catholicism, refined and reinforced by his years at St. John's, was the single most important influence on his intellectual life. To be a Catholic in the 1930s was, as the historian Patrick Allitt puts it, "to be aware of oneself as a member of a minority group set apart from the rest of society by a pattern of beliefs, ritual actions, liturgical practices, food taboos, and even a distinctive view of the nation's history and its place in western civilization." While they might have seemed outnumbered by Protestants, by the 1920s Catholics accounted for some 17 percent of the country's population, making the church the biggest single religious denomination in the United States. With the church firmly established in most American cities, Catholic American culture was more cohesive than ever before. Catholics were notable for their detachment from secular life, and their church still hoped to create a distinctively Catholic environment for its members, making it possible for them to avoid the non-Catholic world altogether. As the Catholic activist Dorothy Day put it, they were "a world apart, a people within a people, making little impression on the tremendous non-Catholic population of the country." Many Catholics appeared content to withdraw entirely from the secular world, retreating to the embrace of a religion rich in mystery and ritual as well as theological rigor and temporal solace.[13]

At the same time, American Catholicism in the 1920s and 1930s was invigorated by a new sense of confidence and expansion, albeit one tempered by bitterness at prejudice and secularism. Abigail McCarthy, for example, felt that "to be a Catholic now meant that one was part of a worldwide community which shared a splendid heritage of arts and letters and in which tremendous intellectual effort was being put into the restructuring of human society." The writings of European Catholics like François Mauriac, Charles Péguy, Hilaire Belloc and Evelyn Waugh attracted a wide following, and the English writer G. K. Chesterton had become a favorite of many Americans with his call for a new Catholic "knighthood." The sense of Catholic renaissance was given added credence and intellectual weight by the spread of neo-Thomism, the revival of Thomas Aquinas and his tradition of rational thought. Neo-Thomism's emphasis on inherent human dignity, natural law and the preeminence of reason struck a chord with many American theologians, encouraging them to apply rational analysis to the social problems of the day and to emphasize the intellectual rigor of Catholicism. Thomistic terms like "organic unity" and "synthetic vision" became the everyday language of the Catholic classroom. The style of neo-Thomism, meanwhile, was intellectual and classical, privileging moderation, clarity and order.[14]

The self-conscious restraint and intelligence of scholastic thought not only matched the young Eugene McCarthy's reserved temperament, it also clearly informed his political thought. In his manifesto *Frontiers in American Democracy* (1960), for instance, he argued that the fundamental assumption of democracy was that "man is rational and morally responsible. It accepts that political life as well as private life is subject to reasoned judgment and to the will of men." Even in McCarthy's own writing style—short, Latinate, cool and skeletal, avoiding personal involvement or colorful description—traces of his neo-scholastic education could still be detected, twenty-five years after he had left college.[15]

Although neo-Thomism provided the context for McCarthy's intellectual formation, the guiding philosophy of St. John's went well beyond mere scholastic revivalism. The university was in the 1930s a hotbed of Catholic thought, encompassing personalism, the liturgical movement, social radicalism, corporatism, medievalism and the rural life movement, all of them infused by a sense of crisis born of the Depression and despair at the plight of the modern world. Personalism, a European movement that attempted to marry Catholic social thought with selected insights from Marx, Nietzsche and Bergson, combined contempt for modern society with the belief that the development of the human personality was paramount. The dignity of the individual therefore transcended any other appeals, especially that of the state, and could best be realized in the communal service of God and one's fellow man. These ideas lay at the heart of St. John University's own principal contribution to Catholic thought: the liturgical movement. German Catholic newcomers to the Midwest had arrived with more education than was typical among immigrants, as well as a rich heritage of congregational activism and liturgical enthusiasm. St. John's, with its German background, quickly found itself at the vanguard of the movement for liturgical reform, principally through the work of the extremely influential Father Virgil Michel. The movement had a strong social content, assuming that the involvement of the individual in the spiritual act of communal worship would in itself promote temporal and economic cooperation.[16]

Many Catholic thinkers, however, went beyond pious spiritual abstractions and into the realm of social justice, and equated communal action in society with communion in the Church, the Mystical Body of Christ. The idea of natural law, which suggested that man was inherently a social animal whose potential was best fulfilled through social interaction, inevitably promoted a Catholic emphasis on community. Neo-Thomist thought held that through a rational understanding of natural law, Catholics could grasp the idea of a divinely ordained social order organized hierarchically down from the Church to the government, the unions and eventually to the individual family. Each component was organically linked to the others and each had its own responsibilities; the principle of subsidiarity meant that none, including the state, could usurp the powers of another, nor could any element shirk its responsibilities through selfish individualism. Two papal encyclicals, *Rerum Novarum* (1891) and *Quadragesimo Anno* (1931), had given Catholic social thought added bite through their uncompromising attacks on the human costs of capitalism, calling for a corporate restructuring of the modern economy, support for moderate trade unions, and a revival of the spirit of medieval guilds. Even the Jesuit magazine *America* criticized "government by a plutocracy" and called American capitalism "a stupid and malicious giant."[17]

Catholic thought did not fit into the usual conservative-progressive dichotomy, and the kind of social teachings to which McCarthy was exposed as a student combined elements of neomedieval Catholic conservatism with ideas and proposals far to the left of conventional Progressive thinking. The crisis of the 1930s gave Catholic social philosophy an even greater air of urgency and radicalism. The appeal of Father Charles Coughlin, the populist "radio priest" who had once been seen as the most articulate voice of Catholic social activism, illustrated the potential for radicalism in the religious ideas of the 1920s and 1930s. However, most Catholic liberals, already sympathetic to the Democratic Party, were more impressed by Franklin Roosevelt and the New Deal. Indeed, Roosevelt himself told Catholic audiences that his programs had been inspired by the papal encyclicals.[18]

Political radicalism, as well as liturgical reform, was central to the ethos of St. John's in the years when McCarthy was a student. Virgil Michel, the intellectual dynamo of the monastery, was committed to a program of social and economic reconstruction on Catholic lines. In 1938, for example, he declared: "Capitalism has reduced hundreds and thousands to a state of chronic malnutrition and even of starvation. Capitalism has starved the souls of millions, even of many whom it made materially rich." It was dying, he insisted, "and should die." The prevailing spirit of secular Americans, he told his students, was "a pagan and unnatural individualism." Only "the social solidarity of the Mystical Body," including enormous redistribution of wealth, could stave off the twin threats of unbridled selfishness and godless Communist collectivism. In practice, this meant that he supported some trade unions and cooperatives, endorsed the efforts of distributists and agrarians, and championed the rural life movement. A new St. John's Institute of Social Study taught Catholic activists how to establish credit unions, cooperatives and rural life associations. The Catholic Worker movement, too, had close links with St. John's: its combination of nostalgic ruralism, anti-Communism, social conscience and religious inspiration appealed to the Minnesota monks, and its founders, Dorothy Day and Peter Maurin, were frequent guests at the university. McCarthy subsequently wrote with wry fondness about his memories of Dorothy Day, while his wife, Abigail, recalled that it had seemed at times "that the Worker was the answer to Christ's call to serve the poor."[19]

The serious young Eugene was greatly impressed with the social theories that he encountered at St. John's. The teachings of Virgil Michel and the other monks percolated down to the students through textbooks, clubs and seminars, and no student could have been unaware of the university's social commitments. Eugene's wife remembered that he was fascinated by the idea of liturgical reform and by the cooperative and rural life movements. Students were encouraged to read the works of fashionable Catholic writers like Jacques Maritain, Emmanuel Mounier, Chesterton and Péguy, all of whom reappeared in McCarthy's speeches thirty years later. According to his teachers, McCarthy was particularly interested in the problems of the day and was "very much under the influence of Virgil Michel's ideas." McCarthy's respect for Father Virgil never waned, and the monk was probably the strongest single influence on his political thought. "He knew where it was, you know," McCarthy later mused. Fifty years later, he still wrote enthusiastically about the monastery's social teaching and initiatives, which he called "a sophisticated, an historically advanced application of the Benedictine commitment to worship and work, not as separable, but as the essence of the creative or re-creative role of man." "Distributive justice," he argued, was still a viable and useful concept.[20]

In fact, the radical influence of the teachings of the 1930s on McCarthy has generally been underestimated. As a teacher in St. Paul in the late 1940s he was something of a missionary for Catholic social thought. One pupil recalled: "The consistent lessons that we drew from his teachings and example were those of social justice and compassion for the poor and oppressed. It was he who introduced us to Dorothy Day and the *Catholic Worker*." In 1950, shortly after his election to the House of Representatives, McCarthy told a college audience of "the need of continued efforts at social reform, and for the Christian participation in such reform movements." The ideas of Father Virgil, he argued, were still relevant in the 1950s: "The social consequences of his teaching are clear. If we participate in the liturgy according to this teaching, we take on full responsibility for our fellow men disregarding national boundaries, differences of race, or of culture." Even in the 1960s, the bookshelves in McCarthy's austere Senate office were filled not with political almanacs but with the works of Aquinas, Augustine and Thomas More.[21]

McCarthy left St. John's in 1935 and spent the next five years as a teacher, a predictable enough course for a bright young man of modest means. After a job at St. John's fell through, McCarthy found himself the nineteen-year-old principal and English teacher of a high school in the small, empty Catholic town of Tintah, Minnesota. A year later he moved on to Kimball, Minnesota, where he again filled the twin roles of school principal and English teacher. Finally, in 1938, he accepted the job of head of English in a larger school in Mandan, North Dakota, where he taught for two years. It was not an especially happy time for McCarthy. "If I were to graph my personal advancement during these two terms," he wrote of the first job, "the line would be as flat as is the topography of the Red River Valley in which Tintah is situated." Later, in Kimball, he learned "humility almost to the point of abjection" as his basketball team was thrashed nineteen times out of twenty.[22]

For a clever and idealistic young man such as McCarthy, isolation in these dusty country towns must have been extremely frustrating. He was, nevertheless, a very successful high school teacher. The Tintah superintendent of schools, for instance, wrote: "As a man and as a teacher and principal, Mr. McCarthy is the finest I have ever worked with." The Mandan superintendent, however, had a few reservations. McCarthy was, he said, "a little shy and diffident in his manner, and does not always get the full measure of results that a man of his ability should." He was also "rather absent-minded about reports and unusual assignments."[23]

It was in Mandan that Eugene met Abigail Quigley, his future wife, who also taught English at the high school. The town was not much of an improvement on Tintah and Kimball, a "bleak town of small frame houses laid out on a grid of wide streets between the Northern Pacific tracks and the bare bluffs." The young teachers often met in discussion groups and, according to Abigail, "argued passionately and furiously about the Spanish Civil War and Roosevelt and quoted the recent *New Republic* or *Nation* or *Atlantic* or *Harper's* to each other." Abigail had been born and raised in the town of Wabasha in south Minnesota. Her father owned and edited the local newspaper and was for a time the town's mayor. Like Eugene, she was a Catholic, serious, bright and highly opinionated. She had come to Mandan after studying in St. Paul, and taught German at the local high school. Abigail first heard of her future husband from a mutual friend, who described him as "a genius, a fine man from a good family . . . Went through college in three years . . . He's at Mass every morning. Never misses devotions." At first she was envious of his seniority and reputation, but as it turned out, she discovered that the enigmatic McCarthy was "too handsome to be true."[24]

McCarthy was still an extremely serious young man who "kept very much to himself." Raphael Thuente, his closest friend in Mandan, remembered most of all his "dissatisfaction with life," regular attendance in church, and interest in "the social order." He was certainly not a great one for romance, and when Thuente suggested going on a weekend excursion with some girls, McCarthy complained: "Why do you always want to take a girl along?" Abigail Quigley, however, was different. After a few months at Mandan, Eugene somehow conquered his shyness and asked her out on a date. In January 1938, he asked her to be his wife.[25]

Practical difficulties, however, including financial problems and the unacceptability of a married woman's continuing to work full-time, prevented Eugene and Abigail from marrying immediately. In 1940 a lifeline presented itself: McCarthy was offered a position teaching education and eco-

nomics at his alma mater, St. John's. In returning to St. John's, McCarthy
was immersing himself again in the atmosphere of spiritual and political
debate that he had left five years before, a world of late-night whisky and
argument among the younger teachers. He taught small classes, especially
after the United States entered the war in December 1941, and coached the
hockey and baseball teams. There seemed little reason to doubt that young
Eugene McCarthy would stay on as a college teacher at the institution
where he had himself been so happy and successful. He was among friends
and like-minded colleagues; he lived close to his family; and he was looking forward to a contented, peaceful life with his bride-to-be. Returning to
St. John's felt like coming home.[26]

CHAPTER TWO

The Education of a Catholic Politician

It would have been easy for Eugene McCarthy to settle down as a teacher at St. John's in the early 1940s. He was popular there and he felt comfortable in its dry, witty and masculine environment. By now he was a tall, lean man, wryly good-humored, but still serious and reserved. Perhaps only Abigail realized that beneath the cool detachment there was a restless and moody young man, frustrated by the banality of his background and the suffocating insularity of his surroundings. She noticed "how different Gene's life of thought was from the world he actually saw and lived in": for example, he knew much of Shakespeare by heart, but confessed that he had never actually seen a proper stage play. Always the cleverest boy in the class, Eugene had never really been challenged, and he struck her as fundamentally dissatisfied with his life and his environment:

> He said that he struggled with a deep disinclination to accept life—a state he later described as being neither "hot or cold" toward it, "an inertia of years." He marked it as beginning with an incident when he was twelve and after a heavy rain had come upon a baby sparrow thrown from its nest to the sidewalk. He stepped on it and watched the life go from it. That was all there was to life, he thought, that faint flicker.[1]

This dissatisfaction was rarely visible to his male friends. It was reflected, however, in McCarthy's extreme piety, which Abigail considered excessive to the point of being self-destructive. Although she too was a practicing Catholic, she was disturbed by his uncompromising, exacting faith: "It was as though he measured everything except the earth itself against an abstract pattern of perfection, and he found that pattern in the teachings of the Church." His criticism was based in part on his rejection of the capitalist world and fervent belief that Christians must be committed to sweeping social justice. His need for vocation meant that "he felt called to *do* something rather than to *be* something"; he was "a restless river seeking a channel." On Good Friday 1941, this tension finally came to a head when Eugene stunned his fiancée with the news that he "felt called to be a priest after all." He had decided to enter the novitiate at St. John's, and proposed that she might consider entering a convent, thereby joining him in his devotion to God.[2]

In 1968 McCarthy dismissed his decision to enter the novitiate as "a mixed sort of case. I was inclined to give it a test. On the other hand, if it didn't really prove out, it doesn't hurt to spend nine or ten months drawn away from it all." In truth, the decision marked the culmination of a long period of soul-searching and demanded an extremely painful separation from his fiancée. To submit himself to the austerity and rigor of the novitiate was not, in fact, a decision that such a serious young man would take lightly. Far from being a period of rest "away from it all," the novitiate was for many men a time of great spiritual trauma, "an interior conversation with God." For Eugene, the novitiate marked his final rejection of the secular world. In a short autobiographical sketch he wrote on entering the monastery, he explained that the preceding years had convinced him "that it was quite impossible for a Catholic to do satisfying work as a teacher in the public school system." He had realized, he said, that "compromise with the counsels and vocation" could last no longer. On the afternoon of St. Benedict's Day, 21 March 1942, his hair tonsured, Eugene McCarthy became Frater (Brother) Conan.[3]

The life of a novice was physically hard and rarely intellectually stimulating. The novices would rise at 4:10 every morning, and one among them would have to get up at 3:30 to ring the abbey bells. One monk later wrote: "We got up before the sun and went to bed as it set; contacts with the wider world were minimal; there was silence, prayer, public and private reading, elaborate and lengthy liturgy, physical labor, and study—always more study." McCarthy's close friend Gunther Rolfson remembered feeling so tired that he would fall asleep while standing in choir. It was a sign of the novices' dedication that they endured such hardships: few of them enjoyed their studies, which included the history of the order, the lives of the saints, and similar topics. For those like Eugene and Gunther who had been teachers, it was mundane stuff. Their studies rarely deviated from neo-scholastic orthodoxy; as another seminarian put it: "There was a deadly and predictable sameness about all those days in all those hard oak chairs, taking all those notes about all those sublime and marvelous realities, natural and supernatural." To make matters worse, Father Basil Stegmann, the novice master in charge of their training, was, in the words of McCarthy's friend Virgil O'Neill, a "hard-nosed German," a stern and ascetic monk who often fell out with his novices. Basil had in fact warned Eugene and Virgil that as lazy, hard-drinking Irishmen, they were "going to have a hard time." In 1943, Basil wrote that the foundations of the Benedictine order were "obedience, love of silence, humility, poverty and stability": not, unfortunately, virtues that observers would come to associate with the willful and opinionated Eugene McCarthy.[4]

There were two reasons for McCarthy's problems during the novitiate. First, he was still in touch with Abigail, who continued to send long letters to him and had not abandoned hope of resuming their relationship. These letters upset him deeply, and McCarthy evidently never quite suppressed his doubts about leaving her for the life of a Benedictine. Indeed, many of the other novices never forgave Abigail for luring him away. Perhaps more significantly, Eugene fell out with Father Basil and was effectively expelled from the novitiate. He was thought to be "intellectually proud," and had in fact openly defied the novice master by smuggling theological periodicals under his habit to read during Mass. Basil would constantly reprimand him for showing off his intelligence, and for reading for personal pleasure rather than for spiritual insight. "If you were always reading," recalled Virgil O'Neill, "that was a bad sign." McCarthy, the best student St. John's had ever had, a high school principal at nineteen, the bright hope of the university, made little effort to disguise his boredom with Basil's discipline; consequently, Basil called him in and advised him to go. In May 1943, less than a year after he had entered the novitiate, McCarthy left. His fellow novices were stunned. Eugene had been a popular, friendly figure, and they had been impressed by his wit and intelligence. "It was like losing a twenty-game winner," one later explained.[5]

McCarthy never spoke about his feelings when he left St. John's, even to Abigail, but it must have been a shattering blow to his pride and idealism. Although he was often criticized throughout his life for his supposed intellectual pride, it was not a fault that he ever recognized. Years later he made a note for a book: "Intellectual pride—always a contradiction—demanding rejection of the one distinctly human faculty—reason or knowledge." He also noted, from Pascal: "One with excess of, like defect of, intellect, is accused of madness. Nothing is good but mediocrity."[6]

McCarthy spent another month at a seminary in Milwaukee before abandoning all his plans for a religious vocation and returning to Watkins. He resumed his relationship with Abigail, but now that he had left the monastery he was no longer exempt from the military draft. The county draft board rejected him for active service because he suffered from severe bursitis in his feet, which left him with a slight limp. Like many bright young midwesterners he had been an intellectual pacifist, even an isolationist, in the late 1930s, and had written with scorn of the "arrogance, presumption and emotion" of those who urged American involvement early in the war. But Pearl Harbor evidently changed his mind: when a teaching job fell through, McCarthy finally volunteered to work for the War Department in Washington, D.C., deciphering Japanese codes for the Signal Corps. In early 1945, he returned to Minnesota, and in June he and Abigail were married. By now they had built up a little circle of like-minded friends, romantic Catholics who clustered around St. John's and earnestly discussed religious issues. McCarthy's best man was Emerson Hynes, who had been in his class at the university and now taught ethics and sociology there. Hynes was a quiet and reserved man, passionately devoted to the rural life movement and Catholic agrarianism, and he was probably McCarthy's closest friend. There were others, a community united, wrote one, by a vague vocation "to found rural Catholic families, to batten on the liturgy at St. John's, to fill their lungs with the intoxicating air."[7]

Despite Eugene's unhappy experience in the abbey, the McCarthys were no less enthusiastic in their devotion to the Catholic rural life movement. "We all thought of our system as having failed us," Abigail wrote. "Gene believed in renewal through the rural life movement and I was ready to assent to whatever he thought right. We would live on a farm—but, of course, a farm like none either of us had ever known, a farm which would become the center of a community of writers and scholars." Rural life was central to the personalist movement: it allowed Catholics to retreat from the sinfulness of secular, bourgeois modernity and to rediscover the authentic spirit of medieval Catholicism. The National Catholic Rural Life Conference had strong links with St. John's, and rural life summer schools were held there six times between 1939 and 1946. The rural life phenomenon also had a radical tinge: the founders of the Catholic Worker movement, for instance, found in it a romantic antimodernism similar to the ideas of European distributists like Chesterton and Belloc. These movements expressed the tensions of the transition from a settled, agricultural, Christian society to a more fluid, consumerist and secular one. In their nostalgia, their rejection of bourgeois conformity and their cultural elitism, they often sounded as much like European archconservatives as they did like American radicalists of the left. Eugene himself read and admired Willis Nutting's agrarian manifesto *Reclamation of Independence.* His vision, according to his wife, was of "the land as a source of freedom and security and as a base of community."[8]

Accordingly, after they were married, Eugene and Abigail bought eighty acres of land in Watkins from his father and proposed to set up a farm of their own, called St. Anne's Farm. The plan was to become the center of a cooperative community, perhaps reopening the local high school with lay Catholic teachers. Their life, wrote Abigail, would be "based on the Benedictine ideal of mixed prayer and work," and they began and ended each day with prayers from the Divine Office. Unfortunately, the year they spent on the farm proved beyond doubt that they were not cut out for agricultural life. Austin McCarthy remembered that they would stay inside with a "mass of books with two typewriters and paper"; he was "not sure just what farming they did." To make matters worse, in April 1946 Abigail gave birth to a stillborn son, Christopher Joseph. Nonetheless, the couple somehow enjoyed their time at the farm and co-wrote an article in *Land and Home,* a rural life periodical, about the experience. Eugene wrote of "the exhilaration of spirit, the sense of rightness, of security" he felt when he first stepped onto his land. Abigail praised "the time and the disposition to prayer, and a sense of proportion and a hierarchy of values" that "a house on a narrow city lot" could never have. All the same, like so many other rural idealists of the day, they were running short of both food and money. At the end of the summer of 1946, a friend suggested that McCarthy should write to the College of St. Thomas, in St. Paul, and offer his teaching services. The college was overburdened with returning veterans and immediately accepted.[9]

McCarthy remained in close contact with the monastic community for the rest of his life, occasionally dropping in to the abbey to discuss politics and religion over coffee or whisky, and received several awards from the university. Although he joked that the ideal religion for a politician was either "a vague religion strongly held, or a strong religion vaguely held," he retained his deep commitment to the Catholic faith. Even as a congressman, he attended Mass every day in his neighborhood church near the Catholic Uni-

versity of America campus. He rarely talked about his faith. In one interview, for a book about religious experience, he confessed to "two or three
experiences of . . . not really transcendence, it's just an 'intensity,' a 'fullness.'" One occasion was "in the pursuit of knowledge"; another "a sort
of spirituality of nature"; and the third "just a personal relationship, like
looking at sleeping children, where you sense that it's not just you and they,
but something more." Intellectual insight, it is clear, was central to his idea
of religious experience: "understanding" was "in a way, an act of worship."
In 1968, pressed to explain the purpose of human existence, he explained
vaguely that it came down "to a conception of some kind of service to
the rest of humanity and, at the same time, a kind of perfection of yourself
in terms of what you think and how much you can grasp and what can
be known."[10]

In fact McCarthy never liked talking about his personal beliefs, and the
rather imprecise quality of his answer probably suggests that he took the
issue much more seriously than did many politicians with neat prepared
responses. Moral and religious issues were, he thought, matters for individual conscience rather than public display or national legislation. He supported freedom of choice regarding birth control, for example, although
he and Abigail personally opposed artificial contraception and relied on the
rhythm method. In the 1970s, although he disapproved of the *Roe v. Wade*
decision, he insisted that it was "nobody's business" what he thought about
abortion, and urged government neutrality on the issue. Although he became
critical of the institutional conservatism of the Church, advising its leaders
to "continually re-examine" its procedures, McCarthy never stopped thinking of himself as a Catholic. The end of his marriage in 1969 encouraged
him to question the relevance of some of the Catholic sacraments, but even
in the late 1980s he continued to urge church leaders to speak out against
the arms race, overconsumption and corporate hegemony, issues reminiscent of his convictions as a young man in the 1930s.[11]

McCarthy's religious education had left an indelible imprint on his personal and political style. The journalist Garry Wills, for example, noted
that, as a senator, McCarthy would casually use phrases like "occasion of
sin" and "rash judgment" that reflected the vocabulary of church and seminary in the 1940s. The future governor of California Jerry Brown worked
for McCarthy in the 1968 campaign and recalled: "He and I would often talk
about theology and ascetical practices that are found in Catholic seminaries and monasteries." He would often, according to Brown, "make jokes
that are only understandable by monks or ex-monks . . . and much of his
phraseology was influenced by Catholic folklore or Catholic theology."[12]

Benedictinism in particular left its mark on McCarthy. His interest in order, stability and the pattern of history was quintessentially Benedictine. Several Catholic journalists noted that his ostentatious humility reflected a seminarian's "boot-training in self-abnegation." His witty, sardonic sense of humor also struck observers as an inheritance from his days teasing his fellows in the abbey refectory. McCarthy's personal style also illustrated what one St. John's monk called a common "temptation to corrosive cynicism." Indeed, the ethos of St. John's was often characterized as a curious mixture of idealism and cynicism; as Eugene's friend Colman Barry put it: "Be kind to people, but lock your doors at night." McCarthy later characterized himself as "ironic rather than satirical; skeptical, not cynical; and optimistic rather than pessimistic, according to the distinction of Chesterton, who wrote that a pessimist was one who saw how bad the state of the world was and despaired of doing anything about it, whereas the optimist saw how bad things were but did not give up hope of change and of improvement."[13]

The 1940s were a propitious time for a Catholic to be entering electoral politics, and the increasing respectability of American Catholicism meant that McCarthy had no cause to disguise its influence upon him. In the aftermath of the Second World War, Catholics were assimilated into the American body politic as never before, ending decades of political and social exclusion. By 1960 there were 35 million Catholics in the United States, between a fifth and a quarter of the national population, concentrated in the cities and middle-class suburbs of the industrial states of the North. Catholic leadership increasingly reflected middle-class aspirations and concerns, and in the 1950s and 1960s the typical prominent Catholic was a lay professional with interests in a broad range of social and cultural issues. Catholic respectability can be gauged by the success of Catholic politicians within the Democratic Party: the likes of John, Robert and Edward Kennedy, Sargent Shriver, Edmund Muskie, Thomas Eagleton and Jerry Brown found that their religion was often a help rather than a hindrance. Eugene McCarthy himself was often taken as the exemplar of the Catholic in politics. In 1949, for example, a Catholic student magazine declared that he represented "the new type of Catholic politician, the intelligent Catholic whose judgments and acts stem from a consistent social philosophy based on the natural law and who is working for the right ordering of society for the good of everyone." Even after McCarthy's religiosity had mellowed, a profile in the late 1950s concluded that he was a "classic example of 'bearing witness' to the Faith." "What Eugene McCarthy is doing," the author wrote, "is bringing Christian principles to politics in this country."[14]

There is no question that McCarthy's politics were fundamentally shaped by the religious and social opinions he had embraced in the 1930s and 1940s. Like his earlier dedication to monastic life, McCarthy's political commitments were founded on his belief in "vocation," the idea that, as Pope Paul VI put it, "in the design of God, every man is called upon to develop and fulfill himself, for every life is a vocation." According to his wife, the young McCarthy was "haunted" by the idea of finding his own correct vocation, and found it in the French novelist Georges Bernanos' description of chivalrous knights, "the protectors of the city, not slaves to it." Indeed, he never really abandoned the idea: in 1955, for instance, he told a Catholic audience that the revival of a spirit of Christian vocation was essential to the reinvigoration of society. Nor did he forget the Benedictine lessons he had absorbed at St. John's. "The important thing," he once reflected, "is that they didn't separate religion and secular life in any artificial way. The two worked together. The idea of responsibility to society was Benedictine." The Christian, he argued, had a duty to engage in political debate and activity, because "in the conflict between good and evil . . . the Christian cannot be indifferent to so important an area of conflict as that of politics."[15]

One of the consequences of McCarthy's Catholic education was that he retained both his suspicion of the modern secular world and his commitment to rebuild it on explicitly Christian lines. Modernity, he told a religious convention in 1952, "has destroyed the essential community and social organizations which were once a fundamental and vital part of the social structure . . . The result has been a fragmentation of society, isolating individuals and placing a terrific strain on the natural society, such as the family." The answer was to "Christianize social institutions, such as the neighborhood, the class to which one belongs, the business and professional community, leisure-time activities, culture, means of communication, and political institutions." There was, he admitted, no such thing as a distinctly Catholic or Christian agenda or political system. Still, he thought that in a Catholic politician there should be at least "some reflection of the whole great body of teaching in the Catholic tradition relating to government and politics and the question of social justice." In fact, he quite explicitly drew a parallel between the liberal agenda of the postwar years and the Catholic inspiration of his youth:

The Catholic's regard for the doctrine of the Mystical Body of Christ should make him more aware of the dignity of men everywhere, should incline him to oppose racial and economic injustice and should open his mind to international cooperation. His response to the command to love his neighbor should be reflected in a willingness to assist others even when they have no claim in justice. His respect for freedom of the will and his certitude of the essential goodness of man's nature should put him on the side of those willing to take risks to advance human rights and civil liberties.[16]

At the same time, McCarthy also defined Catholic politics by what it was not. He took care to distance himself from the increasingly popular evangelical strain of religious politics, and insisted that Catholic politicians should avoid at all costs making "unwarranted appeals to religion." The genuinely Christian politician, he wrote, "should shun the devices of the demagogue at all times, but especially at a time when anxiety is great, when tension is high, when uncertainty prevails, and emotion tends to be in the ascendancy." The politics of emotion were anathema to a man who had been educated in an institution that prized moderation, clarity and restraint.[17]

McCarthy's intellectual development occurred in a cloistered, Catholic environment at a time of great economic misery and social unrest. Like most other young Catholics of his day, he thought that laissez-faire individualism and unbridled secular capitalism were responsible for the various miseries of the Depression, and that Catholic thought offered the most effective middle way between capitalistic excess and godless Communism. Politics, to McCarthy, meant the self-conscious realization of a social philosophy: intellectuals should leave their "protected caves" and "prove the relevance of their ideas to life." For all politicians, he wrote, the fundamental objective must be "to bring about progressive change in keeping with the demands of social justice." This meant that politicians should be unafraid, when necessary, to use the power of the state. When in 1951 McCarthy wrote, "American thought has been strongly influenced by an erroneous, pessimistic concept of the nature and function of the state," he was contrasting American individualism with the corporatist tendencies of the Catholic social tradition. He went on: "Man's need for the state rests in his rational, social nature . . . The state has a positive function, namely to assist man in the pursuit of happiness in the temporal order." Of course, the state had no right to invade personal privacy or curtail personal freedom; rather, it was the function of the state to assist man in his quest for perfection, "to encourage and promote personal liberty as it encourages and promotes public morality." This, McCarthy argued, would be a genuine "welfare state," one that stood proudly in the tradition of the papal encyclicals and fulfilled the papal demands for a political system "in accordance with the demands of distributive justice."[18]

* * *

McCarthy's musings on the role of the Catholic politician and of the state were often published in the periodical *Commonweal,* and several observers thought that he could best be understood as a *"Commonweal* Catholic." The magazine was a highly respected Catholic periodical with an interest in European social thought; its contributors included Chesterton, Belloc, Waugh, Maritain, Mauriac, Bernanos and Graham Greene, as well as Virgil Michel and both Eugene and Abigail McCarthy. As a young congressman, McCarthy was considered "a friend of the magazine." He reflected the educated, liberal attitudes of its readership: the *Commonweal* Catholic tended to support organized labor and the cooperative and consumer movements, and to disapprove of McCarthyism, anti-Semitism and racial discrimination. Like McCarthy, the editors of *Commonweal* saw politics as a viable means of working toward a more just society, emphasizing pragmatic gradualism rather than zealous crusading. The Catholic writer Garry Wills argued that the *Commonweal* Catholic was a distinct social and intellectual type. The typical reader was inspired by the papal encyclicals, neo-Thomism and French Catholic literature, yearned for the romantic nostalgia of Walter Scott and John Ruskin, and was intensely critical of urban materialism. Usually a Democratic voter and a self-styled intellectual with an ostentatious familiarity with ecclesiastical Latin, the average reader combined aesthetic elitism with liberal politics.[19]

McCarthy clearly had many affinities with the *Commonweal* tradition, and it often made sense to think of him as a typical *Commonweal* liberal. But he was not a typical *American* liberal. His abiding interest in the superiority of the medieval world over the modern one, for example, pointed to an aesthetic conservatism very different from the liberalism of his political contemporaries. Like Virgil Michel, McCarthy argued that unbridled individualism and capitalism had brought about the disasters of the 1930s; the western world needed to rediscover the Catholic spirit of the past. He admitted, "I am not advocating any jumping back to the supposedly good old days of a nicely ordered, highly stratified society. We cannot solve our problems by dreaming romantic dreams of a new medievalism." Yet in 1952, as we have seen, he publicly deplored the corrupting effects of modernity. Even thirty years later, when dedicating a book to his late friend Senator Philip Hart, McCarthy acclaimed him as "a man out of his proper time, a man meant for the Age of Faith, or at least for the declining years of that age, when men like Thomas More could make their last defense, beyond the civil law, in religious belief."[20]

McCarthy's medievalism owed much to his educational background. At St. John's his teachers had encouraged their students to venerate the history and culture of Catholic Europe in the Middle Ages, and Catholic boys everywhere were expected to read James J. Walsh's best-seller *The Thirteenth: Greatest of Centuries,* which vaunted the thirteenth century as the supreme moment of human progress and civilization. In the escapist fantasies of Catholic boyhood, gallant God-fearing knights replaced American pioneers as idols and heroes. For Catholic social theorists, too, the Middle Ages offered an idealized, organic alternative model to the corruption of modern society, an inspiration and a rebuke to the contemporary world. In celebrating the achievements of medieval Europe, McCarthy and his fellows also drew inspiration from European social critics such as William Morris, John Ruskin and R. H. Tawney. The influence of Tawney was particularly important: like the critics at St. John's, he argued that modern individualism had destroyed human dignity, law and the family, and had instituted an unjust economic and social order. This was exactly the kind of critique that Eugene McCarthy absorbed as a student and later translated into political action.[21]

This was not, however, a liberal critique of American society. In fact, McCarthy's political philosophy can best be understood in relation to European conservatism rather than American liberalism. Those Americans who shared his interest in medieval Christianity and its lessons for the modern world were conservatives like Richard Weaver and Eric Voegelin rather than liberals like Hubert Humphrey or Walter Mondale. McCarthy's rhetoric in the 1950s calling for a re-Christianization of social institutions, and emphasizing the decline of community and morality in the postindustrial world, was that of a conservative lamenting the passing of tradition, not a liberal confident in the march of progress. This kind of intellectual, organic conservatism, celebrating tradition, religion and institutions, was also very far from the libertarianism or Christian conservatism of the late twentieth century. Its inspiration was not Wall Street or Billy Graham, but Edmund Burke; one scholar defined it as "the dream of an orderly, disciplined, hierarchical society inwardly formed by a sense of the past." Like McCarthy, American conservative intellectuals of the 1950s read European Catholic writers such as John Henry Newman, Chesterton, Belloc and Bernanos; and like McCarthy, they based their arguments on European history, Catholic orthodoxy and the natural law tradition.[22]

Indeed, McCarthy did not disguise his respect for conservative thought. In 1968, for instance, asked whom he most admired, he replied: "I rather admire Edmund Burke for what he said. I don't think he was the best politician around, but he had good ideas." McCarthy, like Burke, had an abiding faith in the value of institutions and traditions. Catholics, he argued, should be particularly quick to the defense of established bodies like the Senate or the Democratic Party. In his memoirs, McCarthy even admitted that he ultimately judged individuals according to their respect for tradition. "I really believe in institutions, you know, that this is a government of institutions and ideas more than of men," he explained in 1987. He had a similar respect for the virtues of prudence, compromise and moderation. In 1954 he wrote: "Prudence may require the toleration of evil in order to prevent something worse, and may dictate a decision to let the cockle grow with the wheat for a time." The politician, he argued, should recognize the importance of gradual, steady change rather than moralistic crusading zeal: "He must be realistic, anticipating that in that [real] world the simple choice between that which is altogether good and that which is altogether bad is seldom given."[23]

Prudence and realism, values associated more with conservative restraint than liberal zeal, were also important elements in the thinking of postwar Christian pessimists like Jacques Maritain and Reinhold Niebuhr. McCarthy often quoted Maritain's advice that the task of ethics was "the mutable application of immutable moral principles even in the midst of the agonies of an unhappy world as far as there is in it a gleam of humanity." Not all social ills, McCarthy argued, were answerable by government legislation, and secular laws should recognize man's irredeemably sinful nature. Even when the moral challenge was an urgent one, as in the question of civil rights, McCarthy's compassion was tempered by his conservatism. "A government cannot run far ahead of the dominant prejudices and customs of its people if its orders and laws are to be fully effective," he wrote in 1963. "We cannot repeal prejudice by law, although laws do have in themselves an important educational effect."[24]

Although McCarthy was often happy to define himself as a liberal in terms of Democratic factional politics, he was not always eager to be associated with the liberal political tradition of buoyant, progressive rationalism associated with statesmen and thinkers like Thomas Jefferson, Woodrow Wilson, John Stuart Mill and John Dewey. In 1957, for instance, he warned: "Optimism can become self-delusion, change an obsession." The liberal, he went on, "may therefore neglect or take lightly the lesson of history and underestimate the value of custom and of tradition . . . In his concern for freedom, the liberal is in danger of forgetting the obligations and restraints that are the price of freedom and of discounting the importance of institutions and their function in the perfecting of persons." Of course, McCarthy did not object to liberal welfare legislation, and counted himself among the more progressive members of the postwar Democratic Party. What he opposed was liberalism as an idea inherited from the nineteenth century, with its attendant notions of secularism, individualism and unbridled capitalism. In fact, it was these "competitive, individualistic, laissez-faire assumptions" that had appalled European conservatives in the nineteenth century and American Catholics in the early twentieth century, and had provoked McCarthy's own brief flight from urban modernity in the 1940s. When McCarthy wrote and spoke scornfully about "the liberals," he did not mean the progressive legislators of the 1950s, but the intellectual heirs of nineteenth-century bourgeois ideology, secular and individualistic.[25]

McCarthy's intellectual heritage is therefore not readily comprehensible in terms of the conventional New Deal liberal-conservative dichotomy. Politically, he stood with the liberals; philosophically, he seemed much more conservative. He was perhaps most comparable in terms of fundamental emphases to the postwar Christian realists Maritain and Niebuhr, both of whom exercised great influence on European and Latin American Christian Democrats. The Catholic Maritain and the Protestant Niebuhr were united by their "moral critique of power." Jacques Maritain, a dogged critic of idealism and subjectivism, was a fervent advocate of neo-Thomistic realism, insisting above all on "practical reason" and "prudence." Reinhold Niebuhr's rejection of sentimentality, utopianism and idealistic enthusiasm, and his concomitant emphasis on irony, pragmatism and order, injected the vital center with an Augustinian pessimism, and gave an intellectual rationale to liberal gradualism.[26]

McCarthy's debt to Niebuhr also suggests a parallel with the neoconservatives of the 1970s. Many neoconservatives paid homage to Niebuhr's seminal manifesto *The Children of Light and the Children of Darkness,* in which he called for a more pessimistic, hard-edged strain of American liberalism. Like McCarthy, neoconservatives such as Daniel Patrick Moynihan cultivated an intellectual style that was formal, literary and allusive as well as a personal style that was often ostentatiously cerebral and classical. But although McCarthy shared many of the goals and assumptions of the neoconservatives, he was never quite a neoconservative himself. His willingness to challenge the orthodoxy of the Cold War, his commitment to the rights of minorities and his support for federal expenditure on a wider welfare state distanced him from most true neoconservatives.[27]

While McCarthy did not quite fit into the liberal or neoconservative tradition, he was not entirely without political bedfellows. As the religion historian David O'Brien observed, McCarthy was closest to the Christian

Democrats of Catholic Europe. McCarthy certainly shared many of the goals of the Christian Democrats, and liked to see himself in a European or Latin American context. In 1961, for example, he attended the third Christian Democratic World Conference in Chile, addressing one session and participating enthusiastically in debates. Abigail McCarthy recalled that they were very close to a number of prominent South American Christian Democrats, including the Chilean leaders Eduardo Frei and Radomiro Tomic. But he might most fruitfully be compared to the Canadian politician Pierre Trudeau. Both McCarthy and Trudeau articulated a political vision rooted in Catholic social thought; both drew on the ideas of neo-Thomism and the papal encyclicals; and both sought to reconcile their convictions about the innate dignity of the individual with their commitment to wider social and economic justice.[28]

If McCarthy often perplexed and irritated contemporary observers, it was frequently because they did not realize that his premises were very different from those of pragmatic New Deal liberals like Hubert Humphrey. Trying to fit McCarthy into the native political traditions of the United States, observers could not understand why he seemed to veer from Franklin Roosevelt to Barry Goldwater in the same paragraph. McCarthy was neither an eccentric liberal nor a frustrated conservative; his political style, assumptions and aims remained relatively consistent throughout his career. He was drawn to Democratic liberalism in the 1940s, as he had been drawn to Chesterton and Burke, by the principles of his Catholic education. And as Eugene and Abigail prepared to wind up their affairs on the farm in August 1946, they were still as strongly and seriously committed as ever to their Catholic principles. If their religious commitments could not be realized on the farm, then they could at least be channeled into teaching and writing. Both Eugene and Abigail looked forward to a long and happy life working alongside intellectuals and students in the state capital, but neither could possibly have imagined how their life was to turn out. "We left the farm that fall for St. Thomas and St. Paul," Abigail wrote later, "and, although we did not know it then, for politics."[29]

CHAPTER THREE

The New Liberalism and the 1948 Election

On 20 September 1946, the student newspaper of the College of St. Thomas announced the arrival of Eugene McCarthy to teach sociology. St. Thomas seemed the ideal environment for the pious young professor. It was a small, liberal, Catholic college overlooking the Mississippi on the western edge of Minnesota's capital. The new academic year found it crammed to the seams with earnest veterans intent on exchanging the benefits conferred by the GI Bill for a Catholic liberal education and the promise of a steady living. Like many other faculty members and married student veterans, the McCarthys lived in the cramped surroundings of "Tomtown," a village of little Quonset huts temporarily established in the campus, each with barely more than two rooms. McCarthy's experience working on the farm was useful for making improvements to their makeshift home. "I hate that man," one colleague announced. "My wife keeps saying, 'If you had a modicum of mechanical ability you could make our place as comfortable as Gene makes theirs.'"[1]

Despite the difficult circumstances, however, Abigail McCarthy recalled that life in Tomtown was "the most carefree and enjoyable we had known." They were, she wrote, surrounded by interesting people: "Gene had the camaraderie of the faculty restaurant at noon, plus the stimulation of the students who were back from the war and of the new faculty members who

came from all over the world." Both McCarthys found the atmosphere of
the city and the academic life invigorating after their months of solitude.
While Abigail taught a course at nearby St. Catherine's College, her alma
mater, her husband soon settled into the routine of teaching. A friend on the
faculty recalled that as a teacher of economics McCarthy was "concerned
more with the distribution of wealth than with its production or consump-
tion," and that after a semester of hearing McCarthy's principles of social
justice, one aspiring young Horatio Alger complained, "Professor, you're
softening us up so we won't be able to go out of here and *compete*!"[2]

There can be little doubt that both McCarthy and his wife believed that
teaching was his vocation and that he would remain, if not necessarily at
St. Thomas, then certainly in the academic world. A year into his career
at St. Thomas they collaborated on an article for *Catholic Youth* entitled
"Satisfaction Guaranteed," urging bright young Catholics to consider teaching as a career. "To real men and women [it] is the most fascinating and
attractive of all professions," they wrote. It was "a very real *vocation* and
not just another job" and an essential bulwark against the increasing secu-
larization of American life. Abigail McCarthy was convinced that her husband's commitment to Catholic education precluded any new change of
direction, the fact that he had already become involved in local politics
notwithstanding. "I foresaw a life of academic distinction and leadership
for him and I was happy," she recalled.[3]

The cramped living conditions that the McCarthys endured in Tomtown
were not unique in St. Paul in the late 1940s. Across the city the demand
for housing outstripped the number of homes available, and the period saw
the beginnings of the chaotic drive to the suburbs that would transform not
only the city itself but also the very nature of midcentury American society
and politics. Nevertheless, many observers claimed that the fundamental
spirit of St. Paul had outlasted the superficial physical changes of the postwar period. "St. Paul is a Boston that never made it out to San Francisco,"
wrote a visiting lecturer in 1962. The Minnesota journalist Albert Eisele
praised its "rich ethnic mix, instinct for politics, intellectual atmosphere,
straight-laced morals, continental flavor, unimaginative wealth, love of the
past and provincial outlook." The physical fact of St. Paul's ethnic mix was
perhaps the most tangible and important of these characteristics. The city's
cultural heritage had been most marked by two groups: the Irish, who had
settled the new city in the 1850s, and the Germans, who had settled in the
downtown and Frogtown neighborhoods in great numbers in the 1880s,
with their own schools, shops and clubs. Other ethnic and national groups
in the city in the late 1940s included Canadians, Jews, Czechs and Slovaks,

Poles, Scandinavians, and Mexicans. McCarthy himself noted in his memoir of 1987 that local union politics were a microcosm of the city's ethnic divisions: carpenters and milk drivers were Scandinavians, metal workers were Germans, machinists were Poles, and so forth. Characteristically, he saw this not as a sign of separation and stratification, but of "order."[4]

The period that McCarthy spent teaching at St. Thomas was a troubled one for St. Paul politics. During the 1930s, Minnesota had been notable for the success of the Farmer-Labor Party, a third-party coalition of farmers and workers that was strongly marked by Scandinavian and Protestant allegiances and by a combination of personal individualism and public idealism. Ever since the heyday of Populism in the late nineteenth century, third parties and protest groups had been common in the states of the upper Midwest, even though they never managed to broaden their appeal across the country as a whole. Farmer-Laborism, then, was a typically midwestern phenomenon, functioning at the same time as an economic protest movement, an education association and a political party. The party attracted both the midwestern farmers' cooperative movement and the increasingly militant urban labor movement, and from the outset the Farmer-Labor Party was itself a coalition, containing "conservatives, moderates, reformers, agrarians, unionists, socialists, and northern and east European ethnics." Its rhetoric came close to socialism. The 1934 platform, for example, insisted that "immediate steps must be taken by the people to abolish capitalism in a peaceful and lawful manner" and demanded that "all the natural resources, machinery of production, transportation and communication shall be owned by the government and operated democratically for the benefit of all the people and not for the benefit of the few." There was, however, quite a difference between the language of the party platform and the performance of the party's leaders when in office. The party's leader and Minnesota's governor from 1931 to 1936, Floyd B. Olsen, enjoyed enormous popularity in the state, but was also more occupied with pragmatic administration than with the radical aspirations of his more extreme supporters. Since the party was from the beginning a coalition, there remained a continual tension between simple goals of reform and a more ambitious program of socialist transformation.[5]

While the moderate wing of the Farmer-Labor Party drew its strength from rural Minnesota and called for liberal reform, the cities tended to produce more radical leaders advocating public ownership. Minnesota's location on the edge both of the Great Lakes and of the undeveloped prairies of the West meant that it contained not only a large farming community but also a significant unionized labor force in the port of Duluth and the mines of the Iron Range in northeastern Minnesota. The more radical Farmer-Labor activists drew upon the European immigrant heritage of working-class self-consciousness, and in the early 1930s the party's moderate leaders often rose to the expectations of their more left-wing supporters. From 1935 onward the party began to attract the active support and participation of Minnesota's Communist Party, based among Finnish and other Scandinavian farmers with socialist family traditions and disgruntled miners on the Iron Range. Together the Communist and Farmer-Labor activists constituted an uneasy "Popular Front," devoted to progressive reform and the defeat of Republican conservatives. This allowed the Communists to wield influence in the institutions of government, but it also required of them a new, moderate strategy, broadening their appeal from the working class to farmers, middle-class professionals and even some progressive businessmen. The fortunes of the Farmer-Labor Party, meanwhile, were threatened by the re-emergence of the Democratic Party as the national party of social and economic change thanks to the popularity of President Franklin D. Roosevelt and the New Deal. This new approach therefore made strategic sense to the moderate Farmer-Labor leaders. Perhaps, they thought, it was better to ally with the Communists than compete with them.[6]

Most voters in St. Paul did not support the Farmer-Labor Party. The city and its suburbs, known as Ramsey County, constituted Minnesota's Fourth Congressional District and formed a bastion of Democratic support in the state, rivaled only by the Great Lakes port of Duluth in northern Minnesota. In contrast to the Farmer-Labor Party, the Democratic organization in Minnesota had been in poor health since the end of the First World War. While the state had consistently voted for Roosevelt since 1932, as a local force the Democratic Party enjoyed only marginal status and was largely kept afloat by the residual loyalties of Irish and German Catholics. As late as the middle 1940s the Democratic Party was still little more than a patronage party drawing its support from urban areas with high concentrations of Catholics, notably St. Paul, Duluth and St. Cloud. Its only other real source of support was among the German and Irish opponents of Prohibition in southern Minnesota. Party leadership rested with the small St. Paul machine and tended, in the words of one historian, to be "middle-class, rather conservative and unimaginative." Most of the state's Protestant voters preferred either the Republican or the Farmer-Labor Party, and between 1918 and 1946 the Democrats won more than 12 percent of the vote for governor on only three occasions. Unlike their Farmer-Labor rivals, they completely failed to articulate issues that would expand their support beyond those groups already tied to them by ethnic or religious loyalty.[7]

The two pillars of political life in St. Paul, both of which supported the local Democratic establishment, were the labor movement and the Catholic Church. The American Federation of Labor, for example, while weak in neighboring Minneapolis, was, through the local Trades and Labor Assembly, perhaps the strongest single force in Ramsey County politics. From as early as 1937, however, the assembly had become the principal forum for St. Paul politicians alarmed at allegations of Communist infiltration into the administration of Elmer Benson, the new Farmer-Labor governor. The Democrats remained staunchly anti-Communist, and thanks mainly to the strength of both the Catholic Church and the labor movement in the city, St. Paul became the focus of opposition to Governor Benson's Popular Front coalition. By 1940 a prototypical coalition had been formed, uniting the more conservative members of the Farmer-Labor Party with Catholic Democrats and anti-Communist elements in the Trades and Labor Assembly. This coalition, which anticipated the eventual merger of the Farmer-Labor and Democratic Parties, united around one single issue: opposition to Communism. As one activist noted, the central alliance was that of "unreconstructed old-time Irish Democrats" and anti-Communist trade unionists; it would provide the institutional strength behind McCarthy's early campaigns in St. Paul.[8]

By the time Eugene McCarthy arrived in St. Paul, the state Democratic and Farmer-Labor Parties had become one united Democratic-Farmer-Labor (DFL) Party, formed as a result of a merger in 1944 that had owed much to pressure from both the Congress of Industrial Organizations and Communists in the Farmer-Labor Party. Even after the merger the various factions could not be persuaded to settle their differences, and the wry remark of one local politician neatly summarized the fault lines of the new party: "For the first time in the history of the world a fusion has been made with the Pope, Martin Luther and the Kremlin." As one historian points out, it was inevitable that the merger of the two parties, joining urban Irish Catholics and rural Scandinavian Lutherans, socialist Farmer-Labor supporters and conservative, middle-class Democrats, would compound rather than soothe their factional difficulties. By the winter of 1946, according to the St. Paul activist and professor Theodore Mitau, the DFL factions had coalesced into two identifiable blocs around the central issue of "the attitude of the Democratic Party . . . toward the political far left."[9]

In Ramsey County, meanwhile, "the factional strife of Farmer-Labor days continued behind a façade of unity," with every public office now the object of competition between the Popular Front and the anti-Communist factions. In 1946, at the Ramsey County DFL convention, the local Popular Front officeholders easily defeated a rival slate organized by a group of Irish Catholic Democrats. In the congressional election in November, meanwhile, the frustrations of the anti-Communists deepened when their candidate suffered a narrow defeat by the Republican Edward Devitt. The twin priorities of the Democratic right wing for 1948 would therefore be to wrest control of the local party from the Popular Front and to recapture the congressional seat from the Republicans.[10]

Red-baiting was a successful political tactic in Minnesota, particularly since the state had a large Catholic population. In 1938 the Republican Harold Stassen defeated Governor Benson, with the state's newspapers claiming that Communists had written the Farmer-Labor Party program. In the aftermath of this disaster, quarreling broke out within the Farmer-Labor Association over the issue of Communist support, with the state committee ordering a purge of Communists from the party, only three years after they had first begun to join it. The Communists' opponents insisted no compromise was possible. "These weren't left-wing liberals," insisted Joseph Dillon, later mayor of St. Paul. "These were Communists." The difference, he implied, was not one of degree, but of basic political legitimacy. One Minneapolis activist even claimed to have been invited by accident to a meeting of the left-wing faction where orders from Moscow were produced urging the immediate capture of the Democratic Party. Arthur Naftalin, a close adviser to Hubert Humphrey and later mayor of Minneapolis, wrote that by the late 1940s "the organization had become, in terms of its controlling elements, virtually a Communist-front group."[11]

This is almost certainly an exaggeration. While Minnesota did have one of the country's most active Communist Party branches, the state party in the 1940s boasted only about three hundred members: enough to wield a significant influence in the DFL, perhaps, but not enough to overwhelm it utterly. As Hubert Humphrey recognized, what made the Communist group so influential in DFL affairs was not underhanded trickery but open hard work: "a steadfastness, a willingness to stay up later than anyone else, to stall a meeting, to grab onto a social issue with broad appeal, to stay together while they divided others." Such qualities, the attributes of any successful political movement, would have to be emulated by any serious competitors.[12]

In the long term, it is clear that events both in the nation and abroad were running in favor of the anti-Communist faction. The end of both the Depression in the United States and the fascist threat in Europe and the Pacific reduced the relevance of the alliance between progressives and Communists, while the growing fear of the Soviet Union renewed old anti-

Communist suspicions. While international events and American foreign policy threatened the integrity of the Popular Front, domestic factors also weighed against it, notably the shift in the national and state CIO against Communism and the increased political engagement of the AFL and the farm cooperative movement, both of which were hostile to Communists. Anti-Communism, moreover, was an increasingly fruitful election issue. In July 1946 a Gallup poll revealed that 36 percent of Americans felt that domestic Communists should be killed or imprisoned. The following month a poll showed that 60 percent of citizens believed that the Soviet Union was bent on world domination and 78 percent thought that Soviet spies were at work to bring down the country. These figures suggested, first, that the days of the Communists in the DFL party were numbered and, second, that for an ambitious young man in the late 1940s, anti-Communism might prove an excellent route to political success.[13]

At the center of the anti-Communist alliance in the Twin Cities were two close personal friends: Hubert Humphrey and Orville Freeman. Humphrey was the son of a North Dakota pharmacist, Freeman the child of Minnesota shopkeepers. Both had been earnest and hardworking students at the University of Minnesota in the late 1930s. In August 1945, promising to clean up the city and curtail crime and corruption, Humphrey had become mayor of Minneapolis. When Freeman agreed to come and work for Humphrey on party organization, the nucleus of the liberal faction was created. Not only was Freeman a brilliant organizer, but as a wounded and decorated marine he could be expected to appeal to the large number of veterans whose support would be crucial in any contest with the left wing or the Republicans. The meetings held by the two men in Humphrey's mayoral office became the central forum for the attempt to wrest control of the party organization from the Popular Front. These meetings, which continued until Humphrey became a senator and decamped to Washington, drew a group of young men who would in later years become influential figures not only in Minnesota politics, but also in the national Democratic Party, including Walter Mondale, Donald Fraser and Eugene McCarthy. Another participant, Theodore Mitau, later explained: "It kind of seemed to be an important moment in American political history for true believers to stand up and be counted, and for men and women who ordinarily had very little political activist interest to get themselves involved in politics."[14]

Two characteristics distinguished the "true believers" from other politically active Minnesotans of the time. First, they were young. Hubert Humphrey wrote that apart from the Minneapolis black community, his first, most earnest supporters were young people. Both William Kubicek and Orville Freeman's wife, Jane, remembered that their opponents would derisively call Humphrey's followers "the diaper brigade." "We were a bunch of smart alecs," Kubicek recalled. "We thought we knew every-thing." This was the other main characteristic of the "diaper brigade": their education. Humphrey, McCarthy, Congressman John Blatnik and Arthur Naftalin were all college teachers before they entered politics. Fraser and the future state governor Karl Rolvaag were the sons of faculty members. Undoubtedly this contributed to the state party's devotion to social and economic issues over the next twenty years. It also mirrored a development in liberal politics in the nation at large; as Steven Gillon has shown, the members of Americans for Democratic Action, the organization which most embodied anti-Communist liberalism in the postwar period, were, like the Minnesota brigade, white, middle class and well educated. The Minnesota liberal was also a forerunner for a type of Democratic activist that would emerge in the 1950s and become prominent in the following decades: the amateur activist, intelligent, affluent, and dedicated to ideas and issues rather than party discipline or electoral success.[15]

The youth of the Humphrey camp inevitably helped to determine its core constituencies. A minor tactical triumph for Freeman and Humphrey was to concentrate on the issue of housing for veterans. As Eugene McCarthy's experience shows, housing was short in the Twin Cities, and returning servicemen and -women were impressed by Freeman's dedica-tion to the issue. Humphrey recognized that his "uneasy" anti-Communist coalition was united above all by opposition to the current DFL Party lead-ership, but he also managed to attract several different groups of supporters: young people, blacks and Jews in the Twin Cities; moderate farm coopera-tive leaders in rural Minnesota; and anti-Communist labor leaders in the northern ports and mines and the cities. The success in building this coali-tion, however, owed much to the personal qualities of Humphrey and Free-man. The latter was keen to recognize the extraordinary personal achievement that was Humphrey's leadership, calling him "the core, the inspiration, the center of this operation, which brought the dynamism and the excitement that attracted people." Such was Humphrey's charismatic influence that it transcended the traditional rivalry between Minneapolis and St. Paul. For Theodore Mitau, who was then working with Eugene McCarthy in Ramsey County, "his words were the words of the party . . . it was a Humphrey party without any question."[16]

Nevertheless, it was the ebullient Humphrey's partnership with the stern ex-marine Freeman that made the alliance such a success. Jane Freeman recalled that her husband "would hang tough, which was always very hard for Humphrey to do," and "was not afraid to say no to people," taking care of the nuts-and-bolts organization while Humphrey traveled the state inspiring his audiences. Likewise, other activists also saw that while Humphrey was the charismatic orator, Freeman was "the organizer of the party," unafraid to make enemies on his friend's behalf. By March 1947, having recruited supporters through ADA and the veterans' groups, their group was ready to declare war on the Popular Front.[17]

To some extent the new liberals drew on an existing midwestern tradition of fervently anti-Communist liberalism, from the pragmatic, moderate progressivism of the Scandinavian settlers to the rhetoric of Robert La Follette. They also drew on the deep hostility to Communists that had been present in parts of the Farmer-Labor Association from the first days of the alliance in 1935. The schism of the 1940s, then, was not a new one. Its resolution, however, would mean two developments in Minnesota politics. First, not only the Communist Party but also virtually any criticism of American capitalism was driven from the arena of practical and popular politics. Liberalism in Minnesota, as elsewhere in the United States, would henceforth be narrower and more complacent, and political debate would effectively be circumscribed. Second, it marked the triumph of a small group of relatively young men and women who would control state politics for a generation. Similar groups of activists were emerging at the same time in other states, but none was as talented or as successful as the Minnesotan group led by Humphrey and Freeman. Their solid base at home, impeccable anti-Communist credentials and experience in the arts of political struggle would propel them to the highest echelons of national party politics.[18]

Since the DFL Party structure was in the hands of its adversaries, the Humphrey group used as its organizational vehicle the new liberal pressure group Americans for Democratic Action (ADA). According to the Duluth organizer Gerald Heaney, the ADA state chapter served as a "vehicle to get people together who were liberal but not [Communist Party] members," raising money from Irish Catholics, steel and auto workers and the anti-Communist International Ladies' Garment Workers Union, who sent out veteran organizers to help the fledgling group. In St. Paul, the city commissioner, John Findlan, an old Democrat opposed to the Communist influence in the DFL Party, aligned his city hall organization with the group. Another boost came from the president of the St. Paul Trades and Labor Assembly, Gerald O'Donnell, who joined the ADA's committee of union leaders in August 1947. To have the support both of city hall and of the local union leaders was a great coup for the ADA in Ramsey County. In fact, according to one historian, the peculiar circumstances of liberal politics in Minnesota, where the official Democratic Party institutions were hostile to anti-Communist liberals, meant that it was the state where the ADA enjoyed its greatest success.[19]

The origins of the ADA lay in the rift that opened in the national liberal movement after the Second World War, between the more radical supporters of Henry Wallace and those who backed the Cold War foreign policy of Harry Truman. By the end of 1946 anti-Communist liberals like Arthur Schlesinger Jr. and trade unionists like Walter Reuther had united around a self-consciously "tough" attitude to foreign policy and the rejection of Communist participation in American politics. For Minnesota's liberals, fighting a bitter internal struggle against the advocates of the Popular Front, the Progressive movement led by Wallace seemed another dangerous manifestation of the threat they already faced at home, and they saw themselves as the vanguard in a national struggle against domestic Communism. In the spring of 1946 Humphrey and Freeman founded a state chapter of ADA with Humphrey as president and Eugenie Anderson as state chairman, and by March 1947 it boasted a hundred members across the state. Its purpose was to articulate their message of anti-Communist liberalism, backed up by Humphrey's inspirational oratory and Freeman's consummate organizational skills. The central issue of the ADA's recruitment drive was the Cold War. Eugenie Anderson remembered that at party meetings she "would be defending the Truman foreign policy, the Truman doctrine for Greece and the aid to Iran and Turkey . . . And, of course, [the Progressives] were denouncing Truman at every one of these meetings. And we would always lose."[20]

Both the Truman Doctrine and the Marshall Plan acted as litmus tests, dividing the DFL movement down the middle. For Hubert Humphrey and his allies, Communism was not merely an external threat but also an insidious internal one, and their hatred of it was based not just on their attitude to Soviet foreign policy but also on their perceptions of the fundamental nature of domestic Communism. Theodore Mitau insisted: "We wanted to keep America and the social democratic tradition, but we knew that could only be done if a very sharp line were drawn between legitimate social protest and protest that was exploited for strategic and tactical reasons by those who seemed to follow what we thought was the Communist Party line in those days." The ADA liberals in Minnesota avoided complicated discussions of the intricacies of foreign affairs, relying instead on the emotive rhetoric of immorality, subversion and appeasement, and from late 1947 until the 1948 primaries the Humphrey wing's approach was based on simple, direct and uncompromising anti-Communism. A poster at the 1948 state convention exemplified the tone of the liberals' campaign: "Will the DFL Party of Minnesota be a clean, honest, decent progressive party?— Or—Will it be a Communist-Front Organization?"[21]

Although still passionately interested in questions of social justice, Eugene McCarthy would probably never have considered becoming active in electoral politics had it not been for the influence of his friends on the St. Thomas faculty. McCarthy was still the shy young professor, someone his wife thought "too idealistic for politics." He met the man who was effectively the inspiration for his political career on registration day at St. Thomas in September 1946. Marshall Smelser was a young historian from St. Louis who, like McCarthy, was devoted to the principles of Catholic social activism. According to Abigail McCarthy, "Marshall shared with Gene an admiration for Benedictinism in history" but "believed in combining Benedictine ideals with the political process." McCarthy himself recalled that Smelser encouraged him to become interested in political action "in a more detached way, as history in the process." They became the center of a little group of like-minded Catholic intellectuals, gathering in the McCarthys' tiny home for "company and good talk" at dinner and sherry parties. Another guest was the political science professor Heinrich Rommen, a refugee from the Nazis who had been head of the social action department of the Catholic People's Union in Germany. Abigail McCarthy remembered that he revealed to them "a whole new world of thinkers and writers," such as the anti-Nazi German theologians of the 1930s, and the sixteenth-century Spanish Jesuit egalitarian Francisco Suárez. McCarthy's exposure to Rommen's ideas reinforced the social commitments he had formed at St. John's. In the most coherent expression of McCarthy's political thought, *Frontiers in American Democracy* (1960), he chose to use a quotation from Rommen to define the ultimate purpose of government: "that of bringing about peaceful change in accordance with the demands of distributive justice."[22]

Whereas McCarthy and Smelser were equal in age and experience, Rommen was an intellectual patron who filled a vacuum in McCarthy's life that had previously been occupied by the monks of St. John's. Larry Merthan, who shared Rommen's office and was later to work for McCarthy in Washington, thought that "Rommen was like a godfather to him. Here was this great international scholar, the first political theorist he'd been exposed to in person, and McCarthy devoured it all. We used to sit at Rommen's feet and talk about how social problems in Germany related to the

U.S. and how we should guard against militarism here." Rommen emphasized the dangers that excessive state power posed to individual liberty,
although his concern for social justice meant that he envisaged a role for
the welfare state greater than that acceptable even to many Democrats. His
suspicion of power, however, was coupled with an enthusiasm for the American political process that amused Abigail McCarthy.[23]

Eugene McCarthy was Rommen's favorite protégé. Another St. Thomas
professor who later worked for McCarthy, Joseph Gabler, recalled: "He
took a great liking to Gene and really encouraged and pushed him." Rommen's insistence on direct political participation, reinforcing the enthusiasm of Marshall Smelser, was crucial in pushing the passionate McCarthy
from contemplation into action. After reading the pope's Christmas message supporting Christian involvement in politics, McCarthy told another
professor friend: "The Pope says we should get into politics. Instead of
griping, we should act." His wife, not for the last time, was simply astonished by his new excitement. At first she thought he saw politics "only
as a laboratory exercise and as a matter of principle." But yet another
St. Thomas professor who was to follow McCarthy to Washington, his old
St. John's colleague Adrian Winkel, had always recognized his yearning for
personal involvement. "Even at St. John's, Abigail," he explained, "Gene
always seemed to want something more direct and more immediate than
teaching."[24]

On one level Eugene McCarthy's growing interest in politics simply
reflected his milieu: his friends, their interests and the intellectual excitement of the crowded colleges after the end of the Second World War. But
McCarthy was also drawn to liberal politics by two personal ideological
commitments, the growing strength of which startled his more placid wife:
first, social activism, and second, anti-Communism. Indeed, rather than
developing new interests, McCarthy was actually finding a new way of artic-
ulating his old commitments. His friend Arleen Hynes, for one, was not
surprised to hear that the quiet professor was becoming involved in politics: it seemed to her simply a natural expression of his Catholic principles.
As a new senator in late 1958, McCarthy was asked why he had gone into
politics and explained that "for a long time" he had been interested in social
legislation, particularly after he had been teaching it in his classes at St.
Thomas. He reflected in his memoirs that "it did seem at the time, as it does
in retrospect, to have been an orderly progression from study and reflection
on political and social problems and thought."[25]

The ADA would naturally appeal to a highly educated, devout, liberal
young man becoming politically active in the late 1940s, and it was Marshall Smelser who first suggested it to McCarthy as the ideal vehicle for

realizing their Christian aspirations. Abigail McCarthy shared their interest in the new organization, admiring its focus on "remedying those evils in society which made people turn to communism." "To Marshall and to Gene," she later wrote, "this line of thought could not have been more congenial. The concern with adequate housing, just wages, care for the aged, job security, and enlightened welfare was in complete harmony with the thinking of the new generation of Catholic social scientists." Later, in *Frontiers in American Democracy,* which represented the culmination of a decade of writing and speaking about the nobility of politics and importance of government, McCarthy made very clear the religious inspiration for his social agenda:

> Man's need for government remains a positive one . . . Government has a positive and natural function to assist man in the pursuit of perfection and of happiness . . .

> The fundamental object of politics is to bring about progressive change in keeping with the demands of social justice . . .

> It is absurd to hold that religion and politics can be kept wholly apart when they meet in the conscience of one man. If a man is religious and if he is in politics, one fact will relate to the other if he is indeed a whole man.[26]

McCarthy's vision of public affairs as the natural expression of religious faith was by no means unique: among his contemporaries in DFL politics, for example, both Humphrey and Mondale were rooted, if not always consciously, in the pietistic, Protestant activism of the Social Gospel. Nor was it unusual in the 1940s to find prominent Catholic Democrats supporting both the New Deal–Fair Deal agendas of social legislation and the Cold War foreign policy of President Truman. If McCarthy's zeal was perhaps unusual—few of his contemporaries, after all, had entered novitiates—his commitments were not.[27]

For McCarthy and his contemporaries at St. John's and St. Thomas, advancing social justice and defeating the advance of Communism went hand in hand. In his memoirs McCarthy chose to downplay his opposition to Communism and the Popular Front in Minnesota. He was struck only, he recalled, by their "incompetence" and "internal, mostly personal conflicts," and concluded: "Minnesota seemed undisturbed by their existence." His wife, though, remembered that McCarthy and his friends were convinced "that the left was attempting to seize the party structure for its own purposes" and had to be stopped. A 1949 interview captured McCarthy's conviction that anti-Communism and social activism were the essential and interdependent duties of the Christian in politics. "Communism's chief weapon against Christians is the charge, and fact, that we have failed and continue to fail in our responsibility as our brothers' keepers," he explained. "The best way to combat Communism is to meet the legitimate criticism, especially in the field of social justice."[28]

These were hardly unusual sentiments for a man of his background. Father Virgil Michel, the intellectual dynamo of St. John's, had called Communism "an all-devouring, godless collectivism . . . certain to crush all human and spiritual values" and praised the radical, pacifist, but anti-Communist *Catholic Worker* as the "most successful antagonist against Communism in this country." The Catholic Church in both Europe and the United States was deeply opposed to the spread of Communism in the 1930s and 1940s, and for American Catholics anti-Communism was not merely an essential church teaching but also an opportunity to dispel suspicions about the depth of their patriotism. Just as papal encyclicals like *Rerum Novarum* had tried to answer Communism with social programs of their own, so the Catholic liberals urged reform as a way to defeat Red agitators at home. Throughout the 1940s the struggle for control of the trade union movement was largely fought between Communists and their sympathizers on one hand, and Catholic liberal unionists, inspired by the papal teachings, on the other. In fact, Truman's shock election victory in 1948 owed much to a record Catholic turnout, in some areas eclipsing even the totals cast for Al Smith in 1928. Truman's blunt assertions of his anti-Communist credentials were instrumental in mobilizing Catholic voters, and it is important to bear in mind that for Eugene McCarthy and his St. Thomas contemporaries in the late 1940s, the anti-Communism of Truman and the liberals was no less attractive than their dedication to domestic reform.[29]

Just as in neighboring Minneapolis, the St. Paul ADA chapter became the central focus of liberal anti-Communist opposition to the Popular Front politicians controlling the DFL organization. "Gene found in ADA a new perspective," wrote his wife. "In it he glimpsed a way of reaching the levers of a society whose wrongs disturbed him deeply." Enthusiasm was the primary qualification for leadership. Theodore Mitau recalled that "Gene McCarthy became the Ramsey County central figure" for the liberal intellectuals. Hubert Humphrey and his circle gave them a warm welcome at the first state chapter meeting in the summer of 1947, and when Smelser nominated his friend for state treasurer the result was the first election victory of McCarthy's political career. Then, in August, his friends elected

McCarthy to another office: temporary president of the Ramsey County ADA. Enthusiasm, commitment and timing had taken him from being an obscure new professor to local head of the most important liberal organization in the country.[30]

McCarthy's relationship with Hubert Humphrey and his Minneapolis organization was characterized from the first, as it would be in years to come, by a mixture of deference and independence. As mayor of the state's largest city, Humphrey was clearly the most important liberal politician in Minnesota and it was essential to secure his patronage. In early 1947 Smelser and McCarthy visited the ebullient mayor, whose advice, according to Smelser, was to move into the local party "with as many like-minded friends as we could muster." McCarthy was personally popular among the Humphrey circle, "recognized early as one of our best leaders" in Eugenie Anderson's words. "When we first started working with him, we thought he was great. He was clever as could be . . . [with] an easy, friendly way about him," recalled Jane Freeman. McCarthy regularly attended the meetings held in Humphrey's office to discuss political strategy, alongside the likes of Orville Freeman and the leading anti-Communist labor leaders. Although he could dispense encouragement, and sometimes money, Humphrey was in no position to win McCarthy's battles in St. Paul for him. The St. Paul activists would have been mortally offended by the idea that they should act as subordinates to Humphrey's Minneapolis operation, and thought of him as an ally rather than a patron. Jane Freeman captured the complicated nature of their relationship when she observed that although the St. Paul liberals waged their own struggles separately, Humphrey's camp did discreetly contribute "some small amount of money" to McCarthy and his friends. From the very beginning of their relationship McCarthy was laboring in Hubert Humphrey's shadow, quietly proud of his own independence from the Minneapolis machine, yet still indebted to him for his aid and encouragement.[31]

The aspiring politicians from St. Thomas faced a tough challenge in 1947, for the remnants of the Popular Front did not intend to cede control of the local Democratic Party without a fight. McCarthy discovered just how hard it was going to be in the county caucuses of April 1947, when he and his friends suffered a humiliating defeat by their better-organized opponents. The battle lines in Ramsey County were clear: on one side stood the old Farmer-Labor leaders and most of the CIO delegates; and on the other, the old Democrats, the city hall organization, a few anti-Communist CIO delegates and the ADA. Every office was now the focus of a contest between the two camps.[32]

His initial shyness notwithstanding, McCarthy was a ready organizer. "Powers behind all sorts of small and large thrones seemed to come flocking into our hut," his wife recalled. Raphael Thuente was astonished by his old friend's enthusiasm at a precinct caucus, where he "simply took over the meeting. He just moved his chair in, put his long legs out and got himself appointed to be a delegate to the county convention." Before the county convention began, Smelser successfully nominated McCarthy as leader of the liberal group, presenting him as "a plain dirt farmer from Watkins, the only candidate who owns a walking plow." The convention itself, however, was a disaster. The right wing, outnumbered two to one on the floor, did not win a single party office. It was not an election year and public interest was very low, which tended to give the advantage to the entrenched forces of the left. But the liberals had not lost heart, and even in defeat Smelser was proud that "Gene McCarthy had emerged our leader against all those who booed the Truman Doctrine and attacked Humphrey as a reactionary lackey of the interests."[33]

The forthcoming presidential election inevitably focused public interest on questions of public policy and political competition. For several years the national Republican Party had been recovering its strength, and memories of Herbert Hoover were rapidly receding. Both the cooperative and labor movements saw a revitalized, anti-Communist Democratic Party as the ideal bulwark against a potential Republican victory and any attempt to dismantle the New Deal. The Taft-Hartley Act of June 1947, enacted by an aggressive Republican congressional majority over Truman's veto, infuriated the labor movement and prompted the Minnesota unions to push for a Democratic victory in 1948. The same period saw the remarkable politicization of Minnesota's farm cooperatives; frightened by Republican threats to make them liable for corporate income tax, they moved into open alliance with the unions.[34]

Meanwhile, the liberal activists, undismayed by the defeats of 1947, continued to work and plan. In early 1948 they agreed to concentrate their energies on the county caucuses, scheduled for the last day in April. They were, in the words of one local newspaper, an alliance of "organized labor and college students as well as the regular conservative group in the party and those interested in eliminating Communist influence from the DFL." As before, Eugene McCarthy was an instrumental figure in the campaign. According to one local union organizer, he "was kind of a natural born leader. He had that kind of something all good leaders have." The work of local activism was a tough slog: stuffing envelopes, knocking on doors, telephoning volunteers, and turning up for interminable meetings. This

was politics as hard labor, not as glamour. The telephone was always ringing in the McCarthys' hut, while the tireless young professor, dramatically
introduced at meetings as "the man who broke the Japanese code," "picked
up a supporter here, two or more there, identified a potential precinct
leader there, and everywhere, of course, were the students." It was an
aggressive as well as a tiring campaign. The vocabulary of weakness,
treachery and subversion was not unusual. "The Communist Party mas-
querading behind the cloak of a third party is out to take over the country,"
warned one pamphlet. "If we win, the party will finally be rid of the Communist and fellow-traveler splinter groups." For his part, Hubert Humphrey,
who was in the early stages of a bruising but successful campaign for the
United States Senate, was in no doubt: "The Wallace program for all its
fine words spells only one thing: appeasement."[35]

The caucuses on April 30 would decide the fate of the Minnesota DFL:
would it become part of the Wallace campaign, or remain a loyal branch of
Truman's Democratic Party? McCarthy's friends, wiser after the previous
year's defeat, used exactly the same tactics for which they had criticized the
Communists and their sympathizers, and packed the caucuses, surprising
the overconfident Wallace faction. "I took my eighty-year-old father, my
brother, his girlfriend, my sister, her boyfriend and several neighbors,"
remembered Larry Merthan. "When we walked in, we had a three to one
majority and I had my sister nominate me as precinct chairman." The result
was a landslide victory. Humphrey himself sent a jubilant report to the
national ADA leadership in Washington the following week, exulting that
the "commies and other left-wingers" had been duly thrashed and noting
that Ramsey County "beautifully illustrated" the scale of the victory, with
the left-wing county chairman defeated in his own precinct. The ADA could
be proud of its role, he added, with the state treasurer, Eugene McCarthy,
instrumental in the triumph. A month later, at the state convention in Brai-
nerd, the left wing walked out of the DFL Party to form the Progressive
Democratic-Farmer-Labor League and leave the old party apparatus in the
hands of Humphrey, McCarthy and their allies.[36]

This struggle, which marked the final defeat of the Popular Front in
Minnesota, was one of the most bitter in the state's history. The campaign
had succeeded above all because of its ruthlessness, and some activists felt
a little guilty that they had contributed to the atmosphere of hysterical anti-
Communism that was to grip the country in the following few years.
"Some of it was darn unpleasant and we had some confrontations and we
were pretty abrasive," admitted Orville Freeman. "We probably went further than we needed to, but we were fighting Communists, and we were

young and very much involved." One writer sympathetic to the Popular Front has argued that the liberals' appeal "was based on old-fashioned red-baiting" and insists that the "purge" had one unquestionable effect: to narrow "the permissible range of political debate within Minnesota." The Wallace supporters were not welcome in Humphrey's new DFL and appeared to drift away from political participation after 1948. "They just vanished. I don't know what happened to them. They just evaporated," remarked William Kubicek. Both sides saw their opponents as illicit and unwanted challengers, and both used harsh and exaggerated rhetoric. Both were devoted to their ideals and determined to fight to the end, using any legitimate political means to control the party organization. The inevitable result was the exclusion of the losers from the party.[37]

No sooner had the battle with the left been won than the anti-Communist coalition in St. Paul temporarily fell apart. The older labor politicians, used to deciding for themselves whom they would present to the voters, were taken aback by the ambitious presumptions of the young liberals. In May 1948 a group of activists approached McCarthy and urged him to run for Congress to prevent a labor candidate from being selected and losing the general election. McCarthy, according to one student leader, was unenthusiastic, but he allowed himself to be persuaded anyway. Abigail McCarthy, however, recalled that her husband rebelled against the labor leaders' insistence that the "college boys" now depart the ring and announced: "I'll run myself if I have to." Marshall Smelser thought his friend was "rushing things" and suggested that instead he study for a Ph.D. in medieval history. Certainly his candidacy was not Abigail's idea: she later admitted that she thought he was interested just "in the philosophical problem of the caucuses," and she "raised hell" with one of his major supporters when she found he was running. It is likely, then, that running for office was Eugene McCarthy's own decision, surprising those who had seen him only as a shy and diffident intellectual. He was now beginning to emerge as a more assertive personality, rejecting his family's objections to his nascent political career. Politics was a means of satisfying his urge for vocation, a vehicle for his pride, and a way of challenging his introverted personality. He also simply enjoyed it; as Larry Merthan put it: "McCarthy loved the business from the start."[38]

The Ramsey County district convention met in June to decide on a nominee, and chose McCarthy. A labor candidate then challenged him in the DFL primary in September. McCarthy and his friends wrote much of their campaign literature themselves and printed it on the St. Thomas mimeograph machines late at night. Adrian Winkel noted that he organized the effort "out of his head and hip pocket." McCarthy won the primary by the closest of margins: 11,270 to 10,717. It was a dramatic night and one vividly remembered by all his friends and supporters. The McCarthy camp was installed at a friend's house, listening to the radio and receiving word from city hall by telephone, and after a long period of close returns, the radio announced that he had fallen 5,000 votes behind with only 3,000 left to count. Looking at her pale husband, Abigail McCarthy felt "a sense of relief," and whispered: "It's all right, Gene, we can go back to working on our rural community." But McCarthy knew the precincts well enough to doubt the veracity of the news, and in a remarkable denouement was leading the assembled company in prayer—saying the rosary, in fact—when the telephone rang with the news that there had been a mistake: he was ahead, and had won.[39]

McCarthy had no less confidence in his ability to defeat Devitt in the general election. The AFL faction in the local party quickly accepted its primary defeat and rallied behind the candidate. McCarthy's campaign style did not alter from the pattern of his primary effort: he remained calm, aloof and confident, with a sharp eye for strategy and a disdain for organizational detail. It was not an expensive campaign. McCarthy later estimated that his team spent $4,000 in total. His family's savings of $1,200 were quickly swallowed up by the campaign, while the Democratic National Committee, stretched by Truman's re-election effort and its own weakness, contributed the princely sum of $150. "If I hadn't needed that $150 so badly, I would have framed it," McCarthy told an interviewer. The St. Thomas newspaper recorded that Professor McCarthy would spend the mornings at Mass and in the classroom, the afternoons preparing his teaching materials and his speeches, and the evenings at public engagements and on the stump. The candidate's speeches were, and would remain, something of an acquired taste. Audiences were often left bemused by his classroom style and taste for the historical allusion. Even McCarthy's friends thought his style "awful": "as dry as any speaker I've ever heard . . . without any humor," commented Joseph Dillon, later mayor of St. Paul, who was seen to fall asleep during McCarthy's addresses.[40]

In this campaign, foreign policy and domestic Communism were no longer important issues. The central issue was the 1947 Taft-Hartley Act, which prohibited the closed shop, allowed states to enact right-to-work laws banning union shops, and restricted wildcat and sit-down strikes and slowdowns. The DFL alliance of unions, farmers, cooperatives and liberals that Hubert Humphrey had organized from 1946 onward was built as much on opposition to the Taft-Hartley Act and the Republican Congress as it was on anti-Communism. The law, McCarthy told the *St. Paul Pioneer Press,* singled out labor for "punitive and discriminatory treatment" and must be repealed immediately. The Taft-Hartley law thus served as political shorthand, permitting McCarthy to paint Devitt as a reactionary dedicated to repudiating the New Deal. A leaflet entitled "What's Wrong with Devitt's Record?" warned that the Republican incumbent opposed social security and favored "benefits to the high income brackets," "class legislation," "higher prices," "exploitation by the big oil companies" and "the public utility monopolies."[41]

In a union town like St. Paul, this was rousing, populist stuff. Devitt himself admitted subsequently that the issue had destroyed his chances of re-election in a district he thought was normally 70 percent Democratic to begin with. In general, McCarthy's positions in the 1948 campaign were those of a quintessential Fair Deal liberal, defending the accomplishments of Roosevelt and promising more under Truman. His filing statement, for example, insisted: "The general coverage of social security must be extended and the program to insure civil rights to all citizens, so courageously sustained at the Democratic Convention, must be as courageously promoted." And in his final radio address at the close of the campaign McCarthy again pledged his support for social security; a strong, though undefined, civil rights program; and repeal of the labor laws, even borrowing Truman's rhetoric to lambaste the "do-nothing" Republican Congress.[42]

After all the excitement of the primary, election night was something of an anticlimax. Early DFL majorities across the state indicated that the party was heading for a smashing victory on an unprecedented scale, and Devitt conceded defeat in the Fourth District before midnight. McCarthy and his wife listened to early radio reports at a friend's house before heading to a victory celebration and then across the Mississippi to Humphrey's home to listen to the news of the mayor's Senate victory: an indication, despite McCarthy's success, of where power and influence really lay in the world of Minnesota liberalism.[43]

November 1948 was not merely a personal victory for Eugene McCarthy. The result in the Fourth District was also a victory for Harry Truman and Hubert Humphrey, for the labor movement and the liberal agenda, and for a particular political style and constituency. Across the nation the election was a success for the Democrats, as the party gained nine seats in the Senate and seventy-five in the House, winning majorities in both houses. The Midwest in particular was kind to Truman: he improved on Roosevelt's 1944 showing in the region by adding Iowa, Wisconsin and Ohio to the Democratic column. The St. Paul newspapers noted that Truman had won the state by 212,000 votes and the county by more than 40,000, a handsome triumph that had made McCarthy's task a good deal easier. The president's margin in St. Paul itself was bigger than anything ever achieved by Roosevelt. It seems probable that Truman's anti-Communism and Cold War foreign policy were crucial in luring Catholics, including Eugene McCarthy, back to the Democratic fold. The Democrats also retained the allegiance of middle-class liberals, thanks to Truman's overtly liberal domestic agenda, and union members, around 70 percent of whom voted for him in 1948. Union votes, in fact, made up 27 percent of the total Democratic vote. In some respects, of course, Truman's was a conservative appeal: he promised simply to defend and overhaul the New Deal state. Even so, his remarkable achievement in 1948 was "to maintain a Democratic coalition that was badly frayed around the edges." McCarthy was both a contributor to and a beneficiary of that success.[44]

But the man to whom McCarthy owed the biggest debt for the 1948 victory was Hubert Humphrey. The day after the election a local newspaper commented: "[McCarthy] probably has DFL standard-bearer HHH to thank for a part of his success," and noted that Humphrey had "campaigned strongly" for McCarthy in St. Paul. Humphrey's closest friend, Orville Freeman, was in no doubt: "Gene McCarthy or any of the rest of us could never have gotten anywhere in politics without Humphrey. The guy who put it all together, the symbol, the figurehead, the guy with the charisma was Humphrey." McCarthy's published recollections of the period make no mention of any assistance from Humphrey or Freeman, and he later told one writer: "They used to consider me a protégé of Humphrey's but I think I had to be introduced to him the night I got elected." His own records, however, indicate that the Humphrey organization made unspecified financial contributions to his cash-strapped campaign. At the end of 1948, Freeman and Humphrey agreed to help pay off McCarthy's campaign debts. "I think this is a worthy investment in the future," Freeman wrote to Humphrey, "for certainly complete loyalty of McCarthy can be of tremendous value to us in many respects."[45]

Not only was McCarthy regarded by Minneapolis liberals as a promising ally, he was also now considered a favorite of the labor movement, and particularly of the CIO. Despite the fact that they had opposed him in the DFL primary, the unions had campaigned aggressively for McCarthy in the general election and considered him a fine candidate. *Congressional Quarterly* noted that the CIO had given McCarthy substantial financial backing in the Fourth District, and the liberal *New Republic* predicted that he would be a strong advocate of labor interests in the Eighty-first Congress. The growing involvement of the trade unions in Democratic Party politics was a reflection of regional change as well as national politics: with the Midwest becoming increasingly urban and industrial, organized labor was more important than ever. Without the political mobilization of the unions and the farm cooperatives in Minnesota, the anti–Popular Front wing of the DFL would have lacked both financial and organizational muscle. At the national level, too, the unions had begun to assume the functions of the Democratic Party's campaign apparatus. The federal agencies set up under the New Deal had taken over many of the traditional patronage and welfare functions of the political parties, and already both the Democratic and Republican Parties were beginning to lose their grip on the loyalties and pocketbooks of their ordinary members. As the intensity of individual union members' commitment to political action began to weaken in the 1940s under the impact of increased affluence and suburbanization, so the union organizations, aiming to compensate for that decline, committed their resources to electoral campaigns. Such was the weakness of the national Democratic Party, in fact, that even under Truman it was beginning to depend on the unions both for funds and for votes.[46]

McCarthy's success as a politician both in Minnesota and nationally owed much to his ability to strike the pose of an apolitical independent while simultaneously mobilizing the core Democratic electorate, for instance with his attacks on the Taft-Hartley Act. As American voters became more affluent, so their intense partisan allegiances began to dwindle, and an appearance of independence was therefore an important asset for a politician hoping to appeal to middle-class audiences. A reporter from the *Minneapolis Tribune,* later herself a member of the Democratic National Committee, interviewed McCarthy shortly after the election and afterward recalled her surprise at what a "nonpolitical type" he was: "He was much too open, much too apolitical, and I wondered why he wanted to be a politician." She immediately understood why he was successful, however, noting that he appealed brilliantly to "young people and the intellectual community." Even at this early stage in his career McCarthy was reluctant to become involved in partisan campaigning that did not directly benefit him. Jane Freeman commented that he evidently "decided early on that '48 campaign that he needed to take care of his own problems and campaign for himself and get himself known and not campaign for other people," and this caused some resentment among the Minneapolis group.[47]

Indeed, McCarthy actively cultivated the image of an intellectual above the partisan fray. His campaign literature trumpeted his "unusual intelligence" and featured endorsements from his St. Thomas students and colleagues, while a newspaper advertisement quoted Mayor John McDonough's pride in "a man who is better fitted, better trained and better educated for the job." The high proportion of students among McCarthy's campaign staff and supporters was a reward for his self-consciously "intellectual" appeal. Since many students in the immediate postwar years were over twenty-one, they were eligible to vote, while younger students worked as campaign volunteers. McCarthy himself nicknamed his campaign "a kind of school project." The student-intellectual wing of McCarthy's constituency anticipated James Q. Wilson's classic description of the Democratic amateurs of the 1950s: "young, well-educated professional people, including a large number of women . . . distinctly middle- and upper-middle class." They were the successors to an older tradition of middle-class reform, going back beyond the Progressives at least as far as the Mugwumps of the 1880s. The historian Richard Hofstadter's lines on the ideal Mugwump leader—"a well-to-do, well-educated, high-minded citizen . . . a conservative in his economic and political views"—also fit Eugene McCarthy, whose liberal principles were, after all, based on a fundamentally conservative approach, that of the devout Catholic with a respect for order and institutions.[48]

The success of Truman, Humphrey and McCarthy, and the failure of Wallace and the Popular Front, marked the resolution of a long debate within the Democratic Party over the meaning of liberal values, the limits of the Fair Deal, and the morality of the Cold War. While the right's triumph foreclosed more radical approaches to American politics, it also defined the liberal agenda for the next two decades. Henceforth liberal standard-bearers such as Humphrey and McCarthy would promote the unfinished agenda of the Fair Deal, with its Keynesian emphasis on full employment and price controls, social security expansion, national health insurance and civil rights. Hand in hand with these domestic commitments went a commitment to the Cold War and anti-Communism that both prepared the ground for the scares of the 1950s and effectively insulated Democratic liberals against them.

Meanwhile, in Minnesota itself, an essentially defensive coalition of recently mobilized trade unions and farm cooperatives was transformed from an alliance to fight Communism into an alliance to maintain the hegemony of the DFL. If the 1948 election confirmed the continuing appeal of the New Deal, it also saw the destruction of the radical strain in Minnesota center-left politics. The state Progressive Party soon collapsed and many of its leaders were never heard from again. The events also demonstrated that anti-Communism in Minnesota was not simply a Cold War phenomenon: its roots were in the factionalism of the 1930s, and as John Earl Haynes argues, while "the Cold War added to the intensity with which both DFL factions pursued their fight, . . . this was only the last battle of a decade-long war."[49]

What had emerged in Minnesota was a liberalism that both rejected the legitimacy of Communism and radicalism in politics and sought to defend the perceived accomplishments of the New Deal. For some historians, this new liberalism was perfectly consistent with the values of the Roosevelt administration, but others, like Alan Brinkley and Ira Katznelson, have argued that the 1948 election marked a new stage in the gradual *repudiation* of the social democratic potential of the middle 1930s. Certainly it seems clear that the resolution of the Democratic schism in Minnesota with the elevation of McCarthy and Humphrey foreclosed any opportunity that social democrats might have had to move center-left politics in the state, and by extension in the nation, away from Keynesian tinkering and toward serious consideration of a comprehensive, federally organized welfare state on European lines. Unlike many of their predecessors in the New Deal administrations, the new liberals did not dream of regulating big business or establishing a centrally planned economy; instead, they essentially accepted the existing contours of the federal state, and channeled their energies into legislation on behalf of vulnerable groups like southern blacks and unemployed workers. Even if McCarthy and Humphrey felt that they were defending the commitments of the Roosevelt era, their refusal to tolerate alternatives to their left meant that there *was* a vital and identifiable difference, if only in terms of tolerance and social democratic potential, between the New and Fair Deals. It would, of course, be wrong to underestimate the distance between the liberals and their Republican adversaries, for example on the Taft-Hartley issue, or even, eventually, on the issue of how the Cold War ought to be fought. All the same, Truman's victory marked the establishment of a new kind of Cold War liberalism. From 1948 onward, both Hubert Humphrey and Eugene McCarthy were not only pledged to work for mild reform at home, they were also dedicated to the struggle against Communism overseas. These two commitments appeared perfectly consistent in the context of the late 1940s, but two decades later, the tension between them would drive the two men into open political combat.[50]

CHAPTER FOUR

The Quiet Congressman

In December 1948 Eugene and Abigail McCarthy left St. Paul for Washington. They took with them their baby daughter Ellen, who had been born in October 1947 and was growing into a bright, inquisitive toddler. Three more children, whom they christened Mary, Michael and Margaret, followed in the next seven years, and McCarthy's waking hours were consumed by the twin duties of congressman and father.

Although he had some regrets about leaving behind his friends at St. Thomas, McCarthy told an interviewer that he was "anxious to put into practice some of my convictions." His new office on the first floor of the Cannon Office Building marked the transition to an altogether different lifestyle from the casual camaraderie of the St. Thomas faculty, although his administrative assistant and right-hand man, Adrian Winkel, was an old friend from St. John's who had also taught sociology alongside McCarthy at St. Thomas and been head of his volunteer committee in the campaigns of 1948. Each long day began with Mass at his local church, and McCarthy reached his office before nine o'clock to begin reading hurriedly through newspapers and letters. The rest of the day, as for all congressmen even in the relatively leisurely days of the 1950s, was a whirl of committee meetings, a hurried lunch, snatched glances at office memoranda and correspondence, and appearances on the House floor. Rarely was he home in time for dinner, and he admitted to a newspaper in 1952 that he saw very little of his three young children. Even during holidays in Minnesota, the article commented, "he doesn't go home just for a rest. There are endless speeches, conferences with the folks at home and discussion of their problems, investigation of public housing sites, and interviews with constituents who need his help." McCarthy was now a public man; his days of privacy were over.[1]

Despite his talent for political organization, McCarthy struck some observers as a gray and introverted figure. The *St. Paul Pioneer Press* commented in February 1949 that the new congressman had "remained pretty much to himself thus far." He was well liked by his Democratic colleagues, however. One Minnesota congressman, John Blatnik, nicknamed him "the Needle" for "his clever comments about someone or something going on on the floor." McCarthy's colleagues thought of him as the state intellectual, "the moral conscience or spiritual adviser of the Minnesota [Democratic] delegation." Despite his popularity, McCarthy evidently made few close friends. "Gene was always kind of a loner," observed his fellow newcomer Wayne Hays of Ohio. "If he had any close friends, I don't know who they were. On the floor, he was always restless. He'd sit with somebody three or four minutes and then move somewhere else." McCarthy was also notable for his cynicism: he once turned to Hays, another former teacher, during a lifeless floor debate and remarked: "This is a hell of a way to make a living, isn't it? But it sure beats teaching." Yet he was not so cynical as to have forgotten his Minneapolis patron. Another Minnesotan noted that he was "extremely close" to Hubert Humphrey and even that the junior senator "was somewhat of an idol of McCarthy's." One arena in which McCarthy did shine was the Democratic baseball team, on which he played first base and regularly tormented their Republican adversaries, to the delight of his home state newspapers. Although her husband worked long and tiring hours, Abigail McCarthy certainly enjoyed the move to the capital and remained there until her death in 2001. Their new friends, she later recalled, were a circle of progressive Catholics and liberal, ADA Democrats: "a coming together of like-minded people," "halcyon days . . . of spontaneous get-togethers and simple associations."[2]

In the 1948 elections, the Democrats had recaptured control of both houses of Congress, and they now commanded majorities of 263–171 in the House and 54–42 in the Senate. As McCarthy explained to the St. Thomas college newspaper, he had high hopes that the Democratic majority would move quickly to push through an extensive program of domestic reform, including "an adequate housing bill, President Truman's civil-rights bill, and a labor relations law to replace the Taft-Hartley Law": in short, roughly the Fair Deal agenda that would dominate liberal platforms for a decade to come. He was to be sorely disappointed. Perhaps the most notable feature of Congress after the Second World War was the implicit coalition between the Republican members and the conservative southern Democrats. Not only did this alliance block liberal legislation, it also held a tight grip on the levers of institutional power in both houses.[3]

McCarthy's frustration at being a powerless outsider, as well as at the evaporation of his hopes for a swift enactment of the Fair Deal, quickly boiled over. The seniority principle, which reserved power for the southern perennials, was, McCarthy told *Minnesota Labor,* "unfair," placing in authority "men who do not subscribe to the party program and, in the present congress, men who did not even support the presidential candidate of the party." The voters, he complained, had approved the Fair Deal in November 1948, but here was the conservative coalition, preferring "to sit tight and prevent any constructive action on domestic issues." Of course, McCarthy was risking little by making such statements. He had been elected, after all, as a liberal, and at that stage it seemed unlikely that he would ever wield much influence in southern Democratic circles. These were not the accusations of a maverick but the clarion cries of a typical liberal, and even of the president himself.[4]

Indeed, the Eighty-first Congress was neither a New Deal nor a Fair Deal Congress, and the liberals' high hopes of November quickly soured when they discovered that power in both the House and the Senate was still in the hands of the conservatives. In 1949 Truman sent to Congress a civil rights bill, an antilynching bill, a bill abolishing the poll tax, a housing bill and a fair employment bill. Only the housing bill became law, and the heart of the Fair Deal died in Congress. This was hardly surprising, since the victory of 1948 had been more of a mandate to defend the New Deal than an endorsement of major new social programs. It was hard to discern any vocal constituency in the country for the kind of agenda McCarthy favored. Nor was there any possible majority in Congress for Truman's proposals, with the Democratic group heterogeneous, diffuse, and disunited. McCarthy's first Congress, then, was a frustrating experience. Even so, in Alonzo Hamby's view, it was still "the most liberal since the great days of the New Deal," both the last hurrah of reform and a first glimpse of the somnolent passivity of politics in the Eisenhower era.[5]

Outside Congress, McCarthy kept a low profile. The journalist Mary McGrory remembered McCarthy in his first years in Washington as "very nice and quiet with very little to say," a man who would settle down and read a book at social gatherings. There was little pressure on McCarthy, coming from St. Paul, to cut a swath through Washington politics; in 1951 he remarked to friends that the scene back home was "very peaceful with nothing to worry about except the inflation, which we will soon have under control." Indeed, McCarthy even admitted to the St. Paul press that he was not particularly motivated to speak much in the House. "The main reason that I have been comparatively quiet on the floor is that I am still studying the situation," he announced. "Any time that I feel I have something of merit to contribute, I will not hesitate to tell it to the other members." This attitude, coupled with his withdrawal from the bonhomie of the House floor, created an impression of laziness and awkwardness that McCarthy was never able to shake. Adrian Winkel recalled that he "was never the kind of Congressman to attend meetings without fail" and that he was disgruntled at his first assignment, to the Post Office Committee, rather than to his preferred choice of Education. McCarthy apparently confided to his assistant "that the most fun of all was being in a campaign—not the work in Congress." As early as 1952 the Minnesota newspapers were commenting on his habit of skipping roll calls and committee meetings in order to give paid lectures, leading to a reputation as a "Tuesday to Thursday" congressman, like the eastern members who decamped for long weekends at home. He would never help with problems or campaigns in the state party, recalled Jane Freeman. "He really *never* did do much of *anything* to help other candidates. He didn't harm them, he didn't speak against them; he just didn't appear or help out."[6]

McCarthy's record in his first two terms in the House, the Eighty-first Congress of 1949–1950 and the Eighty-second Congress of 1951–1952, was a model of liberalism. He was not a maverick, a lone voice or an eccentric. In his first term he voted with the majority of his party on all the key issues identified by *Congressional Quarterly,* and in the following congressional session he voted with his party on nine out of ten key issues. Other congressional scorecards illustrated the strength of his liberalism. During his first session, for instance, McCarthy voted in perfect opposition to the Republican–southern conservative coalition, and during the Eighty-second Congress he voted for increased federal spending and against the "economy" position on all twenty-four occasions the issue was put to the test. Liberal interest groups and the labor unions consistently lauded McCarthy's record. Labor's League for Political Education, a division of the AFL, declared at the end of 1952 that McCarthy had voted "right" on every one of the twenty-one key issues during his first two terms, including the repeal of the Taft-Hartley Act, social security, housing, taxation, price controls and foreign affairs. Both the AFL and the CIO gave McCarthy either perfect or near-perfect ratings during his first four years: he never voted "wrong" more than once in a session.[7]

On the domestic front, McCarthy's devotion to the principles of the Fair Deal was unwavering and frequently formed the basis for his interventions on the House floor. In 1950, for example, he attacked Republican criticisms of the "cooperative" nature of HR 7402, the housing bill for moderate-income families, using uncompromising and unusually charged rhetoric. The bill, he argued, was a response to the "social disorder which has resulted from conduct motivated by avarice and greed, by bald self-interest." A vote for it was a vote for the middle class, "the last protection against the class struggle," while a vote against was "a vote for the money lenders, for those who profit by the exploitation of need . . . who not only refuse to be their brother's keeper, but even undertake to keep others from sharing responsibility and from acting as their brother's keepers." This was a rare instance when McCarthy openly emphasized the religious inspiration behind his political career.[8]

Another example of his overt dedication to the Fair Deal agenda was his open affiliation with the labor movement. In one ten-day period in 1951, for instance, he twice praised the movement's history and mission, lauding its role in casting off "the old economic tyranny" and hailing its record "of honor and of unselfishness." The strength of McCarthy's rhetoric illustrates the extent of the differences between Republicans and liberal Democrats during the Truman years. Although the liberals had rejected the radicalism of the Progressives and the Popular Front, this did not mean that they shared Republican reservations about the role of the state. Liberals such as McCarthy entered the 1950s with a strong faith in the capacity of the federal government to intervene in and even manage not only education, welfare and health services, but also the economy itself. Truman's failure to realize the goals of the Fair Deal meant that after his retirement in 1953, it was to the young liberals that the torch of domestic reform was passed, giving McCarthy and his contemporaries a ready-made agenda for the decade to come. Despite the perceived failure of Truman's later years, McCarthy's respect for him was such that he was the only president treated with great admiration in McCarthy's memoirs.[9]

McCarthy's early career in the House was steady rather than spectacular. He initially served on the Post Office and Agriculture Committees, which hardly allowed him much scope for seizing the limelight. His first two terms yielded a total of five very minor bills enacted into law. His interventions in the House were infrequent but noted by journalists for their wit and references to the classics and philosophy, authorities often beyond the horizons of his peers. He was certainly confident of his rhetorical ability, and a radio debate with Congressman Fred Hartley Jr. about the Taft-Hartley labor law in 1952 attracted a flood of letters of praise. Each congressman was expected to concern himself with a small number of specific issues, on which he could come to be an authority, and McCarthy was no exception, reserving his public remarks for selected areas. One such was the question of social responsibility and the cooperative movement, especially in the realm of housing policy. The example given earlier of McCarthy's rhetoric on this issue was stronger than most, but not uncharacteristic in its focus. The housing bill, McCarthy insisted in June 1949, was a way in which "social responsibility can be expressed in action," and "in the best and oldest American tradition." This recourse to abstract, moral, almost religious principles—"social responsibility"—was typical McCarthy. No issue motivated him so much in his early congressional career as the defense of the cooperatives, an interest which reflected his religious background. Supporting tax exemptions for agricultural cooperatives a year later, he claimed the cooperative principle was "the very essence of democracy, not only in politics, but in every other phase of fruitful living—economic, religious, and social."[10]

McCarthy's assignment to the Agriculture Committee was not particularly useful for a congressman from an urban district, and his colleagues teased him that he was representing "the farmers of Ramsey County." His dissatisfaction was reflected in his occasional absences, and he complained that the committee acted as a vehicle for "special agricultural interests." Through his service on the committee, however, McCarthy became interested in the issue that perhaps best reflected his commitment to social justice: the plight of the migratory Mexican agricultural worker, or "wetback." In May 1951 McCarthy opened his assault on the migratory labor program, declaring in the House that the importation of "poverty-stricken Mexican peons" had driven down farm wages and reduced a million American laborers to "a state of homeless, rootless migrancy." McCarthy and Ohio's Congressman James G. Polk filed a minority report on the annual extension of the migratory labor program, demanding minimum wage standards that would both improve the lot of the Mexicans and help to protect the jobs of American workers. The following year he opposed a cut in funding for patrols of the Mexican border, arguing that only if illegal immigration was kept under control could "a decent legal program for the importation of agricultural labor" be devised. The years following his re-election in 1952 would also see McCarthy return to the subject; although the migrant labor program was never really a major national issue, it was perhaps the one area in which he became a genuine congressional specialist.[11]

There was only one issue that reliably united the Democratic Party's uneasy alliance of southern conservatives, northern liberals and urban machines: foreign policy. Both in Minnesota and in the national Democratic Party, support of Truman's Cold War stance and of the Marshall Plan had become the litmus test of party loyalty. With Communism on the march in Asia, the Republicans had long since abandoned their old isolationism and were becoming increasingly fierce critics of what they saw as Truman's military weakness and appeasement of Soviet interests. Liberal Democrats, meanwhile, felt a moral urge to embrace Truman's crusade against Communism, and under the threat of Republican criticism and the pressure of events overseas they were beginning to abandon the gentler rhetoric of the 1930s and adopt the harsher vocabulary of "toughness" and "realism." Minnesota itself, with its predominantly rural German and Scandinavian population, had in the 1930s been one of the most isolationist states in the Union, but the crucible of the Cold War produced in Humphrey and McCarthy leaders who allied a Wilsonian respect for international institutions with an urgent moral commitment to American intervention abroad.[12]

During McCarthy's first two terms in Congress his visceral opposition to Communism and dedication to the Cold War were plain to see. In an address to the South Dakota Knights of Columbus in 1950, for instance, he articulated the fashionable intellectual pessimism of the day:

> We live in a time which is not merry and bright. Darkness for the modern man seems almost impenetrable. One by one he has seen his lights grow dim and fade. The evils which the nineteenth century thought it was about to destroy forever—the evils of ignorance, of persecution, and of slavery, torture, of all evil, including the fear of evil, and even the fear of fear—all have returned; and like the evil spirit of the parable, once driven out, they have returned sevenfold.[13]

"Our wrestling is not with flesh and blood," he declared; the adversary was an idea, a creed. On the House floor a year later he went further, rejecting the isolationism of Republican conservatives such as Robert Taft as a "failure to recognize the basic evil of communism." Like many other Catholic liberals, he saw reform as one possible solution, and argued: "The best way to combat Communism is to meet the legitimate criticism, especially in the field of social justice." The outbreak of the Korean War in June 1950 pushed McCarthy's rhetoric a step nearer outright belligerence. In August he called for an increase in the armed forces and in military production, and warned that the "whole economy and pattern of living must be adjusted to this semi-wartime basis." Like most liberals, he rallied to the president and never questioned Truman's assumption of executive war powers as he was to question Johnson over Vietnam. "We must undertake to preserve western civilization and the peoples who value it," he told Congress in February 1951. "We must preserve our national honor." In letters to constituents, he urged that the United States "use all of its resources" to "stand against Communism." Explicitly praising the policy of "containing Communism," he argued that Truman was justifiably devoted to "building up military strength at home and in western Europe." "We as a nation must not be blind to the evil which confronts us," McCarthy solemnly warned in December 1951. "We must not underestimate its powers and we must not be guilty of failing to take adequate steps to defend ourselves."[14]

McCarthy and his fellow Democrats were to be victims as well as perpetrators of the anti-Communism of the early Cold War. The issue was domestic internal security: how far could the government go to protect the United States from Communist subversives? McCarthy himself never used the rhetoric of betrayal or subversion, and later recalled that he had felt the domestic threat was "greatly exaggerated." Those Republicans who hunted for traitors and Communists in the corridors of power, like Congressman Richard Nixon and Senator Joseph McCarthy, were, he felt, "not so much Communist baiters as baiters of persons who believed in freedom of speech." In April 1950, shortly after the Republican McCarthy had issued a series of wild allegations of Soviet infiltration into the State Department, Eugene McCarthy criticized his "broadside attack" on the department and its staff, and the "general disregard for basic personal and civil rights" demonstrated by the Communist-hunters. Although he agreed that the issue of espionage was "a legitimate concern," he was never comfortable with the ferocious, unrelenting rhetoric of McCarthyism.[15]

In July 1950 he proposed an amendment to a civil service bill (HR 7439) that would prove extremely controversial. Federal employees who were to be dismissed from sensitive jobs because they had been found to be security risks, he suggested, should be given the chance of employment in other, nonsensitive areas. He explicitly suggested that they "be given preference for re-employment in a department or agency which is not listed as sensitive." The amendment was summarily rejected on a standing vote, 128–21. McCarthy explained decades later that he was motivated by a belief in "the near sacredness of the person" and by Charles Péguy's remark on the Dreyfus case that "if an injustice against one person was allowed to stand unchallenged in a society, [then] the whole of that society would be corrupted." Coming just months after his senatorial namesake's famous speech in Wheeling, West Virginia, alleging the presence of spies in the Truman administration and the State Department, this was a courageous attempt to protect civil service employees vulnerable to dismissal.[16]

In the 1950 congressional election McCarthy's Republican opponent, Ward Fleming, tried to make his civil service amendment into an election issue, accusing him of "pampering" Communists and being part of a "fraternity of feather-heads," but McCarthy easily rode out the storm and won a comfortable victory. Elsewhere, however, the Democrats took a heavy drubbing. In many races local issues were decisive, but there could be no question that the internal security issue had damaged them. Not every Democrat was as insulated as McCarthy against charges of weakness and appeasement.[17]

For some historians the 1950 elections marked a critical development in the public's attitude to the Democrats, as their Republican adversaries now adopted the rhetoric of populist insurgency to attack a perceived liberal elite for its sympathy for Communism. Ironically, the Democrats themselves had done much to legitimize the rhetoric and tactics of anti-Communist hysteria, and Minnesota provided an excellent example of the way in which the liberals had made the politics of anti-Communism respectable. Hubert Humphrey, for instance, had grandly declared: "I would rather be a red-baiter than a traitor." It was the Democrats, after all, who established a federal loyalty program, purged Communists from the party and attacked unions with pro-Communist leaders. By 1952, however, two years after Senator Joseph McCarthy's Wheeling speech, and with the U.N. forces still entrenched in Korea, the Democrats were daily having to fight off accusations of weakness on the Communist issue.[18]

Eugene McCarthy himself faced two challenges: first, a televised debate with the "other" McCarthy; and second, a bitter re-election campaign in which he himself became the target of anti-Communist attack. The television debate with the senator from Wisconsin has become part of Eugene McCarthy's personal mythology, but in fact the debate was a sedate affair, concentrating on Truman's policy in Asia, and had no serious political consequences. McCarthy himself proudly boasted for decades afterward that he had been "the first to challenge Senator McCarthy," but no biographers of Joseph McCarthy or historians of the period have ever considered the debate worthy of mention. According to Eugene McCarthy's memoirs, NBC approached him only "because no one in the Senate would accept the invitation." His wife was "terrified" and recalled their liberal friends, including Hubert Humphrey and Senator Paul Douglas of Illinois, telephoning to urge her to dissuade her husband. Joseph McCarthy certainly spoke to him beforehand, either by telephone or in person, with a surprisingly friendly suggestion that they avoid "an Irish brawl"; perhaps he thought that Eugene would be a difficult adversary. As it turned out, both men were cordial, with the Republican senator addressing the Democratic congressman as "Gene," although the younger McCarthy unswervingly called the elder "Senator." There were no personal attacks, and there was no mention of internal security; instead the two men confined themselves to vague, inoffensive generalizations about foreign affairs. The debate brought McCarthy a brief moment of attention, if only in the television review columns of the Washington papers. This was all good publicity for a congressman seeking re-election, but even the St. Paul newspapers gave it only limited coverage on the inside pages. In fact, Eugene McCarthy was certainly not alone among liberal Catholics in publicly opposing the senator, and stood to lose little by debating him; given Joseph McCarthy's overbearing reputation, anything better than an embarrassing browbeating was likely to ensure him good publicity.[19]

The second challenge McCarthy confronted in 1952 was his campaign for re-election, in which he faced a rich and well-connected Republican neophyte, Roger Kennedy. This, too, became something of a myth for McCarthy's partisans, another story demonstrating the courage and commitment of their hero. In fact, McCarthy was never in serious danger of losing the election. Kennedy commanded the support of most wealthy Minnesota businessmen, hired the most expensive public relations firm in the state, and was related by marriage to the owners of the *St. Paul Pioneer Press and Dispatch* and one of the district's two television companies. His strategy was to intensify Ward Fleming's 1950 charges that McCarthy was weak on the security issue and to proclaim the inadequacy of McCarthy's record in Congress. Kennedy's central claim, propagated through extensive newspaper and television advertisements as well as pamphlets, posters and flyers, was that McCarthy's amendment of July 1950 permitting the preferential federal re-employment of suspected security risks was "a proposal to guarantee government jobs to men and women whose loyalty, or integrity, or morality, was in such serious question as to menace the nation's safety." Only twenty-one fellow congressmen, he pointed out, had backed McCarthy's lunatic scheme; the others had shrunk from the prospect of giving "top preference for government jobs" to people "who endangered our national security in times of war."[20]

For McCarthy and his friends there was an ugly side to Kennedy's campaign. Abigail McCarthy claimed that she saw flyers asking "IS YOUR CONGRESSMAN A TRAITOR?" and that her daughter came home from kindergarten complaining that her father was being called a Communist. Their affluent college friends began to ask that their names be withdrawn from lists of supporters, and her husband, she wrote, was "growing more thin and distraught each day over the attack." McCarthy himself recalled watching a television political commercial in which Kennedy asked two soldiers on leave from Korea: "And how did you feel when you came home and found that your congressman was giving aid and support to the enemy?"[21]

McCarthy mounted an uncompromising defense of his record. In the local newspaper he attacked Kennedy as having "no professional standing or reputation" and denounced his "false and misleading statements," while simultaneously defending his record in Congress as a supporter of "those basic programs initiated under the New Deal." The Republicans, read a McCarthy pamphlet, were "desperate men for whom no lie is too base and who will use any means to gain power over our citizens," even though their attacks would "poison the wells of free speech and honest debate in our community." The argument over McCarthy's internal security amendment actually revealed just how sensitive to criticism he still was. The Republican *Pioneer Press* pointed out that discussion of his record was "all a proper part of campaign discussion": "Naturally each side will argue the interpretation most favorable to him and least favorable to the opposition. But we will get nowhere if all effort to discuss a public man's record is smothered by nothing more than cries of 'smear,' 'libel' and the like." The writer argued, furthermore, that no one was questioning McCarthy's loyalty: it was "nonsense for him to say or intimate that the Republicans accuse him of being pro-Communist."[22]

McCarthy also held a grudge against Warren Burger, an ambitious young Twin Cities lawyer who stood in for Kennedy at a public debate and told McCarthy that his approach to internal security was "using a feather duster where he ought to be using a pick axe." When Burger was nominated to be Chief Justice of the Supreme Court in 1969, McCarthy was one of only three senators to oppose him, making an "almost inaudible" speech explaining that Burger was unfit to hold the office because he had "misrepresented my position" in 1952. Roger Kennedy later apologized to McCarthy for the tone of his campaign, but even he was baffled by McCarthy's animus toward Burger.[23]

Despite the Republican onslaught, McCarthy did not want for friends in 1952. A committee of local theology lecturers and clergymen, for instance, rallied to defend his record, and one, Robert McAfee Brown of Macalester

College, later a prominent professor of religion at Stanford University, told a story that gave added luster to McCarthy's purer-than-thou image. McCarthy was apparently offered $1,100 to use for a "smear sheet" against Roger Kennedy, but he refused it. Brown later wrote: "It was a high moment in my understanding of democracy to see a man whose political life was being threatened, stand up to that concerted opposition and say 'No.'" As Brown's story stands, McCarthy emerges as a man of principle who would put the health of democracy above his own fortunes. But there is, of course, more to it than that. McCarthy himself, reading Brown's story, commented: "I also knew it was bad politics . . . You just lose people if you seem to be using the same smear attack." McCarthy was never on the brink of defeat and certainly never in a position where he needed to resort to risky personal attacks on his opponent's family. McCarthy's old friend William Carlson, now running unsuccessfully as the Democratic candidate for senator, remembered that McCarthy "was so bored with his own campaign he took off with me and campaigned all over the state." This was hardly the behavior of a man on the ropes tempted by desperate measures to win re-election, and as McCarthy implicitly admitted, the story was more a red herring than a dramatic demonstration of his political purity. When the votes were finally counted in November, Kennedy had amassed a smaller percentage than had Ward Fleming two years previously, while McCarthy piled up 61.7 percent of the vote and his largest margin yet.[24]

Kennedy had, of course, attacked him on the one issue on which he could hardly be faulted, his anti-Communism. In a television broadcast, McCarthy reminded the voters that he had "entered politics in an all-out effort to take control of the DFL organization away from the Wallace-ites and the Progressives." President Truman spent a day campaigning in St. Paul and told the crowds that McCarthy had battled all his life "against the bad conditions that breed communism here at home" and "fought staunchly for all our programs to stop the spread of communism abroad." McCarthy also cast himself as the enemy of domestic subversives. "I have supported the un-American activities committee and every basic piece of legislation directed to control subversive activities," he told the local press. To attack McCarthy as soft on Communism was simply not a good campaign tactic.[25]

The final confirmation of McCarthy's anti-Communism came two years later, when Humphrey proposed a bill to outlaw the Communist Party. Supporting the ban made political sense: it ensured he would be completely protected against Republican criticism in the state, which continued despite Kennedy's defeat, and it also reflected the views of his constituents, 74 percent of whom favored the measure. McCarthy did not merely vote for the ban; he made an uncompromising speech on its behalf. On 15 August 1954 McCarthy told the *Minneapolis Tribune* that Humphrey's bill to outlaw the Communist Party "compares with his offer of a civil rights plank to the Democratic Party in 1948." On the floor of the House he explained his admiration for Humphrey's measure: "The Communist Party cannot claim the protection and privileges given to other political parties because of its international conspiratorial character and because of its continued and determined use of the methods of deception, falsehood and subversion." Joseph McCarthy could hardly have put it better.[26]

The historian Michael J. Lacey has argued that the Truman presidency was the single most important period of the modern American political order. Certainly there emerged between 1947 and 1952 a new liberalism, the creed of an intellectual elite vaunting itself as tough and aggressive while repudiating its opponents as weak, unrealistic and effeminate. Historians continue to argue about the extent to which the new liberal ideology represented a betrayal of the commitments of the New Deal. What is perhaps most plausible is that while liberals after 1948 attempted to retain the moral spirit of Roosevelt's programs, their very emphasis on anti-Communism at home and abroad, on economic growth as the panacea of all ills and on the virtues of the market effectively circumscribed and undermined their ambitions. What also emerged was an agenda that Eugene McCarthy and his colleagues would embrace and proclaim for the next ten years: civil rights legislation, federal aid to education, an increase in the minimum wage, support for the labor unions and financial assistance for unemployed workers. The Fair Deal essentially represented the limit of liberal aspirations until the middle 1960s, and the party platforms of 1952, 1956 and 1960 were little more than the 1948 program reheated.[27]

In all this, the Cold War played a central and defining role as the issue that drove the politics of the new postwar order. The series of commitments built by Truman and his special counsel Clark Clifford on the national level, and by activists like Humphrey and McCarthy in the states, united disparate Democratic factions who could agree on the Marshall Plan and aid to Greece. These commitments were imbued with a sense of grim determination, an urge for security and even a sense of existential bleakness that appealed to the Catholic pessimism of Eugene McCarthy and replaced the daring optimism of many New Dealers. Anti-Communism was a vital part of this consensus; it both gave a moral impetus to the liberals' support for the Cold War and encouraged a rigidly bipolar view of world affairs. It was not merely a driving imperative for the likes of Humphrey and McCarthy; it was the very issue on which they built their political careers.[28]

From the outset, however, the coalition of 1948 was an uneasy one. Liberalism itself was never a strictly defined, stable intellectual doctrine, and Truman's Democratic alliance was badly frayed. Even in the late 1930s factional squabbling between north and south, city and country, labor and agriculture, minorities and elites, and liberals and conservatives had threatened to destroy the New Deal coalition. Throughout the 1950s and 1960s the factions of the Democratic and liberal worlds, Populists, Progressives, urban machines, Catholics, unionists, and southerners, bickered among themselves despite their Cold War alliance, especially over issues like civil rights which exacerbated existing tensions of race and class. In Minnesota itself, there remained a minority of voters loyal to the potential of the old Farmer-Labor Party and still susceptible to the appeals of candidates more radical than Truman, Kennedy and Johnson. Not only did later events seem to replay the liberal-Progressive battles of the 1940s, but even the minor rift between the liberals and older labor leaders in St. Paul in the summer of 1948 anticipated the growing tension between labor leaders and the "intellectual" liberals in the late 1960s.[29]

For McCarthy himself, the years from 1947 to 1952 marked an astonishing personal transformation. He began them a diffident young professor at a small Catholic college in St. Paul and ended them a popular and ambitious liberal congressman, elected three times and even suggested by some of his friends in 1952 as a possible senatorial candidate. In politics he had found the vocation denied him at St. John's, and in many ways he was already the Eugene McCarthy of 1968, appealing, as he later remembered, to "students, some old enough to vote, some not, old liberals, and party persons, especially women." Most significantly, he was already acquiring a reputation in the Minnesota party for independence and detachment, never one to "get too involved in wrangles within the party," "not one who really sat around and planned and so forth," according to contemporaries. All the same, he was still a popular figure in the DFL, "always back for the party events"; as Donald Fraser remarked, "it wasn't as if he had run off and taken a different boat." In his keynote address to the 1952 DFL state convention, McCarthy remarked that the political independent had his place, "but his status is a kind of luxury which he can enjoy only because other responsible people are working in party activities." For all his detachment, the McCarthy of the early 1950s was still a good party man.[30]

CHAPTER FIVE

Patronage and Principle in the Eisenhower Era

The atmosphere of the House of Representatives in the 1950s has reminded some observers of Adlai Stevenson's characterization of the diplomatic world: a place of "protocol, alcohol and Geritol." Behind the elaborate courtesies and traditions of the lower chamber and the backslapping camaraderie of the cloakrooms lay the insecurities of driven men and the coldness of political calculation. Even as late as the 1950s the House "could reasonably be described as a part-time institution." Its members would arrive in the January frosts by train or car and leave to avoid the uncomfortable heat and sweat of the summer. As the political scientist Nelson Polsby put it, while the Senate was considered by most observers as a "great forum" and a "publicity machine" for its more eager members, the House was "a large, impersonal and highly specialized machine for processing bills," "a perennially timberless ecology." To make a name in such an institution was hard work, and Eugene McCarthy's eventual success at doing so testified to his political skill. The House was briefly controlled by the Republicans in 1953–1954, and then by the Democrats, but there never existed any workable majority for progressive legislation, and certainly not for the enactment of the Fair Deal agenda or expansion of the New Deal. Throughout this period the life of the chamber was controlled by one man: the Speaker, Sam Rayburn, the champion of accommodation and moderation and the very antithesis of a crusading liberal. McCarthy was enormously impressed by the venerable Speaker. Rayburn, he later wrote, was "so true to the rules of the House and to its traditions that members could never accuse him of unfairness or partisanship." In Rayburn's sedate, hierarchical House "the lines of authority, power and responsibility" were clearly defined; even though they often cut against the liberals, McCarthy had no complaints.[1]

Success and upward mobility in Rayburn's House were won by those politicians who knew how to win and wield influence, and in an institution that placed a premium on deference the pursuit of patronage united representatives across the political spectrum. As early as 1951, a St. Paul newspaper noted that McCarthy had "been getting the little extra attentions which the party leadership usually reserves for a political 'comer,'" with Senator Humphrey cited as his chief patron. Within the House of Representatives itself, McCarthy made his closest congressional friendships among "the Southerners and the Texans," particularly through his friendship with Homer Thornberry and Frank Ikard. The Texan group naturally enjoyed a special status because of their closeness to the Texan Speaker, and even had their own reserved table in the House restaurant. Abigail McCarthy recalled that her husband "used to be asked to sit at this table frequently and became, in a way, a sort of honorary Texan." McCarthy himself remembered that although his northern friends, "kind of the extreme liberals," had their own table, he "used to eat with the Texans once in a while." Some observers, he recalled wryly, used to claim that he was a pawn of the Texans merely "because I had lunch with them."[2]

McCarthy's friendship with Rayburn's delegation, however, did help him to rise through the Democratic ranks. According to the columnist Doris Fleeson, Rayburn, "hot on the scent of a coming man," adopted McCarthy as a liberal protégé and "moved him about rapidly" from committee to committee. Frank Ikard recalled that McCarthy "was clearly identified as a comer" and was so popular with his fellow Texans that they helped raise campaign funds for him in 1952, approaching "people around the country." McCarthy was unquestionably popular with the party leadership. "I have always been proud of you," wrote an admiring House majority leader, John McCormack, after McCarthy had moved to the Senate. Nothing reflected McCarthy's popularity with the powerful more than his elevation to the prestigious Ways and Means Committee in January 1955, at the beginning of his fourth term. Not only was it an integral part of the conservative coalition's control of the House and a powerful revenue committee in its own right, but its Democratic members also formed the party's steering committee. Until then, McCarthy recalled, he had been disappointed by his committee assignments, but his appointment to Ways and Means meant that he had "been accepted by Rayburn."[3]

Despite McCarthy's friendships with conservative southerners like Rayburn, his liberal reputation never wavered. His voting record remained remarkably consistent, but his rhetoric was unmistakably mellowing, reflecting the supposed consensus of the 1950s rather than the grand passions of the New Deal and the early Cold War. In his comfortable 1956 re-election campaign he told the League of Women Voters that his main domestic interests were the conservation of natural resources, civil rights, school aid and tax revision. A profile in *Congressional Quarterly Almanac* shortly after his Senate victory in 1958 noted that his stands "actively put him in the liberal class," citing his votes for low-rent housing, high farm price supports, the 1957 Civil Rights Act and federal aid to schools and the unemployed, as well as his opposition to the McCarran Act, which he felt went too far in its efforts to monitor "subversive activities." Throughout his five congressional terms, McCarthy's party unity scores remained extremely high and his support for federal spending occasionally even eclipsed that of Hubert Humphrey. Between 1953 and 1958 his ADA voting score never dipped below 81 percent and three times reached an unbeatable 100 percent. McCarthy's labor voting record, meanwhile, was outstanding. In his Senate race the AFL-CIO proudly broadcast the fact that between 1949 and 1958 he had voted "right" on every one of the fifty-six designated "key votes." The UAW likewise declared that McCarthy had never once voted contrary to their recommendations, and when at the end of the decade the AFL-CIO Committee on Political Education (COPE) listed the forty crucial votes in House and Senate since 1948, McCarthy's score was a perfect 100 percent.[4]

McCarthy's careful liberalism was best illustrated by his attitude to the increasingly contentious issue of civil rights. Like other Minnesota Democrats, he supported civil rights legislation and the principle of desegregation. In February 1955, for instance, he debated Allen Ellender on the radio and called segregation "inhuman and irrational." He supported making lynching a federal offense and in December 1955 was even hailed by Adam Clayton Powell as a potential "key regional leader" of the civil rights bloc in Congress. In 1958, McCarthy agreed to introduce in the House Paul Douglas's unsuccessful civil rights bill, which would have mandated the federal government to cut off funds to segregated schools. But he was careful not to appear an uncompromising zealot, and in his longest speech on the issue, in 1956, explained that he did not blame "any one person or group" for the "injustice" of segregation. It was, he said, "an historical demonstration of the truth of the biblical statement that injustices of the fathers are visited upon the children." Not one of them, northern or southern, had done enough to eliminate "this evil." Unlike many other liberals, McCarthy had reservations about federal intervention in the South. "These are dangerous methods and means," he admitted, although he still supported them. While McCarthy's support for civil rights was never in doubt, it was never as passionate or overt as that of Hubert Humphrey or Paul Douglas, and he made sure that it never lost him friends among the southern potentates of the House.[5]

The one issue on which McCarthy did stand up alone to make a case was the migrant labor problem. Throughout the early fifties he continued his efforts to improve the lot of the migrants and publicize their difficulties. In April 1953, for instance, he told the House that the issue was "one of the greatest social-economic problems in the United States," calling the workers' plight "truly tragic" and their living conditions "a national disgrace." In 1955, he proposed an amendment to another migrant labor bill which would have prohibited the employment of Mexican migrants unless no domestic workers were available and would have guaranteed them the same wages and conditions. As in 1951, it was rejected.[6]

It was in the mid-1950s that McCarthy's reputation as a better congressman for columnists than for the people of St. Paul began to take hold. He was, recalled the redoubtable Mary McGrory, "wonderful copy." His contributions to House debate wittily lampooned the misfortunes of Eisenhower's cabinet of mediocrities, with the secretary of agriculture, Ezra Taft Benson, a favorite target. Yet as his Minnesota colleague Fred Marshall put it, he was also "a little on the lazy side." According to Marshall, "he could get away with being lazy because of his intelligence and his sense of humor." The Democratic mayor of St. Paul, Joseph Dillon, found that when he pressed for federal projects for the city it was better to approach other Minnesota congressmen and not the district's own representative. McCarthy was, he said, "a good congressman for the country, but not for St. Paul." Even McCarthy's own administrative assistant recalled that he often skipped committee meetings and was easily bored, and while other congressmen kept their staff busy with local problems, McCarthy quipped that a wise politician used his employees "for protection, to go to lunch for you." National coverage of the bright Minnesota liberal was always favorable, however. "In his ten years in the House," commented the *Washington Star* in 1958, "Mr. McCarthy has gained the reputation for serenely cleaving to his principles, no matter what the prevailing political winds. Where other men gnaw their fingernails and temporize in agony, he, with an almost carefree air, has ignored the mode of the moment and spoken and voted his own convictions."[7]

What was "the mode of the moment"? One commentator called the 1950s "a new gilded age," in which an unreal sense of lassitude and serenity, disturbed only by factional bickering, belied the pressing social needs of the day; for another, the decade was "an expensive holiday from responsibility." The mode of the moment was above all determined by its president. Eisenhower, in the historian David Plotke's words, was "a conservative caretaker for the New Deal order," not a political innovator. Eisenhower was reluctant to expand the federal budget to pay for new social programs, but he was also reluctant to roll back the federal state: he famously wrote to his brother Milton that if any party attempted to eliminate the New Deal, "you would not hear of that party again in our political history." Eisenhower's aim, in short, was to develop a new, self-consciously modern conservative party that accepted the legacy of the New Deal, resisted its further expansion, and sought a new alliance between the government and business. The political scientist Stephen Skowronek calls Eisenhower an example of the "pre-emptive" president, unable to repudiate completely the commitments of his predecessors because of the resilience of the political establishment, and in this case unwilling to jeopardize his own personal popularity by potentially controversial innovations. With Eisenhower as caretaker, the transformation of the federal government into a modern welfare state was temporarily postponed, while party politics settled into "a basic equilibrium," soothed by economic prosperity and ideological moderation.[8]

Although controversies over civil rights and cultural freedom were certainly brewing in communities across the nation, the Washington stage in the Eisenhower era was remarkably tranquil. Indeed, by the middle 1950s it appeared that partisan debate was simply an argument between two wings of the same middle-class, moderate consensus. Both Republicans and Democrats seemed to share the same confidence in American society and anxiety about the threat of Soviet Communism. Both shared the same faith that prosperity and economic growth would resolve domestic social problems. To some extent, then, the consensus of the 1950s was "a gigantic deal," with the Republicans grudgingly accepting the new economics and the Democrats moderating their demands for social justice, and with the presidency increasingly becoming the focus of hopes that the national government could manage economic prosperity as well as a successful Cold War.[9]

The leaders of the Democratic Party in Congress, often southern, old and by disposition moderate, reacted to Eisenhower's appeal by emphasizing their own supposedly nonideological bipartisanship. A "prevailing spirit of consensus and accommodation" settled over Congress. The Senate majority leader, Lyndon Johnson, personified the pluralism and pragmatism of the decade. On issues of labor and energy policy and the regulation of business he deferred to conservatives, and on civil rights he argued for compromise. At most Johnson and Rayburn argued merely for greater spending on the old programs; often they were even more supportive of the president than was his own party. The Democratic majority, said Johnson, had "a solemn responsibility to cooperate" with Eisenhower, and their task was "to pass legislation, not to sit around saying principled things." Passing legislation with bipartisan support was Johnson's mission in the Senate, and he had nothing but contempt for the liberal "bomb-throwers" who complicated his task. In 1953 he had discussed with the liberals' hero Adlai Stevenson ways in which the party might back away from excessive liberalism and woo the South. Both Stevenson and Johnson agreed that party unity was paramount, and Johnson felt that the Democrats' congressional gains in 1956, the year of Eisenhower's triumphant re-election, had vindicated his approach. This "go along, get along" strategy was criticized by a liberal minority at the time, and it has been criticized since by liberal commentators. Doris Kearns Goodwin, for instance, argued that Johnson had not only conceded "the right of defining national goals" to the White House, but by neutering the Senate had closed a forum for the discussion of the social problems that would explode in the following decade. Agreeing with Johnson's harshest critic, the Illinois senator Paul Douglas, she charged that his insistence on moderation and cooperation inhibited the development of a healthy opposition and "abdicated the possibility even of stimulating national debate."[10]

McCarthy's own attitude to Eisenhower was one of wry disdain rather than burning opposition. The Democrats had lost the presidency in 1952, he explained, only because "people just got a bit tired of [them]." Far from the Republicans' being the party of economic competence, he argued in 1956, they had allowed the national debt and excise taxes to rise and foreign aid to languish. Partisan mockery came easily to McCarthy: in 1954 he accused the congressional Republicans of "irresponsibility and extremism" in foreign affairs, and relished the way in which they had "handicapped" their own secretary of state through their intemperate attacks on anything that smacked of moderation abroad. McCarthy's support that year for the Communist Control Act, however, illustrated the extent of his agreement on essentials with many Republicans, and with the American voter apparently dulled by prosperity, McCarthy's own zeal for social legislation gradually faded. When his 1954 opponent ran a "back Ike" campaign, McCarthy was unconcerned. "About half of his program was the Democratic program anyhow," he shrugged. "I'm for Ike when he's right."[11]

This halfhearted opposition to Eisenhower reflected liberal uncertainty in what was then thought to be an age of conservatism. New York's Senator Herbert Lehman remarked of his colleagues: "There was an impression among them that they were aliens in an alien land and needed to accommodate themselves to the conservative majority." The election of Eisenhower, the dulling opiate of prosperity and the submergence of the CIO in the AFL had certainly all wounded the cause of social reform. But liberalism also had its inherent weaknesses. It was always unstable, with its advocates continually arguing among themselves. Some wanted above all to preserve the old New Deal coalition in order to expand the welfare state on behalf of the poor; others, the intellectual descendants of the Progressives rather than of the radicals of the 1930s, hoped to use the power of the national government to address so-called quality of life issues such as the environment, civil rights and détente. Liberal sympathizers who respected party unity and were prepared to compromise with southern and conservative demands, as at the conventions of 1952 and 1956, squabbled with Johnson's "bomb-throwers"—the likes of Paul Douglas and Herbert Lehman, who regarded accommodation and moderation as cowardice and perfidy.[12]

It was in the figure of Adlai Stevenson, commonly but erroneously seen as Eugene McCarthy's political mentor, that the contradictions of liberalism and the Democratic consensus were best personified. McCarthy was never part of Stevenson's inner circle, according to Stevenson's friend Arthur Schlesinger Jr., and there exists no correspondence between them. Yet in books published in the 1970s and 1980s McCarthy insisted that Stevenson had been his model, "the purest politician of our time." In the words of his friend George Ball, however, Stevenson was "never a real liberal." He exhibited little enthusiasm for social democratic legislation, and like a latter-day Progressive, was more interested in the possibility of improving the processes of politics and in encouraging "the moral uplift of society itself." On foreign policy he unquestioningly endorsed the premises of the Cold War, supporting the war in Korea and the strategy of unrelenting containment, a more uncompromising approach than that of many of his friends and advisers. He also hesitated to endorse the *Brown v. Board of Education* decision, told Hubert Humphrey that he disagreed with school integration, and privately used the coarsest racial epithets. In the 1956 presidential primaries there were two plausible Democratic candidates more liberal than Stevenson, Estes Kefauver and Averell Harriman.[13]

What is interesting about McCarthy's identification with Stevenson is that Stevenson was not merely not a liberal, he was much closer to being a classical conservative. In 1952 he denied there was any difference between Eisenhower and himself, campaigned as a fiscal conservative and a Cold War hawk, and was labeled by Arthur Schlesinger Jr. as the most conservative Democratic nominee since John W. Davis in 1924. He opposed public housing, farm subsidies and federal aid to education, denounced "socialized medicine" and thought civil rights were the states' responsibility. Only on foreign policy did he agree with President Truman. No wonder that John Stennis claimed him as the candidate of the South in 1956. According to one historian, Stevenson was "more inclined to inaction than action" and became personally "uneasy, sometimes ambivalent," when confronted with liberal activism. For Paul Douglas, he was simply "lacking in human sympathy, particularly for the poor and underprivileged."[14]

Just as Douglas's criticism of Stevenson is reminiscent of the criticisms of Eugene McCarthy in 1968, so Stevenson also anticipated McCarthy's enormous appeal to the liberal middle class *despite* his social agenda. This was above all a question of style. Stevenson was not an intellectual, but his quick mind, wit, charm and thoughtful demeanor meant that "he looked and sounded like [one]." He avoided emotional rhetoric and appealed above all to the intellect; the *New Republic* lauded his "high road of intelligence and reason." His speeches sought to soothe, not to inflame; like McCarthy, he ignored issues of class and economics and emphasized issues of rights and ethics. "Better we lose the election than mislead the people," Stevenson told the 1952 Democratic convention. He was more sensitive to power's limitations than to its possibilities, unenthusiastic about total commitment to an issue or a cause, and endlessly indecisive. Like McCarthy in 1968, he was often accused of "frivolity." Stevenson disliked addressing black, Catholic and Jewish groups, and "simply did not understand the civil rights issue." The same dry wit that impressed affluent white audiences fell flat among black Democratic voters.[15]

Nonetheless, the impact of Stevenson's campaigns on the Democratic organization itself, in the political scientist James Q. Wilson's words, "can scarcely be exaggerated." To a generation of young, educated middle-class activists, Stevenson was an icon, lauded as "genuine," "a true intellectual, and more than that, a true American aristocrat." Wilson argued that Stevenson was instrumental in bringing a new faction of "reformers" into the Democratic Party in the 1950s. The period between 1952 and 1954 saw a wave of idealistic, reformist activity in local Democratic organizations that went unmatched until the late 1960s. For all the apparent tranquillity of the era, a new generation of earnest liberal activists was rapidly rising through the suburban ranks. Stevenson's major legacy, then, was the largest infusion of new blood into the Democratic coalition since the 1930s, with thousands of educated upper-middle-class activists, contemptuous of compromise, zealous in their veneration of wit and reason, joining Democratic reform clubs and the party itself. What attracted them was not so much substance as image, less Stevenson's policies than a pose of intellectual urbanity reminiscent of the "well educated, high-minded," economically conservative, pseudo-aristocratic types who had appealed to Mugwumps and Progressives decades earlier.[16]

McCarthy's most significant contribution to liberal politics during his years in the House was undoubtedly his role in drafting the liberal manifesto of 1957, the blueprint for the highly influential Democratic Study Group. Ever since Stevenson's crushing defeat in the 1956 presidential election, liberal dissidents had been ever more visibly chafing under the restrictions of Johnson and Rayburn. The ADA chairman Joseph Rauh, for example, complained that the Democrats had become "practically indistinguishable from the party they allegedly oppose." The main focus of opposition to the Johnson strategy was Paul Butler, chairman of the Democratic National Committee since 1953, a former ADA member who argued against a campaign of compromise and moderation and urged the party to stake out clear alternative positions. Although he had been the candidate of the South for the position of DNC chairman, Butler increasingly drew his support from the ADA and the liberal, former CIO wing of the AFL-CIO. Dissent in the Senate was growing too; after the 1956 elections, six liberal senators called for a new and aggressive agenda that built on the imagined promise of Stevenson's campaign. The expression of this renascent liberal confidence was the Democratic Advisory Council, founded by Butler within the national committee as an explicit challenge to Johnson's authority and the strategy of allowing "the Republican President to set a pattern" for the Democratic Party. The DAC was funded by wealthy New York liberals, and included not only the likes of Truman, Stevenson, Harriman and Kefauver, but also the leading Minnesota liberals, Hubert Humphrey and Governor Orville Freeman.[17]

Although McCarthy had cultivated good relations with the southern Democrats in the House, his natural colleagues remained his fellow northern and western liberals. During the Eighty-third Congress he had worked closely with Lee Metcalf (Montana) to defeat an anticonservation measure, but their prototypical liberal bloc, including the likes of Frank Thompson Jr.

(New Jersey), Stewart Udall (Arizona), Chet Holifield (California) and John Blatnik (Minnesota), was too informal and disorganized to make any decisive impact on the House, and throughout the following Congress they remained frustratingly unable to secure any positive legislation. Under Rayburn's benign but passive leadership there seemed to be no dynamic opposition to Eisenhower and the Republicans. A sign of the Democratic establishment's torpor was the fact that between 1953 and 1960 the House Democratic caucus held not a single meeting on a substantive issue, compared with over forty held by its Republican counterpart.[18]

In the aftermath of Stevenson's defeat in 1956, the liberals' patience was at an end. Only in 1952, when the Republicans benefited from a popular backlash against Harry Truman, had the Democrats in Congress failed to outstrip their rivals at the polls, but after 1956 their solid majorities in the House were seriously undermined by the collusion between the conservative Democratic leadership and the Eisenhower White House. As McCarthy later explained: "They were letting the platform drift, not even having a test on it because of Eisenhower's threat to veto . . . It was the whole liberal program, housing and healthcare and civil rights." The rationale for the proposed liberal manifesto, he admitted, "was kind of anti-Rayburn," while the direct inspiration came from the 1956 Southern Manifesto, an attack on civil rights signed by most southern Democrats. McCarthy was the prime mover. "[Frank] Thompson did a lot of work, but I guess it's true that I suggested it to Frank and Metcalf," he recalled. Hubert Humphrey certainly believed that the "full credit" belonged to McCarthy and enthusiastically commended him on his "excellent leadership." "This is the kind of thing that ought to be brought to the attention of our party leaders," he wrote. "I am going to do it. I am afraid that you are too modest to do so yourself."[19]

In fact, the actual draft of the manifesto had been a joint effort. McCarthy wrote most of it in early January 1957, with Representatives Metcalf, Holifield and Blatnik contributing individual sections. The manifesto was released to the press on 8 January with twenty-eight signatories; three weeks later the list had grown to eighty. Although these names represented twenty-one states, none were from the Deep South and about three-quarters were from urban areas, reflecting the metropolitan base of liberalism at midcentury. All had been in the House for several terms, but few were committee or subcommittee chairmen or wielded any great legislative influence. Eschewing lofty rhetoric, the manifesto proposed a sober liberal agenda: expanded public works and conservation programs; federal aid for school construction, medical education and housing; increased social security and unemployment benefits; the repeal of the Taft-Hartley Act; a vague commitment to civil rights; increased foreign aid; and steady expenditure on the armed forces. The Democratic platform of 1960 followed a similar pattern.[20]

As the *St. Paul Pioneer Press* noted, what was significant about the manifesto was not its unsurprising content but its implicit and unprecedented challenge to Sam Rayburn. One powerful supporter, Emanuel Celler of New York, the chairman of the Judiciary Committee, told the journal that there was "a grassroots insurgent movement among Democratic liberals in the House." "There is no leadership now in the House," he insisted. "We are no longer going to take it lying down." According to Frank Thompson, the rebels believed that without a firm liberal agenda the Democrats would suffer in the Northeast in 1958 and 1960. McCarthy himself, credited as the "chief spokesman," claimed that this "constructive approach" was no challenge to Rayburn and later recalled, "Rayburn never said anything about it; it wasn't anti-Democratic, which was the real test for Sam Rayburn." According to Representative Richard Bolling, who showed Rayburn a copy of the manifesto, "the old man looked it over and said he didn't disagree with anything in it." McCarthy's standing with the leadership was not in danger, and his stock on the party's left had risen. One union publication rejoiced that "for the first time in many years, an influential group of legislators" had "openly identified themselves with a program of generally liberal objectives."[21]

The principal consequence of the manifesto was the emergence of a loose, informal group of liberal congressmen known to the press as "McCarthy's Mavericks" or "McCarthy's Marauders." They met sporadically and without ceremony, although in early 1957 they established a rudimentary whip system for important votes, headed by the de facto secretary, Frank Thompson. Although the group was characterized by "extreme informality and flexibility," McCarthy was the unquestioned guiding spirit, and strategy meetings took place in his office. "We all looked to Gene as our leader in those days," recalled Metcalf. Adrian Winkel, McCarthy's administrative aide, later commented: "The Marauders was the kind of thing that appealed to him: the organizing of people to have the capacity to influence events is the principal motivating factor in his political life." In June 1957 McCarthy, with funds from the National Committee for an Effective Congress, began organizing a series of meetings, inviting eminent speakers to address audiences of fifteen to twenty liberal congressmen. The group also issued statements on policy or impending legislation: for example, McCarthy himself drafted statements on the civil rights bill in the summer of 1957, urging that the southern-Republican coalition "finally be broken," denouncing "immoral log-rolling at the expense of human rights," and labeling the bill "our primary objective for this session." In November 1957 *Labor's Daily* noted that the group had held strategy meetings "perhaps a dozen times" during the year; it had lent "effective support" to civil rights legislation, public atomic power, and foreign aid; it had avoided antagonizing Rayburn; and in short had "commanded considerable respect and attention from members of Congress." It was this McCarthy-led group that was, in 1959, to become the Democratic Study Group, the primary organized expression of liberal sentiment in the House and a powerful tool in the 1960s for Presidents Kennedy and Johnson. It was this group, moreover, in tandem with liberals in the Senate, which developed and publicized the domestic agenda that was to win the elections of 1958 and 1960 for the Democratic Party.[22]

McCarthy's great skill in the House was his ability to maintain good relations with the southern barons while simultaneously establishing his reputation as the brightest of the young liberals. Liberalism's strength in the Democratic Party appeared to be in decline during the 1950s. At the conventions of 1952 and 1956 the party platforms avoided liberal rhetoric or commitments; the influence of ADA waned to the point that *Time* called it an "albatross"; and the Democratic agenda seemed a tired rehash of the Fair Deal. By staying faithful to the old commitments of 1948, McCarthy was able to carve out his own niche as a northern liberal who could both win elections and work with the center and right of the congressional party. He carefully positioned himself between the Butler-Douglas faction and the Johnson-Rayburn leadership, equally at home with and congenial to both. An additional aspect of his image was his reputation as "the hero of the Catholic intellectuals and reform-minded liberals." Eugene and Abigail McCarthy moved in Catholic intellectual circles in Washington, and their Minnesota friends remarked on the consistency of their Catholic views and relationships. McCarthy retained a keen interest in religious affairs: although most of his letters were barely a paragraph long, he once wrote a four-page reply to one clergyman about the question of U.S. representation at the Vatican. He was an active member of the American liturgical movement and on the board of directors of the National Liturgical Conference, and also gave hundreds of addresses to religious and academic groups throughout the 1950s. "The speeches were pretty cheap speeches," he remembered. "It would free you of the frustration of just sitting around."[23]

McCarthy used the materials for his innumerable speeches and articles for Catholic periodicals as the basis for three books published between 1960 and 1964: *Frontiers in American Democracy* (1960), *The Crescent Dictionary of American Politics* (1962) and *A Liberal Answer to the Conservative Challenge* (1964). Although published in the 1960s, these three books repeated, often word for word, McCarthy's rhetoric of the previous decade. *Frontiers* offered the reader McCarthy's musings on the role of government, the nature of liberalism, the relationship of religion and politics and the inadequacies of President Eisenhower; the *Dictionary* was a judicious and largely unrevealing lexicon of political terminology; and *A Liberal Answer* was an explanation of the superiority of liberalism over moderate conservatism written for the election of 1964. All three were written in McCarthy's exceedingly spare and colorless style, with very rare flashes of irony. The ultradetached tone and extraordinary conciseness of his writing, often so disappointing to readers and reviewers, were still evident in the occasional writings that he dashed off at the beginning of the twenty-first century.[24]

The themes of McCarthy's books, particularly the most discursive, *Frontiers in American Democracy,* suggest that even in the 1950s his liberalism was very different from that of, say, Hubert Humphrey. Its religious dimension, for instance, was explicit to an unusual degree. According to his wife, McCarthy, "always haunted by the idea of vocation, had worked out a philosophy of the vocation of politics which satisfied him." In *Frontiers* he argued that a religious politician, if he were "whole," was necessarily driven by his faith. Neatly justifying both his anti-Communism and his liberalism, he explained that the Christian should be "the first to detect and oppose a truly totalitarian threat or movement, and the last to label every proposal for social reform 'socialistic.'" Similarly, his own detached, dry style was explicable because the Christian "should shun the devices of the demagogue at all times, but especially at a time when anxiety is great." And the ultimate verdict on the politician must be "whether through his decisions and actions he has advanced the cause of justice, and helped at least to achieve the highest degree of perfection possible in the temporal order." His authorities, including Plato, Aquinas, Jacques Maritain and Reinhold Niebuhr, made very clear his debt to the intellectual and religious traditions of the Old World.[25]

McCarthy's definition of liberalism was also unusual. Liberals, he argued, were united not by an agenda but by a common "method or manner of approach to human problems." The liberal was "ideally and characteristically an optimist," confident in human progress, "willing to advocate and to accept change," but not besotted with the new for its own sake. If there were basic elements of liberalism, these were "self-determination," equality, liberty, and the positive role of government. Government had "a posi-tive and natural function to assist man in the pursuit of perfection and of happiness," by "promoting the common good." The common good, he explained, could be divided into material, intellectual and moral goods, moral good being "the mastery of self, the cultivation and possession of those virtues which in the limited order of temporal life are the highest goal." Quoting his old St. Thomas mentor Heinrich Rommen, McCarthy wrote that the purpose of government was "that of bringing about peaceful change in accordance with the needs of distributive justice." The liberal welfare state investing in public housing, social security and unemploy-ment insurance was not merely the ideal vehicle for this, but was "the kind of state to which we have been committed from the beginnings of our national experience and beyond that, from the very beginnings of western civilization."[26]

To claim that the liberal Democratic agenda of the 1950s was the ulti-mate and necessary development of thousands of years of European his-tory may seem rather ludicrous. But it reflected the more conservative side of McCarthy's thought: his desire to ground his beliefs in a pattern of Euro-pean religious history; his elevation of reason above emotion; his venera-tion of institutions; and his emphasis on order. The liberal, he wrote, "need not always advocate something new; he can support elements of the status quo, or he may even advocate a return to conditions known in the past." McCarthy's reverence for institutions remained constant throughout his political life; from *Frontiers* to the end of the century, he repeatedly com-plained that Congress was being ignored and devalued by the president. In *Frontiers,* for instance, he objected that Eisenhower treated Congress "like the board of directors of a corporation." In his memoirs, *Up 'til Now,* he cited Harry Truman and Sam Rayburn as people "who believed in institu-tions, honored them, and strengthened them against attack by persons and ideas," contrasting them with unnamed people "who lacked understanding or respect for institutions, for their directing and stabilizing function in dis-ordered times," and "were willing to corrupt institutions for personal ben-efit or political advantage." The House of Representatives, he argued, was "a good institution" for the twenty years between his departure and the procedural reforms of the 1970s: the cause, he modestly explained, was his own liberal manifesto.[27]

Crusading zeal was not merely something with which McCarthy felt uncomfortable; it was also something he regarded as irrational and insidi-ous. He cited Adlai Stevenson's warning that "only men who confuse them-selves with God" would pretend they knew "the exact road to the Promised

Land." Even Eisenhower, according to McCarthy, was guilty of presenting politics as a "crusade," and he blamed this tendency on the phenomenon of "the innocent" looking for "massive effort" and instant results. McCarthy usually branded his political opponents, however uncharismatic, as "demagogues," the worst insult in his vocabulary. The demagogue, he explained in his *Dictionary,* was concerned not with "truth" but with "his own influence and power"; he was "a threat to orderly democratic government, which depends on a certain measure of tolerance and on reason." Compromise, on the other hand, was far from a dirty word. It was "the mark of human relations" in almost every institution and relationship, not a surrender of principle, but a "concession to reality." To bring about "progressive change in keeping with the demands of social justice," he wrote, "compromise and accommodation are not only called for, they are inevitable." Citing two English statesmen, Lord Morley and Sir Thomas More, to support his case, McCarthy contended that the goal of the politician, through a series of compromises, was to keep an imperfect world "from becoming even less perfect."[28]

In both *Frontiers in American Democracy* and his later books, McCarthy looked to the past rather than the future for guidance and inspiration. Considering McCarthy's religious background, this is hardly surprising. He spent his formative years reading English conservatives like Belloc and Chesterton and living in an institution that looked to Europe, Catholic orthodoxy and natural law philosophy for inspiration. Most conventional liberals, like John Kennedy and Hubert Humphrey, were simply not interested in Catholic theology, and although McCarthy's voting record did not betray his incongruity in such company, his thoughtful philosophical conservatism and eagerness to debate abstract notions of ethics and government marked him out as an unusual figure in the world of postwar liberalism.[29]

By 1957 McCarthy seemed set for a career of success and influence in the House for as long as he wanted. Not one of his four re-election campaigns had been close, and the margin of victory had widened each time.[30] With a secure base in the Democratic stronghold of unionized, Catholic St. Paul and a seat already on the "power" committee of Ways and Means, McCarthy could look forward to seniority in the House and eventually, perhaps, a committee chairmanship of his own. In early 1957 he was offered the chairmanship of ADA, the supreme recognition of his liberal leadership. But McCarthy turned it down. His sights were set on a new challenge, election to the Senate in 1958, and he feared that the ADA post would monopolize his attention and get in his way. To some, including his wife, this was an unwelcome surprise, for he had seemed at home in the House. McCarthy himself later recalled his happy years there: they had "some good issues, you know, enough to keep you occupied." But he was also bored: "You're kind of dictated to by the chairman of the committees and so on, so you just kind of hung around until it was time to vote." He told a Minnesota Democratic organizer, William Kubicek, that "he was getting bored of being a congressman." He even claimed afterward that if his Senate bid had failed, he would have left politics and returned to teaching. In the summer of 1957 Hubert Humphrey had encouraging news for another senatorial aspirant, Eugenie Anderson. McCarthy, he explained, might well quit politics completely in 1958: "He is quite unhappy about his service in the House. It poses serious family problems. His wife, Abigail, is quite unhappy in moving the family back and forth between Washington and St. Paul at least twice a year."[31]

Whether this was true remains doubtful, and the opportunity to run for the Senate in 1958 was certainly tempting. The incumbent Republican senator, Ed Thye, would be up for re-election, and McCarthy knew that the DFL organization was strong and successful enough to give any challenger a fighting chance. In 1956, for instance, Minnesota had given Eisenhower only 54 percent of the vote while re-electing Governor Freeman and five Democratic congressmen. A poll in summer 1958 found that both metropolitan voters and farmers associated with the DFL rather than the Republicans, by margins of 53–24 and 48–33 respectively. Thye himself was perceived as moderate, benign, avuncular and ineffective. He had been a farmer, governor of the state between 1943 and 1947, and senator thereafter. In Harry McPherson's pithy words, he was "a Scandinavian grandfather, . . . methodical and square, rather like Lawrence Welk."[32]

Securing the Democratic nomination for senator was a long and complicated process. Eugenie Anderson, who had worked with Humphrey and Orville Freeman in Minneapolis since the 1940s, was extremely popular among party activists and had served on the Democratic National Committee; she had also been the country's first female ambassador, to Denmark. As 1957 gave way to 1958, however, McCarthy became ever more determined. One friend recalled traveling with McCarthy to a city in southern Minnesota in late 1957:

We were driving along and suddenly he asked me if I had a subscription to *Time* magazine. I said, "Yes, why?" He said, "Did you ever hear of or see a representative being quoted?" I said I couldn't recall and he said, "Do you recall reading the quotations of a senator?" And I said, "Yes, senators are quite frequently quoted."[33]

When the state's lieutenant governor, Karl Rolvaag, declined to run, the way seemed clear. According to the activist Gerald Heaney, the party leaders had agreed that the chance now would fall to McCarthy, even though "there were quite a few in that group who didn't think that Gene McCarthy would be willing to give up what he had in the House for an uncertain run for the United States Senate." Many of them, especially those close to Governor Freeman, were privately backing Anderson. The result was a fight between Anderson and McCarthy that divided both the hierarchy and the party regulars, with the Minneapolis group generally supporting Anderson and the St. Paul organization pushing their congressman. On 1 February McCarthy opened his Senate campaign with a promise to increase "the Senate's influence on foreign policy and administration decisions." An opinion poll put him nineteen percentage points behind Senator Thye.[34]

Since not a single issue divided McCarthy and Anderson, the campaign for the party's endorsement was conducted entirely in terms of regional factionalism and personal loyalty. While McCarthy drew support from metropolitan Catholics and the labor movement, Anderson appealed more to the party's Minneapolis "establishment" and intellectuals and young suburbanites—a curious reversal of McCarthy's usual appeal, owing much to his image as the candidate of labor. McCarthy entered the state convention in May with three of the nine districts solidly behind him: his own; the Iron Range, which had a strong and supportive labor movement; and the Sixth, which included his old haunts around St. John's. It took two ballots for McCarthy to secure the required majority, and the *Minneapolis Tribune* called the battle "one of the fiercest competitions for party endorsement in recent years." The struggle certainly made McCarthy enemies among the DFL, particularly among the "official family" of Governor Freeman. Several observers noted "vestiges of bitterness" and "sounds of dissension": McCarthy's union backers, for instance, were furious that their candidate, whose labor record was second to none, had even had to fight at all, and blamed the "palace guard" clique of Freeman and Humphrey. In subsequent years both McCarthy and some of his associates blamed Freeman and Humphrey for supporting a candidate who would be less of a rival to Humphrey himself. In truth, though, Humphrey had actually encouraged McCarthy to enter the race, urging him in January to "give it all you got." One columnist thought that a McCarthy victory, potentially the first statewide triumph for a Catholic, would reflect well on Humphrey and set him up nicely for a presidential bid in 1960. And both the mayor of Minneapolis and McCarthy's campaign manager agreed that "in those days there [was] really a rather close bond between Hubert and Gene."[35]

By October 1958 the national and local press had begun to cast McCarthy as the favorite against Senator Thye, and in the middle of the month polls showed McCarthy winning 51 percent of the vote to his older opponent's 42 percent. His biggest backers, as ever, were the labor unions; he was one of only five of the thirty Democratic senatorial candidates in 1958 to receive money from the AFL-CIO, the Brotherhood of Railway Trainmen and the Railway Labor Executives' Association. McCarthy's team devised a strategy to campaign against the entire Republican record rather than Thye personally, painting McCarthy as a loyal party man and a dynamic "man in his prime," and focusing on four economic issues: the recession, the problems of small businesses, the cost of living, and the continuing decline in farm income. McCarthy's publicity in 1958 became legendary: his billboards projected the image of a young, handsome and active man with the slogan "Minnesota deserves *two* strong United States Senators," and his radio advertisements, all ending with that same refrain, both drew attention to the Republicans' economic problems and urged: "The two men Minnesota sends to the United States Senate must be the very best the state has to offer. Just being nice or friendly simply isn't good enough. He must be a leader." Thye's campaign, by contrast, relied simply on his own amiable and familiar personal appeal, and his advertising did not even mention the Republican Party by name. McCarthy evidently enjoyed campaigning, and even forty years later his aides could recall some of his witticisms. His style did raise some eyebrows: one profile noted that he took no advice but dispensed it instead, and his friend Maurice Rosenblatt recalled with wry horror that McCarthy's friends implored him "to campaign more than a five day week at the end. And his answer was, 'Look, I'm going to either end up in the United States Senate or teaching. I will not stay in the House.'" He traveled the state with Governor Freeman, who was facing re-election, but he was not unduly interested in his fellow Democrats. When asked to provide a strong endorsement statement for his successor in the Fourth District, McCarthy finally produced eight words: "Looking forward to campaigning with you this fall."[36]

McCarthy had every reason to feel confident on polling day. Although both major newspapers, the *Minneapolis Tribune* and the *St. Paul Pioneer Press,* had endorsed Thye, their praise was lukewarm and neither criticized McCarthy with any great conviction. McCarthy was judged to have a slight edge in the polls, but he was not nearly as well known as the long-serving Republican senator. As one writer put it: "In essence the contest is between the personal popularity of Ed Thye against Gene McCarthy and the hard-hitting Democratic organization." The mild weather of Election Day brought a huge turnout to the polls, with officials being greeted by lines of waiting voters when they arrived to open the polling stations, and the majority favored McCarthy. He was elected to the Senate by 608,847 votes to 535,629, thirteen years after first entering the DFL. The average McCarthy voter, a study later declared, "would have been a low-income, middle-aged Irishman with his home in St. Paul. He should also have belonged to the Catholic Church and a trade union." With nearly a quarter of the state's population comprising German and Irish Catholics, McCarthy's religion, according to *Congressional Quarterly,* "seemed to have helped him more than it hurt him." As one Irish Catholic housewife put it: "McCarthy is a very intelligent conservative. It's too bad he's not a Republican but he has my vote. The only thing I hold against him is the crowd of Democrats he's surrounded by."[37]

McCarthy himself attributed his victory to rural displeasure at Eisenhower's farm program, the problems of economic recession, and "general dissatisfaction with the record of the Republican administration." It was also beyond question that he had been helped by the efforts of Governor Freeman and Hubert Humphrey on his behalf. Freeman privately believed that their commitment to appearing with the less widely known McCarthy had effectively won him the election, and was disappointed at what he saw as McCarthy's ingratitude. McCarthy was, in fact, still extremely dependent on Humphrey and Freeman for support in the state. He also benefited from the angry reaction of Minnesota's farmers against Secretary of Agriculture Ezra Taft Benson's stated purpose of ending the system of federal farm price supports. Throughout the decade, farm surpluses had been driving prices down, and by 1958, Benson's policy of buying up the surplus had proved a fiasco and farmers had fallen into the lowest 20 percent of national earners.[38]

Most of all, however, McCarthy benefited from the national Democratic sweep of 1958. Across the nation voters repudiated Eisenhower's passivity in the face of one of the sharpest economic declines since the Civil War, with unemployment rising to 5.2 million (7.5 percent), heavy job losses in the industrial states of the Northeast and Midwest, and a greater sense of public gloom about the economy than at any time since the Depression. Eisenhower, it seemed, weakened by ill health and advancing years, had lost his touch: since his second inauguration, his approval ratings had fallen from 79 percent to 49 percent. The Democrats could not but profit from his economic misfortunes, the Sherman Adams scandal, the effect of the Soviet *Sputnik* launch, and general weariness with an administration apparently more interested in golf than in government.[39]

McCarthy's victory, then, was part of a trend. What is more, it was the election of 1958, rather than the presidential election of 1960, that reinvigorated Democratic liberalism and marked the beginning of eight years of liberal legislation in Congress. Especially in the states of the Northeast and the industrial Middle West, the pattern of the 1958 results would ensure Democratic and liberal political predominance until the catastrophic reverses of 1966. In the Senate, for example, no party in history had ever won so many seats in a single election: the Democratic margin widened from 49–47 to 65–35. This also meant that the conservative Democratic congressional leadership would find it more difficult to restrain their liberal colleagues. The results, said Pennsylvania's liberal senator Joseph Clark, "exceeded our fondest hopes." Humphrey's aide William Connell commented that the Democratic triumphs in the North meant that the Senate was now virtually "a liberal institution." In 1960, therefore, John Kennedy was not the instigator but the beneficiary of the northern liberal revival. Liberal reform clubs were thriving in populous states such as New York, California, Pennsylvania and Michigan, and the DFL in Minnesota was just one of a number of state parties and local groups that enjoyed unprecedented success between 1956 and 1962 with the same revived and revivified Fair Deal agenda that would become the basis of the New Frontier.[40]

McCarthy himself could hardly have joined the Senate at a more propitious moment. Since his career in the House had been so successful, great things were expected of him. The *Christian Science Monitor,* for instance, observed that he promised to be all the things Republicans scorned—"a professor, a scholar, and worst of all, an egghead"—but also noted that as "a rangy, gentle fellow who specializes in poker-faced humor," he was likely to be a popular figure. The influential columnist Drew Pearson declared the new senator "a tough battle-seasoned House veteran who's sure to become a leader and wear no one's brand," and another commentator, Charles Bartlett, announced, "The new McCarthy is a man to watch." McCarthy was evidently excited about his new role and had high hopes of substantive debate and legislative craftsmanship. It would be "more orderly" than the House, he told one interviewer: "There will be regular roll calls and sessions. There will be more time for study and debate of problems facing our country."[41]

But McCarthy would have to learn to bite his tongue and accept the patronage of his seniors if he was to succeed in the Senate. A stray remark that Lyndon Johnson could be expected to "lean ahead" of the wind of liberal success, for example, almost soured their relationship before McCarthy had even entered the chamber. Hubert Humphrey warned his new colleague that Johnson was "very sensitive" to criticism and was "blowing a gasket," while Johnson told Sam Rayburn to caution his cocksure young protégé. If McCarthy hoped to get ahead in the Senate, he could not afford to alienate the hot-tempered Johnson. It was only a minor row, and one that soon cooled, but it augured ill for the relationship between the sardonic McCarthy and the thin-skinned Texan.[42]

CHAPTER SIX

The Politics of Ambition

T he most common perception of the Senate was that it was, as one observer put it, "the most exclusive gentlemen's club in Washington." Indeed, the cloakroom at the back of the Senate chamber, where most informal wheeling and dealing went on, was furnished exactly like a gentlemen's club, with stuffed leather chairs and discreet phone booths. Even at the beginning of the 1960s, the chamber had the atmosphere of an exclusive institution closed to public scrutiny: voice votes were anonymous and roll calls rare. Television and radio generally did not carry proceedings live, and contemporary admirers lauded the heavy atmosphere of formal courtesy, "this lovely aura of senatorial ethics, which rises like a fragrance to the gallery, oozing through the florid prose of the *Congressional Record,*" as one described it. The Senate, like some isolated, backward tribe fit for anthropological study, was said to be characterized by "folkways": specialization, reciprocity, restraint, institutional pride and politeness. New senators were expected to respect and follow these folkways, to deliver on their promises to their colleagues, to discharge their assignments efficiently, and to observe the boundaries that divided restrained debate from mere attention seeking or violent partisanship.[1]

For Eugene McCarthy, who was not only familiar with the routine and rituals of the House but had spent years in the tightly ordered world of the

Benedictines, the atmosphere of the Senate was highly congenial. It might, he later wrote with heavy irony, be "the last primitive society in the Western world," with its respect for seniority, "occupancy and the territorial imperative"; yet he felt that both its weaknesses and the case for reform were exaggerated. Institutions that had slowly developed over time should not be reformed in haste, and the "reasonable rules of conduct" and emphasis on "a tolerable accommodation" encouraged by Senate traditions should be applauded. Not all liberals agreed with McCarthy. Paul Douglas, for example, thought the Senate folkways were simply "mutual backstabbing and mutual logrolling." For all its gentility, the Senate was also "closed," "inward-looking" and "unequal," "like a small town" in its narrowness and intolerance.[2]

What outraged liberals most was the sheer conservatism of the Senate as an institution. Even McCarthy objected to what was called "the Club," an association of older members, usually southern Democrats or conservative Republicans, that wielded disproportionate influence irrespective of party loyalty. Throughout the 1950s the Senate had been dominated by a bipartisan conservative coalition, bolstered by the seniority principle and the filibuster. It remained opposed to civil rights and congressional reform and firmly supported the military and belligerent anti-Communism abroad. The southern presence on the Democratic Steering Committee remained just short of 50 percent until 1964, even though the national Democratic Party was beginning to fall out of favor in the South. Indeed, the southern domination of senatorial committees actually increased between the mid-1950s and mid-1960s, as more and more southerners filled the top seats on important committees such as Appropriations, Armed Services, Finance and Foreign Relations. Nothing was more important to a senator than committee membership. Far from being Woodrow Wilson's "dim dungeons of silence," the committees were "the Senators' show," an opportunity to grab the limelight and make a name. Not surprisingly, therefore, it was in the committees' membership that the Senate caste system and the dominance of conservatives and the South were most evident. Control of committee assignments was also one way in which the majority leader, Lyndon Johnson, maintained control of his Democratic troops. Ever since 1953, he had been careful to ensure that every Democratic member had at least one major committee seat regardless of his or her own political position. Committee assignments were perhaps the most recognizable feature of Johnson's skillful, informal and bipartisan management of the Senate, which infuriated liberals because it gave them little chance of ever overturning the conservative control of the institution.[3]

Washington was a city that lived for one thing alone: politics. For a senator, there was no escape from the endless discussion of influence and ambition, factions and feuds. "From your orange juice at breakfast to your bourbon nightcap, it's all politics or no politics," Johnson told Hubert Humphrey. "The Senate is not a part-time job." By 1959 the chamber sat for almost the entire year, recessing only in August. Never had the stresses on an individual senator been greater, with fourteen-hour days not uncommon. One contemporary, Fred Harris, recalled that "time for reading and reflection was almost non-existent." Joseph Clark, representing Pennsylvania, expected to receive between 1,000 and 10,000 letters a week and a total of perhaps 110,000 letters a year. One of McCarthy's assistants told an interviewer that in 1948 they received letters; in 1954, telegrams; and in 1959, telephone calls. By the late 1960s, constituents were waiting at the office before the staff had even arrived for the day. Many observers remarked that behind the clichéd façade of the gentlemen's club, senators were lonely and harried men. Edmund Muskie admitted that most days he rarely saw more than one or two of his colleagues; another colleague said that one of the "major frustrations" was that there was simply no time for socializing with other senators. In truth, noted one writer, the Senate was less a club than "a confederation of a hundred baronies," the rulers of which occasionally sallied forth to make speeches or show off at hearings. What made matters worse was that so many senators were, in Hubert Humphrey's words, "prima donnas." Each senator had fought long and hard to become the center of attention and the focus of so many pressures: it was hardly surprising, then, that close friendships were so rare and loneliness so common. In fact, there was no better example of the reserved senator who guarded his privacy from his fellows and regularly retreated to the sanctity of his inner office than Eugene McCarthy.[4]

Accession to the Senate inevitably brought with it a level of prestige hitherto unknown to McCarthy, but if the ambitious new member wanted to wield in the Senate the same influence that he had in the House, that prestige had to be forged anew into power. One avenue was specialization: the six-year term meant that senators could devote their time to a single issue, linking their name to it by speeches, legislation and publications. Notable liberal examples from McCarthy's generation were Edmund Muskie (on the environment) and Edward Kennedy (on health). But perhaps the most fruitful approach was sheer hard work, what one senator called "just year after year of patience—willingness to carry at least your fair share of the work." According to senatorial lore, there were two types of members: "show horses" and "work horses." There was little mileage in being a show horse. The hardworking member could expect his career to advance step by slow step: first, shoring up his base at home, laboring for his constituents, and making allies in Congress; then broadening his outlook, moving onto a policy committee, and becoming an issue specialist; finally, reaching one of the prestigious "power" committees and possibly joining the party leadership. There was no shortcut to success, although friendship with the powerful older southerners was no hindrance to advancement. On the other hand, a liberal Cassandra was unlikely to get ahead. "Fellows who back hopeless causes all the time are also impotent legislators," explained one Democratic member. Some liberals, such as Paul Douglas, despairing of or rejecting the possibility of congressional prominence, chose to address a wider audience and used the chamber as a public soapbox for any number of issues; they rarely earned the respect of their colleagues. Most of all, the criteria for success were personal: the capacity for work, the willingness to take responsibility, perceived "manliness" and toughness. McCarthy had proved in the House that the game of influence was one he could play effectively. Few Senate newcomers in 1959 could have expected so much from their new occupation.[5]

With the Democratic margin in the Senate having risen from two seats to thirty, liberal hopes were high for the Eighty-sixth Congress. Opinion polls showed that the public favored legislative activity on such issues as the school integration crisis, federal aid to education, and unemployment. There were nine new liberal members, including McCarthy, Edmund Muskie (Maine), Philip Hart (Michigan) and Stephen Young (Ohio), and flushed with their recent victories they struck commentators as noticeably "buoyant, self-confident and highly optimistic." In fact, the new class was markedly liberal, young and aggressive; many members had won only narrow victories and were eager to promote their own political fortunes. Still, for some observers the new intake was rather too slick, young and telegenic, a far cry from the populist tub-thumpers of the past. The new liberals, wrote Karl Meyer and Lewis Coser, promised managerial tinkering rather than genuine change, a "bland smile" rather than true grit. The Fair Deal had given way to nothing more than a "Smooth Deal." As McCarthy later recognized, however, the liberal class of 1959 "changed the whole Senate," setting the stage for the civil rights legislation of the 1960s. To Joseph Clark, the Senate was simply "a different place" after 1959. Between 1959 and 1965, meanwhile, another twenty-three northern Democrats entered the Senate, including such eminent names as Edward and Robert Kennedy, George McGovern and Walter Mondale. Even if the querulous liberals never really formed a tightly united and disciplined bloc, their very presence had consequences both for policy and for procedure. The pressure for the Democratic Party to push for progressive reform in Congress was now intense, and most liberals argued that the elections had been a mandate for increased federal spending. Indeed, John F. Kennedy's New Frontier of 1961–1963 would largely be based on the liberals' unsuccessful initiatives on health care, tax cuts, area redevelopment and manpower retraining, all of which were important liberal issues in Eisenhower's final years.[6]

McCarthy's integration into the life of the Senate was far easier and quicker than it had been into the House in 1949. Although close personal friendships between members were rare, Abigail McCarthy recalled that the atmosphere among the new intake was that of "hearty back-slapping humor." McCarthy, as if cultivating the reputation of a maverick, later liked to play down his friendships with other senators, explaining that "you sort of ought to maintain your distance from every Senator." Nonetheless, in the late 1950s he was a popular character. True, he was always a calm, detached figure, intimate only with a few chosen friends such as Senators Hart and Muskie, but in the Senate dining room, he was witty, charming and gregarious company. McCarthy, Hart and Muskie were often bracketed with Mike Mansfield and Edward Kennedy (who joined the Senate in January 1963) as an intimate cluster of Catholic liberals. McCarthy also greatly admired the maverick Oregon senator Wayne Morse. It was McCarthy's intimacy with Hart and Muskie that was most revealing, however. All three were introspective Catholics and had been notably shy when young, a trait which still manifested itself as extreme reserve. McCarthy and Hart were bound together above all by their religion and remained friends in later years despite their disagreements over Vietnam and McCarthy's political behavior. McCarthy and Muskie, however, were both sensitive and essentially withdrawn men whose friendship was eventually broken by ambition. Both were highly intelligent and given to harsh words: McCarthy with quiet malice, Muskie with temperamental fury. They often went golfing together, and on one occasion were fined by the police for illegal bird hunting in Muskie's home state of Maine. They sat in the Senate back row, where they were eventually joined by Edward Kennedy, and, unusually, refused to move forward with seniority. In their first year in the Senate, with their families often away, the three "chummed around together" and "ate a lot of bad food together" on Connecticut Avenue. They were sometimes mocked by their staffs as "homebodies" from the country whose idea of a wild night out was "eating chow mein at the Moon Palace restaurant."[7]

The single most important colleague for any Democratic senator was Lyndon Johnson, the majority leader. Johnson's style was restless, intrusive, charismatic and exhausting, but by 1959 his colleagues had become weary of his manipulation and emphasis on bipartisanship. McCarthy recognized that now that the Democrats enjoyed a handsome majority, Johnson's tactics, and even Johnson himself, were outdated. The very existence of the new generation of liberals was an implicit threat to his authority, and in 1959 the habitual criticisms by Paul Douglas were endorsed by more moderate figures such as Patrick McNamara (Michigan) and Albert Gore (Tennessee), men already established in the chamber and so with little to lose. One of McCarthy's own first acts as a new senator was to support an unsuccessful bid to reform the rules on cloture; in this new environment, opposing Johnson's position was no longer a risk. All this made Johnson's distribution of committee assignments even more significant. In the past he had used the lure of attractive committees and responsibilities to cultivate the likes of Humphrey and Mansfield; now he tried to impress the incoming liberals with his openhandedness.[8]

The class of 1959, therefore, was treated better than any other in the 1950s and 1960s in terms of committee assignments. Eight of the newcomers were placed on so-called prestige committees—for example, Clair Engle (Armed Services) and Gale McGee (Appropriations)—and McCarthy was given perhaps the choicest prize of all, a seat on the Finance Committee. Many of the new boys who had opposed Johnson on the cloture issue were banished to lesser committees, but not McCarthy. For the political analyst William S. White this was a sign that McCarthy was "in a position immensely to forward his career and his region" and was a name "to reckon with in the Senate, and the country, for decades to come." McCarthy's preferential treatment in 1959 intrigued commentators for years thereafter. Why had he fared so well? One obvious reason was that he was, like Johnson, a former Rayburn protégé and had been earmarked as a coming man. Yet evidently he was not a Johnson intimate: they had, of course, fallen out over McCarthy's wisecrack even before he had once entered the chamber, and McCarthy's advertising consultant told his administrative assistant that he was "impressed and slightly surprised" at the assignment "in the light of the Johnson-McCarthy history." The Finance seat was particularly sensitive because Johnson, as a Texan, opposed the constant attempts of Paul Douglas and Albert Gore to cut the oil depletion allowance, a controversial tax loophole which exempted from federal taxation 27.5 percent of the gross income of the oil and gas companies. For Douglas, as for many liberals, support for the allowance was simply incompatible with sincere liberalism. Douglas himself had waited seven years to join the committee and was "ecstatic" that a liberal freshman had been assigned to bolster his cause.[9]

Certainly McCarthy's appointment was a surprise to his fellow liberals. Joseph Clark, for example, was surprised that William Proxmire had once again been overlooked in favor of the more junior McCarthy, and Proxmire himself was furious. McCarthy later recalled that Johnson had made a point of telling the press that "it was a real thing for him to do because he'd bypassed Proxmire," the implication being that McCarthy now owed him a favor. Johnson's notes of a private conversation with McCarthy in January 1960, the only such record extant, make it clear that the majority leader did feel that McCarthy was now in his debt. Arguing against an expansion of the Democratic Policy Committee, Johnson reminded McCarthy that a free and democratic vote would never have put him on Finance, and grumbled: "This son of a bitch Proxmire is after me because of what I did for you. You came in here and I took you before Proxmire." Johnson *had* given McCarthy preference, then, but, as always, he expected a return on his investment. The next five years were to bring McCarthy and Johnson ever closer together, and McCarthy's relationship with Johnson became probably the single most important influence on his future political career.[10]

The suspicion that McCarthy had somehow done a deal with Johnson and the oil interests in order to get his seat on the Finance Committee dogged him throughout his Senate career. In June 1959, in his first real test, McCarthy startled the liberals by failing to support Douglas's attempt to slash the depletion allowance. Douglas had simply assumed that McCarthy would back him, but first McCarthy refused to co-sponsor the amendment, scrawling a big handwritten "no" on his letter, and then he failed to turn up in the Senate for the crucial vote. According to Douglas:

> He said he was going down to the dining room for lunch, but he somehow allowed me to believe that he would be back in time to vote. He was not, but strolled in carelessly after the vote . . . I finally decided that he had been put on the committee after he agreed with the party leaders to go along on depletion and other important points. Indeed, he seemed not to regard taxation as an important matter.[11]

Even forty years later McCarthy groaned at the mention of the subject and dismissed it as "never a big issue." The allowance was "an obsession" for Douglas and his friends, he said; there was no point in bringing it up every session, and no point in voting against it unless they could win. But the oil depletion allowance *was* an important issue—not to the general public, perhaps, but certainly to the Treasury and the oil companies, not to mention liberal pressure groups. Douglas' assistant Howard Shuman later claimed that McCarthy had effectively sold his vote to the charismatic Oklahoma Democrat and defender of the oil interests, Robert Kerr. Shuman maintained that he had discovered the following story:

> When McCarthy came to the Senate, he wanted to be on the Finance Committee. He was told by Johnson that he had to clear it with Kerr who was the number two on the committee, and the oil senator from Oklahoma . . . Kerr said, "There's one thing he's got to do, he's got to vote with us on gas and oil." And McCarthy agreed.[12]

Whether this was truth or gossip is impossible to determine. In 1964 the liberal columnist Drew Pearson printed the allegation that McCarthy had won his seat "only after an advance pledge of loyalty to the oil and gas politicians." In McCarthy's own files are letters to and from Minnesota oil executives referring to a meeting in December 1958, after his election to the Senate and before his assignment to Finance, during which he evidently assured them of his support for the depletion allowance. If it seems hard to imagine that so proud a man as McCarthy would have stooped to a deal with the oil lobby, still the anecdotal evidence means the suspicion can never entirely be dispelled.[13]

Far from entering the Senate as a confirmed maverick, McCarthy was as devoted as any other member to the pursuit of patronage, influence and power. In later years he made a point of claiming that the eccentric and single-minded Wayne Morse had been his model, but there is little evidence for that in his first years as a senator. Unlike Morse, McCarthy never made "a display of systematic independence" from his party. In fact, McCarthy was typical of the 1959 liberal newcomers: when the voting bell sounded, virtually all remained on the inside track rather than defy the leadership and assert their own individuality. Among McCarthy's friends, Edmund Muskie contrived to fall out with Johnson within weeks of joining the Senate, received awful committee assignments and refused to speak to his leader for a year. But even Muskie had nothing but contempt for the likes of Morse and Douglas, who preferred a martyr's defeat to a compromise victory. Philip Hart's wife, Jane, recalled how at a party for the Democratic freshmen, Johnson was raised on the telephone and "one by one, like little boys, they trooped to the phone to say 'Yes, Mr. Leader. No, Mr.

Leader. Of course, Mr. Leader.'" McCarthy's senior colleague, Hubert Humphrey, offered the perfect example of a dedicated liberal who, despite a difficult start in 1949, had nevertheless managed to "get along" with the conservative power brokers; indeed, Humphrey proudly boasted of his preference for compromise over "losing . . . in the name of moral principle or liberal convictions." McCarthy himself, for all his air of casual detachment, was fiercely ambitious. His debut in the Senate held out the prospect of great success to come, and it was not for nothing that columnists and commentators advised their readers that he was the coming man of the liberal wing.[14]

For all his alleged derelictions on the Finance Committee, McCarthy's overall voting record during his first years as a senator was liberal perfection. He voted consistently in favor of increased federal spending, in opposition to the conservative coalition, and in support of the Democratic Party. According to some indices, his record was even better than that of Hubert Humphrey. On civil rights, which was quickly becoming the supreme litmus test for liberalism, McCarthy could not be faulted; he even risked the wrath of the leadership to support a revision of Rule 22, the notorious filibuster rule that had obstructed so much legislation in the past. Although he did not identify himself with the issue to the extent of becoming a recognized leader, McCarthy told the Senate that the question was a "moral" one of "basic human rights," and he wrote an article for the ADA demanding that the Democrats mount a "total" response to meet the "total challenge" of racial discrimination. Until then, he had reserved such rhetoric for his advocacy of anti-Communism abroad. In short, McCarthy's elevation to the Senate, the controversy over the Finance Committee aside, did not affect in any way his steady commitment to ADA liberalism. Indeed, for all that it was ever more technocratic and managerial, political liberalism was also increasingly self-assertive as 1960 approached, with Senate veterans, including not only Clark and Douglas but also Humphrey, Patrick McNamara and John Kennedy, privately challenging Johnson to give the party greater ideological drive. McCarthy himself, a member of the ADA national board, used his status as a senator to call for an end to political homogenization and an aggressive liberal campaign in 1960 on the issues of civil rights, labor reforms, unemployment and the environment.[15]

One of the decisive issues in the elections of 1958 had been the problem of growing unemployment, a product not only of the recession but also of technological change, the decline of heavy industry and the changing demands on the American worker. With 4.7 million workers still out of work in January 1959, the two parties bickered inconclusively over the question of federally funded unemployment insurance, and in March McCarthy proposed an amendment to prolong the current emergency aid package until 1 July, extending payments to 100,000 workers who would otherwise have been without benefits. It failed, but it signaled McCarthy's interest in what was very much an issue of the moment. Northern Democrats and union leaders were demanding that Johnson present an alternative to Eisenhower's passivity, and Patrick McNamara, whose home state of Michigan was particularly hard hit, threatened to become a constant thorn in Johnson's side unless action was forthcoming. It was in response to this pressure that Johnson, on 12 September 1959, agreed to set up a temporary nine-man committee to investigate the problem of unemployment. His critics from the industrial Middle West, McNamara and Clark, were on the committee, but to the astonishment of most observers the chairman was Eugene McCarthy: a pointed rebuke from Johnson to the older senators who had been "tormenting him on the quiet." Even McCarthy was surprised that someone "pretty new in the Senate" should be given such a position. As the political scientist Michael Foley put it, there could be no more striking illustration of "the rapid strides a newcomer could make in the Eighty-sixth Congress"; nor could there be any better indication of McCarthy's own standing as the star of his generation.[16]

McCarthy's stewardship of his committee was characteristically sober, well informed and unexciting, although one newspaper photograph caught him fast asleep while the United Auto Workers boss Walter Reuther was exhibiting a chart of unemployment rates. The minutes of the committee meetings that still exist, however, suggest that the real driving force was Joseph Clark, who pushed the case for field hearings in selected states. Clark certainly knew more about the issue, as was hardly surprising in a senator from suffering Pennsylvania, and it was Clark who argued the case for a federal training and retraining program, subsequently enacted as the Manpower Development and Training Act (1962). McCarthy never quite managed the trick of turning his office into extensive publicity and influence for himself. Occasionally newspapers reported his attacks on the Eisenhower administration on the subject—but only occasionally.[17]

The committee did work hard, however. By the time its report was released on 30 March 1960, it had met twenty-nine times and held twenty-seven full days of hearings in twelve states, involving a host of federal and local officials, academic experts and spokesmen for the unemployed, and amassing four thousand pages of testimony and statements. The final draft of the report was written by McCarthy himself and his staff and called for federal assistance and public works in areas suffering from chronic unemployment, national standards of unemployment insurance, action to fight racial and other discrimination, a youth conservation corps, expanded vocational training and federal funding for retraining the jobless. McCarthy conceded: "It was almost an academic report before we got done with it." For all that it was dry, the report was also "an overwhelming demand for action on behalf of the structurally unemployed": older workers, minorities, school dropouts and residents of depressed areas. Its recommendations added weight to the growing pressure for a more activist federal government in the 1960s, and most found their way onto the 1960 Democratic platform. By 1963 many had found their way into the statute books as part of the New Frontier: area redevelopment, a youth conservation corps, and national vocational training, for example. Samuel Merrick, who served as counsel to the committee and then as congressional liaison officer for the Labor Department under Kennedy and Johnson, later thought that the Manpower Development Act "came into existence because of that committee." McCarthy, he acknowledged, had not been personally responsible, but as "a very hard-working chairman" who knew when to defer to experts, he deserved some of the credit. It was McCarthy's first significant Senate accomplishment—and perhaps also his last.[18]

Most liberal Democrats looked forward to the presidential election of 1960 with justified confidence. In 1959 McCarthy declared that the country needed a vigorous leader who could "meet Communism in the competition of ideas" and increase the economy "at a rate of 10 to 12 percent." There was, however, no one obvious Democratic candidate, although Johnson, Humphrey, Kennedy and even Stevenson were highly favored. With none likely to tie up the nomination well in advance of the convention, this meant that a young and ambitious Democratic senator needed to play his cards carefully if he were to retain the respect of all sides and the confidence of the eventual victor. McCarthy, as a respected liberal Catholic and coming man, would be a useful ally, and there was some speculation in 1959 that he might support his Minnesota patron, Humphrey, or his fellow Catholic, Kennedy. But McCarthy privately mocked all the contenders and told his friends that none were as qualified as he was, an extraordinarily proud assertion for a man who had been a senator for barely a year. He was, he declared, "twice as liberal as Humphrey [and] twice as Catholic as Kennedy," a remark that soon found its way into the press and that he unsuccessfully sought to deny having made. He would, however, have to make a stand sooner or later. Reflecting on the choice, McCarthy later chuckled: "I was for everybody in '60!" In fact, his strategy could hardly have been worse. Of the four main candidates, he ended up supporting, occasionally even at the same time, three of them—but never the eventual winner, Kennedy. To support one Kennedy rival might be regarded as a misfortune; to support all three looked like horrendous political judgment.[19]

McCarthy's first commitment was to the campaign of his senior colleague, Hubert Humphrey. This was essentially unavoidable, and it surprised no one. Humphrey told him that while he needed his help "as never before," he recognized that McCarthy had to "think through very carefully" his involvement in presidential politics, and would respect whatever decision he made. McCarthy agreed to help, not least because he would hardly have won friends in Minnesota by refusing, and devoted most of his energy to campaigning for Humphrey, particularly among Catholic voters, in the primary of neighboring Wisconsin. Some Minnesota Democrats suggested that McCarthy did not work quite as hard as he might have on Humphrey's behalf, but McCarthy did make regular appearances on stages and in the newspapers to push his friend's candidacy, and Humphrey himself lauded him afterward as "one helluva great guy." It was the Humphrey campaign in Wisconsin and West Virginia that for the first time brought McCarthy into direct opposition with Jack Kennedy and the Kennedy family. Several times in the spring of 1960 McCarthy stood in for Humphrey in debates with Kennedy, although they were fairly low-key affairs. On one occasion, Kennedy privately complained to McCarthy about an "outrageous" Humphrey pamphlet attacking his record; McCarthy, deadpan, replied: "Jack, it's not so bad a record for a man from Massachusetts." There was one serious dispute, however, when Kennedy called McCarthy to his Senate office and told him: "Tell Hubert to lay off in West Virginia or we will unload on him." McCarthy later recalled that the Humphrey campaign had infuriated Kennedy by flirting with anti-Catholicism and alleging that his father was buying up votes, while the Kennedys responded with attacks on Humphrey's war record and personal patriotism. In fact, despite the personal friendship between Humphrey and Kennedy, the tone of that campaign did sour relations between the two camps, and many in the Humphrey campaign, including McCarthy, never forgot or forgave the violence of the Kennedys' attacks on Humphrey's patriotism.[20]

The personal relationship between McCarthy and Kennedy is important not only in itself, but also because of its profound consequences for McCarthy's political career. Indeed, McCarthy's blatant hostility to Kennedy in 1960 was as significant a turning point in his career as any other. There was no great personal reason for the two men to become antagonistic; when they were colleagues in the House, their relations had been "casual, friendly, and occasionally social," and McCarthy had been invited to Kennedy's wedding and occasionally to dinner. McCarthy claims today that they were good friends. However, by the late 1950s McCarthy's contemporaries had noticed that he was becoming bitter and contemptuous in his private remarks about his richer and more prominent colleague. During the 1956 Democratic convention he refused to help Kennedy's vice presidential campaign, claiming that Minnesota was too Protestant a state to ever back a Catholic. According to his aide Ted Sorensen, Kennedy began hearing "that McCarthy was around Washington making adverse and nasty comments about [him]." This last point was unquestionably true, as several contemporaries have confirmed. McCarthy, who enjoyed nothing more than mocking his colleagues behind their backs, told friends that Kennedy was shallow, unintelligent, and unequipped for high office, his reputation bloated with his father's money. The columnist and Kennedy confidant Joseph Alsop recalled that during a plane journey in the late 1950s, McCarthy came and sat by him and told him a series of anecdotes about Kennedy's past: "real sort of hate stuff, and nasty hate stuff." According to Alsop, when he protested, McCarthy reacted in haughty fashion: "He rose without a word, returned to his own seat at the front of the plane, and there got out the very largest missal I have ever seen. It held an astonishing collection of long and elaborately decorated Sacred Heart page markers, one of which, I remember, was a meticulous embroidery of the Veil of Saint Veronica. For the rest of the trip, the senator held the missal very high in front of his face so that all would be sure to notice what he was studying." Alsop found that Kennedy was amused rather than outraged by the story. Sorensen remembered: "It was an antipathy on McCarthy's part that none of us ever understood." Ideologically, after all, McCarthy could have had little against Kennedy, whose overall Senate record was as liberal as any, despite the many subsequent claims to the contrary.[21]

McCarthy's unconcealed contempt for Kennedy was rooted not in ideological disagreement but in sheer jealousy. McCarthy's political contemporaries were, to a man, convinced that he wanted to be the country's first Catholic president and resented Kennedy as a threat to his ambitions. With Catholics now nearly 25 percent of the population, it was probable that sooner or later a Catholic would reach the White House, and it seemed to observers that McCarthy was simply not prepared to accept that it could be anyone but himself. After all, who was a better Catholic than the self-consciously pious former novice who attended Mass every day and who supposedly read theology for pleasure? Kennedy, in contrast, seemed to McCarthy a "spoiled rich kid," not only a bad representative of his faith but one whose success would mean the end of his own ambitions. "We thought that if JFK got the presidency it would be the end of Gene," remarked one of his friends.[22]

McCarthy's hostility, then, was partly personal pique and partly political calculation. Of course, he was not the only Catholic to regard Kennedy's elevation as a misfortune. Many Catholic intellectuals felt that Kennedy, hardly a devout man, was an inappropriate candidate to break the religious taboo; the journalist Murray Kempton, for example, wryly remarked: "We have again been cheated of the prospect of a Catholic president." Even so, few of Kennedy's Democratic contemporaries were quite so personal in their opposition. Time and again McCarthy mocked the fact that Kennedy's father was funding his campaign. When Kennedy was besieged by auto-graph hunters at a joint appearance in Detroit, McCarthy loudly remarked: "Pay no attention. The meat is so bad they had to find something to distract them." Why was he so bitter? Perhaps his contemporaries did not quite realize the intensity of McCarthy's ambition or of his frustration that Kennedy was stealing the Catholic banner. At the Democratic convention, McCarthy recklessly told Representative Tip O'Neill: "Actually, I'm the one who should be nominated. Any way you measure it, I'm a better man than John Kennedy. I'm smarter, I'm a better orator, and if they're looking for a Catholic, I'm a better Catholic. Of course, I don't have a rich father." McCarthy could not even contain himself at Kennedy's inaugura-tion; he was, said a watching friend from St. John's, "mad" with jealousy and resentment.[23]

McCarthy had chances to win back favor with the Kennedys during 1960, but he appeared to be plotting a careful course designed to annoy them as much as possible. The Kennedy campaign team noted that the Minnesota delegation to the Democratic National Convention in Los Angeles fell into two camps: the Humphrey-Freeman group, and the "labor–Catholic–Ramsey County (St. Paul) group," the latter being their best hope to sway the state to Kennedy's cause. The problem, according to Ted Sorensen, was that the natural leader of the St. Paul group, McCarthy, was so "anti-Kennedy." McCarthy demonstrated his impeccable anti-Kennedy credentials at the Minnesota delegation caucuses in Los Angeles. The del-egation, nominally for Humphrey, was actually split between Stevenson and Kennedy, and ultimately took no clear position at all. McCarthy was deter-mined to block any move to Kennedy and even publicly rejected the idea before the convention began, citing Kennedy's tactics in West Virginia as justification. At the caucus itself, McCarthy's obstinacy baffled his fellow Minnesotans; one exasperated delegate wondered aloud whether he thought he took his orders directly from his beloved St. Thomas Aquinas or from God. Still, he won the day. Toward the end of the caucus, McCarthy rose and delivered "a quiet but devastating description of Kennedy as a man of no courage." One observer recalled his words:

> Whenever I looked around when we were marching, often to defeat, on a matter of liberal principles, I would not see Jack Kennedy among us leading the pack. And when I looked back over my shoulder to see who was following, he wasn't there either.[24]

The delegates agreed not to switch from Humphrey. Not only did this further displease Kennedy, it also severely damaged, perhaps for good, relations between McCarthy and his old ally Governor Orville Freeman. Freeman had been asked to nominate Kennedy and was mentioned as a possible vice presidential candidate, but McCarthy seemed determined not to help his colleague's cause. Kennedy eventually appointed Freeman secretary of agriculture, and McCarthy's first words on greeting his old ally in Washington in January were typically caustic: "So you got your payoff."[25]

The tangled history of the 1960 Democratic convention has left many questions unresolved, but what is indisputable is that McCarthy successively backed two losing horses in an attempt to stop Kennedy's nomination. Hubert Humphrey had been effectively eliminated as a serious contender in the primaries, so the contest came down to a convoluted convention fight between John Kennedy, Adlai Stevenson and Lyndon Johnson. Stevenson drew his support from northern liberal activists, while Johnson was the candidate of the South and the party's conservative wing. Both Hubert Humphrey and Eugene McCarthy were fond of Stevenson and shared the principles of his liberal supporters; at the same time, both were also personally close to Johnson and could expect preferential treatment from a Johnson administration. Shortly after McCarthy arrived in Los Angeles, he was announced by Robert Kerr as supporting Johnson's candidacy, which McCarthy later explained as "a holding position" in case Stevenson became a candidate. Johnson, of course, was the candidate least palatable to McCarthy's fellow liberals. On the other hand, there had already been allegations that the Humphrey campaign had been a Johnson front, enjoying Johnson's patronage and financial support, and Humphrey did hold secret meetings with Johnson during the convention. Humphrey himself recalled: "Gene and I were about the only two at the time that were considered in the liberal bloc, that were willing to stick our necks out for Lyndon Johnson." Rumors circulated throughout the convention that McCarthy had been lined up as the vice presidential candidate on a Johnson ticket. Before and during the convention newspaper reports claimed that McCarthy was being seen as the ideal northern, Catholic, liberal counterpart to the exuberant Texan. One report even claimed that Humphrey himself had generously told Johnson that his junior colleague would be the ideal running mate: "He's the guy for you. But you've got to promote him."[26]

Adlai Stevenson's campaign at the convention built on his base among upper-middle-class reform activists, typified by the "tall, emaciated young men with thin, wry beards and three-string guitars" and "ascetic, face-washed young Beat ladies in sweaters and dungarees" that Norman Mailer observed outside the arena. As the convention wore on, it became clear that Kennedy could be denied victory on the first ballot only if Stevenson managed to put together a strong liberal campaign. To emerge as the nominee, Johnson would therefore have to promote Stevenson's effort and divide the northern vote, and when both Humphrey and McCarthy abruptly announced that they were supporting Stevenson after all, many observers were convinced that this was simply a cunning ruse on Johnson's behalf. Given that both were liberals, their support for Stevenson was hardly out of character; but given their closeness to Johnson, it seems plausible that they were acting at his request. Not only did McCarthy support Stevenson, he nominated him in front of the convention, in the full glare of the national media. Yet although McCarthy told one correspondent that his ideal Democratic ticket would be the unlikely combination of Stevenson-Kennedy, he was not personally close to Stevenson in 1960. Indeed, according to Johnson's aide Bobby Baker, McCarthy agreed to nominate Stevenson only with Johnson's express permission. Even many of Stevenson's own advisers were never sure whether their candidate's cheerleader was really backing Johnson and hoping to be his vice presidential choice.[27]

McCarthy's famous nomination speech for Stevenson on 13 July was actually yet another example of his debt to Hubert Humphrey, who declined the opportunity and suggested his Minnesota colleague. Although Stevenson's aides privately questioned McCarthy's loyalty to their candidate, he was an excellent choice, appealing to both liberal and Catholic delegates, and of course he accepted. This was his opportunity to make his name in front not only of the Democratic Party hierarchy in the hall, but also of millions following the convention on television. While McCarthy had only a few hours to write the speech, he did not, as has been claimed, deliver it spontaneously; there remain copies of drafts remarkably similar to the speech as delivered. It was given at eight that evening, in front of a national audience that was still unsure whether the nominee would be Stevenson or Kennedy—or Johnson. The crowd had already been whipped up by Stevenson's backers, and McCarthy had to shout to be heard above the din, making him sound all the more passionate. This was very far from McCarthy's usual style and gave a quite erroneous impression of him as a speaker. Similarly, the reaction to the speech, with Stevenson supporters breaking into pandemonium at the final mention of his name, left onlookers with the impression that the normally dry McCarthy was a brilliant tub-thumping orator. Even Kennedy was impressed.[28]

The text of the speech, however, was very typical McCarthy, and the sheer drama of the occasion meant that the actual meaning of his words was overlooked in favor of his declamatory rhythm. Given that McCarthy knew that this was the speech of his life, he came up with a very curious effort. His principal argument was that nobody should be nominated at first: that the race should go to a second ballot, with all the delegates released from their previous commitments. It took sixteen long and wordy paragraphs for McCarthy to explain this, during which he never mentioned, or even alluded to, Stevenson himself. Rather, paragraph after paragraph dwelt on the importance of democratic and open procedures in the balloting, or else disappeared into rambling vagueness, with McCarthy pontificating on the various strains of "demagoguery." Needless to say, few delegates or reporters remembered this part of the speech. At last, just over halfway through, McCarthy produced his candidate, the "one man who did not prophesy falsely." As one writer put it, McCarthy presented Stevenson not with ringing affirmation, but with "a crescendo of negative phrases." He praised Stevenson's virtues: "patience," "tolerance," and "forbearance." What qualified Stevenson above all for the office, he explained, was his very refusal to ask for it: "History does not prove that power is always well used by those who seek it. On the contrary, the whole history of Democratic politics is to this end, that power is best exercised by those who are sought out by the people." After all this, however, McCarthy struck a rich and memorable vein, his voice rising above the growing tumult: "And so I say to you Democrats here assembled: do not turn away from this man. Do not reject this man . . . Do not reject this man who has made us all proud to be called Democrats . . . Do not leave this prophet without honor in his own party. Do not reject this man."[29]

The immediate reaction to the speech was total bedlam—then the delegates nominated Kennedy. McCarthy himself, having supported two losing candidates, watched his own slim hopes of the vice presidency disappear.

He had even lost his claim to be the party's rising Catholic star. Still, the reaction to the speech meant his political capital was not completely spent: he was now seen as "an Adlai Stevenson with sex appeal." He received thousands of complimentary letters, and many observers predicted that he was on the national stage for good. The *St. Paul Dispatch* thought that it might be "the turning point" in McCarthy's life: "It gave him a national platform before a nationwide audience. It could be the first step in making him a national figure." Kennedy invited McCarthy to breakfast the day after the nomination, asking him to open his drive in liberal Connecticut and carry a unity message to the Stevenson Democrats in southern California. McCarthy estimated that he gave sixty speeches in sixteen states for Kennedy during the campaign, and Kennedy showed a deft diplomatic touch of his own after the election by visiting McCarthy in hospital, where he was recovering from pneumonia. All the same, the events of 1960 had unquestionably damaged McCarthy's reputation with the new leader of his party and his country, even if they had won him a wider national following in the process. With Kennedy's platform echoing the liberal agenda of the late 1950s, and the remnants of the New Deal coalition contriving some-how to scrape him past Nixon into the presidency, it seemed that McCarthy would have to abandon any thoughts of high office and content himself with a quiet life in the Senate.[30]

From Kennedy's inauguration in January 1961 to his assassination in November 1963, McCarthy's career was moribund. According to one pro-file written in 1964, McCarthy "virtually withdrew from active politics, not only cut off from the White House, but aloof from the major business of the Senate." He could hardly be bothered even to make the rudimentary ges-tures of support for and loyalty to the new Democratic president; he called the Kennedy clan "Big Brother" and ridiculed Kennedy's speeches among his staff. The president did try to bring McCarthy back into the fold, inviting him to give the administration's speech at the annual journalists' Gridiron Dinner in 1961, for example, and asking him to carry a message to the pope in Rome. Their assistants discussed how the two might be reconciled, and in 1962 a Kennedy trip to Minnesota passed off successfully and marked the beginning of a mild rapprochement. By the end of Kennedy's life McCarthy was even "very generous" about him in private and told one friend that Kennedy was "a man he could talk to, a man who stood for a good number of things he did." After Kennedy was murdered McCarthy paid him handsome tributes; he wrote about him with great respect and maintained in conversation that he and Kennedy had always been the best of friends. But he did not, in truth, enjoy good relations with the Kennedy administration from 1961 to 1963 and was often scathing about the New Frontier. In this he was not alone: other Senate liberals were equally frustrated with the administration's caution, apparent centrism and occasionally clumsy management of Congress. Throughout the period he publicly criticized the White House for its failure to lead on controversial issues, its excessive secrecy and its inattention to Congress. In the *New Republic* in April 1963 he wondered whether "the Administration is not so busy taking soundings that it forgets to sail the ship."[31]

Despite all this sniping at the White House, McCarthy remained a loyal Democrat on the Senate floor. His overall voting record was resolutely liberal throughout the 1960s. Contemporary analyses characterized McCarthy as a committed liberal, consistently voting against the Senate conservatives and for an expanded federal government. A later study by the political scientist Michael Foley ranked 91.2 percent of McCarthy's votes between 1959 and 1970 as "liberal," comparable with Humphrey's (89.5 percent), Muskie's (86.1 percent), McGovern's (90.0 percent) and Robert Kennedy's (92.3 percent). As far as civil rights were concerned, major events such as the clashes in Mississippi and Alabama provoked no great reaction from McCarthy; he had no need to emphasize his outrage over an issue on which his record was already very strong. Far from being an accessory to racism, he unwaveringly supported civil rights legislation and frequently spoke out emphasizing the moral urgency of the issue and urging greater boldness from the White House. Indeed, when McCarthy did rouse himself to speak on contemporary domestic politics, he took positions well to the left of the administration, for instance calling poverty "no longer defensible" and demanding action on issues of welfare and housing. Throughout Kennedy's presidency, meanwhile, McCarthy maintained his interest in the issue of Mexican migrant labor and again lobbied unsuccessfully for legislation to improve the migrants' pay and working conditions. He was not demonstrably deficient in his Senate duties, as was also frequently charged. McCarthy might have been more laid-back, more detached and more playful than his colleagues, but his roll-call participation score in the Eighty-sixth and Eighty-seventh Congresses, covering over eight hundred votes, was a very decent 83.5 percent, just above the average for all Democrats.[32]

One reason that McCarthy did have what one writer called a "slightly suspect" reputation was that his record on the Finance Committee was not that of a crusader. Indeed, while McCarthy understood the intricacies of taxation and finance perhaps better than most of his contemporaries, he evinced little interest in turning this to liberal advantage. He proposed obscure bills to cut taxes on telephone and telegraph companies, to give tax credits for the pension funds of the self-employed, or to slash taxes on the foreign subsidiaries of American corporations, none of which managed to capture the public imagination. Like most other Democrats, he supported Kennedy's major tax cut plan. And although McCarthy voted for Paul Douglas' futile attempt in 1962 to cut the oil depletion allowance, he still refused to think of it as an important issue. In fact, McCarthy may well have felt free to vote with Douglas simply because he knew that the measure had no chance of success. Liberal activists remained astonished by his insouciance about the subject, while McCarthy explained that he favored "some reduction in the $27\frac{1}{2}$ percent depletion allowance, but not the entire removal of it." It continued to annoy him that those supporting the allowance were seen as "immoral and seeking special privilege" while their adversaries were "pure." More than any other issue, this drove a wedge between the sardonic, detached McCarthy and his more zealous liberal colleagues, and the accusations that McCarthy was the pliant representative of "special interests" on the committee continued to intensify in liberal circles as the decade progressed.[33]

With McCarthy's career apparently stalled, his commitment to partisan politics began to dwindle. Between 1960 and 1963 he gradually detached himself from the ADA, finally resigning from the board in February 1963. He later vaguely explained that he disagreed with them over foreign policy; according to the activist Joseph Rauh, the real reason was that he objected to their attacks on Lyndon Johnson. Like many impecunious liberals, he was a favorite on the paid lecture circuit, spending much of his free time outside the Senate and often far from Washington. There seemed no end to the school convocations, banquets, conventions and religious organizations that would pay a senator for a short, formulaic lecture, and McCarthy was even thought to owe his $75,000 house to his popularity as a speaker. His ebbing interest in politics surprised observers: at a lecture at the University of Illinois, for instance, he declined to stay behind and chat with his audience but quickly disappeared to drink whisky and discuss literature with a historian friend. In the Senate itself he struck observers as listless and lazy, content to bask in the shadow of Hubert Humphrey. On the Agriculture Committee he could barely muster even a pretense of interest, and was described by his former ally Orville Freeman, secretary of agriculture, as "totally unresponsive." Even at meetings of the Finance Committee, McCarthy, "to break his boredom," would telephone friends to "chat about nothing."[34]

McCarthy's office was more an oasis of calm and silence than a whirli-gig of activity like other senators' offices, and Hubert Humphrey's staff dubbed it "Sleepy Hollow." As usual, McCarthy came up with a rationale for his dissatisfaction that he repeated for decades to come. It was the sign of a bad senator, he explained, to work too hard, to have an excellent atten-dance record, or to have a staff that was "too efficient." A worthy legislator would not be "wasting time answering roll calls and quorum calls"; he would, like McCarthy, be far above the trivialities of everyday politics. The Senate itself was a far quieter and less exacting arena under the new major-ity leader, Mike Mansfield, than it had been during McCarthy's first two years under Johnson. Mansfield himself was "more amused by McCarthy than impressed by him." McCarthy's studied contempt for its procedures owed less to the atmosphere of the institution than it did to his own irrita-tion at the frustration of his political ambitions.[35]

Although McCarthy's roll call record was good, his Democratic col-leagues were unimpressed by his transformation from bright young star to jaded cynic. Hubert Humphrey, a friend wrote, "could never even under-stand how McCarthy could hang out in his favorite watering place, the Assembly restaurant, day after day, wasting time just gabbing with cronies while there was so much work to be done on the Senate floor or in com-mittee." Worse, Humphrey was "embarrassed" by McCarthy's "constant show of blatant superiority and disdain, not only for the Senate body but for individual senators." On the other hand, McCarthy loved to cultivate the press corps, spending hours in the press gallery composing jokes about his colleagues. One striking example of this attitude was his treatment of the Maine liberal Republican Margaret Chase Smith, who prided herself on her perfect, and unmatched, roll call attendance record. McCarthy had to be persuaded by one of his aides not to ruin her record by calling for a roll call when he knew she was away; even so, he managed to indulge his spite by telling a Maine audience that it was "a terrible record" because Smith had been "wasting [her] time waiting round to vote on trivial bills." His fel-low Democrats found such behavior churlish and inexcusable. From 1961 onward McCarthy's image became increasingly tarnished. One Minnesota Farmer's Union leader recalled that he was "sulky and uncommunicative." Johnson's aide Harry McPherson remembered him "in the Senate restaurant, delivering bons mots about the political situation to infatuated reporters." Senator Herman Talmadge, noting McCarthy's absences from Finance Committee hearings and executive sessions, called him "mentally and physically lazy." And Senator Joseph Tydings recalled: "He would never help on your vital fights. You could never depend on Gene McCarthy."[36]

McCarthy's most serious problem, however, was his future in Minnesota. Few observers thought that the 1964 elections would be a landslide for the Democrats, and McCarthy's re-election was not expected to be easy. The local press noted that he had "made few ripples on the Minnesota political scene." He kept a low profile during the 1962 congressional campaign and was warned by Walter Mondale that local Democrats were complaining that he had made little effort in the state since 1958. Even in St. Paul, only 49 percent of voters recognized McCarthy, compared with 76 percent for Humphrey and 95 percent for Governor Wendell Anderson. He was not unpopular, merely anonymous. Eighteen months before the election, only half of the state electorate approved of his performance as their senator. A White House memorandum reported that Representative John Blatnik expected him to have "re-election trouble": "the Senator has done very little work in [the] state, seldom goes back there on political business, [and] has no taste for a tough campaign." Rumors abounded in Minnesota political circles that he would drop out of the Senate at the end of 1964 in favor of the more sedate life of a college president.[37]

The assassination of President Kennedy in November 1963 completely altered McCarthy's fortunes. With Kennedy dead and Johnson in the White House, McCarthy could once again aspire to be the liberal, Catholic balance on a Democratic national ticket. Just five days after the assassination, his name was being suggested as a possible vice presidential candidate and the ideal partner for Lyndon Johnson in 1964. The obvious front-runners, however, were Robert Kennedy, still the attorney general, and Hubert Humphrey. McCarthy himself admitted that the more experienced and popular Humphrey "would be a stronger candidate," and a newspaper profile noted that McCarthy failed to arouse "the same kind of warmth" as his colleague and suffered from his "relative obscurity." There were other candidates, of course, notably Mike Mansfield and Robert McNamara, but at the end of July 1964 Johnson narrowed the field by eliminating from consideration all the current members of his cabinet, including Kennedy and McNamara. According to press reports, this left the two senators from Minnesota as the remaining possibilities for the vice presidency. The matter would be decided at the Democratic convention in Atlantic City.[38]

McCarthy qualified as a likely candidate not merely because he was a liberal and a Catholic. According to contemporaries close to both men, he was, if anything, closer to Johnson than in 1960, and newspapers named him as one of the few legislators whose judgment Johnson respected.

Humphrey, too, recalled that McCarthy's friendship with Johnson necessarily propelled him near to the top of the list of candidates. Another factor taken surprisingly seriously by observers was the extremely close friendship between Abigail McCarthy and Lady Bird Johnson, who was also fond of Abigail's husband. Abigail even told her Minnesota friends that Lady Bird had assured her that McCarthy would be the candidate. Certainly Johnson and McCarthy cultivated each other from November 1963 onward. In December, for example, McCarthy was invited to an informal dinner at the White House to rewrite Johnson's speech to the United Nations. The records of Johnson's telephone conversations indicate that although the two men were not intimate, they did work closely together: in early 1964 Johnson urged McCarthy to "go after" Barry Goldwater on foreign policy and also entrusted him with keeping the other Democrats on the Finance Committee in line:

> I never have asked you to prove Frank Ikard was right, but he told me one time that if I put my chips on you, he guaranteed the time would come when I would be damned happy you're on there. Now what I want you to do is, outside of Harry Byrd and Albert Gore, I want you to pull together those other Democrats and make them attend the meetings, make them keep their mouths shut . . . and get me a bill out on that floor.[39]

In January 1964, Johnson indicated his high regard for McCarthy by appearing unexpectedly at a Washington benefit dinner for the Minnesotan's re-election campaign. All of these hints suggested not only to McCarthy but to other observers that he was a very serious candidate for the vice presidency, and according to his aide Kenneth O'Donnell, Johnson even urged McCarthy to arrange meetings with regional Democratic barons such as Jesse Unruh and Richard Daley. As one Minnesota contemporary remembered, Johnson "just put the bait out there and really had Gene McCarthy honestly thinking in his own heart that he was going to be vice president."[40]

Interviewed years later about the 1964 election, McCarthy insisted that he "didn't really try" to win the vice presidential nomination, and told one historian: "I was playing a game." This was untrue. His old friends from St. Paul all agreed that he badly wanted to be vice president. Moreover, McCarthy and his friends actually organized an active, although discreet, campaign to win the nomination. At the very beginning of 1964 a small group of his close friends, including several former Stevenson supporters, formed a committee to lobby for his selection, and with financial backing from the liberal philanthropist Stephen Currier they opened a secret office in a Washington town house and hired a campaign manager and a press secretary. A *Newsweek* correspondent who covered McCarthy in 1968 estimated that the vice presidential effort cost some $39,000 and concluded: "He wanted that very much." The committee, which met almost weekly, was sufficiently formal to have its own "guidelines" for promoting McCarthy, and his campaign manager, a party activist from Wyoming, regularly filed reports on his travels and meetings with delegates and local potentates. McCarthy himself worked to rebuild his bridges with the New Frontier officials: his office sent regular digests of speeches and clippings to the White House, and he urged friends to contact Johnson and sing his praises. If this came at the expense of Hubert Humphrey, all the better: McCarthy's strategy depended on painting his senior colleague as too divisive a figure for the national ticket. All the same, despite the fact that the two men were direct rivals, they maintained surprisingly amicable relations, perhaps because each secretly believed that he would inevitably win the day. McCarthy was more confident than he later admitted. He was, he declared, "practically everybody's second choice" and boasted, "My wife is one of Lady Bird's best friends. Everything else being equal, that may be the best reason of all."[41]

His most serious problem, however, was that he was nowhere near as popular as Humphrey with the Democratic rank and file. The unions, for example, were squarely behind Humphrey as their preferred candidate. The liberal *New Republic* called McCarthy "less than a heavyweight" and the *New York Times* endorsed his rival. Both for the general public and for Democratic activists, Humphrey was a well-known and respected political veteran, while McCarthy was a nobody. A national poll of Democratic county chairmen at the beginning of the year saw 185 declare themselves for Humphrey, 166 for Robert Kennedy, and only 28 for McCarthy, placing him behind the likes of Stevenson, Mayor Robert Wagner of New York and Governor Edmund Brown of California. A poll of 40 delegates to the Minnesota DFL convention in July resulted in 36 supporting Humphrey and just 4 preferring his junior colleague. Worst of all, with the convention just weeks away, a Harris poll taken in August showed that of Democratic voters, 54 percent wanted Humphrey; Brown, Wagner, Stuart Symington and Abraham Ribicoff each received the support of 10 percent; and a feeble 6 percent, the lowest score on the list, backed McCarthy. These were not statistics to impress the White House.[42]

A second problem, perhaps equally serious, was that Robert Kennedy and his circle were dead against McCarthy's selection as a Catholic substitute for his murdered brother. McCarthy's team privately conceded this was a liability from the start. Kennedy and his friends were determined that if the attorney general were not to be the candidate, then Humphrey was the most preferable alternative, and McCarthy the least. McCarthy made matters worse by criticizing Kennedy's decision to run for the Senate in New York. "I just don't have any respect for that man at all," Kennedy told Ted Sorensen. By early 1964, according to Kenneth O'Donnell, the Kennedy circle had agreed: "If Bobby is not the candidate, we're all going to go [for] Humphrey." Humphrey himself well knew that he was Kennedy's favored candidate. Johnson was not eager to alienate Robert Kennedy completely, and therefore McCarthy's chances were severely limited by Kennedy's implacable opposition.[43]

The only reason that McCarthy was under consideration at all was the remarkable fact that he was the candidate of the South. A minority of Johnson's advisers was "worried about Hubert and his big red flag of civil rights." McCarthy had spoken eloquently in the Senate on behalf of the 1964 civil rights bill, and had even anticipated the trend of the civil rights movement by warning of the "genuine and designed discrimination against Negroes in many northern cities." He did not, however, have the same associations with civil rights as Humphrey, and southerners regarded him as a more moderate candidate. McCarthy, it was thought, would run better in southern and border states. As Fred Harris, senator from Oklahoma, put it: "He seemed safer, less radical." Abigail McCarthy admitted that "some of the people working for Gene were from the South." Even James Eastland, perhaps the most implacable southern opponent of civil rights in the Senate, pleaded McCarthy's case with Johnson. McCarthy's most important advocate was the governor of Texas, John Connally, whom Johnson regarded as his protégé and whose advice he constantly solicited. On 23 July 1964, Connally and Johnson spoke about the issue at length and with great frankness. Johnson confessed his preferred choice would have been Robert McNamara, "but that's out." Connally urged him to choose McCarthy: "I'd take him simply on the premise that nobody knows him, and he's damn little harm, damn little good." Johnson countered: "But we're not going to carry any Southern states, John, and Humphrey has a lot more appeal in the other states, in the Mid-West." There was another argument against McCarthy, Johnson explained:

> He'll get a lot of smear. He votes the oil and gas companies. He votes for the depletion, and he'll help you a little that way in Texas. But he'll catch you unshirted hell from the Drew Pearsons and [James] Restons, they've already told me.[44]

McCarthy's votes on the Finance Committee certainly discouraged many liberals from supporting his vice presidential candidacy, despite his overall liberal record. In February 1964 he voted both in committee and on the Senate floor against two attempts to cut the oil depletion allowance, his most flagrant transgression thus far of liberal orthodoxy. McCarthy variously explained that the depletion allowance had "been built into the financial structure of wholly responsible industries" and that the existing situation was "the best that could be done." This explanation cut little ice with liberal columnists such as Drew Pearson. It was widely thought that McCarthy had defended the allowance with an eye on southern and specifically Texan support for the vice presidency. Indeed, Johnson told McCarthy, while discussing an unrelated matter, to "tell Russell Long that you helped me with his depletion," and his remark to Connally demonstrates that McCarthy's support for the allowance had not gone unnoticed in the White House. The oil and gas lobbies, after all, were vital contributors to Democratic campaign funds in 1964. There were also persistent rumors that McCarthy's 1964 vote had effectively been bought in exchange for southern campaign funds toward his re-election. One report noted that McCarthy had raised $40,000 in one appearance at the Houston Petroleum Club, principally from the Houston oil businessman and Democratic fund-raiser J. R. Parten. McCarthy's own administrative assistant told a journalist that McCarthy had once received a $50,000 campaign contribution from Robert Kerr, with the implicit understanding that he would give Kerr his vote on the oil issue. McCarthy himself quipped to a journalist: "I ran for President as a penance for all I've done for Bob Kerr and Lyndon and Russell Long." Of course, there is no hard evidence either way; still, it is not difficult to imagine some kind of link between McCarthy's oil vote in February 1964 and his pursuit of the vice presidency six months later.[45]

Although Johnson constantly toyed with the idea of picking McCarthy rather than Humphrey, the senior man was always the likely choice. For one thing, Johnson knew that Humphrey was more likely to remain loyal than was the willful McCarthy. "I [have] got to be sure he won't be running against me four years from now," he told one adviser. Humphrey and Johnson also conducted a long and ultimately successful flirtation; in May, Johnson told him: "I'm trying to build you up. I'm trying to make you the greatest man in the world." Two months later Humphrey promised him: "If your judgment leads you to select me, I can assure you—unqualifiedly, personally, and with all the sincerity in my heart—complete loyalty." Johnson was certainly tempted to defy the conventional wisdom and pick McCarthy, but the potential opposition of the Kennedy camp, not to mention the strongly pro-Humphrey labor unions, was too great an obstacle. Even McCarthy's own backers were less than wholly enthusiastic about him, as Connally's comments demonstrated. Of Johnson's closest advisers, only Walter Jenkins eventually favored McCarthy, and faced with such an over-whelming endorsement of Hubert Humphrey, Johnson was never likely to select the junior man.[46]

By the time of the Atlantic City convention McCarthy was evidently beginning to doubt his own chances, and his campaign contacted the White House for reassurance: "We want to know, we don't want to be sitting on the porch when he goes off with the other girl. And we'll understand." Johnson did not want to break the suspense, however, and so McCarthy arrived in Atlantic City still believing he had a chance of selection. While he and Abigail stayed in a suite near the amphitheater, his campaign team was based in a motel north of the town with a secretarial staff and secret phone line. McCarthy himself was "the most available interviewee" of the con-vention, appearing on television "almost as often as the commercials." On 23 August, Humphrey and McCarthy made a cloying joint appearance on *Meet the Press* to discuss the contest, culminating in a three-way public telephone conversation with President Johnson. "Embarrassing, at a mini-mum," declared the *Washington Post*. All of this activity was in vain, how-ever: Johnson had already made his decision. Three days later, with rumors now overwhelmingly indicating that Humphrey was the man, McCarthy and his wife drafted a telegram to the president announcing his withdrawal from consideration, a last attempt to regain some pride which Johnson never forgave. Johnson piled humiliation on disappointment by instructing McCarthy to deliver the nominating speech for his rival; the result was, unsurprisingly, "barely perfunctory." McCarthy, always a proud man, was unquestionably hurt and humiliated by the whole affair. An old friend from Minnesota recalled that he was "very sarcastic and very bitter" at the state delegation's party for Humphrey, and Abigail refused to attend at all. Edmund Muskie, who spent much of the convention relaxing with McCarthy at his motel headquarters, also remembered that he was "very bitter" at the way Johnson had led him on.[47]

McCarthy's rejection by Johnson was an even greater setback than the presidential campaign of 1960. Humphrey's success left no room for another Minnesotan in presidential politics. McCarthy himself maintained that as he had been "completely passive"—which was not true—he was not in the least disappointed. In fact, it seems quite clear that he never forgave either Johnson or Humphrey, the two men who had been his most generous patrons, for the events of 1964. He had always been jealous of Humphrey;

now jealousy became contempt, as he mocked his subservience to Johnson, his cheerful garrulousness, and even his intellect. More significantly, the disappointment brought the end of the relationship between McCarthy and Johnson. In the words of Johnson's aide George Reedy, it turned "very sour." When McCarthy heard a story that Johnson had wanted to announce his choice at the rostrum with the oblivious Humphrey and McCarthy beside him, he said, "What a sadistic son of a bitch."[48]

With all the publicity from his narrow failure to win the vice presidency, McCarthy's re-election in Minnesota was a simple affair. He hid his disappointment well and struck observers as supremely relaxed and confident, although to the *Minneapolis Star* he sometimes gave the impression "of a remote junior senator, almost only casually interested in the political and economic affairs of his own state." His opponent was a wealthy but obscure Republican moderate rejoicing in the name of Wheelock Whitney III, and McCarthy eventually thrashed him by 931,353 votes to 605,933, or 60.3 percent to 39.2 percent. Across the nation, the Johnson-Humphrey ticket led the Democrats to a 68–32 margin in the Senate and a 295–140 margin in the House, a glorious triumph. Meanwhile, McCarthy returned to the Senate, "his great gifts curdling into bitterness." What neither he nor Humphrey realized was that 1964 marked the high point of liberalism, and a steep decline lay ahead. In the long term, the most significant developments of 1964 were the electoral successes of George Wallace in the north and the pioneering conservative agenda of Barry Goldwater. White working-class voters were already beginning to turn away from the Democratic Party toward a new, aggressive and culturally conservative brand of populism, especially in the South. Almost unnoticed, these developments were a harbinger of the eventual collapse of the liberal coalition under the impact of racial unrest and the Vietnam War. Paradoxically, McCarthy's rejection in 1964 meant that he more than anyone would be supremely placed to benefit four years later.[49]

CHAPTER SEVEN

Rethinking the Cold War

W hen Eugene McCarthy returned to the Senate in January 1965, a promising future lay behind him. Johnson had won the 1964 presidential election by an overwhelming majority and would probably win again in 1968, leaving Humphrey perfectly poised to take over the party leadership in 1972. McCarthy's career in presidential politics was almost certainly over. At the beginning of the new Congress he was elected to the Democratic Steering Committee, the body that assigned Democratic members to the regular standing committees. The committee had been heavily dominated by southerners, and the addition of McCarthy and Patrick McNamara tilted it toward the more moderate liberal element in the party. Although this was a mark of McCarthy's acceptance by the powerful conservative "club," it was no compensation for missing out on the vice presidency. Later in January 1965 he conferred with Lee Metcalf, Ed Muskie and Philip Hart about establishing a Senate version of the Democratic Study Group and told one newspaper: "We plan to have some informal meetings to discuss legislation and matters of mutual interest." Unfortunately, the atomized and self-centered world of the Senate did not lend itself to the establishment of an informal liberal club, and the attempt came to nothing. Instead, McCarthy began to sink into torpor. The *New York Times* portrayed him as a "political scholar-gypsy . . . dropping for a few minutes into a committee hearing and leaving in all-too-apparent boredom, and then retiring to his office, where visitors may find him reading Yeats rather than the *Congressional Record*."[1]

The story of McCarthy in the Senate from 1965 onward, then, was one of frustration. One possible alternative was a move to replace Adlai Stevenson as U.S. ambassador to the United Nations. Stevenson himself was tired of the U.N. and told friends that McCarthy would be his first choice to succeed him. When Stevenson died in July 1965, McCarthy, who as U.N. ambassador would not alienate Democratic conservatives and who had already come so close to the vice presidency, was among the favorites to replace him. The White House aide Jack Valenti even listed McCarthy as the number one possibility in a memorandum to President Johnson, pointing out that "of all the liberals now operating as liberals, he is the most sensible and the most eloquent. Moreover, he is signed on to your program." Johnson instead nominated Arthur Goldberg.[2]

The problem was that McCarthy was fast disappearing from Johnson's circle of friends. Not only was he still bitter about his treatment at Atlantic City, but he had also become friendly with Indiana senator Vance Hartke, who served on the Finance Committee alongside him and had fallen out with the administration. Internal White House memoranda as well as newspaper gossip noted that Hartke and McCarthy were forming an anti-Johnson alliance. In February 1966 one of Johnson's advisers reported that McCarthy himself had not spoken to the president since 1 June 1965, "and even then he only attended a swearing-in ceremony in the Flower Garden." McCarthy and his wife had not been invited to the White House for over six months, quite a departure from the intimacy of 1963 and 1964.[3]

As his programs became more controversial and his political position gradually weaker, Johnson moved to punish those Democrats who publicly opposed his policies, and by 1966 McCarthy, like other erstwhile allies such as Hartke, Mike Mansfield and William Fulbright, had effectively been banished from the presidential circle. In McCarthy's case, however, the rift with the White House was not simply a matter of policy. His reaction to being snubbed in 1964 made it unlikely that he and Johnson could ever again be close, and decades later he still preferred to remember Johnson with contempt as a "barbarian," rather than with affection. In different circumstances, the collapse of their relationship might have been a mere triviality. But what made it significant was the growing opposition, both in the Senate and in the nation, to Johnson's war in Vietnam.[4]

In 1947, McCarthy had made his political debut at the Democratic-Farmer-Labor caucuses in St. Paul as the local spokesman for the Cold War, a "leader against all those who booed the Truman Doctrine." McCarthy's basic commitment to fighting Communism, both at home and abroad, was the defining premise of his foreign policy, underpinned by a pervading intellectual pessimism. The United States, he believed, was a lone champion of freedom in a dark and wicked world. Communism was "a basic evil," its expansion "limited only by the fertility of imagination, the viciousness of will and the power of those who control the totalitarian state." McCarthy also argued that the United States had an explicit responsibility to shoulder the burden of defeating international Communism. In February 1951, with the U.N. troops in Korea in full retreat under the onslaught of the Chinese, he told the House of Representatives: "We must undertake to preserve western civilization and the peoples who value it . . . We must preserve our national honor. This is simply to say that we must accept, as we have in the past, the responsibility that goes with national maturity and power."[5]

Power, it appeared, was not something to be feared, but something to be wielded with enthusiasm. Nor should the United States be too cautious in its commitment to fighting the Cold War; instead, it should use "all of its resources: military, economic, intellectual, and spiritual in order to stand against Communism." This combination of quasi-conservative pessimism and liberal commitment to activism abroad meant that McCarthy neither questioned the premises of the Cold War nor yielded to the temptations of isolationism. With a Democratic president in office, the young congressman was little inclined to challenge the orthodoxy of his party. Nor were his statements on foreign policy particularly original or thoughtful. Still, he was not uncomfortable with aggressive rhetoric. "We as a nation must not be blind to the evil which confronts us," he declared in December 1951. "We must not underestimate its powers and we must not be guilty of failing to take adequate steps to defend ourselves."[6]

The election of Eisenhower in 1952 meant that McCarthy was no longer expected to be an unswerving admirer of the administration's foreign policy. All the same, the Cold War commanded bipartisan support, and as a veteran of the feuds of 1948 McCarthy had no inclination to rethink the assumptions of global anti-Communism. In fact, his energies were directed far more to pursuing influence in the House than to developing a role as a foreign policy critic, and not until the late 1950s did he have much to say about international affairs. Eisenhower's cautious diplomatic stewardship even earned rare and grudging praise from McCarthy in 1954. The president was right on most foreign issues, he told an interviewer, but not on domestic ones. In 1958, asked by the *Nation* to explain the difference between the Democrats and Republicans on foreign policy, McCarthy answered that it was "one of degree rather than of basic disagreement on policy," with the Democrats advocating "a greater stress on programs of technological and economic aid and assistance in international relations." He also criticized President Eisenhower for being insufficiently eager to work alongside other international bodies and to promote development through aid programs. Even in 1951 McCarthy had recognized that the world was too complicated to be reduced to a bipolar struggle between the superpowers. Many members of Congress, he said, "forget that approximately only two out of every twenty people in the world live in the United States and the Soviet Union. Little attention is paid to the other eighteen, they being regarded as pawns in the respective programs of the United States and Soviet Union." He shared other liberals' interest in the developing world, calling for "increasing emphasis on economic aid" and "generosity and imagination in helping impoverished and underdeveloped countries." On issues such as arms control he was happy to follow the lead of Adlai Stevenson—for instance, in 1956 echoing his call for a suspension of hydrogen bomb tests and urging Eisenhower to show more "moral leadership."[7]

Although he agreed that President Eisenhower shared many of his own anti-Communist premises, McCarthy was keen to criticize him for what he called his "hesitation, contradiction, drift and uncertainty" on foreign affairs, and McCarthy spent much of the 1950s berating the administration for its failure to match Soviet military expansion. During the 1954 elections he told a local newspaper: "It is in the interest of the United States to protect non-Communist countries against Communist combination, even to the point of using American troops under certain conditions." In November 1957 a group of six Democratic congressmen, including McCarthy and other prominent young liberals such as Lee Metcalf and James Roosevelt, sent Eisenhower a public letter demanding a "greater sense of urgency" in the American missile program. McCarthy's Senate campaign in 1958 partly relied on the message that the Republicans had administered a feeble and timid foreign policy. He told one audience, "Our military position relative to the Russians has been weakened in part because of our general loss of prestige and loss of support among our allies and, more specifically, because we have fallen behind in the missile and satellite race," claiming that the administration had neglected the "total contest with the Communists" and had "substituted concession for containment."[8]

This was not merely campaign rhetoric, for McCarthy kept it up for three years. In May 1959, for example, he warned that the United States could not "afford to lag behind in missile development and in the perfection of other weapons" and urged that the administration "prepare for limited war." Eisenhower, he mocked, was "afraid to meet" the challenge of Communism. All this did not mean that McCarthy was any more belligerent than his fellows. He was simply a typical liberal Democrat, for whom dynamic action to resist Communism abroad was a necessary and characteristic aspect of his liberalism. In the 1960 campaign he argued that the three objectives of American diplomacy must be to "protect our national integrity," to "preserve our national honor" and to "maintain liberty in the rest of the world." Nowhere did he contemplate the limits of American power or the morality of intervention overseas. "Our policy," he insisted in October 1960, "must be to assist within all possible means the liberation of people who are subject to Communist tyranny."[9]

McCarthy's thinking on foreign issues in the 1950s was not particularly well developed. His public statements and interventions in the House and Senate were concerned more with domestic issues, and he had no reputation as a foreign specialist. In March 1958 a liberal commentator reflected caustically on a McCarthy talk on foreign policy at Princeton. "What he had to say made sense only now and again," remarked the writer, "because only a few scraps and pieces in all his discourse were germane." McCarthy's central message was "We have got to sell our total civilization to the uncommitted peoples of the world," and the writer mocked his "awfully tired" rhetoric of "apostles of freedom."[10]

This did not mean, of course, that McCarthy's approach was especially shallow, more that he was content to repeat the orthodoxy of the day: containment, military expansion, and the proselytizing gospel of American democracy. This aggressive, interventionist outlook was not necessarily a conservative phenomenon: indeed, its emphasis on exporting American models of democracy and capitalism to the outside world owed much to the evangelical, proselytizing zeal of President Woodrow Wilson in the late 1910s. Although McCarthy never acknowledged any debt to Wilson, his background and education certainly meant that he was more open to European and other international influences than many of his fellows. But beyond a general liberal internationalism, McCarthy was so vague that it is difficult to make more specific comments. Certainly there was nothing unusual about his commitment to the Cold War. There was little dissent even in intellectual circles from the assumptions of the day, and as one historian puts it, "in fact, most intellectuals viewed Cold War anticommunism as a fundamental and unquestionable assumption of political life." Compared with the decades that followed, the period from 1948 to 1964 saw a rare bipartisan consensus on foreign policy. Not only did the postwar emphasis on internal security effectively stifle domestic dissent, but most

Democrats and Republicans simply shared the same assumptions about the Cold War and the American duty to provide democratic leadership. McCarthy's dogged fidelity to Cold War orthodoxy both illustrated the prevailing consensus and reflected his own political origins as a dedicated anti-Communist.[11]

When Kennedy became president in 1961, then, McCarthy had no great reputation as a foreign policy specialist. All the same, the very fact of his being in the Senate meant that he was expected to have strong opinions on international matters, and indeed he had campaigned in 1958 with the promise to increase "the Senate's influence on foreign policy and administration decisions." With a rhetorically aggressive Democrat in the White House, McCarthy began to soften his own approach to the Cold War, a change of emphasis rather than assumptions. Perhaps the real threat of nuclear confrontation with the USSR had dulled his appetite for battle; certainly McCarthy abandoned the belligerent style of the late 1950s. The Berlin crisis, for example, was not "beyond negotiating." He supported, with reservations, the establishment of a disarmament agency and the suspension of nuclear testing, and urged increased aid and social reform in South America. He also began to talk for the first time in public about the limits and morality of American foreign policy. In early October 1962 he argued: "We cannot impose international policy at will, no matter how morally right, without taking into account the national interest of other states who are our allies or who, at least, are not actively aligned against us . . . There is a base of moral necessity, of respect for truth, of fidelity to the pledged word, of respect for the rights of other nations and peoples." This was the first time that McCarthy publicly acknowledged the primacy of "moral necessity" over the imperatives of ideological and diplomatic rivalry, and it also marked the end of his aggressive anti-Communist rhetoric. The Cuban missile crisis that unfolded just weeks later drew no reaction from McCarthy, but it takes little imagination to speculate that it helped to accelerate his move away from belligerence toward a more self-consciously ethical foreign policy. In March 1963, for example, he explained: "Morality does not stop at the water's edge. Ethical principles bear strongly on foreign relations. We have never accepted that national interest can ultimately and completely override considerations of right and wrong."[12]

One example of McCarthy's new distaste for American arrogance and aggression was his attitude toward Cuba. The State Department under

Eisenhower had, he thought, shown "insensitivity, frequently bordering on indifference, toward Latin American problems." He accepted that the Cubans could hardly be blamed for their hostility to the United States; as early as 1957 he had bemoaned the American support for Batista and wrote: "We are making serious mistakes not only in Cuba, but in other countries." He never developed this thought into a more rounded critique of American foreign policy, but he did initially approve of Castro and in 1959 welcomed his "new era of peace, justice and stability." The Bay of Pigs invasion in April 1961 not only challenged his ideas about an ethical foreign policy but also shocked him because of its implicit disregard for Congress. It was evident, he concluded, "that the CIA was involved at the time when such involvement was being denied and that the involvement was in violation of our previous commitments and assurances." In May 1962 he complained in an interview that the incident encapsulated Kennedy's contempt for Congress. "In some places the debate is terribly inadequate," he grumbled. "Sometimes it's embarrassing how little we know . . . Take the invasion of Cuba. Who's to decide the invasion of Cuba?"[13]

McCarthy used the issue of American intervention in Cuba to pursue his own growing interest in executive secrecy and the role of the Congress in making foreign policy. McCarthy's interest in the secrecy question stemmed from his institutional conservatism and dated from 1951, when he unsuccessfully proposed that the Speaker nominate three freshman representatives in each successive Congress to a Joint Committee on Atomic Energy, and urged the appointment of a citizens' advisory committee on atomic power and weaponry. The House, he argued, should strip aside the "heavy curtain of secrecy" that had hitherto shrouded the atomic energy program. His failure did not dampen his interest in legislative-executive rivalry; in 1958, for instance, he explained that he wanted to move to the Senate because its "influence on foreign policy and administrative decisions is much more direct than is the influence of the House of Representatives." In May 1959 his obsession with the issue of secrecy found expression in his opposition to the nomination of Lewis Strauss as secretary of commerce. According to McCarthy, Strauss had failed to keep Congress adequately briefed during his stint as chairman of the Atomic Energy Commission and had proved himself "insensitive" to legislative responsibilities. A vote for Strauss, he declared, represented "approval of unwarranted extension of executive secrecy and the independence of the Executive Branch in determination of policy and the administration of laws passed by Congress." This was not simply a matter of partisan politics: the integrity of Congress was at stake. "Congress simply cannot meet its responsibilities with the existing barriers of secrecy [and] the independence of policy declared by the executive branch," he told the Women's National Democratic Club. In the end, the nomination of Strauss was rejected.[14]

No issue, however, encapsulated McCarthy's deepening obsession with government secrecy as much as the independence of the CIA. The bipartisan Cold War consensus meant that there was little political or institutional incentive for congressmen to question intelligence activities or the unrestrained freedom of the intelligence agencies. The subcommittees of the Armed Services and Appropriations Committees that dealt with intelligence matters were "trusting to the point of somnolence" and depended on the friendly relations between their conservative members, such as Richard Russell, Harry Byrd and Styles Bridges, and CIA director Allen Dulles. As a liberal Democrat, McCarthy could not reasonably hope to be selected to join them, and since his factional base in the Congress was his fellow liberals, he actually had little to lose in criticizing the cozy arrangement that protected the CIA from scrutiny. On four separate occasions in the House McCarthy proposed a resolution to establish a Joint Committee on Information and Intelligence to supervise the CIA, with members chosen by the president and the Speaker of the House. On each occasion, of course, he failed, just as a parallel measure in the Senate proposed by Mike Mansfield failed in 1956.[15]

Moving to the Senate did not dull his appetite, and four more attempts followed between 1959 and 1963. McCarthy certainly did not share President Kennedy's fascination with the mystique of the secret agent. In May 1961 he was reported to have told colleagues that the Bay of Pigs incident demonstrated more than ever the need for supervision of the agency. When Kennedy nominated John McCone to replace Dulles as director of the CIA, McCarthy immediately stepped forward to protest. As McCarthy explained, the nominee had tried to dismiss ten scientists from the California Institute of Technology, of which he was a trustee, for supporting a moratorium on nuclear testing. In a flagrant demonstration of his alienation from the Kennedy administration, McCarthy appeared as the solitary witness against McCone before the Armed Services Committee. McCone, he insisted, was incapable of the "objective judgment" necessary to clean up an agency that had secretly intervened in Iran in 1953, Guatemala in 1954 and Cuba in 1961. Needless to say, McCone's nomination was approved over McCarthy's objections. The affair won McCarthy little public attention, but it could hardly have endeared him to the White House. It also marked a hardening of his attitude to the CIA, to executive control of foreign policy and to Kennedy's handling of foreign policy.[16]

For all his enthusiasm to discuss issues like Cuba and the CIA, McCarthy showed little interest in perhaps the most momentous diplomatic development of Kennedy's brief presidency: the decision to triple American aid to South Vietnam and increase the number of American military advisers in the troubled republic from a few hundred to over sixteen thousand. Like most of his contemporaries, McCarthy did not have much to say about Kennedy's Indochina policy. Vietnam was a far-off country of which he knew little. In his first recorded comment on the area, in 1954, he had asserted that the United States should aim "to establish the territorial integrity of non-Communist countries of south-east Asia and should try to strengthen these countries so that they will be able to protect their territory, even if this would involve some military support." He next spoke about the issue eight years later, when he defended Kennedy's escalation of military aid in a letter to a constituent:

> It is rather generally agreed, I believe, that it is very much in our national interest to keep South Viet Nam out of communist hands. It was the best judgment of the President and his military advisers that the deteriorating situation there necessitated a step-up in our military aid and assistance to the democratic forces. I am afraid that many of those who are now criticizing the President for increasing the American troop commitment would be among the first to belabor him if South Viet Nam were lost to the communists.[17]

Vietnam was simply not an issue that greatly occupied McCarthy between 1961 and 1964, and he saw no reason to question the bipartisan consensus. While other senators, notably Wayne Morse, Ernest Gruening and George McGovern, were beginning to question the extent of American involvement in the region, McCarthy was busy working to catch President Johnson's eye. At the end of May 1964 he even issued a press release on the "successes of American foreign policy," hailing the diplomacy of the New Frontier as a cause for "great pride and consolation" and celebrating the "broader responsibilities which reach out and include the entire world—all nations, all races and all continents." McCarthy was still a long way from the emphasis on "the limits of power" with which he was later associated. It is hard not to surmise that the evolution of his thought on foreign policy was as dependent on his own personal fortunes, and his relationship with Johnson, as it was on the American experience overseas.[18]

Just as McCarthy did not question the American commitment to South Vietnam, so he raised no objections when Johnson sought the Gulf of

Tonkin Resolution in order to authorize "all necessary measures to repel any armed attack against forces of the United States and to prevent further aggression." Many Democrats thought that the resolution, if not the alleged confrontation off the North Vietnamese coast, was really a riposte to Barry Goldwater's bellicose rhetoric at the recent Republican convention. "It never occurred to me that we'd stay in Vietnam once the [1964] election was over," remembered George McGovern. "I always thought that the Gulf of Tonkin Resolution was a political ploy to cut the ground from under Goldwater. And that's the way Bill Fulbright sold it to a lot of the liberals in the Senate." The measure passed unanimously in the House, and in the Senate only Wayne Morse and Ernest Gruening opposed it. Johnson successfully persuaded the respected chairman of the Foreign Relations Committee, William Fulbright, to secure the quick passage of the resolution, and there was no real debate about its appropriateness or implications. Fulbright dismissed objections with the explanation that the resolution would in fact *prevent* a wider war: "The last thing we want to do is become involved in a land war in Asia." The measure passed 88–2, a striking illustration of the bipartisan consensus on foreign policy in general and on involvement in Vietnam in particular. Johnson, it was later said, "carried a copy of the Resolution in his back pocket, and was always prepared to produce it as evidence of Congressional support for his Vietnam policies." To have opposed it, which in McCarthy's case would have scuttled his chances for the vice presidency, would have invited criticism for abandoning the president in an hour of emergency. Few senators were prepared to take that risk, and even those who entertained doubts about the resolution, such as Frank Church, Albert Gore and George McGovern, dutifully supported it. Opinion polls suggested that the public agreed: Johnson's approval rating jumped overnight from 42 percent to 72 percent, and support for his handling of the Vietnam issue rose from 58 percent to 85 percent.[19]

McCarthy himself, his mind on the vice presidency, had no doubt that the Gulf of Tonkin Resolution was justified and necessary. "The strength of America," he wrote to his constituents, "is not just the strength of its military power but also the strength of its reputation, honoring its word and keeping its commitment. All of these things were involved in the President's action, which has been sustained by the Congress." On the television show *Face the Nation,* he said, "It was a matter of responding to a direct attack on our ships. The escalation came from the enemy." Johnson, McCarthy thought, must have no doubts about his vice president's commitment to the existing policy on Vietnam. His Minnesota friend Gerald Heaney recalled, "He made it clear that he felt we were committed in Vietnam and we'd have to see it through to the end." McCarthy added that his rival for the vice presidency, Hubert Humphrey, was more likely to abandon that commitment, telling Heaney: "He might be inclined to tell the editor of the *New York Times* that he goes along with it because he has to but that we ought to be doing something different." McCarthy even asked Heaney to point this out to Johnson himself.[20]

In fact, in the short term the Vietnam issue did the Democrats no harm at all. There was little debate about the conflict during the presidential campaign, and few ordinary Americans in 1964 were particularly interested in the subject. When the voters did focus on the issue, at the behest of opinion pollsters, they approved Johnson's policy in overwhelming numbers; only the Second World War had enjoyed so much public support at its outset. Even after his vice presidential hopes had been dashed, McCarthy's fidelity to the administration never wavered. "I do not think we can simply withdraw our forces and abandon the people of South Viet Nam," he wrote, dismissing the idea of neutralization. "Our experience with a supposedly neutral Laos has been none too encouraging." In a debate with his Republican opponent in Minnesota, he even refused to rule out an invasion of North Vietnam. At the end of the year he explained to a Minnesota clergyman that Johnson's policy was the best way of reconciling the twin goals of peace and containment: "I supported the action of the Eisenhower and Kennedy Administrations in this area, and believe that the policy of the Johnson Administration in limiting the action to South Vietnam and keeping the use of force to a minimum is at least the best immediate policy." In short, at the end of 1964 there was no reason to imagine that McCarthy would remain anything other than a wholehearted supporter of the American involvement in Southeast Asia.[21]

In April 1965 McCarthy acquired a seat on the Foreign Relations Committee, one of the most prestigious of all standing committees. To be serving both on Foreign Relations and on Finance was a marvelous achievement for a senator just beginning his second term, and McCarthy told a UPI reporter that the seat was the fulfillment of a long ambition. According to his close friend Edmund Muskie, however, McCarthy took the seat only by chance. As part of the Steering Committee, McCarthy was busy making assignments and offered Muskie the Foreign Relations berth. Muskie declined, because he would have had to forfeit his seniority on other committees, and as he remembered: "Gene said, 'Well, then I'll take it myself.' So you see, he went on the committee as casually as he later came off."[22]

Whether true or not, this story suggests that as early as 1965 McCarthy's friends were conscious of his dwindling interest in the Senate. Still, the committee offered McCarthy a splendid opportunity to develop his interest in foreign policy. Its membership comprised thirteen Democrats and six Republicans, and among the Democrats were men McCarthy already liked and admired, such as William Fulbright, Albert Gore and Vance Hartke. Since the Cold War necessitated American involvement overseas, the committee was more important than ever, and the vagueness of the Constitution regarding presidential authority and foreign policy meant that the committee and the White House were frequently competing for power. One historian has called the Foreign Relations Committee of the 1960s "an extraordinary group of men who dominated much of the news on foreign policy and acquired an influence beyond their numbers." All the same, the competition was one that the White House always seemed to win. By the mid-1960s, most observers agreed that "never in their memories had relations between the executive branch and the Foreign Relations Committee been worse."[23]

The men with whom McCarthy worked on the Foreign Relations Committee unquestionably had a powerful influence on his changing attitude to foreign policy. First, there were the members of the committee staff, "all foreign policy activists with a strong social conscience." McCarthy was closest to two men: Carl Marcy, the chief of staff, a neat, ambitious and intelligent Oregonian; and Pat Holt, a former Texas journalist and the committee's Latin America expert. Both became critics of the Vietnam War and the concentration of executive power. The greatest influence on McCarthy, however, was J. William Fulbright, Democratic senator from Arkansas, who had chaired the committee since 1959. Although a conservative southerner on issues such as race, Fulbright enjoyed the reputation of a sophisticated and intellectually acute observer of foreign affairs. "We had a guy in the Senate who doubled the IQ of any room he entered," recalled one of his aides, the future President Clinton. His critics were less kind. The White House aide Harry McPherson thought that he "seemed to have a stake in losing, in being isolated and right." Fulbright, he wrote, was "bored by the kind of things with which most senators were agreeably concerned . . . [and] skeptical of man's ability to choose a reasonable course."[24]

Ever the self-conscious statesman, Fulbright thought that his committee should be above petty party politics and "take rational, enlightened positions rooted in a realistic internationalism." By 1965 he had become an incisive critic of the anti-Communist consensus. In a speech in March 1964 on "Old Myths and New Realities" he supported the American commitment to South Vietnam, but questioned "the master myth of the Cold War . . . that the Communist bloc is a monolith composed of governments equally resolute and implacable in their determination to destroy the free world." The threat posed by many Communist countries was "little or none." Moreover, the United States must "come to terms, at last, with the realities of a world in which neither good nor evil is absolute and in which those who move events and make history are those who have understood not how much but how little it is within our power to change." This formed the context for his dissent over the war in Vietnam. Similarly, it clearly influenced McCarthy's own thought, not least his book *The Limits of Power* (1967). By that date, of course, Fulbright's thesis had evolved into an attack on "the arrogance of power," a rebuke both to Johnson personally and to unbridled executive power. Like McCarthy, Fulbright was extremely solicitous of congressional prerogatives, and like McCarthy he bemoaned the "unhinging of traditional constitutional relationships." He complained, "The Senate's constitutional powers of advise and consent have atrophied into what is widely regarded as, though never asserted to be, a duty to give prompt consent with a minimum of advice."[25]

It is quite probable that the very fact of being on the Foreign Relations Committee and exposed to the ideas of Fulbright and his staff was a crucial factor in the evolution of McCarthy's thinking, without which he might have remained relatively quiet on Vietnam. From 1965 onward, in fact, the committee became the single most important forum in Congress for criticism of the Vietnam imbroglio, not least because it was the only committee in either house with a chairman who opposed the war. Fulbright's influence can hardly be exaggerated: as one writer put it, "the onset of the committee's anti-war activities coincided with its chairman's public assumption of anti-war views." The institutional framework of a committee devoted to foreign policy and the presence of a large contingent of specialized and idealistic staff assistants also made it easier for members to question the American commitment in Vietnam. A newspaper estimate put the number of doves on the committee in 1967–1968 at eleven members out of nineteen, easily the highest proportion on any congressional committee. By contrast, only one member of the eighteen on the Armed Services Committee opposed the war. The *New York Times* reported in 1968 that at least nine members believed that the United States had overreacted in 1964 and that the administration was now withholding and distorting information about the war. In short, it was hardly surprising that McCarthy, like his colleagues, came to oppose the war. It would in fact have been astonishing had he *not* done so. Whether the opposition of the committee had any great effect is another question entirely. The antiwar commentator I. F. Stone mocked its "cloakroom crusaders, brave in private, cautious in public, fitfully aroused and poorly informed." On the other hand, the open dissent of Fulbright and his fellows undoubtedly publicized and legitimized criticism of the war, and perhaps only McCarthy's 1968 campaign was a comparable example of the way in which dissent could be expressed through conventional political channels.[26]

McCarthy's first major test on the committee came in April 1965, when Johnson sent four hundred American marines to the Dominican Republic to prevent a rebellion by forces loyal to former president Juan Bosch against the current pro-American dictator. Bosch, who had been democratically elected at the end of 1962 and deposed by a junta months later, was far too sympathetic to "leftist" and Communist elements for the Johnson administration's liking, despite his popular mandate. Within a week there were 21,000 American troops in the republic, ostensibly to protect foreign citizens and prevent widespread bloodshed, marking the first open military intervention by the United States in Latin America since the declaration of the Good Neighbor policy in the 1930s. The public overwhelmingly supported Johnson, with only a few dissenting political and intellectual voices such as those of Senator Wayne Morse and the historian Henry Steele Commager.[27]

McCarthy's original reaction was that Johnson's actions were justified, adding that he must "get the troops out as quickly as [he] can." On the other hand, he was not pleased that Johnson had completely excluded Congress and the Foreign Relations Committee from deciding the Dominican policy. As his reaction to the Bay of Pigs suggested, McCarthy was also uneasy with a precedent of armed intervention in the Americas. He had a keen interest in Latin American affairs; he had visited the Third International Christian Democratic Conference in Santiago in 1961 at the behest of President Kennedy and became friendly with Eduardo Frei, who from 1964 to 1970 was a popular reforming president of Chile. McCarthy was consequently not eager to see the United States play the blundering bully in Latin America. At the beginning of June, after the Dominican factions had signed a cease-fire negotiated by the Organization of American States, McCarthy began calling for a congressional investigation of the entire affair, "to know what really happened" and consider establishing guidelines for future crises in the Americas. Why, he asked, had it been necessary to commit American troops? What had been the role of the CIA in the crisis? What was the truth of the president's claim that "some 1,500 innocent people were murdered and shot, and their heads cut off"?[28]

McCarthy's was not a lone voice. The doggedly independent Ernest Gruening had long opposed the military aid program to Latin America. Similarly, McCarthy's friend on the Foreign Relations Committee, the patrician moderate Albert Gore, had reacted to the original pro-American Dominican coup in September 1963 by attacking the "enormous gamble" of using military aid to put "big guns in the hands of irresponsible militaries." In July 1965 the Foreign Relations Committee held nine days of hearings into the whole Dominican issue. The appearance of the undersecretary of state for Latin American affairs, Thomas Mann, who argued that a pro-American military dictatorship was preferable to an anti-American democratic socialist regime, infuriated McCarthy, particularly when Mann dismissed Juan Bosch as a "poet-professor type" manipulated by the Communists. In September Fulbright attacked the Dominican intervention in the Senate, a moment that marked the decisive breach not only between himself and Johnson but also between the Foreign Relations Committee and the White House. "The movement of the future in Latin America is social revolution," he declared. "The United States turned its back on social revolution in Santo Domingo and associated itself with a corrupt and reactionary oligarchy." When the White House launched a verbal counterattack, only McCarthy, Joseph Clark and Wayne Morse were willing to defend Fulbright in public. "The revolution could have been settled without bloodshed," McCarthy told the press. "Are we going to have a State Department policy which calls for U.S. intervention in every Latin American crisis?" On the Senate floor he condemned congressional passivity in the face of an overweening executive: "Our function in the Senate is not merely to find out what the administration policy is and then say yes or no to it—and oftentimes too late. We have a definite responsibility to develop policy ourselves." Although he had already criticized Kennedy over the Bay of Pigs operation, this was the first time McCarthy had defied Johnson over foreign policy. It was a decisive indication that he had chosen to side with Fulbright rather than with his erstwhile ally.[29]

In his memoirs McCarthy wrote that as far as Vietnam was concerned, "1965 was a warning year." In fact, only two other senators were more loyal to Johnson on foreign policy votes during the year. His loyalty to Johnson owed much to the fact that the great majority of the public continued to support the administration. *Time* magazine called the war "the crucial test of American policy and will" and celebrated "the Right War at the Right Time." Opinion polls taken in the spring demonstrated that although the public was not opposed to a negotiated settlement, 79 percent still believed that a Communist victory would mean the fall of all Southeast Asia and that it was "very important" to prevent it. Even so, "Rolling Thunder," the massive bombing campaign against North Vietnam which began on 24 February, alarmed many liberals. Both George McGovern and Frank Church spoke out against it, while Stephen Young and Gaylord Nelson expressed quiet concern. McCarthy's reaction was similar to those of the liberal members of the administration, like Hubert Humphrey, Adlai Stevenson and George Ball. Although he was disturbed by the bombing, he did not publicly condemn it. Dissent in the Senate was largely reluctant: few senators were comfortable criticizing the war effort, and even fewer were prepared to vote against it. In May, for example, only Morse, Gruening and Nelson voted against a defense appropriation of $700 million for Vietnam. True, there was far more dissent than in 1964. Church, Morse and McGovern all supported Charles de Gaulle's call for a negotiated settlement, and Fulbright proposed an experimental bombing halt to encourage the North Vietnamese to the conference table. But there was little major public pressure on Johnson to withdraw from Vietnam, nor was there any great support for such a move within Congress. Indeed, Johnson probably had more to fear from belligerent critics on his right than he did from the cautious and muddled opposition of the liberal dissenters.[30]

The escalation of the war throughout 1965 put McCarthy under increasing pressure to clarify his stance on the issue. His correspondence, for instance, increased heavily, with hundreds of concerned letters, especially from women and clergymen, to which he replied with a standard neutral response explaining the difficulty of the problem and his confidence that Johnson would find a solution. But two events on 18 February 1965 increased his doubts about the administration's policy. That afternoon he and five other Democrats attended a meeting with Vice President Humphrey and McGeorge Bundy, the national security adviser, and were offended by what they perceived as Bundy's "arrogant manner." In the evening, Johnson held a White House reception for between twenty and thirty senators and invited Secretary of Defense Robert McNamara, Secretary of State Dean Rusk and other leading officials to brief the visitors on the success of American policy in Vietnam. Johnson himself, according to Frank Church, "really acted almost like a carnival barker, using all of his persuasive powers . . . and calling upon many a folksy tale to fortify his argument." The president spent an hour castigating Church for his opposition to the bombing. McCarthy, characteristically, complained afterward, "If Frank Church had just surrendered, we all could have gone home half an hour ago." Dean

Rusk, meanwhile, assured the delegation that the regime in South Vietnam was stable and secure. McCarthy remembered: "He said, 'We really have things under control,' that General Khanh had stabilized things and the Buddhists were happy and the Catholics were happy." This was at nine in the evening. The next morning McCarthy awoke to read in the newspaper that the Khanh government had been overthrown at the very moment that Rusk was speaking. "After an experience or two of this kind," McCarthy remarked, "I think you inevitably begin to raise some questions and have some doubts."[31]

Even though McCarthy's position on the war for the remainder of 1965 was one of cautious ambivalence, his distrust of the administration was making him increasingly suspicious of American foreign policy. At the beginning of March Johnson ordered two marine battalions ashore at Da Nang in the first commitment of American combat troops in Indochina. Later that month, paraphrasing and distorting Fulbright, McCarthy made a vague attack on "the new myths used to explain the new realities" of foreign policy, but defended the bombing of North Vietnam: "To the extent that the North aids the Vietcong, our strikes are necessary. But when we are satisfied that all support from the North is cut off and that there is still a real indigenous revolution in South Vietnam, we must reassess the whole problem." The United States, he explained, must eventually be willing to negotiate for the South a genuine neutrality and independence from both American and Communist vassalage. A month later, during an appearance by Dean Rusk before the Foreign Relations Committee, McCarthy supported Fulbright's point that the Gulf of Tonkin Resolution was "outdated" if the administration was planning to send thousands of ground troops to Vietnam. If the White House intended to hide behind the resolution, he warned, Congress should reconsider "the authority which we supposedly gave." He was not ready, however, to join the likes of Morse and Gruening in outright opposition. After all, he still had a reasonable chance of replacing Stevenson at the United Nations, and until that evaporated his public statements remained rather circumspect. The truth was that like most of his peers, McCarthy did not quite know what to think about Vietnam. He told one interviewer: "If we don't have a better policy than the administration does, there is nothing to do but support it. I don't think the administration policy has proved itself right, but I don't think it has proved itself wrong either."[32]

By the beginning of 1966 there were nearly 200,000 American soldiers in Vietnam and the war had become the central topic of conversation in the cloakrooms of the Senate. Polls taken in February and March suggested that more Americans were worried by the war than by crime, race or the cost of living, although the urban riots of the summer would focus attention once more on the problems of race and the cities. During the first half of the year, opposition to the war widened to include respected Cold Warriors such as George Kennan and Generals James Gavin and Matthew Ridgway. Moderate Democrats began privately to question the American commitment, and the protest movement gained adherents, particularly on university campuses. Later in the year the polling analyst Louis Harris concluded that most people wanted "to honor this country's commitment to the South Vietnamese," but "would also like to see the war come to an honorable end as soon as possible." As the political scientist Seymour Martin Lipset put it, ordinary people were "simultaneously doves AND hawks." For McCarthy, the year marked the decisive turning point from grudging cooperation with the administration to outright defiance. He later recalled: "As we moved into 1966, and began to build up troops, as the reports about imminent victory tended to prove false, by that time . . . I was persuaded that the progress, and the course of the war, the escalation, was most dangerous and, at that point, became a very open and continuous critic."[33]

On Christmas Day 1965 Johnson had suspended the bombing of North Vietnam in an attempt to persuade the Communists to negotiate. By late January, however, no discernible progress toward peace had been made. Opinion polls showed that the United States was almost exactly divided over the possibility of resuming the bombing campaign. On 27 January, with the administration expected to renew the bombardment at the end of the month, fifteen Democratic senators sent a public letter to Johnson urging him to prolong the suspension. The instigators of the letter were Hartke, McCarthy, Metcalf, McGovern, Frank Moss of Utah and Quentin Burdick of North Dakota, although they were known to have consulted Fulbright beforehand. According to the *New York Times,* they felt that Johnson was committed "to a course of action which has been unsuccessful in achieving its objectives in the past and threatens disaster in the future." Johnson's public reply was curt and noncommittal, but privately he determined to punish Hartke as an example to the others, openly mocking him as "obstreperous" and dismissing his protégés from federal posts. Johnson had already attempted to prevent the public disagreement over the bombing by ordering his ambassador-at-large Averell Harriman to invite McCarthy, McGovern, Hartke and Burdick to his home for drinks and a lecture. Harriman was convinced that McCarthy "wanted to support the President, but didn't fully understand what was in the President's mind"

and reported that he "had the impression that Gene McCarthy could be persuaded to take leadership in supporting the President's policies." In fact,
McCarthy had not been convinced by Johnson's emissary and later sardon-
ically remarked that Harriman had merely bored them with tales of "how
things had been back in 1941."[34]

Although McCarthy had escaped punishment, he still knew that the letter was an overt declaration of dissent from presidential policy. There was
now nothing to be gained in remaining silent. On the same day that the letter was released, he rose in the Senate to make his first statement on the
war. The burden of proof, he argued, was on the administration to demonstrate that the bombing had been effective. He personally was "not convinced that the resumption of bombing in North Vietnam would advance
the military objectives, or that they would advance our political objectives." Moreover, the whole enterprise lacked an obvious sense of moral
purpose. "The serious problem today," he explained, "is that we are called
upon to make a kind of moral commitment to an objective or to a set of
purposes which we do not clearly understand." McCarthy also suggested
that the bombing issue had led him to rethink the fundamental premises of
American involvement abroad. There must, he said, be "a national debate,
a national discussion, and a real searching of the mind and soul of America." The bombing debate, he concluded, was "a proper point for the beginning of a much deeper and much more extensive discussion not only of
Vietnam, but also of the whole function of America in history during this
second half of the twentieth century."[35]

McCarthy's public skepticism about the war was symptomatic of many
liberals, both in Congress and the nation, who were beginning to rethink
their initial enthusiasm for the American commitment to South Vietnam.
While opposition to the war was muted at first, it increased greatly between
1965 and 1968. The vagueness of much congressional comment on the
war, and the desire of many Democrats to temper their criticism of the policy with praise of the administration, meant that it was never easy to identify clear factions of hawks and doves. Nonetheless, the trend was clear. In
the House, for instance, there were only three open doves in 1966 but
eighteen in 1967, all northern Democrats. By March 1966, according to
one estimate, fifteen members of the Senate had publicly questioned the
administration's policy in Vietnam; two years later, over thirty had done so.
These figures did not include senior Democrats who questioned the war in
private but defended it in public, such as Mike Mansfield and Richard Russell. Until 1966 McCarthy was rarely identified as one of the more outspoken Senate critics of the war. McCarthy was, however, certainly part of the

core group of fifteen or so dissenters that had formed by the spring of 1966. One analysis separates them into four groups: first, Morse and Gruening, the most outspoken and severe critics of the administration; second, Fulbright, McGovern, Church, Young, Nelson, and Gore, all frequent and consistent critics; third, George Aiken, Mike Mansfield, John Sherman Cooper and Joseph Clark, whose dissent was moderate and reluctant; finally, Hartke, Robert Kennedy and McCarthy, who were all less widely recognized as critics of the war. In McCarthy's case, as one scholar puts it, this was "probably because he did not articulate his reservations with the frequency of most of the early critics."[36]

Of these fifteen dissenters, it was notable that eight were members of the Foreign Relations Committee, and indeed the doves were generally distinguished from their fellows by their knowledge and experience of foreign issues. Dissenting senators were likely to represent liberal, middle-class and urban states. They were often from the Midwest, despite the region's low level of dissenting opinion. They were generally junior figures in the Senate, and they usually declared their opposition to the war when their re-election seemed distant. McCarthy, for example, did not have to face the voters again until 1970. The Johnson administration treated the dissenters with little more than contempt: Fulbright and McGovern, for instance, were dismissed by the White House as "dangerous visionaries." And according to Johnson's loyal columnist William S. White, Clark, McCarthy and Hartke were not figures to be taken seriously: they were "simply in a state of dithery horror at the dreadful state of the world of reality."[37]

The outspoken dissent of the Senate doves was essentially reactive, responding to the engagement of American troops in ground combat in Vietnam and the escalation in troop commitments. They had two specific complaints: first, against the bombing of North Vietnam, which they viewed as brutal and unproductive; and second, against the apparent reluctance of the administration to seek a peaceful, negotiated settlement in which the National Liberation Front, the umbrella organization for Communist and nationalist guerrilla groups in the South, might have to play a part. Very few congressional critics called for the immediate withdrawal of all American forces from Vietnam. Their opposition was as much practical as moralistic, arguing that the Vietnamese conflict was not essential to American interests and questioning the validity of common shibboleths like the Munich analogy and the domino theory. Similarly, influential critics of the war from outside Congress, such as Walter Lippmann and George Kennan, objected to the administration's means, not its ends; they commanded great respect from liberals within the Senate. They did not initially rethink their opposition to Communism or their faith in American moral responsibility for the rest of the world. As the historian Charles DeBenedetti put it, they were "liberal internationalists," united by their commitment to international law, supranational organizations and the benefits of foreign aid and free trade. Their stake in the liberal order, meanwhile, meant that they were more likely to resort to persuasion within existing political institutions rather than to challenge those institutions themselves.[38]

McCarthy's own position in 1966 was little different. On 27 February he told the press that the administration had "not worked as hard as it should have in trying to get North Viet Nam to negotiate." The war was not really a Cold War issue but "mostly a Vietnamese problem, with just limited involvement by China and Moscow." Peace talks with the North Vietnamese and the NLF would, he thought, produce an acceptable end to the conflict. Indeed, the inclusion of the NLF in peace negotiations became something of an idée fixe for the congressional dissenters, who harped on the issue again and again as if it alone would provide a lasting solution to the problems of Vietnam. William Fulbright made it the focus of his criticism of the administration, and McCarthy alluded to it incessantly throughout 1966. In March he gave an extended interview to the *Minneapolis Tribune* about the war, and his comments bear repeating in detail:

> This war is not simply an extension of North Vietnamese or Chinese communism. There is a much stronger element of a South Vietnamese civil war to it than the administration states. The Vietcong undoubtedly get some help and direction from Hanoi, but indications are they are not getting much help from China . . . The public and private testimony of this administration has not been realistic. The National Liberation Front is a real political force. We should acknowledge this. It might not produce negotiations, but we should state we are willing to negotiate with them . . . I don't say that the other Southeast Asian countries are stable, but I don't think their fate is as closely related to Vietnam as the administration contends. I don't think China would take over Southeast Asia even if we weren't there . . . A very happy solution would be stabilizing the country like Laos with the National Liberation Front participating in the government without taking it over.

What he and his fellows were complaining about, then, was the administration's basic failure to grasp these simple points. The dissenters, said McCarthy, wanted "explanations of why we have failed and why we haven't negotiated." Whether their strategy for peace was a plausible alternative to either renewed commitment or unilateral withdrawal, however, remains extremely dubious; it is unlikely that the NLF and the South Vietnamese government could have worked together as harmoniously as McCarthy hoped.[39]

The most important influence on McCarthy's approach to Vietnam was the interplay of ideas in the cloakrooms of the Senate. Under Mike Mansfield, there were few institutional constraints on congressional dissent. Mansfield's own relaxed and indulgent style "encouraged Democrats and Republicans alike to speak their minds freely on Vietnam." Senators increasingly had access to information and opinion of all kinds relating to the war through the work of lobbyists, pressure groups and the peace movements. As the January public letter to Johnson suggests, there were repeated attempts to build an effective organization of war critics within the Senate. In early 1966 the dissenters held occasional meetings, loosely chaired by Fulbright and attended even by cautious critics such as Robert Kennedy, to discuss a common approach. The very existence of organized senatorial meetings to discuss opposition to administration foreign policy was, in the context of the Cold War, extraordinary in itself. On the other hand, the organization was always loose and informal. One Senate aide recalled: "They would get together informally once in a while, maybe arrange to get a few Senators on the floor at the same time, but there wasn't anything of a sustained or formal nature." George McGovern remembered that "there were two or three meetings but they weren't organized very well." The dissent, he thought, "was erratic, disorganized—or should I say unorganized." McCarthy himself was contemptuous of the attempts to coordinate opposition to the war: people "just kind of talked around the edges," in his view, and "everybody was kind of playing a different game." This actually applied as much to McCarthy as to anyone. In May 1967, for instance, Frank Church organized a statement from the doves emphasizing that while they urged negotiations, they did not support a unilateral American withdrawal. The letter was a sensible attempt to protect dissenters from charges of disloyalty and thereby to clear the way for future opposition, but McCarthy refused to sign, complaining that it was too "responsive to administration assertions that dissenters give encouragement to the enemy and are discouraging to our own efforts." McCarthy was not alone in this, but the incident was an embarrassing revelation of the weakness of the doves' organization, their internal disagreements, and the subordination of mutual interests to their own private egos and ambitions.[40]

Since the Foreign Relations Committee was the nucleus of opposition to the war in the Senate, it was not surprising that the committee hearings on the war held in January and February 1966 represented a watershed in the deteriorating relationship between the White House and its Democratic critics. Johnson made no secret of his contempt for the hearings, calling them "a lot of sound and poppycock stimulated by the personal needs of William Fulbright," whom he now privately mocked as a Soviet secret agent. The press was divided, with the *New York Times* in favor and the *Washington Post* against, and 45 percent of the public saw them as "unhelpful." With the hearings being screened live on network television, few politically aware Americans could fail to catch at least excerpts on the evening news. The Foreign Relations Committee received over 20,000 letters and telegrams, and Random House published a paperback transcript of the proceedings. McCarthy was a great advocate of the hearings, arguing that they demonstrated that the Senate was "beginning to assume its constitutional and traditional role: to challenge and question the Department of State and the Department of Defense." His own contributions were unspectacular, except for one exchange with Secretary of State Dean Rusk. McCarthy asked Rusk whether the old adage of Generals Eisenhower, Gavin and Ridgway, "that a land war in Asia is unwinnable," had now officially been rejected. Rusk replied with a convoluted discussion of the problems of facing guerrilla tactics. McCarthy cut in: "Well, I don't think that quite answers my question." Rusk answered with bland self-assurance: "I know it didn't, sir." McCarthy's question reflected his conviction that if military and diplomatic experts such as General James Gavin and George Kennan opposed the war, then the administration must be on the wrong track. Both Gavin and Kennan appeared at the hearings and made a tremendous impression on the committee. Gavin's preferred military strategy, in which the United States would defend designated "enclaves," was popular with Fulbright and other doves and commanded McCarthy's support for the next few years.[41]

Although the hearings drew some criticism from dissenters, with the senators characterized as too timid in their treatment of administration officials, they were a genuine "national sensation." As one historian put it, the comments of the more critical senators and witnesses such as Gavin and Kennan "projected to the American people the message that dissent could be politically moderate and responsible." The hearings were the first time that dissent against the war had been so publicly expressed in a conventional political context, and given the publicity they received, their effect should not be ignored. Not the least of their achievements was that unlike the massive demonstrations that followed in years to come, they presented criticism of the Vietnam conflict "in exactly the sort of closed forum most conducive to dignity, moderation and expressions of patriotism."[42]

At the end of February 1966, Wayne Morse proposed that the Senate repeal the Gulf of Tonkin Resolution, which Johnson was using to justify the commitment of troops to Vietnam. On 28 February Fulbright held a meeting of the twelve most prominent doves to discuss a common strategy. Both Fulbright and Robert Kennedy argued that Morse's amendment would attract only about fifteen votes and would appear an embarrassing failure, leaving the White House to crow that Congress supported the war policy. McCarthy disagreed. Fifteen votes, he thought, were better than none. "We've got a wild man in the White House, and we're going to have to treat him as such," he declared. McCarthy now believed that the Gulf of Tonkin Resolution represented a symbol of unjustifiable executive hegemony, and argued that Johnson was asking the Senate "to repudiate its duties under the Constitution." On 1 March, the amendment came to a vote. Only McCarthy, Gruening, Young and a repentant Fulbright supported Morse, who complained that more liberals had not dared "to vote their consciences."[43]

Although McCarthy's vote put him in the company of four of the Senate's most conspicuous doves, he rather eccentrically insisted that he did not agree with their position on the resolution. The vote had come on a motion to kill the Morse amendment, and McCarthy declared that he had voted on purely procedural grounds. The two reasons given to suppress the amendment, irrelevance and a lack of time for debate, he claimed, had not been substantiated. Even more confusingly, he insisted that he would have voted both against the Morse amendment itself and against a rival bid to reaffirm the Gulf of Tonkin Resolution. On the one hand he thought that Johnson's actions in Vietnam were "constitutional and legal without the resolution"; on the other he excused his own vote as a necessary "benchmark along the way against extension of executive power." Not surprisingly, McCarthy's convoluted excuses brought him a good deal of criticism. The *St. Paul Pioneer Press,* for example, concluded that his explanation was "a lot of parliamentary gobbledegook" which served only "to completely confuse the public as to his real views on Vietnam."[44]

Still, that McCarthy was a serious and committed critic of the war was not now in doubt, even though it was hard to detect in this intensely reserved man the kind of private anguish suffered by some of his fellow dissenters. In July 1966 he attacked the decision to bomb the North Vietnamese oil depots, warning that it would bring "a more open commitment by the Communist Chinese" and would "freeze the Soviet Union into support of North Viet-Nam." In McCarthy's eyes, the Vietnam War was not necessarily a wider Cold War conflict already, but it was in danger of becoming one through the aggression of the United States. Autumn saw him venturing out on the lecture circuit. At Washington University in St. Louis, he urged his countrymen to "leave behind an age of innocence and simplicity" and question American "moral isolation." The Vietnam debate required them "to re-examine the role of the United States in history, to put aside such old concepts as manifest destiny and the rather widely accepted idea that America had a mission to sit in judgment on other nations." In December he was invited to give the three Noble Lectures at Harvard and chose the subjects "Religion on Politics," "Morality in Government" and "The Moral Aspects of Foreign Policy." As his wife, Abigail, recalled, "his statements were so abstract and philosophical that they left me as well as the students with a feeling of inconclusiveness." But the trip and the "pessimism, unrest and mounting division within the academic community" left a deep impression on her. At the same time McCarthy made a prophetic forecast:

> The real challenge to the Democratic party in the field of foreign affairs will come in 1968, at which time the Presidential candidate of each party will be called upon to present his proposals for this country within the current of history. Generalizations about the speed of change and how the world has grown smaller, replays of our triumphs, and appeals to our treaties and declarations will then not be acceptable. Both old and new myths which are irrelevant or deceptive will then have to be challenged.[45]

CHAPTER EIGHT

The Limits of Power

I n the congressional elections of November 1966, the Democratic cause took a severe battering at the polls. The Johnson administration was already on a downward spiral: three successive summers of urban riots and the increasing frustration of the civil rights movement were tearing apart the uneasy coalition that had elected Democratic presidents in 1960 and 1964. In July 1966 Johnson's approval rating fell beneath 50 percent and never recovered. The central issue in the 1966 campaign was race, not Vietnam: according to White House polls, eight out of ten voters listed racial problems as their primary concern, and it was the liberal support for civil rights that explained the worrying defection of union members to the Republicans. However, while it was black protest that undermined the assumptions of the Great Society, it was the war that undermined the political coalition that had produced it. By now the war had cost some $21 billion and over five thousand American lives. Johnson's liberal critics were beginning to argue that the war was diverting necessary funds and energy from the Great Society reform projects, wasting money that could be better spent alleviating the problems that caused the riots. In the words of the historian Gareth Davies: "Vietnam deflected the administration from cherished domestic commitments at the very time when the racial crisis at home was lending new urgency to those same commitments." The 1966 elections were a disaster for the Democrats and for liberalism. The Republicans, running a more ideologically moderate campaign than in 1964, gained 47 seats in the House, 3 in the Senate, 8 governorships and 677 state legislature seats. Johnson had lost control of the House to the old Republican-southern Democratic coalition, effectively killing further domestic reform.[1]

For the moment, however, McCarthy and his contemporaries were more interested in the war and how to stop it. Why were they not more successful? Stanley Karnow, for example, calls the congressional doves "long on rhetoric and short on action." Other surveys have also asked "why so few of them saw fit to use their votes against the policy they opposed verbally." One obvious answer is that very few legislators between 1964 and 1968 felt comfortable voting against a war in which American servicemen were currently engaged. It was not uncommon for a senator to vote in support of the administration while publicly stating that he had profound misgivings about its policy. Most dissenters, aware of opinion polls demonstrating support for the war and contempt for its critics, believed that their opposition would hurt them politically and therefore underplayed it when they could. A frequent theme in historical examinations of the war is that Congress "failed not only in its constitutional duty to act as a check on the executive, but also in its representative function of reflecting changing public attitudes towards the war." McCarthy himself later claimed that Congress had acted "like a garden society—just bring up a resolution and we pass it." The implication is that if Congress had been more intimately involved in Vietnam policy in the early years, then the outcome would have been very different. But this is quite clearly nonsense. McCarthy and his fellows were always in a minority in Congress. As one scholar puts it, the record of Congress to 1968 was "one of vigorous, if not zealous, support of the military involvement in Vietnam . . . a record of uncritical acceptance of the Administration's justification of its actions and hasty, almost automatic, near-unanimous compliance with its requests for appropriations and other legislation pertaining to the Vietnam policy." In short, Congress was far more likely to tend toward greater belligerence than greater caution. Like their constituents, most congressmen were hawks rather than doves. Whatever McCarthy might claim, the truth was that he and his fellow critics were in the mid-1960s themselves unrepresentative and unpopular, and their legislative failures were less a sign of timidity or disorganization on their part than an inevitable result of their minority status.[2]

Opposition to the war in the Senate did not take place in a vacuum. It was influenced and informed by discussions in intellectual salons, disturbances on college campuses and arguments in liberal periodicals. For American intellectuals the importance of the Vietnam issue was that it represented the "consummation of twenty years of thinking in a broader context—that of the Cold War." It was an argument about responsibility for foreign policy, the relationship of means and ends, the accountability of government, and the right of dissent. Public opposition to the administration's policy in Vietnam, however, was less a united movement than an uneasy coalition of contradictory and competing forces and interests. Those who opposed the war included isolationists, pacifists, conscientious and selective objectors, libertarians, progressives, liberals and conservatives. Some critics thought that all war was fundamentally immoral; others thought that the administration was guilty only of using ineffective military tactics. Like his Senate colleagues, McCarthy had few links with the more extreme or moralistic peace organizations, and it seems that they had very little impact on him.[3]

One important influence on liberal Democratic dissenters, however, was the National Committee for a Sane Nuclear Policy (SANE), which had been established in 1957 by a group of leading "nuclear pacifists," including Norman Cousins and Norman Thomas, to work for nuclear disarmament and a more progressive foreign policy. Its most notable early effort came in 1962, when the SANE co-chairman and Harvard professor H. Stuart Hughes ran a peace campaign against Ted Kennedy and George Cabot Lodge in the Massachusetts senatorial election and won 50,013 votes. McCarthy was not a member of the group, but the presence of Eleanor Roosevelt and the theologian Paul Tillich among its founders undoubtedly gave it great credibility in his eyes. By the middle 1960s, SANE was concentrating its efforts on the war in Southeast Asia, its aim being to work "within the establishment, particularly among liberal Democratic politicians, to convince them that negotiations should begin in Vietnam."[4]

Like SANE, other reform groups within the liberal community were enjoying a period of renewed vigor in the middle 1960s and were instrumental in popularizing opposition to the war in Vietnam. As early as 1955 the liberal *New Republic* had printed articles by Graham Greene critical of the American presence in Vietnam, and his caustic novel *The Quiet American* met with a warm reception in liberal circles. The *New Republic* had supported Adlai Stevenson in the 1950s and was the voice of Wilsonian internationalism abroad and domestic reform at home. Its readers were young, well educated and affluent, forming what contemporaries called the "new class" or the "constituency of conscience." At the beginning of the 1950s, reform groups had a relatively low membership, but by the middle of the following decade the impact of the Adlai Stevenson campaigns and the civil rights movement had breathed new life into reform activism. In the words of Maurice Isserman and Michael Kazin, the image of the liberal was "that of a youthful and energetic man or woman, knocking on doors or buttonholing strangers on a street corner to collect signatures on a petition for the burning liberal cause of the moment. The egghead was dead; the activist triumphant."[5]

Pressure from these constituencies was vital in pushing McCarthy and other liberals into opposition to the war. The *New Republic* first called for American withdrawal from Vietnam through negotiations with the NLF in 1964, and by the following year most liberal publications had joined the chorus calling for a negotiated settlement rather than increased military commitment. Vice President Humphrey, for years the darling of the liberals, warned Johnson in 1965 that he faced opposition from "Democratic liberals, independents, [and] labor . . . at the grassroots across the country." The increasing radicalization of the ADA, for example, reflected the aggressive resurgence of reform liberalism and the corresponding eclipse of liberal anti-Communism, and in June 1965 the organization co-sponsored a SANE peace march. The shift in liberal attitudes was further reflected in the wave of third-party peace campaigns in the 1966 congressional elections. Peace candidates ran in fifteen states, and in Oregon Howard Morgan, a critic of the war, won 34.5 percent of the vote in a primary against the incumbent, pro-administration Democratic congressman. As one journalist later wrote: "In Maine, Delaware, Kentucky, Washington, Hawaii, California, in almost every state, some movement was afoot. And though there were no peace candidate victories that year except for reelection of a handful of dove Congressmen, a loose, grass-roots political structure for 1968 had begun to develop." In Minnesota, meanwhile, there was widespread unrest about the war. The state chairman, George Farr, later recalled that the prevailing sentiment among ordinary members "was basically anti-war," tempered only by their old loyalty to Hubert Humphrey. By October 1967, Johnson's local approval rating stood at only 38 percent, with 50 percent recorded against him. Only 27 percent backed his handling of the war in Vietnam, while 62 percent registered discontent for one reason or another.[6]

McCarthy had never given the impression of being terribly interested in his constituents, however, and their unease about the war seems to have had little effect on him. Much more important, and perhaps the single most important influence on McCarthy, was the position of his fellow Catholics. The Catholic community had for years been noted for its stalwart support of American foreign policy and the Cold War in particular. There was strong Catholic support at all levels for the war in Vietnam, partly because of the powerful influence of anti-Communism, especially among eastern Europeans, but also because of the publicity given to the Catholic community in South Vietnam. The church hierarchy strongly supported the war. Francis Cardinal Spellman, for example, was an extremely vociferous advocate for the administration and visited American troops in Indochina, telling them: "This war in Vietnam is, I believe, a war for civilization . . . It is a war thrust on us and we cannot yield to tyranny."[7]

But this apparent unanimity barely concealed the deep divisions between liberal and conservative Catholics, whether lay or ordained, regarding the war. Catholicism in the 1960s seemed to be changing in unexpected and controversial ways. The influence of the civil rights movement, the Second Vatican Council and ecumenical and interdenominational organizations brought a renewed engagement with modern political issues and a new commitment to social justice. American Catholicism had a new intellectual curiosity and vigor, and clergymen had more freedom to speak out on controversial political questions. There was a new emphasis on conscience rather than on authority. In 1963 Pope John XXIII issued the encyclical *Pacem in Terris*: if civil authorities contradicted the moral order, he declared, "neither the laws made nor the authorizations granted can be binding on the consciences of the citizens, since *we must obey God rather than men.*"[8]

Catholic critics of the war in Vietnam used not only *Pacem in Terris* but also the theory of the "just war" to support their arguments. A just war, they argued, must have the virtue of proportionality between the means used to prosecute it and the likelihood of achieving just ends. Whatever the benefits, means immoral in themselves could not be used. The bombing of North Vietnam in particular seemed to breach these conventions, and so from 1965 onward liberal Catholic opposition to the war began to intensify. As early as March 1965 the periodical *Commonweal,* in effect the voice of liberal Catholicism, called the bombing and commitment of American marines "essentially aimless, provocative acts that can only lead to the kind of escalation it is in our interest to avoid," and argued that negotiations were "the only intelligent course" open to the United States. Pope Paul VI sent a public letter to world leaders in September 1966 imploring the combatants "in God's name to stop" and insisting, "A settlement should be reached now." In December 1966 *Commonweal* ran an editorial denouncing the war as "unjust," "immoral," "a crime and a sin," and urged the United States to withdraw even at the price of a Communist victory. In January 1967 the *National Catholic Reporter* also denounced the war, arguing that the conflict was "casting away a heritage" and "changing the meaning of America." Two months later a group of Catholic bishops and teachers sent a letter to eight diocesan newspapers asking all American Catholics to think again about the war, citing the "indiscriminate bombing, the needless destruction of human life" and numerous civilian casualties. At the same time, younger Catholics were active in the peace demonstrations and organizations that provided some of the most abiding images of the late 1960s. In fact, it was Catholic opposition to the war in Vietnam that first marked the increasing radicalization of the Catholic clergy in the United States, so that by the 1980s Catholic bishops were among the most passionate voices in the American peace movement.[9]

McCarthy was certainly aware of the unrest in the Catholic intellectual community over the war. His own links with Catholic organizations remained strong, and he and Abigail were both active in the American liturgical movement. He evidently still took great pride in his religious background and associations: in February 1965, for instance, he gave a talk on *Pacem in Terris* in New York during which he bemoaned the "growing separation between reason and life, between means and end, mind and matter, society and the individual, religion and morality." In March 1966 he suggested that William Fulbright invite "theologians from some of the better-known seminaries" to testify in the Vietnam hearings. He took great offense when a White House spokesman referred to members of the National Council of Churches who opposed the war as "alleged churchmen," and later wrote to a Presbyterian clergyman in Minnesota that the war was "becoming more and more a test of a moral and religious commitment of America." The Quakers' lobbyist on Capitol Hill, David Hartsough, remembered that McCarthy was "very receptive" to overtures from religious peace groups and was among a group of congressmen who regularly met church leaders to discuss the war. Hartsough was sufficiently impressed by his meetings with McCarthy to say, "I think we began the process . . . that led to him deciding to run."[10]

The most influential religious peace group was probably Clergy and Laity Concerned About Vietnam (CALCAV), an ecumenical group formed in the spring of 1966. Its members were typically theological liberals with a strong sense of social responsibility, and they included relatively few Catholics. It was a moderate organization, and its primary aim was to encourage the administration to move toward a negotiated settlement. In December 1966 the executive committee called for "American clergymen of all faiths" to descend on Washington for two days of prayer and lobbying beginning on 31 January 1967. The rally was a great success, attracting 2,400 demonstrators, including prominent clergymen such as William

Sloane Coffin, Reinhold Niebuhr and Daniel Berrigan as well as liberal peace activists like Allard Lowenstein, Curtis Gans, Sanford Gottlieb and Leon Shull. McCarthy's old friend Robert McAfee Brown presented a position paper urging the usual liberal solution to the war: a bombing halt and the acceptance of the NLF in peace negotiations. On the afternoon of the first day the demonstrators walked to the Capitol to lobby their representatives. The Minnesota chapter of CALCAV was one of the nation's largest, with a full-time staff and close links with St. John's, and its members were determined to make their views heard. The CALCAV director Richard Fernandez recalled:

> I can still remember going by the doorway of Gene McCarthy's office . . . I could hear the noise. I mean, it was like a football rally. There were about sixty Minnesotans in there. And so I kind of went in. And they were *screaming* at him . . . All these people came in from his state. And he didn't know, he didn't understand, how outraged people were. Respectable people, you know—it wasn't just kids.[11]

Fernandez thought that it was this meeting that turned McCarthy into a dissenter. That was obviously not true, as McCarthy had been speaking against the war for months. The following day, however, McCarthy joined Wayne Morse and Ernest Gruening at the closing session in a packed Presbyterian church on New York Avenue. His speech was less outspoken than theirs, but it was still by far his strongest denunciation of the war, and it was greeted with enthusiastic applause by his audience. His main point was that Christians, and clergymen particularly, had a special responsibility to oppose the war, and he quoted Archbishop Geoffrey Fisher: "Everything which touches on the life of a nation is of concern to a Christian. It does not escape God's judgment by becoming in a party sense 'political.'" It was time, he said, for "a hard and harsh moral judgment on the United States position in Vietnam." It was "a cause that is beyond defense," and Americans must abandon the notion that "morality stops at the entrance to the Central Intelligence Agency." McCarthy concluded his remarks with two quotations chosen to express his moral outrage at the war and to appeal to his clerical and academic audience. The first was the French Catholic poet Charles Péguy's reflection on the Dreyfus case: "One single injustice, one single crime, one single illegality, if officially confirmed, one single hurt done to law and justice, above all if legally, nationally, generally accepted, one single crime breaks, and suffices to tear, the whole social fabric, to dishonor a whole people." He then concluded with the historian

Arnold Toynbee's words on Hannibal: "Nemesis is a potent goddess . . . War posthumously avenges the dead on the survivors, and the vanquished on the victors. The nemesis of war is intrinsic. It did not need the invention of the atomic weapon to make this apparent. It was illustrated, more than two thousand years before our time, by Hannibal's legacy to Rome." He received a standing ovation.[12]

McCarthy thought that his meetings with CALCAV represented "a turning point in the sense that we realized that there were a lot of good responsible people that were willing to make a commitment." Since the CALCAV constituency was moderate and middle class, McCarthy thought "it shocked the Administration; they didn't know how to ridicule it, you know, couldn't brush it off." For the first time he felt that there could be "really serious support" for a peace campaign, what he called an "organized group or identifiable group that the administration couldn't brush off as pacifists or freaks or agitators." Although CALCAV did not command enormous support, the respectability and importance of its members had a great impact on McCarthy. Religious and intellectual leaders, the very people with whom he most liked to associate and felt most comfortable, had now come out against the war and had come to Washington to solicit his help and to applaud his thoughts. His own speech, he later reflected, "was the first big public break of any significance." From now on there could be no turning back from the path of opposition.[13]

At the same time that McCarthy was questioning the administration policy in Indochina, he was also moving farther away from the bipartisan consensus on international affairs in general. The controversy over the war had reopened the old midcentury debate about the Cold War and the role of the United States in the world. McCarthy's long interest in government secrecy and the waning influence of Congress on foreign policy showed no sign of abating. The Johnson presidency, McCarthy later argued, saw "the gradual usurpation of power" by the executive. When he moved onto the Foreign Relations Committee he found a ready ally in William Fulbright, whose "determination to preserve congressional prerogatives in the area of foreign policy had become an obsession," according to Carl Marcy. Fulbright also shared McCarthy's alarm at the freedom and secrecy allowed the CIA. In January 1966, at the same time that he was planning the public letter to Johnson about the bombing of North Vietnam, McCarthy made another effort, his ninth, to establish a subcommittee to control the agency. "Wrapped in its cloak of secrecy," he told the *Saturday Evening Post,* "the

CIA has overthrown foreign governments, violated international law and wrecked a summit conference. The CIA is making foreign policy and assuming the role of the President and Congress. It has taken on the character of an invisible government answerable only to itself. This must stop." His notes for the subsequent Senate debate on the issue referred to CIA interventions in the Bay of Pigs, the Vietnam conflict and almost a dozen different countries, from Iran and Indonesia to Laos and Pakistan. McCarthy worked on his resolution with Carl Marcy and Pat Holt from the Foreign Relations Committee staff, and produced a proposal for an oversight committee with three members apiece from the Appropriations, Armed Services and Foreign Relations Committees. A great deal of wrangling ensued; at last, four months later, the Foreign Relations Committee approved the measure and sent it to the Senate floor. To McCarthy's great displeasure, and despite the best oratorical efforts of William Fulbright, the Senate rejected it, 61–28. As with Mike Mansfield's similar proposal in 1956, it had fallen victim not only to personal and bureaucratic jealousies, but also to the simple fact that most senators believed that intelligence was an executive responsibility. McCarthy reacted bitterly, accusing the majority whip Russell Long of soliciting votes against him on "entirely unrelated" grounds and claiming that Vice President Humphrey and Mike Mansfield had made insufficient efforts on his behalf. Richard Russell and the Senate "club," he complained, suffered from "a psychosis of the inner ring—they feel they have to be more and more exclusive." He was outraged when in February 1967 it was revealed that the CIA had secretly been funding the National Student Association. "Is it all right for the CIA to tell us that 'everything goes'?" he demanded. "This is what Hitler said."[14]

McCarthy was by no means an isolationist. He opposed measures to slash the military aid budget and supported a continued American troop presence in Western Europe. Like William Fulbright and Robert Kennedy, he was a forthright advocate for Israel. He was, however, increasingly critical of the American military and its role in diplomatic policy. A case in point was the sale of arms. In July 1966 he published a piece in the *Saturday Review* calling for a moratorium on arms sales to the developing world, with the United States setting an example to other industrialized nations. McCarthy was not alone in his interest in the issue: in late January 1967 the Foreign Relations Committee released a highly critical report on the "aggressive" arms sales promoted by the Pentagon. McCarthy himself released an accompanying statement arguing that the goal of American diplomacy should be to permit "nations to devote their resources not to weapons of destruction but to the works of peace and social justice."

Unfortunately, the "apparent lack of effective political control" of the sale of arms meant that it had "become a vested interest in the Pentagon and in the arms-supplying industry." The arms issue encapsulated McCarthy's newfound distaste for the orthodoxies of national security, his distrust and contempt for military and political elites, and his growing belief that the United States was no longer a force for peace in the world. When Senators Henry Jackson (Democrat) and John Tower (Republican) sought to restore the Pentagon revolving fund for arms sales, he bitterly called it "the most arrogant proposition we have had for some time . . . an amendment to establish in the Pentagon a kind of Federal Reserve Bank for arms sales around the world." Indeed, the radicalization of McCarthy's rhetoric on the arms sales issue reflected his increasing estrangement from the conventions of the Cold War. In October 1967, for instance, he urged the Senate to "put some kind of a limit on the power of the military-industrial complex to control or unduly influence the foreign policy of this Nation." The McCarthy who talked of "the military-industrial complex" seemed a long way from the McCarthy who had urged a "total contest with the Communists" barely a decade previously.[15]

So, by 1967, McCarthy's dissatisfaction with the war in Vietnam had widened into an interrogation of the old orthodoxies of the previous two decades. This was not necessarily surprising: other Senate critics who were making similar intellectual journeys included George McGovern, Frank Church and even Robert Kennedy. By far the most influential of McCarthy's colleagues, however, was William Fulbright. As early as March 1964 Fulbright had attacked the concept of monolithic world Communism and the simple Manicheanism of the Cold War. By 1966 Fulbright was arguing that Americans tended to "grossly exaggerate" the threat of the Chinese and called for a "general accommodation" with China. Such was Fulbright's influence with younger Democratic dissenters that he quickly found supporters; George McGovern, for instance, urged a new policy of conciliation toward China later that same year. In 1967 Fulbright published *The Arrogance of Power,* a development of his memorable speech of that name and a text that embodied the "limitationist" critique of American policy and power. The book presented the classic liberal opposition to the war, with Fulbright urging an end to the bombing of North Vietnam, the recognition of the National Liberation Front as a prelude to negotiations, and the concentration of American forces in defensive enclaves as General Gavin had earlier argued. It was time, he thought, for a renewed emphasis on the home front, "a redressing of the balance toward domestic affairs after twenty-five years of almost total preoccupation with wars and crises abroad."[16]

There was a conservative element in Fulbright's argument: his authorities, for example, included Burke, Metternich and Castlereagh. But his argument was also an excellent example of the "limitationist" analysis of American diplomacy. Its premise was that the United States was overextended; the dogmatic rigidity of anti-Communism in the 1940s and 1950s had lured successive administrations into a series of commitments abroad that betrayed what he called an "outmoded and mindless" misunderstanding of international affairs. In March 1966, for example, Fulbright argued: "American interests are better served by supporting nationalism than by opposing communism, and . . . when the two are encountered in the same country, it is in our interest to accept a communist government rather than undertake the cruel and all but impossible task of suppressing a genuinely national movement." His own erudition led him, like Ernest Gruening, to draw apocalyptic parallels with the great empires of history; by the late 1960s, according to one biographer, Fulbright was obsessed with the theme of the "tragic fall from power caused by the mindless lust for power." American power and its dangers played a central role in the arguments of liberal dissenters in the late 1960s, and the likes of Robert Kennedy, Church, McGovern, Gore and Mansfield all echoed Fulbright's sentiments. McCarthy's own book on foreign policy, also published in 1967, was titled *The Limits of Power.* Like his colleagues, he rejected a return to isolationism: the United States should maintain its engagement in the wider world, but in a more responsible and self-consciously modest manner. This was not a new approach; the limitationist argument had something of the old Progressive internationalism about it, and the Senate critics of the war actually owed as much to old traditions of ethical diplomacy as they did to new ideas about American overextension and the temptations of power in the age of the Cold War.[17]

In *A Liberal Answer to the Conservative Challenge* (1964), McCarthy had anticipated the conflict between ethical principle and perceptions of national security, noting "increasingly difficult problems of the international common good and what often appears to be a conflict between that good and our own proper national interest." He went on to add: "We cannot always impose international policy at will, no matter how right we may be, without taking into account the judgment and even the national interests of other states." *The Limits of Power* was his foreign policy manifesto: a summary of his position on foreign policy in general and a characteristic presentation of the limitationist argument. Although he rarely used ghostwriters, McCarthy acknowledged in the preface the help of the Foreign Relations Committee staff, another indication of the formative influence on him of that institution. The principal theme of the book, he explained, was "that our foreign policy should be more restrained and, insofar as prudent judgment can determine, more closely in keeping with the movement of history." This was, wrote McCarthy, the argument "which I believe Adlai Stevenson would have made on American foreign policy, had his ideas and his attitudes been translated into political reality." The reference to Stevenson, of course, served several purposes: it was an implicit rebuke to his old rival Johnson; it associated McCarthy with the old liberal cause; and it emphasized the extent to which his thinking was informed as much by temperamental conservatism as by newfound radicalism. All the same, the book offered a fairly predictable survey of American foreign policy and its weaknesses from the point of view of a liberal dissenter within the political elite.[18]

McCarthy presented his readers with both a historical and a geographical tour of American diplomatic relations. The villains of the book were John Foster Dulles and Dean Rusk. Dulles was "moralistic and ideological," while under Rusk foreign relations "could not have been handled more ineptly." The consequence of such mismanagement was that "our potential foreign obligations are almost unlimited," and the United States now occupied "a position of isolated, almost singular responsibility for the whole world." McCarthy did not, however, ask whether his own brand of militant anti-Communism might have played some part in defining American international commitments; instead, he now argued that at the outset of the Cold War the Soviet Union had simply intended to achieve Russia's "traditional aims: the establishment of satellite states on her western frontier and the fragmentation of German power." Since he had removed anti-Communism as a dynamic and reasonable justification for American policy, McCarthy was now able to attack recent initiatives as ludicrously, unaccountably misguided. In Latin America, for example, the United States had been at fault, relying too heavily on military aid and not enough on generous trade agreements. In Western Europe, meanwhile, the United States had for too long played the bully, with "precipitous or punitive policies" and an "insistence upon structures and policies which insure, or are thought to insure, domination of the United States and subordination of others."[19]

McCarthy devoted much of *The Limits of Power* to the same aspects of American foreign policy that he had previously attacked in the Senate and elsewhere. Pentagon arms sales, for instance, had "seriously exacerbated tensions and threatened world peace." The military aid program came "very close in operation to being the military-industrial complex against which President Eisenhower warned just before he left office." He had surprisingly little to say about Vietnam, perhaps because the subject was so controversial. In the paperback edition the chapter on the subject, entitled "In Dubious Battle," lasted just six pages. These contained nothing that was original, merely the same arguments for an enclave strategy, the involvement of the United Nations and negotiations with the NLF that liberal critics had been repeating for two years. The conclusion captured McCarthy's suspicion of power, his emphasis on morality in foreign policy and his rejection of his country's current role in international affairs:

> Throughout history, mighty nations have learned the limits of power. There are lessons to be learned from Athens, from Rome, from sixteenth-century Spain, and from England and France in this century. A nation has prestige according to its merits. America's contribution to world civilization must be more than a continuous performance demonstration that we can police the planet.[20]

The Limits of Power was not a particularly original, perceptive or well-crafted book. Like McCarthy's other publications, it was often underdeveloped, underwritten, oblique and airy. Still, in the fevered political atmosphere of 1967, it received some enthusiastic reviews. As the reviewer in the *Christian Science Monitor* pointed out, however, the finished product betrayed a lack of "time and effort": "Facts are spotty and not meticulously compiled; there are many generalities and some question as to what several chapters were trying to say." For all its weakness, however, the book encapsulated McCarthy's changing attitude to foreign affairs. If its defining feature was its unoriginality, then that in itself emphasized the importance of his debt to Fulbright and his dissenting contemporaries. McCarthy was no maverick. His views were as representative of a widening group of liberal critics as they were a reflection of his own alienation from the president and the administration. McCarthy's own conservative temperament, meanwhile, made him immediately sympathetic to the fashionable critique of American power. As the historian David O'Brien has pointed out, McCarthy's emphasis on moral restraint owed much to his own intellectual foundations: the thought of theologians like Jacques Maritain and Reinhold Niebuhr, for example. Both emphasized restraint as an antidote to the temptations of power. Maritain warned, "The power machine tends ceaselessly to extend itself," while Niebuhr argued, "All power is a peril to justice." Niebuhr blamed American pride and overconfidence for the country's involvement in Vietnam, and urged a negotiated compromise rather than unilateral withdrawal. McCarthy had always been impressed by this "moral critique of power"; now more than ever it appeared an urgent corrective to the arrogance of American policy.[21]

One factor that made it much easier for McCarthy to challenge Cold War orthodoxy and the war in Vietnam was his gradual relegation to the political margins. Since 1964, he had been losing interest in the daily grind of political life. After eight years in the House he had begun to feel restless, and 1967 would mark his ninth year as a senator. His commitment to the sometimes tedious routine of his Senate career was fading. With the Great Society programs on the books, he felt that the agenda of 1948 had been fulfilled: "Now the basic work has been done. You just fight for the administration of the programs. It isn't the same anymore." After all, much of a senator's job was boring, "a series of cameo appearances in the various ritual arenas," as one writer put it. The politician had always to be playing a part: "[He] enters one scene, is coached by a waiting assistant for a few moments, and then performs the role." In March 1967, during the hearings into the misconduct of Senator Tom Dodd, the columnist Drew Pearson noted that reporters were amusing themselves by "clocking McCarthy's ho-hum performance," constructing a little chart that ran from "listless," via "now listening but looks sleepy" and "begins work on some yellow sheets clearly not connected with hearing," to "missing." In 1965 he had entered a hospital for treatment of a urinary infection and finally underwent extensive prostate surgery that left him weak and convalescent for months. It had been a serious scare. "He really thought he was going to die," recalled Larry Merthan. At the same time, Abigail's health was poor and she underwent a hysterectomy. In such circumstances, and with his political career apparently heading nowhere, McCarthy's frustration was understandable.[22]

Still, his friends were disturbed by an increasingly bitter edge to his ruminations. His old friend Representative John Blatnik recalled: "I noticed a real change in him because his comments used to be a beautiful blend of cleverness and meaning with a little nip to them, but now they had a mean thrust. They were delivered with a cynical meanness that just wasn't characteristic of Gene before." Both Blatnik and Senator Gaylord Nelson, a liberal who also opposed the Vietnam War, noted that Humphrey and Johnson were the regular targets of McCarthy's remarks. McCarthy, said Nelson, "said some things that I wouldn't even repeat over the years, even up at the time Hubert died. He was just very negative and I think quite jealous of Hubert." McCarthy's closest political confidant, Philip Hart, despaired of his bitterness and lassitude; even some years later, it upset him to recall his friend's behavior:

> Out of a hundred liberals Gene would be ninety-ninth on my list. He is not worth a damn. I'm the civil rights activist and I know these have been miserable fights. They took work. They took commitment. I never saw McCarthy from one end of the month to the next. Where's he been? What do you identify with him? . . . He is my best friend in the Senate but what do you say when you take that to the country?[23]

McCarthy had never been one for "wasting time answering roll calls and quorum calls." By 1966 he was evidently considering plans to retire from the Senate in 1970 for a more sedate existence, perhaps the presidency of the University of Minnesota, with which he had been linked in the late 1950s. Even as late as September 1967 McCarthy had lunch with friends who found him "really sick of politics, sick of being in the Senate, bored, and we'd had the distinct feeling he was looking for another career, out of politics."[24]

Although McCarthy's commitment might have been wavering, his liberalism was not. His overall voting record was still, to progressives, exemplary. According to the AFL-CIO, between 1960 and 1967 he cast just one wrong vote out of thirty-eight crucial roll calls. In 1965 and 1966 his ADA voting scores were 82 percent and 90 percent. Throughout 1966 and 1967 he voted steadily in favor of expanding the federal government, in support of the Democratic Party, and against the conservative coalition of Republicans and southerners. In 1966, in fact, his attendance record was very good: *Congressional Quarterly Almanac* gave him a roll call participation score of 95 percent. But 1967 saw the halo begin to slip. On minor issues, such as federal controls on labeling and packaging, subsidies to rifle clubs, or funding for the Daughters of the American Revolution, he cheerfully defied liberal expectations by voting with the conservatives. Whereas in 1966 his "opposition to the conservative coalition" score had been a creditable 86 percent, in 1967 it fell to 45 percent, barely half of the scores registered by Mondale, Muskie and the Kennedy brothers. Similarly, his roll call attendance fell to 66 percent, the worst record among Democrats except for two senators stricken by illness and the notorious truant George Smathers. McCarthy was keener on his schedule of speaking engagements, which might net him $1,000 apiece, than on the tedious rituals of roll call votes, and his attendance on Mondays and Fridays was particularly low, perhaps indicating a fondness for long weekends. Still, the AFL-CIO gave him a rating of 100 percent for 1967. Although his attendance was patchy, and his commitment on minor issues shaky, he could still be counted on to vote the liberal line on matters of genuine national importance.[25]

There were, however, two possible blemishes on McCarthy's record that bear investigation. The first was his alleged susceptibility to powerful lobbyists. The question of McCarthy's links to the oil and gas lobby has already been discussed; although it seems impossible to resolve one way or another, the suspicion cannot entirely be dispelled. Certainly his contemporaries were never sure what to believe of McCarthy. In 1978, for instance, Arthur Schlesinger Jr. wrote that McCarthy "had come to seem indolent, frivolous, cynical, [and] also unduly responsive to the legislative requests of the Minneapolis/St. Paul banking community." The British journalist Godfrey Hodgson also thought of McCarthy as "a guy with a slightly smelly reputation for doing deals on the Finance Committee to help the oil industry." Milton Gwirtzman, an assistant to Robert Kennedy who examined McCarthy's voting record for weaknesses in 1968, later commented that "especially on the Finance Committee, he had played interest group politics against the public interest and the liberal Democratic position." Another Kennedy aide, Peter Edelman, recalled that Kennedy thought of McCarthy as "less than totally honest in his politics in the Senate Finance Committee, that he may not have taken bribes, but he had certainly represented the special interests on certain things." The problem, he went on, was that McCarthy had "been sufficiently clever about that that you couldn't pin it on him. Special interests stuff—I went and talked to former Senator [Paul] Douglas for an hour one day. And everything that [Douglas] had said just didn't check out. I mean you just couldn't pin it on McCarthy because McCarthy basically had taken positions within the Committee which were not on record in any way, or at least not on record in any available way."[26]

McCarthy's own finances were meager by senatorial standards: in 1968 he estimated that his assets came to some $30,000. It seems highly unlikely that he was personally corrupt. It is more likely that liberals, particularly those close to Robert Kennedy, were less than impressed with McCarthy's refusal to mix ethics and finance. Serving on the Finance Committee brought with it an inevitable choice between the path of the moral crusader and the path of compromise, and McCarthy unerringly chose the latter. Judging by McCarthy's attitude when questioned about the issue years afterward, he positively enjoyed infuriating the "righteous." Only once did his performance on the Finance Committee attract public criticism, when in December 1966 the *Washington Post* published an exposé of the influence of lobbyists on the recent Foreign Investors Tax Act, passed in the final hours of the Eighty-ninth Congress and known as the "Christmas Tree

Bill" for its plethora of amendments "tailor-made for importuning industries and individual corporations." McCarthy was one of several members, including Hartke, Talmadge and Fulbright, criticized for their malleability.[27]

One other suspicious incident, albeit one that attracted little attention, was McCarthy's vote on Finance in late 1967 against an amendment that would have required the government to buy drugs for Medicare at generic prices, rather than the higher brand-name prices. Larry Merthan, his former legislative assistant, was by now a lobbyist for the giant drug company Charles Pfizer, and some reports suggested that Merthan had persuaded his old employer to do Pfizer a favor. McCarthy never offered a coherent explanation for his vote, but Robert Kennedy's researchers later concluded that there was "no evidence" of anything especially nefarious. Although this was not McCarthy's finest hour, it was not necessarily corrupt or even unusual in a legislature where compromise was the norm. McCarthy was neither a crooked dealmaker nor a moral crusader. His record on the Finance Committee was not his greatest achievement and remains in large part ambiguous, but neither did it make him the worst legislator in the Senate.[28]

The other issue on which McCarthy courted controversy was his vote against abolishing the poll tax as a voting requirement during the debates over the Voting Rights Act of 1965, a decision which later attracted severe criticism. The measure was the one major legislative proposal urged by civil rights leaders that the administration had not included in the bill, and it became Edward Kennedy's own personal project. As Kennedy recognized, the constitutional position was unclear. On the one hand, the Fifteenth Amendment gave Congress the power to enforce the prohibition of discrimination in voting. On the other, in 1962 the administration had chosen to use a constitutional amendment to prohibit poll taxes in federal elections. President Johnson was worried that Kennedy's measure would alienate Republicans; the attorney general, Nicholas Katzenbach, feared it would slow down the bill's progress; and Lawrence O'Brien, the administration's head of congressional relations, thought it was a naïve blunder. Encouraged by Joseph Rauh, Kennedy pressed ahead regardless and lost narrowly, 49 votes to 45. McCarthy was one of a handful of northern Democrats who swung the vote against the bill. According to Kennedy's friend Lester Hyman, Kennedy chased McCarthy down to the Senate dining room in search of his vote and breathlessly begged him to come up and help:

> "I'm having my lunch," Eugene McCarthy said. "But Gene, the vote is going on, now, in the chamber—" "Ted"—McCarthy seemed to be chewing, if possible, even slower than before. "I'm-eating-my-lunch." McCarthy wan-

dered up a little later on, thought over it a moment, cast his vote: against the Kennedy amendment.[29]

To explain his opposition, McCarthy cited Katzenbach's insistence that it was better to wait for a Supreme Court ruling. He did point out, though, that he supported the abolition of the poll tax and literacy tests in voting procedures. As it turned out, Katzenbach was vindicated within the year, and in March 1966 the Supreme Court ruled the poll tax requirement unconstitutional. McCarthy's decision to oppose the amendment was therefore hardly a blow against the civil rights cause, particularly as he made it clear that he supported the thrust and spirit of Kennedy's proposal. Indeed, the attorney general had personally asked him to oppose it, telling him they would win in the Supreme Court and adding: "You can always do it if we fail." But why was it McCarthy who opposed the measure when so many northern liberals voted for it? Even if his vote was far from being a vote against civil rights, and even if Kennedy's case was flawed, it was a striking incident reminiscent of his former disputes with the Kennedy clan. True, McCarthy had done as the administration requested, but most of his usual colleagues had voted with Kennedy. As another Kennedy aide put it: "The only thing is if you look at the people who were voting on each side, he was in bad company and the fellows on Edward Kennedy's side were in good company." McCarthy himself, meanwhile, never understood why liberals thought him culpable, and he never forgave Robert Kennedy for making it an election issue three years later.[30]

From 1966 onward, McCarthy's attention was so focused on foreign affairs that he had relatively little to say about domestic issues. The growing threat of inflation, one of the most significant political developments of the late 1960s, was of little concern to the former economics teacher, and was even "a necessary price to pay for economic growth." In January 1967 he opined that a tax increase to fund both guns and butter was currently unnecessary, but he thought he would support it if the time came. There was no need for alarm, he insisted: "The overall strength of the American economy is such that we can meet predictable demands of the war in Vietnam and also continue our ever-expanding programs designed to meet domestic needs." His casual unconcern was also evident in matters of partisan competition. Most Democrats were horrified at their severe losses in the 1966 elections. McCarthy merely remarked that since most of the Great Society laws were already on the books, perhaps the time was right for new blood. "Maybe it's a good thing all these Republicans were elected," he told the press. "Let them come in and show us what's wrong, and we'll fix it. I mean it."[31]

Even his own commitment to the Great Society, the supreme achievement of Johnson's presidency, was uncertain. In March 1967 he observed
that liberals had been so concerned with the passage of the old legislative
program first advocated in 1948 that they had become "distracted from giving adequate attention to the new problems that were developing." He did
not elaborate further, but one of the new challenges must surely have been
the growing unrest in American inner cities. In 1966 there were riots in
thirty-eight cities, including Chicago and San Francisco, claiming seven
lives. In 1967 there were 164 urban disturbances, and the riots in Newark
and Detroit in July left a total of sixty-six dead. McCarthy, anxious not to
give in to the mood of embittered backlash, on 8 August made a rare but
earnest address on the subject on the Senate floor. Like his most liberal colleagues, such as Walter Mondale, Jacob Javits and Abraham Ribicoff, he
made no concessions to conservatism. This was, he said, a rebellion "by
the poor and the exploited—those who have been denied their part in the
American dream," and it was attributable not to the villainy of the rioters
but to "the scandal of poverty in a land of affluence":

> Most of the persons involved in the riots are Negroes who suffer not only the
> degradation of institutionalized poverty but also the humiliation and frustra-
> tion of discrimination and segregation. It is a mistake, however, to regard the
> riots as racial disorders and to ignore the bitter truth that many people in the
> United States live each day on the brink of despair.[32]

McCarthy's emphasis on poverty rather than on race, although faithful to
the founding spirit of the War on Poverty, was increasingly unfashionable.
At the same time, his emphasis on injustice rather than criminality put him
firmly on the liberal side of the spectrum. The problem for McCarthy and
liberals like him was that the American voter did not agree.[33]

The year 1967, Eugene McCarthy later reflected, was "the point of suspicion and some questioning." His speech to the clergymen of CALCAV on
1 February had been a pivotal moment, hardening his opposition to the war
and inflating his own self-confidence. Later that month, he appeared alongside McGovern, Gruening, Mark Hatfield and Martin Luther King Jr. at a
conference on the war organized by the *Nation* in Beverly Hills. King himself had moved into outright opposition on the issue of Vietnam. McCarthy
was now spending less and less time in the Senate chamber and more time
meandering across the country making mild denunciations of the war and
the administration in front of sympathetic audiences of students or clergy-

men. On 26 February, for instance, he was in California urging a six-month bombing pause and distancing himself from suggestions that Robert Kennedy might replace Lyndon Johnson in 1968. "I would not want to be included in that plan," he insisted. McCarthy still did not want unilateral withdrawal; instead, he argued that American troops should withdraw from designated areas and send in United Nations observers to see how the NLF reacted. The terms of his dissent, however, were changing even though its programmatic content did not. Senators did not have a *right* to dissent, he argued, but a *duty,* a "very special and unique obligation concerning the foreign policy of this country." In May 1967 he told an audience at the Union Theological Seminary in New York that speaking out was not a question of having a "right to dissent" but an "obligation . . . to speak out on matters of great importance to the public good." Unlike many of his colleagues, McCarthy did not appear particularly perturbed by the growth of public protest against the war. He agreed with student protesters that the draft law was anachronistic and unfair, and in 1966 had told one newspaper that the demonstrations were "quite a natural thing . . . There should be demonstrations showing our anxiety and uncertainty."[34]

Had McCarthy been selected as Johnson's running mate in 1964, it is unlikely that he would have become an outspoken opponent of the war. Despite private misgivings, his old colleague and rival Hubert Humphrey exuded public enthusiasm for the conflict. Vietnam, according to Humphrey, was "the place where the family of man has gained the time it needed to finally break through to a new era of hope and human development and justice." "This is our great adventure," he insisted, "and what a wonderful one it is!" Loyal to a fault, Humphrey could barely contemplate abandoning either his anti-Communist commitments or his president and political patron. McCarthy had no such qualms. There was "no historical basis," he said, for the claims that the war was assisting "the containment of communism and the containment of Chinese imperialism." He explained to one constituent:

At the present time I see two possibilities: one, that we permit and encourage the United Nations to assume a much stronger role in the efforts to settle the war; and second, as an alternative, that we gradually reduce our military effort, push pacification within the controlled areas, and attempt negotiations with the National Liberation Front over the uncontrolled areas, preliminary to a settlement with Hanoi.[35]

But by the summer of 1967 it was quite evident that the administration had no intention of paying the slightest attention to McCarthy's advice. For the first time he began to turn his rhetoric on individual members of the administration, a significant step forward from simply questioning their policies.

McCarthy's principal targets in the administration were Nicholas Katzenbach, now undersecretary of state, and Dean Rusk, secretary of state. On 17 August he walked out of a Foreign Relations Committee appropriations hearing after a clash between Katzenbach and Fulbright over the Gulf of Tonkin Resolution. Katzenbach was arguing that the president had the right to make war without a formal declaration, a convention "outmoded in the international arena." He was not impressed by Fulbright's dissent and retorted, "Didn't that Resolution authorize the President to use the armed forces of the United States in whatever way was necessary? Didn't it? What could a declaration of war have done that would have given the President more authority and a clearer voice of the Congress of the United States than that Resolution?" At that, McCarthy got up and walked out. Carl Marcy recalled, "I could see he was distraught, so I got up and followed him out . . . McCarthy and I walked out into the hall, and Ned Kenworthy [a *New York Times* reporter] was there. About all I remember of that conversation was McCarthy saying, 'Someone's got to take them on. And if I have to run for president to do it, I'm going to do it.'" According to Kenworthy, McCarthy said, "This is the wildest testimony I've ever heard. There is no limit to what he says the President can do. There is only one thing to do—take it to the country." What did he mean? McCarthy later explained that Katzenbach and Johnson were proposing a "kind of dictatorship in foreign policy":

> I concluded that if this was really the judgment of the president, then in a way the engagement in Vietnam was secondary and that more important than that was the conception of the role of the presidency in the field of foreign policy . . . I didn't decide then that *I* should run, but I think I decided that there had to be some kind of a showdown challenge to that point of view.[36]

But at the time, few people took McCarthy seriously.

CHAPTER NINE

A Footnote in History: New Hampshire, 1968

B
y 1967, the journalist Stewart Alsop later wrote, Washington, D.C., had become "an unhappy place." He explained: "The old, carefree self-confidence which used to distinguish Washington from other capitals has been replaced by uneasiness, bitterness, and self-doubt, which hang over the city like a noxious fug. Old friends, groping through the fug, suddenly find that they have become enemies." They had been driven apart by one issue above all: the war in Vietnam. It was, remembered George McGovern, "all people talked about at cocktail parties or across the back fence . . . [It] was the transcendent issue in American politics. If you lived in Washington, it was the only issue." For Johnson's liberal critics, his stubborn belligerence symbolized all that was wrong with his faltering administration. As month followed month with no sign of any change in presidential policy, their opposition became ever more strident and they became ever more unwelcome at Washington soirees and in the White House itself. The liberal Republican mayor of New York, John Lindsay, commented that over Washington there hung a heavy atmosphere of "disaffection and betrayal."[1]

This mood of dissatisfaction was central to Eugene McCarthy's bid for the presidency. At the same time, his campaign would have been unthinkable were it not for the mounting personal unpopularity of Lyndon Johnson. In January 1966 Johnson's Gallup approval rating had stood at 61 percent; by October 1967 it had sunk to 38 percent. Johnson's unpopularity was not attributable solely to the war. No opinion poll in 1967 ever put opposition to the war above 32 percent, and an outright majority of Americans always opposed unilateral withdrawal from Vietnam. Indeed, a Gallup poll in October 1967 found that two-thirds of the public still supported the bombing of North Vietnam, and another survey even found that a quarter of respondents favored a nuclear attack on the North. Even so, levels of support for the war were beginning to fall, and in October 1967 one poll found that nearly half of all Americans believed that the original commitment to South Vietnam had been a "mistake." Businessmen were beginning to question the increasing costs of military operations in Indochina, and even *Life* magazine wondered whether the war was "worth winning." Many working-class Democrats felt that the White House should simply "let the gooks fight it out." Meanwhile, many Americans, weary of Johnson's personal style and enthusiasm for domestic reform, were "tired of being improved." The riots in Newark and Detroit, as well as the looming threat of inflation raised by Johnson's demands for tax surcharges, had badly damaged his domestic credibility. Johnson's various commitments, from civil rights and the War on Poverty to the endless war in Vietnam, seemed finally to have dragged him down.[2]

Johnson was also peculiarly vulnerable to a challenge because the national Democratic organization itself had never been weaker. In 1966 it had been badly damaged by the issues of race and crime. Johnson himself had slashed the budget of the national committee and concentrated its resources in the White House. By 1968 no more than a fifth of the population lived in areas with a dominant Democratic Party organization. "Legend to the contrary notwithstanding, when it came to party politics, [Johnson] was not good," recalled Hubert Humphrey. In January 1967 Eugene Wyman, the national committee member for California, warned that unless the party apparatus were rebuilt, there might be "a general disintegration of Democratic organizations throughout the country." But change did not come, and in September 1967, just months before McCarthy announced his candidacy, Lawrence O'Brien told Johnson that the national committee was "not staffed or equipped to conduct a successful presidential election."[3]

Eugene McCarthy's campaign for the Democratic presidential nomination had first been discussed nearly a year before his actual declaration. His close friend Larry Merthan even remembered that McCarthy had first raised the subject in 1964, after Johnson overlooked him for the vice presidency. McCarthy's opposition to Lyndon Johnson therefore not only owed a great deal to personal resentment but also long anticipated the overtures made to him by antiwar groups in 1967. On Christmas Eve 1966, for instance, two of his aides drew up a plan, dubbed "Operation Casa Blanca," to coordinate nationwide efforts for an insurgent campaign in 1968. The most important early influence, however, came from the wealthy liberal veterans of Adlai Stevenson's campaigns in the 1950s, a group which clustered around the New York lawyer Thomas Finletter, secretary of the air force in the Truman administration and a prominent figure in reform circles thereafter. The Stevensonians remembered Johnson as their conservative adversary from the party battles of the 1950s, and were eager to see a liberal restoration. In January 1967, after a series of clandestine meetings, Finletter offered McCarthy $50,000 to set up an office and to begin planning a challenge over the issue of Vietnam. Two months later Finletter and his friends invited McCarthy to a dinner party in New York to persuade him to raise his public profile in preparation for a challenge. Money, McCarthy was told, was not in short supply: the Stevenson veterans had wealthy friends on Wall Street. Although McCarthy was initially enthusiastic, he never wholeheartedly endorsed their plan, and very little came of it. He was not yet ready to take the plunge. Nonetheless, it was now clear to him that should he decide to run in 1968, support and money from the old Stevenson wing would be immediately forthcoming.[4]

The mutiny of the Stevenson group against Johnson's presidency revealed the extent to which the apparently serene coalition of the middle 1960s was in fact torn by ideological and factional divisions. The ADA, for example, was bitterly divided on grounds both of policy and of class. Middle-class reformers, such as Leon Shull and Joseph Rauh, opposed the war and were keen to use the organization either to press Johnson into changing his policy, or to replace him with a more liberal candidate. In October 1967, for instance, the ADA chairman, John Kenneth Galbraith, issued a letter calling for a moderate, liberal solution to the war on lines very similar to those proposed by McCarthy. In particular, the war heightened the growing disenchantment of many reform liberals with the pace and direction of the Great Society, and pushed Johnson's critics toward more radical positions on foreign policy generally and on domestic issues such as race and welfare. The revolt within ADA, and the McCarthy candidacy, thus represented on one level the resurgence of the old Stevensonian reform faction that drew both on a historic tradition of Mugwumpery and Progressivism and also on the contemporary growth of reform clubs in the cities of the North. As Hubert Humphrey's adviser William Connell noted, McCarthy appealed most to "the old adherents of Adlai Stevenson, for whom he was almost a god who could do no wrong." The war, and their opposition to Johnson, united the old Stevensonians with a new breed of ADA reformers who had cut their teeth in the civil rights struggles of the early 1960s. But as McCarthy's campaign would demonstrate, these groups were ultimately held together only by what they stood against, not by any shared program for the future.[5]

On the other hand, labor leaders such as Gus Tyler of the ILGWU and Walter Reuther of the UAW were deeply committed to President Johnson at all costs. Many union leaders had vivid memories of the faction fights against the Communists in the 1940s and shared the Catholic and eastern European heritage of their fiercely patriotic members. At thirteen AFL-CIO conventions in 1967, only 267 out of a total of 3,542 delegates supported withdrawal from Vietnam. Even those older Democrats who privately questioned the war, such as Mayor Richard J. Daley, were appalled by the thought of a public breach with the president, and when the ADA endorsed McCarthy in February 1968, the ILGWU, the United Steelworkers and the UAW all walked out of the organization and exposed the schism between the younger reformers on the one hand and the anti-Communist stalwarts on the other. Of course, there had always been a division between the middle-class reformers and their moderate union allies, but as the historian Steven Gillon has argued, it took the heightened moral climate of the Vietnam War to destroy any middle ground and to drive the two groups irrevocably apart. Joseph Rauh was one of the few ADA leaders who recognized the dangers of such a breach, warning in October 1967 that the rebellion against Lyndon Johnson would break "the liberal-labor-Negro coalition that had elected every liberal President and made possible every liberal advance since the 1930s." Observers were left with a strong sense that an era in liberal politics was drawing to a close. The journalist David Halberstam wrote: "The party has been split for longer than it knows, its divisions deeper than it realizes; the old partners in the coalition have become strange bedfellows and are dreaming very different dreams."[6]

Although little came of McCarthy's meetings with the Finletter group in early 1967, reform liberals did not abandon their search for a candidate to challenge Johnson in 1968. Throughout the summer of 1967 there were persistent rumors that disaffected liberals might launch a challenge to Johnson's renomination. Senators Wayne Morse and Vance Hartke had already publicly called for a new Democratic presidential candidate in 1968. Nobody thought of McCarthy as the obvious choice, and he was one among many Democrats who were encouraged to challenge the president, including Frank Church, George McGovern and Robert Kennedy. One particularly persistent group was the network of young reformers associated with Allard Lowenstein and Curtis Gans. The two men were old friends from the University of North Carolina in the 1950s who had then moved into reform politics and the ADA, recruiting friends and associates through the National Student Association. By Christmas 1966 they were convinced that Johnson must be replaced as the next Democratic nominee by a liberal candidate who would end the war in Vietnam, and in July 1967 Gans called in *ADA World* for a primary challenge to the president. In August 1967 they founded the National Conference of Concerned Democrats, better known as the "Dump Johnson" organization, building up mailing lists of interested contributors and activists, organizing students, and lobbying politicians and officials. Gans and Lowenstein were not radicals; rather, they were younger and more strident reformers who advocated a negotiated settlement in Vietnam, not an immediate American withdrawal. Their liberal backgrounds were illustrated by their chosen recruiting grounds: the National Student Association and the local chapters of the ADA. Throughout the early autumn of 1967 Lowenstein and Gans pestered liberal senators to offer themselves as almost sacrificial primary candidates against Johnson. The problem was that most of the leading Senate doves were facing re-election in 1968 and were reluctant to jeopardize their chances: this group included Church, Morse, Nelson and their favored candidate, George McGovern. McGovern later recalled:

> Very frankly, I felt that none of us had a chance of winning the nomination but I thought the effort was worthwhile. So I suggested they pick a Senator who was not up for election. Just off the top of my head I said, "How about Metcalf, for example, or Gene McCarthy." What happened is that when this group went up to see McCarthy, he surprised both them and me by readily agreeing. Really, I was shocked—pleasantly so—when Gene came over to the Senate floor and said, "Well, I think I am going to go. Thanks for sending those people up. I think I am going to run."[7]

McCarthy did not have great respect for Lowenstein and Gans, and did not tell them that he had made up his mind until a meeting two days later, when he allowed them to implore him for over an hour before he announced that he was prepared to be their candidate.[8]

Even so, it seems fairly clear that McCarthy was not yet fully decided after all and he continued to waver both in public and in private for at least another month, during which he received embassies not only from Lowenstein but also from leading liberals such as Rauh and Galbraith. It is most likely that it was the continued pressure from these older and more influential figures that swung him into making the challenge. Both the White House and the national press were aware that McCarthy was toying with the idea of a presidential bid, and Johnson's adviser John P. Roche told the president: "He has, I hear, told Allard Lowenstein that *if* the 'Dump Johnson' movement can mobilize 'real political support,' he will consider running for President. Characteristically, he isn't going to do any work."[9]

McCarthy spent much of October and November 1967 on the road, addressing college audiences from New England to California and explicitly inviting speculation about his prospects. It is evident from his rhetoric, however, that he still had not made up his mind. At Berkeley, for instance, he told students that a primary challenge was certainly desirable, but added, "I do not know whether we ought to settle on a particular candidate . . . I see the possibility of favorite sons or of politicians urging instructed delegations or uninstructed delegations, if they wish." Similarly, he told the *New York Times* on 2 November that the challenge should be made "at a number of levels—one of resolutions and recommendations for the platform and consideration of instructing the delegations and favorite sons in certain cases." There was, he said, only a "possibility" of a personal primary challenge to the president. Ten days later, he was still admitting that "I have not quite made up my mind."[10]

Even at this late stage, McCarthy was still waiting for somebody else to enter the race—in particular, Robert Kennedy. There had been lively speculation for months that Kennedy might challenge his brother's successor, and in fact many of his advisers were urging him to do so. McCarthy was no great admirer of Robert Kennedy, but he recognized that the younger man was better placed to make the case against the war in the presidential primaries, and he told Lowenstein, "I think Bobby should do it." Indeed, during his months of indecision McCarthy seemed determined to goad Kennedy into throwing his hat in the ring. "There come certain times in politics when the individual I do not think really has the right to anticipate how things are going to be better for him in 1972," he told his audience at Berkeley. In fact, McCarthy not only sent messages to Kennedy about the race through intermediaries such as the journalist Joseph Kraft, but also met him for twenty minutes late in November. According to one of Kennedy's aides, McCarthy told him, "If you get into it, I'll get out," but this is not substantiated by any other report. What is more likely is that McCarthy recognized Kennedy's preeminent claim to carry the antiwar banner, that Kennedy gave McCarthy his tacit approval, and that no commitments were made on either side.[11]

It took Kennedy's friend and adviser John Kenneth Galbraith, the ADA president, to persuade McCarthy that the challenge was his to make. Both Galbraith and his ADA vice president, Joseph Rauh, had given up on the prospect of a Kennedy candidacy, and Galbraith had even flirted with running himself, only to discover, to his evident astonishment, that his Canadian birth made him ineligible. Rauh, meanwhile, had initially opposed the Dump Johnson movement and was terrified of the damage that could be done to the liberal-labor coalition by the younger reformers. He privately admitted that he was "desperately anxious to keep them from controlling Gene's campaign," and had decided to involve himself in the insurgent candidacy in an effort to prevent "[Henry] Wallace or New Left types" from taking it over. It was, in fact, Rauh who persuaded McCarthy to make his initial announcement in Washington and not at a Chicago conference organized by Lowenstein. Neither Galbraith nor Rauh was seriously looking for a potential president. George McGovern recalled: "They were looking for somebody to frighten Johnson into changing his policy. They never thought in terms of actually taking the nomination away from him." But they carried much greater influence with McCarthy than did the younger breed of reformers. Rauh remembered: "I told him that if he made the race, Ken and I would work for him and that, although we could make no commitment for the ADA, we would use our best efforts to get the ADA to support him." Both were senior liberals of long standing, with eminent reputations and powerful connections, and it was probably their encouragement that was ultimately decisive. McCarthy had, after all, publicly declared that the issue was "not the kind of political controversy which should be left to a children's crusade or to those not directly involved in politics." The backing of respected liberal elder statesmen was a different matter entirely, and was all the reassurance he needed. On 11 November, McCarthy flew to Cambridge to address the College Young Democratic conference, and afterward repaired to Galbraith's house, sipped a cup of tea and told him that he had decided to run.[12]

Nothing in his career had suggested that McCarthy might be the type to stand up as a sacrificial candidate, and many observers were astonished that he had decided to enter the race. One Democratic insider speculated that boredom had led him to do it, and told the press, "It's not in his nature to be President. He doesn't even want to be *Senator*!" McCarthy later gave several slightly different explanations of what had provoked him to challenge the president. His principal argument did not concern the morality of the war in Vietnam, but was instead the contention that Johnson "was abusing the Senate." "I was frustrated," he told the journalist Jules Witcover. "You couldn't get the Senate to do anything, which is where the battle should have been fought, primarily." In another interview, in the late 1990s, McCarthy insisted that Johnson "was corrupting the Senate, keeping them from debating . . . If the Senate doesn't do what it should do, why, every Senator has a responsibility to do what the Senate doesn't." He explained elsewhere: "I didn't take this as a wholly personal act on my part. I was acting for the Senate in this historical context against Lyndon Johnson and not for me as a politician." McCarthy also claimed that he was the first to spot the latent potential of the antiwar movement, a phenomenon in which he had not hitherto evinced a great deal of interest. "I thought they had a right to some directed action against the war," he recalled several decades later. In fact, McCarthy seemed to believe he had single-handedly invented the antiwar movement, explaining: "They were the kind of Americans you could brush off, saying, 'Well, they're college kids and radicals and church leaders and . . .' So it wasn't there until we put it to the test."[13]

McCarthy's private expectations were not high. "We didn't think we could win," he recalled. "We wanted to debate the issue of the war. Just by raising it, we thought we could change the picture Johnson tried to paint of unquestioned support." Before he even declared his candidacy, McCarthy had discussed his plans with the eminent Democratic lawyer Thomas Finney. According to Finney:

> Gene's original motive in going into the campaign . . . was as much to assert the utility of the political process to the young people, as it was with the idea that he was going to be successful in any normal political terms as far as his own candidacy . . . He really was trying to provide a political outlet for a deep dissatisfaction, a deep alienation on the part of a lot of people who were not traditionally participants in the political process.[14]

Indeed, at first McCarthy could barely bring himself to admit he was a candidate for the presidency, instead describing his campaign as "a referendum on Vietnam." He told the *Boston Globe* in an interview in December 1968 that his plan had simply been "to test the people." He had expected, he said, to win in Massachusetts, Wisconsin, Oregon and California, and thereby to force Johnson either to change his position on the war or to cede the nomination to Robert Kennedy. The problem, he grumbled, was the intrusion of "too much help and too much financial support."[15]

One other important factor was that McCarthy was under increasing pressure from his family and friends to stand up against the Vietnam War. Both his daughter Mary and his son, Michael, were involved with student peace organizations, and Mary in particular implored her father to oppose the administration. Abigail, meanwhile, was no less concerned about the war, but did not agree that Eugene should be the one to lead the campaign. The religious and moral climate of the McCarthy household was captured in her exchange with her daughter. "Why shouldn't it be someone else?" asked Abigail. Mary replied, "Mother! That is the most immoral thing you have ever said! That's the exact opposite of everything you've taught us to believe." In fact, McCarthy's children were so intent on his running that they were apparently quite prepared to see him sacrifice his career in the process. "Of course, we know this means Daddy can't be Senator any-more," Mary told a family friend. At the same time, moral pressure came from McCarthy's old friends at St. John's. "*Viriliter agite*," one of the monks told McCarthy in late 1967. "Act manfully."

McCarthy's religious background, his friendships with academics and clergymen, his intellectual debt to More and Maritain: all this surely had some impact, however slight. Perhaps there was also a slight sense of guilt; after all, he had hardly made a great moral contribution to American pub-lic life during his twenty-year career. "If you've been around for thirty years posing moral judgments on politics and society, you have got to take a stand. You cannot go on waving your wooden sword forever," he remarked. All the same, he was not especially enthusiastic about this opportunity to test his moral fiber. If Fulbright, Church, Nelson or Kennedy had run, he admitted, he would have happily stepped aside. Even when, twelve months later, McCarthy was being applauded as a hero, the irony of his situation rarely escaped him. In 1969, strolling back to his car with an interviewer after lunch in Washington, he discovered that it had been blocked by a Pepsi truck:

> "Can you drive that thing?" McCarthy asked. I assured him I could not. "Not very resourceful, are you?" he said, and then climbed up behind the wheel and drove off with about 500 gallons of Pepsi. I hoped he was hijacking it for the Senate Dining Room. But he stopped at the end of the block.
>
> "Did you notice that I looked around for someone else to make that run before I made it?" he said not quite solemnly. "I may not have been the best man to make it, but I was the only one willing to try."[17]

As McCarthy himself acknowledged, he was no saint. Although the courage of his decision should not be ignored, many of his more ardent supporters exaggerated his heroism in challenging Johnson for the Demo-cratic nomination. What, after all, did he really have to lose? His standing in the White House was at rock bottom anyway. He had lost much of his interest in the Senate, and privately told friends in the autumn of 1967 that he was "really sick of politics, sick of being in the Senate, bored, and . . . was looking for another career, out of politics." Vice President Humphrey recalled: "Gene told me in December of 1967 that he had lost real interest in the Senate, that he disagreed with the President's policy in Vietnam. He said he had no reason to believe he could make any impact particularly, but he thought it wouldn't hurt to give it a try. Now, maybe he felt stronger than that himself, but he didn't say it to me." Humphrey felt "it was just sort of a lark on his part"; at the same time, Humphrey was "very much upset" that his old ally was in public revolt against the administration. At this stage, of course, the prospect of an electoral showdown between the two Minnesotans seemed extremely unlikely.[18]

For McCarthy, money would not, contrary to some reports, be a problem. The success of the McCarthy campaign depended on the ease with which a few extremely affluent liberal donors could finance their pet causes, a phenomenon unthinkable after the campaign finance reforms of the 1970s. McCarthy had been promised $1 million immediately after he announced his candidacy, and he could expect generous financial backing from the liberal establishment and from businessmen and philanthropists opposed to the Vietnam War. In short, he had nothing to lose and everything to gain. "They say I'm committing political suicide," he remarked after his announcement. "Well, I'd rather do that and face up to the wrongness of the war than die of political old age." As he later explained, he did not ever want to "have to say: 'I should have made myself available in 1968' . . . In addition, when you are fifty, you don't have much time left for courage or for bold action. And especially in politics, if you have no future ambitions, that makes you a very dangerous politician. You might just run for the presidency." This was a last chance to make a mark on history—indeed, a last chance to revenge himself on Lyndon Johnson for the events of 1964. In the summer of 1968, McCarthy told a prominent Massachusetts activist:

> In 1964 I had every right to think Johnson would pick me as his Vice President. All the signals I was getting were very positive . . . I invited my family to come down from Minnesota to Atlantic City to see me accept the nomination of my party as Vice President. Without any notice to me, it was Humphrey.
>
> I vowed I would get that son of a bitch, and I did.[19]

* * *

On 30 November, with wet snow falling outside, McCarthy walked into the Senate Caucus Room and announced his intention to challenge Johnson in four primaries. He stood calmly, with his right hand in his coat pocket, and read his short statement quietly and without a smile. *Newsweek*'s correspondent Richard Stout wrote: "He wore a gray suit. His hair was gray, his eyes were gray, and his face seemed to have a grayness to it. He was all gray, like some sort of essence." McCarthy never once said that he was a candidate for the presidency, or even for the Democratic nomination, and never gave the slightest indication that he thought he could actually defeat the president. In fact, given that his statement focused uniquely on the issue of Vietnam, it seems clear that he intended his candidacy to be perceived as a vehicle for protesting against the war, rather than as a serious bid for office. There was no great substance to the speech. McCarthy refrained from criticizing President Johnson and merely remarked that he was not "for peace at any price, but for an honorable, rational and political solution to the war." Indeed, far from reciting his own credentials for the presidency, McCarthy admitted that he would have been "glad" if Robert Kennedy had run: "If he had, there'd have been no need for me to do anything." He added that Kennedy had made "no commitment to stand aside all the way." "There would surely be nothing illegal or contrary to American politics," he said, "if he or someone else were to take advantage of what I'm doing."[20]

The reaction of McCarthy's Minnesota constituents was largely favorable: an opinion poll found that 60 percent of all respondents, and 57 percent of Democrats, approved of his decision to challenge Johnson, although far fewer agreed with his position on Vietnam. The *St. Paul Pioneer Press*, however, used McCarthy's own words on Vietnam to attack his "costly exercise in futility." *Newsweek*'s Kenneth Crawford thought that McCarthy's candidacy made "no political sense" and was an ungrateful "mutiny" against a president and vice president who had once helped him. In general, however, the national press was kind to McCarthy. As expected, liberal publications such as *Commonweal,* the *Nation* and the *New Republic* praised his courage. "McCarthy . . . restores wit and style to political discourse," declared a *New Republic* editorial. The *New York Times* applauded McCarthy's "thoughtful, responsible" candidacy, which it expected "to clarify the alternatives in Vietnam and usefully contribute to the complex political process by which the American people make up their minds on great issues." *Time* praised him for giving "legitimate dissenters a civilized political voice," and the venerable Walter Lippmann exulted that McCarthy had "come forward as the defender of the American faith . . . the deepest and most cherished values of American political life."[21]

The national opinion polls, on the other hand, were less encouraging.

Only 42 percent of Americans had heard of him, although as the Gallup Report pointed out, this was not too bad a score given that McCarthy was "a relative newcomer to the national political scene." At least, unlike Spiro Agnew in 1968, he was not identified by a baffled public as "some kind of egg." Lyndon Johnson's personal popularity actually seemed to be rising, due not least to his renewed public relations efforts, and in December his approval rating edged above his negative rating for the first time since the summer. A Harris poll pitting McCarthy against Johnson nationwide gave the president a heavy 63 percent to 17 percent advantage, with a large majority also backing the escalation of the war.[22]

That winter, according to one observer, McCarthy was the "most friend-less figure in the United States Congress." Not only were his fellow Democrats reluctant to jeopardize their own careers by backing an outsider against an incumbent president, but his caustic remarks and semi-detached relationship with the Senate in the preceding years had won him few admirers. "The reason there was no great rush by his colleagues to endorse Gene," remarked one anonymous aide, "was that he pissed off everybody by making fun of them." Both Robert Kennedy and John Pastore, for example, privately thought that McCarthy was running merely "to up his lecture fees." Even those who agreed with McCarthy's outspoken dissent, like William Fulbright and George McGovern, hesitated to endorse him. Joseph Clark, who actually opposed the war, even insisted that the Philadelphia ADA cancel McCarthy's invitation to speak at Clark's benefit dinner. In the White House McCarthy's challenge was regarded as a "joke." The presidential aide John Roche quipped that a third of McCarthy's supporters were from New York or California, a third were "Japanese, Swedish or Upper Voltan," and a third "thought he was 'Joe.'" McCarthy's estranged friend Orville Freeman, still secretary of agriculture, concluded: "[He] will be a very small footnote, if a footnote at all, in history."[23]

As it turned out, McCarthy's campaign was rather more than a footnote, and indeed there has been so much written about the campaign that it makes little sense to give a detailed narrative here. McCarthy spent the first two months of 1968 languishing in the polls before rallying on 12 March, contrary to most expectations, to finish a strong second in New Hampshire, with a startling 42.4 percent to Johnson's 49.5 percent. If Republican write-ins were included, McCarthy was within 230 votes of defeating the incumbent president. Four days later, Robert Kennedy joined the race. On 31 March, with McCarthy poised to win an extraordinary victory in the Wisconsin primary, President Johnson addressed the nation and announced his withdrawal from the contest. These first three months represented a quite distinct period in the McCarthy campaign, during which he was perceived not as a potential candidate for the presidency, but as a lone standard-bearer for a cause. His principal opponent, moreover, did not campaign against McCarthy but remained in the Oval Office. This was, then, a very different operation from those McCarthy conducted against Robert Kennedy and Hubert Humphrey later in the year.

McCarthy began the year in the doldrums. His poll ratings were, if anything, falling: at the beginning of February, Gallup reported that Johnson led him 71 percent to 18 percent among Democratic voters. Robert Kennedy, on the other hand, trailed Johnson by only 12 percentage points. "Things couldn't be worse," one supporter complained. "He had more support the day he announced than he does now." In part this was because McCarthy's personal style was not what the national press had either expected or wanted. He delivered his speeches from casual notes rather than from a smoothly prepared text; he carelessly threw away lines that should have brought laughter or applause; and he refused to build to a climax, but would merely stop when he thought he had talked long enough. Addressing a group of New Hampshire Rotarians, recorded the *New York Times,* "he said what he had to say, with some eloquence but no particular flourish, and then he sat down." According to *Time,* McCarthy scratched several dawn appearances at factory gates, explaining that "I'm not really a morning person," and lacked a speechwriter, a secretary and even a typewriter. The columnist Jack Newfield, a zealous admirer of Robert Kennedy, wrote, "Eugene McCarthy's campaign is a disaster . . . McCarthy's speeches are dull, vague and without either balls or poetry. He is lazy and vain . . . It is so inept it almost seems that only a paranoid view of his intentions can explain its failure." Richard Goodwin, who joined McCarthy as a speechwriter in the spring of 1968, watched with horror as McCarthy strolled unnoticed into the largest restaurant in New Hampshire to eat dinner alone. In short, said *Newsweek,* the McCarthy campaign was "now hardly even an embarrassment."[24]

McCarthy's impatience with the rituals of presidential campaigning was palpable. The day after he announced his candidacy, he appeared before Lowenstein's Conference of Concerned Democrats in Chicago and made an almost willfully obscure speech, regaling the delegates with quotations from Charles Péguy on the Dreyfus case and Arnold Toynbee on the Punic Wars, as well as a little lecture on Hannibal and Tiberius Gracchus. *Life* rather kindly called it "oblique" and "academic." The writer Wilfrid Sheed later wondered, "What is this business with quotations?" and concluded, "The people who indulge in it most heavily are generally lightweight schoolmasters and clergymen, intellectual kibitzers and con men . . . For most other politicians, it is just a silly, parvenu form of showing off. For McCarthy, it seemed to serve no purpose at all." In fact, the self-evident explanation was that McCarthy was indeed simply showing off. It was not an isolated incident: he liked to defy the expectations of his supporters. At a New York fund-raiser, McCarthy "came in, shook three hands, and then, apparently overcome by boredom, retired to the bar." In late December McCarthy addressed thousands of students in Bedford, New Hampshire, and delivered an academic address "in his flattest conceivable style." One activist recalled:

> He got a standing ovation when he came in and no one stood when he left . . . I remember I took the Senator immediately from the podium after he finished back to his room in the motel. And I was trying to think of something appropriate to say under the circumstances. And he put his arm around me and said, "I think we really got them that time. I could feel it." I said to myself, "Oh, my God."[25]

McCarthy's supporters were less than delighted with his slow start. Joseph Rauh wrote that McCarthy must "put more fire into the campaign." "I have been doing some work for Gene," he told a friend, "but the organization is *so* bad that it is not an easy matter." Two of McCarthy's major financial backers met him for lunch in Washington and implored him to change his style and "go for the jugular vein." His campaign manager was the ironic and unflappable Blair Clark, a former Harvard classmate of John Kennedy and Robert Lowell who had been vice president and general manager of CBS News and only barely knew his candidate. Clark himself was astonished to be asked to manage the campaign, and he soon lamented to Theodore H. White that McCarthy was "wandering around the country, personally, like a Peter the Hermit" with "no organization, no force in being, nor any understructure whatsoever." Clark later explained:

> The basic thing is that McCarthy did not want a campaign . . . I said to Gene when he asked me to run the campaign and asked me to be chairman, "You should have somebody like Fred Dutton, a guy who has run campaigns and so on, but I'll take over until you can get a Fred Dutton." That was exactly what I said. And he never even looked for one, didn't want one. He didn't want another campaign.[26]

On 5 February the Minnesota Democrat Miles Lord reported to the vice president that McCarthy was "very downcast and tense." His Senate aides

ABOVE: *Eugene McCarthy and Abigail Quigley on their wedding day, 25 June 1945 (Minnesota Historical Society-MHS)*

ABOVE RIGHT: *The rising star from Minnesota's Fourth District, 1954 (Corbis)*

RIGHT: *"Gene is a good boy, but he's in the wrong party." Michael McCarthy dispenses some paternal wisdom, 1958. (MHS)*

LEFT: *Eugene and Abigail McCarthy during his first Senate campaign (MHS)*
BELOW: *The McCarthy family, 1958: (left to right) Ellen, Eugene, Margaret, Michael, Abigail and Mary (MHS)*

LEFT: *Accepting the congratulations of Minnesota Governor Orville Freeman and Ambassador Eugenie Anderson after winning the DFL senatorial endorsement (MHS)*

ABOVE: *On the stump in Minnesota, 1958 (MHS)*
BELOW: *"Any way you measure it, I'm a better man than John Kennedy."*
At Minneapolis airport, 1962, with President Kennedy, Mayor Donald Fraser,
Governor Karl Rolvaag and Senator Hubert Humphrey. (MHS)

ABOVE: *Mary, Ellen and Margaret McCarthy campaign with their father, 1964 (MHS)*
BELOW: *"What a sadistic son of a bitch." In the Oval Office with President Lyndon Johnson, political patron and future adversary, 1964. (Corbis)*

ABOVE: *Friends and rivals: Humphrey and McCarthy at the height of the vice presidential contest, 1964 (Corbis)*
BELOW: *"I got an A in economics and Bobby only got a C." With Robert Kennedy at a Democratic fundraiser, December 1967. (Corbis)*

ABOVE: *On the campaign trail in Manchester, New Hampshire, March 1968 (Associated Press)*
BELOW: *"A triumph of heroic magnitude." 12 March 1968 (Corbis)*

ABOVE: *Meeting privately with President Johnson, 12 June 1968, seven days after Robert Kennedy's assassination (Associated Press)*
BELOW: *Acclaimed by supporters at the Democratic National Convention, Chicago, August 1968 (Corbis)*

ABOVE: *The contenders: McCarthy, Humphrey and Senator George McGovern in Chicago (Corbis)*
BELOW: *"What do they expect me to do? Come on like Al Jolson?" The first of many comebacks: Massachusetts, 1972. (Corbis)*

were "sick of the deal." "He is a lonesome, pathetic figure," Lord wrote. "For goodness sake, counsel everyone not to attack him."[27]

McCarthy did not originally intend to enter the New Hampshire primary, preferring instead to wait for the primary in liberal Wisconsin, and it took several meetings for his staff to persuade him to enter New Hampshire anyway. The polls in the state gave McCarthy barely more than 10 percent, and the loyal Democratic governor predicted that Johnson would "murder" him. McCarthy had little to lose. He subsequently explained that he knew all he had to do was "beat the spread." "We couldn't lose because people thought I was Joe McCarthy," he joked. "We figured we could get 12 percent from people who just missed the [correct voting] aisles." New Hampshire certainly had a reputation as a conservative, hawkish state. It had twice as many registered Republicans as Democrats, and many Democrats were French and Irish Catholic workers who were thought likely to support military action overseas. On the other hand, the southern tier of the state resembled the fringes of Boston, with expanding suburbs inhabited by affluent white professionals: "true McCarthy country," as one account put it.[28]

McCarthy's most conspicuous issue was, of course, the war in Vietnam, and in an article for *Look* magazine, "Why I'm Battling LBJ," McCarthy did not even mention any other issue. At times he emphasized the moral grounds for dissent, telling one audience: "Vietnam did the United States no real harm. It is no threat to our country . . . In the name of God and man, and in the name of America, let the fighting stop." More frequently, however, he argued from grounds of pragmatism. Addressing the "Business Executives Move for Peace" he explained that the war was causing inflation and tax increases as well as undermining the Great Society "in a time of unprecedented need for public expenditure" on domestic programs. He continually repeated that he was not for "peace at any price," but he did expect to be able to withdraw troops within five years. His proposals to end the war were the standard liberal fare that dovish senators had been promoting for two years: an end to the bombing of the North, negotiations with the National Liberation Front, phased troop withdrawals, and a coalition government in Saigon. If this failed, he admitted, the United States might have to consider unilateral withdrawal.[29]

The Communist Tet offensive of January and February 1968 gave McCarthy's statements on the war an added bite. The White House insisted, quite correctly as it turned out, that the offensive was a military failure for the NLF. McCarthy remarked, "I suppose by this logic that if the Vietcong captured the entire country, the Administration would be claiming their total collapse." Although the importance of Tet has perhaps been over-stated, the fact that Johnson had been promising imminent military victory for so long made the Communist offensive look like a staggering reversal, and it was both a great boost for McCarthy and a blow for Johnson. In the following six weeks the president's approval rating fell by 12 percentage points, the proportion of Americans supporting the bombing dropped by 19 points, and for the first time a plurality of respondents told opinion pollsters that the intervention of troops in the South had been a "mistake." At the same time, McCarthy was careful not to position himself as a single-issue zealot. Curtis Gans recalled that McCarthy's volunteers emphasized the issues of "character and leadership" in order to maximize the anti-Johnson vote, whatever the voters' feelings on the war. McCarthy's tele-vision advertising consciously underplayed the peace issue. "The issue in this campaign," he told the camera, "is not Vietnam and not national priority, but really something more basic. It's the question of national lead-ership."[30]

The truth is that from his television commercials it was impossible to tell whether McCarthy was for or against the war. What was clear was that he was certainly not for Lyndon Johnson. The president, he said, had brought Congress to "a state of rebellion and anarchy." He was "erod-ing and weakening certain structures of government and the functions of certain institutions of government." In a clever bid to pick up disaf-fected Kennedy admirers, McCarthy strove to identify his own cause with the presidency of John Kennedy. When Kennedy died, he claimed, the mood of the United States had been one of "youth and confidence and an openness to the future." The "joyless spirit" of 1968, on the other hand, was one of "frustration, of anxiety, of uncertainty." The culprit, according to McCarthy, was none other than President Johnson. He told the television presenter David Frost that thanks to Kennedy's mastery of the economy and "restrained attitude toward the rest of the world," the United States in 1962 and 1963 had been "approaching the ideal." By contrast, Johnson had turned his back on the tradition of Wilson, Roosevelt, Truman and Kennedy and had "dissented from long-standing principles of the party." And therefore, since Robert Kennedy was not running himself, it made perfect sense to endorse a Kennedy restoration by proxy, and so to vote for McCarthy.[31]

Vietnam was not McCarthy's only issue. He complained, "If I don't speak to an audience about my views with reference to Vietnam and the related problems, people say, 'Why don't you speak about that subject?' And if I do, they say, 'Why haven't you broadened the attack?'" His other major issue was the Great Society and the question of domestic expenditure. He argued, for example, that money was being diverted to the war from programs to rebuild the cities, and suggested either tax increases or cuts elsewhere to divert money to urban affairs. Taken at face value, McCarthy's domestic proposals were drastic, to say the least. Americans needed to rethink their "moral and financial priorities" and prepare for heavy increases in spending on health, education, housing, public works and apprenticeship programs. Between two million and three million housing units, for example, were needed in the suburbs to lift black Americans out of the cycle of unemployment. He admitted that this would be expensive, although his figures fluctuated alarmingly from week to week: on 23 January, for example, his housing program would cost $15 billion, but on 2 February, only $6 billion. McCarthy's attitude to the Great Society itself, meanwhile, was extremely ambiguous. On the one hand, he lamented that it had been starved of funds; on the other, he complained that it had been "imposed on people" and "had no moral or intellectual constituents." He told a television panel that as "a kind of hand-out or public welfare approach" it was inconsistent with the New and Fair Deals. It was "defeatist" and not "the kind of constructive program on which you can really build strength in a party or basic strength in society." The tension between McCarthy's liberal and conservative instincts was nicely captured by two excerpts from the same speech:

> We must, for the moment, de-escalate the promises that are being made to our own citizens. Much of the unrest in America today is due, I believe, to the unreasonable expectations that have been generated by the effort to appear to be all things to all men . . .

> We must devise an income distribution system that would guarantee to every American a minimum livable income.[32]

It was perhaps a sign of the extent to which McCarthy was identified with the war issue that no commentators noticed the inconsistency.

Not surprisingly, given the origins of his campaign, McCarthy drew support mainly from two related but not necessarily harmonious groups: Lowenstein's young activists and the old Stevensonians. Many of his advisers, particularly in states like New York, came from the same group of upper-middle-class professionals who had supported Adlai Stevenson. Far from being merely a children's crusade, McCarthy's campaign boasted plenty of Democrats in their thirties or forties, well educated, often members of reform clubs, and long used to working for liberal causes. So closely did McCarthy work with the former Stevensonians that some of his younger and more radical supporters bitterly complained—not that McCarthy appeared to care. Martin Peretz, for example, grumbled that the old liberals were "reflective of the dead hand of American politics . . . the intellectual pastorate for some of the worst incidents of the Cold War." McCarthy's personal style was also extremely reminiscent of Stevenson's cool manner. David Mixner heard McCarthy speak in Cambridge, and later told an interviewer: "At that night I remember, I thought, 'Just like Adlai Stevenson, just like Adlai Stevenson!' "[33]

Mixner himself was a representative of the other major group backing McCarthy: the students. This was a largely unexpected alliance, and *Life* magazine remarked how curious it was to see "'hippies' and housewives working together." In fact, like their elders, most young people and even most students supported the war. Those who did oppose the war, however, were "frustrated, weary, and consumed by a kind of dull rage," as one of them put it. McCarthy's candidacy seemed to represent the answer—not that they cared much about McCarthy himself. Mixner noted: "He could have been a gorilla at that stage." Some estimates of the number of students working for McCarthy have probably been inflated. Ben Stavis, a McCarthy volunteer who later wrote a book about the campaign, claimed that between 5,000 and 10,000 worked in the various state headquarters, and a further 50,000 as canvassers. This seems rather unlikely, especially given that in early March 1968 the *New York Times* reported that "upwards of 500 students" had been canvassing for McCarthy in New Hampshire, with a thousand expected to turn out for the final push from the universities of the Northeast. On the other hand, the sheer numbers of students willing to work for his campaign did take McCarthy and his advisers aback. Busloads of supporters were actually turned away because there was nowhere for them to stay. Perhaps this had slipped McCarthy's mind when he later complained that he "could have used a little help in New Hampshire."[34]

One myth given credence by McCarthy himself was that the back rooms of his headquarters were a "chamber of horrors" containing the "hairies, the freaks and the non-straights" who refused to clean themselves up for Gene. McCarthy simply did not attract that kind of student. Many of his volunteers were already active in student liberal politics. "They were clean-cut kids, they were friends, they were people we had seen from one student conference to another," recalled one. Another volunteer thought they were "student body leaders, student leaders, people with really serious motivation." More radical students were not likely to work for a regular politician like McCarthy. He appealed to graduate students from liberal eastern colleges such as Harvard, Yale, Columbia and Brown; they were, according to the *New York Times*, "serious, sophisticated young people" with strong political commitments. A typically earnest example was the son and name-sake of one of McCarthy's Senate colleagues, Albert Gore, who worked that summer as chairman of Tennessee Youth for McCarthy and attended the Democratic convention in Chicago. Many even called themselves "New Stevensonians." "As far as I could see," concluded one reporter, "there were not that many beards to be shaved."[35]

Not only did McCarthy have plenty of volunteers in New Hampshire, he also had plenty of money. John Kenneth Galbraith found that "money was never raised so easily as for McCarthy," especially in New York and on Wall Street in particular. Palmer Weber, a member of Business Executives Against the Vietnam War, thought that over $2 million had been raised for McCarthy on Wall Street alone, not to mention the large sums contributed by antiwar businessmen to the re-election campaigns of senators such as Fulbright and McGovern. In total, McCarthy's presidential campaign cost some $11 million and was at the time the most expensive Democratic primary campaign in history. He outspent Johnson in New Hampshire and Wisconsin by almost three to one. Robert Kennedy, admittedly in a much shorter period, spent $9 million, and the combined preconvention campaigns of Johnson and Humphrey spent about $5 million. McCarthy's was, then, certainly not a shoestring effort, and only Richard Nixon spent as much as he did. Although much of this money came from a large number of very small contributors, at least $2.5 million of it came from about fifty wealthy donors. Five contributors gave over $100,000 each: they included two liberal philanthropists, two Wall Street executives, and Martin Peretz, a Harvard professor who in the 1970s became the publisher of the *New Republic.* Peretz had married the Singer sewing machine heiress and was a frequent donor to liberal causes; he was later to flirt with neoconservativism and become an enthusiastic cheerleader for his former student Al Gore. In 1968, however, he was one of McCarthy's more radical advisers. Indeed, he even paid for two similarly progressive speechwriters to work for McCarthy, although the candidate rarely bothered to take any notice of their suggestions. Many large contributors had equally strong views on how the campaign should be run, and, given the disorganized nature of the McCarthy operation, the result was a traveling circus of feuding, bickering, and even rival campaign bank accounts. Such was the chaos that Blair Clark admitted that even though funds kept coming in, they were still "always short of money . . . We never could count, never could budget, never could plan on money for a given political operation." And as the campaign went on, the situation deteriorated.[36]

McCarthy's sober personal style initially distressed his friends and supporters. Among reporters, he became notorious for the perverse habit of giving the dullest speeches before the largest audiences, and as the campaign drew on, his rhetoric became ever more encumbered with meaningless qualifiers ('kind of," "perhaps" and so on), obscure classical or theological allusions, and a pervasive sense of vagueness and indirectness. Many observers thought that his low-key monotone betrayed a "passion gap." Actually, this had always been McCarthy's style, although it is plausible that the pressure of the campaign exaggerated his verbal idiosyncrasies before a larger and more critical audience than ever before, making him more dependent than ever on instinctive, mechanical exhibitions of his own cleverness. He refused to accept that the national stage demanded a new style; when Gloria Steinem asked how the New Hampshire primary differed from his congressional campaigns in Minnesota, McCarthy replied: "It doesn't. They're exactly the same." One Senate colleague observed, "The man we know usually can't be heard more than ten feet away when he talks on the Senate floor." There was also in his style a heavy dose of contempt for those who expected something more, especially among the press. "Jesus, Jerry, it sounds like a lecture," one reporter said to McCarthy's administrative assistant Jerry Eller. "It *is* a lecture," he answered. "That's exactly what it is. I don't know why you guys keep coming along."[37]

In truth, McCarthy simply did not believe that aggressive, excited or declamatory rhetoric was appropriate during a period of national crisis. In 1960, for example, he had written: "The Christian in politics should shun the devices of the demagogue at all times, but especially at a time when anxiety is great, when tension is high, when uncertainty prevails, and emotions tend to be in the ascendancy." In March 1968 he told a New Hampshire radio station:

> I haven't really chosen to campaign in that way; that's the way I campaign. I think it's natural to me, and I think also if it weren't, if I had the gift or disposition to campaign in some other way, more violently, perhaps more aggressively, I wouldn't do it because I think that the issues with which we are dealing are the kind that ought to be considered with some reservation, and some restraint—somewhat moderately instead of in the atmosphere of shouting and emotion.[38]

When, after the campaign, the BBC interviewer Robin Day asked why his style was "flat, prosaic and almost deliberately uneloquent," McCarthy explained that there was "a danger really in stirring people up on an emotional basis when there is no place to go." "Sometimes," he said mournfully, "the audience comes to be amused and entertained, and I . . . don't like to do that very often." This attitude perplexed some of his liberal supporters. He was unrepentant, and called his position "the essence of conservatism." Most commentators were intrigued by his sober manner and ignored his profligate spending proposals. Norman Mailer's assessment was particularly striking:

> Everything in McCarthy's manner, his quiet voice, his resolute refusal to etch his wit with any hint of emphasis, his offhand delivery which would insist that remarks about the future of the world were best delivered in the tone you might employ for buying a bottle of aspirin, gave hint of his profound conservatism. He was probably, left to his own inclinations, the most serious conservative to run for nomination since Robert Taft.[39]

The columnist Henry Fairlie called McCarthy "the nearest there is to Calvin Coolidge." Even Barry Goldwater was impressed by McCarthy's performance on the campaign trail, calling him "a gentleman and a scholar who has done things in a calm and reasonable way." If there had to be a Democratic president in 1969, he admitted, "I would pick McCarthy."[40]

What few had anticipated was that McCarthy's style would also work brilliantly on television. Richard Goodwin, who had previously worked with John and Robert Kennedy and Lyndon Johnson, thought he was "masterful." McCarthy's manner was simple, direct, calm and frank. Nobody could believe he was a radical. "They saw that mid-western face and the manner of speaking and everything," Goodwin recalled, "and it was absolutely clear that they were looking at a man that whatever his position on the issues, that in his heart he was conservative." Even better, his manner invited comparison with the "hyperthyroid," "human dynamo" style of Lyndon Johnson, who was not considered a successful television performer. McCarthy's conservative approach worked beautifully in white, hawkish New Hampshire. His calm demeanor was "the personal antithesis of the very idea of social turbulence." By early March some reporters had noticed that he was actually doing rather well. In one factory his company guide said, "I'm amazed. He got the best reception anyone who's ever toured this factory has received." In short, concluded Curtis Gans, McCarthy's style was "perfect."[41]

By polling day on 12 March, the momentum was clearly with McCarthy. Johnson's representatives in the state had committed a series of blunders, and their attacks on McCarthy's patriotism had made no discernible headway. McCarthy's campaign swamped the airwaves with the simple message: "Vote for a man you can believe in. Eugene McCarthy for President." In his election eve broadcast McCarthy spoke calmly and unscripted into the camera for eighteen minutes, asking the voters to forgive him for intruding on their privacy and to "look forward to the restoration of the old spirit of America, but in new contexts, and with new enthusiasm, and with new hope that this country will again be moving as John Kennedy offered to have it move and as in fact he did begin to have it move." Twenty-four hours later, McCarthy was celebrating.[42]

The important thing about the vote for McCarthy in New Hampshire was that it was *not* a vote against the Vietnam War. According to exit polls, most voters were ignorant of his stance on the war; had they known he was a dove, they would have opposed him in greater numbers. A comprehensive survey by the University of Michigan found that three out of every five McCarthy supporters thought that Johnson was mishandling the war in Vietnam because he was not being aggressive enough. If McCarthy's candidacy invited a referendum on the war, then, the result was not quite what he had expected. So why did he do so well? In reality, his vote was an anti-Johnson vote, not an antiwar vote. In the last days before both the New Hampshire and the Wisconsin primaries, his advertising emphasized the question of "leadership," not the war, and thereby exploited Johnson's unpopularity on a range of issues. Voters were tired of Lyndon Johnson, and the desire for change encompassed both conservatives and liberals. As an unknown quantity, McCarthy could hardly fail to profit from Johnson's unpopularity. His surname certainly helped. One elderly voter told the journalist Jack Germond: "He chased all those communists out of the State Department, so I think we can give him a chance." McCarthy's showing in New Hampshire can, in fact, be usefully compared with that of George Wallace among working-class voters in 1964, 1968 and 1972. Both the McCarthy voter and the Wallace voter felt that they were "sending a message" to the regular politicians. Both Wallace and McCarthy benefited from a generalized desire for change: an end to social unrest, tax increases and the stalemate in Indochina. Indeed, had Wallace run in New Hampshire, it is probable that he and not McCarthy would have been the sensation of the season. After all, no less than 18 percent of McCarthy's primary voters ended up supporting Wallace in the general election in November.[43]

All the same, McCarthy's popularity had significant limitations. His

campaign had been notable for the absence of minority groups and organized labor, two crucial components of the Democratic coalition. It was
consequently not surprising that he fared worst in labor-dominated cities
such as Manchester, where his Catholicism proved insufficient to win over
French Catholic union members. He did well, on the other hand, in middle-
class suburbs and college towns. The *New Republic* warned that McCarthy
could not afford to neglect the unions and the minorities, who "in state
after state . . . put up the votes it takes to win." But McCarthy's campaign
remained unshakably white and middle class. In rural Wisconsin, for example, his delegation included nine college professors, but not one farmer. His
strength in New Hampshire and Wisconsin was concentrated in the suburbs. In New Hampshire, he won an unexpected 5,500 Republican votes,
evidence of his appeal to more conservative middle-class voters. A survey
of four hundred McCarthy volunteer leaders suggested that a typical supporter might be a woman in her late thirties, perhaps working in education,
with two or more degrees and a salary around $15,000, three times the
national average.[44]

Some observers saw this as the triumph of a "New Politics," heralding a
new alliance for the Democrats, "a new, postliberal coalition of students,
intellectuals, professionals and ordinary voters." At the same time, it also
clearly reflected the persistence of the Stevensonian tradition in American
politics. Stevenson, especially in 1960 when he contended with Kennedy
for the Democratic nomination, had appealed to liberal students, the "tall
emaciated young men" and "ascetic, face-washed Beat ladies" of Norman
Mailer's account. Stevenson, like McCarthy, won over the middle classes
because of his style, not his message: "his weariness, his civilized stance of
being *above politics, beyond ideology* . . . his personal qualities of reason
and wit." Neither made any pretense of appealing to working-class concerns. McCarthy did not even emphasize his party identification as a
Democrat, and won considerable Republican and independent support in
both New Hampshire and Wisconsin. Some political commentators saw the
dangers of this approach. David Broder, for instance, noted that local
activism for Stevenson had been confined to white middle-class and upper-
class areas, adding that "in states like California, where the Stevenson heirs
are still in control of the Democratic Party, this weakness shows up." As
Broder recognized, the problem for liberals like McCarthy was that bask-
ing in the fervent adulation of these small but enthusiastic middle-class
groups, they might forget to reach out to the millions of blue-collar workers who had formed the bedrock of the New Deal coalition. Ordinary voters had already punished the Democrats for their associations with crime,

urban unrest and profligate spending in the 1966 midterm elections; the main task now was surely to rebuild the alliance of middle-class reformers and blue-collar union members that had worked so well for Roosevelt, Truman and Kennedy. It was certainly not inevitable that working-class voters would abandon the New Deal coalition after Lyndon Johnson's reforms, but the onus was on the leading figures in the liberal movement to reassure blue-collar Americans that they still had a place at the center of the Democratic Party.[45]

None of this, however, could eclipse the fact that McCarthy had pulled off an extraordinary success, first in New Hampshire and then in Wisconsin, where he was poised to deal Johnson a smashing blow until the president withdrew two days before the primary. *Newsweek* called New Hampshire a "triumph of heroic magnitude." For old allies like Hubert Humphrey and Walter Mondale, the result represented not only McCarthy's revenge for the events of 1964, but also a shattering disaster that threatened to undo all their work over the previous four years. "I think Humphrey thought his political career was destroyed," Mondale subsequently recalled. For McCarthy, it was a sweet success, all the more welcome because it was so unexpected. Writing two years later, Richard Scammon and Ben Wattenberg, two Democrats who had worked for President Johnson and whose ideas would later become the blueprint for Democratic neoconservatism, generously concluded: "There is no tarnishing a victory of that magnitude, nor can the velocity of McCarthy's climb to national prominence be deprecated in any way; it was a meteoric ascent rarely matched in American political annals."[46]

CHAPTER TEN

The Road to Chicago

Within two weeks, however, the entire campaign had changed. On 16 March Robert Kennedy declared his candidacy; then, on 31 March, Lyndon Johnson, McCarthy's original target, announced that he would not seek re-election. McCarthy, addressing a Wisconsin college audience while the president was speaking on television, was stunned by Johnson's decision. His reaction was characteristically unemotional; he barely lost his self-possession for an instant. "It's a surprise to me," he said blandly. "Things have gotten rather complicated."[1]

His advisers were at once flabbergasted, ecstatic and horrified; as Theodore H. White put it, "In ten seconds the rationale of their campaign had dissolved." McCarthy could not now run against Johnson as the plucky outsider who had dared to challenge the president, nor could he now run as the embodiment of moral virtue who had defied the odds to make a stand against the war. "He was now simply another Democrat after the prize," said Jack Germond. McCarthy had not expected this; he had not even wanted it. He later told the *Boston Globe* that he had expected to win three or four primaries and then to concede the nomination either to Kennedy or to a repentant Johnson. Kennedy's entrance, he insisted, had ruined things. If he had stayed out, "Bobby could have come in as the unifying force." There was little chance of that now. McCarthy from April 1968 onward faced a struggle for the Democratic nomination not with Johnson but with Robert Kennedy, whose candidacy McCarthy had encouraged the previous autumn. McCarthy could no longer simply run against Johnson; he now had to run *for* himself, a very different prospect. "I think the question becomes one of which of us you think could best administer the government—which of us could best unify the country and provide what is called leadership for the days which are ahead," he told an audience in Indiana on 28 April.[2]

This second campaign would be totally unlike the crusade against Johnson's war. McCarthy now found himself locked in a grueling political struggle with Robert Kennedy as the primary circus moved first to Indiana and then to Nebraska, Oregon and California. Vice President Humphrey, meanwhile, declared his own candidacy on 27 April, too late to enter most of the primaries. Kennedy won in Indiana on 7 May, with 42 percent to McCarthy's 27 percent. A third candidate, Governor Roger Branigin, a stand-in for the administration, won 31 percent. The result gave the Kennedy campaign a welcome boost, but it was still not enough to knock McCarthy out of the race. A week later McCarthy lost again in Nebraska, by 51.5 percent to 31 percent. Oregon, an affluent white state, was more to his liking. A third consecutive loss would have been disastrous, but instead he inflicted the first ever election defeat on a member of the Kennedy family, beating Robert Kennedy on 27 May, by 44.7 percent to 38.8 percent. This meant that California would be decisive. On 4 June the state gave Kennedy a narrow victory, by 46 percent to 42 percent. Just minutes after giving his victory speech, however, Kennedy was assassinated, and the nature of the campaign changed for a second time.

One important difference between McCarthy's first and second campaigns of 1968 was his own personal status. He was no longer an anonymous outsider; instead, he became a well-known, even fashionable, public figure. The *New York Times* now thought he deserved "the respect and gratitude of all who cherish democracy." In fact, after New Hampshire the national press was remarkably generous to McCarthy, and hostile or even skeptical coverage was extremely hard to find. Edgar Berman, the vice president's personal physician and no lover of Eugene McCarthy, later wrote: "Humphrey, who knew the vagaries of a Gene McCarthy candidacy better than almost anyone, watched with mounting amazement as line by line, drink by drink, the press consensus built that poetic Irishman's myth." Liberals and activists took up his cause with a vengeance. "They didn't know McCarthy," Arthur Schlesinger Jr. wryly remembered, "but they were suddenly seized by the notion that here was this man, a poet himself, a friend of poets, that had the courage to lift the banner of opposition to the war. He was a romantic figure, and suddenly came out of nowhere, and everyone could find in him their own visions of what the country needed." As an unknown, McCarthy was also a clean slate. "Our candidate had no past for us; he existed only in the present which we had helped to make," wrote Jeremy Larner. Suddenly he was also the idol of a host of celebrities, from Dustin Hoffman and Paul Newman to Arthur Miller and Igor Stravinsky. Hoffman took McCarthy's eldest daughter, Ellen, as his date to the Oscars, where she declined to wear any shoes, while the actor Leonard Nimoy opined, "I'd certainly like to be like McCarthy. But I'm not sure I am." One observer even recalled that at the Washington opening of *Man of La Mancha*, the orchestra struck up "The Impossible Dream" "as McCarthy entered his box to the thundering applause of a packed house."[3]

McCarthy was a proud man, and the adulation he received in some quarters encouraged him to think even more highly of himself and his campaign. Jules Witcover thought that he became "haughty" with all the praise. McCarthy's ambitions had certainly changed. Kennedy's appearance in the race, rapidly followed by Johnson's withdrawal, provoked McCarthy to change his rhetoric and offer himself, without reservations, as a plausible candidate for the presidency. On 13 March, in the aftermath of New Hampshire, he buoyantly announced for the first time: "I think I can get the nomination." On 23 March McCarthy declared his new intentions:

> We are not really out trying to raise an issue any longer for the attention of the people of this nation because the issue has been raised and the people of this nation are aware of what that issue is and that whole complex of issues. What we are doing is laying down a challenge to control the Presidency of the United States of America.[4]

This speech, rather than McCarthy's initial announcement on 30 November, constituted his real declaration for the presidency. He later acknowledged that he had not entered the campaign intending to aim for the White House. He had known all along, he said, that he might be forced to revise his plans: "I was never quite so naïve as to believe that in the beginning we were simply raising an issue or carrying on an educational program of some kind, because when you identify with Presidential issues and with a contest of this kind, the possibility and the real probability is that these issues become identified with you as they are with the Presidency. So you may have to go on to the campaign, which is what happened to me."[5]

McCarthy admitted that "hours shaking hands or rushing through facto-ries" was not his idea of fun, and confessed to "an inevitable feeling of boredom" at giving the same speech again and again. In interviews later in his life he refused to acknowledge that he had ever wanted to be president or had really tried to win the White House. "Well, I wouldn't say I wanted to," he insisted on one occasion. "Willing is a much stronger motivation, I said, than wanting." Many observers, however, thought that McCarthy both wanted to win and, for a time, genuinely believed that he could win. John Kenneth Galbraith, for instance, noted the effects of "political hope, the most disorienting of drugs" soon after Johnson withdrew. McCarthy, he wrote, "made half-serious references to the things he would do when he got to the White House and hazarded the unserious guess that a couple of hours a day would be sufficient for the job." McCarthy's wife, Abigail, who had initially opposed the idea of the presidential campaign, was startled to real-ize that "Gene really wanted to be president." McCarthy even ended one press conference by inviting reporters to say, "Thank you, Mr. President," which they delightedly proceeded to do. This was very different from his attitude at the beginning of the campaign, and one of his own speechwriters remembered his disappointment that "McCarthy had turned out to be any-thing but the messenger who humbly effaces himself for the sake of his mes-sage, the modest warrior who stands or falls on the virtue of his cause."[6]

As that quotation suggests, there was increasing tension between McCarthy and some of his supporters, exacerbated by the three defeats in Indiana, Nebraska and California. Toward the end of the Wisconsin primary campaign two of his senior staff members had resigned, citing as provoca-tion his position on racial issues. But in fact the problems owed more to the nature of the McCarthy effort. He was becoming tired of his student fol-lowing, and asked Blair Clark: "Why don't you get rid of all these people, and just you and I have a couple of people to hold our coats and go round and talk to people?" Because he had initially been the only candidate to oppose the war, he had attracted a large number of retainers and advisers whose opinions he did not share and who often were a good deal more rad-ical than he was. He ignored most of his speechwriters' suggestions, and said sadly one night, "You're always putting in things you *know* I won't say." McCarthy's casual approach infuriated his more earnest supporters, particularly once they started losing, and many lost their initial enthusiasm for the candidate. On one occasion he gave a talk in Los Angeles before the audience had even arrived; on another, he kept the *New York Times* colum-nist James Reston waiting while he composed a poem about wolverines; and before the debate against Kennedy he warmed up by singing Irish ballads with Robert Lowell. The more he was expected to show his serious-ness, the more casual he became.[7]

The real problem was that the campaign had turned into something very different from what he had originally intended. "Gene really didn't want to have anything you could call a presidential campaign," Clark recalled. At the same time, his advisers, many of whom had widely differing motives and expectations, began falling out among themselves to an extent excep-tional even by the standards of presidential campaigns. This had an effect on the organization of the campaign, so that in Indiana, according to *Time,* "the crack of dawn found Senator McCarthy heading for Whitlow Commu-nity Center where he talked to precisely twelve persons. During the after-noon he visited Kokomo, Peru, Wabash, Marion and Gas City. It was snowing at Peru. Most of his partisans were under the age of fifteen. At one point, his audience consisted of three farmers in a tool shed."[8]

One important factor in changing McCarthy's attitude to the presidential campaign was the entrance of Robert Kennedy, which brought out his most competitive instincts. Although McCarthy and Kennedy were certainly not enemies before 1968, neither were they at all close, nor had Kennedy for-gotten McCarthy's hostility to his brother at the Democratic convention in 1960. McCarthy later estimated that in his entire life he spent no more than three hours in conversation with Kennedy. The two men were tempera-mental opposites: Kennedy intense and impulsive, McCarthy cool and sar-donic. George McGovern and Fred Harris, two senators close to Kennedy, both recalled that Kennedy was extremely suspicious of McCarthy and was disturbed by his success in New Hampshire. The journalist Jack Newfield later wrote that Kennedy looked back bitterly at the events of 1960 and told him, "Gene just isn't a nice person." McCarthy did not think much of Kennedy either. He felt that the Kennedy family had, unpardonably, traded on their Catholicism in order to advance their political interests. Blair Clark remembered that McCarthy resented the Kennedys "as a political phenomenon . . . the rich, highly motivated kids who were going to make it in politics because that's what Daddy wanted them to do." He concluded that McCarthy "had extreme contempt for Bobby Kennedy."[9]

McCarthy never forgave Kennedy for entering the presidential race. "He was a destructive person," he later declared. "Teddy doesn't destroy any-body but himself, but Bobby would destroy other people." Robert Kennedy, he said, had promised him in November that he would not run. McCarthy repeated this allegation again and again over several decades. "We had a commitment from him that he wouldn't come in," McCarthy told Jules Witcover. "He said it publicly, and he said it to me. We shook hands and that was it." This was entirely untrue. In his very first press conference, as we have seen, McCarthy publicly stated that Kennedy had made "no commitment to stand aside all the way." He had also told the *New York Times*: "I told him I was considering entering the primaries myself. I didn't ask him what he was going to do. I just said, 'I'm not worried as to whether I'm a stalking horse for you,' meaning that if Bobby were to enter later on I would not say I'd been tricked. I left it open to him." As late as 16 March, McCarthy told another interviewer: "[Kennedy] made no commitment to me to stay out of the primaries or to support me or stand by me at the convention, so that on that score he's absolutely free to do what he's doing or anything else he might want to do." So, far from it being Kennedy who broke his promise to stay out of the campaign, it was actually McCarthy who reneged on their agreement, and, despite his promise, denounced Kennedy for joining the race.[10]

McCarthy did not bother to disguise his bitterness when Kennedy entered the race. He enjoyed mocking Kennedy for his initial refusal to challenge the president. Kennedy and his supporters, he said, "were willing to stay up on the mountain and light signal fires and bonfires, and dance in the light of the moon. But none of them came down, and I tell you it was a little lonely in New Hampshire. I walked alone." Rarely had a presidential candidate displayed such blatant and public contempt for one of his Senate colleagues. He bragged to journalists: "I got an A in economics and Bobby only got a C." The campaign, he explained, should be about "personality, competence and qualification . . . He plays touch football, I play football. He plays softball, I play baseball. He skates in Rockefeller Center, I play hockey." Most observers felt, probably correctly, that the bitterness between the two men prevented any possibility of an eventual compromise. Mary McGrory, a friend of both candidates, thought that by the end of the California primary the abuse "had reached a point of unprecedented harshness" that would inevitably prevent any rapprochement. Blair Clark recalled that Kennedy even offered McCarthy a deal: they could divide up the primaries between them, and then fight a winner-takes-all campaign in California, with the loser dropping out to support the victor. Clark felt that such a scenario could only benefit the antiwar cause, and that McCarthy might well be able to win; McCarthy, however, refused to countenance even the slightest concession. He never forgave the Kennedy campaign for distributing a pamphlet attacking his Senate record, even though it was no worse, and no more inaccurate, than most political attacks.[11]

Many of Kennedy's supporters were no less bitter in their dislike of the Minnesotan. "We regarded Gene as a dangerous man . . . He raised enthusiasms without following through," one told Arthur Herzog. In May 1968 Kenneth O'Donnell told Hubert Humphrey that Kennedy would back him, rather than McCarthy, if McCarthy won in California. While the primary campaign was in full swing, Humphrey was crossing the country lining up delegate support at the convention. Paradoxically, although Kennedy and McCarthy both opposed the war, they were also both determined to throw their support to Humphrey should they themselves falter. Personal resentment, therefore, was just as important to them as their position on the issues. By the time they reached California, McCarthy's animus toward Kennedy was so great that he publicly declared, "Under no circumstances would I join with Kennedy to stop Hubert Humphrey." McCarthy later admitted that if Kennedy had lived, "I would have given my delegates to Hubert." There was a tactical basis for this, too. Richard Goodwin, who worked for both candidates, thought that "McCarthy could expect a pretty good vote from some of the pro-Humphrey people who had been trying to get Kennedy so he shouldn't attack [Humphrey] . . . because it might alienate voters that he might otherwise get in the primary." What was more, McCarthy simply thought better of Humphrey than he did of Kennedy. As one of his advisers wearily explained: "Look, he just likes Humphrey better. It's a personal thing."[12]

McCarthy thought that he and Kennedy were actually "more or less agreed in terms of the issue," and predicted that voters would choose between them on the basis of "personality, competence and qualification." John Kenneth Galbraith noted that on "trade unions, welfare, social security, on the domestic issues of the time, there was no great difference." When the two candidates met in California for a televised debate, the result was "downright dull," according to *Time*, and even the moderator complained: "There don't seem to be very many differences between you, really." The real differences between McCarthy and Kennedy were in their style and appeal. Kennedy's strategists noted: "McCarthy deliberately cultivates a non-political image . . . he is a professor, man of ideas, inoffensive, safe, witty." Kennedy, on the other hand, traded on his cabinet experience and reputation for unswerving realism. The two men also provoked very different reactions in their audiences. Kennedy's wildly enthusiastic supporters screamed at their candidate's speeches and tore at his clothes; McCarthy's crowds listened in silence to his elliptical addresses on the war. While Kennedy embarked on exhausting street tours and rallies, McCarthy strolled through the local television studios. "There would be two minutes each night of Robert Kennedy being mauled, losing his shoes," wrote David Halberstam, "and then there would be fifteen *free—*

that was painful—minutes of Gene McCarthy talking leisurely and seriously about the issues." Kennedy seemed the candidate of emotion, McCarthy the candidate of reason. This meant that while McCarthy appealed more to middle-aged conservative voters, to some activists he failed "to convey the life-or-death implications, the bleeding human dimension, of his challenge." The *Washington Post* nicknamed the campaign "Evangelist vs. Philosopher," and remarked, "McCarthy speaks in generalities and Kennedy speaks in specifics. He dwells on himself and his moment in history; Kennedy dwells on the tragedy of the poor. McCarthy . . . 'meanders' through his campaign; Kennedy drives on like a sprinter. McCarthy soothes; Kennedy arouses."[13]

McCarthy certainly exhibited an attitude to the presidency that was unusual in a presidential candidate. When the telelvision host Johnny Carson asked him if he would be a "good President," McCarthy replied with a grin, "I think I would be adequate." Before Kennedy entered the race, McCarthy sent Richard Goodwin to tell him he wanted only one term; then Kennedy could take over. "I'm quite serious," he told Goodwin. "The presidency should be a one-term office. Then the power would be in the institution." McCarthy's conception of the presidency often seemed a negative, even passive one. The president, he said, must know "the limitations that must be placed upon the exercise of power in that office." The "basic problem" in American government, he told one audience, was "the concentration of power in the executive." President McCarthy would "spread the burden with the other branches of the government somewhat more equitably." This became a common McCarthy refrain: for the next three decades he wrote again and again of the need for "a responsible presidency rather than a strong presidency" and an office of "limited power." In 1968, however, his interpretation of the presidency was not a fashionable one. One Kennedy aide remarked: "From what he says, he'd turn the conduct of the office over to a committee and go off and read books. That scares the hell out of me." McCarthy's own wife, according to Jerry Eller, "thought he'd be a lousy President. Some morning, she'd say, he'll say: 'What, the Cabinet's meeting again? Let them worry about it; let them work it out.'" Many senior members of ADA were disturbed by his casual attitude to presidential power. Arthur Schlesinger Jr. wrote that McCarthy was the first modern liberal "to run *against* the Presidency," despite the fact that the times seemed to call for strong executive action. Indeed, at times it appeared that McCarthy was reaching back to the old liberal drive to curtail the rise of central power over the individual, an impulse that many in the 1960s saw as conservative rather than liberal.[14]

Although McCarthy and Kennedy were thought to be in broad agreement on most issues, there were important differences of emphasis between them. The war in Vietnam effectively ceased to be an issue after Johnson withdrew, since both McCarthy and Kennedy espoused the liberal "limitationist" position on the war, urging a bombing halt, a coalition government, and so on. Soon after Robert Kennedy entered the contest, however, McCarthy abandoned his previous reliance on John Kennedy's legacy. In New Hampshire McCarthy had insisted that American foreign policy had deteriorated since 1963—in other words, since Johnson replaced Kennedy in the White House. This was no longer appropriate in a race against the late president's brother. By May 1968 McCarthy had completely reversed his position on the Kennedy years, so that the period 1961–1963 was now the source of all the ills that followed. McCarthy now presented himself not as the candidate who would *return* to the past, but as the candidate who would *break* with the past. His advertising proclaimed: "Kennedy was part of the original commitment [to Vietnam] . . . As a member of the National Security Council, he must bear part of the responsibility for our original—and fundamentally erroneous—decision to interfere in Vietnam."[15]

By the time of the Oregon and California primaries, McCarthy was arguing that responsibility for the Vietnam War lay not with Johnson, but with the Eisenhower and Kennedy administrations and their dogmatic Cold War attitudes. More than ever, McCarthy's speeches betrayed his estrangement from the fraying Cold War consensus. In Indiana he warned of "a huge, powerful, and somewhat autonomous military establishment whose influence reaches into almost every aspect of our national life." In California he argued that the United States should recognize Communist China; that Cuba "should be offered the chance to return to the family of nations"; and that Americans should abandon forever the idea of "manifest destiny." He used these issues as a way of attacking Robert Kennedy, turning Kennedy's experience and associations against him, and in San Francisco he drew stark contrasts between them. Vietnam, he declared, "was no accident":

It originated in the containment doctrines of the 1950s . . . America in that period still set for itself a moral mission in which we took it upon ourselves to judge the political systems of other nations and the right to alter those systems if we found them wanting . . . This is why we could move so quickly into the period of the middle sixties and the quicksand of Vietnam. We had been there, after all, in the earlier part of the decade. Troops had been sent then. The first American soldiers had died then. And the process continued and grew naturally, for its premises remained unchanged . . . I am not entirely convinced that Senator Kennedy has entirely renounced that misconception.[16]

To some extent these were the words of his speechwriters: Carl Marcy from the Foreign Relations Committee staff, a tireless critic of executive domination of foreign policy; and Paul Gorman, a congressional speechwriter hired by Richard Goodwin. But McCarthy certainly agreed with them, and they built on his recent record of questioning the old Cold War assumptions. McCarthy's attack was, in fact, the first criticism of Cold War orthodoxy by a major candidate in a presidential campaign since 1948. It explicitly questioned Robert Kennedy's own emphasis on "our right to moral leadership of this planet," and it struck not only at Kennedy's brother, but also at Eisenhower, Dulles, Johnson and Rusk. There could be little doubt that, as Kennedy's biographer Ronald Steel puts it, on foreign policy "McCarthy was by far the more radical candidate."[17]

For all McCarthy's rhetoric, however, the withdrawal of the president from the race meant that foreign policy was no longer really the issue. Both McCarthy and Kennedy were now expected to focus on domestic concerns like poverty, race and crime. An opinion poll published in May 1968 suggested that after Vietnam, what bothered American voters were race relations, crime and the cost of living, in that order. Throughout the campaign against Kennedy, McCarthy's speeches emphasized two themes: first, Vietnam; and second, the interrelated questions of race and the inner cities. He couched this in the rhetoric of a "New Politics," though what he meant by this is not at all clear, perhaps due to the confusion of competing speechwriters. On occasion he defined it in terms of race: it meant "a greater measure of moral commitment" to civil rights and the diffusion of power and responsibility throughout the community in order to "release the black people and the poor of this country from bondage." Sometimes his New Politics veered close to woolly waffle derived partly from his Catholic education, partly from the New Left and partly from fashionable social theories of the day: he wrote, for instance, of the growing "bureaucratic control" that "deprives the individual of all sense of individual initiative, and nourishes the belief that he can do nothing if it is not planned and organized and somehow fitted into a pattern of action." Usually, however, he was really talking about the character of politics itself, and not least about party procedure. He urged, for example, a "New National Democratic Party" with biannual conventions and enlarged machinery to involve the young and minorities. Although McCarthy was vague on the subject, it was in this area that his legacy would be most enduring.[18]

McCarthy's position on domestic issues was unquestionably affected by the more progressive inclinations of his advisers. Indeed, it is likely that his emphasis would have been more conservative had it not been for the fact that his early supporters tended to be from the left wing of the liberal spectrum. On issues such as the cities, housing and a guaranteed annual income, McCarthy's position was well to the left of his own previous commitments. The question of the inner cities was a case in point, and a particularly fashionable issue after the unrest of previous years. McCarthy argued that "a substantial part of the thirty billion dollars now going into Vietnam" should be spent on regenerating urban areas. He promised to "eliminate" welfare through enormous job creation schemes; to provide "income support" for those unable to work; and to entrust important decisions to local organizations, giving the poor "responsibility for their own programs." This, he admitted, required "massive efforts" on the part of the federal government, not to mention "a great commitment of public funds" to be spent on new housing. Kennedy had a very different approach, arguing that the slums should be renovated by private finance and local organizations, not by the national government. While this appealed to the advocates of community action, it also won the support of conservatives and broke with the liberal reliance on federal funding. On this issue, therefore, McCarthy's emphasis on greater government spending clashed with Kennedy's faith in "individual initiative, self-reliance, and business participation."[19]

McCarthy's most notable proposal, however, concerned the question of a guaranteed annual income, something he had never mentioned before 1968. First, he insisted, the federal government must ensure the widespread distribution of free food stamps. Then, it should "assure everybody an annual income sufficient for him to meet his needs." Partly this would involve widening existing provisions, such as the minimum wage and unemployment compensation; but it would also involve the creation of a new "income distribution system," with "built-in incentives for self-improvement." This was not only the first time McCarthy had mentioned the subject, it was also the first time it had been raised in a presidential campaign. McCarthy was certainly under pressure from his younger advisers to embrace the issue. One encouraged him, "[It will be] one of the major liberal issues of the 1970s, and the historical and political ground could now be broken by you." It also reflected the intellectual fashion of the late 1960s. For several years an alliance of spokesmen for the poor, middle-class liberals and poverty lawyers had been arguing that welfare was a legally guaranteed entitlement. By 1968, in fact, the idea of a guaranteed income was attracting admirers from all sides. McCarthy's proposal might not have reflected his previous legislative proposals, but it certainly anticipated the initiatives of the early 1970s—not merely George McGovern's "demogrant," but also President Nixon's Family Assistance Plan, a proposal that McCarthy helped to defeat.[20]

Despite all this rhetoric about housing and welfare, McCarthy's standing was not high among black voters. "McCarthy's okay," a young black taxi driver told Gloria Steinem, "but he doesn't know what it's all about." McCarthy simply did not appeal to black audiences. Some of his staff felt that urban blacks were less interested in the war than in domestic issues, and McCarthy had a reputation as a candidate interested only in the war. A campaign manual produced by his staff on 20 June lamented that "McCarthy is still virtually unknown to the black people" and recommended that he not be presented "as a one-issue peace candidate." Even so, as *Commonweal* pointed out, McCarthy had spoken out on civil rights time and again during the campaign. The problem was that the national press was focusing on his image as the quixotic outsider and ignoring his proposals on employment, health, housing and the like. "His position could not be clearer," the *Commonweal* article concluded, "but it has not gotten across."[21]

McCarthy's position on racial issues was far from conservative. He borrowed from Frantz Fanon and Eldridge Cleaver to describe blacks as "a colonial people, living in our midst." Black poverty was no accident; rather, "black people are poor because they are powerless and powerless because they are black." The "demeaning conditions" and "racist attitudes" inflicted on black Americans were the real causes of urban unrest, and the only answer was a new policy of investment in inner city communities. There must be a program of "new civil rights," concerned not with legal status or voting rights but with "the right to a job," "the right to an education," "the right to health," and "the right to a decent house." Not only should the federal government provide subsidies to establish jobs and businesses in the cities, but it should take radical steps to break down segregation and employment—in other words, the government should move "large numbers of Negro workers and their families to jobs and housing opportunities in the nation's suburbs." This last proposal drew criticism from Robert Kennedy, who asked in their televised debate whether McCarthy seriously expected to "take ten thousand black people and move them into Orange County," a remark much deplored by progressive commentators although it was fairly consistent with Kennedy's intellectual position. If it was a bid to attract conservative votes in Orange County, it failed, since McCarthy easily won the county a few days later. McCarthy, meanwhile, argued that Kennedy intended "merely to rehabilitate the ghetto," leaving it in a "colonial" condition. Some liberal thinkers agreed; James Wechsler, for instance, thought that McCarthy, unlike Kennedy, "was quietly fighting the spreading sickness of separatism."[22]

McCarthy failed to win over black voters because his style was simply wrong. His cultivated detachment often seemed closer to aloofness than to compassion, and many observers felt that he failed to reassure voters who suffered from racial prejudice or economic disadvantage, or both. As one commentator remarked: "McCarthy could not, if life depended on it, act out his compassion for the poor." What was more, he seemed to enjoy defying the calls to make specific appeals to black audiences. Asked why blacks should vote for him, he replied, "I don't know. I haven't really made much of an argument that they should." It is difficult to imagine Robert Kennedy responding in the same way. McCarthy, however, was adamant, insisting, "I will not make racial appeals, to either black or white. I will speak the same to all." He would meet black leaders in private, but he would not make public appeals. In Wisconsin he initially refused even to visit the ghettos, telling his staff, "I don't have to prove myself to anyone, they know my record." One of his supporters remembered: "[He] struck us not only as arrogant toward black voters but as utterly contemptuous of those of us who believed a politician was obligated to go to the people and prove himself." Indeed, when Martin Luther King was assassinated, McCarthy's first reaction was to refuse an invitation to the funeral because there would be "a great big vulgar public spectacle." It took Blair Clark to argue him round. There was, as McCarthy probably recognized, a perfectly good strategic argument to avoid identification with black issues. Many of McCarthy's more conservative suburban supporters, for example in the small towns of Indiana, were disturbed whenever he spoke on civil rights. McCarthy himself later admitted he saw little purpose in it anyway: "It was pointless . . . I couldn't get the Negro votes away from Bobby Kennedy. I could have moved into the ghettos and stayed in them the whole campaign."[23]

The middle-class basis of McCarthy's support was even more apparent in the campaign against Kennedy than it had been against Johnson. He consciously pitched his restrained style to suburban audiences, drawing a contrast with Kennedy and Humphrey and appealing to what he called "a constituency of conscience." "The middle class has always been the greatest force for change," he told one reporter, and he assured his supporters in California: "You're the best and you're the ones that are most needed."

Kennedy, on the other hand, had never been popular with Stevensonian Democrats. McCarthy even remarked that his opponent was "running best among the less intelligent and less educated people in America." Kennedy was certainly perceived as the candidate of the poor and minorities: in Gary, Indiana, for example, black voters accounted for 80 percent of Kennedy's total. As McCarthy's six-point victory in the Oregon primary suggested, the two men had become firmly identified with very different constituencies, with McCarthy winning the suburban middle class and Kennedy "locked into his core constituency of blacks, Hispanics, some blue-collar ethnics, and Camelot sentimentalists."[24]

It was also increasingly difficult for McCarthy to break into other demographic groups. In both New Hampshire and Wisconsin he had polled badly in black and working-class wards, for instance in Manchester and Milwaukee, and consistently failed to impress those Catholics who read the diocesan paper rather than the liberal *Commonweal*. It is striking that in Milwaukee, when he was facing an unpopular president who had just renounced the contest, McCarthy lost the black wards by at least two to one, the Polish wards by more than three to one, and the eastern European and German wards by more than six to one. As the unsympathetic columnist Joseph Kraft pointed out, McCarthy's appeal therefore had severe limitations for any Democrat hoping to put together a victorious coalition. He might well appeal to a growing middle-class constituency, argued Kraft, "but it is not now the majority. The majority now lies with the low and middle income whites lining up around former Vice President Richard Nixon. They are hostile to the people Gene McCarthy represents, and suspicious of their fancy ideas."[25]

In fact, the primary results suggest that both the Kennedy and McCarthy candidacies had severe weaknesses. In Indiana, Kennedy beat McCarthy handily among blacks, Catholics, and urban voters. McCarthy, however, led Kennedy by 35 percent to 27 percent among middle-aged voters; he won 41 percent of those against the war and 26 percent of those supporting it; and he led his bitter rival by a handsome 44 percent to 18 percent among those with a college degree. Neither man, it appears, was capable of breaking out beyond his nucleus of committed supporters. Kennedy, meanwhile, was further crippled by his association with civil rights. McCarthy's canvassers found a strong backlash in low-income and middle-class white neighborhoods against Kennedy, traceable to his identification with black protest. Indeed, McCarthy's showing in Indiana indicates that Kennedy was very far from assembling the kind of neopopulist "black and blue-collar coalition" that he would need to sweep to victory in November. Kennedy won only eleven of the seventy white precincts in the city of Gary. In industrial Lake County, which had supported George Wallace in 1964, he won a mere 34 percent of white votes, and his margin of victory over McCarthy came almost completely from black voters. Similarly, in California, Kennedy won his victory among black and Hispanic voters, while McCarthy did well in small towns, suburbs and agricultural areas outside the Central Valley. As Kennedy's associates William vanden Heuvel and Milton Gwirtzman later wrote: "The more personally identified the white voters were with the racial struggle, the more they identified Kennedy with the black side of it, and turned to his opponents as an outlet for their protest." Far from representing a solution to the challenge of the white working-class backlash against civil rights, Robert Kennedy was perceived as part of the problem. While McCarthy remained locked into his "constituency of conscience," Kennedy was equally handicapped by his associations. As Ronald Steel puts it, he "did not—popular mythology notwithstanding—ride the crest of a black–poor white coalition. There was, in fact, no such coalition."[26]

Had Kennedy lived, his victory in the California primary would not have knocked McCarthy out of the contest. McCarthy and his strategists had, in fact, already calculated that a narrow Kennedy victory would be an ideal result. If McCarthy won, then Kennedy would drop out and his delegates would probably go to Humphrey; but if Kennedy were to win by a slim margin, McCarthy could stay in the race until the convention and then hope to emerge as the compromise choice. Blair Clark, for one, was convinced that McCarthy's strategists had to keep Kennedy in the race and that it was therefore essential that McCarthy be narrowly defeated. What was more, the final primary in two weeks' time would be in New York, the state that Robert Kennedy represented in the Senate. As a perceived carpetbagger, Kennedy had made plenty of enemies in New York's Democratic circles, and many observers felt that since it was also the state in which McCarthy's liberal support was strongest, there was considerable potential for an upset. Kennedy agreed, and told Richard Goodwin that he was willing to make McCarthy secretary of state in order to avoid a bloody fight in New York. In fact, even after the result in California, Hubert Humphrey was easily the most likely nominee, whatever Kennedy's admirers may subsequently have claimed. An approximate delegate count published by *Newsweek* at the end of May put the vice president just 32½ votes from victory. Even Kennedy's own delegate count, shown to him hours before he died, estimated that Humphrey had 994 delegates to his 524½, with McCarthy at 204. Humphrey always led both men in polls of Democratic voters: the last poll taken before Kennedy's death put the vice president at 40 percent, Kennedy at 31 percent and McCarthy at 19 percent. If Kennedy had lived, it seems extremely unlikely that either he or McCarthy could have overtaken Humphrey's delegate lead and defied the power of the union leaders, organization bosses and government officials supporting him. Even supposing Kennedy *had* somehow, very implausibly, won the nomination, it is highly improbable that so divisive a candidate, identified with black voters and minority issues, would have equaled Humphrey's showing against Richard Nixon. As the political scientist David Plotke has pointed out, a more likely prospect is that Kennedy would have run against Nixon in 1972 and done a good deal better than George McGovern, although he would still probably have lost.[27]

What the Kennedy-McCarthy struggle revealed, especially where domestic policy was concerned, was the widening fissure within liberalism over issues of race and class. Paradoxically, Kennedy appeared the more radical candidate because of his emotional associations, despite the fact that many commentators thought his proposals were actually more conservative. The disagreement over welfare in particular indicated the fraying nature of the liberal consensus. For some observers, Kennedy's attacks on welfare and the idea of a guaranteed income, as well as his emphasis on locally run community development projects, drew on a dying political tradition of virtuous, enlightened republicanism. Kennedy's rhetoric certainly strove to unite both liberal and conservative aspirations; at the same time that he argued for an end to the war and a new campaign against poverty, he also attacked the principle of welfare and boasted of his dedication to law and order. McCarthy, meanwhile, gave every appearance of being a patrician conservative while advocating much more radical proposals on welfare, housing and a guaranteed income. Unlike Kennedy, he wanted to break up the residential segregation of the ghettos, and unlike Kennedy, he promised to spend large amounts of public, not private, money to do so. The paradox was that despite their policy differences, it was McCarthy who struggled to put together a slate in Harlem, and Kennedy who had problems organizing a slate in the Manhattan "silk stocking" districts. The failure of McCarthy and Kennedy to unite in 1968 was not, then, merely a question of personal jealousies: it also pointed to a deeper crisis in the liberal coalition.[28]

Kennedy was shot just minutes after his victory speech in California. McCarthy, who was in his hotel bedroom planning a concession speech, was quickly told of the assassination. His reaction did not endear him to his advisers. According to Blair Clark, McCarthy remarked, "He brought it on himself," while Curtis Gans heard him quietly muttering, "Demagoguing to the last." McCarthy later admitted that this was indeed how he felt. Kennedy, he said, had played up his support for Israel in their televised debate: he therefore had only himself to blame for provoking Sirhan Sirhan.[29]

Kennedy's death fundamentally changed the campaign. On 18 June McCarthy won 62 of the 123 elected New York delegates, while his remaining rival, Hubert Humphrey, won only 12. McCarthy now had to overtake Humphrey's daunting lead among the delegates, but the calendar was against him: there were no more presidential primaries. For many of his volunteers, therefore, the campaign was over. McCarthy and Humphrey, meanwhile, began an unrelenting whirl of speeches, tours and appearances, all aimed at persuading the large number of uncommitted Democratic state delegations to endorse their cause. A third candidate also entered the race: George McGovern, who hoped to provide leadership for Robert Kennedy's supporters and to present the case against the war in a more dynamic and heartfelt fashion. The delegate hunt continued for over two months, and then the Democrats assembled in Chicago to nominate their candidate. The convention opened on 26 August in an atmosphere of extreme tension. Two days later, amid scenes of ugly fighting between antiwar demonstrators and Mayor Daley's police, Hubert Humphrey was selected as the presidential nominee, with 1,761½ votes to McCarthy's 601 and McGovern's 146½. McCarthy did not endorse Humphrey until 29 October, a week before the election, and even then his support was lukewarm. In the general election, on 5 November, Humphrey lost to Richard Nixon by just 499,704 votes.

Kennedy's murder not only changed the context of the campaign; it also radically affected the mood. "The fun went out of the campaign so quickly it was hard to remember it had ever been there," wrote Wilfrid Sheed. McCarthy thought privately that the campaign was effectively over. As his aide Tom Finney observed, McCarthy was now cast in a totally new role, "a contender in a two-way race against Humphrey." He had never expected the campaign to be reduced to a direct struggle with his old colleague from Minnesota, and he certainly did not welcome it. McCarthy had despised Kennedy, but Finney noticed that he retained "a residual affection and respect for Hubert Humphrey" which hung like a cloud over his campaign for the next three months. Humphrey's memoirs recorded that he "always considered Gene a friend," although he knew McCarthy often ridiculed

him. Senator Gaylord Nelson remembered that McCarthy was "very negative and I think quite jealous of Hubert," and that he would often mock
Humphrey in private. It seems likely that though the two men were never
close, Humphrey still respected McCarthy's intelligence, while McCarthy
retained at least some of his old fondness for a man who had helped him so
much in the past. After all, McCarthy was much less rude about Humphrey
than he was about most of his other colleagues.[30]

Hubert Humphrey's campaign for the Democratic nomination had begun
the moment that Johnson announced his withdrawal from the race. Not
only did Humphrey cast himself as the natural heir to the liberal tradition,
but he also now stood as the representative of the Johnson administration
and the spokesman for the Great Society. What he called the "politics of
happiness, the politics of purpose, the politics of joy" reflected his own liberal optimism, so unlike McCarthy's philosophical conservatism; meanwhile, Humphrey's emphasis on "maturity," "integrity" and "experience"
reflected a deliberate attempt to distinguish himself from the rebellious and
unpredictable McCarthy. Their personal relationship was, perhaps surprisingly, still intact. The vice president had been careful not to attack his old
associate during the first months of McCarthy's candidacy. They had many
mutual friends, and many of their advisers knew one another well. In early
April, according to Humphrey's personal doctor, McCarthy visited the vice
president and railed against Kennedy, his tactics and his money. In this
account, McCarthy admitted that he was unlikely to win and made a vague
promise to reassess his position "when the time was ripe." Throughout the
campaign against Kennedy, McCarthy consistently refused to turn his fire
on Humphrey and openly admitted that of his two rivals, he preferred his old
ally from Minnesota. Indeed, although his speechwriters prepared a detailed
dossier on Humphrey and carried it with them all summer, McCarthy never
once used it. Abigail McCarthy even traded weekly notes with the vice
president "about health, family, etc."[31]

Throughout the primaries, emissaries from the Humphrey campaign
made regular but mysterious appearances in the McCarthy camp. On 22
April, for example, Humphrey's friend Miles Lord reported that he had just
spent several hours with McCarthy. McCarthy told Lord that he wanted
Humphrey to join the attack on Robert Kennedy. Lord replied that "from
the Vice President's point of view, it would seem to be up to Gene to take
care of Bobby." Lord and McCarthy even discussed McCarthy's finances,
and McCarthy suggested that the "offered help should be held in reserve
for a while." There is little doubt not only that McCarthy and Humphrey
were colluding in the campaign against Kennedy, but also that McCarthy

was receiving financial support from the Humphrey campaign. The White House in fact considered it "imperative" that McCarthy be "adequately financed for a good California campaign to draw off Kennedy votes." As early as 21 March, Miles Lord reported to Humphrey: "They need money badly . . . Kennedy will make the big primaries in Oregon and California much more expensive and [McCarthy] will need more money for that." Four years later, Blair Clark wrote to George McGovern:

> In '68 the McCarthy campaign definitely received money from the Humphrey campaign, or its supporters. I myself was handed $5,000 in cash by a famous lady—I thought it was hers, but after the election Marvin Rosenberg told me it came from him (Humphrey fund-raiser in NY). There was clearly more, maybe much more.[32]

McCarthy's financial obligations to Hubert Humphrey have never been acknowledged by historians of the campaign. But the evidence certainly suggests that McCarthy was taking considerable sums from the vice president's campaign and that stopping Robert Kennedy meant more to him than either the purity of his effort or his commitment to the moral issue of Vietnam.

Kennedy's death meant that McCarthy would have to alter his plans; whatever commitments he had made to Humphrey evidently no longer applied. On the evening of 7 June, three days after Kennedy's death, he visited Humphrey in Washington. Humphrey later wrote a lengthy report of their "friendly conference." McCarthy was evidently exhausted, mentally and physically. He complained vaguely about his wife, the students, and the costs of the campaign, but made no firm promise to support Humphrey at any stage. His feelings are more palpable in the handwritten jottings that Humphrey made during the meeting, which make it clear that McCarthy was in a bitter and miserable mood. While McCarthy was speaking, Humphrey scribbled: "RFK must not be President . . . Must not take Teddy . . . Kids very antagonistic towards me [McCarthy]—much more than HHH knows . . . Kennedys Hate Him." Far from putting pressure on the vice president to change his position on the war, then, McCarthy cut a weary and forlorn figure. Blair Clark has speculated that if McCarthy had been firmer with Humphrey, he might have forced him to break with Johnson earlier and therefore given him more of a chance against Nixon. The fact is, however, that McCarthy was clearly beholden to Humphrey for his help in the primaries and made no effort to disguise his deep depression. Far from concentrating on the issue of Vietnam, he was still obsessed by his feud with the Kennedys, and the only demand he made of Humphrey was that he "must not take Teddy."[33]

Although McCarthy had greatly disliked Robert Kennedy, he was still deeply affected by his death. One journalist noted that the morning after the shooting McCarthy's face was "white and ravaged . . . as if he had possibly spent the worst night in the history of Christendom." Norman Mailer remarked that he seemed "weary beyond belief," and McCarthy's speechwriter Jeremy Larner thought he looked "ravaged and grim—as if he hadn't slept for a week." In fact, McCarthy was not sleeping well, and according to Abigail, he was "deeply depressed . . . Night after night he lay beside me sleepless, staring at the ceiling." Several observers, including John Kenneth Galbraith and Martin Peretz, felt that McCarthy was stricken by guilt. He had taunted Kennedy for months in a heightening atmosphere of tension and excitement, and now Kennedy was dead. To make matters worse, the campaign was also taking an enormous toll on his personal life. Abigail was unwell, had fallen out with his senior advisers, and felt that both she and their children were being ignored by her husband. Their relationship had been strained for some time, and there were persistent rumors that McCarthy was extremely close to some of the women reporters covering his campaign. It did not escape the press that Abigail left the campaign in the early summer, citing health reasons, or that she and her husband were spending most weekends apart.[34]

With campaigning temporarily suspended, McCarthy retired to St. John's for a few days, but even there he had no peace: after a disagreement one night at dinner, one of the monks had to be restrained by the Secret Service from attacking him with a revolver. It was, wrote Abigail, as though even his spiritual home had been "wrested from him" in the madness of the year. Not surprisingly, McCarthy's enthusiasm for the campaign was waning. Blair Clark thought he was "sleep-walking" through the campaign and "had obviously quit." McCarthy told his wife that he was tempted to give up and throw his delegates to another candidate, such as his old comrade Edmund Muskie. "It was bound to be Humphrey," he later reflected. "When Bobby was killed in Los Angeles, it was the end for us. That summer was an exercise in self-abasement."[35]

By the early summer, the divisions and feuds within McCarthy's campaign staff had reached their nadir. One adviser complained that there were "more coups in that McCarthy Washington office than in Saigon." McCarthy's managers, arguing bitterly among themselves over the future direction of the campaign, came and went with bewildering frequency: Gans was dismissed five times, Clark four times, and Finney three times. As one

British report put it, the campaign resembled "something of a girls' boarding school and something of an Oriental court." The attitude of the candidate certainly did not improve matters. Blair Clark remembered arranging a meeting for McCarthy in New York with a group of local Democratic politicians whom the candidate proceeded to treat with "absolute contempt." "Even Caesar could kiss the ass of somebody who would be useful to his cause," said Clark, "but not Gene." McCarthy's general behavior in New York appalled his volunteers. "McCarthy didn't throw cold water on the New York primary," remarked one activist. "He pissed on it." Other accounts told of McCarthy's canceling two meetings with Mayor Daley in Chicago, failing to return telephone calls from influential state governors, and ignoring an offer of endorsement from George McGovern.[36]

On the other hand, it is not true that McCarthy simply gave up campaigning after June 1968. In July, for example, he kept to an exacting schedule of talks and public appearances. By the end of the campaign, he had visited thirty-eight different states and talked to twenty-five state delegations. McCarthy himself felt that his supporters had a "death wish" and "wanted to die in public." Richard Goodwin, a veteran of presidential campaigns, thought that the talk that McCarthy had given up "was due to the fact that for a lot of people it was their only campaign and they had no standards of comparison." What is certain is that by the end of the campaign, few of McCarthy's principal supporters still admired their candidate. He refused the company of the many eminent experts and intellectuals who supported him, such as Galbraith and Daniel Patrick Moynihan, preferring to travel with what Jeremy Larner called "snobs, sycophants, stooges and clowns." Larner was particularly bitter at his candidate's behavior. He claimed, for example, that McCarthy "was fantastically self-righteous about himself and about everything about himself," was "disloyal" and "made nasty remarks about everybody, including his wife." Another volunteer insisted, "He screwed us. We gave him a lot . . . He owed us more than he gave us." There are quarrels in all presidential campaigns, of course. Still, it says something about McCarthy and his effort that twenty years later, his own campaign manager wrote a retrospective with the subtitle "How Gene McCarthy Sank The Peace Movement—And Himself."[37]

The objective of the campaign from June to August was to persuade as many delegates as possible to support McCarthy rather than Humphrey at the convention. Most of the volunteer groups that had accompanied the candidate in the primaries were disbanded, and McCarthy traveled with a smaller entourage in order to give the appearance of greater professionalism and efficiency, issuing regular position papers on every issue from

Vietnam to urban housing. What was never quite resolved was the question of whether the morality of the war should continue to be the central emphasis of the campaign. Thomas Finney, for example, believed that McCarthy should play on a variety of different issues in order to break Humphrey's support into its constituent factions, but this was never tried with any great consistency or efficiency. Moreover, if McCarthy were to succeed, he would need to win the backing of Robert Kennedy's former supporters. But this was never forthcoming. As one journalist put it, the Kennedy camp nurtured a powerful sense of grievance toward McCarthy. Many leading Kennedy supporters had not forgiven McCarthy's taunts in Oregon and California. Frank Mankiewicz, Kennedy's press secretary, was typical. He explained: "I would never have gone to McCarthy. I just didn't think he should be president."[38]

In truth, McCarthy's summer campaign was a shambles. He refused to reach out to the Kennedy supporters, and contrived to alienate as many delegates as he attracted. One British journalist reported that McCarthy would address the delegates "as if they were a particularly stupid bunch of undergraduates not truly interested in his subject." McCarthy's supporters also failed to understand that many delegates were more interested in local issues, and in the Democratic Party itself, than in the Vietnam War. The mayor of Pittsburgh, for example, told one McCarthy adviser, "I'd rather lose with my guy than win with yours." The problem was not that McCarthy was lazy, because he was not lazy at all. The problem was that he cultivated the appearance of laziness, aloofness and unconcern. As Garry Wills observed, this rather oddly became the central thrust of his appeal: "He had arrived at a desire for power whose purity was guaranteed by his unwillingness to take any practical steps towards power. He *should* be President because he would not *try* very hard to be." This was no basis on which to build a successful convention strategy, and on 10 August George McGovern declared that he too would seek the nomination. McCarthy had casually told him on the Senate floor that he had already privately given up but was maintaining his campaign for form's sake, and McGovern felt that he should step into the breach. His campaign, which inherited many of Kennedy's old supporters, was a bitter rebuke to McCarthy: its campaign buttons proclaimed that McGovern was "the real Gene McCarthy," and McGovern publicly criticized his rival's conception of the passive presidency and questioned his "empathy with the guy at the bottom." Although a failure, the campaign did establish McGovern's credentials for 1972. It also permanently soured his relationship with McCarthy.[39]

McCarthy's problems were exacerbated by the fact that he drew support from social types very different from the average Democratic delegate. Throughout the summer he never came close to attracting support beyond his base in the suburban, educated middle class. As Andrew Hacker had observed in *Commentary* several months earlier, the typical delegate was not chosen in a primary, but was a local party loyalist. "Most are year-round county committeemen," he wrote, "quite senior in service and accustomed to going along with the leadership. Very few, especially among the Democrats, have opinions that are in any way ideological and quite a few have no opinions at all on national issues." In Minnesota, recalled one McCarthy activist, local politicians "could not fathom opposing Humphrey." Meanwhile, despite McCarthy's labor record, the union leaders did not find him an impressive candidate and were firmly united behind Humphrey, whom they both liked and trusted. Although the two candidates disagreed over the war, their legislative records on both domestic and foreign issues were virtually identical. McCarthy's position on Vietnam was encapsulated in the peace plank eventually rejected by the convention, a litany of the usual proposals for a bombing pause, a negotiated settlement, new elections and so on. In fact, Lyndon Johnson's private pollster concluded that many Democrats either thought that McCarthy endorsed the bombing or did not know what his position was. What was more, those who did back his candidacy actually *supported* the bombing by 55 percent to 29 percent. The convention delegates probably associated McCarthy as much with the cause of party reform, a subject long dear to the Stevensonian faction, as they did with foreign policy. As the political scientist James Reichley put it, he reminded the regular Democrats "of the hypocritical reformers who chipped away at their political structures, of the sophisticated intellectuals who sneered at their religious and social values, [and] of the disheveled anti-war protestors who scorned their patriotism."[40]

McCarthy's campaign put great emphasis on the question of opinion polls, particularly those comparing the two candidates in a hypothetical showdown with Richard Nixon. A poll taken in California in July, for example, showed Nixon beating Humphrey by 3 percent, but losing to McCarthy by 11 percent. In August the pollster John Kraft prepared a comprehensive report based on 5,500 interviews in ten states to assess the relative appeal of the two Democrats, and concluded: "In all ten states McCarthy runs more strongly than Humphrey." McCarthy would certainly win three states that Humphrey would lose, and in two more he had at least a fighting chance while Humphrey did not. According to Kraft's report, McCarthy would run 15 percent ahead of the vice president in California, 17 percent ahead in Illinois, 20 percent ahead in Oregon and 5 percent ahead in New York, all of which were important electoral battlegrounds. In the final poll before the Democratic convention, meanwhile, Gallup found that Nixon led Humphrey by 16 percent but McCarthy by only 5 percent. Unfortunately for McCarthy, the opinion polls also consistently found that *among Democrats* Humphrey was by far the more popular candidate. One poll concluded that while Humphrey was more popular among Democrats, blacks, Jews and Catholics, McCarthy won over only the independent voters. A detailed national survey taken in July concluded: "McCarthy's appeal is strongest in the West, in suburban and rural areas, among the younger voters, and among the better educated. He is noticeably weak among Negro voters." While McCarthy led Humphrey by 53 percent to 32 percent among independents, the vice president led among Democrats by 53 percent to 39 percent. And Democrats, not independents, were the electorate that would decide the convention.[41]

By the time the convention finally opened on 26 August, McCarthy was "certain" that he would not be nominated. He had already told Thomas Finney that he was tempted to pull out and support a dark horse, perhaps New Jersey governor Richard Hughes or his old friend Edmund Muskie, who would be "a real President." There remained, however, the tantalizing possibility of an alliance with the South to stop Humphrey, the old advocate of civil rights, and McCarthy's aides were keen to strike a deal with the southern establishment. To get the nomination, according to Harry Mc-Pherson, McCarthy was prepared to resubmit the names of Abe Fortas and Homer Thornberry for confirmation to the Supreme Court, and was also "willing to permit President Johnson to name his Vice-Presidential running mate—within reasonable limits." Richard Goodwin, who had returned to McCarthy after Kennedy's death, visited Governor John Connally during the convention and offered to support "a watered-down Vietnam plank and also [to] let the Southerners choose whomever they want for Vice President" if Texas would support McCarthy. If Connally endorsed McCarthy, he would be offered the vice presidency as well as the right to choose some cabinet and judicial nominees. It seems fairly clear that McCarthy himself was unaware of most of the details, and when the plan was presented to him he balked at the idea of Connally as a running mate. The arrangement did make a certain sense. McCarthy had always been close to the Texans, and offered the prospect of a more passive presidency than the hyperactive Humphrey. He had a long congressional history of compromise and accommodation, not to mention close personal links with the South. As Tom Finney reflected, McCarthy's vision was "more compatible with a lot of the leaders in the south than Hubert Humphrey's view of the presidency." Had it not been for his campaign in 1968, in fact, McCarthy might well have remained a southern favorite.[42]

The convention itself did not show McCarthy at his best. Even before it opened he gave the appearance of utter resignation. "Senator McCarthy, your attitude here seems to indicate that you've given up," commented one CBS journalist during a televised interview. When the California delegation arranged a debate between the three Democratic candidates, McCarthy flatly refused to discuss his stance on the war, announcing simply, "The people know my position." Nor was he prepared to work on a convention strategy with his advisers. "It was," said Blair Clark, "a shambles." McCarthy declined to address the convention on the subject of the peace plank or even to examine a draft of the resolution, and spent the period of the vote on Vietnam playing mock baseball with his brother in his hotel suite. The convention, he implied, was a total waste of his time. His wife complained that while other people worked for his cause or demonstrated for peace, McCarthy was sequestered "debating dactyls and spondees" with Robert Lowell.[43]

McCarthy took his final defeat with equanimity, and his reaction to the violence on the evening of the ballot was typically understated: he looked down from his Hilton suite windows and mused that it reminded him of the Battle of Lake Trasimene, an analogy which he subsequently amended to the Battle of Cannae. The essayist Wilfrid Sheed later wrote that "an average citizen looking in would have said, There you are, that's an intellectual for you—making Punic war jokes while Chicago prepares to incinerate." It was as if McCarthy were consciously playing a part, but as Sheed put it, "McCarthy might or might not be an intellectual, but you couldn't prove it by Scipio Africanus."[44]

The following night, however, the Chicago police raided McCarthy's campaign headquarters on the fifteenth floor of the Hilton. This was not quite the brutal, unprovoked attack on innocent idealists that has been described by writers sympathetic to McCarthy. Although the police were excessively aggressive, they were reacting to reports of a constant hail of missiles being hurled down by McCarthy's frustrated volunteers. The speechwriter Paul Gorman recalled: "A lot of things were being thrown out of the window . . . I saw a couple of typewriters being thrown out . . . there was water, and you know, water bombs, and beer." Jane Freeman, who was in charge of the Humphrey hospitality suite, also remembered that the McCarthy staff had been throwing "nasty stuff" from their windows. Humphrey's personal doctor visited the suite after the raid and remarked that there were "more beer drinkers than casualties and certainly no semblance of the battle-station atmosphere reported on television." McCarthy himself, however, was extremely shaken by the incident and spent considerable time comforting his distraught supporters. "It was really a kind of fascist-run convention," he later explained, adding that President Johnson "wanted a fascist take-over of the convention." Indeed, McCarthy even maintained that he might have run as an independent but for his fear of further violence and "Nazi-type stuff."[45]

McCarthy's greatest complaint, however, was that the nomination had been somehow stolen from him. He consistently maintained that "the party regulars sewed up" the nomination and defied the popular will by handing it to his opponent. At first glance, he had a strong case. The voters in the Democratic primaries had cast 38.7 percent of their ballots for McCarthy, 30.6 percent for Kennedy, 7.3 percent for Johnson and only 2.2 percent for Hubert Humphrey. Moreover, over six hundred of the delegates had been selected more than two years before the convention, and in many states there was great hostility to the participation of newcomers in the Democratic caucuses, so that in Missouri, for example, one township caucus was held on a bus speeding along country roads in a successful attempt to prevent McCarthy's supporters from gaining admittance.[46]

On the other hand, there is also a persuasive case that McCarthy was not mistreated at all and that Humphrey's nomination was perfectly justifiable. As early as February 1968, well before any primary had been contested, the journalist Andrew Hacker pointed out that McCarthy would be mistaken to rely on primaries alone. Only fifteen states, he explained, used primaries to select their delegates, with the other thirty-five relying on closed conventions of party regulars. Of the 2,600 delegates to the national convention, a mere 900 would be selected by the primary system. The precedents of Theodore Roosevelt in 1912 and Estes Kefauver in 1952 demonstrated that primary victories were not enough. "Given the obduracy of the primary system," Hacker concluded, "it is not really possible for anyone who enters that maze to emerge as a clear-cut and popular choice for the nomination." Yet as the *New York Times* noted, McCarthy "seemed strangely unworried about the nonprimary states," even though they accounted for the vast majority of the delegates. As the *Times*'s Tom Wicker wrote the day after the New Hampshire primary, the "hard political probability" was always that McCarthy would face the same fate as Kefauver in 1952: "winning the primaries and losing the nomination." McCarthy's effort in the nonprimary states was extremely weak. Successful insurgent candidacies in the same period, such as those of Goldwater in 1964 and McGovern in 1972, succeeded because of their extensive efforts to win delegates in these states.

McCarthy had not learned the lesson of Goldwater's effort four years earlier. His efforts were too little and too late, and Hubert Humphrey won 76 percent of the nonprimary delegates to McCarthy's 16 percent.[47]

Humphrey did not duck the primaries because he was afraid of being beaten. In fact, he simply entered the race too late to contest most of them. He was, quite clearly, the overwhelming choice of most ordinary party members. Even when McCarthy was at his peak, during the Oregon primary, polls showed that Humphrey led him 56 percent to 37 percent among Democratic voters. And even in states where McCarthy had won the primary vote, opinion polls put Humphrey ahead, suggesting that the primaries were an inaccurate reflection of party sentiment. The historian Herbert Parmet concluded: "For all the complaints of the new-politics people about how the traditionalists had controlled the Chicago convention, they did select the candidate most representative of the rank-and-file." Indeed, as Lewis Gould argues, "Humphrey was clearly the strongest nominee the Democrats could have picked in 1968." He was not imposed on the party, as McCarthy's backers claimed. After all, only a small proportion of Democrats had actually voted in the presidential primaries. Since the opinion polls suggested that Humphrey was the overwhelming favorite of the party rank and file, the evidence suggests that McCarthy's supporters had, as one said, "spent too much of our time talking to each other." The playwright Arthur Miller, a McCarthy delegate, sniffed that the party hacks were just not interested in the issues. Richard Scammon and Ben Wattenberg observed, "Exactly why a Carl Albert elected every two years by Oklahomans for two decades is called a party hack—while Arthur Miller who has not exactly made a career of elective politics is a self-proclaimed voice of the people—is something of a mystery." If the convention was "rigged," it was rigged only to reflect the views of most Democrats in the country.[48]

The Democratic nomination system was not inherently hostile to outsiders. John Kennedy, for example, looked beyond the party organization in 1960 to put together a broad liberal coalition in both primary and nonprimary states. As it was, the McCarthy camp, contrary to popular belief, did rather well at the convention. "The insurgent forces, supposedly denied any chances of expression, actually came within 263 votes of passing their platform plank on Vietnam," noted David Broder, "and they actually prevailed on what was to become the convention's most important by-product— the mandate for reform of the procedures for selecting future delegates." McCarthy claimed that he lost "because the political procedure isn't responsive to the will of the people." But the truth was that the procedure quite adequately reflected the will of the Democrats, and McCarthy deserved to lose. His campaign came across as "frighteningly inept"; his organization was chaotic; his public statements were willful and obscure; his view of the presidency smacked of conservatism; he often seemed vindictive and arrogant; and his constituency struck many ordinary Democrats as "a collection of beardies and weirdies and unpredictable poets and intellectuals." He barely ran as a Democrat at all, rarely mentioning the party, its history or its iconic figures, and appealed more to independents than to party loyalists—in one speech at Boston University, for example, he listed the party's achievements in health, education and civil rights without once using the word "Democrat." In fact, he had much less cause for complaint than did Estes Kefauver in 1952, or even George Wallace in 1972. As the political scientist Andrew Busch has argued, comparison with George McGovern's successful campaign in 1972 leads to the conclusion that McCarthy lost for three reasons: first, the difficulty of overcoming an incumbent president and vice president; second, his personal weakness as a candidate; and third, his disorganized and limited efforts in nonprimary states. It is worth remembering that by McCarthy's original standards, he had not failed at all. He had pledged to raise the issue of the war, and indeed he had. As one unsympathetic columnist observed: "Personal ambitions have been thwarted, but they were never said to be important in the first place."[49]

His campaign over, McCarthy retreated to the south of France with his wife and various supporters for a well-deserved rest. It was expected that when he returned in September, he would finally endorse Humphrey for the presidency. The weeks passed, however, and no endorsement was forthcoming. Humphrey himself had anticipated that McCarthy would endorse him in mid-September, after the passions of the convention had died down, and later recollected that before the convention, McCarthy had promised to do so. That McCarthy broke his word seems incontestable. In fact, he even toyed with the idea of running as an independent in the general election, and met several leading supporters in Washington in September to discuss it. At one point in the meeting he exclaimed enthusiastically: "I guess we could win New York, California, Oregon, Minnesota and maybe even Wisconsin," but eventually (and typically) he lost interest. Eventually, on 29 October, barely a week before the election, McCarthy issued a grudging statement. Humphrey's position on the war, the draft, and Democratic Party reform, he said, fell "far short" of what it should be. Still, Humphrey had "a better understanding of our domestic needs and a stronger will to act" than Nixon, and he had more chance than the Republican of "scaling down the arms race and reducing military tensions." Accordingly, McCarthy announced that he would be voting for Humphrey in November. At the same time, however, he declared that he would seek neither the Democratic nomination for the Senate in 1970 nor his party's nomination for the presidency in 1972. He gave various excuses for the delay in endorsing his old ally: he was angry at the violence in Chicago; he thought the endorsement might hurt congressional peace candidates; he was waiting for Humphrey to change his policy; he was a captive of his own movement. Indeed, he even remarked years later that he had been too good to Humphrey: "I went a little further than I thought I should in terms of what I thought he might do about the war." In his memoir *Gene McCarthy's Minnesota,* McCarthy observed that "Hubert was loyal to his friends"; it was a loyalty that in McCarthy's case was clearly not reciprocated.[50]

Most observers were appalled that McCarthy had waited so long to endorse his former rival, and many of Humphrey's closest advisers thought that the delay cost their man the election. More than any other act, it destroyed McCarthy's popularity among senior Democrats in Minnesota. Humphrey lost, after all, by only half a million votes, and even the slightest boost might have brought him closer to victory. He later wrote that in several states where McCarthy was personally popular, such as New Jersey, Illinois and California, "had McCarthy campaigned early and hard for me and the Democratic Party, he might have turned it." Other, more objective observers agreed. Abigail McCarthy, by contrast, argued that the endorsement was irrelevant, and that very few voters cared what McCarthy thought. But this is to miss the point. McCarthy's refusal to endorse Humphrey damaged the vice president's credibility when he needed it most and perpetuated the image of the Democrats as bickering, faction-ridden and incompetent. Humphrey could hardly portray himself as a candidate of national unity if he could not even unite his own party. McCarthy, however, told the *Minneapolis Tribune* that Humphrey should blame himself for his defeat: he should have "changed his position on Vietnam earlier in the campaign." In later years, McCarthy was adamant that he had not let his old friend down. If Humphrey had won, he argued, "they probably would have said it was really clever of McCarthy to hold off." He could not resist the occasional gibe. "If they're willing to take responsibility for the fifteen million votes they lost between '64 and '68," he remarked, "I'll take responsibility for the last 300,000." In his memoirs, however, McCarthy wrote that Humphrey's "not being elected to the presidency was nothing short of tragedy." If so, it was one in which McCarthy's own role had been less than heroic.[51]

In October 1999 the Minnesota ACLU hosted a tribute to McCarthy attended by scores of local dignitaries and veteran activists. The speakers ignored McCarthy's career before 1968, and concentrated exclusively on his presidential campaign. A reporter for the *St. Paul Pioneer Press* wrote admiringly: "Thirty-two years after he challenged a sitting president and the conscience of a nation, the name of Eugene McCarthy still commands respect. This week, it also demands appreciation." Curiously enough, however, of all the guests at the reception McCarthy himself probably took the dimmest view of his own campaign. In 1987, for example, he wrote in an unpublished essay that the effort "probably had little or no effect on how the Vietnam War was conducted and how it finally ended." Its principal result, he thought, was to ensure that no president would assume that he could "carry on a war unaffected by the moral judgment of the people." He concluded that "the events of 1968 and the aftermath demonstrated the instability of liberal judgment, the absence of historical sense in the liberal mind, and the lack of continuity and commitment to liberal political action." Far from being a triumph, therefore, the campaign was instead a tragic turning point. In part this was because he had simply done too well. "We never expected to win," he later recalled. "In fact, if we hadn't done as well as we did, we might have had more impact. If instead of beating Johnson and driving him out, we'd gotten 25 or 30 percent, they would have had to say, 'Well, you got 25 or 30 percent—we can try to accommodate you.'"[52]

For some liberals, McCarthy was a heroic figure. Before the campaign was even over, Daniel Patrick Moynihan was declaring: "McCarthy has done more than merely made us proud to be Democrats, he has made us glad to *be*." The Massachusetts peace activist Jerome Grossman wrote in his autobiography: "Eugene McCarthy . . . is an authentic hero. We can never repay him for his personal sacrifice. For all his political faults, he clearly expressed the righteous indignation so typically American." Many people, however, remembered McCarthy with hostility rather than with admiration. One campaign veteran wrote that McCarthy had "succumbed to hubris" rather than "set aside his pride and lend wholehearted support to Hubert Humphrey." McCarthy, he continued, "confused his own fortune with that of the country. His ego became more important than his message . . . licking his own wounds and pouting was more satisfying than consigning Richard Nixon to oblivion." Even the *New York Times* recorded that his behavior had been "caustic, not particularly generous to opponents, lackadaisical and boring." Many of his fiercest critics were those who knew him best. His old friend Gilbert Harrison, the editor of the *New Republic,* wrote that he had been "lazy," "unresponsive" and "insensitive." Jeremy Larner wrote an entire book arguing that McCarthy was "a man whose concept of his own identity was so precious to himself, and so fragile, that he could not tolerate disagreement or equality, could not, in fact, work directly and openly with others." Blair Clark, who felt that McCarthy had wasted a wonderful opportunity after Kennedy's death, ended the year very unimpressed with his candidate. "Gene was not a great human being," he recalled. "The milk of human kindness curdled before it got anywhere with him. I'm not saying he was mean or anything. In many ways he was a good chap, but he was contorted. I'm not at all hostile to Gene, but he was hopeless at the candidacy."[53]

The election of Richard Nixon marked the end of eight years of liberal administration and the beginning of a new era of relative conservatism in the White House. Had it not been for McCarthy's campaign, it is possible that Johnson or Humphrey might have been elected in November 1968. "I think we elected Nixon," admitted one supporter. "I think the McCarthyites did this and I'm not at all sure that we all didn't think it was a good thing and we were glad to see Humphrey lose." Many of McCarthy's supporters had joined his campaign in order to end the war in Vietnam, but in damaging the cause of Hubert Humphrey, they unwittingly contributed to Nixon's victory and the prolongation of the war until 1973. Humphrey would almost certainly have ended the American involvement in Indochina much faster than Nixon and Kissinger did. Nor did the campaign seem to provoke a great shift in public opinion regarding Vietnam. Although McCarthy did help to make dissent more respectable, his candidacy did not inject any new ideas into the Vietnam debate: instead, he preferred to rehash the old liberal critique of the war. Voters did not in fact treat the election in November as a referendum on Vietnam, and given that they chose Nixon as their next president, it can easily be argued that McCarthy ultimately failed. Blair Clark, for example, admitted:

> Well, it was a gigantic failure of course—it failed in all the obvious things it could have done in my view. It was a safety valve, if you want, for the anguished young and the peacemakers and maybe that had some useful function; but I think the main legacy of it is negative, that an effort that should have done so much more failed. So I think it definitely had a deleterious effect on America.[54]

The real legacy of the McCarthy campaign concerned not foreign policy but domestic politics. Most historians agree that by 1968 the old New Deal political order was giving way to the decentralized, suburban, televised, often conservative politics of the late twentieth century. Individual candidates now prospered at the expense of the old party organizations, and the Democratic Party in particular adjusted badly to the demands of presidential campaigning in a system that emphasized charisma and television appeal rather than legislative experience or organizational fidelity. McCarthy himself had been a product of the old party system, but in 1968 his candidacy anticipated the personality-driven campaigns of the 1970s. His appeal hinged not on his record, but on his personal identity. Jeremy Larner observed that McCarthy "was ready to make his personality the center of his campaign, and to let the cause for which he stood win or lose on the strength of it." So it was that McCarthy's rhetoric avoided mentioning the Democratic Party, its leaders or its record, and focused instead upon himself, his role and his aspirations. He was not the first to do so; Adlai Stevenson had similarly excited enthusiasm not because of his record but because of a personal style and demeanor with which liberal voters could identify. As Peter Steinfels wrote of Daniel Patrick Moynihan: "The intellectual and professorial element is not only critical in shaping his outlook; it is in the foreground, offered as qualification for holding power." The election of Jimmy Carter in 1976 suggested that candidates who emphasized their independence from party structures were more successful than those who made a fetish of party loyalty, and McCarthy was therefore an important pioneer, encouraging the notion that the authenticity and personal charisma of the individual candidate were more important than his record of commitment to the party cause.[55]

At the same time, McCarthy himself was also a revealing example of the way in which liberal Democrats failed to adjust to the political climate of the late 1960s and 1970s. The decline in the Democratic presidential vote between 1964 and 1968 was the greatest electoral disaster of the century, comparable only to the collapse of Herbert Hoover's support in 1932. Yet McCarthy, who was one of the nation's best-known Democrats, barely gave any thought after 1968 to the reasons why the party had lost such a wide swath of voters. Moreover, by concentrating on the question of Vietnam, he lost sight of the issues that won the election for Richard Nixon: crime, drugs, race, and "law and order." Like other liberals, by ignoring these issues he simply conceded them to the Republican right. At the same time, liberal Democrats, desperate to rejuvenate their presidential fortunes, took up new issues that transcended the old ideological consensus. The *New York Times* noted, for instance, that McCarthy had "rejected virtually the whole of postwar American foreign policy . . . and questioned the post-Rooseveltian theory of a strong Presidency." He had also during the primaries proposed domestic measures unthinkable a decade earlier: enormous job creation programs to eliminate welfare; tens of millions of dollars to be spent on inner city housing; and, especially, a national guaranteed income. By the early 1970s other liberals, notably George McGovern and Fred Harris, had embraced or even gone beyond these proposals, asserting what one historian calls "radical notions of income by right" and redefining liberalism as a philosophy of welfare entitlement that many thought contradicted the old emphasis on independence and opportunity. Only during the Clinton administration were the Democrats finally able to shake off their consequent associations with dependence, profligacy and radicalism. If McCarthy and George Wallace both represented different ways of rebelling against the political status quo, then it can certainly be said that Wallace, not McCarthy, represented the wave of the future. Wallace's aggressive, populist appeal could not have been more unlike McCarthy's self-consciously educated and elitist campaign, but it was with Wallace, Nixon and Reagan that the political future lay.[56]

McCarthy's campaign also had profound consequences for the Democratic Party itself, not least the obsession with "New Politics." One correspondent, for example, wrote in *Commonweal* that McCarthy "could become the herald of a new political alignment, embracing the new populism of the black and the poor, the new progressivism of the Middle-West, and the new liberalism of the cities." At the heart of the New Politics was the project to reform the institutional procedures of the Democratic Party and open up the party organization to racial minorities, the young, and middle-class pressure groups, principally through the presidential primary system. This had its origins in the majority report of the Credentials Committee at the Chicago convention, which established a commission to study the procedure for selecting convention delegates. A second project aimed to expand the base of the New Politics movement, especially in universities, through such vehicles as the Vietnam Moratorium of 1969. The institutional outcome of these efforts was the New Democratic Coalition, which aimed to unite the liberal supporters of the Kennedy and McCarthy campaigns after 1968; it later proved to be the nucleus of the organizational apparatus behind George McGovern's primary campaign in 1972. These groups also formed the nucleus of another successful effort twenty years later: the presidential campaign of Bill Clinton. After the Chicago convention, and again in September 1969, young activists gathered for informal meetings in Martha's Vineyard to plan their political strategy, and it was at the second meeting that "a rather lanky, good-looking man . . . [with] wiry hair that grew out like an afro and a tattered, baggy sweater over his jeans" first met many of the political contacts who would work for his election as president in 1992 and thereafter in his two administrations. Indeed, during the 1992 campaign, President George H.W. Bush even argued that Clinton's presence at the meeting of McCarthy veterans was proof of his supposed left-wing tendencies.[57]

The New Politics movement was overwhelmingly middle class, white and affluent. One consequence was that Democratic convention delegates in 1972 were younger and better educated than in 1968, as well as more likely to be female or nonwhite. The reformers were also fiercely moralistic. One woman from suburban Detroit, for example, emerged from a local meeting at which the McCarthy supporters had been outvoted and tearfully told reporters: "They just don't understand. We're morally right." Indeed, some young zealots delighted in the idea of destroying the existing party and then building it anew. "As they gave us no quarter at the convention, so we will give them none," wrote the co-chairman of Youth for McCarthy. "We seek nothing less than the destruction of the political machinery which proved so unresponsive this year. We will dedicate ourselves now to breaking the grip of the old men, the defensive, frightened men who hate all change." This moralistic fervor probably damaged the party far more than it invigorated it. As an activist from Minnesota later admitted: "We tore the country apart and we assured the loss of the presidency; but that was not all. We did damage at the local level; in the process of winning the precinct caucuses, we wiped out labor leaders and everyone who disagreed with us in the three metro districts."[58]

It was certainly not healthy for liberal Democrats to be besotted with their own internal procedures at the expense of broader national questions, and the lack of new programmatic proposals from leading figures after 1968 is evidence of their exaggerated self-absorption. Indeed, most historians have agreed that the reformers ultimately damaged the Democratic Party and the cause of liberalism. Thanks to the party reforms, more attention was given to presidential primaries than ever before, and state delegations were required to make sure that they had the right balance of women, blacks and other minorities. Even if center-right politicians like Edmund Muskie and Henry Jackson, with their financial resources and union backing, had a decent chance of succeeding under the new system, the fact was that these procedural changes excluded regular Democrats from the party conventions, weakened the control of the party organization over the presidential nomination process, and skewed the primaries toward a small group of moralistic, affluent, middle-class voters whose interests were not those of the party electorate as a whole. Certainly the reform movement damaged the organizational capacity of an already weakened national party.

As the roguish Roscoe Conkling had pointed out a century earlier, good intentions were not enough to build up a successful party machine: "Parties are not built up by deportment, or by ladies' magazines, or gush!"[59]

McCarthy's campaign was as much a culmination of a long tradition of middle-class reform as it was the harbinger of a "new politics." An analysis of McCarthy's volunteers demonstrated that they were not "new kinds of people," but were generally educated and affluent, "much like . . . those who have been politically active in other electoral campaigns." From the Mugwumps to the Progressives to the New Dealers to the Stevensonians, there had been a vibrant tradition of high-minded, intelligent and middle-class reformers flocking to erudite and patrician leaders and working for principled political ends. Like the ideal Mugwump leader, McCarthy had been "a well-to-do, well-educated, high-minded citizen" who appeared to put the national interest above his own political career; and like the amateurs of the 1950s, he articulated his political aims in terms of morality and high principle rather than party loyalty and personal advantage. In fact, the New Politics was not new but was the culmination of the reform movements that had been expanding throughout Democratic cities and suburbs for several decades. Independent from the economic concerns of other Democratic voters, and often bitterly opposed to party loyalty and organization for its own sake, it was these groups which provided the backbone for the McCarthy campaign and the subsequent efforts of the New Politics movement to control the Democratic Party. As the liberal consensus began to pull apart in the late 1960s under the impact of Vietnam and racial unrest, with many liberals moving toward social democracy or neoconservatism, the reformers anticipated the development of a new center that would build on the work of the McCarthy campaign, and it was this faith that propelled the campaign of George McGovern in 1972.[60]

Reform liberalism after 1968, however, remained hamstrung because of its inability to reach beyond its middle-class origins. Its advocates rarely addressed the social and economic problems that interested other Democratic voters, and they continued to be absorbed by the kind of moralistic issues that McCarthy had addressed in 1968. Not only did reform liberals turn away from the rhetoric of economic populism, but they were also simply more interested in issues of human rights and clean government than they were in so-called bread and butter problems like unemployment and inflation. One onlooker wrote of a Democratic meeting in Minneapolis: "The issues of race and jobs and economic opportunity had never been

mentioned by the brash young white professional men who had monopo-
lized the meeting up until then. They didn't have to think about things like
that. They didn't have to be concerned with losing an election. The outcome of a political contest would not change their way of life at all." As
Joseph Kraft presciently noted after the Chicago convention, the McCarthy
campaign almost seemed to cultivate an attitude of disdain for what Kraft
called "Middle America." "McCarthy," he remarked, "is almost exclusively
an engine for participation by Americans who think of themselves as better than other Americans—the leader of the Pharisees." McCarthy's emphasis on the educated middle class was typical of the shortsightedness
of those liberals who seemed more interested in moral rectitude than electoral success. Several commentators pointed out during 1968 that his campaign ignored the fact that many Democratic voters were more worried
about economic issues than moral ones, and that there were more votes in
one factory than an entire university faculty. As Arthur Schlesinger Jr.
warned, the danger of the New Politics was that the Democratic Party
would turn into a "semi-precious alliance of college graduates." The consequence was that while the Democratic vote remained steady among
upper-middle-class and professional groups, and grew among blacks, it
fell in other areas: the white South, the white working and lower-middle
classes, and the West. And while the power of the wealthy liberals grew
within the party, the tax burden on their less-affluent counterparts increased,
setting the stage for the tax revolts of the late 1970s and the mass desertion
of the Reagan Democrats in 1980 and 1984.[61]

In the long term, then, the 1968 campaign was a pivotal moment in the
history of both the Democratic Party and modern American liberalism. The
broad liberal consensus that had hitherto bound together middle-class progressives and low-income workers was now in a state of advanced decay.
The old commitments to anti-Communist containment abroad and the realization of the Fair Deal at home were seen as aging relics inappropriate
for the new challenges of the 1970s. While McCarthy's effort had drawn on
the legacy of Stevensonian progressivism, his success among professional
and suburban voters on the East Coast, along the Great Lakes and in the
Pacific Northwest also proved a model for future reformist efforts. In 1980,
for example, John Anderson's studied independence and moderation not
only won the support of McCarthy's own wife and former fund-raisers, but
also appealed to a similar constituency of "college students, Cambridge
professors, young professionals, newspaper editors, Hollywood celebrities,
New York café society, and generally what one commentator dubbed the
'brie and Chablis' set." The so-called neoliberals and "Atari Democrats"

of the following decade, including prominent young politicians such as Gary Hart, Bill Bradley, Paul Tsongas and Michael Dukakis, likewise drew their support from suburban professionals, intellectuals and the media. Like McCarthy in 1968, Gary Hart benefited in the 1984 Democratic primary campaign from the support of middle-class, affluent voters and from Republican and independent votes in the New Hampshire and Wisconsin primaries. In 2000, another "Atari Democrat," Bill Bradley, ran for the presidential nomination. As Louis Menand remarked, he was reminiscent of no one so much as the "austere, elliptical, remote" Eugene McCarthy. Bradley, he wrote, "has the same physical languor, the same hint in his personality of dark and lonely introspection, the same laconic indifference to political glad-handing." Like Hart, like Anderson, like McGovern, like Stevenson, and like McCarthy in 1968, Bradley appealed to comfortable professionals and intellectuals on the East and West Coasts; like McCarthy, he attempted to inject into his campaign a moralistic dedication to principle rather than expediency; and like them all, he ended the campaign a loser.[62]

McCarthy might have lost a lot of friends in Minnesota, but his prospects at the end of 1968 were not at all bad. At the end of the Chicago convention, he had told the peace demonstrators, "We will press forward to get a change of policy on the war, to demilitarize the American foreign policy, to demand selective conscientious objection for this country. We will push forward on poverty, and against racism, in this nation." At a farewell meeting of his staff and supporters, he insisted that they had "not lost the fight." He clearly felt that he still had a political future. Indeed, in late October and November McCarthy campaigned vigorously for liberal Senate candidates such as Morse, Gruening, Church, Fulbright and even the despised McGovern. Few observers paid much attention to his pledge not to run for re-election in 1970: it seemed more of an attempt to distance himself from the party organization than a binding promise. Even if he did retire from the Senate, he could still remain a major political figure and even a presidential contender. *Time,* for instance, noted that McCarthy, "as leader of the government in exile, will remain the conscience for millions of Americans, and a formidable figure that the President, whoever he is, cannot ignore." In late December a Gallup poll found that McCarthy was the tenth most admired man in the country. A year before, most Americans had not even known his name.[63]

For McCarthy and the reform liberals, the outlook for 1972 was extremely bright. While the strength of the party regulars appeared to be on the wane, the reformers had built an extensive network of activists and financial backers across the country, had set in motion the reform of the rules on delegate selection, and were united by the goal of nominating a sympathetic presidential candidate four years hence. It was not inevitable that the candidate should be George McGovern. An opinion poll published in February 1969 suggested that McCarthy's support among both Democrats and independents far outstripped that of McGovern. Ted Kennedy was the overwhelming favorite among Democrats with 45 percent, followed by Humphrey (21 percent), Muskie (17 percent), McCarthy (7 percent) and McGovern (1 percent). Indeed, since even in 1971 McGovern's personal ratings did not rise above 6 percent, McCarthy had every chance of being the Democratic nominee in 1972. As the political strategist Richard Goodwin later put it: "Had he simply stayed in the Senate, spoken out on the issues, made some effort to cultivate the political establishment, then he and not McGovern would have been the party's nominee in 1972. But maybe that's not what he wanted." It was, indeed, never really clear what McCarthy did want, and although he now enjoyed an excellent opportunity to assert his position at the head of the liberal movement, the years after 1968 were to mark the beginning of his slow decline into irrelevance and obscurity.[64]

CHAPTER ELEVEN

The Aftermath of Defeat

J ust after one in the afternoon of 6 November 1968, Hubert Humphrey
went down to the hall of the Leamington Hotel in Minneapolis and,
with tears glistening in his eyes, told his supporters that he had just
telephoned to concede the presidential election to Richard Nixon. It had
been desperately close, and he had lost by less than 1 percent of the popular vote. Humphrey was shattered. "Jesus," he said heavily, looking out
over the Minneapolis skyline. "I think I would have done a good job in the
White House." Hundreds of miles away, in his office in Washington, D.C.,
Eugene McCarthy, who had done as much as anyone to hinder and frustrate
his old friend and had come through for him only at the last minute, sat
sunk in gloom in his Senate office. "It's a day for visiting the sick and bury-
ing the dead," he muttered bleakly to a visiting reporter. "It's gray everywhere, all over the land."[1]

After all the high drama and exhaustion of his own presidential campaign, McCarthy was left with nothing. "It's like the athlete who's been
training all his life for the big race, every nerve stretched, every muscle
tuned—and then there is no race," Abigail McCarthy wrote some years
later in her political novel, *Circles*. "His mind may accept it but his body
will be suddenly drained, I should think, flaccid—suddenly without use for
all that splendid conditioning." Abigail felt that he had come close to a ner-

vous breakdown after the campaign ended. She explained to an interviewer: "No one understands what it is to nurse a man through a defeat. There is a depression of cataclysmic proportions—a loss like a death in the family. He questions how 'wanted' he was." McCarthy certainly found it difficult to come to terms both with defeat and with his new popularity. In January 1969 a national survey of Americans under the age of twenty-four found that McCarthy was their most admired public figure, beating rivals from Che Guevara and Herbert Marcuse to Richard Nixon and Ted Kennedy. As one of his friends later put it, however, he had "never wanted to be anybody's icon." He was both extremely ambitious and intensely private; although he thirsted for recognition and respect, and took offense if they were not forthcoming, he also disliked being the object of his supporters' enthusiasm and expectations. His ambivalence toward the prize he sought, his uneasiness with many of his supporters, and his discomfort with the adulation of the young meant that, according to the liberal commentator James Wechsler, "even in some of his finest hours, he manifested what appeared to be either contemptuousness or indifference to the feelings of those who most cared about him."[2]

The dreary routine of life in the Senate, with its humdrum rituals of votes and debates and hearings, held little appeal for McCarthy after the end of his presidential campaign, not surprising since he had been steadily losing interest in his senatorial responsibilities since the mid-1960s. A month after the election, he received an unexpected offer from the Nixon White House to take the post of ambassador to the United Nations, but since the Republican governor of Minnesota refused to contemplate appointing a Democrat to the Senate to replace him, McCarthy turned it down. He still had a lingering sense of party loyalty. "I wanted to take the office," he later wrote sadly, ". . . but I did not feel that I had a right to give up the [Senate] office to a Republican." It was a shame that he did not take it, since a new job might well have offered him a new lease on life. Instead he settled listlessly back into the florid atmosphere of the Senate, weighed down by the enthusiastic expectations of his liberal followers. It was all too predictable that they would soon be disappointed. At the beginning of January, Ted Kennedy announced that he was challenging Russell Long for the position of Democratic whip in the Senate. It was not, admittedly, the most important office in the country, but it was, in the words of one commentator, "the first real confrontation of the post-election era between liberal and reactionary Democrats." To liberals, Long was a southern racist, a prowar hawk, the tool of the oil interests and a loudmouthed bully, while Kennedy not only had an impeccable voting record but was also regarded as the bright, attractive liberal front-runner for the presidential nomination in 1972. Kennedy won, but McCarthy voted for Long.[3]

As if that were not enough of a shock to his admirers, a week later he announced that he was relinquishing his post on the Senate Foreign Relations Committee in favor of the hawkish Gale McGee. At his own request, McCarthy was placed instead on the obscure backwater that was the Government Operations Committee. The combination of these two supposed transgressions outraged McCarthy's former supporters, and his office was flooded with angry letters and telegrams. "We are so upset," wrote Martin Peretz, whose money had helped to propel his presidential campaign just months before. "We can readily understand that you might feel that you have had it with the nonsense and the nonsensical politicians and press . . . Please don't quit." Mary McGrory, the Washington columnist who had so ardently praised McCarthy in 1968, now declared: "Last year's shining politician became this year's old politician with his vote against Teddy."[4]

According to McCarthy, the two episodes were "non-events." The election for the Democratic whip was "so unimportant that reporters shouldn't bother to ask you how you voted." "I haven't got anything against Russell Long," he said mildly. "I don't see any reason to strike out against him over something this unimportant." In fact, McCarthy had worked closely with Long on the Finance Committee, and according to Washington gossip, oil money had been known to find its way from southern donors to McCarthy through Long. Few of his admirers in the country realized that McCarthy had always been a canny congressional operator, popular with southerners like Long and Sam Rayburn. McCarthy himself joked that his presidential campaign had been "a penance for all I've done for Bob Kerr and Lyndon and Russell Long." It was hardly surprising, either, that he should find a reason to vote against Ted Kennedy when he blamed his late brother for derailing his presidential campaign the previous spring. As for his decision to leave the Senate Foreign Relations Committee, he at first gave a convoluted and implausible explanation about keeping the size of the committee down while still honoring the leadership's commitment to seat McGee, but eventually admitted that he had fundamentally lost heart. The committee, he had decided, was "not very powerful" and since he expected to leave the Senate in 1970, there was not much point in keeping his place. He was tired of fighting hopelessly against the Vietnam War and tired of having to please liberal allies whom he often secretly despised. "The liberals, the ADA and those people, half of them were looking for a reason to get after me," he said later.[5]

Within a few months of Nixon's election, it was obvious to political observers that McCarthy was both bored and unhappy. "He doesn't know what he wants to do," admitted his confidant Jerry Eller. He had never been a political crusader and had hitherto been content to cruise along in the shadows, but now he found himself condemned by liberal allies who had little understanding of his personality, his beliefs or his record in Congress. "I don't like to take pot shots at Eugene McCarthy," announced Allard Lowenstein, "but I'm afraid he's brought it on himself. I remember him historically, but I've forgotten him as a contemporary." "I told you he was no good; why didn't you listen?" one activist wrote to Joseph Rauh, while the *Miami Herald* ran a cartoon showing McCarthy as an overgrown baby sulking in a corner and sucking his thumb. It was certainly true that McCarthy had lost any appetite for congressional politics, not least because the first months of 1969 offered little to interest him. He also lacked any inclination to provide the kind of leadership that the liberals demanded, preferring to spend his days playing tennis, fiddling with his poetry and chatting to friends from outside politics across long lunches at the Assembly restaurant. "Last year I was more outspoken than anybody," he complained to one interviewer in July. "I fought the fight where it should have been fought. What is it that people would have me do now? What is it that people want from me?"[6]

While McCarthy was agonizing about his political future, his wife, Abigail, was becoming increasingly frustrated, urging him to keep his options open and maintain his links with their liberal friends. Relations between the couple had been fraying badly for several years. McCarthy's friends and colleagues observed that, like so many senatorial wives, Abigail always felt marginalized by her husband's staff and resented the fact that her own opinions and requests were usually subordinated to political considerations. She was an intelligent, demanding and strong-willed woman, and McCarthy once remarked to an old friend at St. John's that she was fond of "too many shoulds, woulds, coulds, oughts and musts." From her point of view, the life of a politician's wife was rarely involving and often demeaning, and it was not a life that she would have chosen herself. "The strain began long before the campaign," one friend of the couple later recalled. "Abigail knew it. She had known it for two years, that there was a definite breach, and I think that the fact that she was aware that there was a breach before [meant that] when the campaign came, she was more nervous, more concerned." As the speechwriter Jeremy Larner noted with distaste, Abigail was often the target of McCarthy's cutting remarks, especially as she found it difficult to campaign against her friends Hubert and Muriel Humphrey. The McCarthy family was being torn apart by the anxieties of the campaign. "He did not appear to recognize that other people were there with him," she told an interviewer twenty years later. "He saw it as his lonely venture, and he didn't want the children involved. It broke my heart to see Michael trying so hard to help, and it was sad to see Ellen, who was very shy but wanted so much to be a part of it."[7]

Plagued by ill health, Abigail had dropped out of the campaign in the early summer of 1968. Her husband, meanwhile, continued to tour the country with his entourage, and it did not escape the attention of gossip columnists that he often dined alone with certain female members of the press corps. Political campaigns are notorious breeding grounds for affairs. "On a campaign the roar of the jet plane taking off drowns out the noise of wedding rings being dropped into change purses," commented one Senate aide some years later. Most of the reporters covering the campaign thought that McCarthy was unusually close to two women in the press corps, Shana Alexander and Marya McLaughlin, whom they nicknamed the "little sisters of the press," although McCarthy later denied the rumors. According to one account, during the summer of 1968 a couple returning late one night to their Washington apartment building were startled by a mysterious stranger:

> A shadow, made gigantically grotesque in the dim light, trod down heavily. They braced themselves. The footsteps kept coming. Face to face, a voice pitched low said, "Good evening." In relief the huddled couple answered enthusiastically, "Good evening, Senator." It was Gene McCarthy . . . He had been in the Dresden visiting a lady friend of some consequence in Washington.[8]

Blair Clark was tipped off by a contact at the *Washington Post* that his candidate had been spotted at the Dresden apartments, and later recalled, "I thought this was the makings of a major scandal in the middle of a presidential campaign, so I flew up to Boston . . . and told him this story was all over Washington. He thanked me, I left and that was the end of that." Fortunately for the campaign, nothing came of the rumors.[9]

When his presidential campaign ended, McCarthy returned to his family home in Woodley Park, but his marriage could not be salvaged. In July 1969 the news broke that he had moved into a suite in the Sheraton-Park Hotel and that the longest and most important relationship of his life was over. One rather melodramatic story that circulated in Minnesota was that he had simply walked out of the house one night at dinner and never returned. Newspaper reports suggested that up to the end, Abigail had been trying to keep the marriage alive. "She was willing to pretend there was nothing wrong as long as he didn't force the issue and make it public," one confidant told the press. "But his moving out makes it pretty official." Although Eugene had been pressing her for a divorce for more than a year, Abigail never granted one, and they remained married but separated for the next thirty years. It was a deeply upsetting and traumatic time for their children, with Ellen and Mary in particular being forced to pick sides. Meanwhile, McCarthy himself struggled to continue with his Senate responsibilities even while press speculation was once again linking him with two journalists who had covered his campaign, Shana Alexander of *Life* magazine and Marya McLaughlin, a television correspondent for CBS. Both were talented, attractive and considerably younger than McCarthy, and both were often seen lunching with him on Capitol Hill during the summer of 1969. Most gossip columnists concentrated on his alleged relationship with Shana Alexander, but it was Marya McLaughlin, a devout Catholic, with whom he spent most of the next thirty years. Their relationship was low-key and publicly unacknowledged; although they were close companions, she did not accompany him on his political campaigns, and in later years McCarthy divided his time between his own retreat in rural Virginia and McLaughlin's apartment in Washington, D.C.[10]

It is hard to exaggerate the transformation in McCarthy's life between 1967 and 1969; little wonder, then, that he was both emotionally and intellectually exhausted, or that he should shrink within himself and shun the limelight. "He really went through a great personal crisis," Abigail later explained. "He wanted to cut off everything and that is what he did." McCarthy had always been, if not an insider, then a quiet man who for all his irreverence had always been careful to keep on the right side of the conservative party barons. He had never expected that his presidential campaign would take the course it did; he had allowed himself to dream of winning the highest office in the land, but now he was out in the cold. "He had to be against his party, against his home state, people, for a principle," Abigail told an interviewer. "It was a dividing point in his life—and he had to divide from so much to do it. He cut himself off from so many things that mattered." The experience of defeat, she thought, had deeply wounded her husband, leaving him angry, bitter and distant. Until 1968 McCarthy had been known as a pragmatist, a witty and waspish critic who nevertheless believed in the virtues of compromise and accommodation. Now he rarely hid his contempt for his colleagues and even for politics itself.[11]

During the 1968 campaign Wilfrid Sheed had remarked that so much attention had been paid to McCarthy's days at St. John's that reporters "had him sounding like a thirteenth-century eccentric, a man of crazed frivolity." By the end of the election year, McCarthy the career politician had somehow been forgotten in all the enthusiasm for McCarthy the poet. "One wants to say to the public, Look, I could have been that, if I'd tried; my real gift was always for such and such," Sheed explained. "And some small hobby that was long ago relegated to the attic is brought down and dusted off and perhaps really taken seriously." The obsession with McCarthy's literary experiments was unquestionably misleading; as Sheed put it, even "a banjo-playing senator is a politician first." But McCarthy's poetry made good copy, and as he lost his interest in senatorial politics, so he increasingly spent his time reading and writing verse. He had long enjoyed the company of poets, from Allen Tate and Reed Whittemore to James Dickey and Robert Lowell, and later recalled that he wrote his first poem in a restaurant in 1966: it was about a restaurant critic. In the months after his presidential campaign his poetry drew almost as much attention as his politics: in April 1969 he was one of six poets invited to a prestigious conference on "Poetry and the National Conscience," and in December two of his poems won national awards and were read by Frank Church and Lee Metcalf into the *Congressional Record*. Several published volumes of spare, whimsical verse followed, and in later years some of McCarthy's admirers claimed that he was just as good a poet as any in the country. "Although politics was his vocation, poetry was his real life," explained one of his more earnest devotees. More informed critics did not always agree: a reviewer of *Ground Fog and Night* (1979) called it "a collection of mostly forgettable poems, some of which seem exercises in imitation of Yeats, Stevens, Eliot, Frost or Auden." McCarthy himself admitted that he was not really a poet of the first rank. "Doing something you enjoy doesn't mean you have to aspire to rank with the greats," he told one interviewer. "Stretching from one-dimensionality, using more of yourself expressively—that's benefit enough."[12]

In 1970 McCarthy published his "Lament of an Aging Politician":

> *Stubbornness and penicillin hold*
> *   the aged above me.*
> *My metaphors grow cold and old,*
> *My enemies, both young and bold.*
>
> *I have left Act I, for involution*
> *and Act II. There mired in*
> *   complexity*
> *I cannot write Act III.*[13]

To write Act III, McCarthy would need to pull himself out of his lethargy and work hard to rally the country against the Vietnam War. Instead, as the *St. Paul Pioneer Press* noted: "Not only has McCarthy said nothing about the raging ABM question, but very little about Vietnam. In fact, he has said very little about anything. Since the session started in January, his appearances in the Senate and at committee meetings have been few and brief." Many of the activists who had mobilized against the war in 1968 had lost heart by the following year, especially as Nixon's policy of Vietnamization initially appeared to appease public discontent at American casualties. "I was tired of the whole affair. I was fed up of the war . . . and I was tired of fighting Nixon," the clergyman and peace campaigner William Sloane Coffin later recalled. McCarthy was little different; although he stuck to his demands for a negotiated settlement and a coalition government, he was reluctant to assume the leadership of the movement. "I don't think talking about it helps very much," he told CBS Radio. "I have never been one for fighting the wind really. I am prepared to after the whistle blows and the game starts but I'm not much for warming up on the sidelines."[14]

McCarthy was certainly happy to support and attend the Moratorium demonstrations, which were bankrolled by Martin Peretz and organized by the young New Politics activists who had worked for him in 1968. But when one activist asked him to lead the battle in the Senate to cut off funds for the war, McCarthy replied, "There are plenty of leaders now. Call me sometime when there's no one else to call on. Okay? Well, goodbye." He was right: there were plenty of leaders, and his own contribution to the movement would be lost amid the clamor. By the end of 1969, liberal Democrats were lining up to attack President Nixon's handling of the war in Vietnam. Even Hubert Humphrey and Edmund Muskie had entered the fray, and during 1969 and 1970, an estimated twenty-five members of the Senate and fifty-two members of the House spoke at demonstrations against the war. McCarthy did denounce Nixon's call for "peace with honor"; in February 1970, he appeared before the Foreign Relations Committee and asked: "What, if any, honor has been gained by the death and destruction and social chaos that has gone along with our overwhelming military power and our massive physical presence in Vietnam over the past five years, and what will be gained from the continuation of the war?" Vietnamization, he thought, was a fraud, since the United States "would still have moral responsibility for the war, for continuing it and sustaining it. We will have made of the Vietnamese army, if the Nixon policy is 'successful,' essentially a mercenary army fighting its own people for an unrepresentative government." In his recommendations for a negotiated settlement, however, McCarthy was no different from dozens of other lib-

eral Democrats. Although he spoke out against Nixon's invasion of Cambodia in the spring of 1970, he refused entreaties to lead the opposition in
the Senate. "There's no sense crowding the gate," he said wearily.[15]

Having lost interest in congressional politics, McCarthy became a rare
presence in the Senate chamber, and by 1970 he was bothering to turn up
for only one in three roll calls. His last significant contribution was his role
in the defeat of Richard Nixon's audacious bid to reform the welfare system, the Family Assistance Plan (FAP). Nixon's plan, largely devised by his
liberal adviser on social policy, Daniel Patrick Moynihan, was first aired in
August 1969; it committed the federal government to provide a guaranteed
annual income to every family in the country, reaching $1,600 for a house-
hold of four. Provision was made for work incentives, and all families were
eligible for the FAP until their total income reached the official poverty line
of $3,290. With the FAP in place, the costly apparatus of the War on
Poverty would be dismantled; there would be no need for Aid to Families
with Dependent Children, Model Cities, rent supplements, food stamps
and the whole bureaucratic infrastructure that supported them. These cuts
might appeal to conservatives, but the Family Assistance Plan was hardly a
conservative venture. Nixon was proposing to spend an additional $4.4 bil-
lion on welfare in 1971, while the number of welfare recipients was projected to rise from 10 million to 22 million. Although it made little or no
provision for families without children or poor northerners who already
claimed benefits from their state governments, it would especially help
"the poorest of the poor": black families in the South with several children.
As one commentator put it, despite its flaws the FAP "promised a degree of
income and power redistribution remarkable for American legislation," and
promised to be a remarkable coup for President Nixon. "His proposals,"
commented the *Richmond News-Leader,* "have left the liberal supporters
of Hubert Humphrey and Eugene McCarthy gasping at an audacity their
leaders never dared."[16]

In 1968 Eugene McCarthy had been the first politician to campaign for
the presidency promising "an income distribution system that would guarantee to every American a minimum livable income." The notion of welfare as a legally guaranteed entitlement, funded and provided by the federal
government, was extremely fashionable among academics, social workers
and politicians at the end of the decade. For liberal Democrats, the issue of
a guaranteed income offered not only an opportunity to develop a new
social agenda to replace the commitments of the Fair Deal and the Great
Society, but also the chance to promote their own progressive credentials in
the lead-up to the 1972 presidential primaries. Senator Fred Harris, for
example, who had decided to campaign for the nomination as a born-again

populist, was promising to redistribute 2 percent of GNP through a guaranteed income in order to "bring everyone in the country up to a minimum standard of living and employment." For ambitious liberals like Harris, the prospect of Richard Nixon's taking the credit for a guaranteed income plan was personally repellent and a potential political disaster. As the Kennedy strategist Frank Mankiewicz put it: "The liberals and the welfare community, by and large, cannot take the Nixon reforms emotionally, and cannot afford them politically."[17]

The FAP passed comfortably through the House of Representatives and in April 1970 was sent to the Senate Finance Committee for approval. The plan had already come under fierce attack, partly from conservatives who disliked the idea of a guaranteed annual income, but also from the National Welfare Rights Organization (NWRO), a short-lived alliance of local welfare groups headed by the flamboyant George Wiley, a former chemistry professor and civil rights activist. Most of the NWRO's 20,000 members were the so-called aristocracy of welfare recipients: black mothers who lived in northern ghettoes and received Aid to Families with Dependent Children. Since they were already covered by federal programs, they stood to gain little from Nixon's plan. Even though millions of other poor families, especially in the South, would be covered under the FAP for the first time, Wiley and his organization set their hearts against it. The proposed benefits, they insisted, must be raised from $1,600 to an unlikely $5,500 per household; meanwhile, the provisions to encourage work must be deleted, since they constituted "an act of political repression" and "illfare for poor people." Other New Politics groups scrambled to follow suit. Few ambitious liberals wanted to antagonize the interest groups that might prove influential in determining the party's presidential nominee in 1972, and they therefore lined up to denounce the FAP. According to Whitney Young, the head of the National Urban League, the plan was "a web of vengeful fantasies," while Fred Harris insisted that "instead of raising families out of poverty, [it] would mean for many a sad plunge into the lower depths of even greater poverty." Young wanted the proposed benefits to be raised to $6,500; Harris suggested that a figure of $3,600, costing the government some $20 billion a year, was more appropriate. These alternatives never had the slightest chance of being accepted by the White House. "They were demanding economic ruin," a disillusioned Daniel Patrick Moynihan later wrote. "But they did not know this, or if they knew it they did not care. The defeat of FAP became for many on the liberal left a truly impassioned cause . . . [and] it evoked an increasingly hysterical and irrational response."[18]

On 30 April, the day after the Family Assistance Plan had been sent to the Finance Committee, McCarthy rose to make a rare appearance in the Senate. Not only had he been one of the first politicians to support the idea of a guaranteed income, but he also had close links with the welfare lobby through his presidential campaign in 1968. Moynihan saw McCarthy as the chief "sympathizer and sponsor" of the NWRO cause, and his suspicions were confirmed when McCarthy told the Senate that he was introducing his own "Adequate Income Act." This alternative plan followed the NWRO recommendations to the letter. The system established by the War on Poverty was, he said, "inefficient" and "often demeaning and discriminatory." Work incentives, which were "not conducive to [the] freedom and self-respect of those who must use the system to survive," would have no place in McCarthy's welfare bill, while the $1,600 benefit provided by the FAP was "too low to be adequate for families." Instead, McCarthy followed Wiley in demanding an income of $5,500 for a family of four, to be given "without exception, whether they work or not." If this was unrealistic, he remarked curtly, then "the same may be said about the amounts provided under the proposals of President Nixon."[19]

Moynihan was appalled. McCarthy's plan, he thought, pandered to the wildest excesses of the New Politics coalition and abandoned reason altogether. An analyst from the Department of Labor told him, "The inflationary impact of these developments, not to mention the social and political disruption they might cause, would be severe. In short, the direct and indirect cost implications of this proposal are simply too large for it to be taken seriously as a viable legislative program." It would, Moynihan concluded, "have created a massive work disincentive for almost the entire population. A family of four would have needed to do absolutely nothing to obtain an income of $2.75 for the average working year of 2,000 hours." McCarthy's plan stood no chance of being enacted into law, but that was not the point. Although he had already confirmed his intention to leave the Senate at the end of the year, he was already beginning, albeit haphazardly, to reach out to the New Politics groups that might be able to secure him the presidential nomination in 1972. Since the antiwar movement was rallying behind his rival George McGovern, McCarthy's close association with the NWRO and northern black organizations made perfect political sense. His Adequate Income Act immediately became, in Moynihan's words, "almost a talisman of advanced liberalism."[20]

It was an indication of McCarthy's uncertainty during his last two years in the Senate that while he refused to assume a leadership role in the fight against the Vietnam War, he was still very happy to become the champion of the NWRO campaign against the Family Assistance Plan. Until the late 1960s he had never been closely associated with the issue of welfare and was perceived as a sensible, careful liberal rather than a "bomb-thrower" like Paul Douglas or George McGovern, but in the general rush to court the New Politics groups before the 1972 primaries, he positioned himself as the most uncompromising of all the FAP's opponents on the left. Southern blacks, the poorest social group in the nation, stood to make great gains from Nixon's proposed reforms, but McCarthy was adamant that if the plan did not live up to the impossible standards of George Wiley, it should not pass. As the historian Gareth Davies points out, McCarthy and his fellow liberals could have argued that a new welfare system should guarantee *work*, not income, an alternative that would certainly have had stronger public appeal and more attraction for conservatives. But McCarthy was, it appears, interested only in scoring easy points and impressing his new constituency, and was now prepared to do whatever it took to discredit Nixon's plan.[21]

In November, Russell Long announced that the Finance Committee would not accept testimony from the NWRO, and so McCarthy decided that he would host unofficial hearings of his own in the Senate Office Building. Before 1968, he would never have dreamed of making such a blatantly rebellious gesture, but since his Senate term had only weeks to run, he had nothing to lose; in addition, it was bound to improve his reputation on the left of the Democratic Party. McCarthy's NWRO hearings were, in Davies's words, "to prove disastrous for the cause of welfare reform." They also ranked among the most bizarre hearings ever held in the Senate, providing a platform for the welfare mothers assembled by the NWRO to hurl a stream of insults at various senators and members of the Nixon administration. The transcripts of the hearings had to be censored for release. However, since support for the NWRO had by this point become a litmus test for liberal virtue, there was no shortage of Democratic senators keen to endorse McCarthy's enterprise, including Edmund Muskie, George McGovern, Fred Harris, Lee Metcalf, Harold Hughes and Albert Gore. As one commentator put it, most liberals "commended McCarthy's initiative and probably wished they had thought of it themselves."[22]

On 18 November, the first day of the hearings, George Wiley opened the NWRO testimony by calling the Family Assistance Plan "a sham . . . that will only harass, degrade, demean and further deteriorate the situation of the poor people of this country." He then ushered in a series of black mothers, all on welfare, to express their contempt for the plan, but to the embarrassment of the politicians present the mothers proved unpredictable witnesses. Beulah Sanders, for example, branded Senator Abraham Ribi-coff "a nut" whose mother and wife ought to be "picking up trash" from the streets, while Roxanne Jones criticized "Tricky Dick and all his sportsmen telling us now we have to leave our children and go to work on some slave labor job and join the slave market, or else." Mrs. Jones did, however, praise McCarthy's avoidance of "bullshitting." The real master of cere-monies was not McCarthy but Wiley, who, in the words of Mary McGrory, "floated around the room in his iridescent, multi-colored dashiki, and beamed as the ladies made their uninhibited remarks about their absent senators." Russell Long, a savage critic of the NWRO, did come to listen to the first few witnesses, but left too early to hear the remarks of one mother from Louisiana, who, according to McCarthy, declared, "I'm sorry that lit-tle old Senator Long has gone . . . He sits around drinking that expensive whisky and talking about us poor folks . . . He's got more black half broth-ers and sisters than I have!" Perhaps fortunately, the court reporter was par-tially deaf, and even McCarthy himself later admitted that "it was kind of a comedy," with some senators cringing beneath their desks to avoid being harangued by the mothers. The second day of hearings was, if anything, even worse. One woman announced that she had "visited Teddy Kennedy just this morning and he can kiss my ass," while the witness speaking for Nebraska called Senator Roman Hruska a "loose-lipped mediocrity" and declared that Hruska and his fellow Nebraskan, Carl Curtis, were "buck-passing cats . . . [who] shoot more shit than Bull Durham."[23]

Beneath their gaudy spectacle, though, the NWRO hearings carried an unmistakable political message. Although he admitted that there had been a strong element of farce in the proceedings, McCarthy later praised the "great testimony" of the welfare mothers, whose visceral opposition to the FAP was precisely what the liberals wanted to hear. One woman told the panel, to cries of "Yeah! Yeah!" from the audience, that they wanted only "the kind of jobs that will pay $10,000 or $20,000 . . . We aren't going to do anybody's laundry or babysitting except for ourselves." Another insisted, "You can't force me to work! You'd better give me some-thing better than I'm getting on welfare. I ain't taking it." This was the justi-fication McCarthy needed. "With the welfare mothers opposing it, it makes it easy to vote against," he explained. The FAP was, he declared at the hear-ings, a "Family Destruction Plan" that discriminated against single parents, since "the mother with young children will be forced to take work rather than devote herself to her family." Two days later, the Finance Committee rejected the plan. Six conservative senators voted against it, and they were joined by three liberals: McCarthy, Harris and Gore. In the eyes of most observers, McCarthy's campaign against the FAP had been the decisive factor in turning the other liberals against it. Fred Harris, for example, has been undecided until he attended McCarthy's hearings. Not only had McCarthy made himself the congressional champion of the welfare lobby, but in giving the NWRO free rein to denounce the plan, he had made it virtually impossible for any ambitious Democratic liberal to support it.[24]

If the liberals had supported the Family Assistance Plan, then it might well have survived the predictable conservative onslaught on it in the Senate. Instead, McCarthy helped to ensure the defeat of the most ambitious welfare scheme proposed by any modern president. Most historians agree that the FAP offered a genuine opportunity to improve the lot of the nation's poorest citizens. Liberals like McCarthy distrusted the plan not only because it had been drafted by the Nixon administration but also because it emphasized values like efficiency and hard work that they associated with conservatism. In fact, if it had passed, the plan would have enshrined in American law the progressive principle of a federally guaranteed annual income; it would also, in Davies's words, have had "a dramatic impact on malnutrition and poverty, particularly in the South, where the income of the typical eligible nonwhite family would have increased by more than $1,200." By fighting against the FAP, McCarthy and his fellow presidential aspirants were putting their own political ambitions ahead of the interests of their poorest countrymen. Not for nothing does the conservative commentator Walter Williams call the liberal attacks on the FAP "ugly, mean affairs marked by special interest group and constituency politics, congressional posturing and moralism, and the sad spectacle of the near-poor pitted against the more poor." McCarthy never regretted his opposition to the FAP, and remained proud of his role in the colorful NWRO hearings. The only victors in the affair, however, were affluent liberal politicians like McCarthy and Harris. "In the end," write Vincent and Vee Burke, "the anti-reform liberals scorned the gains that were possible, sacrificing help for millions of America's poorest children in an effort to show that they were . . . 1,000 percent pure, more loyal than others to the poor." As James Patterson puts it in his history of poverty in the United States, the defeat of the plan "marked the end of the most ambitious effort for welfare reform in the forty years since the creation of the welfare state in 1935." The abiding legacy of McCarthy's final year in the Senate was therefore the destruction of a plan that might have done much to improve the lives of the most vulnerable citizens in the nation.[25]

McCarthy's term in the Senate was due to expire at the end of 1970, and he had been thinking about retiring for several years, largely because he was bored and saw little future for himself in Congress. When endorsing Hubert Humphrey in October 1968, he had publicly announced that he would not run for re-election to the Senate. "Before I got into the presidential race," he explained to David Frost a year later, "I had more or less decided that this would be my last term in the Senate." It was not, however, a simple matter of abandoning the Senate for a simple, contemplative retirement in Minnesota, because like many ambitious politicians, McCarthy found it difficult to imagine life outside the political arena. Although he had lost interest in the intricate rituals of Senate life, he had not entirely lost his interest in politics itself, and it appears that by the time of the fight against the Family Assistance Plan he had begun to regain some of his old enthusiasm. He later admitted that had it been left to him, he "would probably have stayed on in the Senate"; it was, however, too late to change his mind since he was now publicly committed to retirement.[26]

If McCarthy had decided to run again in 1970, he would not have gone unchallenged. Hubert Humphrey was still immensely popular in Minnesota, and McCarthy had alienated plenty of his own constituents by his apparent disloyalty in 1968 and unpredictable conduct thereafter. "It would have been a bloody fight out there between the Humphrey people and my people," he later told an interviewer. As early as March 1969, newspaper reports claimed that labor leaders were encouraging Humphrey to challenge McCarthy for the DFL nomination if he ran again, and an opinion poll in April showed not only that Humphrey was much more popular among Democratic voters, but that McCarthy would even struggle to defeat a Republican opponent. "There has been a strong feeling in the DFL that Humphrey could win the DFL endorsement next year, even if McCarthy tried for a third term," reported the *St. Paul Pioneer Press* in July. Humphrey was not a bitter man by nature, but he told Edgar Berman that he had lost his old respect for McCarthy: "He fooled me for a long time. As I've said many times, the only tender a politician has to offer is his word and Gene's currency is devalued even in Washington. He's a strange man."[27]

During the early months of 1969, the two men warily circled one another, with Humphrey waiting impatiently for confirmation that McCarthy was going to leave his Senate seat. McCarthy seemed to enjoy baiting his former friend. "Tell those Democrats if they keep quiet and don't get too mean with me I may not run and let them have the job," he told an intermediary in May. "If they keep yelling at me, I will come back and run, just to beat them . . . I think they could beat almost anyone else, but not almost anyone else plus me." But the truth is that he was hurt by the speculation that Humphrey was planning to run and beat him, as Humphrey's friend and adviser Jim Rowe reported:

Gene said very quietly to me that "Humphrey and his people shouldn't make remarks about they don't care whether I run or not in Minnesota." McCarthy said this might well force him into the race and he might run as an Independent candidate. I said my observation was that "Hubert has been very good about this in general." McCarthy said yes that was true. I suppose none of us have any illusions left about the unpredictable McCarthy and it probably doesn't matter very much what the Humphrey people do or don't do.[28]

McCarthy, understandably, did not relish the prospect of facing Humphrey in a DFL primary, and on 25 July 1969 he confirmed his intention to retire. "Hubert needs the job worse than I do anyway," he remarked privately. Humphrey, meanwhile, reacted to the news with typically garrulous enthusiasm, reportedly shouting, "It's a resurrection! I'm as high as a kite! I'm on the run! I'll win in a walk!"[29]

For the first time since 1948, McCarthy now faced the prospect of life outside Congress. While Humphrey coasted to an easy victory in November 1970, McCarthy was busy fighting the Family Assistance Plan, his last contribution to congressional politics. On 21 December, his Minnesota colleague Walter Mondale, whom McCarthy was later to deride mercilessly, organized a touching tribute to him in the Senate. McCarthy sat "looking slightly embarrassed" in a corner of the chamber while an array of Democrats lined up to praise him and bid their farewells. As David Broder remarked in the *Washington Post,* the tributes were "unusually honest" and "restrained by the suspicion that McCarthy might not resist the temptation to deflate the pomposity of the occasion by one last wisecrack." Mondale began by praising McCarthy for his courage in 1968, even though he himself had worked hard for Hubert Humphrey. "For this act of singular courage," Mondale said, "every Member of this body, every citizen of the nation, and, indeed, virtually everyone in the world owes him an enormous debt." Perhaps the most personal farewell came from Edmund Muskie, who fondly recalled that he, McCarthy and Philip Hart had been "summer bachelors together in those early summers when the Senate labored while our families went home." The three had enjoyed, Muskie said, "special ties of friendship and of value," always sitting together at the back of the chamber, and he concluded:

I have regarded Gene as a friend, not as a political friend or a senatorial friend, but as a friend. I enjoyed his company. He was comfortable to be with. But he could also be uncomfortable. He was congenial, but he could also be withdrawn. He was a man of many moods, often preferred to be alone. He did not solicit friendship. But his friendship was the rewarding friendship of a man with great capacity for understanding and sympathy.[30]

As Muskie was to discover two years later, however, McCarthy did not share his feelings.

In his tribute to McCarthy published in the *Washington Post,* David Broder reflected that he had been "a frustrating, maddening man to cover." "We have reported him badly," Broder wrote, "because at almost every important point, we have misunderstood his purpose and misrepresented his motives . . . In retrospect, one suspects this was often the case because we were unable to see or reluctant to admit that he was operating on insights and reflections that were much deeper than we could comprehend." This was a generous verdict, and not untypical: many reporters thought that McCarthy was not inconsistent or incoherent, but rather unfathomably profound. In December 1970, however, it was not clear that he had left any substantial congressional legacy. Although he had been an instrumental founder of the Democratic Study Group, his legislative accomplishments were few, and by the middle of his second term in the Senate he had a reputation for laziness and indifference. Eight Democratic senators from the "Class of 1958" won a third term in 1970; all were committee chairmen by 1974, with the exceptions of Philip Hart, who was famously unambitious, and Robert Byrd, the majority whip. If he had worked hard at his Senate career and fought for a third term, McCarthy could have expected similar influence and responsibility. Bored as he was of senatorial duties, he would still have had a convenient focus for his political energies and personal drive. Instead, he left the Senate with vague ambitions of running again for the presidency in 1972 and left most of his admirers bewildered and disappointed. The verdict of one Minnesota academic who later switched his allegiance to George McGovern was typical: "I cannot understand how he could abandon a useful career to indulge himself in a fancied talent for poetry . . . He destroyed any opportunity to have influence on the issues before the country by giving up his Senate seat. To remain in the Senate was the only way to retain his stature; I think he lost his marbles." But McCarthy was determined to plow a lonely furrow, as he wrote in his poem "The Aardvark":

> *I am alone*
> *in the land of the aardvarks.*
> *I am walking west*
> *all the aardvarks are going east.*[31]

For all McCarthy's interest in poetry, politics was his real vocation. As he later admitted, even when he declined to run for re-election in 1970 he was considering the possibility of an independent presidential challenge in 1972, when he expected the Democrats to nominate an orthodox candidate like Hubert Humphrey or Edmund Muskie. In the meantime, he was at something of a loose end, living on his own in Washington, D.C., but still not psychologically divorced from the world of Democratic politics. He subsequently wrote that he had been "slightly disappointed" not to be offered a directorship by any financial institution in Minnesota; nor, he complained, was he "asked to be a consultant, or even to teach or lecture at the University of Minnesota." No doubt his reputation for unreliability and his well-publicized rift with Hubert Humphrey had damaged his cause on both counts.[32]

One offer that did materialize came from the University of Maryland at College Park, where at the end of 1971 McCarthy taught an undergraduate seminar on "Literature and Politics" and delivered weekly lectures on "Poetry and Poetics," albeit with mixed results. McCarthy himself admitted that although he enjoyed his lunches with the Maryland professors, he was "slightly intimidated" by the students; it was a long time since he had last taught undergraduates in St. Paul after the Second World War. He was allowed to teach pretty much whatever he liked: in the poetry lectures, for example, he simply discussed his own favorite modern writers like Vernon Watkins, George Seferis and James Dickey. The syllabus for "Literature and Politics" was even more skewed toward McCarthy's own continuing political preoccupations; while students were encouraged to read Machiavelli, Tolstoy, Brecht and Ibsen, they were also assigned the works of Eldridge Cleaver, Norman Mailer's book *The Armies of the Night* and the film *Dr. Strangelove*, as well as the Russian poetry with which McCarthy had recently become fascinated. When a *New York Times* reporter attended one of his lectures, she noted that his typically obscure jokes elicited little response from his bemused listeners. Lecturing on poetry was very different from delivering a prepared political address. McCarthy seemed nervous and underprepared, rambling from allusion to anecdote, and the reporter commented that he "could be reading from the *Congressional Record,* his voice drops so low, his tone so diffident, seeming bored, but actually not so." At the end of the lecture, none of the questions were about poetry. "What's your reaction to the move on the part of McGovern's backers to get you and Lindsay to support him?" was a typical example.[33]

McCarthy's interest in the Democratic nomination to challenge President Nixon was indeed well known to newspaper readers during the summer and autumn of 1971. Even though he had left the Senate, he still had good reason to be optimistic. The New Politics faction within the Democratic Party was far stronger in 1971 than it had been three years earlier, with an extensive web of activists and clubs across the nation, a favorable system of electing convention delegates already in place, and a single shared goal: the nomination of an antiwar reform liberal to face Richard Nixon. The party regulars, meanwhile, had been struggling to attract money and interest since Humphrey's defeat in 1968, while the labor movement was divided among three or four potentially successful presidential contenders. With at least twenty primaries scheduled for 1972, the reform liberals could expect considerable success; their supporters, after all, were more organized and assiduous voters than those of their more conservative rivals. It was certainly not clear in the months before the campaign started in earnest that their candidate would be George McGovern; even at the end of 1971, his poll ratings among Democrats fluctuated between 3 percent and 6 percent. Although McCarthy had abandoned front-line politics, his own ratings remained healthier. In October 1969, for example, he was placed fourth among all possible Democratic candidates, with 10 percent; in May 1970, he was fifth, with 9 percent. Had McCarthy exerted himself, it is perfectly plausible that he and not McGovern might have emerged as the candidate of the reform liberals in 1972, not least because he still had wealthy friends on Wall Street who could be expected to pay for another campaign. It was hardly surprising that he might want to try again, especially after coming so close in 1968. He had, after all, nothing better to do and nothing to lose. "Every day on the campaign trail is a little drama of its own," the *Minneapolis Tribune* noted in 1968, "full of action and suspense. Campaigning, like war, may be hell, but it is also escape of the most exhilarating and demanding, draining and reviving kind."[34]

One enthusiastic advocate of McCarthy's cause in 1972 was President Nixon himself. If McCarthy ran, so Nixon thought, he would attract liberal support, reopen the Democratic wounds of 1968, lose the nomination to a candidate from the center or right of the party, and then run a divisive independent campaign that could only improve Nixon's chances of winning re-election. "We would like to have McCarthy in the race," Nixon told his staff in August 1971, asking Henry Kissinger to "build up the idea . . . [that the] only man . . . who has the intellectual capability on the Democratic side is McCarthy and isn't it a shame that he really doesn't have a chance and all the rest." A month later he asked his chief of staff H. R. Haldeman to "finance and contribute both to McCarthy and to the black thing." Five million dollars, he speculated, would be enough for McCarthy to make an unsuccessful bid for the nomination and then run an independent liberal campaign. Henry Kissinger, who still had links to the liberal and intellectual communities in New York and California, was Nixon's designated operative in the effort to promote McCarthy's chances. "I've been building McCarthy like crazy on the West Coast," Kissinger announced proudly in September 1971. But McCarthy later remarked that no White House money had actually been forthcoming. "I never saw any of it!" he said wistfully. "I was never approached . . . they never approached me with a bag full of money." They did not need to. McCarthy had already made up his mind to run.[35]

In July 1971 McCarthy convened a meeting of various friends and supporters at the St. Regis Hotel in New York, where they spent no less than six hours discussing the possibilities for a campaign to win the nomination the following year. The cast was much the same as in 1968, an uneasy alliance of McCarthy's old Senate staff and a younger group of antiwar reform activists, as well as men like Howard Stein, Martin Peretz and Arnold Hiatt who had financially backed McCarthy three years earlier. As the reform activist Anne Wexler put it, "it was clear . . . that whatever money was needed would be available"; it was also evident that McCarthy was interested not in another "educational campaign" but in eventual victory. "He's running like hell," another supporter told the *Washington Post*. Since many of the activists had worked closely with McCarthy in 1968, they had understandable doubts about his commitment to the task, but these were allayed when at the end of the meeting McCarthy enthusiastically telephoned Andrew Young and Jesse Jackson to ask for their support in winning the black vote, a remarkable change from his behavior in the previous campaign. Young and Jackson were important to McCarthy because, as prominent black clergymen and activists, they were thought to command the allegiance of the Democrats' black constituency. When McCarthy visited the Southern Christian Leadership Conference convention in August, it was clear that he was experimenting with a new approach. His stance on the Family Assistance Plan and open support for the NWRO had already improved his standing among northern black activists; his plan for 1972 was to reach out to the black vote while retaining his strength among reform liberals, middle-class independents, antiwar activists and young people. Andrew Young was one early enthusiast; McCarthy, he thought, was capable of "putting together the big-city urban-ethnic blocs" to create a new liberal coalition that could sweep to victory in November.[36]

In characteristic fashion, McCarthy did not launch his campaign with a ringing announcement of his platform and intentions. Instead, on 25

October 1971, he released to the press the text of a letter he was sending out to the liberal activists and fund-raisers who had supported him in 1968. According to the letter, he intended "to establish very soon a formal campaign committee," although the office for which he was running was not actually specified. He would campaign for "an immediate end to the shooting war" in Vietnam, accompanied by "a political settlement and arrangements for the withdrawal of troops," and reform of the political process itself, the details of which were not disclosed. As in 1968, he criticized the general commitments of the Cold War as well as the conflict in Vietnam. "The whole militaristic thrust of our foreign policy," he said, "continues to be . . . a principal obstacle to significant action to meet the domestic needs of our country: the needs of the poor, of our cities, and of our environment." The other Democratic candidates, "announced and unannounced, have offered little more than warmed-over New Deal programs or quantitative increases in Nixon proposals." What McCarthy meant by attacking "New Deal programs" was unclear; it appeared that he was repudiating the legacies of Roosevelt and Truman and arguing for an entirely new approach to domestic policy, but his own new ideas were never fully explained. It was certainly an odd way to enter the presidential race and earned McCarthy little publicity, almost as though he was reluctant to make an open bid for the office for fear of looking ridiculous if failed. As it was, his conduct over the next few months was very peculiar, and it was not clear even to his own supporters whether he was really running or not. In December he filed as a candidate in the Massachusetts primary. "In Massachusetts, I suppose, I am a candidate," he said mournfully. He told journalists that his plan was to run "primary by primary and state by state." There would not, he confidently predicted, be a winner on the first ballot at the convention; he hoped to have a power base of his own and either to win on a later ballot or, at least, to swing the nomination to a candidate of his choice. This approach made McCarthy very unusual among modern Democratic presidential contenders; not only was he even more elliptical than in 1968, but he openly admitted that he would consider throwing his support to another candidate if a suitable reform liberal emerged. He would also, he said, reserve the right to run as an independent if he felt like it. It was hardly surprising that the press gave him less attention than they gave more committed candidates like Edmund Muskie, George McGovern and John Lindsay. McCarthy's evasions were even beginning to earn him sustained ridicule in some quarters. The *St. Paul Pioneer Press,* for example, accused him of showing "symptoms of Stassenitis," with the caveat that unlike the perennial Republican candidate Harold Stassen, a fellow Minnesotan, Eugene McCarthy "could never in any way be described as a 'nice' fellow."[37]

Many Democratic strategists, following Richard Scammon and Ben Wattenberg, argued that the best way for the party to regain its dominant position in presidential politics was to "drive toward the center of the electorate," appealing to urban working-class union members and what Scammon and Wattenberg called "Middle America." This was, in essence, the approach that had worked so well in the 1970 congressional elections, and it was associated with those presidential candidates thought to represent the center of the Democratic Party, especially Edmund Muskie and Henry Jackson. Few Democratic candidates, however, had much to say about the problems of race, class and inflation that bothered blue-collar voters, and few had developed new ideas for reforming or rebuilding the domestic programs of the Great Society.[38]

Eugene McCarthy's program provided a typical example of the stagnation of liberalism after 1968. Initially his proposed platform was almost exactly the same as the one he had presented in the final months of his last campaign, and during the opening months of 1972 it shifted further to the left, albeit in the vaguest possible way. On the issue of the Vietnam War, for instance, McCarthy called for a coalition government in South Vietnam and a negotiated settlement, just as he had four years earlier, the only difference being that he was now even more confident of success. With a coalition government, he told one interviewer, "I think that one could end all hostilities in about twenty-four hours." His approach to domestic issues was even more lavish and ambitious than it had been in 1968, although McCarthy's various spending proposals were rarely defined in detail. His remedy for the inflation that had afflicted the American economy since 1966 was characteristically unclear; rather than choose between Keynesian and monetarist solutions, he explained that "the theories and recommendations of the monetarists do have application and also those of the Keynesians," leaving his audience none the wiser.[39]

It is, of course, quite normal for politicians to pledge themselves to enormously ambitious but ultimately vague spending programs, but McCarthy went much further than any of his rivals. Many of his suggestions would not only have required millions of dollars in additional spending at a time when the federal government was struggling to cut costs, but would also have represented a radical overhaul of American government and political culture. He promised, for instance, "a new assertion of the right of every child to a proper education, even if it means overriding or even eliminating present school systems." A McCarthy administration would fund "the creation of entirely new systems by which the poor, through their own representatives, can serve their own needs"; he also offered "a commitment to provide a job for everyone who wants work, even if the government has to create these jobs or compel private privileged corporations to provide them"; and he promised "a program to provide health and medical care for all, even though this requires changes in the doctor's concept of his profession and in the practice of medicine." This would, if realized, have left the United States with a welfare state not only unmatched in American history but also in the democratic world. As in 1968, McCarthy also promised a guaranteed annual income for all Americans. As observers of his efforts to defeat the FAP might have expected, McCarthy's plan was suitably munificent. To "provide the poor of this country with a decent standard of living in agreement with the National Welfare Rights Organization's proposals," he offered a minimum of $6,000 per family, without ever quite explaining how this enormous and potentially crippling commitment was to be financed. This was, of course, far more lavish than the much-derided "demogrant" that George McGovern proposed later in the campaign; like some of McCarthy's more frivolous commitments, such as his promises to decriminalize marijuana and to release half of all the prisoners in the nation, it also clearly reflected McCarthy's desire to appeal to the left of his party.[40]

McCarthy's task in 1972 was much harder than it had been four years earlier. This time he was not a valiant crusader facing an unpopular president but merely one ambitious Democrat among many. Nor could he rely on the peace issue to promote his cause among middle-class liberals. Most liberal and moderate Democrats had by January 1972 moved to embrace McCarthy's own position, making it difficult for him to stand out from the crowd. Edmund Muskie, for instance, had promised "as close to an immediate withdrawal from Vietnam as possible"; George McGovern was calling for the withdrawal of all Americans troops by June 1972; and even Hubert Humphrey thought that the "most urgent, immediate need is to end the war and do it now." Muskie's rise was a serious threat to McCarthy's hopes, because the senator from Maine was a sober, unthreatening, Catholic liberal who had belatedly become a public critic of the war and struck many of McCarthy's old supporters as a more plausible contender. Most of the senior office holders and strategists in McCarthy's 1968 campaign had already declared their allegiance to Muskie. When McCarthy asked the Connecticut activist Anne Wexler to return to his colors, she "turned him down cold." "I was for Muskie," she later recalled. "I mean, I wanted to win."[41]

The candidacy of George McGovern, meanwhile, posed an even more difficult problem, since McGovern was a genuine antiwar populist with an impeccable liberal record, a pleasant and unassuming personality, and a reputation for seriousness, sincerity and sheer hard work. Most of the local volunteers who had once lionized McCarthy had by early 1972 switched to supporting McGovern, and he had also won over McCarthy's old fund-raisers, Stewart Mott and Martin Peretz. Even McCarthy's former campaign manager, Blair Clark, was now the co-chairman of McGovern's primary campaign, and when SANE endorsed McGovern rather than McCarthy, it was clear that the South Dakotan was the anointed candidate of the liberal antiwar movement. "McGovern's not in it just to raise issues," one veteran of 1968 commented. "McGovern's in it to win."[42]

The early signs were not promising. When McCarthy had appeared at a picnic in Madison, Wisconsin, in 1968, some 15,000 people had turned up. He returned to a similar event in September 1971 and found fewer than a hundred waiting for him. The old magic, it seemed, had deserted him. "A tired man in a rumpled tan raincoat arrived in Duluth late Tuesday," ran one report in the *St. Paul Dispatch* in February 1972, "met briefly with a small group of followers in a store-front office and went to a hotel for a short night's sleep before catching an early-morning plane to Chicago." Every campaign stop brought the inevitable flood of questions about his reluctance to endorse Humphrey, his behavior after his return to the Senate and his decision to retire from Washington politics in 1970. "Where have you been for four years?" asked one student at the University of Wisconsin. McCarthy wearily explained that he "didn't drop out, and it disturbs me that people keep saying I did." As he saw it: "After 1968, there was no place to go, it was over." For most of his old supporters, however, this was not a satisfactory answer. One young activist from Wisconsin explained: "I worked like hell for him last time, but I haven't made up my mind yet about this time. Frankly, I'm leaning heavily towards Senator George McGovern."[43]

Privately McCarthy was disappointed with the students' reaction. "What do they expect me to do?" he complained. "Come on like Al Jolson?" The fact was that by early 1972, most liberal activists regarded McCarthy as a fundamentally frivolous, unpredictable and haughty candidate who had given up the fight after his defeat four years earlier. His personal idiosyncrasies were all the more apparent because he was no longer seen as the gallant martyr for a noble cause, or the brave underdog facing overwhelming odds. He did not attract the hordes of volunteers who had come to New Hampshire in 1968, and neither did he employ a team of skilled and experienced political consultants like Richard Goodwin or Tom Finney. Instead, the campaign, essentially a series of lectures and speaking appearances, was organized by his former administrative assistant, Jerry Eller, and his old secretary, Jean Stack. It was not a model of smooth professional efficiency; on one occasion, McCarthy invited a group of reporters to meet him at a restaurant on the North Side of Chicago for lunch, but when the press corps arrived, they discovered that the establishment in question was closed, as it always was on Mondays. The veteran political observer Theodore H. White passed a "dimly lit" McCarthy storefront in Milwaukee during the Wisconsin primary. It was, he wrote, a "melancholy" spectacle: he saw "piles of unused literature and pamphlets and several silent phones. Two young girls stood by. Otherwise, empty."[44]

McCarthy's first major test of the 1972 campaign was the Massachusetts Citizens' Caucus, held on 15 January in the assembly hall of Holy Cross College in Worcester, Massachusetts. Sponsored by reform organizations and liberal groups like Mass PAX, Citizens for Participation in Political Action, the National Youth Caucus and the Coalition of Black People, the caucus was a quintessential example of high-minded reform politics in action. As one commentator put it, "the participants included peace activists, Cambridge intellectuals, quarrelling local factions, Nobel laureates, Kennedy followers and Kennedy haters, and an assortment of delegates committed to a variety of other causes." The purpose of the caucus was to nominate a liberal candidate around whom all the reformers in the state would unite; if McCarthy were defeated here, it would be very difficult to project himself as the liberal choice in 1972. Many of the organizers, like Jerome Grossman and Richard Goodwin, were veterans of McCarthy's effort in 1968, and if McCarthy could hold off the challenge of George McGovern, John Lindsay and Shirley Chisholm, then perhaps he could revive his campaign. Only McCarthy and Chisholm bothered to attend, and the night before the vote, to the cheers of his teenage supporters, McCarthy confidently told reporters, "You'll see how serious I am after tomorrow's caucus."[45]

On the evening of the caucus, 2,600 activists arrived to cast their ballots. McGovern won 62 percent of the vote; Chisholm finished second with 23 percent; and McCarthy and Lindsay trailed disconsolately behind with 13 percent and 2 percent respectively. It was, wrote one McGovern aide, "a devastating blow" for Eugene McCarthy's candidacy. Not only had he lost to McGovern, an old rival whose national ratings stood at a mere 3 percent, he had also lost to Chisholm, a black congresswoman whom few commentators regarded as a serious contender. Since McCarthy had already promised to abide by the decision of the caucus, he was now barred from running in Massachusetts; instead, McGovern would bear the liberal standard in the state. As McCarthy admitted to CBS after the result, the "active liberals" clearly preferred his South Dakotan opponent. "I think I still have my troops," he said mournfully. "The officers have deserted, however." His supporters, meanwhile, were already abandoning ship. The Mass Pax activist Jerome Grossman, who had worked hard for McCarthy four years previously, wasted little time in discarding his candidate. Massachusetts's liberals, he said, "no longer believe in McCarthy's leadership quotient." One anonymous reformer told the *New York Times*: "If he can't win in that group, where can he win?"[46]

That night was a watershed in McCarthy's political career, both a terrible setback to his hopes of winning the nomination in 1972 and an unmistakable signal that his credibility among liberal Democrats had collapsed. Even though a Gallup poll of Democratic supporters published a week later still put him ahead of McGovern by 8 percent to 3 percent, McCarthy's weak showing had, as one Minneapolis newspaper remarked, "ripped away whatever cloak of credibility his candidacy had." At the end of January the caucus of the New Democratic Coalition, the quintessential white, educated, suburban reform organization, voted to endorse George McGovern. McCarthy won only 10 percent of the ballot, finishing behind John Lindsay. His career as the darling of the liberals was over. The national press ignored his campaign, and the early primaries passed him by. Most observers expected him to withdraw gracefully into the shadows.[47]

Despite the fact that McGovern was pulling off a series of impressive results in the primaries, however, McCarthy was not ready to shuffle off the stage. Instead, he turned his attentions to Edmund Muskie, his old golfing partner and close Senate friend. At Chicago in 1968 McCarthy had pondered withdrawing from the race for the nomination and throwing his delegates to Muskie as a dark horse; no doubt he knew that although the senator from Maine publicly supported administration policy in Vietnam, he had private misgivings about the war. McCarthy had also telephoned Muskie just before the convention, hinting that if he managed to snatch the presidential nomination, he would be strongly tempted to offer his old friend the second place on the Democratic ticket. At this stage, therefore, the two men were still good friends. At the convention, however, Muskie had accepted Hubert Humphrey's offer of the vice presidential nomination, thereby implicitly associating himself not with McCarthy and the peace campaigners but with the Johnson administration and the war. McCarthy never forgave him, and relegated Muskie to the ranks of his enemies. "While I was in Grant Park," he bitterly remarked to a New York audience in January

1972, "Hubert Humphrey was at the convention hall, with George McGovern on his left and Edmund Muskie on his right." At the very beginning of the campaign he even publicly released the text of a letter he had sent to Muskie warning him that he was out for revenge:

> In Chicago, you opposed my candidacy and my position on the war, and the Maine delegation—I must assume with your approval and support, since you have never publicly or privately indicated anything else—voted against not only me but against my position on ending the war in Vietnam . . . What happened in that year and since bears significantly on what I will do in 1972. As you follow my activities in the coming months, as you say you will, it is important to keep this in mind.[48]

By the end of February, McCarthy had abandoned any attempt to project himself as a serious competitor to George McGovern on the left of the party. He threw himself instead into an attempt to win just one primary: Illinois, which all the other contenders had, in effect, decided to leave to the overwhelming favorite in the state, Edmund Muskie. With his dry, thoughtful manner and pragmatic liberal reputation, the senator from Maine had once been the Democratic front-runner, and remained the opponent that President Nixon most feared, but by the spring his campaign was floundering. McCarthy was hardly in the mood for charity. "I wanted to challenge Muskie," he later explained to an interviewer. "Muskie had behaved pretty badly in '68." This was not merely political; it was personal. Washington gossip columnists even claimed that McCarthy had taken to calling his old friend "the latest Polish joke."[49]

McCarthy spent some $260,000 on his campaign against Muskie in the Illinois preferential primary, more than two-thirds of his entire outlay on the 1972 presidential race. Most of this money came from old liberal supporters and fund-raisers like Martin Peretz and Stewart Mott, and it was poured into a largely negative media blitz against Muskie. The notorious Committee to Re-elect the President also appears to have contributed funds to McCarthy's Illinois effort. McCarthy's slogan, "McCarthy vs. Muskie, March 21," was simple and personal, and the candidate spent the three weeks before the primary crossing the state to issue denunciations of his old colleague. Rather than presenting new ideas of his own, he was instead content to run an adversarial campaign devoted to destroying Muskie's reputation and positions. Muskie was "an incarnation of what's wrong with the Democratic Party today." "You just don't know where he stands on the issues," McCarthy explained coldly. "He represents the unimaginative, survivalist and dug-in position of the party." Muskie's economic plan would, McCarthy said mockingly, "take about forty years to cure the problems facing this nation today." He had "made no proposals to prevent crime or eliminate the conditions of poverty, congestion and unemployment that cause crime." Above all, he had "led . . . the opposition" to McCarthy's peace proposals in 1968.[50]

For McCarthy to take such a negative approach was unusual; earlier in his career he had fought relatively restrained campaigns, even when his patriotism was attacked by Republican opponents in the early 1950s. Most of the reporters who followed him in Illinois, however, commented that McCarthy seemed remarkably happy and comfortable in his quest to "stop Muskie." He was, noted one writer, "spending heavily in the media and campaigning in an energetic way hardly anyone could remember his doing before." Another correspondent who had covered his campaign in 1968 reported that McCarthy moved around Illinois with an unusually "broad and easy smile and confident gait." The *New Republic* observed:

> Where in 1968 he barely endured question and answer sessions that followed most speeches, he now stays on until every question has been asked. He doesn't seem bored; he doesn't mind answering the same question twice . . . He accepts invitations for radio talk shows that encourage viewers to call in questions. He travels from campus to campus, drawing overflow crowds. He lingers after the rally to socialize with small groups of devotees . . . He allows bowling to be scheduled at the end of a busy day, because that's where you find working class voters at night. His manner is gentle, patient . . . It's a bit freaky for a reporter who followed McCarthy in 1968.[51]

Evidently McCarthy found it refreshing, even liberating, to conduct a purely negative campaign after four years wearily defending himself against the complaints of his former supporters. There is little doubt, too, that he felt genuinely aggrieved that Muskie had accepted Humphrey's offer of the vice presidential spot, and so the Illinois campaign represented sweet satisfaction for a bitter grudge. With no McGovern in the field, he had a free run against a candidate of the Democratic center, and to some extent the campaign was a replay of the struggle against Humphrey in 1968. McCarthy's supporters and advisers were in the main veterans of the old campaign; many admitted that it was their "last fight" on behalf of McCarthy and expected to switch to McGovern after the primary was over. The result, however, was further evidence of McCarthy's decline in popular esteem. On 21 March, Illinois's Democratic electorate voted in favor of

Muskie by 63 percent to 37 percent. McCarthy put a brave face on the results as he addressed his workers in the Plaza Hotel in Chicago, announcing that he was "quite content and satisfied," that the defeat marked "a significant beginning on an important campaign" and that he was now planning primary campaigns in New York and California, where he hoped to win enough delegates to stand as a strong candidate at a deadlocked convention. Given that McCarthy had actually outspent his rival, and that Muskie was already slipping badly in the national polls after a series of mishaps in the early primaries, this was not by any means a good result for McCarthy and destroyed any slight hopes he might still have entertained for the presidential nomination. It seems likely that those liberal, well-educated Democrats who supported him in Illinois saw him as simply a stand-in for McGovern; it is also likely that McGovern himself, had he run, would have done much better against the flagging Muskie. Although McCarthy made a show of announcing his projected cabinet choices at the end of the month, which included an eccentric mixture of historians, Democratic senators and personal friends, the promised primary efforts in New York and California never materialized. His campaign, which had cost almost half a million dollars, was over.[52]

On 6 June, after an extremely close and bitter campaign, George McGovern defeated Hubert Humphrey in the final and decisive Democratic primary in California. Four years after rejecting Eugene McCarthy, the party had selected a liberal presidential candidate with a platform very close to that presented by the McCarthy campaign in 1968. The new party procedures and the strength of the New Politics organizations certainly favored McGovern in 1972, but he was also quite clearly more successful than McCarthy both in reaching out to working-class and black primary voters and in projecting an image of compassion, commitment and sheer hard work. It was not surprising that a man with McCarthy's highly developed sense of pride and self-worth should feel a twinge of jealousy that another man had won the nomination on a very similar platform to his own, especially since he had little regard for McGovern and had never forgiven him for his late entrance into the contest in 1968. To McCarthy, the South Dakotan was an unimaginative mediocrity, a stooge for the Kennedy camp who had "stolen the anti-war movement," and worthy of contempt simply because he was a Methodist. Weeks before the decisive California primary, Blair Clark warned McGovern:

I think it likely that McCarthy will try to make trouble for us in California. I think he has a real animus against you, compounded of envy and wrong-headed hostility over what you did in '68 . . . [the liberal journalist Harry] Ashmore said in private McCarthy is very bitter about you (as I know he unreasonably is); Ashmore says he says things like that your tax program will "destroy capitalism" in the US! And he accuses you of copping out on marijuana!

My own view is that Gene's principles are a façade and that he really prefers Humphrey.[53]

As it turned out, McCarthy did grudgingly endorse McGovern in California, no doubt motivated in part by antipathy toward Humphrey and his circle. When issuing the endorsement, McCarthy suggested that McGovern might like to make him secretary of state or secretary of the Treasury; even so, he could not resist adding that if McGovern's platform did not meet his expectations, he reserved the right to run as an independent candidate. Nor did he throw his delegates to McGovern; instead, even at the convention, he insisted on being treated as a possible contender for the nomination. As in the campaign against Muskie, McCarthy evidently derived enormous pleasure from defying the expectations of his old liberal colleagues. "McCarthy is looking splendid," noted Norman Mailer at the Democratic National Convention in Miami Beach. "He has never appeared more handsome, more distinguished and more a philosopher prince."

> He takes great pleasure in teasing one of his total of four delegates who is a good young woman from Chicago but aware to a fault of her own lacks.
>
> "Oh, my God," she says, "I'm just the wife of a butcher. I can't put you in nomination."
>
> "Well, you may have to," he says with as much pleasure as if he were President of Notre Dame and had just told an All-American he will have to read the works of Immanuel Kant before trying to go on to the priesthood.[54]

The Miami Beach convention was the last major Democratic gathering at which McCarthy appeared as a serious and influential political figure, but as Mailer's story suggests, he was increasingly flirting with absurdity and eccentricity, no doubt partly as compensation for his own electoral failure. Addressing the platform committee, he insisted that the Democratic Party reflect the positions he had taken four years earlier, and suggested that they "take a look at the [Humphrey] platform" for "an example of the kind of platform we should not write." In fact the Miami Beach platform was the most liberal adopted by the Democratic Party since the Second World War: it included commitments to withdraw American troops from Vietnam; to cut military spending; to introduce amnesty for draft evaders, gun control legislation and reform of the electoral system; and to establish a national guaranteed income. In the words of the political historian Kenneth Baer, it was "a clear exposition of New Politics liberalism." For McCarthy, however, it was still not enough. He was especially disgruntled that party strategists had begun drafting it before hearing his testimony to the platform committee; to the sensitive McCarthy, this was an outrageous affront. Shortly after details of the platform were released to the press, McCarthy publicly complained that it did not advocate the legalization of marijuana or immediate and unconditional amnesty for draft evaders. He was, then, one of that very small minority of Americans who felt that on the issues of "acid and amnesty," McGovern was too conservative. It is hard to avoid the suspicion that no platform would have been good enough for McCarthy. John Connally even suggested to Richard Nixon that the president might be able to secure McCarthy's public endorsement, "if we could get him a seat on the PBL board, or the FCC." In the event, no deal was made, and McCarthy did campaign for McGovern later in the year, although with little obvious enthusiasm.[55]

In subsequent years McCarthy denied that he had been a serious candidate in 1972, and blamed his ultimate failure on the Democratic Party and the reformed rules for presidential nominations. His primary rivals had done nothing "to clarify the issues" but had instead relied "on a conglomerate of minority interests as the way to victory." The reform faction had, he claimed, betrayed him and decamped to the McGovern campaign, where "with the help of new rules and procedures, they controlled a convention and a campaign which effectively alienated one third or more of the traditional Democratic voters." There is little doubt that the introspective debate about party reform wounded the Democrats at a point when they might have done better to ponder wider questions of social and economic policy; nor is there much doubt that the exultant reformers neglected the union leaders and working-class voters whose support was vital for the general election campaign. This was not, however, the reason that McCarthy's own candidacy had been so overwhelmingly rejected. In attacking the McGovern campaign, he conveniently forgot that his own platform was far more radical than anything the South Dakotan ever proposed. Voters searching for a candidate who championed marijuana, amnesty and enormous welfare handouts, or a candidate who tailored his appeal to middle-class reformers and northern black activists, would have done better to look at McCarthy than McGovern. Nor were there any grounds for McCarthy's insistence that the new party procedures had helped McGovern at the expense of other candidates; in fact, McCarthy himself had as much to gain as anyone from the new rules. The truth was that McCarthy had fought a campaign that, though well financed, was negative, aimless and badly organized, and he consequently found himself a marginal figure. He no longer had a seat in the Senate, his standing with Democratic activists was not high, and he had broken off his friendships with senior party leaders. His conduct in 1972 had not done much to restore his battered reputation, and he had little future in Democratic politics.[56]

CHAPTER TWELVE

The Long Exile

Richard Nixon's landslide victory in the 1972 election left many Democratic liberals at a loss, and McCarthy was among them. Under a McGovern administration he could at least have hoped for an ambassadorship or some vague position of influence, but instead he had nothing. McCarthy was effectively alone, with no Senate office, no staff, few speech engagements and little public attention. He was, he later admitted, "confused—I didn't know what to do or where to go." An opportunity for a new start in a world outside politics had already presented itself, however, in the form of a job offer from a publishing house. In October 1972 McCarthy told an interviewer that he was planning to take an apartment in New York and work for Simon & Schuster as a senior editor three or four days a week. In typical fashion, he did not exude great enthusiasm about the appointment, although he was confident that it would be easy enough. "I think anyone who's written a book wants to be an editor," he explained. "All you have to do is think of a book and find an author and then criticize what he's done. It may be an escape that won't be satisfying, but anyhow I may try it—it's a little bit like being God." These sentiments did not, oddly, deter the Simon & Schuster board, and by January 1973 McCarthy was ensconced in New York preparing for his new life. He had also secured a post at the New School for Social Research in lower Manhattan, where he was to be the first Adlai E. Stevenson Professor of Political Science, teaching courses on The Future of Liberalism and Politics and Literature. He still had many friends and supporters in the city, and New York's liberal intellectuals welcomed him with open arms, throwing a lavish "coming out party" for the former senator at the Library for the Performing Arts. As one newspaper put it, he had moved out of the shadows of Washington, D.C., and was now "traveling in New York's liberal chic circles."[1]

This was not quite true: McCarthy never entirely threw himself into his new existence, and he maintained an office in Washington, where he spent much of the week with a couple of assistants working on a forthcoming book of political commentary. He did not completely neglect his responsibilities in New York, however. Every now and again he would stroll into his Simon & Schuster office cubicle twenty-eight floors above Rockefeller Center to pass an eye over the piles of nonfiction manuscripts accumulated on his untidy desk; on Wednesday nights he headed down to the New School to address four hundred students on the future of liberalism; and on Thursdays he ran his politics and literature seminars for twenty graduate students. One of McCarthy's authors at Simon & Schuster was F. E. Peters, a distinguished historian of the Middle East. Peters later wrote that although he and his editor enjoyed the odd desultory conversation about baseball, there was no evidence that McCarthy had ever looked at his manuscript. Instead, after a decent interlude, McCarthy simply passed it along for publication, without a single editorial change or suggestion. This pleasant and undemanding life could not, unfortunately, last forever. McCarthy's contract with the New School eventually expired, while his employers at Simon & Schuster were evidently underwhelmed by his commitment. Nine months after McCarthy joined the company, they announced that the association would terminate in January 1974. There had, according to the New York Times, been "persistent reports in high publishing circles" that his employers were displeased with his attitude; they had hoped that his fame and reputation in liberal circles would make him a powerful "acquiring editor." "But if he has brought off any such coups," the Times commented dryly, "they have gone unpublicized by his superiors at Simon & Schuster."[2]

A career in publishing, with occasional stints as a visiting professor at one of New York's universities, might well have appealed to many former politicians in McCarthy's position. The problem was that he did not find the life of an editor sufficiently satisfying to devote much time and effort to it. As events were to prove, McCarthy simply could not shake off his interest in politics, and he was still determined to avenge the slights he felt he had suffered since 1964. Humphrey, Muskie, McGovern and the rest were still showing up at the Senate every morning, and McCarthy evidently regretted that he was not joining them in the world that he knew and loved best. He was, said his friend and former fund-raiser Martin Peretz, "very frustrated being on the sidelines," "isolated" and "restless." Humphrey, who found it difficult to maintain a grudge, generously encouraged McCarthy to come and lunch with him in the Senate, but that was hardly the answer. Even in the summer of 1973, while he was working at Simon & Schuster and the New School, there were reports that he was thinking of resuscitating his political career. Running for the Senate from Minnesota was clearly impossible, since the DFL had two popular and successful incumbents in Humphrey and Mondale. Some observers suggested that he might launch an unlikely campaign for the Senate from another state: New York, perhaps, or even New Hampshire. But two days after Simon & Schuster announced that McCarthy was leaving the company, the news broke that he had decided to explore his chances of being elected to the House of Representatives in 1974 from Minnesota's Sixth District, the flat, rural stretch of central Minnesota where he had been born.[3]

McCarthy's flirtation with the Sixth District was one of the most humiliating episodes in his career. The Republican incumbent, Representative John Zwach, had already announced that he would not seek re-election in 1974, and the debacle of Watergate certainly offered an excellent opportunity to the eventual Democratic candidate. But very few people in Minnesota could take McCarthy's candidacy seriously. "No kidding, Gene for Congress?" read the headline on the *Minneapolis Star* editorial page. "For something comparable," explained the local columnist Jim Klobuchar, "imagine Socrates succeeding Mr. Chips in the next semester." It seemed unimaginable that the man who had deposed President Johnson and stood as the national champion of Democratic liberalism could be considering running as the representative of Minnesota's small towns and prairies. "Are the 6th District and Eugene McCarthy ready for each other?" Klobuchar wondered. "Can a man who unhorsed Lyndon Johnson, deflated Senate windbags, electrified the Georgetown cocktail league and occasionally showed up for roll calls find contentment campaigning in Mudgett and Pulaski? Have Pierz, Motley and Milaca read Mr. McCarthy's poem 'Lament of an Aging Politician'? Is there a boom in Stearns County for poet-philosophers?"[4]

Most local officials, meanwhile, had not forgiven McCarthy for his treatment of Hubert Humphrey and were aghast to hear that he was planning a comeback. They already had a potential candidate, Richard Nolan, a twenty-nine-year-old local man who had narrowly lost to Zwach in 1972 and was thought to deserve a second chance. "Rick has earned the right to run again," commented one of McCarthy's 1968 veterans, now a member of the DFL executive committee. "I just can't see any reason for Gene to go in there and muddy the waters." The chairman of the Stearns County DFL organization agreed. "As far as I know," he remarked, "there's no great enthusiasm or excitement about McCarthy." McCarthy was, however, unde-terred, and at the end of October he arrived in the state for a four-day tour of the Sixth District. His objective was "more complicated" than merely standing up for the farmers of central Minnesota. He explained that the real issue was "How do we make the government operate properly?" and that the House of Representatives was now "the best immediately available instrument" to move the United States "along the way to solving some of its most fundamental problems." If another ten senior politicians moved into the House, McCarthy claimed, it would become the most significant political forum in the country. After all, he pointed out, John Quincy Adams had spent seventeen years in Congress after leaving the White House, and there was therefore no good reason why the voters of Min-nesota should prevent Eugene McCarthy from emulating him.[5]

This did not, unfortunately, go down well among the rural, conservative voters of the Sixth District. McCarthy might have been born in the area, but he had left in the early 1940s and now spent his time in Washington and New York. Nor did his somewhat woolly prognostications about national priorities seem to reflect the bread-and-butter concerns of farmers threat-ened by the persistent economic problems of the age of stagflation. The tour was not a success, especially since McCarthy was the only potential candidate who managed to miss an important fund-raising event in Mille Lacs County. His nomination, commented one Mille Lacs activist, would be "a tragedy. I haven't spoken to anybody who likes him. They're old timers that I've talked to and they all feel the same way." When McCarthy arrived in the little town of Marshall, he was welcomed by an editorial in the local newspaper with the headline "Senator McCarthy Is Living in the Past." At a Democratic lunch meeting the same day, one speaker criticized his bid as "untimely and divisive at a time when this largely rural district could return to the DFL fold," while the state DFL director declared herself "very much opposed" to McCarthy's nomination.[6]

By the end of the tour, a triumphant political return for the prodigal son in November 1974 looked extremely unlikely. McCarthy described the local reaction as "rather restrained and passive." Although it "wasn't Palm Sunday, it wasn't really bad either." In truth, it could hardly have been worse. Even though he had dozens of friends and relatives in the district, he was perceived as an opportunistic carpetbagger and the man who had betrayed Hubert Humphrey. At the end of November, an opinion poll found that both Democratic and Republican voters would prefer to see a younger candidate elected from the Sixth District the following year. Only one in four of all DFL supporters welcomed the possibility of a McCarthy comeback. With no great issues on which to base his campaign, and facing the overwhelming opposition of the local party organization, McCarthy backed down. On the day that the poll was published, he admitted to the Minnesota journalist Albert Eisele that he had given up hope. As usual, he denied that he had ever been very interested in the enterprise in the first place. "Good God, you know, I'm not very enthusiastic about it—you don't have to be told that," he insisted. "I wasn't very enthusiastic about it in the beginning." Even so, there was no disguising the fact that he had suffered an embarrassing rebuff at the hands of the constituency on which his entire political career had been founded, the ordinary Democratic voters of his home state.[7]

For all his literary and academic pretensions, Eugene McCarthy was a politician above all else. Politics had been his career for most of his adult life, and the reason he seemed so restless and unsatisfied in the early 1970s was that he was quite simply lost in and frustrated by life outside the political arena. His failure to appeal to the voters of Minnesota's Sixth District in 1973 made it very clear that any political comeback would have to be made outside the state, and McCarthy's attention therefore switched back to the national stage. The Nixon administration was in terminal decline, afflicted by the cancer of Watergate, but although the Democrats swept the board in the 1974 congressional elections, they had still not quite come to terms with the problems of the Great Society or the tensions of race and class that still threatened to tear apart their electorate. Nor had Democratic liberals developed a new agenda to replace the Fair Deal commitments of 1948; instead, the party was effectively led by the same old warhorses: Hubert Humphrey, Henry Jackson, Ted Kennedy and the rest. There was no obvious new contender for the presidential nomination in 1976, and most observers expected the field to look very much as it had in 1972. At one Washington reception, McCarthy remarked in all seriousness to Edgar Berman: "You know, I think Hubert and I are the only team which could pull this party together in '76." Not even McCarthy, however, could have foreseen a scenario in which he might be a plausible contender for the

Democratic presidential nomination to face Gerald Ford. True, in appearance he was growing old gracefully, "more whitely flown of mane, more pirouetting of stance" than ever, as Garry Wills put it in 1976. But although he certainly looked presidential, he no longer had many friends and supporters in Congress or the Democratic Party. One indication of his fall from grace was a minor incident in June 1976. When he had entered the Senate in 1959, his closest friends had been his fellow Catholic newcomers Edmund Muskie and Philip Hart. The mild-mannered Hart, probably McCarthy's most intimate friend in politics, was due to retire at the end of 1976 and Muskie arranged a small dinner party for him that summer. Ted Kennedy and Thomas Eagleton, two other Catholic liberals, were invited, and so was Abigail McCarthy. But McCarthy himself was not. This was a world in which he was no longer welcome.[8]

McCarthy had toyed with the idea of running as an independent presidential candidate both in 1968 and 1972, only to reject it on both occasions. Now that he had no prospects inside the Democratic Party, however, an independent campaign seemed much more attractive. If the Democrats swung back to the right in 1976 and nominated an anti-Communist hawk like Henry Jackson, there might well be scope for a third-party liberal to win a healthy percentage of the final vote. McCarthy had nothing to lose, and if all went well, he stood to rebuild his reputation among Democratic liberals and in the country at large. At best, he might even stake a claim as a serious Democratic contender in 1980; at worst, he would at least win some decent publicity for his books and lecture tours. The political order of the New Deal was giving ground before a new style of politics, based on the televised appeal of individual candidates to suburban voters, and party affiliation mattered less than ever before. In 1968, a Harris poll found that 16 percent of voters identified themselves as "independent"; in 1973, the corresponding figure was 28 percent. Running as an independent candidate, then, was perhaps not such an eccentric idea.[9]

The first newsletters advertising "McCarthy 76" were sent out in March 1973 by Ronald Cocome, a young activist who had been the state chairman of McCarthy's campaign in Illinois the previous year. In August 1974, almost a year after his ambitions to represent Minnesota's Sixth District had evaporated, McCarthy announced the formation of the Committee for a Constitutional Presidency, or CCP, an independent organization dedicated to the nomination of an independent presidential candidate who would offer "realistic choices" and break with the "dogma" of the two major parties in 1976. It was actually a shoestring organization, partly funded by liberal philanthropists like McCarthy's friend William Clay Ford, the Ford Motor

Company heir and owner of the Detroit Lions, and by McCarthy's own lecture fees. McCarthy presented himself as the "temporary chairman" of the
CCP, and insisted that he would be happy if the organization found a different candidate, but the records of the committee make it very clear that it
was designed simply to give his intended presidential campaign "some
credible identity," as one of his assistants put it. McCarthy was the only
politician quoted in the newsletters of the CCP, which were sent out to sub-
scribers and supporters from September 1974. Even McCarthy's teaching
plans at the State Univesity of New York at Purchase, where he was giving
two courses in the fall of 1974, reflected his enthusiasm for an independent
presidential challenge. Students taking Professor E. McCarthy's course on
Political and Governmental Institutions were confronted in their final
examination with the question "Give three reasons why an independent
Presidential challenge—that is one outside the two party structures—may
be desirable." The possibility that such a challenge might not be considered
desirable had evidently not occurred to Professor McCarthy.[10]

As always, McCarthy's time was largely devoted to minor speaking
engagements and occasional articles for newspapers and liberal periodicals, most of which contained little that was especially original. Throughout 1975, however, his attention was also focused on the courts, where the
CCP was contesting the legality of the 1974 amendments to the Federal
Election Campaign Act. Under the provisions of the act, which was essentially a response to the corruption of the 1972 Nixon campaign, there were
to be strict limits on campaign contributions and spending, while for the
first time candidates would also have access to federal campaign subsidies.
McCarthy's co-plaintiffs in the suit, which became known as *Buckley v.
Valeo,* were a motley crew of liberals, libertarians and conservatives, including the Conservative-Republican Senator James Buckley of New York, the
liberal philanthropist Stewart Mott, the New York Conservative Party,
the New York Civil Liberties Union, the Mississippi Republican Party and
the Libertarian Party. For many of the plaintiffs, the law was unconstitutional because its financial restrictions infringed the right to free speech.
McCarthy, meanwhile, furiously insisted that it was "an insurance policy
for the incumbent parties," to the extent of offering their nominees
$20 million each in federal subsidies; it therefore threatened to deprive him
of his opportunity for a well-financed independent campaign. After all, as
he pointed out, his campaign in 1968 had been possible only through the
generosity of a few rich donors; under the terms of the 1974 legislation, it
would have been unthinkable. "It is the same as saying we are going to
have two established religions," he grumbled. "It makes it almost impossi-

ble to have an effective challenge to the two established parties." On
30 January 1976, the Supreme Court handed down a verdict upholding the
provisions of the campaign law regarding public disclosure, limits on campaign contributions and federal subsidies. The limits on overall campaign
spending, however, were struck down, along with the Federal Election
Commission as it was then constituted. But this was not a victory for
McCarthy and his fellow plaintiffs, and he likened it to "telling people
we're going to give you freedom of religion, and then saying you have two
choices, Episcopal or Anglican." The two-party monopoly had not been
broken, and McCarthy faced an uphill task in trying to displace it.[11]

The battle against the Federal Election Campaign Act marked the
beginning of one of McCarthy's abiding interests in his later years: the
sanctity of the Constitution and the importance of historic institutions in
American political life. In his manifesto *The Hard Years,* published in
1975, he argued that the framers of the Constitution had not foreseen the
development of political parties. "At times," he wrote, "there has been no
order, no equity, no justice, and very little reason in the way political parties have operated in this country." The problems in the United States,
meanwhile, could "be met in large part by a return to the procedures set
forth in the Constitution." This might include, for example, a return to the
original principle of an electoral college, untainted by party affiliation,
selecting the president of the United States. Although this was a new hob-
byhorse for McCarthy, it was evident that he had never lost the fundamentally conservative faith in institutions that had been instilled in him at St.
John's in the late 1930s. Now that he no longer needed to appeal to Democratic voting blocs, he fell back on the more conservative aspects of the
European Catholic ideas of his youth. The derelictions of the two major
parties and the unconstitutionality of modern American politics became
obsessions for McCarthy after 1974, allowing him to appeal to a small
minority of middle-class reformers who were interested less in the grubby
details of welfare and political economy than in high-minded questions of
morality and good government. But not only did his fascination with these
issues set him apart from other liberal politicians, it also appealed to his
own intense regard for tradition and institutions. The contempt for modernity that had animated the young Benedictine in the corridors of St. John's
had never entirely disappeared. The same Catholic ideas that had driven
him toward liberalism in the late 1940s were now guiding him toward an
obsessive conservatism unrestrained by electoral realities or the necessities
of political advancement. Guaranteed the financial support of a handful of
liberals nostalgic for the great days of 1968, free of the need to worry about

the intricacies of effective legislation, the expectations and requirements of his constituents or the ambitions and priorities of his colleagues, McCarthy could indulge himself. More than ever, in his own mind and those of his supporters, he was a lone voice of reason preaching in a mad world.[12]

McCarthy's bitter attacks on the Federal Election Campaign Act did not impress many commentators. As the conservative columnist George Will saw it, when McCarthy claimed that no election since 1796 had been constitutional because the parties had interfered with the sanctity of the electoral college, he was "carrying strict construction of the Constitution to the point of parody." When he insisted that Harry Truman had been the last "constitutional President," he was "using hyperbole of the sort that was once beneath him." As Will pointed out, McCarthy's obsession with campaign procedures and the Constitution looked "suspiciously like mere excuses for a campaign which will enable him to punish Democrats for leaving him a prophet without honor in his own party." Having been scorned by his party in 1968 and 1972, McCarthy was in no mood for forgiveness, and throughout the next few years he focused his attentions on the Democrats, not the Republicans. In January 1975, before an audience of four hundred supporters in Madison, Wisconsin, he publicly announced his decision to run as an independent presidential candidate the following year. The Democrats, he said, were the party of "hedge and compromise." "When a party is consistently so wrong on important issues," he insisted, "so timid and late on others, and has twice lost presidential elections to Richard Nixon, one must ask whether it serves much purpose any longer."[13]

McCarthy claimed in January 1975 that he had been invited to run by the Committee for a Constitutional Presidency, although the CCP had in fact been a front for McCarthy's ambitions from the outset. Like Jimmy Carter, his much-derided opponent in 1976, McCarthy was a self-selected candidate, running on the basis of his own personality and intellect rather than any identifiable faction or cause. For the major Democratic and Republican candidates, from Morris Udall and Jimmy Carter to Gerald Ford and Ronald Reagan, the central issues of the day were integrity in government, détente, inflation and unemployment. As a self-anointed candidate, however, McCarthy was at liberty to talk about whatever he pleased, and he therefore made little effort to disguise his own nostalgic obsessions. In one interview he explained that he judged his opponents by three standards: their record on the Vietnam War; their reaction to the 1968 Democratic convention; and their position on the Federal Election Campaign Act. As for the social commitments of his youth, it appeared that he had now risen above such trifling considerations. "They say, 'He had a good domestic record,'" he commented of his Democratic rivals. "Hitler had a good domestic record, you know. So did Mussolini. They were for health insurance, all those things."[14]

McCarthy could not, however, avoid taking positions on domestic policy, and he amused himself by drafting an uncompromising platform that frequently broke with orthodox political assumptions. "We are not really suffering from an energy crisis in this country," he explained. "We still have more energy than we know what to do with, and we are overconsuming what we have." The problems of the economy, meanwhile, indicated "the need for new interpretations, new theory." "We are beyond Keynes," he wrote in 1975. But this did not mean that, like many conservatives in the 1970s, McCarthy was a convert to the monetarist theories of Milton Friedman and the Chicago School, with their emphasis on limited government and the primacy of the free market. Instead, he rediscovered the language of American populism, insisting that the national economy had become "a kind of corporate feudalism" in which every American was beholden to one corporation or another. In *The Hard Years,* he spent six pages developing an elaborate, if not entirely convincing, parallel between modern corporations and late-medieval baronies, and concluded that it was time for "a significant challenge to the political, economic, and social power of the corporations." Having established this premise, McCarthy then sat back and admired his own logic instead of developing specific proposals to sharpen his populist appeal. His economic agenda included limited wage-price controls; selective credit controls; cuts in spending on the military, national highways and the space program; legislation to restrict the size and speed of cars; and the reduction of the workweek to four days in order to cut unemployment. He offered no single message to grab the public imagination, but rather a random collection of contradictory ideas, rarely supported by statistical evidence or economic theory. His ideas were not wholly without merit, but they never amounted to a sustained intellectual analysis of American economic woes in the mid-1970s, and neither did they convince voters that McCarthy had the answer to the problem of stagflation.[15]

On some issues McCarthy took a position that was clearly well to the left of the Democratic presidential aspirants. Even though George McGovern had in 1972 been pilloried by the right as the candidate of "acid, amnesty and abortion," McCarthy still argued that marijuana should be decriminalized and sold under government regulation. He avoided the controversial question of busing with the statement that as president he would support the decision of the courts, and he thought that the federal govern-ment should remain neutral on the issue of abortion. Religious intolerance on questions of morality and conscience was never part of McCarthy's Catholicism; he despised those religious conservatives who imposed their rigid morality on others, and although he never used birth control himself, he had no objection to those who did. Such an undemonstrative and undogmatic approach to religious issues looked increasingly old-fashioned in a decade noted for the revival of conservative, evangelical Protestantism, especially in the South, as a cultural and political force. The success of Jimmy Carter, who claimed to have been "born again," illustrated the potential of evangelical politics, but McCarthy had never liked to trumpet his religious values, and he refused to adapt to the expectations of modern audiences. On international issues, meanwhile, he still clung to the themes of 1968 and 1972, attacking the "increasing militarization of our foreign policy" and "the military-industrial-academic establishment." McCarthy's long and consistent record of international anti-Communism was forgot-ten. "In the roughly twenty-three years since the Korean War," he declared, "the order of values in our foreign policy has been military first, then eco-nomic and material, and only in the last position, conceptions of individual rights and of society. The emphasis must be reversed." Specific details of McCarthy's approach were, however, hard to come by. The United States, he said, ought to support NATO, Japan and Israel and take the lead in dis-armament negotiations; but as for détente, relations with the Soviet Union and China, and the Cold War in the developing world, he had little to add.[16]

Some of McCarthy's ideas, like the reduction of the workweek or legis-lation to restrict automobile use, drew mild praise from the national press. None of his proposals, however, caught the public mood, and his platform communicated a general impression of vagueness, eccentricity and intel-lectual indolence. At one appearance at the University of Minnesota, he refused to explain his own proposals but spent most of his speech attacking the Ford and Carter campaigns. He was, said one reporter, "unwilling or unable to focus on some of the questions that were asked of him": when, for instance, he was asked about American imperialism in the developing world, he "gave a rambling response that led quickly into the subject of corporate responsibility and a few barbs directed at the nation's auto manu-facturers." McCarthy spent most of the campaign railing against the 1974 campaign legislation and demanding a return to the strictest possible inter-pretation of the Constitution, an obsession that bewildered many of his old Washington friends. *Congressional Quarterly* concluded that his campaign was "largely an effort to undermine the two-party system," and McCarthy described it as a bid to restore a "back to basics presidency." He later told an interviewer that the campaign was "an effort really to undo the Federal Election Law," although this was clearly not quite true, since he had begun planning the campaign before the legislation was even passed. He had always been suspicious of moralistic reformers, not surprisingly given his veneration for tradition and institutions, but since 1972 this had intensified into institutional conservatism of the most obsessive kind. The election campaign act, he later claimed, "was essentially like what existed when Hitler was elected in Germany." Nixon's abolition of the military draft had destroyed the old notion of republican military service and created a "volunteer (mercenary) army." Even passing legislation to deal with social injustice and political corruption now appeared iniquitous to McCarthy. "There have been many proposals for new laws to end all abuses," he noted. "We already have too many laws. The real need is to have a President who will say, 'I will honor the Constitution and my oath of office. I will protect the political rights of all Americans.'" The cry of "reform," he wrote, was "a standard item in the catalog of demagoguery."[17]

Not surprisingly, conservative observers were amused and intrigued to hear such statements from the erstwhile darling of the liberals. The British journalist Peregrine Worsthorne, for instance, told the *Washington Post* that McCarthy was "a true—which is to say, British—Conservative," giving Americans "the advice which any sensible man gives a hysteric: calm down first and then let's see what has to be done." The intellectual roots of McCarthy's ideas could be traced back to his Benedictine training and the Catholic social thought of the 1930s, but it is hard to imagine that he would have moved so far toward strict constitutional conservatism if he had stayed in the Senate and maintained friendly relations with his old Democratic allies. This was no doubt a matter of personal pique as much as philosophical conviction. All the same, McCarthy's move away from welfare liberalism and social democracy also suited the mood of the times. The old commitments to Keynesian management, economic growth and federally sponsored reform were seen as unfashionable in an age of inflation, stagnation and distrust of government, and those liberals who held fast to the values of the Fair Deal and Great Society, like Hubert Humphrey or Ted Kennedy, were regarded as hoary old buffaloes living in the past. "Today liberals are in retreat," observed *Time* magazine in April 1976. "They are unmoored and fragmented, a variegated group that has traditionally coalesced around a strong leader and a compelling cause—and now has neither." Mo Udall, the surviving liberal candidate in the Democratic primaries, had at that stage failed to win a single primary. Even Udall, though, had "taken to dropping their label," calling himself "a progressive, a description he says sounds less negative." The image of liberalism had been severely battered by the racial divisions of the late 1960s, the supposed irresponsibility of the Great Society, the national trauma of Vietnam and controversial cultural issues like abortion and pornography. As the sociologist Jonathan Rieder put it, Americans in the mid-1970s associated liberalism with "profligacy, spinelessness, malevolence, masochism, elitism, fantasy, anarchy, idealism, softness, irresponsibility, and sanctimoniousness." In this context, McCarthy's emphases on limits, restraint and tradition looked not unlike the themes articulated by intellectual neoconservatives like Daniel Patrick Moynihan and Irving Kristol, who were beginning to move away from the Democratic Party and into the Reagan camp. Like McCarthy, they distrusted federal power and innovation, celebrated institutional tradition and disliked the evangelical populism of Jimmy Carter. McCarthy himself was not a true neoconservative: he was never a part of their close circle, he repudiated their intense attachment to the Cold War and he shrank from their forays into social conservatism. As a pessimistic liberal disenchanted by Carter's Democratic Party, however, hostile to reform and confident of his own intellectual and moral superiority, he was not alone.[18]

McCarthy's presidential effort in 1976 was not a luxurious business. It cost an estimated $442,491, a little more than the campaign of the Libertarian candidate, Roger MacBride, and a little less than the Communist campaign run by Gus Hall. McCarthy's financial backers were, in general, old friends and donors from the 1968 and 1972 campaigns like the philanthropist Stewart Mott and the film stars Paul Newman and Joanne Woodward. The largest donor was William Clay Ford, who had been backing McCarthy since 1968 and had helped to set up the Committee for a Constitutional Presidency. In February 1976 Ford even agreed to serve as McCarthy's stand-in running mate, provided that he did not have to give any interviews. McCarthy was delighted, calling his candidate "a lot better . . . than those who have been offered over the last twelve years or so," neatly swiping at Hubert Humphrey at the same time that he praised his own man. The *New York Times* quipped that McCarthy's selection was "a stroke of statesmanship," winning him "access to a $100 million bankroll . . . the pro football vote and the support of careless readers," but unfortunately Ford lasted a mere five days on the ticket. It turned out that in several vital states, a stand-in candidate needed to be a legal resident of the state, and Ford gave up his position to protect McCarthy's place on the ballot. McCarthy commented that he hoped "Mr. Ford might be free" when he came to make his "final decisions about the Vice President and the Cabinet" in November.[19]

As for the general public, they remained apathetic about McCarthy's candidacy, and opinion polls put his support at between 3 percent and 10 percent. Those who backed him were, according to surveys, likely to be young, well-educated voters who considered themselves liberals, and doubtless many of them still saw him as the champion of the peace movement in 1968. Of three volunteers profiled by one newspaper in October, two were in their twenties and the third had worked for McCarthy in 1968 and 1972; all three explained their allegiance in terms of their dislike of Ford and Carter rather than their admiration for McCarthy's policy proposals. McCarthy's friend Michael Rubino, a former CIA employee who accompanied him on the campaign trail, later recalled that their volunteers tended to be well-educated, metropolitan professionals. "Some of them," he added, "were a bit quirky." McCarthy's campaign manager Ronald Cocome explained: "We're looking for quality, not quantity. It's not numbers that count but intensity of commitment."[20]

In the spring of 1976 the *New York Times* columnist and former Nixon speechwriter William Safire bumped into McCarthy at a small regional airport. "What are you doing these days, Gene?" he asked him. "Running for president," McCarthy cheerfully replied. As Safire explained to his readers: "That was embarrassing: when a man is seriously running for president, acquaintances should be aware of his occupation." The problem for McCarthy was that since he was no longer perceived as a serious candidate, it was extremely difficult to attract public attention, even though his name and reputation ensured that he was frequently the subject of rather bewildered profiles in major newspapers and magazines. What was more, the life of an independent presidential candidate was less than lavish. McCarthy drove to appearances or paid for commercial flights, accompanied by a handful of curious reporters, and rarely secured a mention on the network news. He had an office in Washington, D.C., staffed by his former administrative assistant and his former secretary, and one speechwriter and research assistant. The hordes of camp followers who had swarmed around him in 1968 were now a memory; Michael Rubino, who shared McCarthy's tastes for whisky, poetry and whimsy, remarked that the campaign entourage was "practically him and me." Even when McCarthy broadcast a five-minute commercial on network television, the final scenes of passionate young crowds shouting, "We want Gene! We want Gene!" were clearly borrowed from footage of the 1968 California primary.[21]

The campaign was essentially a lecture tour, albeit a nostalgic, melancholic, quixotic one. At one appearance at a community college in Illinois, McCarthy was talking to a writers' group when heavy rain began pelting the tin roof over his head, making it impossible for the audience to hear what he was saying. "It's all right," he said, when his host suggested he wait for the rain to end. "*I* can hear." Where McCarthy had once sought to win tens of thousands of votes, he now tried to sway audiences of twenty or ten or even one. The journalist Jules Witcover captured the scene as McCarthy left the tin hut:

> Driving back from Oakton late at night, he sat hunched and tired in the front seat of a Volkswagen and restrainedly responded to a string of questions from a Northwestern University student who was considering active support but wanted assurances on where McCarthy stood. As the questions were posed, the answers came more testily, but they came, until the student was taken to his residence in Evanston. Only then was McCarthy driven to his downtown Chicago hotel.

All too often his reception was humiliating rather than inspiring. In July 1976, a group of enthusiastic supporters scheduled a rally in a suburban Maryland ballpark with a seating capacity of 1,500. "Fewer than 100 voters turned up," reported the *New York Times,* "and Mr. McCarthy found himself speaking indoors in a cinderbox hall to an audience accommodated in four rows of folding chairs."[22]

Since McCarthy's supporters tended to be self-proclaimed liberals, in public meetings he took care to attack the Republican and Democratic candidates in equal measure. In private and in interviews, however, the extent of his bitterness toward his old party was unmistakable. President Ford's calm, sober, unpretentious style aroused little hostility in McCarthy, and he commented that Ford had "a slightly better constitutional conception of the office than Jimmy Carter has." In his memoirs, McCarthy announced that Ford had run "a reasonably competent administration," which was high praise indeed by his standards, implying that he ranked Ford second only to Truman among postwar presidents. He was less indulgent toward the Democrats and the liberal organizations that supported them. When the political reform group Common Cause invited McCarthy to join the other candidates in pledging to uphold certain standards of integrity, responsiveness and accountability, the McCarthy campaign manager Ronald Cocome told their chairman "to take your enclosed standards and stuff them in your ear." As for Jimmy Carter, McCarthy thought that he had "the same wrong ideas about what to do for the country as the Northern liberals in the Democratic Party have."[23]

Having decided to run against the Democrats, McCarthy was bound to criticize them whatever the circumstances, but the fact that their eventual ticket consisted of Jimmy Carter and Walter Mondale made matters easier for him. Carter was everything that McCarthy despised, an ostentatiously religious evangelical Protestant and a folksy populist who promised to clean up the corruption in Washington. McCarthy thought that Carter was "demagogic in just about everything"; he called Carter's religious beliefs "rather vague" and at one point described him as "the pet redneck" of the Democratic liberals. Walter Mondale, who was Humphrey's closest ally and political heir, fared little better. His generous tribute to McCarthy in December 1970 had long been forgotten; in 1973, when Mondale had been thinking of running for the presidency himself, McCarthy pledged to give him "at least the support that he gave me in '68": in other words, none at all. Soon after Mondale was selected as Carter's running mate, McCarthy told reporters that while his former colleague was not fit to be president, he was "well qualified" for the meaningless job of vice president. "I've watched Walter for quite a long time," he explained. "I wouldn't say he was untrustworthy. Walter never betrayed you. But it was awfully hard to say when he made a commitment." Mondale, McCarthy said solemnly, had "the soul of a vice president."[24]

Even by the standards of a presidential campaign, McCarthy's attacks on Carter and Mondale were unusually contemptuous. Not only did he disagree with them, he made it quite clear that he had no respect for them whatsoever. Democratic strategists, however, were worried less by McCarthy's insults than by the possibility that in a close election he might take enough liberal votes from Carter to throw several important states into Ford's hands. McCarthy had adopted what he called a "sleet belt" strategy, concentrating on New England, the urban states of the Northeast like New York and Pennsylvania, and progressive states like Minnesota, Wisconsin and Oregon. From the outset his campaign suffered from the severe disadvantage that the electoral system was skewed against independent candidates: sixteen states prohibited independent candidates from being on the presidential ballot, while in other states an independent challenger needed as many as 150,000 signatures to win a place on the ballot. Most of McCarthy's campaign funds, in fact, were spent on legal challenges to put him on the ballot; while in most states the ACLU or other independent organizations filed as co-plaintiffs, in others he had to pay the entire legal bill himself. Two weeks before the election, he had won a place on the ballot in thirty states with a total of 356 electoral votes, and as the race between Ford and Carter grew tighter, the Democrats became increasingly worried. Opinion polls estimated his support in New York, Illinois, Ohio and Pennsylvania at around 7 percent, and the danger that he might cost Carter not only victory in these states but also the presidency was, according to the Democratic national chairman Robert Strauss, "real and . . . of more than passing interest." "Will Gene Be the Spoiler?" asked *Time* magazine. When one young reporter asked him the same question, McCarthy contemptuously replied: "Oh, you can do better than that. That's a question you get in Peoria."[25]

As the campaign drew to a close, the unlikely figure of Norman Mailer was dispatched to meet McCarthy at La Guardia Airport with an offer of the ambassadorship to the United Nations should McCarthy withdraw and Carter win the election. McCarthy turned it down, and an organized Democratic attack on his campaign predictably followed. The veteran civil rights campaigner Joseph Rauh wrote in the *Washington Post* that through his "negativism and his anti-government campaign" McCarthy had betrayed the ideals of 1968. On 30 October both the *Nation* and the *New Republic* printed full-page advertisements, paid for by the Carter campaign and urging liberals not to waste their vote on McCarthy. The text carried the signatures of more than forty activists who had worked for McCarthy in 1968, including his former speechwriter Jeremy Larner; his former student coordinator, Sam Brown; and a collection of liberal reformers including Michael Harrington, Anne Wexler and Joe Duffey. "McCarthy says he doesn't care if his votes help re-elect Ford," read the advertisements. "We do. We are not cynical enough to believe both candidates and the groups they represent are alike." On the same day, Brown published a piece in the *New York Times* attacking McCarthy for his lack of "a coherent ideology," "long-term commitment" or concern for the problems of "ordinary people." In response, one of McCarthy's volunteers took "Judas" Brown a package of three dollars in dimes, amounting to thirty pieces of silver, and a note reading, "In case Carter forgot." McCarthy's aide and close friend Jerry Eller, who had worked with most of the signers eight years previously, dismissed their appeal: "They had a modest amount of courage in their pre-menopausal stage, but now they wear suits and ties . . . They have an investment in the liberal Democratic establishment." McCarthy himself was understandably irritated that his old supporters had, as he saw it, traded their principles for the prospect of jobs in the White House. "Maybe I should just announce for Ford," he remarked.[26]

The last weeks of the campaign were difficult for McCarthy. Not only did he follow a grueling schedule in very little comfort, but he was also coming under almost daily assault from old liberal allies ridiculing him as an eccentric, treacherous nonentity. The *New Republic,* owned by his friend Martin Peretz, supported him as a "responsible choice" in the tradition of Robert La Follette and Norman Thomas, but no major publications followed suit, and as voters switched back to Carter or Ford, his already meager poll ratings began to decline. McCarthy was now lowering his horizons: 5 percent of the popular vote, he said, would be sufficient to justify his campaign and indicate public dissatisfaction with the two major parties. He spent the day of the election, 2 November 1976, relaxing with his eldest daughter, Ellen, in a spa in California and then flew back alone that night to Washington, where he was greeted by a handful of reporters but no supporters. Told that he was predicted to win about 1 percent of the vote, "he merely nodded his head as he rode the escalator down to the waiting car." The final results did not make glorious reading. After a campaign lasting nearly two years, he had won 756,691 votes and no states, amounting to 0.9 percent of the total. By far his best performance (3.9 percent) was in Oregon, where in happier times he had been the first Democrat to defeat one of the Kennedy brothers in an election, and he also won more than 2.5 percent in Massachusetts, Arizona and Colorado. Even in his birthplace of Watkins, what the local mayor called McCarthy's "hippy ideas" had fallen flat, and he was beaten almost five to one by Jimmy Carter.[27]

The Democrats' fears that McCarthy would "spoil" the election had not been realized. McCarthy's efforts did, however, cost Carter twenty electoral college votes in three states, Oregon, Maine and Iowa. In each of these states, Ford won with an extremely narrow majority because McCarthy drew liberal voters away from Carter: in Oregon, for example, Ford's majority was 1,713, while McCarthy won 40,296 votes. The real story, however, was in New York, where the Democrats had spent more than $50,000 in mounting legal challenges to the petitions filed to place McCarthy on the ballot. Thanks to these challenges, McCarthy's name was not on the New York ballot. If it had been, the evidence suggests that Gerald Ford would have won the presidential election. Opinion polls consistently put McCarthy's support in the state at over 5 percent, and given the closeness of the eventual result, it seems likely that he would have taken enough votes from Carter to hand Ford New York, its forty-one electoral votes and the presidency. In denying Carter the White House, McCarthy would doubtless have ensured himself a disreputable place in Democratic folklore as a spoiler and a traitor. Since he was not on the New York ballot, however, this did not happen, and instead the disappointed McCarthy was left to rail against the media and the electoral system in his final press conference three days after the election.[28]

In his last letter to supporters, McCarthy insisted that his legal campaigns to win a place on the ballot in states like Michigan, Florida, Missouri and Tennessee, all of which had previously prevented independent candidates from running, were "major victories" that were "most significant for the future of American politics." There was a good deal of truth in this. Thanks to McCarthy's legal challenges, courts in fifteen states had struck down parts of their electoral laws, and in the end his name appeared in the ballot in twenty-nine states. As Michael Novak noted in the *Washington Star,* this was "no small deed," since it "made it possible for third-party candidates to run a national campaign." Had it not been for McCarthy's challenge in 1976, future independent candidates like John Anderson, Ross Perot and Ralph Nader would have found it immeasurably more difficult to compete in a presidential election. McCarthy had established the ground for future independent candidates. "He fought a great fight, mostly out of sight and behind the scenes, in the courts," wrote an admiring Novak. "He extended our liberties and our possibilities as a people." Unfortunately for McCarthy, however, very few political commentators in the aftermath of the election agreed with these sentiments. His old friend Mary McGrory, for instance, admitted that she had found his campaign "very embarrassing" and thought he had "frittered away a considerable reputation." In the *New York Times,* Anthony Lewis wrote that it would be "one of the special blessings of the 1976 election if it marks the end of Eugene McCarthy's presence in American politics. He played a great role in 1968, but has since become a spoiled child who yearns literally to be a spoiler." Back in Minnesota, meanwhile, the *St. Paul Pioneer Press* reflected that McCarthy's message had been "one long litany of complaint." As one editorial pointed out, McCarthy had won much more coverage in the press than any other independent candidate, including long profiles in the major New York and Washington newspapers. "For sheer nerve," it continued, "few have equaled Gene. Here was a man whose candidacy was totally self-proclaimed. He was nominated by no party and no convention. He won no primary, nor even came close. Yet he had the gall to cry 'foul' when the networks ignored his demands to be included in the Ford-Carter debates." In short, the editorial writer concluded, "McCarthy might have done better sticking to poetry."[29]

McCarthy was now in his early sixties, still tall and handsome with a thick mane of white hair, and after the hard slog of the 1976 presidential campaign he appeared to be subsiding gently into retirement, having kicked the political habit once and for all. In 1978 he moved into a two-hundred-year-old stone farmhouse in the hamlet of Woodville in Rappahannock County, Virginia, at the foot of the Blue Ridge Mountains, an idyllic rural retreat ninety minutes' drive from the gossipy pressures of Washington, D.C. Visitors approaching his farmhouse bumped along a narrow country lane that finally became a rocky dirt track before emerging in front of his house. The surrounding acres of peaceful pasture were fringed by the mountains and dotted with little pools and woods. It was hard to imagine a more dramatic contrast with the fevered, driven climate of Democratic factionalism; it was as though McCarthy had decided to separate himself physically as well as psychologically from the world of politics and power. His tastes were relatively modest, and he could indulge them by combining his $40,000-a-year Senate pension with an annual retainer as a director of the publishing house Harcourt Brace Jovanovich and his fees for a weekly column in the *Washington Star,* regular lecture tours and book sales. Between 1977 and 1982 he published six more books: a discussion of Alexis de Tocqueville, a book of children's stories, a volume of poetry, a diatribe against the electoral system, a collection of political essays and a slim collection of poems and anecdotes about his boyhood. Lecture fees accounted for about a third of McCarthy's total income, and he appeared on college campuses at least four or five times a month. In one especially busy month in early 1979, for example, he gave talks in Washington, Oregon, Utah, Georgia, Minnesota, Nevada and Connecticut, not to mention a four-day visit to the Soviet Union.[30]

Although McCarthy still maintained a town house in Georgetown as a combined office and apartment, where he spent two days a week, he thought of his farmhouse in Woodville as home and spent much of his time pottering about his garden, walking in the countryside and hammering out newspaper articles on his old typewriter. "I chop a little wood but I'm not that primitive," he told one interviewer. "I have a small garden. It's all right if you're writing books." He also had the opportunity to catch up with his reading, his tastes inclining more to newspapers, magazines and the occasional book of poetry than to fiction, biography or history. Three of his four children, as well as Marya and Abigail, lived in the Washington area, so he did not feel lonely, and the conservative columnist James J. Kilpatrick was an affable neighbor who could be relied upon to drop in for a glass of whisky and a chat. After the alarums and excursions of his presidential campaign, McCarthy relished the experience of settling in a quiet rural community of hunters, carpenters, moonshine makers and even a few friendly pot-smoking hippies who kept an eye on his house whenever he was away. It was, all in all, a gentle life, allowing him plenty of time for reflection by the fireside in the company of his beloved Australian shepherd dog, Molly. "It's just me and the dog," McCarthy admitted. "I'll watch the news at night, and then take a good long walk with the dog. Then I'll come back and read for a while. Then I turn in for the night. My life is kind of quiet."[31]

On 13 January 1978, after a long and agonizing struggle against cancer, Hubert Humphrey died. He had been McCarthy's oldest political ally and his closest rival, a fellow liberal from the North Star State who came unbearably close to winning the presidency ten years earlier and could well have done so if McCarthy had acted differently. Unlike most of his friends, Humphrey had long since forgiven McCarthy for the events of 1968 and was always keen to meet his old associate from Minnesota for a drink and a chat about the old days in the DFL. They met for the last time at a fundraising dinner in December 1977, and Humphrey confessed that he wished they could have had one more public meeting together, as they had in their Senate years. "You could give the philosophy and the jokes," he told McCarthy, "and I could give the issues and the pep talk. The guest speaker would not even want to come on, and everyone there would be happy."[32]

The truth was that the liberal hour had passed. In 1974 a new generation of Democrats had swept into Congress with little interest in the commitments of the Fair Deal and the Great Society; as one newcomer, Senator Gary Hart, had put it, "We're not a bunch of little Humphreys." Four years later, with Humphrey dead and Jimmy Carter pursuing a conservative economic agenda barely recognizable as old-fashioned liberalism, even the fragile ties of nostalgic affiliation between McCarthy and the Democratic Party had been cut. While his attitude to Humphrey had been a complicated blend of respect, affection, jealousy and resentment, his feelings about Mondale and Carter were much simpler. So frequently did McCarthy repeat his quip about Mondale's having the "soul of a vice president" that the St. Paul Pioneer Press ran a long piece attacking the "arrogant, bitter" McCarthy for his "scurrilous" denigration of his old Senate colleague. He continued to hold Jimmy Carter, meanwhile, in the lowest possible regard. "I am not surprised by Carter's ineptness and inadequacy as President," McCarthy wrote in March 1979. "In 1976, I thought he was the most unqualified person to run for President in the last forty years. Carter had no record in foreign policy, no understanding of the structural problems affecting our political economy and no real understanding of the workings of the federal bureaucracies . . . Unless he had been hiding his genius, he was almost certain to be inadequate." Asked by the *Washington Post* to fill in a "report card" for the president, McCarthy gave him 2 out of 6 for "quality of work," 2 for maturity and 3 for intelligence, and suggested that Carter's particular talents were "prayer in public," "moralizing" and "looking enthusiastic as he takes telephone calls screened by Walter Cronkite." Under "disappointments," McCarthy wrote, "None. I found little in his record as governor, or what he offered in the campaign, to establish a basis for subsequent disappointment."[33]

McCarthy regarded the Carter-Mondale administration as a betrayal of Democratic principles, even though he had himself moved away from the party earlier in the decade. His own unyielding philosophical conservatism was reflected neither in the White House nor in the rival Democratic camp of Senator Ted Kennedy, and he began flirting with other, more obscure political groups like the Libertarians. In 1980 the major presidential candidates were joined by an independent challenger, Congressman John Anderson, a sober and serious Republican progressive who appealed not only to the educated, suburban middle classes but also to many of McCarthy's own friends and former supporters, like Martin Peretz and Stewart Mott. In his "utter lack of passion," his cool, cerebral speaking style and his studied disdain for the ritualistic politics of Carter and Reagan, Anderson reminded many observers of McCarthy in 1968, and McCarthy admitted that he was torn between supporting Anderson; the Libertarian candidate, Ed Clark; and the Citizens' Party candidate, Barry Commoner. What McCarthy did next, however, amazed political observers and appalled his friends. On 23 October 1980 he formally endorsed not Anderson, as had been expected, but Ronald Reagan. According to McCarthy's statement, Reagan had a "clear concept of the meaning of the office" and had "run a more dignified and becoming campaign" than Carter. McCarthy announced that Reagan's economic plan, although "an oversimplification of Adam Smith's economic ideas," was "structurally, and economically, sounder than the Carter program," and even on foreign policy he rated Reagan more highly than Carter, arguing that he was more likely to reach a comprehensive deal on nuclear disarmament. It was not, he admitted, a very enthusiastic endorsement, but then he hadn't been "very enthusiastic about any candidate for the presidency since Adlai Stevenson." "Including yourself?" a reporter asked. "Probably least enthusiastic about myself," McCarthy replied with a grin.[34]

McCarthy's support for Reagan in 1980 horrified most Democrats. Reagan was not merely a Republican; he was a conservative who was widely thought to pose a serious threat to the legacy of the New Deal and who was perceived by many liberals as a genuine menace to world peace. The Republicans were predictably delighted, and Reagan himself commented that the endorsement, coming from a man "who has a feeling for people and compassion and so forth," would "give some people confidence that I don't eat my young." Many of the neoconservatives had also endorsed Reagan, but the desertion of the tragic hero of 1968 was a stunning shock to liberal observers. McCarthy's independent campaign in 1976 had been bad enough, but for most Democrats, this was the ultimate betrayal. "Clean Gene Did What?" read the headline in the *St. Paul Pioneer Press*. "He's a merchant," commented one angry DFL veteran. "And anything he can do to maintain his visibility and peddle his poetry, that's what he'll do." For years to come, McCarthy would have to defend himself against Democratic charges of apostasy and treachery, but, true to form, he could hardly contain his mischievous glee at having defied his old friends and colleagues. As he laughingly explained in subsequent interviews, it was "a very negative endorsement," based on the fact that Carter "had really done great harm to the Democratic Party" and was "against everything it stood for." In McCarthy's eyes, any candidate would have been better in 1980 than the hated incumbent. "Carter's economic program had to be stopped," he insisted. "When you get to 12 and 13 percent inflation, you're headed for the deep rocks. And Carter was a complete failure in nuclear arms and dealing with the Russians . . . He was totally inept. He couldn't even get SALT II, which was a nothing agreement."[35]

While most Democrats thought that party loyalty transcended all other considerations, McCarthy remained unrepentant. "I'm not sorry," he said defiantly two years later. "But I thought the Carter thing had to be stopped . . . I was not happy about what Reagan was going to do. I never really endorsed his economics . . . I supported Reagan only as against Jimmy Carter. As soon as he was elected, I turned on him." The determining factor, McCarthy said, had been Carter's decision to boycott the Moscow Olympics: "When he did that, I said this has got to stop pretty soon. I mean, that's the kind of thing a third-rate country does." There were rumors that McCarthy had asked for the position of ambassador to the United Nations in return for the endorsement, but the job was never forthcoming. Although McCarthy never held back from criticizing the Reagan administration, he usually spoke of "Ronald" with amused affection. "Jimmy," on the other hand, deserved only the utmost contempt. "The terrible thing," McCarthy mused, "is that the difference between Carter and Reagan was that there were some gaps in Carter's ignorance."[36]

To Democratic activists in his home state of Minnesota, McCarthy's endorsement of Reagan was the crowning transgression in a long litany of betrayal. He certainly appeared to have given up on the Democrats for good: in 1981, for example, he branded them "the party of little other than the Department of Health, Education and Welfare." But, four years after his last campaign had ended, McCarthy was beginning to wonder whether he was quite ready for retirement. Reagan, after all, was five years older than he was, and there was no reason why a sexagenarian veteran might not aspire to political office. McCarthy's last foray into Minnesota politics in 1973 had been little short of a disaster, and his mind turned to the prospect of a last campaign to redeem his reputation and win back his rightful place in the Senate. So it was that in September 1981, visitors to the Minnesota State Fair were startled to see the familiar figure of Eugene McCarthy wandering the state fairground, shaking hands and signing autographs and generally behaving like a candidate once again. That McCarthy, who still lived in Woodville, Virginia, seriously thought he could rally support in the state of Hubert Humphrey and Walter Mondale was extraordinary enough, but he was in breezy form. "I've suggested to Democrats that if they'll forgive me for being right, I'll forgive them for being wrong," he explained. Some observers concluded that McCarthy had finally lost touch completely with political reality: one cartoon in the *Minneapolis Star* showed tourists walking along a line of state fair stalls, from Hilda the Fat Lady and Zira the Snake Woman to Bongo the Ape Man and Eugene McCarthy for Senator. But McCarthy was undeterred. For one thing, he was confident that this time he had a message that would attract young supporters in their thousands and sweep him to victory, first in the Democratic primary and then in the 1982 Senate election against the popular Republican incumbent, David Durenberger. He would campaign as a champion of the nuclear freeze movement.[37]

Détente between the United States and the Soviet Union had effectively ended in the mid-1970s, and during the Carter administration, relations between the two superpowers had deteriorated to the extent that popular fears of a third world war were once again widespread. Both Carter and Reagan spent more on defense than their predecessors, and both were committed to stationing Pershing and Cruise missiles in Western Europe, to the horror of peace campaigners at home and abroad. By 1982, the nuclear freeze movement, which drew on the legacies of the antiwar campaigns of the 1960s and the environmental movements of the 1970s, had captured the imagination of a new generation of student activists as well as the reform wing of the Democratic Party. Liberal fund-raisers like Stewart Mott and Howard Stein, both of whom had financially supported McCarthy in 1968, were now backing local referendum campaigns as well as antinuclear congressional candidates, and McCarthy's belief that he could once again emerge as the standard-bearer of a revived peace movement was not entirely fanciful, even though he did not have a long record of commitment to the issue of nuclear disarmament. His platform as a candidate for the DFL Senate nomination rested upon his demand for "a nuclear freeze with the Soviet Union and . . . *immediate* reductions in our nuclear arsenal." He would prove, he claimed, that the campuses could again be "stirred up" by a liberal peace campaigner, and at one college in Minnesota he demanded "an absolute confrontation" between students and the administration on the lines of the demonstrations against the Vietnam War. So his proposed campaign schedule would concentrate on the state's universities and colleges, where McCarthy planned to assemble an army of young supporters to match his beardless brigades in New Hampshire fourteen years before. "I'm going to suggest that perhaps they owe me a vote," he said confidently.[38]

From his first appearance at the state fair in September 1981, however, it had been obvious that McCarthy was not popular with voters in Minnesota and that his prospective primary campaign would end in disaster. Unfortunately, McCarthy had grown used to defying the advice of colleagues and commentators, and he therefore eagerly pressed on. The campaign began badly with a press conference in St. Paul in March 1982. McCarthy began by explaining that his long absence from elective office was a strength, not a weakness. "Having stood apart from it for twelve years," he insisted, "I'll be able to come back to the Senate and say, 'Look, I've been looking at you from the outside, and now I want to tell you how to operate.'" On arrival in Washington, he proposed to encourage his colleagues to re-examine "the whole conception of the role of the Senate," and then to turn it into a powerful institution on the lines of the Senate in republican Rome. The bewildered journalists, however, were more interested in McCarthy's endorsement of Reagan than his thoughts on ancient Rome, and a series of exchanges followed in which McCarthy found himself defending Reagan's economic agenda and record in Central America. He dismissed the Democrats themselves, the very organization to which he was hoping to appeal, as "a party that's in utter disarray, that's lost its way both nationally and locally, particularly on national issues," and when pressed about his decision to live in Virginia and not in Minnesota, he defended himself by blaming the inadequacies of the local press. "I haven't been physically living here, true," he said coldly. "If I'd been here, reading Bill Sumner [the editorial writer of the *St. Paul Pioneer Press*] and what comes out in the *Minneapolis Star,* I'd be much less prepared to represent Minnesota in the Senate."[39]

Not surprisingly, his decision to run did not impress local commentators. An editorial in the much-maligned *Minneapolis Star* commented that his plan to lecture the Senate on the need to emulate the Romans was "a bit absurd, even sad," and added, "Couple that with his whimsical reluctance to attack the Reagan administration in any meaningful way and his flim-flamming when asked about his endorsement of Reagan in the presidential campaign and it seems incredible that any DFL voter—other than the cadre of McCarthy true believers—could possibly vote for him." The *Rochester Post-Bulletin,* meanwhile, ran a cartoon showing the "McCarthy for Senate" headquarters, adorned by an enormous banner reading, "Vote McCarthy: He'll Get Us Out of Vietnam!"[40]

McCarthy's platform generally consisted of the same ideas that he had proposed in 1976. "We might suggest they read all my books," he told a campaign aide. "Once I put it in a book, I believe everybody has seen it." In reality, however, 21 percent of Minnesota voters had no idea who he was, while 35 percent looked unfavorably on his candidacy. His approval rating in the state was a pitiful 15 percent, easily the lowest of any public figure, and he was the only prospective candidate in 1982 to have more detractors than supporters. His commitment was frequently questioned: at one press conference, a reporter spotted that McCarthy's watch was still set to Eastern Daylight Time, even though he was on the third day of a swing through southern Minnesota, which is in the Central Time Zone. "The time on the watch suggested that three days is about all the man plans to spend in the Midwest," wrote another local journalist, who also suggested that the campaign was a publicity stunt to improve the sales of McCarthy's latest collection of poems and reminiscences. At a rally in Minneapolis, one local Democrat spoke for many when he called McCarthy's campaign "an embarrassment to Minnesota." As in 1973, the local organization already had a candidate; this time it was the thirty-four-year-old Mark Dayton, the heir to a department store fortune who had married a Rockefeller and was a prominent friend and financial supporter of Walter Mondale. McCarthy claimed, in all seriousness, that their contest would be "a test of who has the better ideas, greater energy and greater commitment to hard work for the people of this state," but nobody thought he had the slightest chance of beating Dayton. The financial gulf between them reached ludicrous proportions: by the end of July, McCarthy had spent $90,000 to Dayton's $3.1 million. As the *Pioneer Press* put it, while Dayton traveled "in private airplanes with a well-paid entourage, McCarthy was led around Duluth by a volunteer who was tempting fate even to be seen with the man."[41]

Both his opponent and the conventional rituals of campaigning were, in McCarthy's eyes, far beneath him. At one debate between the two Democratic candidates, McCarthy spent much of his time slouched listlessly in his chair and according to an onlooker "even lapsed—for a few minutes toward the end of the two-hour program—into a near nap-like state." In June, the DFL state convention endorsed Dayton with 947 votes on the first ballot. It was the first time McCarthy had been a candidate at a state convention since he beat Eugenie Anderson for the senatorial endorsement in 1958. On this occasion, however, matters turned out rather differently: he managed to win precisely eight votes. Needless to say, he had declined to turn up at the convention in Duluth, despite the offer of a hotel suite from the DFL party chairman. To compete for the endorsement, as McCarthy scornfully put it, would be like Bjorn Borg's having to compete in a qualifying tournament in order to be invited to Wimbledon. Instead he stayed at home in Virginia with his dog. When he finally emerged from his seclusion, it was to launch another series of attacks on the Minnesota press, his opponent and the Democratic Party. Dayton, he claimed, had bought "control of the party" with his department store fortune. In McCarthy's eyes, he was just another unthinking, unimaginative Great Society liberal. "I've observed people like him who come to Congress," McCarthy explained.

> They have a great concern for the poor and destitute, sort of a Christmas basket approach. They want to help the poor. It makes them feel good. And also, they sort of like to increase the number of the poor, but they always work it from the bottom up. They'll say more food stamps and rent subsidies and fuel subsidies and rebates and a negative income tax. But they don't have any real understanding, I think, of how people live who are in between, who have to meet mortgages and pay tuition and things of that kind.[42]

This was McCarthy the conservative, rather than McCarthy the liberal champion of the National Welfare Rights Organization. Perhaps this was not the best strategy to win the support of the progressive voters of the DFL, but it is also likely that McCarthy voiced such opinions precisely because he knew it annoyed them. His own remedies for poverty and destitution, however, remained a mystery, because he announced that he would be answering no more press questions about the "issues." Instead, he ordered reporters to go away and read his books; he would be handing out a quiz on their contents at his next appearance.[43]

By now his campaign had degenerated into little more than an exhibition of contemptuous eccentricity. The *Minneapolis Star Tribune* observed that McCarthy had taken to giving "a verbal pounding" to "everyone in reach" and was behaving like "a common scold." Much to McCarthy's amazement, Democratic regulars, union members and students were all united in their preference for Dayton. "Just logically," he remarked, "you'd figure that nobody would vote for Mark Dayton over me if they had a choice, if they were concerned at all about the problems facing the country." He did not give up, however, but spent the next two months touring Minnesota, making unpredictable speeches and generally annoying the Democratic hierarchy. McCarthy even managed to derail a senior citizens' athletics meeting in Duluth when he appeared to win the shot-put event with a controversial toss that was more "throw" than "put." Finally, on 14 September, he was put out of his misery, as Dayton casually piled up a three-to-one margin in the Democratic primary. While McCarthy's defeat had been entirely predictable, even he was amazed that so many Democrats still bore a grudge against him for Humphrey's defeat in the 1968 election. "They practically blame me for his death," McCarthy said sadly. "The party thing is very tough." When the result finally came through, McCarthy refused to admit that it marked the end of his ambitions, explaining: "This was a punctuation mark in my political career. It was a little more than a colon but a little less than a period." All the same, he was "through" with the DFL for good. "I thought I should give them one more chance," he said. "But I think this ends my relationship with the DFL in Minnesota."[44]

There was to be no triumphant comeback for McCarthy in his home state. Instead, he subsided reluctantly back into his retirement in Woodville, writing articles and poems, chopping wood, chatting affably to his neighbors and walking his dog. In 1983, on Labor Day, he suffered a mild heart attack and spent three weeks in the hospital, but he made a full recovery and was soon telling reporters that he would be fit enough for another presidential campaign. In the event, he decided to give the campaign trail a rest in 1984, and watched with interest from the sidelines as Ronald Reagan defeated Walter Mondale in a landslide. He was still no admirer of Mondale, and commented that Reagan was just as good "without knowing the issues." All McCarthy would say about his own preference was that he had voted absentee and hoped that his ballot was "lost in the mail." As before, he spent most of his time writing books and articles and traveling to campus lectures, albeit at a gentler pace more suited to the lifestyle of a man of seventy. Every few years he would publish a new book of essays or political commentary, although in most cases they failed to attract great attention from either the press or the public. As his own friends admitted, he was too lazy and self-assured to work hard at a book, and whenever editors suggested revisions his reaction was usually to look for a new editor. From *The View from Rappahannock* (1984) and *Up 'til Now* (1987) to *A Colony of the World* (1992) and *No-Fault Politics* (1998), the failure of McCarthy's books to win a wider audience mystified their author. "I'm a little frustrated that my brilliant ideas aren't spread to the world, or the Senate, or to anywhere else," he remarked in 1987. "It's not just that I'm not heard. It's just that some of those things are so important that I think they should be obvious to a lot of people."[45]

For many readers, however, the books flopped because they were not really very good. McCarthy tended to repeat himself, often borrowing anecdotes, arguments and entire passages from one book to use in another; his style was as dry, lackluster and obscure as ever; and there was little evidence to suggest wide reading or deep thinking on his part. Working in the solitude of his study in Woodville, McCarthy was free to indulge himself, even though his basic ideas had changed little since 1976. He recommended the abolition of the two-party system and the vice presidency as well as the restoration of the electoral college as a genuine deliberative body; he attacked both the expansion of the federal bureaucracy and the role of multinational corporations in American life; he complained that immigrants were turning the United States into a bilingual society and demanded that the Japanese and the western Europeans pay a defense tax to compensate for the American troops protecting them from Soviet attack. The United States, he argued, had become the "colony of the world," with its economy at the mercy of foreign financiers, its military spread expensively all over the globe and its language and borders under threat from Hispanic and East Asian migrants.

Such ideas might be eclectic and irreverent, but they were also vague, unconnected and undefined, and McCarthy rarely cited evidence to support his propositions. With his general and bitter hostility to reformers of all kinds, contempt for modern politicians and enduring self-regard, McCarthy risked sounding like a bitter, misanthropic old man, harping on the same themes again and again. He received some awful reviews. In 1980, the *New Republic* called his book *The Ultimate Tyranny* "vague," "rambling" and "excruciating." Seven years later, the *Washington Post*'s reviewer declared that *Up 'til Now* was "a terrible book . . . full of sloppy writing, egregious errors of fact, barbs at his enemies and poetry for his friends." In 1998, the *American Spectator* noted that *No-Fault Politics* was "marred by an indistinct thesis, lazy thinking, and a general sloppiness," as well as being riddled with "factual errors," misquotations and outbreaks of "ludicrous hyperbole" that were "symptoms of a general indiscipline." Not only did McCarthy lack "the historical depth he feigns," but his ideas were "stretched so thin as to become nearly invisible."[46]

Most people would have been content with a life of pastoral sequestration such as McCarthy enjoyed in his quiet farmhouse in Virginia. "He fits in real well to this rural scene out here," reported one of his neighbors in 1987. "He gets a lot of pleasure out of going down to the general store on Sunday mornings and listening to all the hunting stories and dog stories. He and I usually take a walk down the stream and see what the beavers are doing in the back of Hawthorne Farm here." But McCarthy himself was not satisfied. In 1975 he had written that "the effect of a good and becoming exit is not to be discounted. A truly great actor, it is said, is marked by his exits. At best they should be such that, although his going may not have been noticed, his having gone becomes evident." Thirteen years later, he proceeded to ignore his own advice in the most public way possible. To the embarrassment and disbelief of his old friends, he decided to run for the presidency again.[47]

As early as 1972, Stewart Alsop had suggested that McCarthy was "a classic example of Stassenization," a condition afflicting a politician who, like the former Minnesota governor Harold Stassen, "feels an ungovernable compulsion to become a Presidential candidate even when it is inconceivable that he will ever become President." Why McCarthy, who had once been a serious and respected politician, insisted on doing this was a mystery to most of his former colleagues. One explanation was that his visibility as a presidential candidate helped to boost his stock as a lecturer and to improve the sales of his books, although in the latter case there was little discernible effect. McCarthy himself admitted, "There are worse things a campaign could do than get people to read one's books." Perhaps more significantly, McCarthy evidently had a personal stake in presenting himself as a perennial candidate. He liked the attention that the campaign trail brought, even if his audiences were often meager, and he relished the opportunity to irritate the press and the Democrats. One of his friends, Maurice Rosenblatt, perceptively remarked that McCarthy had "a rejection wish. He wants to reject others and to be rejected by them." This might seem odd, given McCarthy's history, for when he was rejected by the Benedictines in 1943, or by Lyndon Johnson in 1964, he had taken it very badly indeed. But it was as if rejection now gave his life meaning. Every few years he gave the Democratic Party or the nation "another chance," and every time they overlooked him. To McCarthy, failure was the definitive proof that he was a cut above the other candidates and even above the contest itself. His rejection inevitably proved that his ideas were too clever, too courageous and too difficult for the electorate and the party. If he had simply accepted his retirement, he would have been just another failed politician, but by defying the entreaties of his friends and the advice of the columnists, he proved that he was not just different, but better.[48]

In 1988 McCarthy reached a new low, campaigning as the presidential candidate of the Consumer Party. The party had only four thousand members, mostly anti-establishment middle-class eccentrics in Pennsylvania, Michigan and New Jersey, and its chairman had approached McCarthy about running as their candidate against Bush and Dukakis. McCarthy was keen to find a ticket from which he could advance his ideas, so the two joined forces. He declared his candidacy in June in front of Independence Hall in Philadelphia, before a tiny audience of friends and die-hard supporters. Only one of the major television networks carried the news, but no one took McCarthy seriously. "I'm hopeful some other groups will come in," McCarthy said optimistically. "We've had some calls from the National Unity people—they're a sort of Anderson organization. And maybe independent groups around the country. I don't know about the Socialists and Vegetarians. The Peace and Freedom people might come in. I don't think they have a candidate. They're a pretty wild bunch."[49]

The Minnesota newspapers, embarrassed that one of the state's political legends had sunk to such depths, pronounced his campaign "sad" and "futile." "No backdrop could have masked the foolishness of some of his remedies," commented the *Philadelphia Inquirer*. The campaign was not a success. "Eugene McCarthy is running for President, and almost nobody cares," was the verdict of one journalist, who watched a tiny group of followers "meet McCarthy at the train station, take him to stand behind a battered folding table for a curbside press conference nearly drowned out by growling buses, [and] drop him at the airport where he walks away unnoticed." McCarthy was on the ballot in only four states, Pennsylvania, Michigan, New Jersey and Minnesota; he himself admitted that he was tempted to vote for Dukakis, a self-described liberal with good reason to be proud of his record as a technocratic governor of Massachusetts. The very word "liberalism," however, had by now become an electoral albatross, popularly associated with crime, social elitism and fiscal irresponsibility, and George Bush eagerly exploited the identification. The result was another shattering blow for Democratic morale, as Dukakis, who had once led the race by seventeen points, suffered a spectacular electoral collapse and won just eleven states. As for McCarthy, his final showing did not trouble the statisticians.[50]

Even that was not enough for him. Four years later, with the Democrats searching for a candidate to win back the White House for the first time since 1976, the seventy-six-year-old McCarthy threw his hat in the ring, announcing that he was ready for "a personal confrontation with the Bush Administration." This was his last campaign, a characteristic blend of the witty, the irritating and the shambolic. His platform, which was woolly in the extreme, included such McCarthy staples as a reduction in the work-week, a huge import duty on Japanese and European products to pay for the American military, a capital levy of 20 percent on the wealthiest Americans, and the usual promises to abolish the vice presidency and the direct popular election of the president. The McCarthy campaign headquarters was a desk in the home of his friend Mike Barr, and while other candidates ensured that their telephone numbers contained the digits 1992, McCarthy's campaign line was a nostalgic 202-543-1968. His big campaign send-off, a $50-a-head poetry recital in an Irish bar on Capitol Hill, drew barely twenty people, all friends of the candidate.[51]

Still, McCarthy was not prepared to go down without a fight. So many years had passed since his last campaign for the Democratic presidential nomination that most voters and party officials remembered him not with anger and resentment but with a kind of vague bemusement. In February a pack of reporters, chewing over the latest revelations about Bill Clinton's sex life, spotted an old man in a New Hampshire hotel restaurant, standing forlornly "as if expecting someone to hail him, to wave him over, to invite him to sit down and talk about old times." But nobody did, and instead he sat down at a table alone and stared at a menu. "Jeez," one of the journalists said. "Didn't that used to be Gene McCarthy?" It did. "Nobody knows I'm running," McCarthy admitted in one interview. "I like campaigning if you can really talk about issues, but nobody knows I'm out there." Still, matters could have been worse. While Paul Tsongas was toasting victory in the New Hampshire primary, and Bill Clinton was declaring himself the "Comeback Kid," McCarthy was celebrating a triumph of his own. In the Republican primary, Harold Stassen had won 206 votes; in the Democratic contest, McCarthy won 211. He was, at least, the leading Minnesotan in the race, and he lasted longer than Tsongas.[52]

In March, to the astonishment of most observers, he somehow managed to win more than 15,000 votes in the Louisiana primary and, incredibly, managed to finish second behind Clinton in twenty-eight northern parishes. Nobody could quite explain how this had happened, especially as he had never campaigned in the state, and it was generally seen as a bizarre aberration. McCarthy himself was understandably delighted, although he suspected that the Louisiana voters had mistaken him for Joseph McCarthy. He left the race with an appearance later that month at a debate in New York, between the two remaining candidates, Clinton and Jerry Brown, held in a cavernous theater in downtown Buffalo. "This is the highest-ranking Democratic organization that's let me talk to them for twenty years," McCarthy announced at the outset. "I've got a lot of things to say." He then spent much of the debate, in the words of one report, "doodling on a pad," occasionally rousing himself to issue the usual denunciations of Robert Kennedy, Jimmy Carter and other villains. As Clinton and Brown looked on uncomfortably, McCarthy also attacked George Bush as "a traveling salesman" and added that he had "done more to destroy the English language than Karl Marx." It was a characteristically unconventional note on which to end his final campaign in Democratic politics.[53]

The 1992 campaign really was McCarthy's last electoral effort. He spent most of the following decade in Woodville, still publishing an article or delivering a lecture every now and then. Old adversaries like Humphrey and Muskie were dead, and many of McCarthy's old contemporaries had finally forgiven his various supposed misdemeanors, so he found himself regularly being invited to 1968 reunion dinners or award ceremonies. His alma mater gave him the "Armor of Light" award in 1998, the highest honor that St. John's can bestow, for "the Benedictine light he has brought to the world," and the lavish banquet to celebrate the occasion was the highlight of the monastery's calendar that summer. As he entered his eighties, his mind was still as sharp as ever, and he even made an appearance in 1997 before the Senate Rules Committee to testify on the proposed McCain-Feingold campaign finance act. McCarthy, said the *Star Tribune,* "peppered his testimony . . . with historical references and yarns that kept committee members and spectators chuckling," as he called for the abolition of the two-party system. He also had an easy solution for the problem of the foreign donations raised by Clinton and Gore in 1996, recommending to the amusement of the committee that other countries "can give as much to our government as the CIA gives to theirs."[54]

The 1990s also brought personal sadness, however. Since their parents' separation, the McCarthy children had done very well for themselves. Ellen worked as an administrator in the House of Representatives; Mary taught law at Yale; Michael was a doctor and medical journalist in Seattle; and Margaret became a veterinarian in Massachusetts. In July 1990, Mary, who had worked so passionately for her father's campaign in 1968, died of cancer, at the age of just forty-one. Eight years later, Marya McLaughlin, McCarthy's companion since his separation from Abigail, died of meningitis, and in February 2001, Abigail succumbed to breast cancer. Since 1969 she had carved out her own very successful career as a novelist, campaigner on women's issues and columnist for *Commonweal* magazine. As their son Michael put it, the separation had given her "a chance to develop her career in another way, and she did very well." The old bitterness between Eugene and Abigail had long since ebbed away; not only had McCarthy signed his Senate pension over to his wife, but they had preserved a good friendship and often saw each other on holidays. "I've come to think of Gene as a relative," she explained in 1987.[55]

As for McCarthy himself, he enjoyed relatively good health for a man of advancing years. His father, after all, had been hale and hearty well into his nineties, and Eugene had evidently inherited his longevity. In the summer of 1997 he had a serious scare when anti-inflammatory medication for a pinched nerve in his back seriously damaged the lining of his stomach. An initial operation repaired the stomach ulcer but created problems of its own, making it very difficult for him to digest food and necessitating yet more surgery. Initial reports were gloomy, but McCarthy had made a career of defying those who tried to write him off: by the end of the year he was cheerfully up and about, rather more delicate than before but otherwise unimpaired. By the end of the decade, the tributes were flowing thick and fast, especially from Minnesota, where his reputation had finally begun to recover from the debacle of his 1982 contest against Mark Dayton. In 1998 the Democratic congressman Bruce Vento, who represented the Fourth District, successfully proposed that the post office in downtown St. Paul be named after the city's most famous political representative, and in December a crowd of over a hundred people, including Senator Paul Wellstone and Governor Arne Carlson, crowded into the post office lobby to listen to a typically impish McCarthy address, including the now standard attack on the Kennedy family and a demand for President Clinton's impeachment on the grounds that McCarthy was "tired of him." In October 1999 the Minnesota Civil Liberties Union arranged three days of tributes to McCarthy's "historic and courageous career," during which various prominent political figures in the state queued up to praise a man they evidently regarded as a Democratic legend, although McCarthy confided to the present author that the adulation was a little over the top. The *Pioneer Press* described the occasion as "an affectionate last hurrah," but McCarthy had no inten-tion of leaving the stage just yet, or even of ruling out a potential political comeback.[56]

In January 2000 McCarthy made a nostalgic return to New Hampshire, supporting the Democratic candidacy of Vice President Al Gore, who had been one of his volunteers in 1968 as well as the son of one of his fellow liberal dissenters in the Senate. Indeed, as the twenty-first century began he remained in good form, still publishing the odd article and issuing occa-sional broadsides against contemporary political leaders and old adver-saries like Robert McNamara and Jimmy Carter. He was not impressed by President George W. Bush, whom he considered a "pretender," and dis-liked many of the national security measures introduced after the terrorist attacks on the World Trade Center and the Pentagon in September 2001. "De Tocqueville said you'll find you'll lose the freedoms you're supposed to be defending by setting up your defenses against losing them, and that's what's involved in the stuff that Bush is doing," he said. "We haven't lost any of our liberties to the Iraqis yet, but we've had our own liberties cur-tailed." Eighteen months later, when Bush ordered the invasion of Iraq in order to depose his father's old adversary Saddam Hussein, McCarthy was again skeptical. "This is a faith-based war," he remarked. "The worst thing is faith-based religion." As for the Democrats, McCarthy dismissed them with characteristic contempt. "I think the party's a wreck," he told one interviewer.[57]

McCarthy's career after the failure of his struggle with Hubert Hum-phrey for the presidential nomination had been a study in frustration. His quixotic enterprises attracted little public attention and confirmed the gen-eral impression that he was an unruly, disloyal eccentric who had squan-dered his own reputation in a series of self-indulgent campaigns that never ended in victory and had little impact on American politics and society. This was a harsh verdict—but not, perhaps, an entirely unwarranted one. And yet even as he approached ninety, with so many old friends and rivals long since dead, McCarthy remained as breezily self-confident and caustic as ever. He even refused to rule out another bid for national office. By the time of his eighty-seventh birthday, in March 2003, he was spending much of his time in quiet retirement in the Georgetown, a smart residential home for the elderly in Washington, D.C. "My father lived to be ninety-eight," he gleefully declared, "so I can threaten people for another ten years." He still liked to potter down to his farmhouse in Woodville now and again, and enjoyed his days reading and meandering about the countryside, or occa-sionally driving down to the nearest little settlement to have coffee, buy the newspaper and chat with the local townsfolk. It was a gentle life, and not so very different from the days of his childhood back in Watkins eighty years before, when little Eugene McCarthy had played with his kite and his toy animals in a world almost unimaginably distant from the troubles of the new century.[58]

EPILOGUE: THE LIBERAL'S PROGRESS

After Eugene McCarthy left the Senate in December 1970, his reputation entered a long and apparently irreversible decline, thanks almost entirely to his own arrogant and unconventional behavior. The inevitable comparisons with Harold Stassen were unfair to a man with twenty years of public service and a legendary presidential campaign behind him, but they reflected the common perception of McCarthy as egocentric, frivolous and psychologically flawed. Yet the contrast with McCarthy's career in the House of Representatives, where he had been a professional, respectable and dedicated Democratic politician, could hardly have been more striking. He was never quite the quintessential Democratic liberal, because his intellectual roots in Catholic radicalism and European conservatism meant that his basic philosophical assumptions were often very different from those of his political contemporaries. Indeed, McCarthy's intellectual background helps to explain the apparent contradictions of his political philosophy and his uneasy relationship with conventional American liberalism. His early years, in fact, saw him embrace a kind of Catholic politics that was very different from the machine politics of the cities or the reactionary conservatism of the 1960s. This older, more European brand of political Catholicism emphasized social justice and the redistribution of wealth as well as the usual respect for tradition and the limits of power. After McCarthy entered politics in 1948, the more idealistic aspects of this agenda were diluted by his understandable ambition and eagerness to advance his own career in the Democratic Party. But they never entirely disappeared, and in McCarthy's opposition to the Vietnam War and his 1968 presidential campaign, as well as his subsequent independent campaigns, there were palpable traces of his old radical idealism.

The other important legacy of McCarthy's Catholicism was his fervent opposition to Communism, which endured until the Vietnam War. It was this commitment, together with his interest in improving the welfare state, that defined his entrance into postwar politics. As an ambitious, intelligent man with a dry wit and a talent for organization, McCarthy was an excellent political candidate. It took the particular circumstances of Democratic politics in Minnesota in the late 1940s, however, to tear him away from his teaching career and into the U.S. House of Representatives. Liberalism in 1948 was delicately poised. The alliance between the Popular Front and the anti-Communist New Dealers, complicated in Minnesota by the existence of the Farmer-Labor Party, had always been uneasy and was now at an end. Like other young men and women who came to politics after 1945, McCarthy believed that anti-Communism and moderate social democracy could be combined to define a new liberalism that would defend the New Deal and drive Democratic politics toward a successful future. For McCarthy, like his colleagues Hubert Humphrey and Walter Mondale, anti-Communism and the Cold War played central roles in this new vision of Democratic liberalism.

This was the same approach that President Truman adopted to win re-election in 1948; it provided the intellectual justification for Americans for Democratic Action and other liberal organizations on the fringe of the Democratic Party; and, in the form of the Fair Deal, it was at the heart of McCarthy's liberalism during the 1950s. Representing St. Paul in Congress until 1958, McCarthy never questioned the Cold War or the basic illegitimacy of Communism at home. His domestic policy positions, from his support for migrant workers and civil rights to the liberal manifesto of 1957 and leadership of the embryonic Democratic Study Group, were circumscribed by the limits of the Fair Deal. While McCarthy's personal qualities were promoting him up the political ladder, his substantive attitudes remained unchanged. Like more senior liberal Democrats, such as Hubert Humphrey and John Kennedy, he criticized President Eisenhower not for his fundamental assumptions but for his air of casual passivity. In the election campaigns of 1958 and 1960, McCarthy and his colleagues argued that more dynamism, more growth, and more aggression were required to thwart Soviet interests abroad and to promote economic expansion, the rights of labor and increased equality at home. Although McCarthy's dislike of emotional rhetoric and his emphasis on prudence and gradualism meant that he was never closely associated with the civil rights movement, his record in the late 1950s was eminently liberal and demonstrated an unbroken continuity with the themes and commitments of 1948.

The Democratic victories of 1958–1964 permitted the enactment of the old Fair Deal proposals on domestic issues from unemployment and regional poverty to desegregation and voting rights. McCarthy, however, spent much of this period in the doldrums. He had gambled on opposing Kennedy in 1960, and had lost. Similarly, in 1964 the collapse of his vice presidential ambitions left him weary, bitter and frustrated. Paradoxically, at the same time as liberalism was at its peak of power and influence, McCarthy's own career was in decline. This meant that when the conflict in Vietnam became a controversial issue, he was outside the favored circle of Johnson's White House and had little to lose by opposing the expansion of the war. Like most other liberals, McCarthy had initially approved of Johnson's actions in Vietnam. But his Cold War fervor had mellowed during the anxious and perilous years of the Kennedy administration. Membership of the Foreign Relations Committee, and close personal links with critics of American policy such as J. William Fulbright and Wayne Morse, made opposition to the war relatively easy and natural for McCarthy. Thanks to the influence of Fulbright in particular, McCarthy was coming to question the more simplistic orthodoxies of Cold War policy and the assumptions behind American involvement in Southeast Asia. He was not, however, a maverick or a pioneer. Other liberals had objected to the conflict earlier and with greater passion. With the enactment of the Great Society and the engagement of American forces in Vietnam, liberalism itself was on the point of change. Its old commitments were in question: new activists, bloodied in the civil rights struggles of the 1960s, had joined the Democratic Party, and its advocates were searching for a new direction to take the liberal cause into the 1970s. At the same time that liberals were questioning the old orthodoxies of the Cold War, however, the electoral coalition on which they relied was under severe strain. Ever since the heyday of the New Deal, the Democratic alliance had been marked by deep tensions between North and South, white and black, the cities and the countryside, and affluent reformers and blue-collar workers. By the end of the Johnson presidency the rift between the Democrats' different constituencies was greater than ever.

These tensions found their expression in McCarthy's presidential challenge in 1968. The campaign, originally conceived as a token effort to raise the issue of the war and to assuage liberal dissatisfaction with Lyndon Johnson, united both the old Stevensonian reform liberals and the younger, more impatient breed of activists who had emerged in the preceding decade. McCarthy himself was unclear what he intended the campaign to achieve, and during the campaign his emphasis changed from restoring the values of the Kennedy administration to abandoning liberal Cold War orthodoxy in favor of an undefined "New Politics." The ambiguity of McCarthy's rhetoric in fact belied the instability of liberalism in 1968. The contest between McCarthy and Robert Kennedy demonstrated that the liberal coalition was sharply divided on lines of class and color. Affluent white voters preferred McCarthy, despite his more radical proposals; Kennedy remained the darling of urban blacks, despite his emphasis on law and order. After Kennedy's assassination, Hubert Humphrey inherited much of his support and easily won the nomination, since McCarthy never broke through to win votes outside his liberal middle-class base. Unlike McCarthy, Humphrey made no attempt to challenge the orthodoxies of the 1940s and 1950s: he stuck to the rhetoric of the Fair Deal, basing his campaign on a defense of the welfare state and the Cold War. The divisive impact of race on Democratic politics meant that this appeal was weaker than ever, and McCarthy was right to argue that recycling the old liberal nostrums would not be enough to win elections in the 1970s. His own remedy represented a move to the left: a national guaranteed income, increased federal spending on welfare and the cities, and a withdrawal from anti-Communist containment in the developing world. Other liberals, particularly George McGovern, were to adopt similar proposals in the early 1970s. Like McCarthy, they were not able to attract support beyond the educated, suburban middle class. The coalition of interests that had embraced the Fair Deal agenda in 1948 could no longer be rallied by liberal calls for growth, equality and solidarity, and thanks to the civil rights reforms of Kennedy and Johnson, the national Democratic Party was already losing white support in the southern states that had once been its heartland. Perhaps if they had enthusiastically embraced the language and appeal of militant, egalitarian economic populism the Democrats could have retained their strength among white voters in the South, but given the increasing affluence of the Sun Belt, even this would have been extremely difficult to pull off. The transformation in McCarthy's own political identity from a Cold Warrior and protégé of the unions to the self-consciously intellectual champion of a middle-class, moralistic northern elite therefore reflected a wider transformation in the fortunes and viability of Democratic liberalism.

* * *

In 1835 Alexis de Tocqueville, one of McCarthy's literary favorites, wrote:

> I confess that in America I saw more than America; I sought there the image
> of democracy itself, with its inclinations, its character, its prejudices, and its
> passions, in order to learn what we have to fear or to hope from its progress.

The life of Eugene McCarthy is not only the story of one man's progress
from a small town on the flat plain of central Minnesota to the corridors of
power in Washington, D.C.; it is also the story of American politics in
the postwar era, reflecting broad social and historical trends as well as the
contingencies of an individual life. Indeed, the life and career of Eugene
McCarthy tells us much about the rise and fall of postwar liberalism. In
1948, for instance, his first campaign coincided with the beginning of the
postwar liberal order, making it easy for a socially concerned Catholic anti-
Communist to succeed in politics. In 1958, his bid for election to the Senate came as part of a triumphant liberal sweep as the country repudiated the
passivity of the Eisenhower administration in favor of a more dynamic,
activist approach. When McCarthy won re-election to the Senate six years
later, it was against the background of more Democratic successes in the
Johnson landslide of 1964. From about 1966 onward, however, it became
evident that the liberal tide had peaked. McCarthy's presidential challenge,
his most famous moment, was made possible only because the administration and the cause of reform were faltering, and the chaos of his campaign
anticipated the turmoil and factionalism within the Democratic Party
between 1968 and 1976. McCarthy's personal frustration after 1968 owed
much to the fact that the energies of liberalism were spent and its future
direction uncertain, and had he remained in the Senate like his contemporaries Muskie, McGovern, and Fulbright, he would probably have found
the 1970s frustrating and would have been unlikely to retain his seat in
1982. As it was, the inconsistencies of his perennial campaigns, his articles
and his books all suggested the confusion of a man whose liberal commitments seemed anachronistic in the world of Carter, Reagan and Clinton.
By the time McCarthy finally accepted that his political career was over
and retired to a quiet life in Virginia, liberalism was no longer a force in
American presidential politics, and at the beginning of the twenty-first century, it was a rare and courageous politician indeed who referred to himself
as a liberal.

Yet the vagaries of McCarthy's political career are also easily explicable in terms of his own personal qualities and failings. His rise from obscurity to the Senate and the verge of the vice presidency owed much to his own intelligence, skill as a campaigner, and ability to rise through the ranks of the Democratic Party. Similarly, his decline into retirement and disappointment after 1968 had much to do with his irresponsibility, obstinacy and, above all, his pride. When McCarthy was a young man, he told his fiancée, Abigail, that "he felt called to *do* something rather than to *be* something." He was, she said, "a restless river seeking a channel." He would later insist that intellectuals must venture out into society and "prove the relevance of their ideas to life." The lesson of St. John's, with its emphasis on activism and experimentation, was that thinking and writing were not enough: a man would be judged on his actions and achievements. For those in politics, he wrote, the fundamental goal must be "to bring about progressive change in keeping with the demands of social justice." By these standards, McCarthy's career was not a stunning success. Intelligent, handsome, articulate and idealistic, he was capable of great things. He was probably naturally cleverer than Humphrey, Johnson or John Kennedy; he shared their liberal values, but he achieved only a fraction of what they did. In terms of legislation, McCarthy's legacy was thin compared with those of Humphrey, Muskie or Ted Kennedy. Unlike Fulbright, he did not inject any new ideas into the political debate; unlike McGovern or Mondale, he never won the presidential nomination of his party. He gave his name to no major bills and left little mark on American domestic policy. For all his natural gifts, McCarthy demonstrably failed to fulfill his true political potential.[1]

Perhaps it was never likely that a man with McCarthy's great sensitivity and arrogance could have reached the very highest level of American politics, but in the late 1950s, when he was celebrated by commentators as the coming man of the liberal movement, it certainly looked possible that he might one day win a place on a presidential ticket. Even in 1968, if he had only swallowed his personal pride and worked hard to rally his fellow Democrats behind him, he might have been able to snatch the presidential nomination. As it was, he remained one of the most famous and quixotic losers in American political history. Yet this was not because of a lack of aptitude, but because of a failure of application. The contrast with Hubert Humphrey, a less talented but more generous man in so many respects, could not be more striking. The 1968 campaign, of course, had a major impact on American politics, and many ordinary people still remember McCarthy's crusade against the Vietnam War with enormous affection, so his place in political history is ensured. Of course, it is often all too tempting for biographers to make lofty pronouncements about the weaknesses of their subjects. Yet the ultimate verdict must surely be that a promising and important career, which could have yielded so many benefits for the Democratic Party, the liberal cause and the American electorate, was thrown away through a combination of misplaced pride and unrelenting jealousy. It is, after all, doubtful whether the idealistic young man who took life so seriously as a Benedictine novice in the 1940s would have been satisfied with being remembered for heroic nonachievement. There is not always honor in failure.

ACKNOWLEDGMENTS

This book began life at the end of 1998 as a doctoral dissertation at the University of Cambridge, and it is a pleasure to acknowledge the many debts I have incurred since then.

Had it not been for the generous cooperation of Senator Eugene McCarthy himself, my work would have been both much more difficult and much less rewarding. He endured hours of questions with patience and good humor, and he also kindly granted me permission to read his employment files at the University of St. Thomas. Although I have often been critical of Senator McCarthy's record, I hope that what I have written gives a fair account of his years of public service and political engagement.

I am extremely grateful to my supervisor, Tony Badger, for all his generosity and support over the last six years. I would also like to thank Steve Spackman, who supervised my master's dissertation at the University of St. Andrews and has sent me pages of trenchant criticism and advice ever since. My thanks also go to John A. Thompson and Alan Brinkley, who examined my Ph.D. dissertation and recommended it to the present publisher. Michael O'Brien and Gayle Graham Yates were kind enough to read and comment on individual chapters, and I have benefited from the advice of numerous eminent historians on both sides of the Atlantic, among them Dan Carter, William Chafe, Martin Conway, Gareth Davies, William Gibbons, Steven Gillon, Lawrence Goldman, Lewis Gould, Alonzo Hamby, Iwan Morgan, Eugene Papôt, David Plotke and Harvard Sitkoff.

In its early days at Cambridge, this project was funded by the Arts and Humanities Research Board, the Lyndon Baines Johnson Foundation, the Sara Norton Fund and the Fellows of Jesus College, Cambridge. My fellow graduate students became so familiar with the life and career of Eugene McCarthy that they could easily have written rival books of their own, and it is a particular pleasure to thank Simon Hall, Andrew Preston, Nat Millett and Adam Smith for their vigorous criticisms and amusing companionship.

I was fortunate to be able to present my thoughts on Eugene McCarthy to numerous research seminars, conferences and colloquia at the universities of Cambridge, Sheffield, Keele and East Anglia, and I am grateful not only for the hospitality of my hosts but also for the thoughtful suggestions of my fellow historians. The history department of the University of Sheffield granted me a period of study leave to finish the book, and I would especially like to acknowledge the friendship and encouragement of my colleagues in the North American section: Robert Cook, Hugh Wilford and Joe Street. And I would also like to thank the sixteen students who took my class on the Age of Nixon while I was putting the finishing touches to this book. Their infectious and irreverent enthusiasm provided a welcome distraction from the bureaucratic rigors of academic life, although I fear they now know far more about Richard Nixon than is good for them.

It would have been impossible to complete this book without the assistance of the staff of all the libraries and archives in Britain and the United States where I conducted my research, among them Steve Nielsen at the Minnesota Historical Society, Anne Kenne at the University of St. Thomas and Brother David Klingeman at St. John's Abbey. The archivists at the Lyndon Johnson Library in Austin were more than usually helpful, and I owe a particular debt to Allen Fisher. At Georgetown University, the Lauinger Library special collections staff generously allowed me to browse at will through the boxes of unprocessed McCarthy papers. I am also indebted to the staff of the John F. Kennedy Library in Boston; the Schlesinger Library at Radcliffe in Cambridge, Massachusetts; the Oral History Research Office at Columbia; the Mudd Memorial Library at Princeton; the St. Paul Public Library; the Library of Congress; and the University Libraries at Cambridge and Sheffield.

I am very grateful to the monks of St. John's Abbey for their openness and cooperation, particularly Abbot Timothy Kelly, Abbot John Eidenschink, Father Fran Hoefgen, Father Hilary Thimmesh, as well as Sister Arleen Hynes. I would also like to thank all my other interviewees, especially Carol Connolly, David Lebedoff and the late Abigail McCarthy and Blair Clark. Donald and Arvonne Fraser were good enough to allow me to examine their papers at the Minnesota Historical Society; Kay Bonner Nee allowed me to rummage through her old files; Mike Hazard sent me a copy of his documentary film of McCarthy; and Albert Eisele and Godfrey Hodgson were great sources of advice and addresses. I am also grateful to Norman Sherman for his long and thoughtful correspondence, and to Michael Rubino for his hospitality and his excellent tea.

On my return to England, Ann Holton kindly helped me to transcribe my interview tapes. My brother Alex also lent a hand with the transcriptions, although it would be fair to say that in his case the results were rarely predictable. A man who hears the words "the governor of Illinois—his name escapes me," and then writes "the governor of Illinois, Nallas Gazeby," is not, perhaps, the most reliable of assistants.

I have been extremely fortunate to benefit from the hospitality of many friends and colleagues, especially Simon Hall, Andrew and Fran Preston, Joe Guinan and Jennifer Cooper, Simon Hooper and Lauren Stewart, Kaele Stokes and James Davis, Nathan Bavidge and Vicky Scahill, and Edward Meek and Roger Moore. In Minnesota, Gayle and Wilson Yates were tremendously hospitable and made exceptional efforts on my behalf. Martin O'Neill, however, deserves special mention for putting me up for two weeks in his nightmarishly small room at Harvard. In January 2000 he accompanied Joe Guinan, Don Conklin and me on an expedition to New Hampshire for the presidential primary; our encounters with Senators Bill Bradley, Bob Kerrey and John McCain, not to mention Alan Keyes, Gary Bauer and various other implausible characters, will live long in the memory.

Working with Andrew Miller, my engaging and incisive editor at Knopf, has been particularly enjoyable. My thanks also go to his assistant, Amber Hoover, to the copy editors, designers and publicists, and to the publisher, Sonny Mehta, all of whom were enormously patient with their very naïve and awkward English author. And I am also grateful to my literary representatives, Andrew Wylie and Michal Shavit of the Wylie Agency.

By far my greatest debt, however, is to my parents. Before I began work on this biography, they had almost no interest in American political history and had certainly never heard of Eugene McCarthy. But they have nevertheless been unstinting sources of encouragement and support, and it is with immense gratitude that I dedicate this book to them.

NOTES

The following endnotes are provided for all the quotations and documentary references in the text, as well as for assertions of fact that are not common knowledge. The notes are generally gathered together at the end of each paragraph, but in the case of particularly lengthy quotations, I have placed a note immediately after the extract in question.

ABBREVIATIONS

AUST   Archives of the University of St. Thomas, St. Paul, Minn.
COL   Columbia University Oral History Research Office, New York City
DFL   Democratic-Farmer-Labor Party
EJM   Eugene McCarthy Papers
JFK   John F. Kennedy Presidential Library, Boston, Mass.
LBJ   Lyndon Baines Johnson Presidential Library, Austin, Texas
MHPA   McCarthy Historical Project Archive, Georgetown University, Washington, D.C.
MHS   Minnesota Historical Society, St. Paul, Minn.
SJU   St. John's Abbey and University Archives, Collegeville, Minn.

PROLOGUE

1. *New York Times,* 13 and 14 March 1968.

CHAPTER ONE
The Watkins Wonder

1. Larry McCaffrey to author, 21 January 2000; Albert Eisele, *Almost to the Presidency: A Biography of Two American Politicians* (Blue Earth, Minn.: 1972), pp. 28–31; Eugene McCarthy, unpublished, untitled, and undated manuscript beginning "The summers of 1932 and 1933," "Miscellaneous, 1977–1993," Box 3, Accession 15044, EJM, MHS; and "Two Grandfathers," in Eugene J. McCarthy, *Gene McCarthy's Minnesota Memories of a Native Son* (Minneapolis, 1982), p. 10; Eugene McCarthy to Thomas McCarthy, 8 November 1968, "Family history," Box 3, Accession 12758, Minnesota Historical Society, St. Paul. For anecdotes about McCarthy's grandparents, see McCarthy, "The summers of 1932 and 1933," "Miscellaneous, 1977–1993," Box 3, Accession 15044, EJM, MHS; and Abigail McCarthy, *Private Faces/Public Places* (Garden City, NY: 1972), pp. 42–43, 63–64. Eugene's maternal grandmother died before he was born, but he remembered his grandfather Chris Baden as a serious-minded

blacksmith "with German hands." See the poem "Two Grandfathers," in E. McCarthy, *Gene McCarthy's Minnesota*, p. 10; also McCarthy, "The summers of 1932 and 1933," "Miscellaneous, 1977–1993," Box 3, Accession 15044, EJM, MHS. On the Irish side, Mary Harbinson lived with the family in Watkins and died at the age of ninety-six, after Eugene had left college: see A. McCarthy, *Private Faces/Public Places*, pp. 42, 63; Eisele, *Almost to the Presidency*, p. 31. Michael McCarthy senior, however, also died before Eugene was born.

2. Eisele, *Almost to the Presidency*, p. 28; "Autobiography of Fr. Conan, OSB," unpublished manuscript written by Eugene McCarthy on entering the novitiate, 1942, in "Eugene McCarthy: Clippings," SJU; Eisele, *Almost to the Presidency*, p. 28; author interview with Mary Beth Yarrow, 27 April 2000, New York City; "Mother," in E. McCarthy, *Gene McCarthy's Minnesota*, p. 33; A. McCarthy, *Private Faces/Public Places*, pp. 42–43.

3. McCarthy, "Father," undated and unpublished manuscript, "Miscellaneous, 1977–1993," Box 3, Accession 15044, EJM, MHS; *New York Post*, 1 March 1968; Eisele, *Almost to the Presidency*, pp. 28–32; "Wisdom," in E. McCarthy, *Gene McCarthy's Minnesota*, p. 24; A. McCarthy, *Private Faces/Public Places*, p. 44. Anna died in 1945. Her husband lived to be ninety-seven and died in 1973, by which time his son was sufficiently famous for the news to be reported in the *New York Times*, 15 June 1973.

4. *New York Post*, 1 March 1968; E. J. McCarthy, "Watkins," in Frank B. Lamson, *Condensed History of Meeker County, 1855–1939* (n.p.: 1939), pp. 105–106; Patrick J. Casey, *The First Hundred Years: A History of Meeker County* (n.p.: 1968), p. 103; *Meeker County Memories* (Litchfield, Minn.: 1987), pp. 75–78; "Autobiography of Fr. Conan, OSB," in "Eugene McCarthy: Clippings," SJU; interview with Eugene McCarthy by Robert Rohlf, *Northern Lights and Insights* 268: *Eugene McCarthy*, video recording (Hennepin County, Minn.: 1993), Audio-Visual Collection, MHS; A. McCarthy, *Private Faces/Public Places*, p. 49; Eisele, *Almost to the Presidency*, p. 31.

5. Mary T. Hanna, *Catholics and American Politics* (Cambridge, Mass.: 1979), p. 86; *New Republic*, 8 June 1959; Charles R. Morris, *American Catholic: The Saints and Sinners Who Built America's Most Powerful Church* (New York: 1998), pp. 66–67; Philip Gleason, *Keeping the Faith: American Catholicism Past and Present* (Notre Dame, Ind.: 1987), p. 43; D. Jerome Tweton, *Depression: Minnesota in the Thirties* (Fargo, N. Dak.: 1981), p. 39; Casey, *The First Hundred Years*, pp. 142, 178; John H. Fenton, *Midwest Politics* (New York: 1966), p. 77; Daniel J. Elazar, Virginia Gray, and Wyman Spano, *Minnesota Politics and Government* (Lincoln, Neb.: 1999), p. 155; Lamson, *Condensed History of Meeker County*, pp. 137–138; Casey, *The First Hundred Years*, pp. 155–163.

6. *Hibbing Daily Tribune*, 4 March 1961, in "Scrapbook 8," Box 2, Accession 11455, EJM, MHS; "Clothes," in E. McCarthy, *Gene McCarthy's Minnesota*, p. 27; *New York Post*, 1 March 1968; "Ending," in McCarthy, *Gene McCarthy's Minnesota*, p. 32.

7. McCarthy, "A Town and Its People," undated and unpublished manuscript, "Miscellaneous, 1977–1993," Box 3, Accession 15044, EJM, MHS; Yarrow interview; *New York Post*, 1 March 1968; A. McCarthy, *Private Faces/Public Places*, p. 41; Eisele, *Almost to the Presidency*, pp. 27–30; E. McCarthy, *Gene McCarthy's Minnesota*, p. 35; McCarthy, "Autobiography of Fr. Conan, OSB," in "Eugene McCarthy: Clippings," SJU; McCarthy to Geoffrey Norman, 26 August 1977, "Newspapers and Magazine Articles," Box 2, Accession 13290, EJM, MHS; McCarthy, *Gene McCarthy's Minnesota*, pp. 60–73; *St. Paul Pioneer Press*, 12 July 1982; "The Day Time Began," in Eugene J. McCarthy, *Other Things and the Aardvark* (Garden City, N.Y.: 1970), pp. 46–49; "The Diagonal Dark Path," in Eugene J. McCarthy, *Ground Fog and Night: Poems* (New York: 1979), pp. 26–27; McCarthy to John K. Sherman, 30 October 1963, "General: Questionnaires, 1962–1963," Box 288, EJM, MHS; McCarthy, "The summers of 1932 and 1933," "Miscellaneous, 1977–1993," Box 3, Accession 15044, EJM, MHS; McCarthy, "Church and School," undated and unpublished manuscript, "Miscellaneous, 1977–1993," Box 3, Accession 15044, EJM, MHS.

8. *New York Post*, 1 March 1968; Eisele, *Almost to the Presidency*, p. 33; Eugene J. McCarthy,

untitled essay in Colman J. Barry and Robert L. Spaeth, eds., *A Sense of Place: St. John's of Collegeville* (Collegeville, Minn.: 1987), pp. 103–109; Colman J. Barry, *Worship and Work: St. John's Abbey and University, 1856–1980* (Collegeville, Minn.: 1980), pp. 25–55, 293–294; Vincent Tegeder, "The Benedictines in Frontier Minnesota," *Minnesota History* 32 (1951): 34–43; Dom David Knowles, *The Benedictines* (New York: 1930), p. 67; Dom Hubert van Zeller, *The Benedictine Idea* (Springfield, Ill.: 1959), passim.

9. Andrew M. Greeley, untitled essay in Barry and Spaeth, eds., *A Sense of Place*, p. 75; Emeric A. Lawrence, untitled essay in ibid., p. 124; Albert Eisele, untitled essay in ibid., pp. 45–46; A. McCarthy, *Private Faces/Public Places*, pp. 25–26; *St. John's Record*, 21 January 1988, SJU.

10. Author interview with Father Vincent Tegeder, 21 March 2000, St. John's Abbey, Collegeville, Minn.; Eisele, *Almost to the Presidency*, p. 34; Official Transcript of Eugene J. McCarthy, 30 August 1946, Confidential Employment File, AUST; *St. John's College Yearbook 1935*, p. 34, in "Clippings: Eugene McCarthy," SJU; "Confidential Employment Relating to Eugene J. McCarthy," Bureau of Recommendations, College of Education, University of Minnesota, undated, Confidential Employment File, AUST; *St. John's Record*, 15 June 1935, SJU; Father Dunstan Tucker to Ronda Stevens, 29 January 1970, in "Clippings: McCarthy, Eugene J.," SJU; "Father Dunstan Tucker," unpublished draft, fall 1974, "Newspapers and Magazines," Box 2, Accession 13290, EJM, MHS; McCarthy, "Education," undated and unpublished manuscript, "Miscellaneous, 1977–1993," Box 3, Accession 15044, EJM, MHS; Eisele, *Almost to the Presidency*, p. 34.

11. Father Dunstan Tucker to Ronda Stevens, 29 January 1970, "Clippings: McCarthy, Eugene J.," SJU; *New York Post*, 2 March 1968; Eisele, *Almost to the Presidency*, p. 35; E. McCarthy, *Gene McCarthy's Minnesota*, p. 69; A. McCarthy, *Private Faces/Public Places*, pp. 115–116; William M. Halsey, *The Survival of American Innocence: Catholicism in an Era of Disillusionment, 1920–1940* (Notre Dame, Ind.: 1980), pp. 169–170; *Let's Play Hockey*, 13 November 1987, in "Clippings: McCarthy, Eugene J.," SJU.

12. *St. John's College Yearbook, 1935*, p. 34, in "Clippings: Eugene McCarthy," SJU; Eisele, *Almost to the Presidency*, p. 34; A. McCarthy, *Private Faces/Public Places*, p. 68; McCarthy, "Autobiography of Fr. Conan, OSB," in "Clippings: Eugene McCarthy," SJU; *New York Post*, 1 March 1968; Father Dunstan Tucker to Ronda Stevens, 29 January 1970, "Clippings: McCarthy, Eugene J.," SJU; Tegeder interview.

13. Patrick Allitt, *Catholic Intellectuals and Conservative Politics in America* (Ithaca, N.Y.: 1993), p. 7; James Davison Hunter, *Culture Wars: The Struggle to Define America* (New York: 1991), pp. 69, 72; John T. McGreevy, *Parish Boundaries: The Catholic Encounter with Race in the Twentieth-Century Urban North* (Chicago: 1996), p. 5; Greg Tobin, "Introduction," in Greg Tobin, ed., *Saints and Sinners: The American Catholic Experience Through Stories, Memoirs, Essays, and Commentary* (New York: 1999), p. xv; Morris, *American Catholic*, pp. 160–164; ibid., p. 174.

14. Morris, *American Catholic*, p. 158; Robert A. Slayton, *Empire Statesman: The Rise and Redemption of Al Smith* (New York: 2000); A. McCarthy, *Private Faces/Public Places*, p. 100; Halsey, *Survival of American Innocence*, pp. 2, 11, 138–168; John Macquarrie, *Twentieth Century Religious Thought* (London: 1963), pp. 278–299; David O'Brien, *American Catholics and Social Reform: The New Deal Years* (New York: 1968), p. 7; James Terence Fisher, *The Catholic Counterculture in America, 1933–1962* (Chapel Hill, N.C.: 1989), p. 105; Gleason, *Keeping the Faith*, pp. 23–26, 140.

15. John M. Mulder, "Eugene McCarthy and His Theology of Civil Religion," *Dimension: Theology in Church and World* (Fall 1968): 108–125, in "Articles on McCarthy," Box 2, Accession 12758, EJM, MHS; Eugene J. McCarthy, *Frontiers in American Democracy* (Cleveland: 1960), p. 23. Interestingly, McCarthy's closest friend in the Senate, Philip Hart, had also been educated in the scholastic style, by Jesuits in his case, and showed similar signs of personal moderation, reserve, and intellectualism. See Michael O'Brien, *Philip Hart: The Conscience of the Senate* (East Lansing, Mich.: 1995), p. 12.

16. Paul B. Marx, *Virgil Michel and the Liturgical Movement* (Collegeville, Minn.: 1957), pp. 49–105, 186; R. W. Franklin and Robert L. Spaeth, *Virgil Michel: American Catholic* (Collegeville, Minn.: 1980), p. 20. On the personalist writers Emmanuel Mounier, Léon Bloy, Jacques Maritain, Charles Péguy, and Henri Bergson, see Joseph Amato, *Mounier and Maritain: A French Catholic Understanding of the Modern World* (University, Ala.: 1975), esp. pp. 1–12; Fisher, *Catholic Counterculture,* pp. 44–46; Kenneth L. Grasso, "Beyond Liberalism: Human Dignity, the Free Society, and the Second Vatican Council," in Kenneth L. Grasso, Gerard V. Bradley, and Robert P. Hunt, eds., *Catholicism, Liberalism, and Communitarianism: The Catholic Intellectual Tradition and the Moral Foundations of Democracy* (Lanham, Md.: 1995), pp. 29–58; and Christopher Wolfe, "Subsidiarity: The 'Other' Ground of Limited Government," in Grasso et al., eds., *Catholicism, Liberalism, and Communitarianism,* pp. 81–96.

17. McGreevy, *Parish Boundaries,* p. 24; John W. Cooper, *The Theology of Freedom: The Legacy of Jacques Maritain and Reinhold Niebuhr* (Macon, Ga.: 1985), p. 10; Mary M. Keys, "Personal Dignity and the Common Good: A Twentieth-Century Thomistic Dialogue," in Grasso et al., eds., *Catholicism, Liberalism, and Communitarianism,* p. 187; Morris, *American Catholic,* pp. 149–152; Gleason, *Keeping the Faith,* p. 22; Alan Brinkley, *Voices of Protest: Huey Long, Father Coughlin, and the Great Depression* (New York: 1982), pp. 87, 129–130; Robert Booth Fowler, *Enduring Liberalism: American Political Thought Since the 1960s* (Lawrence, Kans.: 1999), p. 240; D. O'Brien, *American Catholics and Social Reform,* pp. 13–18; Michael Kazin, *The Populist Persuasion: An American History* (New York: 1995), pp. 116–117, 126; Hunter, *Culture Wars,* p. 79; McGreevy, *Parish Boundaries,* p. 43.

18. Fisher, *Catholic Counterculture,* pp. 75–76; D. O'Brien, *American Catholics and Social Reform,* pp. 41, 51, 104, 121–122, 140; A. James Reichley, *Religion in American Public Life* (Washington, D.C.: 1985), p. 220; George Q. Flynn, *American Catholics and the Roosevelt Presidency, 1932–1936* (Lexington, Ky.: 1968), pp. 17–19, 42–51, 89; Allitt, *Catholic Intellectuals and Conservative Politics,* p. 32.

19. *Commonweal,* 29 April 1938; Marx, *Virgil Michel,* p. 66, 178–179, 244, 304–312, 368; Franklin and Spaeth, *Virgil Michel: American Catholic,* pp. 10–11, 20, 35, 109; O'Brien, *American Catholics and Social Reform,* pp. 190–191; author interview with Father Hilary Thimmesh, 15 March 2000, St. John's Abbey, Minn.; Lawrence essay in Barry and Spaeth, eds., *A Sense of Place,* p. 121; A. McCarthy, *Private Faces/Public Places,* p. 98; McCarthy essay in Barry and Spaeth, eds., *A Sense of Place,* p. 105. On the Catholic Worker movement, see Fisher, *Catholic Counterculture,* pp. 1–41; Marx, *Virgil Michel,* pp. 177, 375; McGreevy, *Parish Boundaries,* p. 65; Morris, *American Catholic,* pp. 143–144; Tobin, "Introduction," in Tobin, ed., *Saints and Sinners,* pp. 4–5; William A. Au, *The Cross, the Flag, and the Bomb: American Catholics Debate War and Peace, 1960–1985* (Westport, Conn.: 1985), pp. 19–22; Charles A. Meconis, *With Clumsy Grace: The American Catholic Left, 1961–1975* (New York: 1979), pp. 1–16.

20. Author interview with Father Godfrey Diekmann, St. John's Abbey, Minn., 16 March 2000; Tegeder interview; A. McCarthy, *Private Faces/Public Places,* pp. 68–70; Franklin and Spaeth, *Virgil Michel: American Catholic,* p. 146; Lawrence essay in Barry and Spaeth, eds., *A Sense of Place,* p. 121; Eisele, *Almost to the Presidency,* p. 34; *New York Post,* 2 March 1968; transcript of interview with Eugene McCarthy, by R. W. Franklin, 14 April 1982, in "Eugene McCarthy: Clippings," SJU; McCarthy essay in Barry and Spaeth, eds., *A Sense of Place,* pp. 104–106.

21. *Commonweal,* 23 February 1968; Commencement Address at Mount St. Scholastica College, undated 1950, "McCarthy Speeches 1950–1955," Box 12, Accession 12240, EJM, MHS; *New York Times,* 30 August 1968.

22. McCarthy was paid an annual salary of $900 in Tintah, $1,100 in Kimball, and $1,800 in Mandan: see McCarthy, "Autobiography of Fr. Conan, OSB," in "Eugene McCarthy: Clippings," SJU.

23. "Confidential Employment Relating to Eugene J. McCarthy," Bureau of Recommendations, College of Education, University of Minnesota, undated, Confidential Employment File,

AUST; Faculty Record, St. Thomas College, 12 April 1947, Confidential Employment File, AUST; Eisele, *Almost to the Presidency,* pp. 36–37.

24. A. McCarthy, *Private Faces/Public Places,* pp. 8–15, 20, 31; interview in *Good Housekeeping,* August 1968, in "Articles on McCarthy," Box 2, Accession 12758, EJM, MHS.

25. Eisele, *Almost to the Presidency,* p. 38; A. McCarthy, *Private Faces/Public Places,* pp. 37–40, 65–66, 72–73.

26. Father Dunstan Tucker to Ronda Stevens, 29 January 1970, in "Clippings: McCarthy, Eugene J.," SJU. McCarthy's record as a hockey coach was the worst in the history of the university: the team won only one of its seven games.

CHAPTER TWO

The Education of a Catholic Politician

1. A. McCarthy, *Private Faces/Public Places,* pp. 54, 38.

2. A. McCarthy, *Private Faces/Public Places,* pp. 57, 75, 94–96, 79–80.

3. *New York Post,* 1 March 1968; author interview with Father Virgil O'Neill, 15 March 2000, St. John's Abbey, Minn.; Thimmesh interview; McCarthy, "Autobiography of Fr. Conan, OSB," in "Eugene McCarthy: Clippings," SJU; author interview with Father Gunther Rolfson, 16 March 2000, St. John's Abbey, Minn.

4. Simeon J. Thole, untitled essay, in Barry and Spaeth, eds., *A Sense of Place,* pp. 245–249; Rolfson and O'Neill interviews; James Patrick Shannon, *Reluctant Dissenter: An Autobiography* (New York: 1998), p. 31; Basil Stegmann, *The Benedictines* (Collegeville, Minn.: 1943), pp. 7–8.

5. Diekmann, O'Neill, and Rolfson interviews; Alpha Smaby, *Political Upheaval: Minnesota and the Vietnam War Protest* (Minneapolis: 1987), p. 426.

6. A. McCarthy, *Private Faces/Public Places,* pp. 92, 96; Eisele, *Almost to the Presidency,* pp. 39–40.

7. McCarthy never wrote about his brief stint in Washington, and it evidently had little influence upon him. Perhaps more significantly, his mother died in the spring of 1945, and this may have freed him to marry Abigail: see A. McCarthy, *Private Faces/Public Places,* pp. 87, 102–103, 107; Eisele, *Almost to the Presidency,* pp. 40–41; author interview with Sister Arleen Hynes, 15 March 2000, St. John's Abbey, Minn.; Thimmesh interview; Arno A. Gustin, untitled essay in Colman J. Barry, ed., *A Sense of Place II: The Benedictines of Collegeville* (Collegeville, Minn.: 1990), p. 87; *Commonweal,* 21 October 1938; Betty Wahl Powers, untitled essay in Barry and Spaeth, eds., *A Sense of Place,* pp. 131–133. Her husband, the novelist J. F. Powers, was another leading member of this circle and knew the McCarthys well. See the novels of J. F. Powers, *Morte D'Urban* (New York: 1962) and *Wheat That Springeth Green* (New York: 1988).

8. A. McCarthy, *Private Faces/Public Places,* p. 40; Amato, *Mounier and Maritain,* p. 130; Halsey, *Survival of American Innocence,* p. 64; Hynes interview; Barry, *Worship and Work,* p. 288; Fisher, *The Catholic Counterculture,* pp. 92, 41–42; Robert L. Dorman, *The Revolt of the Provinces: The Regionalist Movement in America, 1920–1945* (Chapel Hill, N.C.: 1993), pp. 107–109; A. McCarthy, *Private Faces/Public Places,* pp. 109–110; Willis Nutting, *Reclamation of Independence* (Nevada City, Calif.: 1947). In the South, meanwhile, cultural and political objections to modernism were being similarly reflected in the Southern Agrarian movement and the work of writers such as Allen Tate and Donald Davidson: see Christopher Lasch, *The New Radicalism in America, 1889–1963: The Intellectual as a Social Type* (New York: 1963), p. 297; Allen Guttman, *The Conservative Tradition in America* (New York: 1967), pp. 148–157.

9. A. McCarthy, *Private Faces/Public Places,* pp. 108–111, 117–118, 125; Hynes interview; *New York Post,* 1 March 1968; *Land and Home,* September 1947; A. McCarthy, *Private Faces/ Public Places,* pp. 131–132.

10. William Cofell, untitled essay in Barry and Spaeth, eds., *A Sense of Place,* p. 19; *St. John's Record,* 29 June 1964, SJU; *St. John's Magazine,* Winter 1988, SJU; "President's Medal Presentation" file, Box 8, Accession 15044, EJM, MHS; Eugene J. McCarthy, *Required Reading: A Decade of Political Wit and Wisdom* (New York: 1988), pp. 136–137; author interview with Michael Rubino, 12 May 2000, Bethesda, Md.; *The Voice of St. Jude,* January 1952, in "Magazine Articles About McCarthy, 1949–1956," Public Relations Files, Box 275, EJM, MHS; Terrance A. Sweeney, *God and . . .* (Minneapolis: 1985), pp. 58, 60; David Frost, *The Presidential Debate, 1968* (New York: 1968), p. 36.

11. *Catholic Bulletin,* 25 November 1960, in "Scrapbook 7," Box 2, Accession 11455, EJM, MHS; *The Wanderer,* 11 July 1985, in "Clippings: McCarthy, Eugene J.," SJU; A. McCarthy, *Private Faces/Public Places,* pp. 81, 177; "Statement on Abortion," 2 April 1976, "Issues: 1972, 1976," Box 7, Accession 15044, EJM, MHS; *Los Angeles Times,* 20 September 1976; Eugene Kennedy, *Believing* (Garden City, N.Y.: 1974), pp. 103–105; *St. Cloud Times,* 13 July 1988, in "Clippings: McCarthy, Eugene J.," SJU.

12. Garry Wills, "Memories of a Catholic Boyhood," in Tobin, ed., *Saints and Sinners,* p. 229; oral history interview of Edmund G. Brown Jr. by unspecified interviewer, 11 August 1969, Oral History Collection, MHPA, pp. 13–15.

13. Halsey, *Survival of American Innocence,* p. 122; Wilfrid Sheed, "Eugene McCarthy: The Politician as Professor," *New American Review* 5 (January 1969): 162, in "Articles on McCarthy, 1968–1969," Box 3, Accession 12758, EJM, MHS; Garry Wills, *The Kennedy Imprisonment* (Boston: 1981), pp. 100–101; Diekmann interview; *New York Times Magazine,* 10 December 1967; Alberic Culhane, untitled essay, in Barry, ed., *A Sense of Place II,* p. 41; *Washington Star,* 3 December 1967; Eugene J. McCarthy, *Complexities and Contraries: Essays of Mild Discontent* (New York: 1982), p. xi.

14. McGreevy, *Parish Boundaries,* pp. 68–83, 85; Lawrence H. Fuchs, *John F. Kennedy and American Catholicism* (New York: 1967), p. 151; Hanna, *Catholics and American Politics,* p. 210; *Today* 4:7 (April 1949), in "Scrapbook 1," Box 1, Accession 11455, EJM, MHS; *Davenport Witness,* 5 June 1958, in "Political: McCarthy, Articles About," Box 263, EJM, MHS.

15. Francis Canavan, "The Image of Man in Catholic Thought," in Grasso et al., eds., *Catholicism, Liberalism, and Communitarianism,* p. 17; A. McCarthy, *Private Faces/Public Places,* pp. 199–201; Address to the National Newman Club Federation Convention, 3 September 1955, "Political: McCarthy Speeches," Box 263, EJM, MHS; *St. Cloud Times,* 26 July 1988, in "Eugene McCarthy: Clippings," SJU; Eugene McCarthy, "The Christian in Politics," 1954, reprinted in Patrick Jordan and Paul Baumann, eds., Commonweal *Confronts the Century: Liberal Convictions, Catholic Tradition* (New York: 1999), pp. 63–66. Note that both here and elsewhere, McCarthy used the words "Catholic" and "Christian" as synonyms. Indeed, he often reused articles and speeches, merely substituting one word for the other depending on the intended audience.

16. *Catholic Times,* 28 March 1952, in "Scrapbook 1," Box 1, Accession 11455, EJM, MHS; *New Republic,* 8 June 1959; *Catholic Messenger,* 27 November 1958, in "McCarthy, Senator Eugene: Clippings," AUST; Statement for inclusion in *Catholic Register,* Eugene McCarthy to John B. Ebel, 22 December 1961, "General: Articles, 1959–1963," Box 303, EJM, MHS.

17. *New York Times,* 13 June 1960; Eugene McCarthy, "The Christian in Politics," in Jordan and Baumann, eds., Commonweal *Confronts the Century,* p. 66.

18. A. McCarthy, *Private Faces/Public Places,* p. 67; Eugene J. McCarthy, "The Intellectual's Place in American Government," *Texas Quarterly,* Winter 1965, pp. 117–124, in "General: Articles, undated," Box 303, EJM, MHS; *Commonweal,* 18 May 1961; Address to Loretta Heights College Conference, 6 March 1956, "Political: Demands of Democracy," Box 264, EJM, MHS; *Commonweal,* 7 November 1952. McCarthy contrasted the papal idea of a welfare state with what he saw as Eisenhower's stolid passivity in the late 1950s: see *New York Times,* 19 October 1959.

19. Sheed, "Eugene McCarthy," pp. 159–160; Peter Steinfels, "Introduction," in Jordan and Bau-

mann, eds., Commonweal *Confronts the Century,* pp. 15–29; Morris, *American Catholic,* pp. 278–279; Garry Wills, *Bare Ruined Choirs: Doubt, Prophecy, and Radical Religion* (Garden City, N.Y.: 1972), pp. 39–60. Wills noted that the *Commonweal* Catholic often thought of himself as above the ordinary pieties of the local parish and would slip off at weekends to some monastery or other (the example he gives is St. John's) for intellectual and spiritual stimulation. He would be doggedly anti-bourgeois and anti-modern, as Wills put it, "the voice of a theological Dwight Macdonald, at war with spiritual Mid-Cult": pp. 39–40.

20. Commencement Address at Mount St. Scholastica College, undated 1950, "McCarthy Speeches, 1950–1955," Box 12, Accession 12240, EJM, MHS; *Catholic Times,* 28 March 1952, in "Scrapbook 1," Box 1, Accession 11455, EJM, MHS; E. McCarthy, *Complexities and Contraries,* dedication.

21 Fred Hughes, untitled essay in Barry and Spaeth, eds., *A Sense of Place,* pp. 96–99; Wills, *Bare Ruined Choirs,* p. 20; Halsey, *Survival of American Innocence,* pp. 66–70; McGreevy, *Parish Boundaries,* p. 43; Gleason, *Keeping the Faith,* pp. 13–20, 22; Au, *The Cross, the Flag, and the Bomb,* pp. 10–11. McCarthy's best man, Emerson Hynes, wrote an article for *Commonweal* in 1948 on "Religion and Capitalism" that explicitly drew on Tawney's manifesto *Religion and the Rise of Capitalism* (London: 1926). See *Commonweal,* 23 January 1948.

22. George H. Nash, *The Conservative Intellectual Movement in America Since 1945* (New York: 1976), pp. 49–80; E. J. Dionne, *Why Americans Hate Politics* (New York: 1992), pp. 154–155; *Catholic Times,* 28 March 1952, in "Scrapbook 1," Box 1, Accession 11455, EJM, MHS; James P. Young, *Reconsidering Liberalism: The Troubled Odyssey of the Liberal Idea* (Boulder, Colo.: 1996), pp. 235–236; Guttman, *Conservative Tradition in America,* pp. 39, 175.

23. Frost, *Presidential Debate, 1968,* p. 31; text of NBC radio address, "The Political Life of American Catholics," 21 August 1960, "Political: Minnesota, Economy, Employment," Box 263, EJM, MHS; McCarthy, *Up 'til Now,* p. xii; McCarthy interview on CBS *Nightwatch,* 23 April 1987, recording in Box 8, Accession 15044, EJM, MHS; *Commonweal,* 1 October 1954; address to the Blessed Sacrament Sodality, Washington, D.C., 3 April 1957, "Political: McCarthy Speeches and Remarks on Floor," Box 263, EJM, MHS.

24. Cooper, *Theology of Freedom,* p. 34; *America,* 11 April 1959, in "Political: Speeches and Releases, 1959–1969," Box 13, Accession 11455, EJM, MHS; McCarthy to Scott Donaldson, 4 June 1963, "Political: Comments, General, 1963," Box 272, EJM, MHS.

25. Address at St. Olaf College, Northfield, Minn., 3 October 1957, "Political: McCarthy Speeches and Remarks on Floor," Box 263, EJM, MHS; Young, *Reconsidering American Liberalism,* p. 135.

26. For "the moral critique," see Cooper, *Theology of Freedom,* p. 166. For Maritain, see John M. Dunaway, *Jacques Maritain* (Boston: 1978), pp. 65, 86; Cooper, *The Theology of Freedom,* pp. 34–39. See also Amato, *Mounier and Maritain,* pp. 62, 135–138; Gleason, *Keeping the Faith,* p. 13; Kenneth L. Grasso, "Catholic Social Thought and the Quest for an American Public Philosophy," in Grasso et al., eds., *Catholicism, Liberalism, and Communitarianism,* pp. 1–14; Michelle Watkins and Ralph McInerny, "Jacques Maritain and the Rapprochement of Liberalism and Communitarianism," in Grasso et al., eds., *Catholicism, Liberalism, and Communitarianism,* pp. 151–172. For Niebuhr, see Ronald H. Stone, *Reinhold Niebuhr: Prophet to Politicians* (Nashville, Tenn.: 1972), pp. 84–173; Fowler, *Enduring Liberalism,* p. 24; Richard Pells, *The Liberal Mind in a Conservative Age: American Intellectuals in the 1940s and 1950s,* 2nd ed. (Middletown, Conn.: 1985), p. 136; Mary McAuliffe, *Crisis on the Left: Cold War Politics and American Liberals, 1947–1954* (Amherst, Mass.: 1978), p. 65.

27. While McCarthy did not agree with most neoconservatives on matters of policy, he certainly shared their faith in order and tradition, as well as their contempt for Jimmy Carter and much of the remaining liberal wing of the Democratic Party: see Peter Steinfels, *The Neoconservatives* (New York: 1979), p. 70; John Ehrman, *The Rise of Neoconservatism: Intellectuals and Foreign Affairs, 1945–1994* (New Haven, Conn.: 1995), pp. 4–8.

28. David O'Brien, *The Renewal of American Catholicism* (New York: 1972), pp. 178–181; "Senator Eugene McCarthy Reports," 22 September 1961, "Public Relations: Newsletters," Box

277, EJM, MHS. Eduardo Frei was the president of Chile from 1964 to 1970. Radomiro Tomic was the Christian Democratic candidate against Salvador Allende in 1970. Abigail McCarthy subsequently wrote: "It was easy to fall into discussions with the Christian Democrats. They had the same questions we had long asked about capitalism and the technological revolution which had enriched many but left the poor poorer than ever. They had the same interests in the distribution of land and wealth and the necessity for the restructuring of society." See A. McCarthy, *Private Faces/Public Places*, pp. 248, 252. On Trudeau, see the brief essay in Michael Bliss, *Right Honorable Men: The Descent of Canadian Politics from Macdonald to Mulroney* (Toronto: 1995), pp. 245–275.

29. A. McCarthy, *Private Faces/Public Places*, pp. 131–132.

CHAPTER THREE

The New Liberalism and the 1948 Election

1. *The Aquin*, 20 September 1946, AUST; A. McCarthy, *Private Faces/Public Places*, pp. 131–132; Eisele, *Almost to the Presidency*, p. 41; undated memorandum, Eugene J. McCarthy Confidential Employment File, AUST. McCarthy's application and contract details are in "Confidential Information Relating to Eugene J. McCarthy," Bureau of Recommendations, College of Education, University of Minnesota, undated, Eugene J. McCarthy Confidential Employment File, AUST; *Harper's Magazine*, June 1964.

2. Eisele, *Almost to the Presidency*, pp. 72–74; Ward M. Winton, "Eugene McCarthy: His Years at the College of St. Thomas," unpublished manuscript, undated, in "Miscellaneous, 1969–1971," Box 5, Accession 15044, EJM, MHS, p. 7; A. McCarthy, *Private Faces/Public Places*, p. 138; *Harper's Magazine*, June 1964.

3. *Catholic Youth*, September 1947; A. McCarthy, *Private Faces/Public Places*, p. 147.

4. Virginia Brainard Kunz, *St. Paul: Saga of an American City* (Woodland Hills, Calif.: 1977), pp. 161–163; Barbara Stuhler, *Ten Men of Minnesota and American Foreign Policy, 1898–1968* (St. Paul, Minn.: 1973), p. 195; Eisele, *Almost to the Presidency*, p. 71; Kunz, *St. Paul*, pp. 174, 180–182; McCarthy, *Up 'til Now*, p. 8.

5. Eisele, *Almost to the Presidency*, p. 48; Millard L. Gieske, *Minnesota Farmer-Laborism* (Minneapolis: 1979), pp. 3–4, 20; John H. Fenton, *Midwest Politics* (New York: 1966), pp. 84–85; Tweton, *Depression*, p. 51; G. Theodore Mitau, *Politics in Minnesota* (Minneapolis: 1961), pp. 13–15; Laura K. Auerbach, *Worthy to Be Remembered: A Political History of the Minnesota Democratic-Farmer-Labor Party, 1944–1984* (Minneapolis: 1984), pp. 13–20. See also Arthur Naftalin, "A History of the Minnesota Farmer-Labor Party," unpublished Ph.D. dissertation, University of Minnesota, 1948, although it is excessively partisan. There were also parallels with the Canadian Cooperative Commonwealth Federation: see Alan Whitehorn, *Canadian Socialism: Essays on the CCF-NDP* (Toronto: 1992). For two different views of the socialist tendencies of the Farmer-Labor movement, see Carl Solberg, *Hubert Humphrey: A Biography* (New York: 1984), p. 80; David Plotke, *Building a Democratic Political Order: Reshaping American Liberalism in the 1930s and 1940s* (Cambridge, U.K.: 1996), p. 175.

6. Gieske, *Minnesota Farmer-Laborism*, pp. 16–20; Elazar, et al., *Minnesota Politics and Government*, pp. 7, 15; Hubert H. Humphrey; *The Education of a Public Man* (London: 1976), p. 69; John Earl Haynes, *Dubious Alliance: The Making of Minnesota's DFL Party* (Minneapolis: 1984), pp. 3–4; G. Theodore Mitau, "The Democratic-Farmer-Labor Party Schism of 1948," *Minnesota History* (Spring 1955), 187–188; Haynes, *Dubious Alliance*, p. 15; Gieske, *Minnesota Farmer-Laborism*, pp. 234–235.

7. Auerbach, *Worthy to Be Remembered*, p. 27; Fenton, *Midwest Politics*, p. 77; Gieske, *Minnesota Farmer-Laborism*, p. 16; Haynes, *Dubious Alliance*, p. 43; John A. Edie, "The Split in the Minnesota Democratic Farmer-Labor Party, 1946 to 1948," unpublished B.A. thesis, Princeton University, 1980, p. 15; Elazar et al., *Minnesota Politics and Government*, pp. 24, 155.

8. Eisele, *Almost to the Presidency*, pp. 71–72; Haynes, *Dubious Alliance*, p. 54; author interview

with Jane Freeman, 7 March 2000, Minneapolis; Haynes, *Dubious Alliance,* pp. 31–32, 38; Gieske, *Minnesota Farmer-Laborism,* p. 287; oral history interview of G. Theodore Mitau, by Arthur Naftalin, 22 August 1978, Minneapolis, Hubert H. Humphrey Oral History Project, MHS, p. 12.

9. Haynes, *Dubious Alliance,* pp. 44, 113; Naftalin, "A History of the Farmer-Labor Party," p. 382; Edie, "The Split in the Minnesota DFL," p. 20; Fenton, *Midwest Politics,* p. 90; Humphrey, *Education of a Public Man,* p. 84; Mitau, "The Democratic-Farmer-Labor Party Schism of 1948," pp. 187–194.

10. Haynes, *Dubious Alliance,* pp. 117, 142; John Earl Haynes, "Liberals, Communists, and the Popular Front in Minnesota: The Struggle to Control the Political Direction of the Labor Movement and Organized Liberalism," unpublished Ph.D. dissertation, University of Minnesota, 1978, p. 421.

11. Plotke, *Building a Democratic Political Order,* p. 329; Seymour Martin Lipset and Gary Marks, *It Didn't Happen Here: Why Socialism Failed in the United States* (New York: 2000), pp. 219–235; Tweton, *Depression,* p. 69; Haynes, *Dubious Alliance,* p. 36; Eisele, *Almost to the Presidency,* p. 77; author interview with William Kubicek, 20 January 2000, Minneapolis; Naftalin, "History of the Farmer-Labor Party," p. 347.

12. Auerbach, *Worthy to Be Remembered,* p. 25; Humphrey, *Education of a Public Man,* p. 104. Both Elmer Benson and John M. Jacobson, the director of the regional CIO Political Action Committee, agreed in later interviews that Communists were working alongside them, but maintained that they were only one small, often ineffectual element: see Edie, "The Split in the Minnesota DFL," pp. 33–35.

13. Haynes, *Dubious Alliance,* pp. 6, 156, 162; Sean J. Savage, *Truman and the Democratic Party* (Lexington, Ky.: 1997), pp. 47–48.

14. See J. Freeman interview; oral history interview of Orville Freeman, by Arthur Naftalin, 16 January 1978, Minneapolis; Eisele, *Almost to the Presidency,* pp. 49–60; Humphrey, *Education of a Public Man,* pp. 59–104; Solberg, *Hubert Humphrey,* pp. 87–123; Author interview with Gerald Heaney, 4 March 2000, St. Paul; Mitau oral history, p. 9. Both Humphrey and Mondale served as vice president and were unsuccessful nominees of the Democratic Party for president. Freeman became governor of Minnesota and was secretary of agriculture from 1961 to 1969. Fraser, a congressman and later mayor of Minneapolis, chaired the much-maligned Democratic Party reform commission in the early 1970s and rewrote the rules and constitution of the national party.

15. Humphrey, *Education of a Public Man,* p. 76; J. Freeman interview; Kubicek interview; typescript of interview with Gerald Heaney, by Arthur Herzog, undated, Folder 8, Part 1, Box 50, National Files, MHPA; Elazar et al., *Minnesota Politics and Government,* p. 20; Fenton, *Midwest Politics,* pp. 87–88; Steven M. Gillon, *Politics and Vision: The ADA and American Liberalism, 1947–1985* (Oxford: 1987), p. ix; James Q. Wilson, *The Amateur Democrat: Club Politics in Three Cities* (Chicago: 1966), especially pp. 13 ff. Humphrey was popular with black voters because of his vociferous support for civil rights: see Jennifer A. Delton, *Making Minnesota Liberal: Civil Rights and the Transformation of the Democratic Party* (Minneapolis: 2002).

16. Freeman interview; Humphrey, *Education of a Public Man,* pp. 75–76, 108; Orville Freeman oral history, pp. 1–2; Mitau oral history, p. 14; Frasers interview; Kubicek interview; Heaney interview; oral history interview of Jack Jorgenson, by Arthur Naftalin, 1 August 1978, Hubert H. Humphrey Oral History Project, MHS, p. 10.

17. Freeman, Frasers, and Kubicek interviews; Haynes, *Dubious Alliance,* p. 164.

18. Nye, *Midwestern Progressive Politics,* p. 306; Steven M. Gillon, *The Democrats' Dilemma: Walter F. Mondale and the Liberal Legacy* (New York: 1992), p. 49; Haynes, "Liberals, Communists, and the Popular Front," p. 858; Fenton, *Midwest Politics,* p. 91; Gary Paul Hendrickson, "Minnesota in the McCarthy Period, 1946–1954," unpublished Ph.D. dissertation, University of Minnesota, 1981, pp. 91, 96.

19. Typescript of Heaney interview, Folder 8, Part 1, Box 50, National Files, MHPA; oral history of Gerald Heaney, by Arthur Naftalin, 11 August 1978, Duluth, Hubert H. Humphrey Oral History Project, MHS, p. 9; Frasers interview; J. Freeman interview; oral history interview of Eugenie Anderson, by Arthur Naftalin, 14 July 1978, Hubert H. Humphrey Oral History Project, MHS, p. 53; Haynes, "Liberals, Communists, and the Popular Front," pp. 478, 485; Herbert S. Parmet, *The Democrats: The Years After FDR* (New York: 1976), p. 74.

20. Gillon, *Politics and Vision,* pp. 12–16; McAuliffe, *Crisis on the Left,* pp. 5–8; Haynes, *Dubious Alliance,* pp. 139, 151; Eisele, *Almost to the Presidency,* p. 64; Humphrey, *Education of a Public Man,* p. 108; Solberg, *Hubert Humphrey,* p. 117; E. Anderson oral history, p. 46.

21. Hendrickson, "Minnesota in the McCarthy Period," p. 100; McAuliffe, *Crisis on the Left,* pp. 7, 11–12; Edie, "The Split in the Minnesota DFL," p. 45; Mitau oral history, p. 9; Hendrickson, "Minnesota in the McCarthy Period," p. 105; Auerbach, *Worthy to Be Remembered,* p. 32.

22. A. McCarthy, *Private Faces/Public Places,* p. 151; Eisele, *Almost to the Presidency,* pp. 72, 75; A. McCarthy, *Private Faces/Public Places,* p. 139; E. McCarthy, *Up 'til Now,* p. 4; *Harper's Magazine,* June 1964; Ward M. Winton, "Eugene McCarthy: His Years at the College of St. Thomas," pp. 1–4, in "Miscellaneous, 1969–1971," Box 5, Accession 15044, EJM, MHS; A. McCarthy, *Private Faces/Public Places,* pp. 139, 142; E. McCarthy, *Frontiers in American Democracy,* p. 110. Rommen was one of the most important Catholic intellectual exiles teaching in the United States in the 1940s: his works include *The Natural Law: A Study in Legal and Social History and Philosophy* (reprint, Indianapolis: 1998); and *The State in Catholic Thought* (St. Louis: 1945).

23. Eisele, *Almost to the Presidency,* pp. 76, 74; A. McCarthy, *Private Faces/Public Places,* p. 141.

24. Eisele, *Almost to the Presidency,* p. 74; A. McCarthy, *Private Faces/Public Places,* pp. 150–151. Before his death in 1967, Rommen told friends he had been disappointed by McCarthy's performance in the Senate and by his protégé's books: see Eisele, *Almost to the Presidency,* p. 76.

25. Hynes interview; *Ave Maria Catholic Home Weekly,* 13 December 1958, pp. 5–10, in "Articles by McCarthy," Box 1, Accession 12758, EJM, MHS; McCarthy, *Up 'til Now,* p. 5.

26. A. McCarthy, *Private Faces/Public Places,* p. 139; E. McCarthy, *Frontiers in American Democracy,* pp. 28, 37, 57.

27. Gillon, *Democrats' Dilemma,* p. 78; Donald F. Crosby, *God, Church, and Flag: Senator Joseph McCarthy and the Catholic Church, 1950–1957* (Chapel Hill, N.C.: 1978), p. xii.

28. E. McCarthy, *Up 'til Now,* p. 42; A. McCarthy, *Private Faces/Public Places,* p. 145; *Today Magazine,* April 1949, pp. 3–4, in "Scrapbook 1, 1948–50," Box 1, Accession 11455, EJM, MHS.

29. Marx, *Virgil Michel and the Liturgical Movement,* pp. 66, 375; Crosby, *God, Church, and Flag,* esp. pp. 1–24; Kazin, *Populist Persuasion,* pp. 137–154; Allen Yarnell, *Democrats and Progressives: The 1948 Presidential Election as a Test of Postwar Liberalism* (Berkeley, Calif.: 1974), p. 109.

30. Haynes, *Dubious Alliance,* pp. 155–157, 186; A. McCarthy, *Private Faces/Public Places,* p. 140; Mitau oral history, p. 10; *St. Paul Pioneer Press,* 9 August 1947.

31. A. McCarthy, *Private Faces/Public Places,* p. 145; *Harper's Magazine,* June 1964; Eisele, *Almost to the Presidency,* pp. 65, 72–73; J. Freeman interview.

32. Haynes, *Dubious Alliance,* p. 117.

33. A. McCarthy, *Private Faces/Public Places,* p. 145; Eisele, *Almost to the Presidency,* p. 73; Haynes, *Dubious Alliance,* pp. 165–166; Haynes, "Liberals, Communists, and the Popular Front," pp. 508–509; *Harper's Magazine,* June 1964.

34. Haynes, *Dubious Alliance,* p. 147; Haynes, "Liberals, Communists, and the Popular Front," pp. 446–447, 458.

35. A. McCarthy, *Private Faces/Public Places,* p. 145; *St. Paul Pioneer Press,* 2 May 1948; Haynes, *Dubious Alliance,* p. 186; Haynes, "Liberals, Communists, and the Popular Front," pp. 600–601; Eisele, *Almost to the Presidency,* pp. 76–77; A. McCarthy, *Private Faces/Public Places,* pp. 148–149; Mitau, "The Democratic-Farmer-Labor Party Schism," p. 191; Hen-

drickson, "Minnesota in the McCarthy Period," pp. 96, 100; Edie, "The Split in the Minnesota DFL," p. 7; "Message to DFL Liberals," undated, early 1948, "DFL Caucuses," Box 25, Mayoralty Files, Hubert H. Humphrey Papers, MHS.

36. Eisele, *Almost to the Presidency,* p. 78; Hendrickson, "Minnesota in the McCarthy Period," pp. 96–97; *Minneapolis Tribune,* 2 May 1948; *Minneapolis Star,* 1 May 1948; *St. Paul Dispatch,* 1 May 1948; "Report to National ADA on DFL precinct caucuses," 10 May 1948, "DFL caucuses," Box 25, Mayoralty Files, Hubert H. Humphrey Papers, MHS; Mitau, "The Democratic-Farmer-Labor Party Schism," p. 192; Haynes, *Dubious Alliance,* pp. 186–187; Haynes, "Liberals, Communists, and the Popular Front," pp. 601–603.

37. O. Freeman oral history, p. 3; Edie, "The Split in the Minnesota DFL," p. 97; Hendrickson, "Minnesota in the McCarthy Period," pp. 105–106; Kubicek interview; Haynes, *Dubious Alliance,* p. 187.

38. *New York Post Magazine,* 28 February 1968; A. McCarthy, *Private Faces/Public Places,* p. 151; *Harper's Magazine,* June 1964; Eisele, *Almost to the Presidency,* pp. 78, 80; typescript of interview with Austin McCarthy, by Lael Herzog, undated, Folder 14, Part 1, Box 50, National Files, MHPA; typescript of interview with Larry Merthan, pp. 19–21, by Arthur Herzog, undated, Folder 7, Part 1, Box 50, National Files, MHPA.

39. *St. Paul Pioneer Press,* 13 June 1948; *St. Paul Dispatch,* 17 and 18 June 1948; Kubicek interview; A. McCarthy, *Private Faces/Public Places,* pp. 151–153; Eisele, *Almost to the Presidency,* pp. 79–81; Haynes, "Liberals, Communists, and the Popular Front," p. 669; typescript of interview with Gerald Heaney, by Arthur Herzog, undated, Folder 8, Part 1, Box 50, National Files, MHPA, p. 1; *St. Paul Dispatch,* 15 September 1948; "Scrapbook 1," Box 1, Accession 11455, EJM, MHS; Haynes, "Liberals, Communists, and the Popular Front," p. 720; A. McCarthy, *Private Faces/Public Places,* pp. 152–153; Mitau oral history, p. 13; Heaney interview.

40. *Harper's Magazine,* June 1964; Eisele, *Almost to the Presidency,* pp. 80–81; *Davenport Witness,* 5 June 1958, in "Political: McCarthy, Articles About," Box 263, EJM, MHS; E. McCarthy, *Up 'til Now,* p. 10; *The Aquin,* 15 October 1948, AUST; Eisele, *Almost to the Presidency,* pp. 76, 82; J. Freeman interview.

41. Taylor E. Dark, *The Unions and the Democrats: An Enduring Alliance* (Ithaca, N.Y.: 1999), p. 20; Haynes, *Dubious Alliance,* p. 205; *St. Paul Pioneer Press,* 26 October 1948; *Minneapolis Tribune,* 27 October 1948; pamphlet, "What About the Taft-Hartley Act?," Eugene J. McCarthy Confidential Employment File, AUST; untitled poster, "Political: 1948 Campaign Finance," Box 259, EJM, MHS; pamphlet, "What's Wrong with Devitt's Record?," "McCarthy, Senator Eugene" clippings file, AUST.

42. Eisele, *Almost to the Presidency,* p. 83; text of filing statement, 3 August 1948, "Political: 1948 campaign," Box 259, EJM, MHS; *Minnesota Labor,* 11 February 1949, in "Scrapbook 3," Box 1, Accession 11455, MHS; *St. Paul Dispatch,* 1 November 1948.

43. *Minneapolis Star,* 3 November 1948; Haynes, "Liberals, Communists, and the Popular Front," p. 2; Eisele, *Almost to the Presidency,* p. 83. For the local reaction to McCarthy's victory, see *St. Paul Dispatch,* 3 November 1948, and *The Aquin,* 5 November 1948, AUST.

44. Savage, *Truman and the Democratic Party,* p. 138; Zachary Karabell, *The Last Campaign: How Harry Truman Won the 1948 Election* (New York: 2000), p. 258; *St. Paul Pioneer Press,* 23 November 1948; *Saturday Evening Post,* 22 January 1949; Pells, *Liberal Mind in a Conservative Age,* pp. 113–115; Savage, *Truman and the Democratic Party,* p. 140; Alonzo L. Hamby, *Man of the People: A Life of Harry Truman* (New York: 1995), p. 465. Truman had gained a good deal from the confused Republican position on farm price supports, as well as from the Taft-Hartley controversy. See *New York Times,* 28 October 1948; Parmet, *The Democrats,* p. 80; Karabell, *Last Campaign,* p. 207; Savage, *Truman and the Democratic Party,* p. 140; Hamby, *Man of the People,* pp. 459–460.

45. *Minneapolis Star,* 3 November 1948; Eisele, *Almost to the Presidency,* p. 70; Solberg, *Hubert Humphrey,* p. 129; Ross K. Baker, *Friend and Foe in the U.S. Senate* (New York: 1980), p. 153;

Arthur Naftalin to McCarthy, 8 September 1948, "Political: 1948 Campaign Finance," Box 259, EJM, MHS; Orville Freeman to Hubert Humphrey, 21 December 1948, "Humphrey Correspondence, 1948–1950," Box 1, Orville Freeman Papers, MHS. McCarthy also received money from typical Democratic donors like the AFL, the CIO, and the United Auto Workers.

46. *Congressional Quarterly Weekly Report,* 29 October 1948; *New Republic,* 27 December 1948. See also "Political: 1948 Campaign Finance," Box 259, EJM, MHS; Nye, *Midwestern Progressive Politics,* p. 356; Crosby, *God, Church, and Flag,* p. 10; McAuliffe, *Crisis on the Left,* pp. 10–13; Byron E. Shafer, "Partisan Elites, 1946–1996," in Byron E. Shafer, ed., *Partisan Approaches to Postwar Politics* (New York: 1998), p. 82; Haynes, "Liberals, Communists, and the Popular Front," pp. 841–843; J. David Greenstone, *Labor in American Politics* (New York: 1969), pp. 4, 9, 206; John F. Bibby, "Party Organizations, 1946–1996," in Shafer, *Partisan Approaches to Postwar Politics,* p. 151; Shafer, "Partisan Elites," p. 87.

47. *Minneapolis Tribune,* 6 November 1948; *New York Post,* 29 February 1968; Eisele, *Almost to the Presidency,* p. 84; J. Freeman interview.

48. Ward M. Winton, "Eugene McCarthy: His Years at the College of St. Thomas," in "Miscellaneous, 1969–1971," Box 5, Accession 15044, EJM, MHS, pp. 3–5; *St. Paul Pioneer Press,* 26 October 1948; Eisele, *Almost to the Presidency,* pp. 80–81; E. McCarthy, *Up 'til Now,* pp. 8–9; Wilson, *Amateur Democrat,* p. 13; Richard Hofstadter, *The Age of Reform: From Bryan to FDR* (New York: 1955), pp. 140–141.

49. Pells, *Liberal Mind in a Conservative Age,* pp. 56–59, 72; Haynes, "Liberals, Communists, and the Popular Front," pp. 4–5, 766, 831, 843, 858. Some veterans of the Progressive Party returned to political involvement through McCarthy's presidential campaign in 1968: see, for instance, materials in Folder 11, Box 2, James Youngdale Papers, MHS.

50. Haynes, *Dubious Alliance,* p. 212; Plotke, *Building a Democratic Political Order,* p. 347; Alan Brinkley, *The End of Reform: New Deal Liberalism in Recession and War* (New York: 1995), pp. 269–270; Ira Katznelson, "Considerations on Social Democracy in the United States," *Comparative Politics* 11 (October 1978): 77–99; Ira Katznelson, "Was the Great Society a Lost Opportunity?," in Fraser and Gerstle, *Rise and Fall of the New Deal Order,* pp. 185–212. For discussions of the differences between the New and Fair Deals, see Plotke, *Building a Democratic Political Order,* p. 347; and Brinkley, *End of Reform,* pp. 269–270.

CHAPTER FOUR
The Quiet Congressman

1. *The Aquin,* 17 December 1948, AUST; *Minneapolis Tribune,* 6 November 1948; *The Aquin,* 12 November 1948, AUST; *The Voice of St. Jude,* January 1952, and *Jubilee,* August 1953, both in "Magazine Articles About McCarthy, 1949–1956," Public Relations Files, Box 275, EJM, MHS.

2. *St. Paul Pioneer Press,* 1 February 1949; Eisele, *Almost to the Presidency,* pp. 110–111; *The Aquin,* 19 May 1951, AUST; Eugene McCarthy to Don J. Bober, 23 June 1952, "Fair Trade," Box 2, EJM, MHS; A. McCarthy, *Private Faces/Public Places,* pp. 164–166. Blatnik, a stolid and experienced labor stalwart, represented the mining area of the Iron Range. Hays was a more colorful figure, perhaps best known for the remarkable sex scandal that ended his career decades later.

3. *The Aquin,* 17 December 1948, AUST; *Minnesota Labor,* 26 August 1949, in "Scrapbook 1," Box 1, Accession 11455, EJM, MHS.

4. "GOP-Dixiecrat Coalition Hit by McCarthy," undated 1949, in "Scrapbook 1," Box 1, Accession 11455, EJM, MHS.

5. Booth Mooney, *The Politicians: 1945–1960* (Philadelphia: 1970), p. 88; McAuliffe, *Crisis on the Left,* p. 49; Savage, *Truman and the Democratic Party,* p. 151; Plotke, *Building a Democratic Political Order,* pp. 247–248, 254, 346; Alonzo L. Hamby, "The Vital Center, the Fair Deal, and the Quest for a Liberal Political Economy," *American Historical Review* (June 1972): 653–678; Randall W. Strahan, "Partisan Officeholders, 1946–1996," in Shafer, ed., *Par-*

tisan Approaches to Postwar Politics, p. 15; Hamby, *Man of the People,* pp. 493, 506; Alonzo L. Hamby, "The Mind and Character of Harry S. Truman," in Michael J. Lacey, ed., *The Truman Presidency* (Cambridge, U.K.: 1989), p. 45; Plotke, *Building a Democratic Political Order,* pp. 247–248, 254, 346; Kevin Boyle, *The UAW and the Heyday of American Liberalism* (Ithaca, N.Y.: 1985), p. 68.

6. Typescript of interview with Mary McGrory, by Arthur Herzog, undated, Folder 7, Part 1, Box 50, National Files, MHPA, pp. 77–79; McCarthy to Herman Schauinger, 23 January 1951, Folder 1, "Correspondence, 1948–1971," Schauinger Papers, Georgetown University, Washington, D.C.; *St. Paul Dispatch,* 14 March 1949; transcript of interview with Adrian Winkel, by Lael Herzog, undated, Folder 14, Part 1, Box 50, National Files, MHPA; *Minneapolis Star,* 9 February 1952; J. Freeman interview. Freeman's allegation was an exaggeration. In 1952, for example, McCarthy took time off from his own campaign to help his friend William Carlson; see Eisele, *Almost to the Presidency,* p. 118.

7. The key congressional issues included social security, foreign aid, housing, rent control, and the Korean crisis. His "party unity" score, meanwhile, in the Eighty-first Congress was a very high 91 percent, while in the Eighty-second it rose to the astonishingly loyal total of 97 percent. See *Congressional Quarterly Weekly Report,* 4 November 1949, p. 1389; 18 November 1949, p. 1442; 6 July 1951, p. 1001; 16 November 1951, p. 1669; *Congressional Quarterly Almanac 1949,* pp. 50–51; *Congressional Quarterly Almanac 1950,* pp. 38–39, 61; *Congressional Quarterly Almanac 1951,* p. 65; *Congressional Quarterly Almanac 1952,* p. 69; *Congressional Quarterly Weekly Report,* 1 February 1952, p. 73; Bulletins, "Federal Spending Facts," Council of State Chambers of Commerce, 20 November 1951 and 22 September 1952, "Political: 82nd Congress, Records," Box 259, EJM, MHS; "House Voting Record 1947–1952," Labor's League for Political Education, undated, "Political: 82nd Congress, Records," Box 259, EJM, MHS; "Vital Issues and Votes," UAW-CIO, 2 January 1950, "Political: 82nd Congress, Records," Box 259, EJM, MHS; *Congressional Quarterly Weekly Report,* 10 February 1950, p. 157; 20 October 1950, p. 1172; 7 March 1952, p. 187; 17 October 1952, p. 1003.

8. "Record of Eugene J. McCarthy: 81st Congress, 1st and 2nd Sessions, 1948–1950," pp. 62–64, 5 October 1949, Box 7, Accession 12240, EJM, MHS; "Record of Eugene J. McCarthy: 81st Congress, 1st and 2nd Sessions, 1948–1950," pp. 91–94, 22 March 1950, Box 7, Accession 12240, EJM, MHS.

9. McCarthy to William J. Pacher, 24 September 1951, "Publicity 1951," Box 15, EJM, MHS; *Minnesota Labor,* 14 September 1951, in "Scrapbook 1," Box 1, Accession 11455, EJM, MHS; Iwan W. Morgan, *Eisenhower Versus "The Spenders": The Eisenhower Administration, the Democrats, and the Budget, 1953–1960* (New York: 1990), pp. 25–27; Haynes, *Dubious Alliance,* p. 212; Hamby, "The Vital Center, the Fair Deal, and the Quest for a Liberal Political Economy," pp. 653, 671; E. McCarthy, *Up 'til Now,* pp. 107–111.

10. Untitled memorandum on McCarthy record, 1949–1954, undated, "Political: 1954 Campaign," Box 259, EJM, MHS; *Congressional Quarterly Almanac 1950,* pp. 520, 537; *Minneapolis Star,* 9 February 1952; "Taft-Hartley Act 1952" folder, Box 6, EJM, MHS; "McCarthy Record, 81st, 1st and 2nd," 28 June 1949, Box 194, EJM, MHS; "Record of Eugene J. McCarthy: 81st Congress, 1st and 2nd Sessions, 1948–1950," 15 August 1950, Box 7, Accession 12240, EJM, MHS; *Congressional Quarterly Almanac 1950,* pp. 161, 193. McCarthy's successful bills concerned issues such as postal rates and salaries, police injury compensation, and the right of appeal for reservists recalled to the ranks.

11. Transcript of interview with Adrian Winkel, by Lael Herzog, undated, Folder 14, Part 1, Box 50, National Files, MHPA; McCarthy to K. K. McMillan, 7 November 1951, "Agriculture," Box 1, EJM, MHS; Hynes interview; "Record of Eugene J. McCarthy: 82nd Congress, 1st session, 1951," Appendix, pp. 62–64, 2 May 1951, Box 7, Accession 12240, EJM, MHS; McCarthy to Clara A. Hardin, 16 May 1951; McCarthy to Edward Schaefer (*Minneapolis Star*), 26 July 1951; John W. McCormack to McCarthy, 11 May 1951: all in "Agriculture," Box 1, EJM, MHS; *Congressional Quarterly Almanac 1952,* p. 113; *Minneapolis Star,* 9 February 1952.

12. Hendrickson, "Minnesota in the McCarthy Period," p. 100; Pells, *Liberal Mind in a Conserva-*

tive Age, p. 11; McAuliffe, *Crisis on the Left*, pp. 19–20; Stuhler, *Ten Men of Minnesota*, pp. 10–14.

13. *Kaysee News* (Yankton, S. Dak.), 28 May 1950, "Scrapbook 1," Box 1, Accession 11455, EJM, MHS.

14. *Congressional Record*, 13 February 1951, pp. 1291–1292; "From Campus to Congress," *Today Magazine*, April 1949, pp. 3–4, in "Scrapbook 1," Box 1, Accession 11455, EJM, MHS; Crosby, *God, Church, and Flag*, p. 20; *St. Paul Dispatch*, 30 August 1950; McCarthy to Edward J. Schuster, 10 January 1951, "State Department and Korean Situation," Box 5, EJM, MHS; McAuliffe, *Crisis on the Left*, p. 34; *Congressional Record*, 13 February 1951, pp. 1291–1292; McCarthy to E. T. Kane, 6 March 1951, "Communism," Box 2, EJM, MHS; McCarthy to A. C. Hubbell, "Foreign Policy," Box 2, EJM, MHS; *St. Paul Dispatch*, 13 December 1951.

15. E. McCarthy, *Up 'til Now*, pp. 41, 43; Newsletter, 15 April 1950, "Political: Minnesota, 4th District," Box 2, Senatorial Files, Hubert H. Humphrey Papers, MHS.

16. "Record of Eugene J. McCarthy: 81st Congress, 1st and 2nd Sessions, 1948–1950," pp. 107–123, 12 July 1950, Box 7, Accession 12240, EJM, MHS; *Congressional Quarterly Almanac 1950*, pp. 399–400; McCarthy, *Up 'til Now*, p. 38; A. McCarthy, *Private Faces/Public Places*, p. 188.

17. *St. Paul Pioneer Press*, 7 October 1950; McCarthy to Walter S. Rosenberry III, 23 January 1951, "Internal Security Act, 1950–1951," Box 3, EJM, MHS; Hendrickson, "Minnesota in the McCarthy Period," pp. 118–119; Hamby, *Man of the People*, p. 550.

18. Kazin, *Populist Persuasion*, p. 4; Hendrickson, "Minnesota in the McCarthy Period," p. 100. At the national level, not only was it President Truman who initiated loyalty hearings and investigations for Communists in 1947, but it was also the ADA that made anti-Communism an issue in 1948. Even a historian sympathetic to the liberals, David Plotke, agrees that "the Democratic campaign against the Communist Party and Popular Frontism in 1947–1949 helped prepare the way for McCarthyism, even if most Democratic liberals rejected McCarthy": see Plotke, *Building a Democratic Political Order*, p. 319; Yarnell, *Democrats and Progressives*, p. 107; Hendrickson, "Minnesota in the McCarthy Period," pp. 86, 144, 159, 168; McAuliffe, *Crisis on the Left*, p. 12. Arthur Schlesinger Jr., the founder and intellectual dynamo of the ADA, has disagreed with this interpretation: see, for instance, *Times Literary Supplement*, 22 September 2000. Not all Democrats were as comfortable as Humphrey and McCarthy with the party's institutionalization of anti-Communism. George McGovern, for instance, never repudiated his fondness for Henry Wallace and disliked "the direction the Democratic Party was taking," while, as we have seen, Orville Freeman later wondered whether they had gone too far: see Yarnell, *Democrats and Progressives*, p. 104; O. Freeman oral history, p. 3.

19. McCarthy, *Up 'til Now*, pp. 45–46; A. McCarthy, *Private Faces/Public Places*, pp. 185–186; *Washington Star*, 24 June 1950; Eisele, *Almost to the Presidency*, pp. 112–114; *St. Paul Pioneer Press*, 23 June 1952; Crosby, *God, Church, and Flag*, pp. 53–54, 69, 84, 236–242.

20. "Scrapbook 1," Box 1, Accession 11455, EJM, MHS; Kennedy campaign pamphlet, undated, "Political: 1952 campaign," File 1, Box 259, EJM, MHS; pamphlet, "The Truth About the McCarthy Amendment," undated [but clearly 1952], "Political: 1950 Campaign," Box 259, EJM, MHS; Hendrickson, "Minnesota in the McCarthy Period," p. 127.

21. A. McCarthy, *Private Faces/Public Places*, pp. 189–192; Eisele, *Almost to the Presidency*, p. 115. There is no mention of such an aggressive commercial in contemporary reports; the only evidence for it is in McCarthy's memoirs, published thirty years later: *Up 'til Now*, p. 39.

22. *St. Paul Pioneer Press*, 24 October 1952; pamphlet, "The Truth About the McCarthy Amendment," undated [but clearly 1952], "Political: 1950 Campaign," Box 259, EJM, MHS; *St. Paul Pioneer Press*, 1 November 1952.

23. A. McCarthy, *Private Faces/Public Places*, p. 191; *St. Paul Pioneer Press*, 22 October 1952; Eisele, *Almost to the Presidency*, pp. 113–117.

24. A. McCarthy, *Private Faces/Public Places*, pp. 192–195; Ward M. Winton, "Eugene

McCarthy: His Years at the College of St. Thomas," in "Miscellaneous 1969–1971," Box 5, Accession 15044, EJM, MHS, pp. 6–7; *Christianity and Crisis,* 19 January 1953, in Box 4, Richard T. Stout Papers, Georgetown University, Washington, D.C.; *Congressional Quarterly Weekly Report,* 24 October 1952; Eisele, *Almost to the Presidency,* p. 118; Hendrickson, "Minnesota in the McCarthy Period," p. 127. According to Abigail McCarthy, who confirmed the incident, the smear sheet had been prepared by newspaper and television reporters and was "an expose of the publishing family [to which Kennedy was related] and its tactics": see A. McCarthy, *Private Faces/Public Places,* p. 195.

25. Text of telecast, 11 September 1952, "Political: 1952 Campaign," File 2, Box 259, EJM, MHS; *Minneapolis Star,* 28 October 1952; *St. Paul Pioneer Press,* 24 October 1952; McCarthy to Donald L. Stofle, 10 May 1968, "Legislative: General: McCarthy Voting Record, 1967," Box 229, EJM, MHS; Eisele, *Almost to the Presidency,* pp. 112–118; A. McCarthy, *Private Faces/ Public Places,* pp. 189–198.

26. Solberg, *Hubert Humphrey,* pp. 157–159; McAuliffe, *Crisis on the Left,* pp. 132–140; Hendrickson, "Minnesota in the McCarthy Period," pp. 4–13; *Congressional Quarterly Weekly Report,* 1 January 1964; November 1953 opinion poll quoted in Hendrickson, "Minnesota in the McCarthy Period," p. 138; *Minneapolis Tribune,* 15 August 1954; *Congressional Record,* 17 August 1954, p. 14803; *St. Paul Pioneer Press,* 18 August 1954.

27. Michael J. Lacey, "The Truman Era in Retrospect," in Lacey, ed., *The Truman Presidency,* pp. 1–18; Brinkley, "The New Deal and the Idea of the State," in Steve Fraser and Gary Gerstle, ed., *The Rise and Fall of the New Deal Order, 1930–1980* (Princeton, N.J.: 1989), pp. 32–55; Alan Brinkley, *End of Reform,* pp. 3–11, 269–270; Alan Brinkley, *Liberalism and Its Discontents* (Cambridge, Mass.: 1998), pp. 37–62, 94–110; Iwan W. Morgan, *Beyond the Liberal Consensus* (London: 1994), p. 8; Katznelson, "Considerations on Social Democracy in the United States," pp. 77–99; Ira Katznelson, "Was the Great Society a Lost Opportunity?," pp. 185–212; Alonzo L. Hamby, *Liberalism and Its Challengers: From FDR to Bush,* 2nd ed. (New York: 1992), pp. 91–92; Arlene Lazarowitz, *Years in Exile: The Liberal Democrats, 1950–1959* (New York: 1988) p. 57. The conservatism of this agenda should not be exaggerated: even so, as Ira Katznelson points out, the expansion of the federal state recommended by Democratic liberals in the 1950s was determined by the interests of the dominant elites of which they were a part: see Katznelson, "Considerations on Social Democracy in the United States," pp. 91–93.

28. Nicol C. Rae, "Party Factionalism, 1946–1996," in Shafer, ed., *Partisan Approaches to Postwar Politics,* p. 66; Morgan, *Beyond the Liberal Consensus,* p. 1; Parmet, *The Democrats,* pp. 37–38; Hamby, "The Liberals, Truman, and FDR," p. 867; McAuliffe, *Crisis on the Left,* pp. 59–62, 147; Plotke, *Building a Democratic Political Order,* p. 291; Gillon, *Democrats' Dilemma,* p. 38; Hendrickson, "Minnesota in the McCarthy Period," pp. 106–107; Pells, *Liberal Mind in a Conservative Age,* p. 97; Gillon, *Politics and Vision,* p. 116. Arthur Schlesinger Jr. disagrees with this thesis: see *Times Literary Supplement,* 22 September 2000. The rise of Richard Nixon, who based his early career on similar issues, offers an interesting parallel. See Irwin F. Gellman, *The Contender: Richard Nixon: The Congress Years, 1946–1952* (New York: 1999).

29. Rae, "Party Factionalism, 1946–1996," pp. 45, 57; Brinkley, *End of Reform,* p. 270. The names of Wallace's supporters in 1948, figures such as Leonard Bernstein, Ben Shahn, Norman Mailer, and Arthur Miller, reappeared in lists of McCarthy and Robert Kennedy's celebrity backers in 1968. Shahn designed McCarthy's campaign logo, Mailer wrote a book about the Chicago convention, and Miller was a McCarthy delegate from Connecticut.

30. *St. Paul Dispatch,* 30 May 1951; McCarthy, *Up 'til Now,* pp. 8–9; Freeman, Heaney, and Frasers interviews; keynote address to DFL state convention, St. Paul, 31 May 1952, "Political: 1952 Campaign," File 2, Box 259, EJM, MHS.

CHAPTER FIVE
Patronage and Principle in the Eisenhower Era

1. Mark Green, *Who Runs Congress?* 3rd ed. (New York: 1979), p. 207; Myra McPherson, *The Power Lovers: An Intimate Look at Politics and Marriage* (New York: 1975), pp. 16, 20; Alan Ehrenhalt, *The United States of Ambition: Politicians, Power, and the Pursuit of Office* (New York: 1991), p. 13; Nelson W. Polsby, "Strengthening Congress in National Policymaking," in Nelson W. Polsby, ed., *Congressional Behavior* (New York: 1971), pp. 6–7; Morgan, *Eisenhower Versus "The Spenders,"* p. 3; John C. Donovan, *The Policy Makers* (New York: 1970), p. 61; E. McCarthy, *Up 'til Now,* pp. 11–13; D. C. Hardeman and Donald C. Bacon, *Rayburn: A Biography* (Austin, Texas: 1987).

2. Ehrenhalt, *United States of Ambition,* pp. 25, 31; *Minneapolis Star,* 9 February 1951; A. McCarthy, *Private Faces/Public Places,* pp. 169–170; author interview with Eugene McCarthy, 12 October 1999, Washington, D.C.

3. "Nation Eyes Thye-McCarthy Race," undated 1958, "Political: McCarthy, Articles About," Box 263, EJM, MHS; Eisele, *Almost to the Presidency,* p. 120; John McCormack to McCarthy, 13 April 1959, "Legislative Files: Finance: Tax: McCarthy Memo on Taxation," Box 56, EJM, MHS; *New York Times,* 16 July 1956; Eisele, *Almost to the Presidency,* p. 119; Donovan, *The Policy Makers,* p. 66; McCarthy, *Up 'til Now,* pp. 30–31; McCarthy interview.

4. McCarthy to League of Women Voters, 25 July 1956, "Political: Campaign Questionnaires, 1956," Box 260, EJM, MHS; *Congressional Quarterly Almanac 1958,* pp. 742–743; *Congressional Quarterly Almanac 1952,* p. 69; *Congressional Quarterly Almanac 1954,* pp. 34–35; *Congressional Quarterly Almanac 1958,* pp. 772–773; "Senator McCarthy's voting record," 11 April 1968, "ADA," Box 44, Part 1, National Files, MHPA; *Congressional Quarterly Weekly Report,* 22 October 1954, p. 1298; Auerbach, *Worthy to Be Remembered,* p. 41; Eisele, *Almost to the Presidency,* p. 122; "How Your Senators and Representatives Voted, 1947–1956," AFL-CIO COPE, "Political: Voting Record, 1947–1956, AFL-CIO," Box 313, EJM, MHS; *UAW Solidarity,* 27 October 1958, in Box 262, EJM, MHS; "Voting Record in the House and Senate on the Key Issues as Designated by COPE, 1948 to 1968," "COPE Voting Record EJM," Box 11, Part 2, National Files, MHPA.

5. *St. Paul Pioneer Press,* 16 February 1955; McCarthy to Meridel Le Sueur, 1 November 1955, "Judiciary: Civil Rights," Box 22, EJM, MHS; *Congressional Record,* 16 December 1955, p. 1300; Paul Douglas to McCarthy, 6 February 1958, "Legislative: Civil Rights, 1958," Box 193, EJM, MHS; *Congressional Record,* 20 July 1956, p. 13753; Statement on Floor of House, 20 July 1956, "Political: McCarthy Speeches and Remarks in Floor," Box 263, EJM, MHS.

6. *Congressional Record,* 15 April 1953, pp. 3148–3157; *Congressional Quarterly Almanac 1953,* p. 117; "McCarthy Record: 84th Congress, 1st and 2nd Sessions," pp. 48–57, in Box 194, EJM, MHS; *Congressional Quarterly Almanac 1955,* p. 184.

7. Author interview with Mary McGrory, 17 September 1999, Washington, D.C.; Eisele, *Almost to the Presidency,* pp. 120–121; Transcript of interview with Adrian Winkel, by Lael Herzog, undated, Folder 14, Box 50, Part 1, National Files, MHPA; Green, *Who Runs Congress?,* p. 236; *Washington Star,* 2 February 1958.

8. Ronald Berman, *America in the Sixties: An Intellectual History* (New York: 1968), p. 2; David S. Broder, *The Party's Over: The Failure of Politics in America* (New York: 1972), p. 5; Plotke, *Building a Democratic Political Order,* p. 348; Robert Griffith, "Dwight D. Eisenhower and the Corporate Commonwealth," *American Historical Review* 87:1 (February 1982): 87–122; Kenneth S. Baer, *Reinventing Democrats: The Politics of Liberalism from Reagan to Clinton* (Lawrence, Kans.: 2000), p. 14; Stephen Skowronek, *The Politics Presidents Make: Leadership from John Adams to George Bush* (Cambridge, Mass.: 1993), pp. 43–44; Morgan, *Eisenhower Versus "the Spenders,"* pp. 16–19, 39.

9. Godfrey Hodgson, *In Our Time: America from World War II to Nixon* (London: 1976), pp. 75–82, 100; William E. Leuchtenburg, *A Troubled Feast: American Society Since 1945,* 2nd ed. (Glenview, Ill.: 1983), p. 19.

10. Michael Foley, *The New Senate: Liberal Influence on a Conservative Institution, 1959–1972* (New Haven, Conn.: 1980), p. 21; Lazarowitz, *Years in Exile,* p. 123; Robert A. Caro, *Master of the Senate,* vol. 3, *The Years of Lyndon Johnson* (New York: 2002), passim; Doris Kearns, *Lyndon Johnson and the American Dream* (London: 1976), p. 153; Morgan, *Eisenhower Versus "the Spenders,"* p. 33; Parmet, *The Democrats,* p. 101; Lewis L. Gould, "Never a Deep Partisan: Lyndon Johnson and the Democratic Party," in Robert A. Divine, ed., *The Johnson Years,* vol. 3: *LBJ at Home and Abroad* (Lawrence, Kans.: 1994), pp. 22–23; Boyle, *UAW and the Heyday of Liberalism,* pp. 83–84; Foley, *New Senate,* pp. 22–23; Kearns, *Lyndon Johnson and the American Dream,* pp. 159, 383–384; Paul H. Douglas, *In the Fullness of Time: The Memoirs of Paul H. Douglas* (New York: 1972), pp. 196–221.

11. *Christian Science Monitor,* 28 September 1956; *Congressional Record,* 12 May 1954, p. 6458; Lazarowitz, *Years in Exile,* pp. 95, 119; Allen J. Matusow, *The Unraveling of America* (New York: 1986), p. 6; Eisele, *Almost to the Presidency,* p. 118.

12. McAuliffe, *Crisis on the Left,* p. 79; John Frederick Martin, *Civil Rights and the Crisis of Liberalism: The Democratic Party, 1945–1976* (Boulder, Colo.: 1979), p. 121; Jeff Broadwater, *Adlai Stevenson and American Politics: The Odyssey of a Cold War Liberal* (New York: 1994), p. 167; Gillon, *Politics and Vision,* pp. ix, 58; Lazarowitz, *Years in Exile,* p. 17.

13. Author interview with Arthur Schlesinger Jr., 4 May 2000, New York City; Eugene J. McCarthy, *The Hard Years: A Look at Contemporary America and American Institutions* (New York: 1975), pp. 212–213; Broadwater, *Adlai Stevenson and American Politics,* p. 77; Lazarowitz, *Years in Exile,* pp. 53, 69–84; Broadwater, *Adlai Stevenson and American Politics,* pp. 91, 140; John Patrick Diggins, *The Proud Decades: America in War and in Peace, 1941–1960* (New York: 1988), p. 306; Mooney, *The Politicians,* p. 241; Parmet, *The Democrats,* p. 127. Stevenson clearly found his liberal reputation a little surprising; in 1952 he asked an ADA delegate, "What do you want from me? I don't agree with your programs," and in 1957 he privately attacked "our intolerant northern liberals that irritate me so much." See Boyle, *UAW and the Heyday of Liberalism,* pp. 85–86; Martin, *Civil Rights and the Crisis of Liberalism,* p. 145.

14. Diggins, *Proud Decades,* p. 126; Broadwater, *Adlai Stevenson and American Politics,* pp. 119, 124; Lazarowitz, *Years in Exile,* p. 56; Martin, *Civil Rights and the Crisis of Liberalism,* pp. 144, 94; Lazarowitz, *Years in Exile,* p. 33.

15. Oral history interview of Carl Auerbach, by Arthur Naftalin, 13 July 1978, Hubert H. Humphrey Oral History Project, MHS, p. 13; Pells, *Liberal Mind in a Conservative Age,* pp. 394–395; Martin, *Civil Rights and the Crisis of Liberalism,* pp. 99–100; Lazarowitz, *Years in Exile,* p. 54; Broadwater, *Adlai Stevenson and American Politics,* pp. 139, 116; Lazarowitz, *Years in Exile,* p. 57; Martin, *Civil Rights and the Crisis of Liberalism,* p. 107; Parmet, *The Democrats,* p. 96; Martin, *Civil Rights and the Crisis of Liberalism,* pp. 95–96; Mooney, *The Politicians,* p. 149; Parmet, *The Democrats,* p. 124.

16. Wilson, *Amateur Democrat,* pp. 52–54; Alan Ware, *The Breakdown of Democratic Party Organization, 1940–1980* (Oxford: 1985), p. 76; Parmet, *The Democrats,* p. 147; Hofstadter, *Age of Reform,* pp. 140–143.

17. Mooney, *The Politicians,* p. 241; Parmet, *The Democrats,* p. 118; Lazarowitz, *Years in Exile,* pp. 128–131; Parmet, *The Democrats,* pp. 105–107, 148–149; Foley, *New Senate,* p. 23; Joseph S. Clark, *Congress: The Sapless Branch* (New York: 1964), p. 2; Martin, *Civil Rights and the Crisis of Liberalism,* pp. 20, 27; Gould, "Never a Deep Partisan," p. 23; Lazarowitz, *Years in Exile,* p. 121–122, 139.

18. Kenneth Kofmehl, "The Institutionalization of a Voting Bloc," *Western Political Quarterly* 17 (June 1964): 257–258; Bernard DeVoto, *The Easy Chair* (Boston: 1955), p. 342; Mark F. Ferber, "The Formation of the Democratic Study Group," in Polsby, *Congressional Behavior,* p. 250; Thomas P. Murphy, *The New Politics Congress* (Lexington, Mass.: 1974), pp. 121–122.

19. McCarthy interview; Eisele, *Almost to the Presidency,* pp. 122–123; A. McCarthy, *Private Faces/Public Places,* pp. 216–217; McCarthy, *Up 'til Now,* pp. 47–48; Parmet, *The Democrats,* p. 203; Hubert Humphrey to McCarthy, 17 January 1958, "Political: Commendations, 1956–1957," Box 260, EJM, MHS.

20. McCarthy to Lee Metcalf, 21 December 1956, "McCarthy Bills: Proposed Program," Box 34, EJM, MHS; Kofmehl, "The Institutionalization of a Voting Bloc," p. 258; oral history of John Blatnik, by Joseph E. O'Connor, 4 February 1966, Washington, D.C., John F. Kennedy Library, Boston; Kofmehl, "The Institutionalization of a Voting Bloc," p. 259; *Congressional Quarterly Weekly Report*, 11 January 1959, p. 59; *Congressional Quarterly Weekly Report*, 22 February 1957, pp. 224–225; *Congressional Quarterly Almanac 1957*, p. 48.

21. *St. Paul Pioneer Press*, 9 January 1957; *Congressional Quarterly Weekly Report*, 22 February 1957, p. 224; McCarthy interview; Eisele, *Almost to the Presidency*, p. 123; press release, International Union of Mine, Mill, and Smelter Workers, 22 January 1957, "McCarthy Bills: Proposed Program," Box 34, EJM, MHS.

22. Kofmehl, "The Institutionalization of a Voting Bloc," pp. 260–262; Ferber, "The Formation of the Democratic Study Group," p. 250; *Washington Post*, 28 March 1957; Eisele, *Almost to the Presidency*, pp. 123–124; transcript of interview with Adrian Winkel, by Lael Herzog, undated, Folder 14, Box 50, Part 1, National Files, MHPA; John Nuvern to McCarthy, 3 June 1957, "McCarthy Bills: Proposed Program," Box 34, EJM, MHS; McCarthy to Harold C. Hinton, 18 June 1957, "McCarthy Bills: Proposed Program," Box 34, EJM, MHS; George E. Agree to Frank Thompson, 30 October 1957, "Liberals: Miscellaneous," Box 34, EJM, MHS; "Statement for Liberal Democrats," 30 May 1957, "Miscellaneous Statements," Box 194, EJM, MHS; draft of statement on civil rights, 12 August 1957, "Liberals: Civil Rights," Box 34, EJM, MHS; "Statement by Democratic Representatives on Civil Rights," 14 August 1957, "Miscellaneous Statements," Box 194, EJM, MHS; *Labor's Daily*, 15 November 1957, in "Newspaper Clippings, 1958," Box 305, EJM, MHS; Ferber, "The Formation of the Democratic Study Group," p. 249; Morgan, *Eisenhower Versus "the Spenders,"* p. 32; Parmet, *The Democrats*, p. 203. In 1958, for example, it was McCarthy who introduced in the House Senator John F. Kennedy's bill to establish federal standards for the states' unemployment compensation systems, a measure which enjoyed wholehearted support from the AFL-CIO at a time of recession and unemployment and which, though unsuccessful, helped Democratic candidates in the North in 1958. See *New York Times*, 3 March 1958, 13 March 1958; *Congressional Quarterly Weekly Report*, 11 April 1958, p. 49; *Congressional Quarterly Weekly Report*, 18 April 1958, p. 479; "Labor Looks at the 85th Congress," AFL-CIO, undated, "Political: Congressional," Box 262, EJM, MHS; Morgan, *Eisenhower Versus "the Spenders,"* p. 115; see also extensive materials in "McCarthy Clips: Economy, Unemployment, Taxes," Box 263, EJM, MHS; and in "Legislative: McCarthy Bills: HR 10570," Box 31, EJM, MHS.

23. Lazarowitz, *Years in Exile*, pp. 43, 89, 103–111; Barbara Sinclair, *The Congressional Realignment, 1925–1978* (Austin, Texas: 1982), p. 73; A. McCarthy, *Private Faces/Public Places*, p. 215; Crosby, *God, Church, and Flag*, p. 53; A. McCarthy, *Private Faces/Public Places*, pp. 163–165; Hynes interview; author interview with Father Raymond Pedrizetti, 14 March 2000, St. John's Abbey, Minn.; McCarthy to Reverend A. G. Lewis, 23 January 1952, "Clark appointment," Box 4, EJM, MHS; *St. John's Alumni Supplement* 71:15 (14 November 1958), in "Political: Minnesota Editorials," Box 262, EJM, MHS; McCarthy interview.

24. Eugene J. McCarthy, *Frontiers in American Democracy;* Eugene J. McCarthy, *Dictionary of American Politics* (New York: 1962); Eugene J. McCarthy, *A Liberal Answer to the Conservative Challenge* (New York: 1964).

25. A. McCarthy, *Private Faces/Public Places*, p. 199; McCarthy, *Frontiers in American Democracy*, p. 57, 60–62, 9. McCarthy told an interviewer in 1982 that *Frontiers* was "sort of the translation into politics . . . of the things I had thought about and learned I suppose at St. John's and after." See transcript of interview with Eugene McCarthy, by R. W. Franklin, 14 April 1982, in "Eugene McCarthy: Clippings," SJU.

26. McCarthy, *Frontiers in American Democracy*, pp. 67–68; McCarthy, *A Liberal Answer to the Conservative Challenge*, p. 10; McCarthy, *Frontiers in American Democracy*, pp. 28–29, 115–119.

27. McCarthy, *Frontiers in American Democracy*, pp. 68, 98; McCarthy, *Up 'til Now*, pp. xi, 48.

28. McCarthy, *Dictionary of American Politics*, p. 41; McCarthy, *Frontiers in American Democracy*, pp. 36–39, 45; McCarthy, *Dictionary of American Politics*, p. 31; transcript of address to Blessed Sacrament Sodality, "Political Responsibility in a Democracy," 3 April 1957, Washington, D.C., "Political: McCarthy Speeches and Remarks," Box 263, EJM, MHS. Although other liberals, such as Stevenson and Humphrey, also proclaimed the merits of political accommodation, surely McCarthy was the only one to elevate it into an almost religious requirement. See Martin, *Civil Rights and the Crisis of Liberalism*, p. 95; Humphrey, *Education of a Public Man*, p. 136.

29. Guttmann, *Conservative Tradition in America*, p. 175; Irving Louis Horowitz, *Ideology and Utopia in the United States, 1956–1976* (New York: 1977), pp. 135–138.

30. He won by 59,930 votes to 39,907 in 1950; 98,015 - 60,827 in 1952; 81,651 - 47,933 in 1954; and 103,320 - 57,947 in 1956.

31. Lawrence C. Dodd, "Congress and the Quest for Power," in Lawrence C. Dodd and Bruce I. Oppenheimer, eds., *Congress Reconsidered* (New York: 1977), pp. 271–273; Joseph Rauh to McCarthy, 8 February 1957; McCarthy to Rauh, 19 February 1957; "ADA: 1957," Box 39, EJM, MHS; A. McCarthy, *Private Faces/Public Places*, p. 216; McCarthy interview; Kubicek interview; McCarthy interview; Hubert Humphrey to Eugenie Anderson, 29 July 1957, "Humphrey, Hubert H., July 1955–December 1958," Box 7, Eugenie Anderson Papers, MHS. Another associate of Humphrey and Anderson wrote that McCarthy's wife wanted him to go back to Minnesota for family reasons: see Max Kampelman to Eugenie Anderson, 9 September 1957, "Anderson Campaign for DFL Endorsement, US Senate 1958: General Correspondence, Oct 1957–April 1958," Box 13, Eugenie Anderson Papers, MHS.

32. *New York Times*, 8 November 1956; G. Theodore Mitau, *Politics in Minnesota* (Minneapolis: 1966), p. 29; Harry McPherson, *A Political Education: A Washington Memoir* (Boston: 1988), p. 79.

33. Eisele, *Almost to the Presidency*, pp. 124–125.

34. Heaney interview; Heaney oral history, pp. 35–37; J. Freeman interview; Heaney oral history, p. 37; *Minneapolis Tribune*, 2 February 1958; *New York Times*, 2 February 1958.

35. Transcript of interview with Gerald Heaney, undated and unattributed, Folder 8, Box 50, Part 1, National Files, MHPA; Frasers interview; Farr interview; Heaney interview; Kubicek interview; Max Kampelman to Eugenie Anderson, 17 April 1958, "Anderson Campaign for DFL Endorsement, U.S. Senate 1958: General Correspondence, Oct. 1957–April 1958," Box 13, Eugenie Anderson Papers, MHS; *New York Times*, 27 April 1958; *St. Paul Pioneer Press*, 25 May 1958; McCarthy interview; Heaney interview; *Minneapolis Tribune*, 26 May 1958; *St. Paul Pioneer Press*, 26 May 1958; *St. Paul Dispatch*, 26 May 1958; *Statesman*, 4 June 1958, in "Political: Convention," Box 262, EJM, MHS. There were also allegations of anti-Catholic prejudice directed against McCarthy: see, for instance, author interview with Matthew Stark, 21 October 1999, Minneapolis; Eisele, *Almost to the Presidency*, p. 127; McCarthy interview; Hubert Humphrey to McCarthy, 17 January 1958, "Political: Humphrey 1958," Box 261, EJM, MHS; "Only the Religious Issue," Joseph Alsop, undated, in "Political: National Comment on 1958 Campaign," Box 263, EJM, MHS; Heaney oral history, p. 40.

36. *Congressional Quarterly Weekly Report*, 7 November 1958, p. 1406; "Conference Report," White, Herzog, and Nee, 10 June 1958, "White, Herzog, and Nee: Advertisers," Box 313, EJM, MHS; Alpha Smaby, *Political Upheaval: Minnesota and the Vietnam War Protest* (Minneapolis: 1987), p. 438; Heaney interview; author interview with Warren Spannaus, 8 December 1999, Minneapolis; Eugene McCarthy 60-Second Campaign Spots 1958 (especially Spot 2.2), Oral History Collection, MHS; *New Republic*, 27 October 1958; McCarthy interview; Farr interview; Heaney interview; *St. Paul Dispatch*, 5 November 1958; oral history interview of Maurice Rosenblatt, by Betty Key, 4 February 1970, Oral History Collection, MHPA; *New York Times*, 6 November 1958; Eisele, *Almost to the Presidency*, p. 128. Intriguingly, the Catholic senator from Massachusetts, John F. Kennedy, promised McCarthy that he too would contribute funds, but according to McCarthy's aide Gerald Heaney he delivered "nothing but a

bunch of words," a failure that McCarthy would not quickly forget. See John T. Galvin to Mary McGrory, 7 April 1958, Box 261, EJM, MHS; Heaney interview. Kennedy's factotum Theodore Sorensen insists that he did contribute financially and was shocked at McCarthy's ingratitude: see oral history interview of Theodore Sorensen, by Larry J. Hackman, 21 March 1969, New York City, Robert F. Kennedy Oral History Project, JFK, pp. 5–6. There is no documentary record of such a contribution, though of course that does not mean that none was made.

37. *St. Paul Pioneer Press,* 22 October 1958; *Minneapolis Tribune,* 2 November 1958; *St. Paul Pioneer Press,* 30 October 1958; *Congressional Quarterly Weekly Report,* 17 October 1958, p. 1324; *New York Times,* 5 November 1958; *Minneapolis Tribune,* 6 November 1958; Mitau, *Politics in Minnesota,* p. 109; Eisele, *Almost to the Presidency,* p. 129; Fenton, *Midwest Politics,* p. 107; *Minneapolis Star,* 23 May 1958; *Congressional Quarterly Weekly Report,* 4 September 1959, pp. 1210–1213; Fenton, *Midwest Politics,* p. 103.

38. McCarthy to Samuel C. Brightman, editor, *Democratic Digest,* 12 November 1958, "McCarthy, Eugene: General, 86th Congress," Box 127, File 2, Papers of the Democratic National Committee, LBJ; oral history interview of Orville Freeman, by Charles T. Morrissey, 22 July 1964, Washington, D.C., Oral History Collection, JFK, p. 13; Orville Freeman to Merritt E. Freeman, 7 November 1958, "1958 Correspondence: Personal 1," Box 6, Orville Freeman Papers, MHS; J. Freeman interview; Heaney interview; oral history interview of James G. Patton, by Ed Edwin, September 1979, Washington, D.C., COL, part 2, volume 1, pp. 70–71; *New York Times,* 19 October 1958; Morgan, *Eisenhower Versus "the Spenders,"* p. 17; Diggins, *Proud Decades,* pp. 132–133, 323; Charles Alexander, *Holding the Line: The Eisenhower Era, 1952–1961* (Bloomington, Ind.: 1975), p. 39; Sinclair, *Congressional Realignment,* p. 81.

39. Morgan, *Eisenhower Versus "the Spenders,"* pp. 93, 99, 100; Alexander, *Holding the Line,* p. 242; Diggins, *Proud Decades,* p. 319; Foley, *New Senate,* p. 26; Robert Dallek, *Lone Star Rising: Lyndon Johnson and His Times, 1908–1960* (New York: 1991), p. 537.

40. Sinclair, *Congressional Realignment,* p. 178; Foley, *New Senate,* p. 25; Dallek, *Lone Star Rising,* p. 538; Robert Mann, *The Walls of Jericho: Lyndon Johnson, Hubert Humphrey, Richard Russell, and the Struggle for Civil Rights* (New York: 1996), pp. 236–238; Parmet, *The Democrats,* p. 193.

41. *Christian Science Monitor,* 8 November 1958; Eisele, *Almost to the Presidency,* p. 130; *Catholic Bulletin,* 5 December 1958, in "McCarthy, Senator Eugene" Clippings File, AUST.

42. Hubert Humphrey to McCarthy, 1 May 1958, "Political: Hubert H. Humphrey," Box 262, EJM, MHS; Rowland Evans and Robert Novak, *Lyndon B. Johnson: The Exercise of Power* (London: 1967), p. 203.

CHAPTER SIX
The Politics of Ambition

1. Donald R. Matthews, *U.S. Senators and Their World* (Chapel Hill, N.C.: 1960), p. 13; H. McPherson, *A Political Education,* p. 17; Adam Clymer, *Edward M. Kennedy: A Biography* (New York: 1999), p. 44; Bernard Asbell, *The Senate Nobody Knows* (Garden City N.Y.: 1978), pp. 8–9; Matthews, *U.S. Senators and Their World,* pp. 94–103; Norman J. Ornstein, Robert L. Peabody, and David W. Rohde, "The Changing Senate: From the 1950s to the 1970s," in Dodd and Oppenheimer, eds., *Congress Reconsidered,* p. 7; R. K. Baker, *Friend and Foe in the U.S. Senate,* p. 45.

2. McCarthy, *Hard Years,* pp. 20–21, 28; McCarthy, *Up 'til Now,* pp. 53–56; Matthews, *U.S. Senators and Their World,* p. 100; Barbara Sinclair, *The Transformation of the U.S. Senate* (Baltimore: 1989), pp. 8, 208.

3. McCarthy, *Up 'til Now,* p. 56; Foley, *New Senate,* p. 9; Randall B. Ripley, *Power in the Senate* (New York: 1969), pp. 60, 64; Joseph S. Clark, *The Senate Establishment* (New York: 1963), p. 13; Matthews, *U.S. Senators and Their World,* pp. 147–149; Donovan, *The Policy Makers,* p. 66; Fred R. Harris, *Potomac Fever* (New York: 1977), p. 59; Sinclair, *Transformation of the U.S. Senate,* p. 13; Matthews, *U.S. Senators and Their World,* p. 123; James L. Sundquist,

"Congress and the President: Enemies or Partners?," in Dodd and Oppenheimer, eds., *Congress Reconsidered*, p. 237; Martin, *Civil Rights and the Crisis of Liberalism*, p. 160. On "the Club" see Robert Mann, *Legacy to Power: Senator Russell Long of Louisiana* (New York: 1992), pp. 149–160; oral history interview of Howard E. Shuman, by Donald A. Ritchie, 22 July–22 October 1987, Senate Historical Office, Washington, D.C., pp. 104–106; and for critical views, see Clark, *Senate Establishment*, p. 10; Clark, *Congress: The Sapless Branch*, p. 113; Douglas, *In the Fullness of Time*, pp. 197, 213.

4. Edgar Berman, *Hubert: The Triumph and Tragedy of the Humphrey I Knew* (New York: 1979), p. 55; F. Harris, *Potomac Fever*, p. 59; Ehrenhalt, *United States of Ambition*, p. 13; Clark, *Congress: The Sapless Branch*, p. 56; Green, *Who Runs Congress?*, p. 241; Rochelle Jones and Peter Woll, *The Private World of Congress* (New York: 1979), p. 6; R. K. Baker, *Friend and Foe in the U.S. Senate*, p. 140; Richard Dougherty, *Goodbye, Mr. Christian: A Personal Account of McGovern's Rise and Fall* (Garden City, N.Y.: 1973), p. 85; Humphrey, *Education of a Public Man*, p. 146; Asbell, *Senate Nobody Knows*, p. 80; Foley, *New Senate*, p. 173.

5. Ornstein et al., "Changing Senate," p. 7; Garry Wills, *Lead Time: A Journalist's Education* (Garden City, N.Y.: 1983), p. 118; Matthews, *U.S. Senators and Their World*, p. 94; Sinclair, *Transformation of the U.S. Senate*, p. 16.

6. Sinclair, *Congressional Realignment*, p. 178; Foley, *New Senate*, pp. 51, 175; Sinclair, *Transformation of the U.S. Senate*, pp. 32, 49; Morgan, *Eisenhower Versus "the Spenders*," p. 126; Irving Bernstein, *Promises Kept: John F. Kennedy's New Frontier* (New York: 1991), p. 286.

7. R. K. Baker, *Friend and Foe in the U.S. Senate*, p. 17; A. McCarthy, *Private Faces/Public Places*, p. 227; McCarthy interview; R. K. Baker, *Friend and Foe in the U.S. Senate*, pp. 27, 161, 166–167; McGrory interview; author interview with Albert Eisele, May 2000, Washington, D.C.; Mason Drukman, *Wayne Morse: A Political Biography* (Portland, Ore.: 1997), pp. 342–343; M. O'Brien, *Philip Hart*, p. 150; Theo Lippman Jr. and Donald C. Hansen, *Muskie* (New York: 1971), pp. 105, 201, 213; R. K. Baker, *Friend and Foe in the U.S. Senate*, p. 124; H. McPherson, *A Political Education*, p. 10; oral history interview of Edmund S. Muskie, by Arthur Naftalin, 4 August 1978, Washington, D.C., Hubert H. Humphrey Oral History Project, MHS, p. 18; R. K. Baker, *Friend and Foe in the U.S. Senate*, pp. 164–167.

8. John G. Stewart, "Two Strategies of Leadership: Johnson and Mansfield," in Polsby, ed., *Congressional Behavior*, pp. 64–68; McCarthy interview; Foley, *New Senate*, p. 27; Jeff Shesol, *Mutual Contempt: Lyndon Johnson, Robert Kennedy, and the Feud That Defined a Decade* (New York: 1997), p. 14; Murphy, *New Politics Congress*, p. 94; Francis R. Valeo, *Mike Mansfield, Majority Leader: A Different Kind of Senate, 1961–1976* (Armonk, N.Y.: 1999), p. 18; Clark, *Congress: The Sapless Branch*, p. 9; Mooney, *The Politicians*, p. 305; *Congressional Record*, 12 January 1959, pp. 461–462; Sinclair, *Transformation of the U.S. Senate*, p. 34; Eisele, *Almost to the Presidency*, p. 130; Mann, *Walls of Jericho*, p. 240; "Westerners to Fore in Senate," undated clipping, "National Comment on 1958 Campaign," Box 263, EJM, MHS. For Johnson as majority leader, see Caro, *Master of the Senate*.

9. William Nee to Dick Boo, 25 February 1959, "Politics, Miscellaneous," Box 264, EJM, MHS; Douglas, *In the Fullness of Time*, pp. 427–438; Shuman oral history, pp. 104–106.

10. Clark, *Senate Establishment*, p. 127; Mooney, *The Politicians*, p. 305; McCarthy interview; "Résumé of conversation between Senator Johnson and Senator Gene McCarthy," 12 January 1960, "1961 Congressional File: McC," Box 265, Vice Presidential Congressional Files, Lyndon Baines Johnson Vice Presidential Files, LBJ.

11. Jeremy Larner, *Nobody Knows: Reflections on the McCarthy Campaign of 1968* (New York: 1969), pp. 72–75; Arthur Herzog, *McCarthy for President* (New York: 1969), pp. 62–64; Paul Douglas to McCarthy, 14 May 1959, "Legislative: Finance: Tax: Depletion Allowance 1959–1960," Box 54, EJM, MHS; *Congressional Quarterly Weekly Report*, 3 July 1959, p. 927; Douglas, *In the Fullness of Time*, p. 433.

12. McCarthy interview; *New York Times Magazine*, 10 December 1967; Shuman oral history, pp. 582–583.

13. *Washington Post*, 20 August 1964; John C. Reidy, Minnesota Petroleum Council, to McCarthy,

2 January 1959, and McCarthy to Reidy, 2 February 1959, in "Legislative: Finance: Tax: Depletion Allowance 1959–1960," Box 54, EJM, MHS. For more on McCarthy's record on the Finance Committee, see *New York Times,* 22 May 1959, 26 June 1959, 16 June 1960; *Congressional Quarterly Almanac 1959,* pp. 200–202; *Congressional Quarterly Weekly Report,* 2 July 1959, p. 919; *Congressional Quarterly Almanac 1960,* p. 363; *Congressional Quarterly Weekly Report,* 17 June 1960, p. 1065; *St. Paul Dispatch,* 29 June 1960; McCarthy to Harold G. Anderson, 5 July 1960, "Legislative: Finance: Tax: DuPont Company," Box 55, EJM, MHS; Douglas, *In the Fullness of Time,* p. 460.

14. McCarthy, *Up 'til Now,* pp. 96–99; Drukman, *Wayne Morse,* pp. 4–5; Asbell, *Senate Nobody Knows,* pp. 117–118; Muskie oral history, p. 8; Lippman and Hansen, *Muskie,* pp. 100–101; Foley, *New Senate,* pp. 194–196; M. O'Brien, *Philip Hart,* p. 79; Humphrey, *Education of a Public Man,* pp. 135–137; "Westerners to Fore in Senate," undated clipping, "National Comment on 1958 Campaign," Box 263, EJM, MHS; *Look,* 26 April 1960.

15. *Congressional Quarterly Almanac 1959,* pp. 90–92, 127, 146, 149; *Congressional Quarterly Almanac 1960,* pp. 86–88, 123, 135; *Congressional Quarterly Weekly Report,* 2 January 1959, p. 16; *Minneapolis Star,* 7 January 1959; *Congressional Quarterly Almanac 1959,* p. 213; *Congressional Record,* 10 March 1964, p. 4744; "Looking 25 Years Ahead at Civil Rights," "Tribute to David L. Lawrence Program," p. 5, ADA Roosevelt Dinner, 18 February 1959, "Articles by McCarthy," Box 1, Accession 12758, EJM, MHS; Morgan, *Eisenhower Versus "the Spenders,"* p. 139; Gillon, *Politics and Vision,* pp. 123–125; David Burner, *Making Peace with the Sixties* (Princeton, N.J.: 1996), p. 93; "Scrapbook 5" and "Scrapbook 7," Box 2, Accession 11455, EJM, MHS.

16. *New York Times,* 26 March 1959; Bernstein, *Promises Kept,* p. 160; Clark, *Congress: The Sapless Branch,* p. 11; Morgan, *Eisenhower Versus "the Spenders,"* p. 141; Lyndon Johnson to McCarthy, 15 September 1959, "McCarthy," Box 367, Correspondence with Democratic Senators, 1957–1959, Papers of the Democratic Leader, Lyndon Baines Johnson Senate Papers, 1949–1961, LBJ; *Congressional Quarterly Almanac 1959,* p. 224; *New York Times,* 17 September 1959; James L. Sundquist, *Politics and Policy: The Eisenhower, Kennedy, and Johnson Years,* Rev. ed. (Washington, D.C.: 1973), pp. 78–80; Eisele, *Almost to the Presidency,* p. 130; McCarthy interview; Foley, *New Senate,* p. 127.

17. *Detroit Free Press,* 13 November 1959; *St. Paul Pioneer Press,* 6 October 1959; *Duluth News-Tribune,* 11 October 1960; "Minutes of majority members meeting of Special Committee on Unemployment," 15 September 1959, and "Minutes of executive session of Special Committee on Unemployment," 17 September 1959, in "Political: Minutes of Committee Meetings," Box 264, EJM, MHS; Bernstein, *Promises Kept,* pp. 182–183, 186–187; *New York Times,* 15 December 1959 and 27 December 1959; Press release, "Long-term Unemployed Are Neglected, McCarthy Says," 8 December 1959, "August–December 1959," Box 11, Accession 11455, EJM, MHS.

18. "Minutes of executive session of Special Committee on Unemployment," 16 March 1960, "Political: Minutes of Committee Meetings," Box 264, EJM, MHS; oral history interview of Philip Booth, by Shirley Riordan, 9 April 1981, San Diego, Unemployment Insurance Project, COL, p. 38; McCarthy interview; drafts of report, Box 312, EJM, MHS; United States Senate Committee on Unemployment Problems, *Unemployment Problems* (Washington, D.C.: 1960); Emerson Hynes interview, in *Ave Maria,* 14 May 1960, courtesy of Sister Arleen Hynes; *Congressional Quarterly Weekly Report,* 1 April 1960, p. 594; *Congressional Quarterly Almanac 1960,* p. 297; Sundquist, *Politics and Policy,* p. 81; Morgan, *Eisenhower Versus "the Spenders,"* p. 142; Press release, "McCarthy Unemployment Committee Set Standards for National Action," 1963, "Political: Elections: Senate," Box 269, EJM, MHS; Sundquist, *Politics and Policy,* p. 83; Donovan, *Policy Makers,* pp. 93–94; Eisele, *Almost to the Presidency,* pp. 133–134.

19. *Albert Lea Daily Tribune,* 24 September 1959, in "Scrapbook 5," Box 1, Accession 11455, EJM, MHS; oral history interview of Senator Maurine Neuberger, by Ann M. Campbell, 12

February 1970, Washington, D.C., Oral History Collection, JFK, p. 6; Eisele, *Almost to the Presidency,* p. 134; McCarthy interview; oral history interview of Katie Louchheim, by Larry J. Hackman, 24 April 1968, Washington, D.C., Oral History Collection, JFK, p. 9; McCarthy interview.

20. Hubert Humphrey to McCarthy, 12 March 1959, "Active Memberships: ADA," Box 5, Accession 12491, EJM, MHS; McCarthy interview; *New York Times,* 14 July 1959; O. Freeman oral history, p. 3; *St. Paul Pioneer Press,* 9 February 1960 and 12 February 1960; *New York Times,* 27 March 1960 and 3 April 1960; Humphrey, *Education of a Public Man,* pp. 472–473; McCarthy interview; E. McCarthy, *Up 'til Now,* p. 135; O. Freeman oral history, p. 7; oral history interview of Joseph L. Rauh Jr., by Paige Mulhollan, 1 August 1969, Oral History Collection, LBJ, p. 10.

21. E. McCarthy, *Up 'til Now,* p. 131; A. McCarthy, *Private Faces/Public Places,* pp. 238–239; Paul Henggeler, *The Kennedy Persuasion: The Politics of Style Since JFK* (Chicago: 1995), p. 59; McCarthy interview; C. David Heymann, *RFK: A Candid Biography* (London: 1998), p. 111; Sorenson oral history, pp. 5–6; oral history interview of Marie Ridder, by Betty Key, 9 February 1970, Oral History Collection, MHPA, p. 5; notes of interview with Theodore Mitau, by Arthur Herzog, Folder 7, Box 50, Part 1, National Files, MHPA; Humphrey, *Education of a Public Man,* p. 237; Joseph W. Alsop, with Adam Platt, *I've Seen the Best of It: Memoirs* (New York: 1992), pp. 421–422; oral history interview of Joseph Alsop, by Roberta W. Greene, 10 June 1971, Washington, D.C., Oral History Collection, JFK, pp. 37–38; J. Alsop, *I've Seen the Best of It,* pp. 421–422; Jim F. Heath, *Decade of Disillusionment: The Kennedy-Johnson Years* (Bloomington, Ind.: 1975), pp. 23–24; Lazarowitz, *Years in Exile,* p. 157; David Burner and Thomas R. West, *The Torch Is Passed: The Kennedy Brothers and American Liberalism* (New York: 1984), p. 158; Parmet, *The Democrats,* p. 168.

22. Notes of interview with Joseph Gabler, by Lael Herzog, Folder 14, Box 50, Part 1, National Files, MHPA; Eisele interview; J. Freeman interview; oral history interview of Geri Joseph, by Arthur Naftalin, 14 July 1978, Hubert H. Humphrey Oral History Project, MHS, p. 33.

23. Morris, *American Catholic,* p. 256; Wills, *Bare Ruined Choirs,* p. 80; Eisele, *Almost to the Presidency,* pp. 140, 149; Tip O'Neill, with William Novak, *Man of the House: The Life and Political Memoirs of Speaker Tip O'Neill* (New York: 1987), p. 202; Pedrizetti interview.

24. Memorandum, "Minnesota," Theodore Sorensen to John Kennedy and Sargent Shriver, 31 May 1960, "Minnesota: Delegates, 60 Convention, 5/27/59–6/8/60," Box 949, Pre-Convention Political Files, 1959–1960, 1960 Campaign: Campaigns by State, John F. Kennedy Pre-Presidential Papers, JFK; oral history interview of D. B. Hardeman, by John Luter, 3 January 1970, Washington, D.C., part 3, p. 1443, Eisenhower Administration Project, COL: oral history interview of Eugenie Anderson, by Larry J. Hackman, 11 March 1973, Red Wing, Minn., Oral History Collection, JFK, pp. 13–14; J. Freeman interview; *New York Times,* 15 May 1960; *Minneapolis Tribune,* 20 May 1960; *Holiday,* June 1962; J. Freeman interview; unidentified clipping, 28 June 1960, "Scrapbook 7," Box 2, Accession 11455, EJM; Norman Sherman to author, 21 February 2000.

25. O. Freeman oral history, p. 9; J. Freeman interview; McCarthy interview.

26. *New York Times,* 12 July 1960; McCarthy, *Up 'til Now,* pp. 137–138; Maurice Isserman and Michael Kazin, *America Divided: The Civil War of the 1960s* (Oxford: 2000), p. 60; Rauh oral history, pp. 1–2, 16–17; Parmet, *The Democrats,* p. 175; oral history interview of Hubert H. Humphrey, by Joe B. Frantz, 17 August 1971, Oral History Collection, LBJ, p. 43; *Detroit Free Press,* 22 June 1960; *Minneapolis Tribune,* 10 July 1960; Eisele, *Almost to the Presidency,* p. 152; Dallek, *Lone Star Rising,* p. 573.

27. Norman Mailer, *Some Honorable Men: Political Conventions, 1960–1973* (Boston: 1976), p. 29; oral history interview of John Sharon, by John Luter, 17 July 1969, Washington, D.C., pp. 89–90, Adlai E. Stevenson Oral History Project, COL; Merle Miller, *Lyndon: An Oral Biography* (New York: 1980), p. 245; Shesol, *Mutual Contempt,* p. 39; McCarthy to William H. Slavick, 12 July 1960, "Political: Miscellaneous," Box 264, EJM, MHS; Schlesinger inter-

view; Eisele, *Almost to the Presidency,* p. 154; Bobby Baker, with Larry L. King, *Wheeling and Dealing: Confessions of a Capitol Hill Operator* (New York: 1978), p. 122; Hardeman oral history, p. 143; Shuman oral history, pp. 124–126; oral history of William McCormick Blair Jr., by John Luter, 10 June 1969, Washington, D.C., pp. 58–59, Adlai E. Stevenson Oral History Project, COL; oral history interview of Newton Minow, by Kenneth S. David, 26 May 1967, Glencoe, Ill., pp. 76–77, Adlai E. Stevenson Oral History Project, COL.

28. Oral history interview of Senator A. S. (Mike) Monroney, by John Luter, 11 June 1969, Washington, D.C., p. 39, Adlai E. Stevenson Oral History Project, COL; oral history interview of Senator A. S. (Mike) Monroney, by Dorothy Pierce McSweeney, 26 February 1969, Oral History Collection, LBJ, Part 2, pp. 11–12; Sharon oral history, pp. 88–89; M. Miller, *Lyndon,* p. 247; Humphrey, *Education of a Public Man,* p. 231; Monroney oral history (COL), p. 42; oral history interview of Mrs. Ernest Ives, by John Luter, 19 April 1969, Southern Pines, N.C., vol. 2, p. 35, Adlai E. Stevenson Oral History Project, COL; Monroney oral history (COL), pp. 39–40; oral history interview of Katie Louchheim, by John T. Mason Jr., 18 April 1973, Washington, D.C., pp. 65–66, Adlai E. Stevenson Oral History Project, COL; *Washington Daily Globe,* 8 August 1960; undated speech drafts, Eugene McCarthy Manuscript Collection 1960, Library of Congress, Washington, D.C.; *New York Times,* 14 July 1960; Harris Wofford, *Of Kennedys and Kings: Making Sense of the Sixties* (Pittsburgh: 1992), p. 50; Eisele, *Almost to the Presidency,* p. 155; *New York Times,* 14 July 1960; Mailer, *Some Honorable Men,* p. 33; Kenneth P. O'Donnell and Dave Powers, with Joe McCarthy, *Johnny, We Hardly Knew Ye: Memories of John Fitzgerald Kennedy* (Boston: 1970), p. 186.

29. The text of the speech is in the *New York Times,* 14 July 1960; see also Eisele, *Almost to the Presidency,* p. 155. See also the drafts in the Eugene McCarthy Manuscript Collection 1960, Library of Congress, Washington, D.C.

30. *New York Times,* 14 July 1960; Eisele, *Almost to the Presidency,* p. 159; *St. Paul Dispatch,* 18 July 1960; *St. Paul Pioneer Press,* 14 August 1960; *New York Times,* 29 August 1960; Schlesinger interview; Joseph E. Cerrell to McCarthy, 18 November 1960, "Political: 1960 Campaign: Folder 5," Box 313, EJM, MHS; *New York Post,* 7 October 1960; *New York Times,* 26 November 1960; Eisele, *Almost to the Presidency,* p. 160.

31. *The Economist,* 8 August 1964, pp. 553–554; undated handwritten note, "Political: Communism," Box 266, EJM, MHS; Eisele, *Almost to the Presidency,* p. 162; E. McCarthy, *Up 'til Now,* p. 144; oral history interview of Father Francis X. Murphy, interview 5, by Peter Jessup, 24 September 1981, Washington, D.C., COL, vol. 3, p. 296; Larry Merthan to Ralph Dungan, special assistant to the president, 8 October 1962, "McCarthy, Senator Eugene," Box 1781, Name File, White House Central Files, Presidential Papers of John F. Kennedy, JFK; transcript of interview with Kenneth O'Donnell, "1968 campaign: McCarthy, Eugene," Box W-54, Arthur M. Schlesinger Papers, JFK; E. McCarthy, *Up 'til Now,* p. 147; A. McCarthy, *Private Faces/Public Places,* pp. 240–242; Ridder oral history, p. 5; E. McCarthy, *Hard Years,* pp. 191–192; Heath, *Decade of Disillusionment,* p. 144; Foley, *New Senate,* pp. 43–44; Burner and West, *Torch Is Passed,* p. 187; *Rochester Daily Post-Bulletin,* 14 January 1961, in "Scrapbook 8," Box 2, Accession 11455, EJM, MHS; *Houston Post,* 18 May 1962, in "Scrapbook 9," Box 2, Accession 11455, EJM, MHS; *Minneapolis Star,* 21 June 1963; *New Republic,* 6 April 1963.

32. *Congressional Quarterly Almanac 1961,* pp. 628, 635; *Congressional Quarterly Almanac 1962,* p. 722; *Congressional Quarterly Almanac 1963,* p. 747; Foley, *New Senate,* pp. 287–293; "McCarthy States Need for Further Civil Rights Action," 29 January 1962, "Jan–July 1962," Box 11, Accession 11455, EJM, MHS; "McCarthy Sees Civil Rights Action as National Commitment," 28 October 1963, "July–Dec. 1963," Box 11, Accession 11455, EJM, MHS; "Additional Civil Rights Legislation a Necessity—McCarthy," 10 January 1964, "Jan.–June 1964," Box 11, Accession 11455, EJM, MHS; "McCarthy Cites Moral Basis of Civil Rights," 29 June 1964, "Jan.–June 1964," Box 11, Accession 11455, EJM, MHS; *St. Paul Dispatch,* 15 May 1961; *Congressional Quarterly Almanac 1961,* pp. 133–138; *Congressional Quarterly Weekly*

Report, 15 September 1961, p. 1574; *New York Times,* 12 September 1961, 13 September 1961, and 17 September 1961; *Congressional Quarterly Weekly Report,* 19 June 1962, p. 1085; *New York Times,* 16 August 1963; "The McCarthy Voting Record," undated, "Political: McCarthy Record," Box 269, EJM, MHS.

33. Author interview with Godfrey Hodgson, 25 February 1999, Oxford, U.K.; *New York Times,* 26 June 1962, 1 September 1962, and 8 September 1962; *Congressional Quarterly Weekly Report,* 24 August 1962, p. 1406; *University of Washington Daily,* 23 January 1963, in "Scrapbook 10," Box 3, Accession 11455, EJM, MHS; *New York Times,* 19 March 1963; *Congressional Quarterly Weekly Report,* 7 September 1962, p. 1514; Stanley K. Sheinbaum to McCarthy, 12 January 1961, "Legislative: Finance Committee: Tax; Depletion Allowance, 1961," Box 67, EJM, MHS; transcript of "Washington Viewpoint," WWDC Radio, Westinghouse Broadcasting Co., 7 February 1961, "Forums," Box 1, Accession 12758, EJM, MHS; Gwirtzman oral history, p. 136; oral history interview of Joe Rauh, by A. Delman, 10 June 1969, Oral History Collection, MHPA, p. 9; oral history interview of Peter Edelman, by Larry Hackman, 15 July 1969, Washington, D.C., Oral History Collection, JFK, Part 1, pp. 49–50, and Part 2, p. 259; *The Economist,* 8 August 1964. These interviews may well reflect the speakers' support for Robert Kennedy in 1968 and consequent antipathy to McCarthy.

34. McCarthy to Violet M. Gunther, ADA national director, 12 February 1963, "Political: ADA," Box 266, EJM, MHS; *St. Paul Pioneer Press,* 27 October 1964; Rauh oral history, MHPA, p. 8; Seymour K. Freidin, *A Sense of the Senate* (New York: 1972), p. 48; F. Harris, *Potomac Fever,* pp. 69–70; Asbell, *Senate Nobody Knows,* p. 243; Larry McCaffrey to author, 20 January 2000; oral history interview of Francis R. Valeo, by Donald A. Ritchie, 3 July 1985–11 March 1986, Senate Historical Office, Washington, D.C., pp. 809–810; Eisele, *Almost to the Presidency,* p. 165; Norman Sherman to author, 17 January 2000.

35. Eisele, *Almost to the Presidency,* p. 175; Eugene McCarthy, *Required Reading: A Decade of Political Wit and Wisdom* (New York: 1988), pp. 28–29, 114–115; Valeo, *Mike Mansfield,* pp. 108–109; Stewart, "Two Strategies of Leadership: Johnson and Mansfield," pp. 74–76; Valeo oral history, p. 440.

36. E. Berman, *Hubert,* pp. 245–247; Norman Sherman to author, 17 January 2000; oral history interview of Alwyn Matthews, by Michael L. Gillette, 23 October 1974, Oral History Collection, LBJ, Interview 1, pp. 42–43; *Milwaukee Journal,* 8 July 1961, in "Political: Voting Records," Box 267, EJM, MHS; author interview with Harry McPherson, 19 October 1999, Washington, D.C.; R. K. Baker, *Friend and Foe in the U.S. Senate,* p. 207; Patton oral history, p. 73; H. McPherson, *A Political Education,* p. 199; oral history interview of Herman E. Talmadge, by Jack Nelson, 2 August 1974, Lovejoy, Ga., Southern Intellectual Leaders Project, Interview 2, p. 92, COL; oral history of Joseph Tydings, by Roberta W. Greene, 8 May 1973, Washington, D.C., p. 58, Oral History Collection, JFK.

37. *Rochester Post-Bulletin,* 2 March 1963, in "Scrapbook 10," Box 3, Accession 11455, EJM, MHS; Walter Mondale to McCarthy, 27 June 1962, "Political: Elections," Box 265, EJM, MHS; Willard N. Beaudin to McCarthy, 1 November 1962, "Political: Governorship Race," Box 267, EJM, MHS; William J. Nee to McCarthy, 21 December 1961, "Political: William J. Nee," Box 267, EJM, MHS; *Minneapolis Tribune,* 13 January 1963; Chuck Daly to Lawrence O'Brien, 5 March 1963, Box 19, White House Staff File of Lawrence F. O'Brien, Congressional Liaison File, Presidential Papers of John F. Kennedy, JFK; *Mankato Free Press,* 12 March 1963, "Scrapbook 10," Box 3, Accession 11455, EJM, MHS.

38. *New York Times,* 27 November 1963 and 16 December 1963; *Christian Science Monitor,* 27 December 1963; *New York Times,* 31 July 1964.

39. McPherson interview; Frasers interview; oral history of Walter Jenkins, by Joe B. Frantz, 24 August 1971, Interview 2, p. 8, Oral History Collection, LBJ; *Minneapolis Star,* 29 November 1963; *Newsweek,* 7 September 1964; *The Nation,* 16 November 1964; Humphrey, *Education of a Public Man,* p. 298; Lyndon B. Johnson, *The Vantage Point: Perspectives of the Presidency, 1963–1969* (New York: 1971), p. 428; A. McCarthy, *Private Faces/Public Places,* p. 258; Irv-

ing Bernstein, *Guns or Butter: The Presidency of Lyndon Johnson* (Oxford: 1996), p. 139; J. Freeman interview; Joseph oral history, MHS, p. 41; oral history interview of Kenneth O'Donnell, by Paige Mulhollan, 23 July 1969, pp. 58–59, Oral History Collection, LBJ; Evans and Novak, *Lyndon B. Johnson,* p. 392; Eisele, *Almost to the Presidency,* pp. 201–202; transcript of telephone conversation between President Johnson and McCarthy, 6 January 1964, 7:46 p.m., Citation 1204, Recordings of Telephone Conversations, White House Series, Recordings and Transcripts of Conversations and Meetings, LBJ; transcript of telephone conversation between President Johnson and McCarthy, 4 February 1964, 12:52 p.m., Citation 1882, Recordings of Telephone Conversations, White House Series, Recordings and Transcripts of Conversations and Meetings, LBJ.

40. Eisele, *Almost to the Presidency,* p. 202; O'Donnell and Powers, *Johnny, We Hardly Knew Ye,* p. 251; *Chicago Daily News,* 24 August 1964; Jon Margolis, *The Last Innocent Year: America in 1964—The Beginning of the "Sixties"* (New York: 1999), p. 275; oral history interview of Miles Lord, by Arthur Naftalin, 22 February 1978, Minneapolis, Hubert H. Humphrey Oral History Project, MHS, p. 8.

41. McCarthy interview on CBS *Nightwatch,* 23 April 1987, recording in Box 8, Accession 15044, EJM, MHS; E. McCarthy, *Up 'til Now,* pp. 156–157; Solberg, *Hubert Humphrey,* p. 246; notes and clippings from interviews with Adrian Winkel, Gerald Heaney, Herman Schauinger, and Theodore Mitau, by Lael Herzog, Folder 14, Box 50, Part 1, National Files, MHPA; correspondence in "Political: Vice Presidential Candidacy: National Committee," Box 2, Accession 12491, EJM, MHS; Eisele, *Almost to the Presidency,* pp. 206–207; Richard T. Stout, *People* (New York: 1970), pp. 100–101; oral history interview of Richard T. Stout, by Betty Key, 13 January 1969, Oral History Collection, MHPA; "Some Guidelines of the Committee on McCarthy," undated, Folder 1, Box 5, Papers of J. Herman Schauinger, Georgetown University, Washington, D.C.; correspondence in "Political: Vice Presidency: General," Box 2, Accession 12491, EJM, MHS; *Boston Globe,* 26 May 1964; *Washington Post,* 20 August 1964; Lawrence F. O'Brien, *No Final Victories* (Garden City, N.Y.: 1974), p. 176; oral history interview of Ted Van Dyk, by Arthur Naftalin and Norman Sherman, 21 June 1978, Hubert H. Humphrey Oral History Project, MHS, pp. 3–4; Heaney interview; transcript of interview with Gerald Heaney, by Lael Herzog, undated, Folder 8, Box 50, Part 1, MHPA; Douglass Cater to Lyndon Johnson, 19 August 1964, "Memos to the White House Staff, May–November 1964," Box 13, Files of S. Douglass Cater, White House Aides' Files, White House Central Files, LBJ; *Minneapolis Weekly Mirror,* 25 July 1964, in "Scrapbook 33," Box 7, Accession 11455, EJM, MHS; *New York Times,* 16 August 1964; *Washington Post,* 20 August 1964; *New York Times,* 27 August 1964; Eisele, *Almost to the Presidency,* p. 210; *Baltimore News-American,* 23 March 1964, in "Scrapbook 32," Box 7, Accession 11455, EJM, MHS.

42. Boyle, *UAW and the Heyday of American Liberalism,* p. 194; Mann, *Walls of Jericho,* p. 434; *New Republic,* 20 June 1964; *New York Times,* 18 August 1964; *Minneapolis Tribune,* 3 January 1964; *Hibbing Daily Tribune,* 29 July 1964, in "Scrapbook 15," Box 3, Accession 11455, EJM, MHS; *Washington Post,* 3 August 1964.

43. "Balance Sheet on Possible Candidates for the Vice Presidential Nomination," undated, "Political: Vice Presidency: General," Box 2, Accession 12491, EJM, MHS; *Minneapolis Star,* 17 August 1964; Sorensen oral history, p. 6; oral history interview of Kenneth O'Donnell, by Paige Mulhollan, 23 July 1969, Oral History Collection, LBJ, pp. 58–59; oral history interview of Hubert H. Humphrey, by Larry J. Hackman, 30 March 1970, Oral History Collection, JFK, pp. 18–19; recording of telephone conversation between President Johnson and Kenneth O'Donnell, 14 August 1964, 5:14 p.m., Citation 4930, Recordings of Telephone Conversations, White House Series, Recordings and Transcripts of Conversations and Meetings, LBJ; Johnson conversation with Bill Moyers, 8:02 p.m., 31 July 1964, in Michael Beschloss, *Taking Charge: The Johnson White House Tapes, 1963–1964* (New York: 1998), p. 489.

44. N. Miller, *Lyndon,* pp. 386–387; *Congressional Record,* 23 April 1964, pp. 8357–8358; and 19 June 1964, p. 14008; *Newsweek,* 27 July 1964; *New York Times,* 17 August 1964 and 27 August

1964; F. Harris, *Potomac Fever*, p. 154; A. McCarthy, *Private Faces/Public Places*, p. 267; recording of telephone conversation between President Johnson and James Eastland, 22 August 1964, 6:21 p.m., Citation 5130, Recordings of Telephone Conversations, White House Series, Recordings and Transcripts of Conversations and Meetings, LBJ; Evans and Novak, *Lyndon B. Johnson*, p. 449; Solberg, *Hubert Humphrey*, p. 244; recording of telephone conversation between President Johnson and John Connally, 23 July 1964, 5:31 p.m., Citations 4322–4323, Recordings of Telephone Conversations, White House Series, Recordings and Transcripts of Conversations and Meetings, LBJ.

45. *St. Paul Pioneer Press*, 7 February 1964; *Congressional Quarterly Almanac 1964*, p. 666; McCarthy to Maurice Kreevoy, 3 March 1964, "Legislative: Finance: Tax: Oil Depletion, 1964," Box 110, EJM, MHS; McCarthy to Drew Pearson, 21 August 1964, "McCarthy, Eugene," Box G261(2), Drew Pearson Papers, LBJ; Pearson to McCarthy, undated August 1964, "McCarthy, Eugene," Box G261(2), Drew Pearson Papers, LBJ; transcript of telephone conversation between President Johnson and McCarthy, 6 January 1964, 7:46 p.m., Citation 1204, Recordings of Telephone Conversations, White House Series, Recordings and Transcripts of Conversations and Meetings, LBJ; Clark, *Congress: The Sapless Branch*, p. 47; *Atlantic Monthly*, September 1969; Don E. Carleton, *A Breed So Rare: The Life of J. R. Parten, Liberal Texas Oilman, 1896–1992* (Austin, Texas: 1998); Eisele interview; Hersh, *Education of Edward Kennedy*, p. 291.

46. Johnson conversation with James Rowe, 5:56 p.m., 30 July 1964, in Beschloss, *Taking Charge*, p. 486; Bernstein, *Guns or Butter*, p. 139; Johnson conversation with Hubert Humphrey, 2:14 p.m., 2 May 1964, in Beschloss, *Taking Charge*, p. 340; Johnson conversation with Hubert Humphrey, 6:46 p.m., 30 July 1964, in Beschloss, *Taking Charge*, p. 340; Ted Van Dyk to Bill Connell, 14 August 1964, "Memos, June–December 1964," Box 1, William Connell Papers, MHS; *Minneapolis Star*, 14 August 1964; Sorensen oral history, interview 2, by Larry Hackman, 23 July 1970, New York, p. 36; O'Donnell oral history, p. 59; Miller, *Lyndon*, p. 387; Robert Dallek, *Flawed Giant: Lyndon Johnson and His Times, 1961–1973* (Oxford: 1998), p. 137; Mann, *Walls of Jericho*, p. 486. Senior establishment figures such as Walter Lippmann and McGeorge Bundy also favored Humphrey rather than McCarthy: see McGeorge Bundy to President Johnson, 21 August 1964, National Security File, Memos to the President, McGeorge Bundy memos, Vol. 6, Box 2, LBJ. I am indebted to Andrew Preston for bringing my attention to this document.

47. McCarthy interview; notes of interview with Herman Schauinger, by Lael Herzog, undated, Folder 14, Box 50, Part 1, National Files, MHPA; Stout, *People*, p. 102; *St. Paul Dispatch*, 25 August 1964; transcript of *Meet the Press*, NBC, 23 August 1964, "Political: Election: Senate," Box 269, EJM, MHS; recording of telephone conversation between President Johnson and Hubert Humphrey [and McCarthy], 23 August 1964, 6:35 p.m., Citation 5139, Recordings of Telephone Conversations, White House Series, Recordings and Transcripts of Conversations and Meetings, LBJ; *Washington Post*, 24 August 1964; A. McCarthy, *Private Faces/Public Places*, p. 272; Dallek, *Flawed Giant*, p. 158; *Time*, 4 September 1964; Bernstein, *Guns or Butter*, p. 142; Eisele, *Almost to the Presidency*, pp. 217–218, 221; Muskie oral history, p. 18; Lippman and Hansen, *Muskie*, p. 110.

48. McCarthy interview; Shuman oral history, pp. 125–126; oral history interview of Rowland Evans, by Norman Sherman, 9 August 1978, Washington, D.C., p. 11, Hubert H. Humphrey Oral History Project, MHS; recording of oral history interview of Gaylord Nelson, by unspecified interviewer, 28 July 1978, Washington, D.C., Hubert H. Humphrey Oral History Project, MHS; Eisele interview; Smaby, *Political Upheaval*, p. 433; Reedy oral history, p. 26; Evans and Novak, *Lyndon B. Johnson*, p. 461; William Vanden Heuvel and Milton Gwirtzman, *On His Own: Robert Kennedy, 1964–1968* (Garden City, N.Y.: 1970), p. 286.

49. *Minneapolis Star*, 27 October 1964; *Minneapolis Tribune*, 27 September 1964, 4 November 1964; *New York Times*, 1 November 1964; Spannaus interview; *Congressional Quarterly Almanac 1964*, p. 1043; *New York Times*, 5 November 1964; Gould, "Never a Deep Partisan,"

p. 25; Lewis Chester, Godfrey Hodgson, and Bruce Page, *An American Melodrama: The Presidential Campaign of 1968 (New York:* 1969), p. 84; Thomas Byrne Edsall and Mary D. Edsall, *Chain Reaction: The Impact of Race, Rights, and Taxes on American Politics* (New York: 1991), pp. 39, 49.

CHAPTER SEVEN

Rethinking the Cold War

1. *New York Times,* 8 January 1965; *Minneapolis Tribune,* 13 January 1965; F. Harris, *Potomac Fever,* p. 71; *New York Times,* 17 October 1967.

2. Oral history interview of Senator William Benton, by Kenneth S. Davis, 15 June 1967, New York City, p. 15, Adlai E. Stevenson Oral History Project, COL; *Washington Post,* 22 July 1956; Broadwater, *Adlai Stevenson and American Politics,* p. 232; *St. Cloud Daily Times,* 23 July 1965, "General: Clippings: Foreign Policy," Box 305, EJM, MHS; Jack Valenti to President Johnson, 15 July 1965, "McCarthy, Eugene J.: 1/1/65–12/31/65," Box 210, Name File, White House Central Files, LBJ; Dallek, *Flawed Giant,* p. 234.

3. Harry McPherson to Jack Valenti, 20 August 1965, "Eliot Janeway," Box 41, Office Files of Harry McPherson, White House Aides' Files, White House Central Files, LBJ; Henry H. Fowler to President Johnson, 27 August 1965, "McCarthy, Eugene J.: 1/1/65–12/31/65," Box 210, Name File, White House Central Files, LBJ; *Washington Post,* 20 January 1966, 8 March 1966, and 21 March 1966; Memorandum to President Johnson, "Concerning your question on contacts w/ Sen. McCarthy," 10 February 1966, "1 February 1966," Box 28, President's Appointment File, LBJ.

4. William Conrad Gibbons, *The United States Government and the Vietnam War: Executive and Legislative Roles and Relationships, Part 4, July 1965–January 1968* (Princeton, N.J.: 1995), p. 158; E. McCarthy, *Up 'til Now,* pp. 153, 166.

5. *Harper's Magazine,* June 1964; "Record of Eugene J. McCarthy, 82nd Congress, 1st session, 1951," 13 February 1951, Box 7, Accession 12240, EJM, MHS; *Congressional Record,* 13 February 1951, pp. 1291–1292.

6. McCarthy to E. T. McKane, 6 March 1951, "Communism," Box 2, EJM, MHS; *St. Paul Dispatch,* 13 December 1951.

7. *Minneapolis Tribune,* 9 October 1954; McCarthy to Carey McWilliams, 4 March 1958, "Questionnaires," Box 41, EJM, MHS; untitled press release on aid to India, 23 May 1951, "India," Box 3, EJM, MHS; McCarthy to Caryl Grefe, 5 January 1960, "Legislative: Foreign Relations: Foreign Aid, 1959–1960," Box 57, EJM, MHS; text of McCarthy speech in Milwaukee, 20 October 1956, "Political: McCarthy Speeches and Remarks," Box 263, EJM, MHS.

8. *Washington Post,* 19 October 1958; *Minneapolis Tribune,* 9 September 1954; *New York Times,* 25 November 1957; excerpts from speech at University of Minnesota, 10 October 1958, "Articles and Press Releases, 1958 Campaign," Box 3, Accession 12758, EJM, MHS.

9. "Senator McCarthy Addresses Minneapolis Memorial Day Program," 30 May 1959, "Press Releases, Jan.–July 1959," Box 11, Accession 11455, EJM, MHS; *Albert Lea Daily Tribune,* 24 September 1959, in "Scrapbook 5," Box 1, Accession 11455, EJM, MHS; *New Orleans Times-Picayune,* 1 May 1960, in "Scrapbook 7," Box 2, Accession 11455, EJM, MHS; *St. Paul Pioneer Press,* 13 October 1960.

10. *The Nation,* 22 March 1958.

11. Stuhler, *Ten Men of Minnesota and American Foreign Policy,* pp. 5, 14; Irving Kristol, "Consensus and Dissent in U.S. Foreign Policy," in Anthony Lake, ed., *The Vietnam Legacy* (New York: 1976), pp. 80–101; Godfrey Hodgson, "The Establishment," *Foreign Policy* 10 (Spring 1973): 3–40; Robert R. Tomes, *Apocalypse Then: American Intellectuals and the Vietnam War, 1954–1975* (New York: 1998), p. 37; Kristol, "Consensus and Dissent," pp. 2–5; Walter A. Zelman, "Senate Dissent and the Vietnam War, 1964–1968," unpublished Ph.D. dissertation, UCLA, 1971, pp. 17–18.

12. *Minneapolis Tribune,* 2 February 1958; *St. Paul Pioneer Press,* 6 July 1961; McCarthy to Mrs. Elmer Harvey, 18 September 1961, "Legislative: Foreign Relations: Disarmament 1961," Box 69, EJM, MHS; McCarthy to Mrs. Harlan M. Smith, 6 December 1962, "Legislative: Foreign Relations: Disarmament 1962," Box 109, EJM, MHS; press release, "McCarthy Discusses Ethical Aspects of Foreign Policy," 10 October 1962, "Aug.–Dec. 1962," Box 11, Accession 11455, EJM, MHS; press release, "McCarthy Says Man Can Give Form and Direction to History," 28 March 1963, "Jan.–June 1963," Box 11, Accession 11455, EJM, MHS.

13. McCarthy to Murray D. Comer, 7 April 1960, "Legislative: Foreign Relations: Cuba, 1959–1960," Box 57, EJM, MHS; McCarthy to Sidney J. Luft, 30 August 1957, "Foreign Affairs; Miscellaneous," Box 34, EJM, MHS; McCarthy to Mrs. Matt Leifeld, 21 March 1959, "Legislative: Foreign Relations: Cuba, 1959–1960," Box 57, EJM, MHS; McCarthy to J. G. McKeon, 20 September 1961, "Legislative: Foreign Relations: Cuba, 1961," Box 69, EJM, MHS; *Houston Post,* 18 May 1962, in "Scrapbook 9," Box 2, Accession 11455, EJM, MHS.

14. Text of H.R. 5830, 10 October 1951, "Committee on Atomic Energy," Box 2, EJM, MHS; *Congressional Quarterly Almanac 1951,* p. 642; *St. Paul Pioneer Press,* 29 October 1951; *Rochester Post-Bulletin,* 1 February 1958, in "McCarthy Senate Announcement," Box 263, EJM, MHS; *New York Times,* 12 May 1959, 29 May 1959, 13 June 1959; *Congressional Quarterly Almanac 1959,* p. 667; press release, "Controversies over Appointments Not 'Personality Clashes,' McCarthy Says," 14 May 1959, "Jan.–July 1959," Box 11, Accession 11455, EJM, MHS. See also LeRoy Ashby and Rod Gramer, *Fighting the Odds: The Life of Senator Frank Church* (Pullman, Wash.: 1994), p. 118; Drukman, *Wayne Morse,* p. 201; Robert D. Johnson, *Ernest Gruening and the American Dissenting Tradition* (Cambridge, Mass.: 1998), p. 230.

15. John T. Elliff, "Congress and the Intelligence Community," in Dodd and Oppenheimer, eds., *Congress Reconsidered,* pp. 193–206; Frances Wilcox, *Congress, the Executive, and Foreign Policy* (New York: 1971), p. 86; Godfrey Hodgson, *All Things to All Men: The False Promise of the American Presidency* (London: 1980), p. 38; William Conrad Gibbons, *The United States Government and the Vietnam War: Executive and Legislative Roles and Relationships: Part 1, 1945–1960* (Princeton, N.J.: 1986), p. 331; Rhodri Jeffreys-Jones, *The CIA and American Democracy* (New Haven, Conn.: 1988), p. 153; "McCarthy Record on Bills for CIA," undated, "Legislative: CIA Floor Fight Notebook, 1966," Box 309, EJM, MHS; "McCarthy Bills, 1953–1954," Box 194, EJM, MHS; "McCarthy Record, 84th Congress, 1st and 2nd Sessions," p. 100, Box 194, EJM, MHS; *Congressional Quarterly Weekly Report,* 10 February 1956, p. 154; Gibbons, *The U.S. Government and the Vietnam War: Part 1,* p. 330.

16. "McCarthy Record on Bills for CIA," undated, "Legislative: CIA Floor Fight Notebook, 1966," Box 309, EJM, MHS; "Legislative: McCarthy Bills, 1960–1961," Box 195, EJM, MHS; *New York Times,* 3 May 1961; *Washington Star,* 16 October 1961; *Washington Star,* 17 January 1962; *New York Times,* 19 January 1962; *New York Times,* 22 January 1962; *Congressional Record,* 29 January 1962, pp. 925–946; *New York Times,* 15 March 1963.

17. *Minneapolis Tribune,* 9 September 1954; McCarthy to Robert Schwank, 2 April 1962, "Legislative: Foreign Relations: Southeast Asia, 1962," Box 109, EJM, MHS.

18. Robert Sam Anson, *McGovern: A Biography* (New York: 1972), pp. 151–152; press release, "Senator McCarthy Traces Successes of American Foreign Policy," 31 May 1964, "Jan.–June 1964," Box 11, Accession 11455, EJM, MHS.

19. Fredrik Logevall, *Choosing War: The Lost Chance for Peace and the Escalation of War in Vietnam* (Berkeley, Calif.: 1999), pp. 196–205; Edwin E. Moïse, *Tonkin Gulf and the Escalation of the Vietnam War* (Chapel Hill, N.C.: 1996); oral history interview of George McGovern, by Arthur Naftalin, 29 July 1978, Washington, D.C., p. 20, Hubert H. Humphrey Oral History Project, MHS; Randall Bennett Woods, *Fulbright: A Biography* (Cambridge, U.K.: 1995), p. 354; Logevall, *Choosing War,* p. 204; Zelman, "Senate Dissent and the Vietnam War," p. 91; Tom Wells, *The War Within: America's Battle over Vietnam* (Berkeley, Calif.: 1994), p. 11; Nancy Zaroulis and Gerald Sullivan, *Who Spoke Up? American Protest Against the War in Vietnam, 1963–1975* (Garden City, N.Y.: 1984), pp. 22–23; Tomes, *Apocalypse Then,* p. 107.

20. Press release, "Senator McCarthy Comments on Senate Resolution," 6 August 1964, "Legislative: Foreign Relations: Southeast Asia, 1964," Box 120, EJM, MHS; transcript, *Face the Nation,* CBS, 9 August 1964, "Political: McCarthy Statements," Box 269, EJM, MHS; Heaney interview; Heaney oral history, pp. 64–66; Eisele, *Almost to the Presidency,* p. 209.

21. Adam Garfinkle, *Telltale Hearts: The Origins and Impact of the Vietnam Antiwar Movement* (New York: 1995), p. 58; Valeo, *Mike Mansfield,* p. 173; Rhodri Jeffreys-Jones, *Peace Now! American Society and the Ending of the Vietnam War* (New Haven, Conn.: 1999), p. 15; McCarthy to Philip Armstrong, 1 October 1964, "Legislative: Foreign Relations: Southeast Asia, 1964," Box 120, EJM, MHS; *Minneapolis Star,* 13 October 1964; McCarthy to the Rev. Donald Woodward, 14 December 1964, "Legislative: Foreign Relations: Southeast Asia, 1964," Box 120, EJM, MHS.

22. *St. Paul Pioneer Press,* 27 April 1965; *St. Paul Dispatch,* 12 May 1965; Lippman and Hansen, *Muskie,* p. 182.

23. Zelman, "Senate Dissent and the Vietnam War," p. 218; Wilcox, *Congress, the Executive, and Foreign Policy,* p. 21. See also Robert David Johnson, "Congress and the Cold War," *Journal of Cold War Studies* 3:2 (Spring 2001): 94–95.

24. Woods, *Fulbright,* pp. 247–248, 264; oral history interview of Carl M. Marcy, by Donald A. Ritchie, 14 September to 16 November 1983, Senate Historical Office, Washington, D.C., pp. 201–202; oral history interview of Pat Holt, by Donald A. Ritchie, 9 September to 12 December 1980, Senate Historical Office, Washington, D.C., p. 213; Freidin, *A Sense of the Senate,* pp. 66–67; Woods, *Fulbright,* p. 244; David Maraniss, *First in His Class: The Biography of Bill Clinton* (New York: 1995), p. 88; H. McPherson, *A Political Education,* p. 35.

25. Woods, *Fulbright,* pp. 248, 263; Eugene Brown, *J. William Fulbright: Advice and Dissent* (Iowa City, Iowa: 1985), pp. 53–55; Dallek, *Flawed Giant,* p. 105; Zelman, "Senate Dissent and the Vietnam War," p. 11; John Ehrman, *The Rise of Neoconservatism: Intellectuals and Foreign Affairs, 1945–1994* (New Haven, Conn.: 1995), p. 22.

26. Michael P. Rosenberg, "Congress and the Vietnam War: A Study of the Critics of the War in 1967 and 1968," unpublished Ph.D. dissertation, New School for Social Research, New York, 1973, p. 85; Zelman, "Senate Dissent and the Vietnam War," p. 242; Rosenberg, "Congress and the Vietnam War," pp. 72, 194; *New York Times,* 25 February 1968; *New York Review of Books,* 26 January 1967.

27. Dallek, *Flawed Giant,* pp. 262–268; Piero Gleijes, *The Dominican Crisis: The 1965 Constitutional Revolt and American Intervention* (Baltimore: 1978); Charles DeBenedetti, with Charles Chatfield, *An American Ordeal: The Antiwar Movement of the Vietnam Era* (Syracuse, N.Y.: 1990), p. 112.

28. *St. Paul Dispatch,* 12 May 1965; A. McCarthy, *Private Faces/Public Places,* p. 252; *Minneapolis Tribune,* 11 June 1965; *New York Times,* 13 June 1965; Eisele, *Almost to the Presidency,* p. 260.

29. R. Johnson, *Ernest Gruening and the American Dissenting Tradition,* p. 229; Eisele, *Almost to the Presidency,* p. 260; Brown, *J. William Fulbright,* pp. 69–73; Woods, *Fulbright,* p. 387; *Duluth News-Tribune,* 17 September 1965, in "Scrapbook 19," Box 5, Accession 11455, EJM, MHS; Stuhler, *Ten Men of Minnesota and American Foreign Policy,* p. 209; *Latin American Times,* 1 October 1965, in "Scrapbook 18," Box 5, Accession 11455, EJM, MHS; Eisele, *Almost to the Presidency,* pp. 260–261.

30. McCarthy, *Up 'til Now,* p. 170; *Congressional Quarterly Almanac 1965,* p. 1103; Terry H. Anderson, *The Movement and the Sixties: Protest in America from Greensboro to Wounded Knee* (Oxford, U.K.: 1995), pp. 136–137; Robert Dallek, "Lyndon Johnson and Vietnam," *Diplomatic History* 20:2 (Spring 1996): 147–162; David Steigerwald, *The Sixties and the End of Modern America* (New York: 1995), p. 114; Anson, *McGovern,* pp. 155–157; Melvin Small, *Johnson, Nixon, and the Doves* (New Brunswick, N.J.: 1988), p. 34; Broadwater, *Adlai Stevenson and American Politics,* p. 220; Zaroulis and Sullivan, *Who Spoke Up?,* p. 43; Garfinkle, *Telltale Hearts,* p. 77; Woods, *Fulbright,* pp. 367–369; Donovan, *The Policy Makers,* p. 74.

31. "Legislative: Foreign Relations: Southeast Asia, 1965," Box 125, EJM, MHS; Eisele, *Almost*

to the Presidency, p. 258; George S. McGovern, *Grassroots* (New York: 1977), p. 106; Ashby and Gramer, *Fighting the Odds,* pp. 193–194; William Conrad Gibbons, *United States Government and the Vietnam War: Executive and Legislative Roles and Relationships, Part 3, January–July 1965* (Princeton, N.J.: 1989), pp. 128–129; Ashby and Gramer, *Fighting the Odds,* p. 196; undated interview with Eugene McCarthy for *Cold War* (CNN) at <http://www.hfni. gsehd.gwu.edu/~nsarchiv/coldwae/interviews/episode-13/mccarthy1.html>, 2 August 2003; Gibbons, *United States Government and the Vietnam War, Part 3,* p. 129; Eisele, *Almost to the Presidency,* p. 258; E. McCarthy, *Up 'til Now,* p. 170.

32. *St. Paul Pioneer Press,* 14 March 1965; Gibbons, *United States Government and the Vietnam War, Part 3,* p. 241; *St. Paul Pioneer Press,* 12 May 1965.

33. Wells, *War Within,* p. 73; Small, *Johnson, Nixon, and the Doves,* p. 62; DeBenedetti, *An American Ordeal,* pp. 142, 162; transcript of question and answer session at Indiana University, 18 April 1968, "Speeches: April 1968," Box 12, Accession 11455, EJM, MHS.

34. Dallek, *Flawed Giant,* p. 350; *New York Times,* 27 January 1966, 28 January 1966; E. McCarthy, *Up 'til Now,* pp. 172–73; *New York Times,* 29 January 1966; Stanley Karnow, *Vietnam: A History* (London: 1984), p. 499; Eisele, *Almost to the Presidency,* p. 263; W. Averell Harriman to McGeorge Bundy, 4 February 1966, Box 439, Special Files: Public Service, Kennedy-Johnson Administrations, 1958–71, W. Averell Harriman Papers, Library of Congress, Washington, D.C.; E. McCarthy, *Up 'til Now,* p. 173; *Insight on the News,* 20 March 2000, at <http://www.insightmag.com/archive/200002264.shtml>, 23 November 2001. I am indebted to Andrew Preston for bringing my attention to the Harriman letter.

35. "McCarthy *Congressional Record* Remarks," Book 3, 27 January 1966, pp. 1247–1249, Box 7, Accession 12240, EJM, MHS; Gibbons, *United States Government and the Vietnam War, Part 4,* p. 158; Parmet, *The Democrats,* p. 265.

36. Sinclair, *Congressional Realignment,* p. 116; Zelman, "Senate Dissent and the Vietnam War," p. 19; Zaroulis and Sullivan, *Who Spoke Up?,* p. 27; *The Nation,* 10 October 1966; Zelman, "Senate Dissent and the Vietnam War," pp. 125–129.

37. Zelman, "Senate Dissent and the Vietnam War," p. 132; Sinclair, *Congressional Realignment,* p. 124; Rosenberg, "Congress and the Vietnam War," pp. 57, 106; Zelman, "Senate Dissent and the Vietnam War," p. 57; Dallek, "Lyndon Johnson and Vietnam," p. 150; Woods, *Fulbright,* p. 375; *Washington Post,* 7 July 1966.

38. Zelman, "Senate Dissent and the Vietnam War," pp. 136, 142–143; DeBenedetti, *An American Ordeal,* p. 91; David W. Levy, *The Debate over Vietnam* (Baltimore: 1991), p. 71; Tomes, *Apocalypse Then,* p. 151; *New York Review of Books,* 7 July 1966; Craig W. Cutbirth, "A Strategic Perspective: Robert F. Kennedy's Dissent on the Vietnam War, 1965–1968," unpublished Ph.D. dissertation, Bowling Green State University, 1976, pp. 71–72; Arthur M. Schlesinger Jr., *Robert Kennedy and His Times* (New York: 1978), pp. 793–797; DeBenedetti, *An American Ordeal,* pp. 13–18; Tomes, *Apocalypse Then,* p. 57; Charles Kadushin, *The American Intellectual Elite* (Boston: 1974).

39. *Minneapolis Tribune,* 27 February 1966; Woods, *Fulbright,* pp. 408, 421; *Pittsburgh Post-Gazette,* 9 March 1966, in "Scrapbook 21," Box 5, Accession 11455, EJM, MHS; McCarthy to the Rev. Lee H. Ball, Methodist Federation for Social Action, 11 April 1966, "Legislative: Foreign Relations: Vietnam, April 1966," Box 207, EJM, MHS; *Washington Post,* 2 May 1966; *Minneapolis Tribune,* 27 March 1966.

40. Valeo, *Mike Mansfield,* p. 207; Wells, *War Within,* pp. 258–259; R. Johnson, *Ernest Gruening and the American Dissenting Tradition,* pp. 274–275; Cutbirth, "A Strategic Perspective," p. 91; Gibbons, *United States Government and the Vietnam War, Part 4,* p. 347; Zelman, "Senate Dissent and the Vietnam War," pp. 58–59, 189; oral history interview of George McGovern, by Paige Mulhollan, 30 April 1969, Oral History Collection, LBJ, pp. 13–14; McCarthy interview; *St. Paul Pioneer Press,* 21 May 1967; Ashby and Gramer, *Fighting the Odds,* p. 226.

41. Kearns, *Lyndon Johnson and the American Dream,* p. 326; Dallek, *Flawed Giant,* p. 367; Wells, *War Within,* p. 69; Woods, *Fulbright,* pp. 409–410, 405; Ibid., p. 405; Wells, *War Within,* p. 69; press release, "Sen. McCarthy Says Vietnam Hearings Have Been Helpful, Must Con-

tinue," 13 February 1966, "Jan.–June 1966," Box 11, Accession 11455, EJM, MHS; "Hearings Before Committee on Foreign Relations on S. R. 2793 (Supplemental Foreign Assistance, Fiscal Year 1966: Vietnam)," Proceedings of Senate Committee on Foreign Relations, 89th Congress, 2nd Session, Volume 1, 28 January 1966, pp. 32–33, in Box 13, Accession 12240, EJM, MHS; Woods, *Fulbright,* p. 404; McCarthy to David M. Cain, 17 October 1966, "Legislative: Foreign Relations: Vietnam, April 1966," Box 207, EJM, MHS; E. McCarthy, *Up 'til Now,* p. 174.

42. *New York Review of Books,* 26 January 1966; Brown, *J. William Fulbright,* p. 75; Garfinkle, *Telltale Hearts,* p. 89; Levy, *Debate over Vietnam,* p. 135.

43. *Washington Post,* 9 March 1966, 10 March 1966; Gibbons, *United States Government and the Vietnam War, Part 4,* pp. 255–257; "McCarthy *Congressional Record* Remarks," Book 3, 31 January 1966, pp. 1515–1516, Box 7, Accession 12240, EJM, MHS; Zelman, "Senate Dissent and the Vietnam War," p. 98; press release, "Sen. McCarthy Says Resolutions Undermine Presidential Powers," 1 March 1966, "Jan.–June 1966," Box 11, Accession 11455, EJM, MHS.

44. *St. Paul Pioneer Press,* 3 March 1966; *Washington Post,* 6 March 1966; McCarthy to James A. Foy, 10 March 1966, "Legislative: Foreign Relations: Vietnam, Morse Amendment," Box 207, EJM, MHS; Eisele, *Almost to the Presidency,* pp. 263–264. McCarthy's façade of parliamentary obscurantism was probably designed to allow him to support the Morse amendment without earning the reputation of an extreme dove: the unfortunate consequence was instead the reputation of an extreme pedant.

45. *Congressional Quarterly Weekly Report,* 8 July 1966, p. 1433; press release, "McCarthy Asks Re-examination of Foreign Policy," 20 September 1966, "July–Dec. 1966," Box 11, Accession 11455, EJM, MHS; A. McCarthy, *Private Faces/Public Places,* pp. 281–283; press release, "Senator McCarthy Delivers Noble Lectures at Harvard," 30 November 1966, "July–Dec. 1966," Box 11, Accession 11455, EJM, MHS; *Saturday Review,* 5 November 1966.

CHAPTER EIGHT

The Limits of Power

1. Steigerwald, *The Sixties and the End of Modern America,* p. 114; John A. Andrew, *Lyndon Johnson and the Great Society* (Chicago: 1998), p. 75; Lewis L. Gould, *1968: The Election That Changed America* (Chicago: 1993), p. 12; Gareth Davies, *From Opportunity to Entitlement: The Transformation and Decline of Great Society Liberalism* (Lawrence, Kans.: 1996), p. 124; Valeo, *Mike Mansfield,* p. 212; Zelman, "Senate Dissent and the Vietnam War," p. 153; Davies, *From Opportunity to Entitlement,* p. 131; Irving Bernstein, *Guns or Butter,* pp. 410–411; Davies, *From Opportunity to Entitlement,* p. 145; Parmet, *The Democrats,* p. 245.

2. Karnow, *Vietnam,* p. 505; Rosenberg, "Congress and the Vietnam War," pp. 32, 37; R. Johnson, *Ernest Gruening and the American Dissenting Tradition,* p. 290; Rosenberg, "Congress and the Vietnam War," p. 144; John Dumbrell, "Congress and the Antiwar Movement," in John Dumbrell, ed., *Vietnam and the Antiwar Movement* (Aldershot, U.K.: 1989), p. 101; Wilcox, *Congress, the Executive, and Foreign Policy,* p. 8; Wells, *War Within,* p. 42; Rosenberg, "Congress and the Vietnam War," p. 192; Dumbrell, "Congress and the Antiwar Movement," p. 108.

3. Tomes, *Apocalypse Then,* p. 3; DeBenedetti, "Lyndon Johnson and the Antiwar Opposition," pp. 24–26; Charles DeBenedetti, "On the Significance of Citizen Peace Activism: America, 1961–1975," *Peace and Change* 9:2 (Summer 1983): 6–20; Levy, *Debate over Vietnam,* pp. 46–76.

4. Jerome Grossman, *Relentless Liberal* (New York: 1996), pp. 34–39; Hersh, *Education of Edward Kennedy,* p. 170; Clymer, *Edward M. Kennedy,* p. 42; Irwin Unger, *The Movement: A History of the American New Left, 1959–1972* (New York: 1974), p. 13; Milton S. Katz, "Peace Liberals and Vietnam: SANE and the Politics of 'Responsible' Protest," *Peace and Change* 9:2/ 3 (Summer 1983): 21–23.

5. Tomes, *Apocalypse Then,* p. 64; Isserman and Kazin, *America Divided,* p. 125.

6. Ware, *Breakdown of Democratic Organization,* p. 76; Tomes, *Apocalypse Then,* pp. 100, 147; Solberg, *Hubert Humphrey,* p. 273; Dallek, "Lyndon Johnson and Vietnam," p. 151; Katz, "Peace Liberals and Vietnam," p. 23; Stout, *People,* p. 56; Farr interview; David Lebedoff, *Ward Number Six* (New York: 1972); *Minneapolis Tribune,* 4 October and 8 October 1967.

7. Levy, *Debate over Vietnam,* pp. 96–100; Mitchell K. Hall, *Because of Their Faith: CALCAV and Religious Oposition to the Vietnam War* (New York: 1990), p. 40; Reichley, *Religion in American Public Life,* p. 250; Au, *The Cross, the Flag, and the Bomb,* p. 179; Hanna, *Catholics and American Politics,* p. 41; Levy, *Debate over Vietnam,* p. 98; Shannon, *Reluctant Dissenter,* p. 114.

8. Hall, *Because of Their Faith,* pp. 6–7; McGreevy, *Parish Boundaries,* p. 143; Garfinkle, *Telltale Hearts,* p. 51 (italics in original); Meconis, *With Clumsy Grace,* p. 6.

9. Au, *The Cross, the Flag, and the Bomb,* p. 42; *Commonweal,* 10 March 1965; Shannon, *Reluctant Dissenter,* p. 114; Jordan and Baumann, eds., Commonweal *Confronts the Century,* pp. 178–181; *Commonweal,* 23 December 1966 and 22 September 1967; Au, *The Cross, the Flag, and the Bomb,* p. 96; Shannon, *Reluctant Dissenter,* p. 115; Wills, *Bare Ruined Choirs,* pp. 125–126; Peter Collier and David Horowitz, *Destructive Generation: Second Thoughts About the Sixties* (New York: 1989), p. 259; Zaroulis and Sullivan, *Who Spoke Up?,* p. 57; Au, *The Cross, the Flag, and the Bomb,* p. xv; Garfinkle, *Telltale Hearts,* pp. 34–41.

10. *St. John's Alumni Supplement* 71:15 (14 November 1958); in "Political: Minnesota Editorials, 1958 Campaign," Box 262, EJM, MHS; *St. Paul Catholic Bulletin,* 22 February 1965, in "Scrapbook 18," Box 5, Accession 11455, EJM, MHS; *St. Paul Pioneer Press,* 20 March 1966; E. McCarthy, *Up 'til Now,* p. 178; McCarthy to Stanley Schlick, United Presbyterian Church Synod of Minnesota, 29 March 1967, "Legislative: Foreign Relations: Vietnam, March 1967," Box 219, EJM, MHS; Wells, *War Within,* pp. 75–77.

11. Hall, *Because of Their Faith,* pp. 1–27, 33; "Agenda for mobilization," 31 January–1 February 1967, "CALCAV," Box 1, National Files, MHPA; Wells, *War Within,* p. 119; Richard Cummings, *The Pied Piper: Allard K. Lowenstein and the Liberal Dream* (New York: 1985), p. 332; Hall, *Because of Their Faith,* p. 34; *Washington Star,* 1 February 1967; Wells, *War Within,* pp. 120–121; Hall, *Because of Their Faith,* p. 38.

12. Tape recording of address to CALCAV, 1 February 1967, Box 3, Eugene McCarthy collection, Audio-Visual Collection, MHS; text of address to CALCAV, 1 February 1967, "Press releases, January–June 1967," Box 11, Accession 11455, EJM, MHS; tape recording of address to CALCAV, 1 February 1967, Box 3, Eugene McCarthy collection, Audio-Visual Collection, MHS; *Minneapolis Tribune,* 2 February 1967; *New York Times,* 2 February 1967; Hall, *Because of Their Faith,* p. 37.

13. McCarthy interview; Wells, *War Within,* p. 121; McCarthy interview.

14. Ehrman, *Rise of Neoconservatism,* p. 23; Tomes, *Apocalypse Then,* pp. 27–29; press release, "McCarthy Asks Re-examination of Foreign Policy," 20 September 1966, "July–Dec 1966," Box 11, Accession 11455, EJM, MHS; McCarthy, *Hard Years,* p. 22; Woods, *Fulbright,* pp. 389, 430; Jeffreys-Jones, *CIA and American Democracy,* p. 153; *Saturday Evening Post,* 4–11 January 1964, in "Scrapbook 14," Box 4, Accession 11455, EJM, MHS; undated memorandum, "Legislative: CIA Floor Fight Notebook, 1966," Box 309, EJM, MHS; Marcy oral history, pp. 203–204; Holt oral history, p. 213; Wilcox, *Congress, the Executive, and Foreign Policy,* pp. 85–86; *New York Times,* 21 January 1966, 25 January 1966, 26 April 1966, 13 May 1966, and 18 May 1966; *Congressional Quarterly Weekly Report,* 4 February 1966, p. 326; *Congressional Quarterly Weekly Report,* 20 May 1966, p. 991; *New Republic,* 28 May 1966; *Congressional Quarterly Weekly Report,* 22 July 1966, pp. 1580–1587; *Congressional Quarterly Almanac 1966,* pp. 620–622; Wilcox, *Congress, the Executive, and Foreign Policy,* p. 86; Elliff, "Congress and the Intelligence Community," p. 196; Eisele, *Almost to the Presidency,* p. 267; *New York Times,* 16 February 1967.

15. *New York Times,* 4 September 1966; *Congressional Quarterly Almanac 1966,* p. 436; Parmet, *The Democrats,* p. 265; *Washington Star,* 4 June 1967; *St. Paul Pioneer Press,* 22 June 1967; Wilcox, *Congress, the Executive, and Foreign Policy,* p. 139; *Saturday Review,* 9 July 1966;

New York Times, 30 January 1967; *Congressional Quarterly Weekly Report,* 17 February 1967, p. 250; *Congressional Quarterly Almanac 1967,* pp. 679–697; *Congressional Record,* 5 October 1967, pp. S14320–S14324.

16. Zelman, "Senate Dissent and the Vietnam War," p. 138; Brown, *J. William Fulbright,* pp. 77, 86; McGovern, *Grassroots,* p. 100; Woods, *Fulbright,* pp. 412, 441.

17. William L. O'Neill, *Coming Apart: An Informal History of America in the 1960s* (New York: 1971), p. 324; Brown, *J. William Fulbright,* pp. 89–104; Woods, *Fulbright,* p. 416; Stuhler, *Ten Men of Minnesota and American Foreign Policy,* pp. 218–220; Levy, *Debate over Vietnam,* p. 171.

18. E. McCarthy, *A Liberal Answer to the Conservative Challenge,* p. 126; Eugene McCarthy, *The Limits of Power* (New York: 1968), pp. 11–12.

19. E. McCarthy, *Limits of Power,* pp. 29, 35, 21, 117, 113, 123.

20. E. McCarthy, *Limits of Power,* pp. 66, 62, 149–154, 181.

21. *Christian Science Monitor,* 9 November 1967; *New York Times,* 18 October 1967; *New Republic,* 28 October 1967; Woods, *Fulbright,* p. 451; D. O'Brien, *Renewal of American Catholicism,* pp. 179–180; Cooper, *Theology of Freedom,* pp. 32, 97, 166; Stone, *Reinhold Niebuhr,* pp. 195, 243.

22. Stout, *People,* p. 108; J. McIver Weatherford, *Tribes on the Hill* (South Hadley, Mass.: 1985), pp. 206–209; *Washington Post,* 25 March 1967; Eisele, *Almost to the Presidency,* p. 259, 257.

23. Eisele, *Almost to the Presidency,* p. 257; untranscribed recording of oral history interview of Gaylord Nelson, 28 July 1978, Washington, D.C., Hubert H. Humphrey Oral History Project, MHS; transcript of interview with Philip Hart by Arthur Herzog, undated, p. 87, Folder 7, Box 50, Part 1, National Files, MHPA.

24. E. McCarthy, *Required Reading,* pp. 114–115; Abigail McCarthy to Myrtle Cain, 7 December 1966, "Correspondence, 1960–1969," Box 1, Myrtle Cain Papers, MHS; oral history interview of Marie Ridder, by Betty Key, 9 February 1970, p. 4, Oral History Collection, MHPA.

25. "Voting Record in the House and Senate as Designated by COPE 1948 to 1968," "COPE Voting Record," Box 11, Part 2, National Files, MHPA; "Senator McCarthy's Voting Record," 11 April 1968, "ADA," Box 44, Part 1, National Files, MHPA; "Senator Eugene McCarthy and ADA," undated, "ADA Support, 1967–1968," Box 1, National Files, MHPA; Joseph Rauh to Eva Levy, 7 May 1968, "District of Columbia: McCarthy for President," Box 33, Joseph L. Rauh Papers, Library of Congress, Washington, D.C.; *Congressional Quarterly Almanac 1966,* pp. 991–1043, 1408–1413; *Congressional Quarterly Almanac 1967,* pp. 97–99, 106–160; Stout, *People,* p. 107; "McCarthy's Voting Record," Box 59, Subject Files, 1968 Campaign Research Files, Robert F. Kennedy Papers, JFK; William P. McDonald and Jerry G. Smoke, *The Peasants' Revolt: McCarthy 1968* (Mount Vernon, Ohio: 1969), p. 11.

26. Schlesinger, *Robert Kennedy and His Times,* p. 888; Hodgson interview; oral history interview of Milton Gwirtzman, by Roberta W. Greene, 4 April 1972, New York, Oral History Collection, JFK, p. 136; oral history interview of Peter Edelman, by Larry Hackman, Oral History Collection, JFK: Interview 1, 15 July 1969, Washington, D.C., pp. 49–50; Interview 2, 29 July 1969, Washington, D.C., p. 259.

27. Stout, *People,* p. 108; McCarthy interview; *Washington Post,* 25 December 1966.

28. Eisele, *Almost to the Presidency,* p. 275; "McCarthy's Voting Record," Box 59, Subject Files, 1968 Campaign Research Files, Robert F. Kennedy Papers, JFK.

29. Larner, *Nobody Knows,* p. 70; Clymer, *Edward Kennedy,* pp. 66–69; Mann, *Walls of Jericho,* p. 470; Hersh, *Education of Edward Kennedy,* p. 291.

30. *Congressional Record,* 10 May 1965, pp. 9713–9715; Clymer, *Edward Kennedy,* p. 69; Mann, *Walls of Jericho,* pp. 471–473; McCarthy interview; Edelman oral history, Interview 5, 3 January 1970, Washington, D.C., p. 67; oral history interview of David Burke, by Larry J. Hackman, 8 December 1971, New York, Oral History Collection, JFK, p. 27. Kennedy's campaign strategists, however, regarded McCarthy's civil rights record as "almost impeccable": see "McCarthy's Voting Record," Box 59, Subject Files, 1968 Campaign Research Files, Robert F. Kennedy Papers, JFK.

31. *Minnesota Daily,* 4 November 1966; *St. Paul Pioneer Press,* 8 January 1967; Jules Witcover, *The Year the Dream Died: Revisiting 1968 in America* (New York: 1997), p. 17; *Washington Post,* 10 December 1966.

32. *Crookston Daily Times,* 6 March 1967, "Scrapbook 25," Box 6, Accession 11455, EJM, MHS; press release, "McCarthy Says Nation Must Deal with Injustices as Well as Study Riot Causes," 8 August 1967, "Aug.–Dec. 1967," Box 11, Accession 11455, EJM, MHS; *Congressional Quarterly Weekly Report,* 8 September 1967, p. 1752; Davies, *From Opportunity to Entitlement,* p. 194.

33. Davies, *From Opportunity to Entitlement,* pp. 44–47.

34. Tape recording of address to SANE, 9 December 1968, Box 3, Eugene McCarthy Audio-Visual Collection, MHS; *New York Times,* 26 February 1967; *Minneapolis Tribune,* 26 February 1967; *Daily Californian,* 27 February 1967, in "Scrapbook 25," Box 6, Accession 11455, EJM, MHS; McCarthy to Dave Erickson, 12 May 1967, "Legislative: Foreign Relations: Vietnam, May 1967, III," Box 219, EJM, MHS; *Minneapolis Tribune,* 6 March 1967; "McCarthy *Congressional Record* Remarks," Book II, 15 May 1967, p. S6851, Box 7, Accession 12240, EJM, MHS; press release, "McCarthy Says Obligation to Speak Out on Great Issues Needs More Emphasis than Right to Dissent," 23 May 1967, "Jan.–June 1967," Box 11, Accession 11455, EJM, MHS; *Sacramento Union,* 29 March 1966, in "Scrapbook 21," Box 5, Accession 11455, EJM, MHS.

35. Solberg, *Hubert Humphrey,* p. 312; *St. Paul Pioneer Press,* 16 June 1967; McCarthy to Emily Bergen, 4 October 1967, "Legislative: Foreign Relations: Vietnam, October 1967," Box 219, EJM, MHS.

36. Author interview with Nicholas Katzenbach, 6 February 1999, London; Gibbons, *United States Government and the Vietnam War, Part 2,* p. 333; Woods, *Fulbright,* p. 475; Zelman, "Senate Dissent and the Vietnam War," p. 96; Marcy oral history, p. 201; Arthur Herzog, *McCarthy for President* (New York: 1969), p. 29; Stout, *People,* pp. 70–71; McCarthy interview in *America Is Hard to See* (Pyramid Films: 1970), Audio-Visual Collection, MHS.

CHAPTER NINE

A Footnote in History: New Hampshire 1968

1. Stewart Alsop, *The Center: People and Power in Political Washington* (New York: 1968), p. 349; McGovern oral history, MHS, p. 25; Andrew, *Lyndon Johnson and the Great Society,* p. 75.

2. Presidential Job Approval Ratings, Gallup Organization, at <http://www.ropercenter. uconn.edu/>, 23 November 2001; Rosenberg, "Congress and the Vietnam War," pp. 138–139, 187; Charles DeBenedetti, "Lyndon Johnson and the Antiwar Opposition," in Divine, ed., *Vietnam, the Environment, and Science,* Vol. 2, *The Johnson Years,* p. 39; Karnow, *Vietnam,* pp. 502–503; Wells, *War Within,* p. 137; John P. Roche, "The Impact of Dissent on Foreign Policy: Past, Present, and Future," in Lake, ed., *Vietnam Legacy,* p. 129; Dallek, *Flawed Giant,* p. 399; Bernstein, *Guns or Butter,* pp. 367–369; Davies, *From Opportunity to Entitlement,* p. 174.

3. Sidney M. Milkis, *The President and the Parties: The Transformation of the American Party System Since the New Deal* (New York: 1993), p. 179; Lewis L. Gould, "Never a Deep Partisan," pp. 1–52; David Plotke, "Party Reform as Failed Democratic Renewal in the United States, 1968–1972," *Studies in American Political Development* 10:2 (Fall 1996): 238–239; Dallek, *Flawed Giant,* p. 335; Milkis, *President and the Parties,* p. 189; Lewis L. Gould, *1968: The Election That Changed America* (Chicago: 1993), p. 17.

4. McCarthy interview; oral history of Larry Merthan, by Arthur Herzog, undated, Folder 7, Box 50, Part 1, National Files, MHPA, pp. 19–21; Eisele, *Almost to the Presidency,* pp. 270–271; Stout, *People,* p. 59; Larry Merthan to McCarthy, 24 January 1967, "Political Files: Miscellaneous by Date, 1966–1969," Box 4, Accession 12491, EJM, MHS; oral history interview of Maurice Rosenblatt, by Betty Key, 4 February 1970, Oral History Collection, MHPA, pp. 6–7;

notes of interview with Russell Hemenway, by Arthur Herzog, undated, Folder 7, Box 50, Part 1, National Files, MHPA, p. 10; Stout, *People,* pp. 59–60. Finletter did later work for McCarthy's campaign and set up the Citizens for McCarthy organization in New York: see *Washington Star,* 22 April 1968.

5. Gillon, *Politics and Vision,* pp. 211–241; Foley, *New Senate,* pp. 55–58; Martin, *Civil Rights and the Crisis of Liberalism,* p. 248; Davies, *From Opportunity to Entitlement,* p. 185; Lanny J. Davis, *The Emerging Democratic Majority: Lessons and Legacies from the New Politics* (New York: 1974), p. 27; Irwin Unger and Debi Unger, *Turning Point: 1968* (New York: 1988), pp. 317–318; William Connell to Marvin Watson, 17 November 1967, Folder 1, "Congressional Attitudes and Statements 1/66–11/67," Section 7F(1), Box 102(1), Vietnam Country File, National Security Files, LBJ.

6. Dark, *The Unions and the Democrats,* p. 66; Jeffreys-Jones, *Peace Now!,* p. 20; Adam Cohen and Elizabeth Taylor, *American Pharaoh: Mayor Richard J. Daley—His Battle for Chicago and the Nation* (Boston: 2000), p. 445; Gillon, *Politics and Vision,* pp. 175–223; Boyle, *The UAW and the Heyday of Liberalism,* pp. 232–236; Gillon, *Politics and Vision,* p. 202; David Halberstam, "McCarthy and the Divided Left," *Harper's Magazine,* March 1968, pp. 32–44.

7. Zelman, "Senate Dissent and the Vietnam War," p. 321; author interview with Curtis Gans, 15 May 2000, Washington, D.C.; oral history interview of Allard Lowenstein, by Larry J. Hackman, 23 April 1969, Washington, D.C., Oral History Collection, JFK; oral history interview of Sam Brown, by Betty Key, 1969, pp. 5–15, Oral History Collection, MHPA; oral history interview of Sam Brown, by William Chafe, 29 May 1990, Berkeley, California, pp. 1–11, Allard K. Lowenstein Oral History Project, COL; oral history interview of Steve Cohen, by William Chafe, 8 January 1991, Washington, D.C., pp. 1–4, Allard K. Lowenstein Oral History Project, COL; oral history interview of Harold Ickes, by William Chafe, 10 December 1990, New York City, p. 22, Allard K. Lowenstein Oral History Project, COL; oral history interview of Marge Sklencar, by Elizabeth Key, 3 September 1969, pp. 1–7, Oral History Collection, MHPA; William H. Chafe, *Never Stop Running: Allard K. Lowenstein and the Struggle to Save American Liberalism* (New York: 1993); David Halberstam, "The Man Who Ran Against Lyndon Johnson," *Harper's Magazine,* December 1968, pp. 50–66; Charles Kaiser, *1968 in America: Music, Politics, Chaos, Counterculture, and the Shaping of a Generation* (New York: 1988), pp. 23–45; George Rising, *Clean for Gene: Eugene McCarthy's 1968 Presidential Campaign* (Westport, Conn.: 1997), pp. 50–57; Milton Viorst, *Fire in the Streets: America in the 1960s* (New York: 1979), pp. 403–404; David Mixner, *Stranger Among Friends* (New York: 1996), pp. 35–40; Richard Cummings, *The Pied Piper: Allard K. Lowenstein and the Liberal Dream* (New York: 1985), pp. 323–339; Ronald Radosh, *Divided They Fell: The Demise of the Democratic Party, 1964–1996* (New York: 1996), pp. 58–59; Ickes oral history, p. 22; Mixner, *Stranger Among Friends,* p. 38; oral history of George McGovern, by Paige Mulhollan, 30 April 1969, pp. 25–26; Oral History Collection, LBJ.

8. Eisele, *Almost to the Presidency,* pp. 278–279.

9. Grossman, *Relentless Liberal,* pp. 41–42; oral history interview of Gilbert Harrison, 7 June 1969, p. 2, Oral History Collection, MHPA; John P. Roche to President Johnson, 19 October 1967, "PL2: Elections: Campaigns, 1967," Box 77, Confidential File, White House Central Files, LBJ.

10. *New Republic,* 25 November 1967; text of address, 26 October 1967, "Berkeley Speech Folder," Box 11, Accession 11455, EJM, MHS; *New York Times,* 3 November 1967; *Minneapolis Star,* 11 November 1967.

11. Schlesinger, *Robert Kennedy and His Times,* pp. 861–904; Evan Thomas, *Robert Kennedy: His Life* (New York: 2000), pp. 343–361; Joseph A. Palermo, *In His Own Right: The Political Odyssey of Senator Robert F. Kennedy* (New York: 2001); Witcover, *Year the Dream Died,* p. 27; text of address, 26 October 1967, "Berkeley Speech Folder," Box 11, Accession 11455, EJM, MHS; oral history interview of Joseph Kraft, by Roberta W. Greene, 7 March 1970, Washington, D.C., pp. 29–30, Oral History Collection, JFK; oral history interview of Peter

Edelman, Interview 1, 15 July 1969, Washington, D.C., p. 52, Oral History Collection, JFK; oral history interview of Bob Healy, by Arthur Herzog, undated, Folder 1, Box 50, Part 1, National Files, MHPA; Vanden Heuvel and Gwirtzman, *On His Own,* p. 287.

12. Galbraith interview; Joseph Rauh to Mildred Ann Myerson, 15 December 1967, "ADA: June–December," Box 11, Papers of Joseph S. Rauh, Library of Congress, Washington, D.C.; oral history interview of George McGovern, by Larry J. Hackman, 17 July 1970, Washington, D.C., pp. 17–21, Oral History Collection, JFK; Joseph Rauh to Jerry Eller, 23 January 1969, "ADA Endorsement of Senator McCarthy for President," "ADA, 1968–1970," Box 11, Rauh Papers; *New York Times,* 12 November 1967; Galbraith interview; Sam Brown oral history, p. 19.

13. *New York Post,* 29 February 1968; press release, "McCarthy Charges Administration Ignores or Violates Intent and Purpose of US Constitution," 23 October 1967, "Aug.–Dec. 1967," Box 11, Accession 11455, EJM, MHS; Witcover, *Year the Dream Died,* p. 38; undated interview with Eugene McCarthy for *Cold War* (CNN) at <http://www.hfni.gsehd.gwu.edu/~nsarchiv/coldwar/interviews/episode-13/mccarthy1.html>, 7 October 2003; "The Summer of Our Discontent," *The APIC Keynoter* 89:3 (Winter 1989), p. 10, in "1988 Campaign Articles," Box 6, Accession 15044, EJM, MHS; Wells, *War Within,* p. 223; interview with McCarthy for *Cold War.*

14. *The Washingtonian,* August 1986, in "Miscellaneous Articles, 1961–1991," Box 4, Accession 15044, EJM, MHS; oral history interview of Thomas Finney, by Betty Key, 13 February 1970, pp. 9–10, Oral History Collection, MHPA.

15. Oral history interview of Richard Goodwin, by Werner Peters, 10 January 1970, p. 8, Oral History Collection, MHPA; *Boston Globe,* 15 December 1968.

16. *New York Post,* 2 March 1968; David English, *Divided They Stand* (London: 1969), p. 67; Witcover, *Year the Dream Died,* p. 32; *Good Housekeeping,* August 1968, in "Articles on McCarthy," Box 2, Accession 12758, EJM, MHS; oral history interview of Elsa Chaney, by unspecified interviewer, dated "January or February 1969," pp. 1–2, Oral History Collection, MHPA; notes of interview with Father Dunstan Tucker, by Lael Herzog, Folder 14, Box 50, Part 1, Oral History Collection, MHPA; undated clipping [February 1968], "Political and Miscellaneous, 1968–1979," Box 3, Accession 12758, EJM, MHS.

17. McCarthy interview; *Look,* 1 April 1969.

18. Oral history interview of Marie Ridder, by Betty Key, 9 February 1970, p. 4, Oral History Collection, MHS; oral history interview of Hubert Humphrey, by Larry J. Hackman, 30 March 1970, p. 41, Oral History Collection, JFK; Humphrey, *Education of a Public Man,* p. 376; Solberg, *Hubert Humphrey,* p. 313.

19. Hamby, *Liberalism and Its Challengers,* p. 279; Steven M. Gillon, *"That's Not What We Meant to Do": Reform and Its Unintended Consequences in Twentieth-Century America* (New York: 2000), pp. 200–234; Herbert E. Alexander, *Financing the 1968 Election* (Lexington, Mass.: 1971), pp. 8, 36–39; *Atlantic Monthly,* January 1968; *Look,* 25 June 1968; McPherson interview.

20. Stout, *People,* p. 81; *New York Times,* 1 December 1967; *Christian Science Monitor,* 1 December 1967.

21. *Minneapolis Tribune,* 17 December 1967; *St. Paul Pioneer Press,* 1 December 1967; *Newsweek,* 13 November 1967; *New Republic,* 9 December 1967; *New York Times,* 1 December 1967; *Time,* 8 December 1967; *Newsweek,* 18 December 1967.

22. *The Gallup Report,* 6 December 1967, in "McCarthy, Eugene," Box 181, Office Files of Frederick Panzer, White House Aides' Files, White House Central Files, LBJ; George C. Herring, *LBJ and Vietnam: A Different Kind of War* (Austin, Texas: 1994), p. 148; Presidential Job Approval Ratings, Gallup Organization, at <http://www.ropercenter.uconn.edu/>, 23 November 2001; *Newsweek,* 11 December 1967. For Spiro Agnew as an egg, see Chester et al., *An American Melodrama,* p. 539.

23. *The Observer* (London), 3 December 1967; *The Washingtonian,* August 1986, in "Miscellaneous Articles 1961–1991," Box 4, Accession 15044, EJM, MHS; Peter Collier and David Horowitz, *The Kennedys* (New York: 1984), p. 400; Mike Manatos to President Johnson, 14

November 1967, "McCarthy, Eugene, 1/1/67–12/31/67," Box 210, Name File, White House Central Files, LBJ; William C. Berman, *William Fulbright and the Vietnam War: The Dissent of a Political Realist* (Kent, Ohio, 1988), p. 90; McGovern oral history, MHS, p. 27; Stout, *People,* p. 142; L. O'Brien, *No Final Victories,* p. 215; Small, *Johnson, Nixon, and the Doves,* p. 265; Eisele, *Almost to the Presidency,* p. 304.

24. *Newsweek,* 5 February 1968; *New Republic,* 25 November 1967; *New York Times,* 8 February 1968; *Time,* 22 March 1968; *Village Voice,* 28 December 1967; Richard N. Goodwin, *Remembering America: A Voice from the Sixties* (New York: 1988), p. 490; *Newsweek,* 29 January 1968.

25. Address to the Conference of Concerned Democrats, 2 December 1967, "Press releases, 1967–1969," Box 11, Accession 11455, EJM, MHS; *Life,* 19 February 1968; Sheed, "Eugene McCarthy," pp. 154–164; Chester et al., *An American Melodrama,* p. 92; oral history interview of Gerry Studds, by Robert Terry, 30 January 1969, p. 8, Oral History Collection, MHPA.

26. Joseph Rauh to Mildred Ann Myerson, 15 December 1967, "ADA: June-December," Box 11, Rauh Papers; Joseph Rauh to Robert S. Morris, 19 January 1968, "McCarthy, Eugene," Box 38, Rauh Papers; oral history interview of Arnold Hiatt, by unspecified interviewer, undated, side 2, p. 1, Oral History Collection, MHPA; author interview with Blair Clark, 18 April 2000, New York City; oral history interview of Blair Clark, by Betty Key, 28 March 1969, pp. 1–2, Oral History Collection, MHPA; Kaiser, *1968 in America,* pp. 52–53; memorandum, "On Eugene McCarthy," 29 December 1967, "Notes: Chapter 3: Eugene McCarthy," Box 32, "Notes on *The Making of the President 1968,*" Theodore H. White Papers, JFK; Clark interview.

27. Hubert Humphrey to William Connell, 5 February 1968, "Memos, Jan.–Feb. 1968," Box 3, William Connell Papers, MHS.

28. Clark interview; oral history interview of David Hoeh, by unspecified interviewer, 30 January 1969, p. 30, Oral History Collection, MHPA; *Time,* 22 March 1968; transcript of panel "1968 and the Presidency: Dumping Johnson—Were Journalists a Catalyst?," Freedom Forum Newseum, 30 April 1998, at <http://www.freedomforum.org/newseumnews/specialprograms/1968transcript2–1.asp>, 23 November 2001; Unger and Unger, *Turning Point: 1968,* p. 332.

29. *Look,* 6 February 1968; *Congressional Quarterly Weekly Report,* 8 March 1968, p. 488; "McCarthy Discusses Economic Costs of War," 18 January 1968, "Jan. 1968," Box 12, Accession 11455, EJM, MHS; *America,* 16 December 1967; *Congressional Quarterly Weekly Report,* 15 December 1967, p. 2574; transcript of question and answer session, Stanford University, 15 January 1968, "Jan. 1968," Box 12, Accession 11455, EJM, MHS; "Eugene McCarthy on the Record," March 1968, "Speeches: Public Excerpts," pp. 3–5, Box 4, Accession 15044, EJM, MHS.

30. "McCarthy Accuses Administration of Self-Deception," 3 February 1968, "Feb. 1968," Box 12, Accession 11455, EJM, MHS; Peter Braestrup, *Big Story: How the American Press and Television Reported and Interpreted the Crisis of Tet 1968* in *Vietnam and Washington,* rev. ed. (Garden City, N.Y.: 1978), pp. 465–507; Karnow, *Vietnam,* p. 559; Rosenberg, "Congress and the Vietnam War," pp. 138–139; DeBenedetti, *An American Ordeal,* p. 211; Gans, quoted in transcript of panel "1968 and the Presidency: Dumping Johnson–Were Journalists a Catalyst?," Freedom Forum Newseum, 30 April 1998, at <http://www.freedomforum.org/newseumnews/specialprograms/1968transcript2–1.asp>, 23 November 2001; text of commercial 49, NH-1m-5, "McCarthy Presidential Campaign—Paid Television Advertising," Television Advertising Finding Aid, MHPA.

31. Carol E. Rinzler, ed., *Frankly McCarthy* (Washington, D.C.: 1969), p. 18; *Congressional Quarterly Weekly Report,* 15 December 1967, p. 2573; *Look,* 6 February 1968; address to the Conference of Concerned Democrats, 2 December 1967, "Press releases 1967–1969," Box 11, Accession 11455, EJM, MHS; Frost, *The Presidential Debate, 1968,* p. 26; "Johnson Dissents from Democratic Foreign Policy," 14 January 1968, "Jan. 1968," Box 12, Accession 11455, EJM, MHS.

32. Speech to the Jacobi Society, Washington, D.C., 3 February 1968, "Feb. 1968," Box 12, Accession 11455, EJM, MHS; *America,* 16 December 1967; "McCarthy Calls for Massive Housing

Program," 15 December 1967, "Aug.–Dec. 1967," Box 11, Accession 11455, EJM, MHS; "Vietnam War Undermines Great Society," 11 January 1968, "Jan. 1968," Box 12, Accession 11455, EJM, MHS; transcript of question and answer session, Atlanta Press Club, 23 January 1968, "Jan. 1968," Box 12, Accession 11455, EJM, MHS; transcript of question and answer session, Portland State College, 2 February 1968, "Feb. 1968," Box 12, Accession 11455, EJM, MHS; *Washington Star,* 3 December 1967; transcript, *Issues and Answers,* ABC Television, 7 January 1968, "PAF 4—Democratic Party—Eugene McCarthy, 1968," Box 1064, Vice Presidential Files, Hubert H. Humphrey Papers, MHS; "McCarthy on State of the Union," 18 January 1968, "Jan. 1968," Box 12, Accession 11455, EJM, MHS.

33. Oral history interview of Sarah Kovner, by unspecified interviewer, 1 April 1969, p. 1, Oral History Collection, MHPA; *New York Times Magazine,* 31 March 1968; Davis, *Emerging Democratic Majority,* p. 27; Martin Peretz to Eugene McCarthy, 22 December 1967, "Personal Correspondence," Martin Peretz papers, in Box 43, National Files, MHPA; oral history interview of David Mixner, by Betty Key, January 1969, p. 14, Oral History Collection, MHPA. For a close study of a typical McCarthy worker, see Melvin Small, "Otto Feinstein, the McCarthy Campaign in Michigan, and Campus Activism During the Cold War," in David L. Anderson, ed., *The Human Tradition in the Vietnam Era* (Wilmington, Del.: 2000), pp. 175–194.

34. *Life,* 23 December 1968; David Caute, *The Year of the Barricades: A Journey Through 1968* (New York: 1988), p. 21; R. W. B. Lewis, "McCarthy and the College Students," in Joseph Frank, ed., *The New Look in Politics: McCarthy's Campaign* (Albuquerque, N.Mex.: 1969), p. 19; Mixner oral history, p. 13; Stanley Hyman, *Youth in Politics* (New York: 1972), p. 115; *New York Times,* 4 March 1968; Clark interview; *St. Paul Pioneer Press,* 9 March 1969.

35. David C. Hoeh, *1968, McCarthy, New Hampshire: I Hear America Singing* (Rochester, Minn.: 1998), pp. 419–420; McCarthy speech at Marquette University, Wisconsin, 22 March 1968, "March 1968," Box 12, Accession 11455, EJM, MHS; Sklencar oral history, p. 28; oral history interview of Cynthia Samuels, by William Chafe, 10 September 1990, New York City, p. 15, Allard K. Lowenstein Oral History Project, COL; *New York Times Magazine,* 31 March 1968; *The McCarthy Advance* 1:5 (18 July 1968), in "Eugene McCarthy 8/1/1968," Box 111, Office Files of Frederick Panzer, White House Aides' Files, White House Central Files, LBJ; *Washington Post,* 27 December 1999; *Time,* 22 March 1968; *New York Times Magazine,* 31 March 1968.

36. Galbraith interview; John Kenneth Galbraith, *A Life in Our Times: Memoirs* (Boston: 1981), p. 492; oral history interview of Palmer Weber, Volume 2, Interview 6, by Andor Skotnes, 10 June 1985, Charlottesville, Va., pp. 345–346, American Entrepreneurs Project, COL; H. Alexander, *Financing the 1968 Election,* pp. 30–34, 69, 44, 50; author interview with Martin Peretz, 11 February 2000, Cambridge, Mass.; Weber oral history, p. 351; Radosh, *Divided They Fell,* p. 27; Clark interview.

37. *New York Times,* 22 January 1968 and 30 August 1968; clipping from *New York* magazine, undated, "Articles on McCarthy," Box 2, Accession 12758, EJM, MHS; *Christian Science Monitor,* 8 January 1968; Halberstam, "McCarthy and the Divided Left," pp. 32–44.

38. McCarthy, *Frontiers in American Democracy,* p. 61; transcript of WBZ radio interview, 7 March 1968, "Forums File," Box 1, Accession 12758, EJM, MHS.

39. Transcript of BBC interview, 8 March 1970, "Jan 1970–June 1971," Box 5, "McCarthy: By and About," MHPA; Herzog, *McCarthy for President,* p. 180; Norman Mailer, *Miami and the Siege of Chicago* (Harmondsworth, U.K.: 1969), p. 116.

40. *New Republic,* 6 November 1976; *Time,* 5 April 1968; McDonald and Smoke, *Peasants' Revolt,* p. 13.

41. Goodwin oral history, pp. 9–10; Goodwin, *Remembering America,* p. 505; *Wall Street Journal,* 15 July 1968; Richard M. Scammon and Ben J. Wattenberg, *The Real Majority: An Extraordinary Examination of the American Electorate* (New York: 1971), p. 105; *New Republic,* 2 March 1968; Gans interview.

42. *Time,* 22 March 1968; *Newsweek,* 25 March 1968; text of commercial 42, NH-10s-1, "McCarthy Presidential Campaign—Paid Television Advertising," Television Advertising Finding Aid, MHPA; transcript of WKBG-TV broadcast, 11 March 1968, in William J. Nee,

"McCarthy Presidential Campaign 1968: Comprehensive Report," pp. 14–21. I am grateful to Kay Bonner Nee for allowing me to examine this and other advertising materials.

43. *New York Times,* 15 March 1968; *Time,* 22 March 1968; *Washington Post,* 3 October 1969; Scammon and Wattenberg, *Real Majority,* pp. 91–111, 121; *New York Times,* 17 March 1968; Germond, *Fat Man in a Middle Seat,* pp. 74–75; A. James Reichley, *The Life of the Parties: A History of American Political Parties* (New York: 1992), p. 339; Hoeh, *1968, McCarthy, New Hampshire,* p. 93; David Lebedoff, *The New Elite: The Death of Democracy* (New York: 1981), p. 110.

44. Ben Stavis, *We Were the Campaign: New Hampshire to Chicago for McCarthy* (Boston, 1969), pp. 47–48; *Time,* 22 March 1968; *New Republic,* 16 December 1967; Unger and Unger, *Turning Point: 1968,* p. 484; Parmet, *The Democrats,* p. 249; Stout, *People,* p. 126.

45. *Commonweal,* 29 March 1968; Mailer, *Some Honorable Men,* p. 20; *Commonweal,* 9 September 1960; Irving Howe, quoted in Jack Newfield, *Bread and Roses Too* (New York: 1971), p. 23; Parmet, *The Democrats,* pp. 267–268; *Washington Post,* 13 May 1968.

46. *Newsweek,* 25 March 1968; Solberg, *Hubert Humphrey,* p. 319; Scammon and Wattenberg, *Real Majority,* p. 107.

CHAPTER TEN
The Road to Chicago

1. Herzog, *McCarthy for President,* pp. 119–120.

2. Memorandum, "Wisconsin Primary: Chrono.: McCarthy Campaign," 3 April 1968, "Notes: Chapter 3: Eugene McCarthy," Box 32, "Notes on *The Making of the President 1968,*" Theodore H. White Papers, JFK; Germond, *Fat Man in a Middle Seat,* p. 77; *Boston Globe,* 15 December 1968; transcript of press conference, Durbin Hotel, Rushville, Ind., 28 April 1968, "1968 Press Conferences and TV Appearances," Box 6, Accession 15044, EJM, MHS.

3. *New York Times,* 10 March 1968; Germond, *Fat Man in a Middle Seat,* p. 74; E. Berman, *Hubert,* p. 143; Schlesinger interview; Jeremy Larner, *Nobody Knows,* p. 71; *Time,* 31 May 1968; press release, "Entertainer in State to Promote McCarthy Campaign," 26 April 1968, "April 1968," Box 12, Accession 11455, EJM, MHS; *Los Angeles Times,* 13 May 1968; Barbara Howar, *Laughing All the Way* (New York: 1973), p. 244.

4. Witcover interview; *New York Times,* 14 March 1968; Seymour Martin Lipset to Martin Peretz, 20 March 1968, "Personal correspondence," Martin Peretz Papers, in Box 43, National Files, MHPA; speech at Pfister Hotel, Milwaukee, Wis., 23 March 1968, "March 1968," Box 12, Accession 11455, EJM, MHS.

5. Speech at Adams High School, South Bend, Ind., 5 May 1968, "May 1968," Box 12, Accession 11455, EJM, MHS.

6. *Miami Herald,* 7 April 1968, in "1968 Campaign Articles," Box 5, Accession 15044, EJM, MHS; McCarthy interview; Galbraith, *A Life in Our Times,* p. 497; Smaby, *Political Upheaval,* p. 424; transcript of press conference, Jamesville, Wis., 20 March 1968, "March 1968," Box 12, Accession 11455, EJM, MHS; Larner, *Nobody Knows,* p. 17.

7. *New York Times,* 27 March 1968; *Congressional Quarterly Weekly Report,* 29 March 1968, pp. 664–665; Clark interview; *New Yorker,* 2 March 1968; E. McCarthy, *Year of the People,* p. 83; oral history interview of Paul Gorman, by Werner Peters, January 1970, p. 26, Oral History Collection, MHPA; Shull oral history, p. 27, COL; oral history interview of Jeff Greenfield, by Roberta W. Greene, 5 January 1970, New York City, pp. 53–55, Oral History Collection, JFK; oral history of Richard Weidman, by William Chafe, 7 April 1989, Albany, N.Y., p. 35, Allard K. Lowenstein Oral History Project, COL; *Time,* 24 May 1968; *Washington Post,* 2 June 1987; Gorman oral history, p. 40.

8. Clark interview; *Time,* 3 May 1968. For the feuding among McCarthy's staff, see Gans interview; Clark interview; Rosenblatt oral history, p. 10, 16; A. McCarthy, *Private Faces/Public Places,* p. 381; Larner, *Nobody Knows,* p. 78; Stout, *People,* pp. 241–248.

9. *Boston Globe,* 22 December 1968; McGovern oral history, pp. 18–21, JFK; F. Harris, *Potomac Fever,* p. 136; Edelman oral history, Interview 2, by Larry Hackman, 29 July 1969, Washington, D.C., p. 258; Bruce E. Altschuler, "Kennedy Decides to Run, 1968," *Presidential Studies Quarterly* 10:3 (Summer 1980): 348–352; Jack Newfield, *Robert Kennedy: A Memoir* (London: 1970), p. 191; Collier and Horowitz, *The Kennedys,* p. 400; Thomas, *Robert Kennedy,* p. 357; *Christian Science Monitor,* 8 January 1968; Jean Stein and George Plimpton, eds., *American Journey: The Times of Robert Kennedy* (London: 1971), p. 236; Clark interview.

10. Undated interview with Eugene McCarthy for *Cold War* (CNN) at <http://www.hfni.gsehd. gwu.edu/~nsarchiv/coldwar/interviews/episode-13/mccarthy1.html>, 7 October 2003; *New York Times Magazine,* 13 November 1977; *The Washingtonian,* August 1986, in "Miscellaneous Articles, 1961–1991," Box 4, Accession 15044, EJM, MHS; Witcover, *Year the Dream Died,* p. 110; *New York Times,* 1 December 1967; *New York Times Magazine,* 10 December 1967; transcript of interview by David Schoumacher, 16 March 1968, "March 1968," Box 12, Accession 11455, EJM, MHS.

11. *New York Times,* 17 March 1968; Rinzler, ed., *Frankly McCarthy,* p. 19; transcript of press conference, Jamesville, Wis., 20 March 1968, "March 1968," Box 12, Accession 11455, EJM, MHS; *Minneapolis Tribune,* 7 June 1968; *Washington Post,* 17 July 1988. For Kennedy's anti-McCarthy advertising see pamphlet "A Time to Pause," in "RFK: Identified Smears," Box 47, National Files, MHPA; and "McCarthy's Record as a Congressman and a Senator," "Voting Record," Box 11, Part 1, National Files, MHPA.

12. Herzog, *McCarthy for President,* p. 214; oral history interview of Adam Walinsky, Volume 6, Interview 10, by Roberta W. Greene, 4 December 1974, New York City, pp. 517–518, Oral History Collection, JFK; Humphrey oral history, p. 44, JFK; *New York Times,* 4 June 1968; *Washington Post,* 1 November 1970; Goodwin oral history, pp. 26–27, MHPA; *Ramparts,* 10 August 1968, in "Articles on McCarthy," Box 2, Accession 12758, EJM, MHS.

13. Transcript of press conference, Jamesville, Wis., 20 March 1968, "March 1968," Box 12, Accession 11455, EJM, MHS; Galbraith interview; *Time,* 7 June 1968; *New York Times,* 2 June 1968; Michael Novak memorandum, "Thoughts on Debate," undated, "Campaign 1968: Eugene McCarthy," Box 2, Senate Subject File, 1965–1968, Adam Walinsky Papers, JFK; David Halberstam, *The Unfinished Odyssey of Robert Kennedy* (New York: 1969), p. 204; Ronald Steel, *In Love with Night: The American Romance with Robert Kennedy* (New York: 2000), p. 152; *Washington Post,* 26 May 1968.

14. Transcript of *Tonight Show,* NBC Television, 26 June 1968, "June 1968," Box 12, Accession 11455, EJM, MHS; Goodwin, *Remembering America,* p. 509; "Eugene McCarthy on the Record," March 1968, "Speeches: Public Excerpts," Box 4, Accession 15044, EJM, MHS, title page; transcript of question and answer session, New Albany, Ind., 26 April 1968, "Speeches: Q and A Periods," Box 6, Accession 15044, EJM, MHS; McCarthy, *Hard Years,* pp. 13–14; Stuhler, *Ten Men of Minnesota and American Foreign Policy,* p. 213; oral history interview of Jerry Eller, by Arthur Herzog, undated, "Folder 7," Box 50, Part 1, National Files, MHPA, pp. 112–113; oral history of Leon Shull, by Beth Laube, 21 October 1969, p. 17, Oral History Collection, National Files, MHPA; Schlesinger, *Robert Kennedy and His Times,* p. 960.

15. Memorandum, "Vietnam and the JFK Legacy," unattributed, undated, "McCarthy, Eugene J.: Quotations," Box 59, Research Division, Subject Files, 1968 Presidential Campaign National Files, Robert F. Kennedy papers, JFK; Kathleen Hall Jamieson, *Packaging the Presidency: A History and Criticism of Presidential Campaign Advertising* (New York: 1984), p. 224.

16. *Ramparts,* 10 August 1968, in "Articles on McCarthy," Box 2, Accession 12758, EJM, MHS; *New York Times,* 23 April 1968; *New York Times,* 23 May 1968; "Beyond the Cold War: Senator McCarthy on Foreign Policy," 14 August 1968, "Press releases, 1968," Box 12, Accession 11455, EJM, MHS.

17. Woods, *Fulbright,* p. 489; oral history interview of Paul Gorman, by Werner Peters, January 1970, pp. 6, 31, Oral History Collection, MHPA; Steel, *In Love with Night,* pp. 177–178.

18. *Los Angeles Times,* 26 May 1968; speech at Americana Hotel, New York, 13 June 1968, "June

1968," Box 12, Accession 11455, EJM, MHS; *Fellowship,* September 1968, in "Articles by McCarthy," Box 1, Accession 12758, EJM, MHS; statement issued at Sacramento, Calif., 12 August 1968, "August 1968," Box 12, Accession 11455, EJM, MHS.

19. Speech to Colorado State Democratic Convention, 13 July 1968, "July 1968," Box 12, Accession 11455, EJM, MHS; position paper on "Cities," 28 July 1968, "Speeches and releases, 1959–1969," Box 13, Accession 11455, EJM, MHS; "A Housing Program for the Nation's Cities," 14 August 1968, "Speeches and releases, 1959–1969," Box 13, Accession 11455, EJM, MHS; Steel, *In Love with Night,* pp. 125–126. Kennedy had already sponsored such a scheme in the Bedford-Stuyvesant neighborhood of New York.

20. Position paper on "Hunger," 11 July 1968, "Speeches and releases, 1959–1969," Box 13, Accession 11455, EJM, MHS; *New Republic,* 3 August 1968; "Eugene McCarthy on the Record," March 1968, "Speeches: Public Excerpts," p. 10, Box 4, Accession 15044, EJM, MHS; Peter Barnes to McCarthy, 8 March 1968, "Manuscript of EJM Book," Box 46, Part 2, National Files, MHPA; Isserman and Kazin, *America Divided,* p. 195; Davies, *From Opportunity to Entitlement,* p. 211.

21. Clipping from *New York* magazine, undated, "Articles on McCarthy," Box 2, Accession 12758, EJM, MHS; Scammon and Wattenberg, *Real Majority,* pp. 98–100; oral history interview of Clinton Deveaux, by William Chafe, 31 October 1990, Atlanta, p. 26, Allard K. Lowenstein Oral History Project, COL; Kovner oral history, p. 27, MHPA; summer campaign manual, III:1.1, 20 June 1968, "Summer Political Activities," Box 36, National Files, MHPA; *Commonweal,* 10 May 1968.

22. *Washington Post,* 28 July 1968; speech at Sheraton-Schroeder Hotel, Milwaukee, 30 March 1968, "March 1968," Box 12, Accession 11455, EJM, MHS; *Washington Post,* 28 July 1968; speech at Boston University, 11 April 1968, "Magic File," Box 3, Accession 12758, EJM, MHS; speech at Sheraton-Schroeder Hotel, Milwaukee, 30 March 1968, "March 1968," Box 12, Accession 11455, EJM, MHS; background paper, "Civil Rights: Vision of Hope and Reconciliation," 29 April 1968, "Speeches and releases, 1959–1969," Box 13, Accession 11455, EJM, MHS; "Eugene McCarthy on the Record," March 1968, "Speeches: Public Excerpts," Box 4, Accession 15044, EJM, MHS; Schlesinger, *Robert Kennedy and His Times,* p. 979; *Washington Post,* 20 May 1968; "Statement on June 1st Debate," 2 June 1968, "June 1968," Box 12, Accession 11455, EJM, MHS; *The Progressive,* August 1968, in "Articles by McCarthy," Box 1, Accession 12758, EJM, MHS.

23. Sheed, "Eugene McCarthy," p. 160; McDonald and Smoke, *Peasants' Revolt,* p. 5; Stout, *People,* p. 214; *Washington Post,* 19 April 1968; Davis, *Emerging Democratic Majority,* pp. 33–34; Blair Clark, quoted in Stein and Plimpton, eds., *American Journey,* pp. 257–258; *New York Times,* 5 May 1968; *Boston Globe,* 24 December 1968.

24. Byron E. Shafer, "Partisan Elites, 1946–1996," in Shafer, ed. *Partisan Approaches to Postwar Politics,* pp. 106–107; speech at Pfister Hotel, Milwaukee, Wis., 23 March 1968, "March 1968," Box 12, Accession 11455, EJM, MHS; *Ramparts,* 10 August 1968, in "Articles on McCarthy," Box 2, Accession 12758, EJM, MHS; Schlesinger, *Robert Kennedy and His Times,* p. 959; Larner, *Nobody Knows,* p. 93; Vanden Heuvel and Gwirtzman, *On His Own,* pp. 348–349; Steel, *In Love with Night,* p. 179; Garry Wills, "Waiting for Bobby," *New York Review of Books,* 10 February 2000, pp. 18–20.

25. *Commonweal,* 26 April 1968; *Newsweek,* 15 April 1968; *St. Louis Post-Dispatch,* 3 June 1968, in "Columnists: Kraft, Joseph," Box 12, Press Division, National Headquarters Files, 1968 Presidential Campaign Files, Robert F. Kennedy Papers, JFK.

26. H. Alexander, *Financing the 1968 Election, p.* 70; Steel, *In Love with Night,* pp. 173–176; *New Republic,* 11 May 1968; Steel, *In Love with Night,* p. 175; Brian Dooley, *Robert Kennedy: The Final Years* (Keele, U.K.: 1995), p. 38; Vanden Heuvel and Gwirtzman, *On His Own,* p. 379, 348–349; Steel, *In Love with Night,* p. 187.

27. Oral history interview of Edward Costikyan, by Jonathan Blank, 22 April 1970, p. 42, COL; oral history interview of Thomas McCoy, by unspecified interviewer, undated, p. 13, Oral His-

tory Collection, MHPA; Steel, *In Love with Night,* p. 192; Costikyan oral history, p. 43; oral history interview of Donald Wilson, by Roberta W. Greene, 2 July 1970, New York City, p. 36, Oral History Collection, JFK; Steel, *In Love with Night,* pp. 187, 192; Goodwin, *Remembering America,* p. 537; Thomas, *Robert Kennedy,* p. 388; Dennis Dean Wainstock, "The 1968 Presidential Campaign and Election," unpublished Ph.D. dissertation, University of West Virginia, 1984, p. 352; Vanden Heuvel and Gwirtzman, *On His Own,* pp. 390–392; Scammon and Wattenberg, *Real Majority,* p. 142; Plotke, "Party Reform as Failed Democratic Renewal in the United States," p. 246.

28. Anderson, *The Movement and the Sixties,* p. 205; Steel, *In Love with Night,* pp. 184, 194; Michael J. Sandel, *Democracy's Discontent: America in Search of a Public Philosophy* (Cambridge, Mass.: 1996), p. 299; Michael Knox Beran, *The Last Patrician* (New York: 1998); Steel, *In Love with Night,* p. 165; oral history interview of John F. English, Interview 4, by Roberta W. Greene, 3 February 1970, New York City, Oral History Collection, JFK, pp. 137–138.

29. Clark interview; undated note, "1968 Campaign: McCarthy, Eugene," "*Robert Kennedy* Background Materials," Box W-54, Papers of Arthur M. Schlesinger Jr., JFK; Kaiser, *1968 in America,* p. 216. Kaiser interviewed McCarthy in March 1986 and reflected that McCarthy had "the distinction of being the only person to pin the blame for the shooting directly on the victim."

30. *Atlantic Monthly,* September 1968; McCarthy interview; Finney oral history, pp. 14–15; Humphrey, *Education of a Public Man,* p. 375; untranscribed recording of oral history interview of Gaylord Nelson, 28 July 1978, Washington, D.C., Hubert H. Humphrey Oral History Project, MHS; oral history interview of Rowland Evans, by Norman Sherman, 9 August 1978, Washington, D.C., p. 11, Hubert H. Humphrey Oral History Project, MHS.

31. Solberg, *Hubert Humphrey,* pp. 331–332; E. Berman, *Hubert,* p. 166; Grossman oral history, p. 4; Larner, *Nobody Knows,* p. 136; Abigail McCarthy to Kathleen Louchheim, undated [summer 1968], Box 4, Papers of Kathleen S. Louchheim, Library of Congress, Washington, D.C.; A. McCarthy, *Private Faces/Public Places,* p. 497.

32. Miles Lord to Hubert Humphrey, 22 April 1968, "Personal PAF: McCarthy," Box 9-1, 1968 Campaign File, Hubert H. Humphrey Papers, MHS; I. N. Sprague to Marvin Watson, 21 March 1968, Reel 504, Series A (Office Files of Marvin Watson), Part II (White House Aides), *Political Activities of the Johnson White House, 1963–1969* (Frederick, Md., 1987); McPherson interview; Miles Lord to Hubert Humphrey, 21 March 1968, "Personal PAF: McCarthy," Box 9-1, 1968 Campaign File, Hubert H. Humphrey Papers, MHS; Blair Clark to George McGovern, 12 May 1972, "McCarthy, Eugene," Box 15, Selected Correspondence 1972, George McGovern Papers, Seeley G. Mudd Manuscript Library, Princeton University.

33. Memorandum for the Record, Hubert Humphrey, 7 June 1968, Reel 10, Series A, Part I (White House Central and Confidential Files), *Political Activities of the Johnson White House;* handwritten notes, 7 June 1968, "Personal PAF: McCarthy," Box 9-1, 1968 Campaign File, Hubert Humphrey Papers, MHS; Clark interview; *Washington Post,* 17 July 1988.

34. *Atlantic Monthly,* September 1968; Mailer, *Miami and the Siege of Chicago,* p. 93; Larner, *Nobody Knows,* p. 127; A. McCarthy, *Private Faces/Public Places,* p. 497; Galbraith, *A Life in Our Times,* p. 499; *Washington Post,* 2 June 1987; Eisele interview; *New York Times,* 16 June 1968; A. McCarthy, *Private Faces/Public Places,* p. 403; M. McPherson, *Power Lovers,* p. 245; Smaby, *Political Upheaval,* p. 424; *New York Times,* 16 June 1968; *Washington Daily News,* 22 August 1969.

35. A. McCarthy, *Private Faces/Public Places,* p. 420; Witcover, *Year the Dream Died,* p. 270; Kathleen Hughes, *The Monk's Tale: A Biography of Godfrey Diekmann, OSB* (Collegeville, Minn.: 1991), p. 293; Eisele interview; *Washington Post,* 17 July 1988; Clark interview; A. McCarthy, *Private Faces/Public Places,* p. 420; *Washington Post,* 2 June 1987; *Boston Globe,* 15 December 1968; *Village Voice,* 27 January 1972.

36. Chester et al., *An American Melodrama,* pp. 458–459; Clark interview; Harold Ickes quoted in Eisele, *Almost to the Presidency,* p. 340; *Washington Post,* 17 July 1988.

37. Schedule for July 1968 in Box 12, Accession 11455, EJM, MHS; Stout, *People,* p. 288; McCarthy interviewed for unfinished pilot documentary *Eugene McCarthy: From New Hampshire to Chicago,* late 1990s, courtesy of Mary Beth Yarrow; Goodwin oral history, p. 48; Larner, *Nobody Knows,* p. 144; notes of interview with Jerome Grossman, by Lael Herzog, undated, Folder 14, Box 50, Part 1, National Files, MHPA; clipping from *New York* magazine, undated, "Articles on McCarthy," Box 2, Accession 12758, EJM, MHS; oral history of Jeremy Larner, by Delman, 4 June 1969, Oral History Collection, MHPA, pp. 19–20; transcript of interview with Jeremy Larner, by Arthur Herzog, undated, Folder 7, Box 50, Part 1, National Files, MHPA; *Harper's Magazine,* December 1968; *Washington Post,* 17 July 1988.

38. *The Economist,* 17 August 1968; summer campaign manual, 20 June 1968, "Summer Political Activities," Box 36, National Files, MHPA; Finney oral history, p. 10; Herzog, *McCarthy for President,* p. 204; *New York Post,* 22 July 1968, in "McCarthy Press Clips, 1967–1968," Box 9, Accession 12491, EJM, MHS; oral history interview of Frank Mankiewicz, Interview 3, by Stephen Goodell, 5 May 1969, p. 16, Oral History Collection, LBJ.

39. English, *Divided They Stand,* p. 307; *Commonweal,* 23 August 1968; *The Economist,* 31 August 1968; oral history interview of Thomas McCoy, undated, Oral History Collection, MHPA, p. 19; Wills, *Kennedy Imprisonment,* p. 100; McGovern, *Grassroots,* p. 118; McGovern oral history, pp. 28–29, LBJ; *Playboy,* August 1971; *New York Times,* 27 August 1968, 30 August 1968; Anson, *McGovern,* p. 193; Blair Clark to George McGovern, 12 May 1972, "McCarthy, Eugene," Box 15, Selected Correspondence 1972, George McGovern Papers, Seeley G. Mudd Manuscript Library, Princeton University.

40. *Commentary,* February 1968; Smaby, *Political Upheaval,* p. 147; Boyle, *UAW and the Heyday of American Liberalism,* p. 232; Jeffreys-Jones, *Peace Now!,* p. 194; Dark, *The Unions and the Democrats,* pp. 80–81; memorandum, Stuart Eizenstat to Delegate Section, undated, "PAF-1968 Camp-VIId: Candidates: McCarthy, Misc. 1," Box 1–2, 1968 Campaign, Hubert H. Humphrey Papers, MHS; *New York Times,* 18 August 1968; Benjamin I. Page and Michael A. Brody, "Party Voting and the Electoral Process: The Vietnam War Issue," *American Political Science Review* 66:3 (September 1972): 979–996; Fred Panzer to President Johnson, 21 August 1968, "PL-McCarthy, Eugene," Box 26, Subject File, White House Central Files, LBJ; *Congressional Quarterly Weekly Report,* 16 August 1968, p. 2178; Reichley, *Life of the Parties,* p. 342.

41. *San Francisco Chronicle,* 19 July 1968, "Polls: McCarthy," Box 45, Part 2, National Files, MHPA; "John F. Kraft, Inc. Report of Surveys in Ten States," August 1968, "Articles About McCarthy," Box 2, Accession 12758, EJM, MHS; *Gallup Report,* 20 August 1968, "Polls," Box 19, Part 1, National Files, MHPA; *New York Times,* 9 July 1968; National Public Affairs Survey, International Research Associates, 13 August 1968, Box 1, Hubert Humphrey Campaign Poll Data, MHPA, p. 4; *Gallup Report,* 7 August 1968, "Polls," Box 19, Part 1, National Files, MHPA.

42. McCarthy, *Year of the People,* p. 210; McCoy oral history, p. 20; Harry McPherson to President Johnson, 12 August 1968, "Eliot/Michael Janeway," Box 41, Office Files of Harry McPherson, White House Aides' Files, White House Central Files, LBJ; memorandum by Jim Jones, 25 August 1968. "PL-McCarthy, Eugene," Box 26, Subject File, White House Central Files, LBJ; Eisele, *Almost to the Presidency,* p. 349; Finney oral history, p. 18.

43. Transcript, *Face the Nation,* CBS, 25 August 1968, "August 1968," Box 12, Accession 11455, EJM, MHS; *New York Times,* 28 August 1968; Clark interview; Herzog, *McCarthy for President,* p. 274; Humphrey, *Education of a Public Man,* p. 491; John A. Farrell, *Tip O'Neill and the Democratic Century* (Boston: 2001), p. 257; *Washington Post,* 1 November 1970.

44. Sheed, "Eugene McCarthy," pp. 154–164.

45. Chester et al., *An American Melodrama,* pp. 660–661; Gorman oral history, pp. 58–59; Cohen and Taylor, *American Pharaoh,* pp. 480–481; Freeman interview; E. Berman, *Hubert,* p. 188; *Chicagoland,* 23 August 1978, in "Newspaper Columns, Magazine Articles and Essays, Jan. 1 1977–Jan. 31, 1980," Box 1, Accession 15044, EJM, MHS; undated interview with

Eugene McCarthy for *Cold War* (CNN) at <http://www.hfni.gsehd.gwu.edu/~nsarchiv/coldwar/interviews/episode-13/mccarthy1.html>, 7 October 2003; *Minneapolis Star Tribune*, 26 August 1996.

46. *The APIC Keynoter* 89:3 (Winter 1989): 4–24, in "1988 Campaign Articles," Box 6, Accession 15044, EJM, MHS; Plotke, "Party Reform as Failed Democratic Renewal," p. 245; Ralph M. Goldman, *Search for Consensus: The Story of the Democratic Party* (Philadelphia: 1979), p. 226; Clymer, *Edward Kennedy*, p. 123.

47. *Commentary*, February 1968; *New York Times*, 14 March 1968; Andrew E. Busch, *Outsiders and Openness in the Presidential Nominating System* (Pittsburgh: 1997), pp. 84–85; William R. Keech and Donald R. Matthews, *The Party's Choice* (Washington, D.C.: 1976), pp. 198–199.

48. Scammon and Wattenberg, *Real Majority*, pp. 123, 135; Lebedoff, *New Elite*, p. 69; Parmet, *The Democrats*, p. 267; Gould, *1968: The Election That Changed America*, p. 165; Davis, *Emerging Democratic Majority*, p. 42; Scammon and Wattenberg, *Real Majority*, pp. 154–155.

49. Plotke, "Party Reform as Failed Democratic Renewal," p. 232; *Atlantic Monthly*, March 1974; *Wall Street Journal*, 30 August 1968; Parmet, *The Democrats*, pp. 267–268; Keech and Matthews, *Party's Choice*, p. 96; Busch, *Outsiders and Openness*, pp. 134, 97; *Wall Street Journal*, 30 August 1968.

50. Clark interview; *New York Times*, 19 September 1968; *Congressional Quarterly Weekly Report*, 9 May 1969, p. 689; English, *Divided They Stand*, p. 378; Byron G. Allen to McCarthy, 16 August 1968, "EJM: By and To," Box 46, Part 1, National Files, MHPA; William Benton to McCarthy, 30 September 1968, "EJM: By and To," Box 46, Part 1, National Files, MHPA; Lord oral history, p. 16; *The Progressive*, March 1969, in "Articles by McCarthy 1968/1969," Box 3, Accession 12758, EJM, MHS; Humphrey, *Education of a Public Man*, pp. 5, 377; Humphrey oral history, p. 57, JFK; Berman oral history, p. 25; Berman, *Hubert*, p. 206; Eisele, *Almost to the Presidency*, p. 343; Chester et al., *An American Melodrama*, p. 827; "Statement of Senator McCarthy," 29 October 1968, "Sept.–Dec. 1968," Box 12, Accession 11455, EJM, MHS; *New York Times*, 30 October 1968; E. McCarthy, *Year of the People*, pp. 227–228; *Emphasis Magazine*, June 1982, in "Correspondence and Clippings 1968, 1979–1982," Correspondence File, Box 2, Accession 13290, EJM, MHS; *Washington Post*, 1 June 1987; "The Summer of Our Discontent," *The APIC Keynoter* 89:3 (Winter 1989): 14, in "1988 Campaign Articles," Box 6, Accession 15044, EJM, MHS; E. McCarthy, *Gene McCarthy's Minnesota*, p. 134.

51. *Washington Post*, 30 October 1968; Farr, Freeman, and Naftalin interviews; Humphrey, *Education of a Public Man*, p. 377; Freidin, *A Sense of the Senate*, p. 116; oral history of Joseph Cerrell, by Dennis O'Brien, 13 June 1969, Los Angeles, p. 34, Oral History Collection, JFK; Patton oral history, Part II, Volume I, pp. 75–76; Smaby, *Political Upheaval*, p. 424; Plotke, "Party Reform as Failed Democratic Renewal," pp. 276–277; *Minneapolis Tribune*, 10 November 1968; McCarthy interview on CBS *Nightwatch*, 23 April 1987, recording in Box 8, Accession 15044, EJM, MHS; *New York Times*, 1 April 1971; E. McCarthy, *Up 'til Now*, p. 95.

52. *St. Paul Pioneer Press*, 21 October 1999; "The Political Significance of the 1968 Presidential Campaign," unpublished essay, undated, "Correspondence, August 1987," Box 1, Accession 14399, EJM, MHS; undated interview with Eugene McCarthy for *Cold War* (CNN) at <http://www.hfni.gsehd.gwu.edu/~nsarchiv/coldwar/interviews/episode-13/mccarthy1.html>, 7 October 2003. McCarthy did not, of course, actually *beat* Johnson until the president had already withdrawn. Even McCarthy himself sometimes forgot that he had actually lost in New Hampshire.

53. *Commentary*, May 1968; Grossman, *Relentless Liberal*, p. 120; *Minneapolis Star Tribune*, 8 April 1996; *New York Times Magazine*, 25 August 1968; *New Republic*, 25 October 1969; Larner, *Nobody Knows*, p. 33; Clark interview; *Washington Post*, 17 July 1988. To be fair to McCarthy, not all of his staff agreed with the more hostile verdicts. Richard Goodwin remained convinced that McCarthy was "personally amiable, often hilariously witty, [and] easy to work with . . . not only an ideal candidate, but the most original mind I have ever known in politics": see Goodwin, *Remembering America*, p. 492.

54. Herzog oral history, p. 36; Garfinkle, *Telltale Hearts,* p. 160; Page and Brody, "Party Voting and the Electoral Process," pp. 979–996; Clark interview.

55. Morgan, *Beyond the Liberal Consensus,* pp. 1–57; Plotke, "Party Reform as Failed Democratic Renewal," pp. 223–288; Larner, *Nobody Knows,* p. 16; Wilson, *Amateur Democrat,* pp. 52–55; Steinfels, *The Neoconservatives,* p. 109; Ware, *Breakdown of Democratic Party Organization,* p. 141; Matusow, *Unraveling of America;* Thomas Ferguson and Joel Rogers, *Right Turn: The Decline of the Democrats and the Future of American Politics* (New York: 1986); Gillon, *Democrats' Dilemma.* While McCarthy in 1968 and McGovern in 1972 both spoke for an organized faction within the party, Carter in 1976 represented no cause but himself, and his victory therefore marked the triumph of "self-nomination." See Ehrenhalt, *United States of Ambition,* p. 36.

56. Plotke, "Party Reform as Failed Democratic Renewal," pp. 250–251; Scammon and Wattenberg, *Real Majority,* p. 39; Edsall and Edsall, *Chain Reaction,* p. 52; *New York Times Magazine,* 25 August 1968; "Eugene McCarthy on the Record," March 1968, "Speeches: Public Excerpts," Box 4, Accession 15044, EJM, MHS, p. 10; speech to Colorado State Democratic Convention, 13 July 1968, "July 1968," Box 12, Accession 11455, EJM, MHS; position paper on "Cities," 28 July 1968, "Speeches and releases, 1959–1969," Box 13, Accession 11455, EJM, MHS; "A Housing Program for the Nation's Cities," 14 August 1968, "Speeches and releases, 1959–1969," Box 13, Accession 11455, EJM, MHS; Davies, *From Opportunity to Entitlement,* esp. pp. 2–7, 219–243; Sandel, *Democracy's Discontent,* p. 288; Kazin, *Populist Persuasion,* pp. 233–260.

57. *Commonweal,* 9 August 1968; Plotke, "Party Reform as Failed Democratic Renewal," pp. 224, 256; Milkis, *President and the Parties,* p. 15; Shafer, *Quiet Revolution,* pp. 13–40; Lebedoff, *New Elite,* p. 71; Davis, *Emerging Democratic Majority,* pp. 37–38; Radosh, *Divided They Fell,* p. 134; see also *The Progressive,* April 1969; *Atlantic Monthly,* April 1969; Stephen C. Schlesinger, *The New Reformers* (Boston: 1975); Mixner, *Stranger Among Friends,* p. 88; Maraniss, *First in His Class,* pp. 183–184; Ken Olsen to Larry O'Brien, 18 September 1968, "Martha's Vineyard Conference Report," Box 49, National Files, MHPA; *Minneapolis Star Tribune,* 10 October 1992.

58. Byron E. Shafer, *The Quiet Revolution: The Struggle for the Democratic Party and the Shaping of Post-reform Politics* (New York: 1983), p. 124; Morgan, *Beyond the Liberal Consensus,* p. 125; Mailer, *Miami and the Siege of Chicago,* p. 89; *Newsweek,* 2 September 1968; *Commonweal,* 4 October 1968; Smaby, *Political Upheaval,* p. 342.

59. Thomas Byrne Edsall, *The New Politics of Inequality* (New York: 1984), p. 58; Shafer, *Quiet Revolution,* pp. 7–8, 127–129; Plotke, "Party Reform as Failed Democratic Renewal," pp. 223, 235, 280; Matthew Josephson, *The Politicos, 1865–1896* (New York: 1938), p. 226.

60. Mary Anderson Donaghy, "Who Were the People?: An Analysis of Data Obtained from the Grass-Roots Workers in Eugene McCarthy's 1968 Presidential Campaign," unpublished M.A. thesis, American University, 1973, pp. 54, 105; Hofstadter, *Age of Reform,* pp. 140–143; Wilson, *Amateur Democrat,* pp. 2–5; Ware, *Breakdown of Democratic Party Organization,* p. 67; Parmet, *The Democrats,* p. 264; Davies, *From Opportunity to Entitlement,* p. 169.

61. Lebedoff, *Ward Number Six,* 64; Stout, *People,* p. 125; *Newark Evening News,* 9 October 1968, in "McCarthy Press clips, 1967–1968," Box 9, Accession 12491, EJM, MHS; *Harper's Magazine,* March 1968; *Commentary,* February 1968; Stout, *People,* p. 385; Thomas Byrne Edsall, "The Changing Shape of Power: A Realignment in Public Policy" in Fraser and Gerstle, eds., *Rise and Fall of the New Deal Order,* p. 278; Plotke, "Party Reform as Failed Democratic Renewal," p. 240.

62. Davis, *Emerging Democratic Majority,* p. 212; Mark Bisnow, *Diary of a Dark Horse: The 1980 Anderson Presidential Campaign* (Carbondale, Ill.: 1983), p. 161; Elizabeth Drew, *Portrait of an Election: The 1980 Presidential Campaign* (New York: 1981), pp. 147–157; Jack W. Germond and Jules Witcover, *Blue Smoke and Mirrors: How Reagan Won and Carter Lost the Election of 1980* (New York: 1981), p. 234; John F. Stacks, *Watershed: The Campaign for the*

Presidency, 1980 (New York: 1981), pp. 159, 173, 222; Lebedoff, *New Elite,* pp. 122–124; Dionne, *Why Americans Hate Politics,* p. 139; Randall Rothenburg, *The Neoliberals: Creating the New American Politics* (New York: 1984), p. 247; Leonard Williams, *American Liberalism and Ideological Change* (DeKalb, Ill.: 1997), pp. 50–52; Dionne, *Why Americans Hate Politics,* p. 123, 309; Rae, "Party Factionalism, 1946–1996," p. 57; Busch, *Outsiders and Openness,* p. 146; *New York Review of Books,* 2 December 1999; *New York Review of Books,* 9 March 2000.

63. "Remarks by Senator Eugene J. McCarthy, Grant Park, Chicago," 29 August 1968, "Press Releases 1968," Box 12, Accession 11455, EJM, MHS; "Remarks by Senator Eugene McCarthy to McCarthy Delegates, Staff and Volunteers," 29 August 1968, "Press Releases 1968," Box 12, Accession 11455, EJM, MHS; *New York Times,* 27 October 1968; "Summary of McCarthy Campaigning for Congressional Candidates, 1968," 25 March 1972, "Political Record and Misc., 1969–1975," Box 3, Accession 12758, EJM, MHS; *Time,* 6 September 1968; *New York Times,* 29 December 1968; *The Gallup Report,* 6 December 1967, in "McCarthy, Eugene," Box 181, Office Files of Frederick Panzer, White House Aides' Files, White House Central Files, LBJ.

64. Davis, *Emerging Democratic Majority,* pp. 69–70; *New York Times,* 13 February 1969; Davis, *Emerging Democratic Majority,* p. 100; Goodwin, *Remembering America,* p. 491.

CHAPTER ELEVEN
The Aftermath of Defeat

1. Solberg, *Hubert Humphrey,* p. 406; *New York Times,* 7 November 1968.

2. Abigail McCarthy, *Circles: A Washington Story* (Garden City, N.Y., 1977), p. 233; M. McPherson, *Power Lovers,* pp. 249–250; *Fortune Magazine,* January 1969; Connolly interview; *The Progressive,* March 1969, in "Articles by McCarthy 1968/1969," Box 3, Accession 12758, EJM, MHS.

3. *Time,* 20 December 1968; E. McCarthy, *Up 'til Now,* pp. 111–112; *The Progressive,* March 1969, in "Articles by McCarthy 1968/1969," Box 3, Accession 12758, EJM, MHS; Hersh, *Education of Edward Kennedy,* pp. 359–361; Clymer, *Edward Kennedy,* pp. 131–132.

4. *New York Times,* 11 January 1969; Anne and Martin Peretz to McCarthy, 9 January 1969, "Legislative: General: Martin Peretz," Box 243, EJM, MHS; *Minneapolis Star,* 22 January 1969.

5. *New York Times,* 19 January 1969; *Time,* 10 January 1969; Hersh, *Education of Edward Kennedy,* pp. 291, 360; *New York Times,* 19 January 1969; McCarthy interview.

6. *New York Times Magazine,* 20 July 1969; Cummings, *Pied Piper,* p. 385; *The Progressive,* March 1969, in "Articles by McCarthy 1968/1969," Box 3, Accession 12758, EJM, MHS; *Minneapolis Star,* 22 January 1969; *New York Times Magazine,* 20 July 1969.

7. Confidential author interviews; oral history of Marie Ridder, by Betty Key, 9 February 1970, p. 7, Oral History Collection, MHPA; Larner oral history; Ridder oral history; Connolly interview; Smaby, *Political Upheaval,* pp. 424–425.

8. A. McCarthy, *Private Faces/Public Places,* p. 404; *Washington Daily News,* 22 August 1969; *Duluth News-Tribune,* 5 January 1969; M. McPherson, *Power Lovers,* p. 165; author interviews and correspondence; Ridder oral history, p. 7; M. McPherson, *Power Lovers,* p. 254; Friedin, *A Sense of the Senate,* pp. 116–117.

9. Clark interview.

10. Confidential author interviews and correspondence; *Washington Post,* 21 August 1969; *Parade,* 28 September 1969; *Los Angeles Times,* 3 December 1968; Shana Alexander to Otis Chandler, 6 December 1968, "Political Files: Miscellaneous by Date, 1966–1969," Box 4, Accession 12491, EJM, MHS.

11. Smaby, *Political Upheaval,* p. 425; M. McPherson, *Power Lovers,* p. 254; Smaby, *Political Upheaval,* p. 425; M. McPherson, *Power Lovers,* p. 253.

12. Sheed, "Eugene McCarthy," pp. 154–164; McCarthy interview; *Minneapolis Star Tribune,* 12 April 1997; *Washington Star,* 18 April 1969; *Congressional Record,* 6 December 1969, p.

S15991; *Congressional Record,* 10 December 1969, p. E10531; *Minneapolis Star Tribune,* 12 April 1997; *Los Angeles Times,* 27 May 1979; "How to Lead Many Reich Lives in One Lifetime," undated article by Sheila Webber, Box 3, Accession 15044, EJM, MHS.

13. "Lament of an Aging Politician," in E. McCarthy, *Other Things and the Aardvark,* p. 6.

14. *St. Paul Pioneer Press,* 21 April 1969; DeBenedetti, *An American Ordeal,* p. 294; Transcript of CBS Radio *Capitol Cloakroom,* 7 May 1969, "Capitol Cloakroom," Box 12, Accession 11455, EJM, MHS.

15. McCarthy press release, 2 October 1969, "1969" folder, Box 12, Accession 11455, EJM, MHS; Ken Hurwitz, *Marching Nowhere* (New York, 1971), pp. 30–31, 114; DeBenedetti, *An American Ordeal,* p. 253; undated clipping from *Wall Street Journal* [1970], Box 5, Accession 15044, EJM, MHS; Garfinkle, *Telltale Hearts,* p. 175; Jeffreys-Jones, *Peace Now!,* p. 87; "Testimony of Senator McCarthy Before Committee on Foreign Relations Hearings on Vietnam Policy Proposals," 19 February 1970, "1970" folder, Box 12, Accession 11455, EJM, MHS; McCarthy statement on Cambodia, 12 May 1970, "Legislative: Foreign Relations: Cambodia 1970," Box 249, EJM, MHS; undated clipping from *Wall Street Journal* [1970], Box 5, Accession 15044, EJM, MHS.

16. Eisele, *Almost to the Presidency,* p. 409; Davies, *From Opportunity to Entitlement,* pp. 213–216; Donovan, *Policy Makers,* pp. 174–175; James T. Patterson, *America's Struggle Against Poverty* (Cambridge, Mass.: 1981), p. 193; Steinfels, *The Neoconservatives,* p. 148; Moynihan, *Politics of a Guaranteed Income,* p. 256.

17. "McCarthy on State of the Union," 18 January 1968, "Jan. 1968," Box 12, Accession 11455, EJM, MHS; Vincent Burke and Vee Burke, *Nixon's Good Deed: Welfare Reform* (New York: 1974), p. 153; Davies, *From Opportunity to Entitlement,* p. 219; Richard Lowitt, *Fred Harris: His Journey from Liberalism to Populism* (Lanham, Md.: 2002); Davies, *From Opportunity to Entitlement,* p. 223.

18. Isserman and Kazin, *America Divided,* pp. 195–196; Moynihan, *Politics of a Guaranteed Income,* pp. 327–335; Davies, *From Opportunity to Entitlement,* pp. 222–223; Moynihan, *Politics of a Guaranteed Income,* pp. 334–335; Patterson, *America's Struggle Against Poverty,* p. 195; Davies, *From Opportunity to Entitlement,* pp. 227, 224; Moynihan, *Politics of a Guaranteed Income,* p. 250.

19. Moynihan, *Politics of a Guaranteed Income,* p. 337; *Congressional Record,* 30 April 1970, p. S6386.

20. Moynihan, *Politics of a Guaranteed Income,* pp. 337–338, 250.

21. Davies, *From Opportunity to Entitlement,* pp. 241–242.

22. Moynihan, *Politics of a Guaranteed Income,* p. 532; Davies, *From Opportunity to Entitlement,* pp. 228–229; McCarthy interview; *Washington Star,* 20 November 1970.

23. Transcript, "Hearings on Family Assistance Plan," 18 November 1970, in "Welfare Hearings: Transcripts: HR 16311," Box 7, Accession 12612, EJM, MHS; *Washington Star,* 20 November 1970; McCarthy interview; transcript, "Hearings on Family Assistance Plan," 19 November 1970, pp. 6, 48, 69, 74–75, in "Welfare Hearings: Transcripts: HR 16311," Box 7, Accession 12612, EJM, MHS.

24. Burke and Burke, *Nixon's Good Deed,* pp. 161–163, 153; Statement at Special Hearings on Administration Welfare Program, 18 November 1970, "1970" folder, Box 12, Accession 11455, EJM, MHS; Burke and Burke, *Nixon's Good Deed,* p. 153; Moynihan, *Politics of a Guaranteed Income,* pp. 532–533; Davies, *From Opportunity to Entitlement,* p. 229.

25. Burke and Burke, *Nixon's Good Deed,* pp. 161–163, 153; Statement at Special Hearings on Administration Welfare Program, 18 November 1970, "1970" folder, Box 12, Accession 11455, EJM, MHS; Burke and Burke, *Nixon's Good Deed,* p. 153; Moynihan, *Politics of a Guaranteed Income,* pp. 532–533; Davies, *From Opportunity to Entitlement,* p. 229, 223; Williams, quoted in Patterson, *America's Struggle Against Poverty,* p. 194; McCarthy interview; Burke and Burke, *Nixon's Good Deed,* p. 137; Patterson, *America's Struggle Against Poverty,* p. 196.

26. Tape recording of *David Frost Show,* 24 November 1969, Box 4, Eugene McCarthy collection, Audio-Visual Collection, MHS; McCarthy interview.

27. Undated interview with Franklin La Cava, "Interview Transcripts," Box 4, Accession 15044, EJM, MHS; *New York Times,* 3 March 1969; *Time,* 14 April 1969; *St. Paul Pioneer Press,* 25 July 1969; E. Berman, *Hubert,* p. 207.

28. Miles Lord to Hubert Humphrey, 16 May 1969, "VIP Correspondence, 1969–1970: Eugene McCarthy," Box 2, Supplementary Files, Hubert H. Humphrey Papers, MHS; Jim Rowe to Hubert Humphrey, 14 July 1969, "McCarthy, Eugene J., 1969," Box 6, William Connell Papers, MHS.

29. *St. Paul Pioneer Press,* 25 July 1969; Miles Lord to Hubert Humphrey, 16 May 1969, "VIP Correspondence, 1969–1970: Eugene McCarthy," Box 2, Supplementary Files, Hubert H. Humphrey Papers, MHS; Solberg, *Hubert Humphrey,* p. 456.

30. *Washington Post,* 29 December 1970; *St. Paul Pioneer Press,* 22 December 1970; *Congressional Record,* 21 December 1970, pp. 20858–20868.

31. *Washington Post,* 29 December 1970; Jones and Woll, *Private World of Congress,* p. 102; Smaby, *Political Upheaval,* p. 319; "The Aardvark," in E. McCarthy, *Other Things and the Aardvark,* p. 80.

32. Undated interview with Franklin La Cava, "Interview Transcripts," Box 4, Accession 15044, EJM, MHS; E. McCarthy, *Up 'til Now,* p. 81.

33. McCarthy to University of Maryland English Office, 2 June 1971, "University of Maryland," Box 4, Office Files 1968–1973, Accession 790115, MHPA; course outline, "English 479: Literature and Politics," 16 September 1971, "University of Maryland," Box 4, Office Files 1968–1973, Accession 790115, MHPA; *New York Times,* 24 October 1971.

34. Davis, *Emerging Democratic Majority,* pp. 69–70; Theodore H. White, *The Making of the President 1972* (London, 1974), p. 71; Davis, *Emerging Democratic Majority,* p. 100; *Minneapolis Tribune,* 28 May 1968.

35. Transcripts of Oval Office conversations, 9 August 1971 and 14 September 1971, reprinted in Stanley I. Kutler, ed., *Abuse of Power: The New Nixon Tapes* (New York: 1997), pp. 26–27, 32–34; McCarthy interview.

36. *New York Times,* 23 July 1971; *Washington Post,* 23 July 1971; *Washington Star,* 26 July 1971; *Washington Post,* 8 August 1971.

37. *New York Times,* 23 July 1971; *Washington Post,* 23 July 1971; *Washington Star,* 26 July 1971; *Washington Post,* 8 August 1971; circular letter, 25 October 1971, "1972 Campaign Articles," Box 6, Accession 15044, EJM, MHS; *New York Times,* 18 December 1971; *St. Paul Pioneer Press,* 24 December 1971.

38. Scammon and Wattenberg, *Real Majority,* pp. 78, 232–233; Plotke, "Party Reform as Failed Democratic Renewal," p. 280.

39. Scammon and Wattenberg, *Real Majority,* pp. 78, 232–233; Plotke, "Party Reform as Failed Democratic Renewal," p. 280; *Chicago Tribune,* 11 January 1972; "McCarthy on the Issues—Vietnam War," undated, "Index of McCarthy Releases, Jan. 1970–July 1972," Box 1, Office Files 1968–1973, MHPA; *Congressional Quarterly Weekly Report,* 23 July 1971, pp. 1578–1579.

40. "A Platform for 1972," 30 March 1972, "Issues 1972, 1976," Box 7, Accession 15044, EJM, MHS; "McCarthy on the Issues—Welfare Reform," 15 March 1972, "Index of McCarthy Releases, Jan. 1970–July 1972," Box 1, Office Files 1968–1973, MHPA; "Position Paper: Guaranteed Income, 1972," undated, McCarthy 1972 File, Nee Collection; *Village Voice,* 27 January 1972; "A Platform for 1972," 30 March 1972, "Issues 1972, 1976," Box 7, Accession 15044, EJM, MHS.

41. DeBenedetti, *An American Ordeal,* p. 323; Davis, *Emerging Democratic Majority,* pp. 71, 89–90; Wexler interview.

42. S. Schlesinger, *New Reformers,* p. 39; Herbert Alexander, *Financing the 1972 Election* (Lexington, Mass.: 1976), p. 298; Katz, "Peace Liberals and Vietnam," p. 33; White, *Making of the President 1972,* p. 98.

43. *Minneapolis Tribune,* 19 September 1971; *St. Paul Dispatch,* 16 February 1972; *New York Times,* 19 February 1972.

44. *Village Voice,* 27 January 1972; *Congressional Quarterly Weekly Report,* 23 July 1971, p. 1574; *New York Times,* 19 February 1972; White, *Making of the President 1972, p.* 107.

45. S. Schlesinger, *New Reformers,* p. 121; Hunter S. Thompson, *Fear and Loathing: On the Campaign Trail, '72* (London: 1994), p. 62; S. Schlesinger, *New Reformers,* p. 122.

46. Dougherty, *Goodbye, Mr. Christian,* p. 103; S. Schlesinger, *New Reformers,* p. 121; Thompson, *Fear and Loathing,* pp. 62–63; *New York Times,* 17 January 1972.

47. *New York Times,* 23 January 1972; *Minneapolis Tribune,* 17 January 1972; S. Schlesinger, *New Reformers,* pp. 113, 125.

48. McCoy oral history, p. 20; Muskie oral history, p. 27; Eisele interview; R. K. Baker, *Friend and Foe in the U.S. Senate,* pp. 164–165; *Village Voice,* 27 January 1972; McCarthy to Edmund Muskie, 3 January 1972, "Correspondence with Members of Congress," Box 1, Office Files 1968–1973, MHPA.

49. *The APIC Keynoter* 89:3 (Winter 1989): 16, in "1988 Campaign Articles," Box 6, Accession 15044, EJM, MHS; *Minneapolis Star,* 13 August 1971.

50. H. Alexander, *Financing the 1972 Election,* pp. 202–203, 61; *Washington Post,* 21 March 1972,13 March 1972, 14 March 1972; untitled press release, 10 March 1972, "1972 Releases," Box 5, Office Files 1968–1973, MHPA.

51. James K. Perry, *Us and Them: How The Press Covered the 1972 Election* (New York: 1973), p. 120; *Christian Science Monitor,* 20 March 1972; *New Republic,* 18 March 1972.

52. *New York Times,* 21 March 1972, 23 March 1972; Davis, *Emerging Democratic Majority,* p. 150; *New York Times,* 31 March 1972; H. Alexander, *Financing the 1972 Election,* p. 98.

53. Solberg, *Hubert Humphrey,* pp. 432–434; Busch, *Outsiders and Openness,* p. 97; McCarthy interview; Eisele interview; Anson, *McGovern,* p. 193; Blair Clark to George McGovern, 12 May 1972, "McCarthy, Eugene," Box 15, Selected Correspondence 1972, McGovern Papers, Mudd Library, Princeton.

54. Untitled press release, 22 May 1972, "1972 Releases," Box 5, Office Files 1968–1973, MHPA; Mailer, *Some Honorable Men,* p. 344.

55. Transcript of Democratic Party Platform Committee Testimony, 24 June 1972, "Presidential Campaign 1972 Speech Transcripts," Box 29, Unnumbered and Unprocessed Files, MHPA; Baer, *Reinventing Democrats,* pp. 24–25; unpublished article submitted to *Democratic Review,* October 1974, "Newspaper and Magazine Articles," Box 2, Accession 13290, EJM, MHS; *New York Times,* 5 July 1972; H. R. Haldeman, *The Haldeman Diaries: Inside the Nixon White House* (New York: 1994), entry for 8 September 1972, p. 502; Dougherty, *Goodbye, Mr. Christian,* p. 235.

56. E. McCarthy, *Hard Years,* pp. 78–79; E. McCarthy, *Required Reading,* pp. 41–43; Shafer, *Quiet Revolution,* p. 524; Edsall, *New Politics of Inequality,* p. 58; Plotke, "Party Reform as Failed Democratic Renewal," pp. 223–288.

CHAPTER TWELVE

· *The Long Exile*

1. Interview with Eugene McCarthy by Robb Mitchell, *Northern Lights and Insights 38: Eugene McCarthy,* video recording (Hennepin County, Minn.: 1988), Audio-Visual Collection, MHS; *New York Times,* 14 October 1972, 9 January 1973; *Minneapolis Tribune,* 13 January 1973; *Washington Star,* 14 February 1973.

2. *Los Angeles Times,* 18 February 1973; "Where Are My Other Twelve Minutes?," F. E. Peters, online at <http://pages.nyu.edu/~fep1/regis2.html>, 8 October 2003; *New York Times,* 11 September 1973.

3. *St. Paul Pioneer Press,* 14 June 1973; Humphrey to McCarthy, 6 August 1974, "VIP Correspondence, 1973–1979," Correspondence File, Box 2, Accession 13290, EJM, MHS.

4. *Minneapolis Star,* 13 September 1973, 26 September 1973.

5. *Minneapolis Star,* 5 October 1973; *Minneapolis Tribune,* 27 October 1973; *New York Times,* 28 October 1973.

6. *Minneapolis Star,* 23 October 1973; *Minneapolis Tribune,* 28 October 1973; *St. Paul Dispatch,* 24 October 1973.

7. *St. Paul Pioneer Press,* 26 October 1973; *Minneapolis Tribune,* 29 November 1973; *St. Paul Pioneer Press,* 30 November 1973.

8. *Time,* 5 April 1976; E. Berman, *Hubert,* p. 247; Wills, *Lead Time,* p. 117; Asbell, *Senate Nobody Knows,* pp. 411–412.

9. *New Republic,* 21 September 1974; Morgan, *Beyond the Liberal Consensus,* pp. 1–57.

10. "CCP History" folder, Box 20, Unnumbered and Unprocessed Files, MHPA; *New York Times,* 27 August 1974, 12 July 1975; Jordan Miller to McCarthy, 7 June 1974, "CCP History," Box 20, Unnumbered and Unprocessed Files, MHPA; Committee for a Constitutional Presidency, *Committee Comments* 1:1 (September 1974), "Open Politics Reports," Box 20, Unnumbered and Unprocessed Files, MHPA; examination paper, "Political and Governmental Institutions, Fall 1974," undated, "Teaching Files: State University of New York at Purchase, 1974 History Course," Box 32, Unnumbered and Unprocessed Files, MHPA.

11. Herbert E. Alexander, *Financing the 1976 Election* (Washington: 1979), pp. 16–18; E. McCarthy, *Contraries and Complexities,* pp. 123–127; *New York Times,* 12 December 1974; H. Alexander, *Financing the 1976 Election,* pp. 17–19, 30–31; *Time,* 9 February 1976.

12. E. McCarthy, *Hard Years,* pp. 168–169.

13. *St. Paul Dispatch,* 17 September 1974; *New York Times,* 13 January 1975; *Wall Street Journal,* 13 February 1975.

14. Ehrenhalt, *United States of Ambition,* p. 36; *Washington Watch* 4:20 (14 May 1976), "Washington Watch," Box 7, Accession 15044, EJM, MHS.

15. Pamphlet, "If you wonder what other Presidential candidates will be saying ten or fifteen years from now—Listen to what Gene McCarthy is saying today," "Political and Miscellaneous, 1968–1979," Box 3, Accession 12758, EJM, MHS; E. McCarthy, *Hard Years,* pp. 151, 61–67, 163–164.

16. Marijuana laws statement, 23 February 1976, "Issues 1972, 1976," Box 7, Accession 15044, EJM, MHS; busing statement, 17 March 1976, "Issues 1972, 1976," Box 7, Accession 15044, EJM, MHS; abortion statement, 2 April 1976, "Issues 1972, 1976," Box 7, Accession 15044, EJM, MHS; E. McCarthy, *Required Reading,* pp. 141–144; on birth control, see interview with McCarthy in *The Wanderer,* 11 July 1985, "Clippings: Eugene McCarthy," SJU; E. McCarthy, *Hard Years,* p. 49; see McCarthy statements, 29 April 1975 and 4 December 1975, SANE Evaluation, "Political Record and Miscellaneous, 1969–1975," Box 3, Accession 12758, EJM, MHS.

17. *Minneapolis Tribune,* 26 October 1976; *Congressional Quarterly Weekly Report,* 16 October 1976, p. 2973; *Candidates 76* (Washington, D.C.: 1976), p. 88; McCarthy interview on CBS *Nightwatch,* 23 April 1987, recording in Box 8, Accession 15044, EJM, MHS; E. McCarthy, *Required Reading,* pp. 59–60; pamphlet, "If you wonder . . . ," "Political and Miscellaneous, 1968–1979," Box 3, Accession 12758, EJM, MHS; E. McCarthy, *Required Reading,* p. 75.

18. *Washington Post,* 1 August 1976; *Time,* 5 April 1976; Donald W. Carson and James W. Johnson, *Mo: The Life and Times of Morris K. Udall* (Tucson, Ariz.: 2001); Kazin, *Populist Persuasion,* p. 246; Steinfels, *The Neoconservatives,* pp. 274, 294; Ehrman, *Rise of Neoconservatism,* p. 99.

19. H. Alexander, *Financing the 1976 Election,* pp. 175, 435, 827; *Minneapolis Tribune,* 6 February 1976; *New York Times,* 8 February 1976, 12 February 1976.

20. *Time,* 25 October 1976; *Congressional Quarterly Weekly Report,* 16 October 1976, p. 2973; *Christian Science Monitor,* 28 October 1976; Rubino interview; *Candidates 76,* p. 85.

21. *New York Times,* 27 May 1976; Rubino interview; *New York Times,* 19 September 1976.

22. *Atlantic Monthly,* September 1975; Jules Witcover, *Marathon: The Pursuit of the Presidency, 1972–1976* (New York: 1977), p. 183; *New York Times,* 10 July 1976.

23. *Congressional Quarterly Weekly Report,* 16 October 1976, p. 2973; E. McCarthy, *Up 'til Now,*

p. 203; *New York Times,* 11 January 1976; *Los Angeles Times,* 6 February 1976; *Congressional Quarterly Weekly Report,* 16 October 1976, p. 2973; *New York Times,* 24 October 1976.

24. Transcript of NBC *Meet the Press,* "March 1976–December 1976," Box 8, "McCarthy: By and About," MHPA; *Chicago Sun-Times,* 21 October 1976; *New York Times,* 26 July 1976; *St. Paul Pioneer Press,* 26 October 1973; *Minneapolis Tribune,* 9 October 1976; *Chicago Sun-Times,* 21 October 1976.

25. *Candidates 76,* p. 85; H. Alexander, *Financing the 1976 Election,* pp. 438–439; *New York Times,* 10 September 1976; *Time,* 25 October 1976; *Washington Post,* 30 October 1976.

26. Rubino interview; McCarthy interview; *Washington Post,* 27 October 1976; *The Nation* and *New Republic,* 30 October 1976; *New York Times,* 30 October 1976; Witcover, *Marathon,* p. 630; *Washington Post,* 17 October 1976, 30 October 1976.

27. *New Republic,* 23 October 1976; *New York Times,* 4 November 1976; *Minneapolis Tribune,* 3 November 1976; *Congressional Quarterly Weekly Report,* 18 December 1976, pp. 3335–3336; *St. Paul Pioneer Press,* 3 November 1976.

28. Martin Schram, *Running for President, 1976: The Carter Campaign* (New York: 1977), p. 365; H. Alexander, *Financing the 1976 Election,* p. 444; *The Progressive,* January 1977; H. Alexander, *Financing the 1976 Election,* p. 440; Stacks, *Watershed,* p. 167; transcript of National Press Club news conference, 5 November 1976, "March 1976–December 1976," Box 8, "McCarthy: By and About," MHPA.

29. "Dear Friends" letter, January 1977, Folder 73, "Campaign Material 1976," Box 3, Leslie W. Higbie Papers, Lauinger Library, Georgetown University; H. Alexander, *Financing the 1976 Election,* p. 439; *Washington Star,* 12 December 1976; McGrory interview; *New York Times,* 4 November 1976; *St. Paul Pioneer Press,* 3 November 1976.

30. *Minneapolis Tribune,* 23 May 1982; *Minneapolis Star Saturday Magazine,* 14 April 1979.

31. *Chicago Tribune,* 5 May 1982; *Christian Science Monitor,* 21 December 1977; *Minneapolis Star Saturday Magazine,* 14 April 1979.

32. Solberg, *Hubert Humphrey,* p. 456; E. McCarthy, "Memories of Hubert," in *Gene McCarthy's Minnesota,* p. 131. For a more hostile account of their last meeting, see E. Berman, *Hubert,* p. 267.

33. *Washington Post,* 4 November 1974; *St. Paul Pioneer Press,* 12 September 1978; *Los Angeles Times,* 4 March 1979; *Washington Post,* 22 July 1979.

34. E. McCarthy, *Up 'til Now,* pp. 226–230; *Los Angeles Times,* 8 September 1979; Lebedoff, *New Elite,* pp. 122–124; *New York Times,* 10 October 1980; Bisnow, *Diary of a Dark Horse,* p. 161; Drew, *Portrait of an Election,* pp. 147–157; Germond and Witcover, *Blue Smoke and Mirrors,* p. 234; Stacks, *Watershed,* pp. 159, 173, 222; "Statement by Honorable Eugene McCarthy," "Democrats for Reagan and Bush," press release, 23 October 1980, Box 2, Accession 15044, EJM, MHS.

35. *New York Times,* 22 October 1980; *St. Paul Pioneer Press,* 24 October 1980; McCarthy interview on CBS *Nightwatch,* 23 April 1987, recording in Box 8, Accession 15044, EJM, MHS; *Red Wing Republican Eagle,* 7 July 1982, in "Correspondence and Clippings, 1979–1982," Correspondence File, Box 2, Accession 13290, EJM, MHS.

36. *Emphasis Magazine,* June 1982, in "Correspondence and Clippings, 1979–1982," Correspondence File, Box 2, Accession 13290, EJM, MHS; Schlesinger interview; McCarthy interview.

37. *Minneapolis Star,* 18 August 1981; *St. Paul Pioneer Press,* 4 September 1981; Brandl interview; *Minneapolis Star,* 1 September 1981.

38. Ferguson and Rogers, *Right Turn,* pp. 150–151, 166; David S. Mayer, *A Winter of Discontent: The Nuclear Freeze and American Politics* (New York: 1990); "Platform of Senator Eugene McCarthy," July 1982, Box 3, Accession 15044, EJM, MHS; *Chicago Tribune,* 5 May 1982; *Minneapolis Star Tribune,* 23 April 1982; *Emphasis Magazine,* June 1982, in "Correspondence and Clippings, 1979–1982," Correspondence File, Box 2, Accession 13290, EJM, MHS.

39. *Minneapolis Tribune,* 19 March 1982.

40. *Minneapolis Star,* 22 March 1982; *Rochester Post-Bulletin,* 27 April 1982, in "McCarthy Clips: Out-state, 1982," Nee Collection.

41. *Philadelphia Inquirer,* undated clipping, in "Correspondence and Clippings, 1979–1982," Correspondence File, Box 2, Accession 13290, EJM, MHS; Minnesota Poll, undated [mid-1982], in "1982 Clippings," Nee Collection; *Mankato Free Press,* 24 July 1982, in "McCarthy Clips: Out-state, 1982," Nee Collection; *Philadelphia Inquirer,* undated clipping, in "Correspondence and Clippings, 1979–1982," Correspondence File, Box 2, Accession 13290, EJM, MHS; *Minneapolis Tribune,* 19 March 1982; *Minneapolis Star Tribune,* 14 July 1982; *St. Paul Pioneer Press,* 22 August 1982.

42. *Biwabik Times,* 13 May 1982, in "McCarthy Clips: Out-state, 1982," Nee Collection; *St. Paul Pioneer Press,* 5 June 1982; *Minneapolis Star Tribune,* 10 June 1982; *Emphasis Magazine,* June 1982, in "Correspondence and Clippings, 1979–1982," Correspondence File, Box 2, Accession 13290, EJM, MHS.

43. *Minneapolis Star Tribune,* 10 June 1982.

44. *Minneapolis Star Tribune,* 14 June 1982; *St. Paul Pioneer Press,* 22 August 1982; *Philadelphia Inquirer,* undated clipping, in "Correspondence and Clippings, 1979–1982," Correspondence File, Box 2, Accession 13290, EJM, MHS; *St. Paul Pioneer Press,* 16 September 1982.

45. *Los Angeles Times,* 7 October 1983; *St. Paul Pioneer Press,* 31 October 1984; *Minneapolis Star Tribune,* 15 March 1987.

46. *New Republic,* 10 May 1980; *Washington Post,* 21 April 1987; *The American Spectator,* August 1998; and see the following books, all by Eugene J. McCarthy: *The View from Rappahannock* (McLean, Va.: 1984); *Up 'til Now: A Memoir* (New York: 1987); *Required Reading: A Decade of Political Wit and Wisdom* (New York: 1988); *Nonfinancial Economics: The Case for Shorter Hours of Work* (New York: 1989); *The View from Rappahannock II* (McLean, Va.: 1989); *A Colony of the World: The United States Today* (New York: 1992); *No-Fault Politics: Modern Presidents, the Press, and Reformers* (New York: 1998).

47. *Washington Post,* 2 June 1987; E. McCarthy, *Hard Years,* p. 100.

48. *Newsweek,* 3 January 1972; *Minneapolis Star Tribune,* 3 November 1988; *Washington Post,* 2 June 1987.

49. *Minneapolis Star Tribune,* 2 June 1988; *Chicago Tribune,* 30 June 1988.

50. *Minneapolis Star Tribune,* 5 June 1988; *St. Paul Pioneer Press,* 11 June 1988; *Philadelphia Inquirer,* 2 June 1988.

51. *New York Times,* 7 October 1991; McCarthy Platform 1992, undated, "Campaigns 1992," Box 7, Accession 15044, EJM, MHS; *Boston Globe,* 19 December 1991.

52. *Los Angeles Times,* 12 April 1992.

53. *Minneapolis Star Tribune,* 13 March 1992; *New York Times,* 14 March 1993; *New York Times,* 22 March 1992.

54. *St. John's Magazine,* Winter 1998, SJU; *Minneapolis Star Tribune,* 15 May 1997.

55. *St. Paul Pioneer Press,* 2 February 2001; *Washington Post,* 2 June 1987; author interviews.

56. *Minneapolis Star Tribune,* 15 November 1997; *Minneapolis Star Tribune,* 11 December 1998; *St. Paul Pioneer Press,* 21 October 1999.

57. *Seattle Post-Intelligencer,* 17 January 2000; *Rappahannock News,* 6 March 2003; *The Hill,* 2 April 2003.

58. *Minneapolis Star Tribune,* 15 April 2003.

EPILOGUE

The Liberal's Progress

1. A. McCarthy, *Private Faces/Public Places,* pp. 94–96; Eugene J. McCarthy, "The Intellectual's Place in American Government," *Texas Quarterly* (Winter 1965): 117–124, in "General: Articles, undated," Box 303, EJM, MHS.

BIBLIOGRAPHY

PRIMARY SOURCES

A. MANUSCRIPTS

St. Paul, Minn.
Minnesota Historical Society

The McCarthy papers in the Minnesota Historical Society cover the period 1948–1992 and are divided into two sections. The first (Boxes 1–314) covers McCarthy's congressional career from 1948 to 1970. The second (Accessions 11455 to 15044, as below) is a miscellaneous collection of personal and political papers from the 1940s to the 1990s.

Eugene McCarthy Papers
    Boxes 1–314
        Executive Files
        Legislative Files
        Public Relations Files
        Political Files
    Accession 11455
    Accession 12240
    Accession 12491
    Accession 12612
    Accession 12758
    Accession 13290
    Accession 14399
    Accession 15044

Abigail McCarthy Papers
Eugenie Anderson Papers
Audio-Visual Collection
    Eugene McCarthy Collection
Myrtle Cain Papers
William Connell Papers
Democratic-Farmer-Labor Party State Central Committee Papers

Arvonne Fraser Papers
Donald Fraser Papers
Orville Freeman Papers
Hubert Humphrey Papers
    Mayoralty Files, 1945–1948
    Senatorial Files, 1949–1964
    Vice Presidential Files, 1965–1968
    1968 Campaign Files
    Supplementary Files
Geri Joseph Papers
Barbara Stuhler Papers
James Youngdale Papers

St. Paul, Minn.
Archives of the University of St. Thomas

Eugene McCarthy Collection
    Confidential Employment File
    Clippings File

Collegeville, Minn.
St. John's Abbey and University Archives

Eugene McCarthy Collection
    Clippings File
    Newspaper Articles File

Minneapolis, Minn.
Personal Collection of Kay Bonner Nee

Nee Report on Campaign Advertising, 1968
McCarthy 1972 File
Miscellaneous Clippings File, 1972–1992
McCarthy Clips, Out-State, 1982
1982 Clippings File

Austin, Texas
Lyndon Baines Johnson Presidential Library

Lyndon Baines Johnson Papers
    Pre-Presidential Papers
        Lyndon Baines Johnson Archives, 1931–1968
            LBJA Congressional File
        Senate Papers, 1949–1961
            Senate Master Files, 1953–1961
            Correspondence with Democratic Senators, 1957–1959
            Congressional Files, 1959–1960
        Vice Presidential Papers, 1961–1963
            Vice Presidential Master Files
            Vice Presidential Congressional Files
        White House Central Files
            Subject File
            Name File

Confidential File
White House Aides' Files
    Office Files of Ceil Bellinger
    Files of S. Douglass Cater
    Office Files of Mike Manatos
    Office Files of Harry McPherson
    Office Files of Frederick Panzer
National Security File
    Vietnam Country File
    Memos to the President
    Files of Walt W. Rostow
Special Files, 1927–1973
    Congressional Favors File
President's Appointment File
Democratic National Committee Papers, 1960–1968
Series I
Series II
Drew Pearson Papers
Recordings and Transcripts of Conversations and Meetings
    Recordings of Telephone Conversations—White House Series, 1964

Boston, Mass.
John F. Kennedy Presidential Library

John Fitzgerald Kennedy Papers
    Pre-Presidential Papers
        1960 Campaign: Campaigns by State
    Congressional Liaison File
        Papers of Mike Manatos
        White House Staff File of Lawrence O'Brien
    White House Central Files
        Name File
Robert Francis Kennedy Papers
    Attorney General Papers, 1961–1964
        Condolences, 1963–1964
    Presidential Campaign Papers, 1968
        National Headquarters Files
            Press Division
            Research Division
Milton Gwirtzman Papers
    Publications: *On His Own*
        Subject File
Frank Mankiewicz Papers
    McGovern 1972 Campaign
        Alphabetical Subject File
Arthur M. Schlesinger Jr. Papers
    Robert Kennedy and His Times
        Background Materials
Adam Walinsky Papers
    Senate Subject File, 1965–1968
Theodore H. White Papers
    Notes on *The Making of the President 1968*

Cambridge, Mass.
Schlesinger Library, Radcliffe

Mary Abigail McCarthy Papers

New Haven, Conn.
Sterling Memorial Library, Yale University

Chester Bowles Papers
    Accession 628, Series I
Walter Lippmann Papers
    Accession 326, Series III

Princeton, N.J.
Mudd Manuscript Library, Princeton University

    George McGovern Papers
        Selected Correspondence, 1972
        Accession 71A 3482

Washington, D.C.
Lauinger Library, Georgetown University

This collection holds the papers of McCarthy's presidential campaigns of 1968, 1972 and 1976. The papers are extremely disorganized and most have never been processed or catalogued. Since there are no coherent catalogues or finding aids, I have divided them for reference purposes into different categories according to the scribbled markings on the tops of the boxes. At the time of writing, there were plans to move the collection to the library of the University of Minnesota.

    McCarthy Historical Project Archive
        National Files 1968
        Office Files 1968–1973, Accession 790115
        1972 File
        McCarthy Papers, Acquisition 9.82
        McCarthy: By and About
        Unnumbered and Unprocessed Files
        McCarthy Microfilm Collection
        McCarthy Television Advertising Collection
    Leslie W. Higbie Papers
    Hubert Humphrey Campaign Poll Data
    J. Herman Schauinger Papers
    Richard T. Stout Papers

Washington, D.C.
Library of Congress

    Eugene McCarthy Manuscript Collection, 1960
    Averell Harriman Papers
        Special Files: Public Service, Kennedy-Johnson Administrations
    Kathleen S. Louchheim Papers
    Joseph Rauh Papers

B. INTERVIEWS AND ORAL HISTORIES

Author interviews

Charles Backstrom, 16 October 1999, Minneapolis
John Brandl, 7 December 1999, Minneapolis
Blair Clark, 18 April 2000, New York City
Carol Connolly, 9 December 1999, St. Paul
Albert Eisele, 7 May 2000, Washington, D.C.
George Farr, 17 January 2000, St. Paul
Arvonne and Donald Fraser, 3 December 1999, Minneapolis
Jane Freeman, 7 March 2000, Minneapolis
John Kenneth Galbraith, 11 February 2000, Cambridge, Mass.
Father Godfrey Diekmann, 16 March 2000, Collegeville, Minn.
Curtis Gans, 15 May 2000, Washington, D.C.
Jeff Greenfield, 31 January 2000, Concord, N.H.
Gerald Heaney, 4 March 2000, St. Paul
Godfrey Hodgson, 25 February 1999, Oxford, U.K.
Sister Arleen Hynes, 15 March 2000, Collegeville, Minn.
Nicholas Katzenbach, 6 February 1999, London, U.K.
William Kubicek, 20 January 2000, Minneapolis
David Lebedoff, 19 January 2000, Minneapolis
Abigail McCarthy, 18 October 1999, Washington, D.C.
Eugene McCarthy, 12 and 13 October 1999, Washington, D.C.
Mary McGrory, 17 October 1999, Washington, D.C.
Harry McPherson, 19 October 1999, Washington, D.C.
Arthur Naftalin, 7 December 1999, Minneapolis
Kay Bonner Nee, 8 March 2000, Minneapolis
Doris O'Donnell, 28 February 1999, telephone interview
Father Virgil O'Neill, 15 March 2000, Collegeville, Minn.
Father Raymond Pedrizetti, 14 March 2000, Collegeville, Minn.
Martin Peretz, 11 February 2000, Cambridge, Mass.
Father Gunther Rolfson, 16 March 2000, Collegeville, Minn.
Michael Rubino, 12 May 2000, Bethesda, Md.
Arthur Schlesinger Jr., 4 May 2000, New York City
Warren Spannaus, 8 December 1999, Minneapolis
Howard Stein, 23 April 2000, New York City
Janet Stein, 23 April 2000, New York City
Father Vincent Tegeder, 15 March 2000, Collegeville, Minn.
Father Hilary Thimmesh, 15 March 2000, Collegeville, Minn.
Anne Wexler, 14 October 1999, Washington, D.C.
Jules Witcover, 10 May 2000, Washington, D.C.
Mary Beth Yarrow, 27 April 2000, New York City

Author correspondence

Shana Alexander, 16 February and 4 May 2000
Albert Eisele, 7 and 8 February 2000
Jerome Grossman, 17 April 2000
Larry McCaffrey, 20, 21, and 22 January 2000
James Shannon, 24 March 2000
Norman Sherman, 17 January, 19 January, 21 January, 24 January, 26 January, 31 January,
    11 February, 21 February, and 25 February 2000

Oral histories

Austin, Texas
Lyndon Baines Johnson Presidential Library
Oral History Collection

Robert S. Allen, 30 May 1969
Hubert Humphrey, 17 August 1971
Walter Jenkins, 24 August 1971
Frank Mankiewicz, 5 May 1969
Alwyn Matthews, 23 October 1974
George McGovern, 30 April 1969
A. S. Monroney, 26 February 1969
Kenneth O'Donnell, 23 July 1969
Joseph Rauh, 1 August 1969
George Reedy, 14 February 1972

Austin, Texas
Lyndon Baines Johnson Presidential Library
Senate Historical Office Oral Histories

Pat Holt, 9 September to 12 December 1980
Carl Marcy, 14 September to 16 November 1983
Howard E. Shuman, 22 July to 22 October 1987
Francis R. Valeo, 3 July 1985 to 11 March 1986

Boston, Mass.
John F. Kennedy Presidential Library
Oral History Collection

Joseph Alsop, 10 June 1971
Eugenie Anderson, 11 March 1973
John Blatnik, 4 February 1966
David Burke, 8 December 1971
Frank Burns, 17 April 1970
Joseph Cerrell, 13 June 1969
Cesar Chavez, 28 January 1970
John Cogley, 20 February 1968
Fred Dutton, 18 November 1969
Peter Edelman, 15 July 1969, 29 July 1969, 8 August 1969, 12 December 1969, and 3 January 1970
John English, 25 November 1969 and 3 February 1970
Thomas K. Finletter, 7 May 1965
Orville Freeman, 22 July 1964
Elizabeth Gatov, 25 June 1969
Jeff Greenfield, 10 December 1969 and 5 January 1970
Milton Gwirtzman, 4 April 1972
Hubert Humphrey, 30 March 1970
Joseph Kraft, 7 March 1970
Katie Louchheim, 24 April 1968
Allard Lowenstein, 23 April and 2 December 1969
Burke Marshall, 19 and 20 January 1970
George McGovern, 17 July 1970

Maurine Neuberger, 12 February 1970
Steve Smith, 16 April 1970
Theodore Sorensen, 21 March 1969
Frank Thompson, 10 March 1965
Joseph Tydings, 8 March 1973
Richard Wade, 13 December 1973
Adam Walinsky, 4 December 1974 and 3 July 1978
Donald Wilson, 19 June 1970 and 2 July 1970

New York, N.Y.
Columbia University Oral Research Office
Carnegie Corporation Project

Eli Evans, 10 March 1970
Alan Piper, 10 March 1970

New York, N.Y.
Columbia University Oral Research Office
Eisenhower Administration Project

D. B. Hardeman, 3 January 1970

New York, N.Y.
Columbia University Oral Research Office
American Entrepreneurs Project

Palmer Weber, 10 June 1985

New York, N.Y.
Columbia University Oral Research Office
Individual Interviews

Edward Costikyan, 22 April 1970
Ben Davidson, 10 November 1977
Donald Harrington, 22 April 1977
Roger Hilsman, 3 March 1981
Father Francis Murphy, 24 September 1981
James G. Patton, 11 September 1979
Robert Wagner, 8 August 1979

New York, N.Y.
Columbia University Oral Research Office
Allard K. Lowenstein Oral History Project

Howard Berman, 15 November 1990
Jerry Brown, 23 November 1990
Sam Brown, 29 May 1990
Steve Cohen, 8 January 1991
Clinton Deveaux, 31 October 1990
Richard Flacks, 13 December 1988
Barney Frank, 25 April 1989
Gary Hart, 11 December 1988

Harold Ickes, 10 December 1990
Sara Kovner, 15 November 1988
Fowler W. Martin, 15 October 1988
Jack Newfield, 9 December 1990
Joseph Rauh, 8 June 1988
Steven Roberts, 19 December 1990
Cynthia Samuels, 10 September 1990
Leon Shull, 11 February 1992
Richard Weidman, 7 April 1989

New York, N.Y.
Columbia University Oral Research Office
Southern Intellectual Leaders Project

Herman Talmadge, 2 August 1974

New York, N.Y.
Columbia University Oral History Research Office
Adlai E. Stevenson Oral History Project

William Benton, 15 June 1967
William Blair, 10 June 1969
Mrs. Ernest Ives, 19 April 1969
Katie Louchheim, 18 April 1973
Newton Minow, 26 May 1967
A. S. Monroney Sr., 11 June 1969
A. S. Monroney Jr., 11 June 1969
John Sharon, 17 July 1969

New York, N.Y.
Columbia University Oral Research Office
Unemployment Insurance Project

Philip Booth, 9 April 1981

New York, N.Y.
Columbia University Oral Research Office
Washington Press Club Foundation: Women in Journalism

Mary McGrory, 4 August 1991

St. Paul, Minn.
Minnesota Historical Society
Hubert H. Humphrey Oral History Project

Byron Allen, 10 August 1978
Eugenie Anderson, 14 July 1978
Carl Auerbach, 13 July 1978
Edgar Berman, 31 August 1978
Rowland Evans, 9 August 1978
Orville Freeman, 16 January 1978
Gary Hart, 20 September 1978

Gerald Heaney, 11 August 1978
Jack Jorgenson, 1 August 1978
Geri Joseph, 14 July 1978
Harry Kelly, 20 June 1978
Miles Lord, 22 February 1978
George McGovern, 29 July 1978
Theodore Mitau, 22 August 1978
Edmund Muskie, 4 August 1978
Gaylord Nelson, 28 July 1978
Joe Rauh, 22 August 1978
Ted Van Dyk, 21 June 1978

Washington, D.C.
Lauinger Library, Georgetown University
McCarthy Historical Project Archive Oral History Collection

James Abourezk, 3 September 1969
Jerry Brown, 11 August 1969
Sam Brown, unspecified date
John Callahan, 23 May 1969
Elsa Chaney, dated "January or February 1969"
Blair Clark, 28 March 1969
Tom Finney, 13 February 1970
Richard Goodwin, 10 January 1970
Paul Gorman, January 1970
Sanford Gottlieb, 12 March 1969
Jerome Grossman, 22 July 1969
Gilbert Harrison, 7 June 1969
Arthur Herzog, 5 June 1969
Arnold Hiatt, unspecified date
David Hoeh, 30 January 1969
Sarah Kovner, 1 April 1969
Jeremy Larner, 4 June 1969
Allard Lowenstein, unspecified date
Patrick Lucey, 4 June 1969
Tom McCoy, unspecified date
David Mixner, January 1969
Mary Naughton, 20 May 1969
Bill Nee, February 1969
Kay Nee, February 1969
Vance Opperman, 29 May 1969
Joe Rauh, 10 June 1969
Marie Ridder, 9 February 1969
Maurice Rosenblatt, 4 February 1970
Leon Shull, 21 October 1969
Marge Sklencar, 3 September 1969
Richard Stout, 13 January 1969
Gerry Studds, 30 January 1969

C. PRINTED PRIMARY SOURCES

Political Activities of the Johnson White House, 1963–1969: Part One: White House Central and Confidential Files. Microfilm, ed. Paul L. Kesaris: Frederick, Md., 1987.
Political Activities of the Johnson White House, 1963–1969: Part Two: White House Aides. Microfilm, ed. Paul L. Kesaris: Frederick, Md., 1987.

D. VIDEO MATERIALS

Held in the audiovisual collection of the Minnesota Historical Society:

Interview with Eugene McCarthy by Robb Mitchell, *Northern Lights and Insights 38: Eugene McCarthy* (Hennepin County, Minn.: 1988).
Interview with Eugene McCarthy by Robert Rohlf, *Northern Lights and Insights 268: Eugene McCarthy* (Hennepin County, Minn.: 1993).

SECONDARY SOURCES

A. BOOKS

Alexander, Charles. *Holding the Line: The Eisenhower Era, 1952–1961.* Bloomington, Ind., 1975.
Alexander, Herbert. *Financing the 1968 Election.* Lexington, Mass., 1971.
———. *Financing the 1972 Election.* Lexington, Mass., 1976.
———. *Financing the 1976 Election.* Washington, D.C., 1979.
Alexander, Shana. *The Feminine Eye.* New York, 1970.
Allitt, Patrick. *Catholic Intellectuals and Conservative Politics in America.* Ithaca, N.Y., 1993.
Alsop, Joseph W., with Adam Platt. *I've Seen the Best of It: Memoirs.* New York, 1992.
Alsop, Stewart. *The Center: People and Power in Political Washington.* New York, 1968.
Amato, Joseph. *Mounier and Maritain: A French Catholic Understanding of the Modern World.* University, Ala., 1975.
Anderson, David L., ed. *The Human Tradition in the Vietnam Era.* Wilmington, Del., 2000.
Anderson, Terry H. *The Movement and the Sixties: Protest in America from Greensboro to Wounded Knee.* Oxford, 1995.
Andrew, John A. *Lyndon Johnson and the Great Society.* Chicago, 1998.
Anson, Robert Sam. *McGovern: A Biography.* New York, 1972.
Asbell, Bernard. *The Senate Nobody Knows.* Garden City, N.Y., 1978.
Ashby, LeRoy, and Rod Gramer. *Fighting the Odds: The Life of Senator Frank Church.* Pullman, Wash., 1994.
Au, William A. *The Cross, the Flag, and the Bomb: American Catholics Debate War and Peace, 1960–1985.* Westport, Conn., 1985.
Auerbach, Laura K. *Worthy to Be Remembered: A Political History of the Minnesota Democratic-Farmer-Labor Party, 1944–1984.* Minneapolis, 1984.
Baer, Kenneth S. *Reinventing Democrats: The Politics of Liberalism from Reagan to Clinton.* Lawrence, Kan., 2000.
Baker, Bobby, with Larry L. King. *Wheeling and Dealing: Confessions of a Capitol Hill Operator.* New York, 1978.
Baker, Ross K. *Friend and Foe in the U.S. Senate.* New York, 1980.
Baker, Russell. *Our Next President: The Incredible Story of What Happened in the 1968 Elections.* New York, 1968.
Barone, Michael. *Political Coalitions and the Democratic Party: A World Turned Upside Down.* Washington, D.C., 1981.

————. *Our Country: The Shaping of America from Roosevelt to Reagan.* New York, 1990.

Barry, Colman J. *Worship and Work: St. John's Abbey and University, 1856–1980.* Collegeville, Minn., 1980.

————, ed. *A Sense of Place II: The Benedictines of Collegeville.* Collegeville, Minn., 1990.

Barry, Colman J., and Robert L. Spaeth, eds. *A Sense of Place: St. John's of Collegeville.* Collegeville, Minn., 1987.

Baskir, Lawrence M., and William A. Strauss. *Chance and Circumstance: The Draft, the War, and the Vietnam Generation.* New York, 1978.

Beran, Michael Knox. *The Last Patrician.* New York, 1998.

Berman, Edgar. *Hubert: The Triumph and Tragedy of the Humphrey I Knew.* New York, 1979.

Berman, Larry. *Lyndon Johnson's War: The Road to Stalemate in Vietnam.* New York, 1996.

Berman, Paul. *A Tale of Two Utopias: The Political Journey of the Generation of 1968.* New York, 1996.

Berman, Ronald. *America in the Sixties: An Intellectual History.* New York, 1968.

Berman, William C. *William Fulbright and the Vietnam War: The Dissent of a Political Realist.* Kent, Ohio, 1988.

Bernstein, Irving. *Promises Kept: John F. Kennedy's New Frontier.* New York, 1991.

————. *Guns or Butter: The Presidency of Lyndon Johnson.* Oxford, 1996.

Beschloss, Michael. *Taking Charge: The Johnson White House Tapes, 1963–1964.* New York, 1998.

Bisnow, Mark. *Diary of a Dark Horse: The 1980 Anderson Presidential Campaign.* Carbondale, Ill., 1983.

Bliss, Michael. *Right Honorable Men: The Descent of Canadian Politics from Macdonald to Mulroney.* Toronto, 1995.

Boyle, Kevin. *The UAW and the Heyday of American Liberalism.* Ithaca, N.Y., 1985.

Braestrup, Peter. *Big Story: How the American Press and Television Reported and Interpreted the Crisis of Tet 1968 in Vietnam and Washington.* Rev. ed., Garden City, N.Y., 1978.

Brezik, Victor B. *One Hundred Years of Thomism.* Houston, 1981.

Brinkley, Alan. *Voices of Protest: Huey Long, Father Coughlin, and the Great Depression.* New York, 1982.

————. *The End of Reform: New Deal Liberalism in Recession and War.* New York, 1995.

————. *Liberalism and Its Discontents.* Cambridge, Mass., 1998.

Broadwater, Jeff. *Adlai Stevenson and American Politics: The Odyssey of a Cold War Liberal.* New York, 1994.

Broder, David S. *The Party's Over: The Failure of Politics in America.* New York, 1972.

————. *Changing the Guard: Power and Leadership in America.* Harmondsworth, U.K., 1980.

Brown, Eugene. *J. William Fulbright: Advice and Dissent.* Iowa City, Iowa, 1985.

Burke, Vincent, and Vee Burke. *Nixon's Good Deed: Welfare Reform.* New York, 1974.

Burner, David. *Making Peace with the Sixties.* Princeton, N.J., 1996.

Burner, David, and Thomas R. West. *The Torch Is Passed: The Kennedy Brothers and American Liberalism.* New York, 1984.

Busch, Andrew E. *Outsiders and Openness in the Presidential Nominating System.* Pittsburgh, 1997.

Candidates 76. Washington, D.C., 1976.

Capps, Walter. *The Unfinished War: Vietnam and the American Conscience.* Boston, 1982.

Carey, Patrick W., ed. *American Catholic Religious Thought.* Mahwah, N.J., 1987.

Carleton, Don E. *A Breed So Rare: The Life of J. R. Parten, Liberal Texas Oilman, 1896–1992.* Austin, Texas, 1998.

Caro, Robert A. *The Years of Lyndon Johnson: Master of the Senate.* New York, 2002.

Carson, Donald W., and James W. Johnson. *Mo: The Life and Times of Morris K. Udall.* Tucson, Ariz.: 2001.

Carter, Dan T. *The Politics of Rage: George Wallace, the Origins of the New Conservatism, and the Transformation of American Politics.* New York, 1995.

Casey, Patrick J. *The First Hundred Years: A History of Meeker County.* N.p., 1968.

Caute, David. *The Year of the Barricades: A Journey Through 1968.* New York, 1988.

Chafe, William H. *Never Stop Running: Allard K. Lowenstein and the Struggle to Save American Liberalism.* New York, 1993.

———. *The Unfinished Journey: America Since World War II.* 3rd ed., New York, 1995.

Chalmers, David M. *And the Crooked Places Made Straight: The Struggle for Social Change in the 1960s.* Baltimore, 1996.

Chester, Lewis, Godfrey Hodgson, and Bruce Page. *An American Melodrama: The Presidential Campaign of 1968.* New York, 1969.

Childs, Marquis. *Witness to Power.* New York, 1975.

Christian, George. *The President Steps Down.* New York, 1970.

Clark, Joseph S. *The Senate Establishment.* New York, 1963.

———. *Congress: The Sapless Branch.* New York, 1964.

Clymer, Adam. *Edward M. Kennedy: A Biography.* New York, 1999.

Cockburn, Alexander, and Jeffrey St. Clair. *Al Gore: A User's Manual.* New York, 2000.

Cohen, Adam, and Elizabeth Taylor. *American Pharaoh: Mayor Richard J. Daley—His Battle for Chicago and the Nation.* Boston, 2000.

Colainni, James. *The Catholic Left: The Crisis of Radicalism Within the Church.* Philadelphia, 1967.

Collier, Peter, and David Horowitz. *The Kennedys.* New York, 1984.

———. *Destructive Generation: Second Thoughts About the Sixties.* New York, 1989.

Conkin, Paul. *Big Daddy from the Pedernales: Lyndon Johnson.* Boston, 1986.

———. *The Southern Agrarians.* Knoxville, Tenn., 1988.

Cooper, John W. *The Theology of Freedom: The Legacy of Jacques Maritain and Reinhold Niebuhr.* Macon, Ga., 1985.

Crabb, Cecil V., and Pat M. Holt. *Invitation to Struggle: Congress, the President and Foreign Policy.* Washington, D.C., 1980.

Crosby, Donald F. *God, Church, and Flag: Senator Joseph McCarthy and the Catholic Church, 1950–1957.* Chapel Hill, N.C., 1978.

Cummings, Richard. *The Pied Piper: Allard K. Lowenstein and the Liberal Dream.* New York, 1985.

Dallek, Robert. *Lone Star Rising: Lyndon Johnson and His Times, 1908–1960.* New York, 1991.

———. *Hail to the Chief: The Making and Unmaking of American Presidents.* New York, 1996.

———. *Flawed Giant: Lyndon Johnson and His Times, 1961–1973.* Oxford, 1998.

Daniels, Robert V. *The Year of the Heroic Guerrilla: World Revolution and Counterrevolution in 1968.* New York, 1989.

Dark, Taylor E. *The Unions and the Democrats: An Enduring Alliance.* Ithaca, N.Y., 1999.

Davies, Gareth. *From Opportunity to Entitlement: The Transformation and Decline of Great Society Liberalism.* Lawrence, Kan., 1996.

Davis, Lanny J. *The Emerging Democratic Majority: Lessons and Legacies from the New Politics.* New York, 1974.

DeBenedetti, Charles. *The Peace Reform in American History.* Bloomington, Ind., 1980.

DeBenedetti, Charles, with Charles Chatfield. *An American Ordeal: The Antiwar Movement of the Vietnam Era.* Syracuse, N.Y., 1990.

Delton, Jennifer A. *Making Minnesota Liberal: Civil Rights and the Transformation of the Democratic Party.* Minneapolis, 2002.

Depoe, Stephen. *Arthur M. Schlesinger Jr. and the Ideological History of American Liberalism.* Tuscaloosa, Ala., 1994.

DeVoto, Bernard. *The Easy Chair.* Boston, 1955.

Diggins, John Patrick. *The Proud Decades: America in War and in Peace, 1941–1960*. New York, 1988.

——, ed. *The Liberal Persuasion: Arthur Schlesinger and the Challenge of the American Past*. Princeton, N.J., 1997.

Dionne, E. J. *Why Americans Hate Politics*. New York, 1992.

Divine, Robert A., ed. *Foreign Policy, the Great Society, and the White House*. Vol. 1, *The Johnson Years*. Lawrence, Kan., 1987.

—— ed. *Vietnam, the Environment, and Science*. Vol. 2, *The Johnson Years*. Lawrence, Kan., 1987.

——, ed. *LBJ at Home and Abroad*. Vol. 3, *The Johnson Years*. Lawrence, Kan., 1994.

Dodd, Lawrence C., and Bruce I. Oppenheimer, eds. *Congress Reconsidered*. New York, 1977.

Donaldson, Gary A. *Truman Defeats Dewey*. Lexington, Ken., 1998.

Donovan, John C. *The Policy Makers*. New York, 1970.

Donovan, Robert J. *Conflict and Crisis: The Presidency of Harry S. Truman, 1945–1948*. New York, 1977.

——. *Tumultuous Years: The Presidency of Harry S. Truman, 1949–1953*. New York, 1982.

Dooley, Brian. *Robert Kennedy: The Final Years*. Keele, U.K., 1995.

Dorman, Robert L. *The Revolt of the Provinces: The Regionalist Movement in America, 1920–1945*. Chapel Hill, N.C., 1993.

Dougherty, Richard. *Goodbye, Mr. Christian: A Personal Account of McGovern's Rise and Fall*. Garden City, N.Y., 1973.

Douglas, Paul H. *In the Fullness of Time: The Memoirs of Paul H. Douglas*. New York, 1972.

Drew, Elizabeth. *American Journal: The Events of 1976*. New York, 1977.

——. *Portrait of an Election: The 1980 Presidential Campaign*. New York, 1981.

Drukman, Mason. *Wayne Morse: A Political Biography*. Portland, Ore., 1997.

Dumbrell, John, ed. *Vietnam and the Antiwar Movement*. Aldershot, U.K., 1989.

Dunaway, John M. *Jacques Maritain*. Boston, 1978.

Edsall, Thomas Byrne. *The New Politics of Inequality*. New York, 1984.

——. *Power and Money: Writing About Politics, 1971–1987*. New York, 1988.

Edsall, Thomas Byrne, and Mary D. Edsall. *Chain Reaction: The Impact of Race, Rights, and Taxes on American Politics*. New York, 1991.

Ehrenhalt, Alan. *The United States of Ambition: Politicians, Power, and the Pursuit of Office*. New York, 1991.

Ehrman, John. *The Rise of Neoconservatism: Intellectuals and Foreign Affairs, 1945–1994*. New Haven, Conn., 1995.

Eisele, Albert. *Almost to the Presidency: A Biography of Two American Politicians*. Blue Earth, Minn., 1972.

Elazar, Daniel J., Virginia Gray, and Wyman Spano. *Minnesota Politics and Government*. Lincoln, Neb., 1999.

Ellis, Marc H. *Peter Maurin: Prophet in the Twentieth Century*. New York, 1981.

English, David. *Divided They Stand*. London, 1969.

Evans, Rowland, and Robert Novak. *Lyndon B. Johnson: The Exercise of Power*. London, 1967.

Fairlie, Henry. *The Kennedy Promise: The Politics of Expectation*. Garden City, N.Y., 1973.

Farber, David. *Chicago '68*. Chicago, 1988.

——, ed. *The Sixties: From Memory to History*. Chapel Hill, N.C., 1994.

Farrell, John A. *Tip O'Neill and the Democratic Century*. Boston, 2001.

Fenton, John H. *Midwest Politics*. New York, 1966.

Ferguson, Thomas, and Joel Rogers. *Right Turn: The Decline of the Democrats and the Future of American Politics*. New York, 1986.

Fisher, James Terence. *The Catholic Counterculture in America, 1933–1962*. Chapel Hill, N.C., 1989.

Fite, Gilbert C. *Richard B. Russell Jr.: Senator from Georgia*. Chapel Hill, N.C., 1991.

Flynn, George Q. *American Catholics and the Roosevelt Presidency, 1932–1936.* Lexington, 1968.

Foley, Michael. *The New Senate: Liberal Influence on a Conservative Institution, 1959–1972.* New Haven, Conn., 1980.

Fontenay, Charles L. *Estes Kefauver.* Knoxville, Tenn., 1980.

Fowler, Robert Booth. *Enduring Liberalism: American Political Thought Since the 1960s.* Lawrence, Kan., 1999.

Franck, Thomas M., and Edward Weisband. *Foreign Policy by Congress.* New York, 1979.

Frank, Joseph, ed. *The New Look in American Politics: McCarthy's Campaign.* Albuquerque, N.Mex., 1968.

Franklin, R. W., and Robert L. Spaeth. *Virgil Michel: American Catholic.* Collegeville, Minn., 1980.

Fraser, Ronald, ed. *1968: A Student Generation in Revolt.* New York, 1988.

Fraser, Steve, and Gary Gerstle, eds. *The Rise and Fall of the New Deal Order.* Princeton, N.J., 1989.

Freidin, Seymour K. *A Sense of the Senate.* New York, 1972.

Frost, David. *The Presidential Debate, 1968.* New York, 1968.

Fuchs, Lawrence H. *John F. Kennedy and American Catholicism.* New York, 1967.

Fulbright, J. William. *The Arrogance of Power.* New York, 1987.

———. *The Crippled Giant: American Foreign Policy and Its Domestic Consequences.* New York, 1972.

Galbraith, John Kenneth. *A Life in Our Times: Memoirs.* Boston, 1981.

Gallup, George, and Jim Castelli. *The American Catholic People.* Garden City, N.Y., 1987.

Garfinkle, Adam. *Telltale Hearts: The Origins and Impact of the Vietnam Antiwar Movement.* New York, 1995.

Gellman, Irwin F. *The Contender: Richard Nixon—The Congress Years, 1946–1952.* New York, 1999.

Germond, Jack W. *Fat Man in a Middle Seat: Forty Years of Covering Politics.* New York, 1999.

Germond, Jack W., and Jules Witcover. *Blue Smoke and Mirrors: How Reagan Won and Carter Lost the Election of 1980.* New York, 1981.

Gibbons, William Conrad. *The United States Government and the Vietnam War: Executive and Legislative Roles and Relationships. Part 1, 1945–1960.* Princeton, N.J., 1986.

———. *The United States Government and the Vietnam War: Executive and Legislative Roles and Relationships. Part 2, 1961–1964.* Princeton, N.J., 1988.

———. *The United States Government and the Vietnam War: Executive and Legislative Roles and Relationships. Part 3, January–July 1965.* Princeton, N.J., 1989.

———. *The United States Government and the Vietnam War: Executive and Legislative Roles and Relationships. Part 4, July 1965–January 1968.* Princeton, N.J., 1995.

Gieske, Millard L. *Minnesota Farmer-Laborism.* Minneapolis, 1979.

Gillon, Steven M. *Politics and Vision: The ADA and American Liberalism, 1947–1985.* Oxford, 1987.

———. *The Democrats' Dilemma: Walter F. Mondale and the Liberal Legacy.* New York, 1992.

———. *"That's Not What We Meant to Do": Reform and Its Unintended Consequences in Twentieth-Century America.* New York, 2000.

Gitlin, Todd. *The Sixties: Years of Hope, Days of Rage.* New York, 1987.

Gleason, Philip. *Keeping the Faith: American Catholicism Past and Present.* Notre Dame, Ind., 1987.

Gleijes, Piero. *The Dominican Crisis: The 1965 Constitutional Revolt and American Intervention.* Baltimore, 1978.

Goldman, Eric F. *Rendezvous with Destiny: A History of Modern American Reform.* New York, 1952.

———. *The Tragedy of Lyndon Johnson.* London, 1969.

Goldman, Ralph M. *Search for Consensus: The Story of the Democratic Party.* Philadelphia, 1979.

———. *Dilemma and Destiny: The Democratic Party in America.* Lanham, Md., 1986.

Goodwin, Richard M. *Remembering America: A Voice from the Sixties.* New York, 1988.

Gould, Lewis L. *1968: The Election That Changed America.* Chicago, 1993.

Grasso, Kenneth L., Gerard V. Bradley, and Robert P. Hunt, eds. *Catholicism, Liberalism, and Communitarianism: The Catholic Intellectual Tradition and the Moral Foundations of Democracy.* Lanham, Md., 1995.

Green, Mark. *Who Runs Congress?* 3rd ed., New York, 1979.

Greenstone, J. David. *Labor in American Politics.* New York, 1969.

Grossman, Jerome. *Relentless Liberal.* New York, 1996.

Gruening, Ernest. *Many Battles: The Autobiography of Ernest Gruening.* New York, 1973.

Gullan, Harry I. *The Upset That Wasn't: Harry S. Truman and the Crucial Election of 1948.* Chicago, 1998.

Guttman, Allen. *The Conservative Tradition in America.* New York, 1967.

Halberstam, David. *The Unfinished Odyssey of Robert Kennedy.* New York, 1969.

———. *The Best and the Brightest.* New York, 1972.

Haldeman, H. R. *The Haldeman Diaries: Inside the Nixon White House.* New York, 1994.

Hall, Mitchell K. *Because of Their Faith: CALCAV and Religious Opposition to the Vietnam War.* New York, 1990.

Halsey, William M. *The Survival of American Innocence: Catholicism in an Era of Disillusionment, 1920–1940.* Notre Dame, Ind., 1980.

Halstead, Fred. *Out Now! A Participant's Account of the Movement in the United States Against the Vietnam War.* New York, 1991.

Hamby, Alonzo L. *Beyond the New Deal: Harry Truman and American Liberalism.* New York, 1973.

———. *Liberalism and Its Challengers: From FDR to Bush.* 2nd ed., New York, 1992.

———. *Man of the People: A Life of Harry Truman.* New York, 1995.

Hamilton, Ian. *Robert Lowell: A Biography.* New York, 1982.

Hanna, Mary T. *Catholics and American Politics.* Cambridge, Mass., 1979.

Hardeman, D. C., and Donald C. Bacon. *Rayburn: A Biography.* Austin, Texas, 1987.

Harris, David F. *Dreams Die Hard: Three Men's Journey Through the Sixties.* San Francisco, 1993.

Harris, Fred R. *Potomac Fever.* New York, 1977.

Harris, Louis. *The Anguish of Change.* New York, 1973.

Hartz, Louis. *The Liberal Tradition in America.* New York, 1955.

Haynes, John Earl. *Dubious Alliance: The Making of Minnesota's DFL Party.* Minneapolis, 1984.

Hayward, Stephen F. *The Age of Reagan: The Fall of the Old Liberal Order, 1964–1980.* New York, 2001.

Heath, Jim F. *Decade of Disillusionment: The Kennedy-Johnson Years.* Bloomington, Ind., 1975.

Henggeler, Paul. *In His Steps: Lyndon Johnson and the Kennedy Mystique.* Chicago, 1991.

———. *The Kennedy Persuasion: The Politics of Style Since JFK.* Chicago, 1995.

Hernon, Joseph Martin. *Profiles in Character: Heroism and Hubris in the U.S. Senate, 1789–1990.* London, 1997.

Herring, George. *America's Longest War: The United States and Vietnam, 1950–1975.* New York, 1986.

———. *LBJ and Vietnam: A Different Kind of War.* Austin, Texas, 1994.

Hersh, Burton. *The Education of Edward Kennedy.* New York, 1972.

Herzog, Arthur. *McCarthy for President.* New York, 1969.

Heymann, C. David. *RFK: A Candid Biography*. London, 1998.

Hodgson, Godfrey. *In Our Time: America from World War II to Nixon*. London, 1976.

———. *All Things to All Men: The False Promise of the American Presidency*. London, 1980.

———. *The World Turned Right Side Up*. New York, 1996.

Hoeh, David C. *1968, McCarthy, New Hampshire: I Hear America Singing*. Rochester, Minn., 1998.

Hofstadter, Richard. *The Age of Reform: Bryan to FDR*. New York, 1955.

Horowitz, Irving Louis. *Ideology and Utopia in the United States, 1956–1976*. New York, 1977.

Howar, Barbara. *Laughing All the Way*. New York, 1973.

Howe, Irving. *A Margin of Hope: An Intellectual Biography*. New York, 1982.

Hughes, Emmet John. *The Ordeal of Power: A Political Memoir of the Eisenhower Years*. London, 1963.

Hughes, Kathleen. *The Monk's Tale: A Biography of Godfrey Diekmann, OSB*. Collegeville, Minn., 1991.

Humphrey, Hubert H. *The Education of a Public Man*. London, 1976.

Hunter, James Davison. *Culture Wars: The Struggle to Define America*. New York, 1991.

Hurwitz, Ken. *Marching Nowhere*. New York, 1971.

Hyman, Stanley. *Youth in Politics*. New York, 1972.

Isserman, Maurice. *If I Had a Hammer: The Death of the Old Left and the Birth of the New Left*. New York, 1987.

Isserman, Maurice, and Michael Kazin. *America Divided: The Civil War of the 1960s*. Oxford, 2000.

Jamieson, Kathleen Hall. *Packaging the Presidency: A History and Criticism of Presidential Campaign Advertising*. New York, 1984.

Javits, Jacob. *Javits: The Autobiography of a Public Man*. Boston, 1981.

Jeffreys-Jones, Rhodri. *The CIA and American Democracy*. New Haven, Conn., 1988.

———. *Peace Now! American Society and the Ending of the Vietnam War*. New Haven, Conn., 1999.

Johnson, Lyndon B. *The Vantage Point: Perspectives of the Presidency, 1963–1969*. New York, 1971.

Johnson, Robert D. *Ernest Gruening and the American Dissenting Tradition*. Cambridge, Mass., 1998.

Jones, Rochelle, and Peter Woll. *The Private World of Congress*. New York, 1979.

Jordan, Patrick, and Paul Baumann, eds. Commonweal *Confronts the Century*. New York, 1999.

Josephson, Matthew. *The Politicos, 1865–1896*. New York, 1938.

Judis, John B. *William F. Buckley Jr.: Patron Saint of the Conservatives*. New York, 1990.

Kadushin, Charles. *The American Intellectual Elite*. Boston, 1974.

Kaiser, Charles. *1968 in America: Music, Politics, Chaos, Counterculture, and the Shaping of a Generation*. New York, 1988.

Kaiser, David. *American Tragedy: Kennedy, Johnson, and the Origins of the Vietnam War*. Cambridge, Mass., 2000.

Karabell, Zachary. *The Last Campaign: How Harry Truman Won the 1948 Election*. New York, 2000.

Karnow, Stanley. *Vietnam: A History*. London, 1984.

Kaufman, Robert Gordon. *Henry M. Jackson: A Life in Politics*. Seattle, 2000.

Kazin, Michael. *The Populist Persuasion: An American History*. New York, 1995.

Kearns, Doris. *Lyndon Johnson and the American Dream*. London, 1976.

Keech, William R., and Donald R. Matthews. *The Party's Choice*. Washington, D.C., 1976.

Kennedy, Eugene C. *Believing*. Garden City, N.Y., 1974.

Kennedy, Robert F. *To Seek a Newer World*. London, 1968.

Klein, Alexander. *Natural Enemies: Youth and the Clash of Generations.* Philadelphia, 1969.

Knowles, Dom David. *The Benedictines.* New York, 1930.

Kopkind, Andrew. *The Thirty Years' Wars.* London, 1995.

Kovler, Peter B., ed. *Democrats and the National Idea: A Bicentennial Appraisal.* Washington, D.C., 1992.

Kunz, Virginia Brainard. *St. Paul: Saga of an American City.* Woodland Hills, Calif., 1977.

Kutler, Stanley I., ed. *Abuse of Power: The New Nixon Tapes.* New York, 1997.

Lacey, Michael J., ed. *The Truman Presidency.* Cambridge, U.K., 1989.

Ladd, Everett Carl, Jr., and Charles D. Hadley. *Transformations of the American Party System: Political Coalitions from the New Deal to the 1970s.* New York, 1975.

Lader, Lawrence. *Power on the Left: American Radical Movements Since 1946.* New York, 1979.

Lake, Anthony, ed. *The Vietnam Legacy.* New York, 1976.

Lamson, Frank B. *Condensed History of Meeker County, 1855–1939.* N.p., 1939.

Larner, Jeremy. *Nobody Knows: Reflections on the McCarthy Campaign of 1968.* New York, 1969.

Lasch, Christopher. *The New Radicalism in America, 1889–1963: The Intellectual as a Social Type.* New York, 1963.

———. *The Agony of the American Left.* New York, 1969.

Lazarowitz, Arlene. *Years in Exile: The Liberal Democrats, 1950–1959.* New York, 1988.

Lebedoff, David. *Ward Number Six.* New York, 1972.

———. *The New Elite: The Death of Democracy.* New York, 1981.

Lehman, John. *The Executive, Congress, and Foreign Policy.* New York, 1976.

Leuchtenberg, William E. *A Troubled Feast: American Society Since 1945.* 2nd ed., Glenview, Ill., 1983.

———. *In the Shadow of FDR: From Harry Truman to Bill Clinton.* 2nd ed., Ithaca, N.Y., 1993.

Levy, David W. *The Debate over Vietnam.* Baltimore, 1991.

Lewis, Findlay. *Mondale: Portrait of an American Politician.* New York, 1984.

Lippman, Theo, Jr., and Donald C. Hansen. *Muskie.* New York, 1971.

Lipset, Seymour Martin, and Gary Marks. *It Didn't Happen Here: Why Socialism Failed in the United States.* New York, 2000.

Logevall, Fredrik. *Choosing War: The Lost Chance for Peace and the Escalation of War in Vietnam.* Berkeley, Calif., 1999.

Lowi, Theodore. *The End of Liberalism: The Second Republic of the United States.* 2nd ed., New York, 1979.

Lowitt, Richard. *Fred Harris: His Journey from Liberalism to Populism.* Lanham, Md., 2002.

Macquarrie, John. *Twentieth Century Religious Thought.* London, 1963.

Mailer, Norman. *Miami and the Siege of Chicago.* Harmondsworth, U.K., 1969.

———. *Some Honorable Men: Political Conventions, 1960–1973.* Boston, 1976.

Mann, Robert. *Legacy to Power: Senator Russell Long of Louisiana.* New York, 1992.

———. *The Walls of Jericho: Lyndon Johnson, Hubert Humphrey, Richard Russell, and the Struggle for Civil Rights.* New York, 1996.

Maraniss, David. *First in His Class: The Biography of Bill Clinton.* New York, 1995.

Margolis, Jon. *The Last Innocent Year: America in 1964—The Beginning of the "Sixties."* New York, 1999.

Martin, John Bartlow. *Adlai Stevenson and the World.* Garden City, N.Y., 1977.

Martin, John Frederick. *Civil Rights and the Crisis of Liberalism: The Democratic Party, 1945–1976.* Boulder, Colo., 1979.

Marx, Paul B. *The Life and Work of Virgil Michel.* Washington, D.C., 1957.

———. *Virgil Michel and the Liturgical Movement.* Collegeville, Minn., 1957.

Matthews, Donald R. *U.S. Senators and Their World.* Chapel Hill, N.C., 1960.

Matusow, Allen J. *The Unraveling of America.* New York, 1986.

Mayer, David S. *A Winter of Discontent: The Nuclear Freeze and American Politics.* New York, 1990.

Mayer, George H. *The Political Career of Floyd B. Olsen.* St. Paul, Minn., 1987.

McAuliffe, Mary. *Crisis on the Left: Cold War Politics and American Liberals, 1947–1954.* Amherst, Mass., 1974.

McCarthy, Abigail. *Private Faces/Public Places.* Garden City, N.Y., 1972.

———. *Circles: A Washington Story.* Garden City, N.Y., 1977.

McCarthy, Eugene J. *Frontiers in American Democracy.* Cleveland, 1960.

———. *Dictionary of American Politics.* New York, 1962.

———. *A Liberal Answer to the Conservative Challenge.* New York, 1965.

———. *The Limits of Power.* New York, 1968.

———. *The Year of the People.* Garden City, N.Y., 1969.

———. *Other Things and the Aardvark.* Garden City, N.Y., 1970.

———. *The Hard Years: A Look at Contemporary America and American Institutions.* New York, 1975.

———. *America Revisited: 150 Years After Tocqueville.* Garden City, N.Y., 1978.

———. *Ground Fog and Night: Poems.* New York, 1979.

———. *The Ultimate Tyranny: The Majority over the Minority.* New York, 1980.

———. *Complexities and Contraries: Essays of Mild Discontent.* New York, 1982.

———. *Gene McCarthy's Minnesota: Memories of a Native Son.* Minneapolis, 1982.

———. *The View from Rappahannock.* McLean, Va., 1984.

———. *Up 'til Now: A Memoir.* New York, 1987.

———. *Required Reading: A Decade of Political Wit and Wisdom.* New York, 1988.

———. *Nonfinancial Economics: The Case for Shorter Hours of Work.* New York, 1989.

———. *The View from Rappahannock II.* McLean, Va., 1989.

———. *A Colony of the World: The United States Today.* New York, 1992.

———. *Mr. Raccoon and His Friends.* Rev. ed. Chicago, 1992.

———. *No-Fault Politics: Modern Presidents, the Press, and Reformers.* New York, 1998.

———. *Selected Poems.* Rochester, Minn., 1999.

McCarthy, Eugene J., and James J. Kilpatrick. *A Political Bestiary.* New York, 1978.

McDonald, William P., and Smoke, Jerry G. *The Peasants' Revolt: McCarthy 1968.* Mount Vernon, Ohio, 1969.

McGinniss, Joe. *The Selling of the President, 1968.* New York, 1970.

McGovern, George S. *Grassroots.* New York, 1977.

McGreevy, John T. *Parish Boundaries: The Catholic Encounter with Race in the Twentieth-Century Urban North.* Chicago, 1996.

McPherson, Harry. *A Political Education: A Washington Memoir.* Boston, 1988.

McPherson, Myra. *The Power Lovers: An Intimate Look at Politics and Marriage.* New York, 1975.

McQuaid, Kim. *The Anxious Years: America in the Vietnam-Watergate Era.* New York, 1989.

Meconis, Charles A. *With Clumsy Grace: The American Catholic Left, 1961–1975.* New York, 1979.

Meeker County Memories. Litchfield, Minn., 1987.

Milkis, Sidney M. *The President and the Parties: The Transformation of the American Party System Since the New Deal.* New York, 1993.

Miller, James. *Democracy is in the Streets: From Port Huron to the Siege of Chicago.* Cambridge, Mass., 1994.

Miller, Merle. *Lyndon: An Oral Biography.* New York, 1980.

Mitau, G. Theodore. *Politics in Minnesota.* Minneapolis, 1961.

Mitchell, Stephen A. *Elm Street Politics.* New York, 1959.

Mixner, David. *Stranger Among Friends.* New York, 1996.

Moïse, Edwin E. *Tonkin Gulf and the Escalation of the Vietnam War.* Chapel Hill, N.C., 1996.

Mooney, Booth. *The Politicians, 1945–1960.* Philadelphia, 1970.

Morgan, Ann Hodges. *Robert S. Kerr: The Senate Years.* Norman, Okla., 1977.

Morgan, Iwan W. *Eisenhower Versus "The Spenders": The Eisenhower Administration, the Democrats, and the Budget, 1953–1960.* New York, 1990.

———. *Beyond the Liberal Consensus.* London, 1994.

Morris, Charles R. *American Catholic: The Saints and Sinners Who Built America's Most Powerful Church.* New York, 1998.

Moynihan, Daniel Patrick. *The Politics of a Guaranteed Income: The Nixon Administration and the Family Assistance Plan.* New York, 1973.

Murphy, Thomas P. *The New Politics Congress.* Lexington, Mass., 1974.

Nash, George H. *The Conservative Intellectual Movement in America Since 1945.* New York, 1976.

Newfield, Jack. *Robert Kennedy: A Memoir.* London, 1970.

———. *Bread and Roses Too.* New York, 1971.

Nutting, Willis. *Reclamation of Independence.* Nevada City, Calif., 1947.

Nye, Russell B. *Midwestern Progressive Politics.* East Lansing, Mich., 1959.

O'Brien, David. *American Catholics and Social Reform: The New Deal Years.* New York, 1968.

———. *The Renewal of American Catholicism.* New York, 1972.

O'Brien, Lawrence F. *No Final Victories.* Garden City, N.Y., 1974.

O'Brien, Michael. *Philip Hart: The Conscience of the Senate.* East Lansing, Mich., 1995.

O'Connell, Marvin R. *McElroy: A Novel.* New York, 1980.

O'Donnell, Kenneth P., and Dave Powers, with Joe McCarthy. *Johnny, We Hardly Knew Ye: Memories of John Fitzgerald Kennedy.* Boston, 1970.

O'Neill, Tip, with William Novak. *Man of the House: The Life and Political Memoirs of Speaker Tip O'Neill.* New York, 1987.

O'Neill, William L. *Coming Apart: An Informal History of America in the 1960s.* New York, 1971.

Orfield, Gary. *Congressional Power: Congress and Social Change.* New York, 1975.

Palermo, Joseph A. *In His Own Right: The Political Odyssey of Senator Robert F. Kennedy.* New York, 2001.

Papôt, Eugene. *Tussen Twijfel en Geloof: Het Politieke Leven van Eugene McCarthy.* Entschede, Netherlands, 1999.

Parmet, Herbert S. *Eisenhower and the American Crusades.* New York, 1972.

———. *JFK: The Presidency of John F. Kennedy.* New York, 1983.

———. *The Democrats: The Years After FDR.* New York, 1976.

———. *Richard Nixon and His America.* Boston, 1990.

Patterson, James T. *America's Struggle Against Poverty.* Cambridge, Mass., 1981.

———. *Grand Expectations: The United States, 1945–1974.* Oxford, 1996.

Pells, Richard. *The Liberal Mind in a Conservative Age: American Intellectuals in the 1940s and 1950s.* 2nd ed., Middletown, Conn., 1985.

Perlstein, Rick. *Before the Storm: Barry Goldwater and the Unmaking of the American Consensus.* New York, 2001.

Perry, James K. *Us and Them: How The Press Covered the 1972 Election.* New York, 1973.

Petrocik, John R. *Party Coalitions: Realignments and the Decline of the New Deal Party System.* Chicago, 1981.

Piehl, Mel. *Breaking Bread: The Catholic Worker and the Origins of Catholic Radicalism in America.* Philadelphia, 1982.

Plotke, David. *Building a Democratic Political Order: Reshaping American Liberalism in the 1930s and 1940s.* Cambridge, U.K., 1996.

Polsby, Nelson W., ed. *Congressional Behavior.* New York, 1971.

———. *The Consequences of Party Reform.* New York, 1983.

Powers, J. F. *Morte D'Urban*. New York, 1962.
———. *Wheat That Springeth Green*. New York, 1988.
Prochnau, William W., and Richard W. Larsen. *A Certain Democrat: Senator Henry Jackson— A Political Biography*. Englewood Cliffs, N.J., 1972.
Quigley, Thomas E. *American Catholics and Vietnam*. Grand Rapids, Mich., 1968.
Radosh, Ronald. *Divided They Fell: The Demise of the Democratic Party, 1964–1996*. New York, 1996.
Rae, Nicol C. *The Decline and Fall of the Liberal Republicans: 1952 to the Present*. Oxford, 1989.
Reichley, A. James. *Religion in American Public Life*. Washington, D.C., 1985.
———. *The Life of the Parties: A History of American Political Parties*. New York, 1992.
Rieselbach, Leroy N. *Congressional Politics*. New York, 1973.
Rinzler, Carol, ed. *Frankly McCarthy*. Washington, D.C., 1969.
Ripley, Randall P. *Power in the Senate*. New York, 1969.
Rising, George. *Clean for Gene: Eugene McCarthy's 1968 Presidential Campaign*. Westport, Conn., 1997.
Rommen, Heinrich. *The State in Catholic Thought*. St. Louis, 1945.
———. *The Natural Law: A Study in Legal and Social History and Philosophy*. Reprint. Indianapolis, Ind., 1998.
Rothenburg, Randall. *The Neoliberals: Creating the New American Politics*. New York, 1984.
Sandel, Michael. *Democracy's Discontent: America in Search of a Public Philosophy*. Cambridge, Mass., 1996.
Savage, Sean J. *Truman and the Democratic Party*. Lexington, Ky., 1997.
Scammon, Richard M., and Ben J. Wattenberg. *The Real Majority: An Extraordinary Examination of the American Electorate*. New York, 1971.
Schandler, Herbert. *The Unmaking of a President: Lyndon Johnson and Vietnam*. Princeton, N.J., 1977.
Schlesinger, Arthur M., Jr. *The Vital Center*. Boston, 1949.
———. *Robert Kennedy and His Times*. New York, 1978.
———. *A Life in the Twentieth Century: Innocent Beginnings, 1917–1950*. Boston, 2000.
Schlesinger, Stephen C. *The New Reformers*. Boston, 1975.
Schram, Martin. *Running for President, 1976: The Carter Campaign*. New York, 1977.
Schulzinger, Robert D. *A Time for War: The United States and Vietnam, 1941–1975*. Oxford, 1997.
Shafer, Byron E. *The Quiet Revolution: The Struggle for the Democratic Party and the Shaping of Post-reform Politics*. New York, 1983.
———, ed. *Present Discontents: American Politics in the Very Late Twentieth Century*. Chatham, N.J., 1997.
———, ed. *Partisan Approaches to Postwar Politics*. New York, 1998.
Shannon, James Patrick. *Reluctant Dissenter: An Autobiography*. New York, 1998.
Shaw, Malcolm, ed. *Roosevelt to Reagan: The Development of the Modern Presidency*. London, 1987.
Shesol, Jeff. *Mutual Contempt: Lyndon Johnson, Robert Kennedy, and the Feud That Defined a Decade*. New York, 1997.
Sinclair, Barbara. *The Congressional Realignment, 1925–1978*. Austin, Texas, 1982.
———. *The Transformation of the U.S. Senate*. Baltimore, 1989.
Skowronek, Stephen. *The Politics Presidents Make: Leadership from John Adams to George Bush*. Cambridge, Mass., 1993.
Slayton, Robert A. *Empire Statesman: The Rise and Redemption of Al Smith*. New York, 2000.
Smaby, Alpha. *Political Upheaval: Minnesota and the Vietnam War Protest*. Minneapolis, 1987.
Small, Melvin. *Johnson, Nixon, and the Doves*. New Brunswick, N.J., 1988.

Small, Melvin, and William Hoover. *Give Peace a Chance.* Syracuse, N.Y., 1992.

Solberg, Carl. *Hubert Humphrey: A Biography.* New York, 1984.

Stacks, John F. *Watershed: The Campaign for the Presidency, 1980.* New York, 1981.

Stavis, Ben. *We Were the Campaign: New Hampshire to Chicago for McCarthy.* Boston, 1969.

Stebenne, David. *Arthur Goldberg: New Deal Liberal.* New York, 1996.

Steel, Ronald. *In Love with Night: The American Romance with Robert Kennedy.* New York, 2000.

Stegmann, Basil. *The Benedictines.* Collegeville, Minn., 1943.

Steigerwald, David. *The Sixties and the End of Modern America.* New York, 1995.

Stein, Jean, and George Plimpton, eds. *American Journey: The Times of Robert Kennedy.* New York, 1970.

Steinem, Gloria. *Outrageous Acts and Everyday Rebellions.* New York, 1983.

Steinfels, Peter. *The Neoconservatives.* New York, 1979.

Stern, Sydney Lodensohn. *Gloria Steinem: Her Passions, Politics and Mystique.* Secaucus, N.J., 1997.

Stone, I. F. *Polemics and Prophecies, 1967–1970.* New York, 1970.

Stone, Richard H. *Reinhold Niebuhr: Prophet to Politicians.* Nashville, Tenn., 1972.

Stout, Richard T. *People.* New York, 1970.

Strout, Richard Lee. *TRB: Issues and Perspectives on the Presidency.* New York, 1979.

Stuhler, Barbara. *Ten Men of Minnesota and American Foreign Policy, 1898–1968.* St. Paul, Minn., 1973.

Sundquist, James L. *Politics and Policy: The Eisenhower, Kennedy, and Johnson Years.* Rev. ed., Washington, D.C., 1973.

―――. *Dynamics of the Party System: Alignment and Realignment of Political Parties in the United States.* Rev. ed., Washington, D.C., 1983.

Sweeney, Terrance A. *God and . . .* Minneapolis, 1985.

Tawney, R. H. *Reform and the Rise of Capitalism.* London, 1926.

Thomas, Evan. *Robert Kennedy: His Life.* New York, 2000.

Thompson, Hunter S. *Fear and Loathing: On the Campaign Trail '72.* London, 1994.

Tobin, Greg, ed. *Saints and Sinners: The American Catholic Experience Through Stories, Memoirs, Essays, and Commentary.* New York, 1999.

Tomes, Robert R. *Apocalypse Then: American Intellectuals and the Vietnam War, 1954–1975.* New York, 1998.

Tweton, D. Jerome. *Depression: Minnesota in the Thirties.* Fargo, N.D., 1981.

Unger, Irwin. *The Movement: A History of the American New Left, 1959–1972.* New York, 1974.

―――. *The Best of Intentions: The Triumphs and Failures of the Great Society Under Kennedy, Johnson, and Nixon.* New York, 1996.

Unger, Irwin, and Debi Unger. *Turning Point: 1968.* New York, 1988.

United States Senate Committee on Unemployment Problems. *Unemployment Problems.* Washington, D.C., 1960.

Valelly, Richard M. *Radicalism in the States: The Minnesota Farmer-Labor Party and the American Political Economy.* Chicago, 1989.

Valeo, Francis R. *Mike Mansfield, Majority Leader: A Different Kind of Senate, 1961–1976.* Armonk, N.Y., 1999.

van Zeller, Dom Hubert. *The Benedictine Ideal.* Springfield, Ill., 1959.

Vanden Heuvel, William, and Milton Gwirtzman. *On His Own: Robert Kennedy, 1964–1968.* Garden City, N.Y., 1970.

Viorst, Milton. *Hustlers and Heroes: An American Panorama.* New York, 1971.

―――. *Fire in the Streets: America in the 1960s.* New York, 1979.

Walton, Richard J. *Henry Wallace, Harry Truman, and the Cold War.* New York, 1976.

Ward, Brian, and Anthony J. Badger, eds. *The Making of Martin Luther King and the Civil Rights Movement.* New York, 1996.

Ware, Alan. *The Breakdown of Democratic Party Organization, 1940–1980*. Oxford, 1985.

Wattenberg, Martin P. *The Decline of American Political Parties, 1952–1980*. Cambridge, U.K., 1984.

Weatherford, J. McIver. *Tribes on the Hill*. South Hadley, Mass., 1985.

Weil, Gordon L. *The Long Shot: George McGovern Runs for President*. New York, 1973.

Weisband, Edward, and Thomas M. Franck. *Resignation in Protest: Political and Ethical Choices Between Loyalty to Team and Loyalty to Conscience in American Public Life*. New York, 1975.

Wells, Tom. *The War Within: America's Battle over Vietnam*. Berkeley, Calif., 1994.

White, Theodore H. *The Making of the President 1960*. New York, 1961.

———. *The Making of the President 1964*. London, 1965.

———. *The Making of the President 1968*. London, 1969.

———. *The Making of the President 1972*. London, 1974.

Whitehorn, Alan. *Canadian Socialism: Essays on the CCF-NDP*. Toronto, 1992.

Whittemore, Katharine, ed. *The Sixties: Recollections of the Decade from* Harper's Magazine. New York, 1995.

Wilcox, Francis. *Congress, the Executive, and Foreign Policy*. New York, 1971.

Williams, Leonard. *American Liberalism and Ideological Change*. DeKalb, Ill., 1997.

Williams, William Appelman. *The Tragedy of American Diplomacy*. Cleveland, 1959.

Wills, Garry. *Bare Ruined Choirs: Doubt, Prophecy, and Radical Religion*. Garden City, N.Y., 1972.

———. *The Kennedy Imprisonment*. Boston, 1981.

———. *Lead Time: A Journalist's Education*. Garden City, N.Y., 1983.

———. *Under God: Religion and American Politics*. New York, 1990.

Wilson, James Q. *The Amateur Democrat: Club Politics in Three Cities*. Chicago, 1966.

Witcover, Jules. *Eighty-five Days: The Last Campaign of Robert Kennedy*. New York, 1969.

———. *Marathon: The Pursuit of the Presidency, 1972–1976*. New York, 1977.

———. *Crapshoot: Rolling the Dice on the Vice Presidency*. New York, 1992.

———. *The Year the Dream Died: Revisiting 1968 in America*. New York, 1997.

Witker, Kristi. *How to Lose Everything in Politics Except Massachusetts*. New York, 1974.

Wittner, Lawrence S. *Rebels Against War: The American Peace Movement, 1933–1983*. Philadelphia, 1984.

Wofford, Harris. *Of Kennedys and Kings: Making Sense of the Sixties*. Pittsburgh, 1992.

Woods, Randall Bennett. *Fulbright: A Biography*. Cambridge, U.K., 1995.

Yarnell, Allen. *Democrats and Progressives: The 1948 Presidential Election as a Test of Postwar Liberalism*. Berkeley, Calif., 1974.

Young, James P. *Reconsidering Liberalism: The Troubled Odyssey of the Liberal Idea*. Boulder, Colo., 1996.

Zaroulis, Nancy, and Gerald Sullivan. *Who Spoke Up? American Protest Against the War in Vietnam, 1963–1975*. Garden City, N.Y., 1984.

B. ARTICLES AND ESSAYS

Altschuler, Bruce. "Kennedy Decides to Run, 1968." *Presidential Studies Quarterly* 10 (Summer 1980): 348–352.

Anderson, Terry H. "The New American Revolution: The Movement and Business." In David Farber, ed., *The Sixties* (Chapel Hill, N.C., 1994), pp. 175–205.

Berkowitz, William. "The Impact of Antiwar Demonstrators." *Social Science Research* 2:1 (March 1973): 1–14.

Bibby, John F. "Party Organizations, 1946–1996." In Byron E. Shafer, *Partisan Approaches to Postwar Politics* (New York, 1998), pp. 142–185.

Brinkley, Alan. "The New Deal and the Idea of the State." In Steve Fraser and Gary Gerstle, eds., *The Rise and Fall of the New Deal Order* (Princeton, N.J., 1989), pp. 32–55.

———. "The Problem of American Conservatism." *American Historical Review* 99 (April 1994): 409–429.

Canavan, Francis. "The Image of Man in Catholic Thought." In Kenneth L. Grasso et al., eds., *Catholicism, Liberalism, and Communitarianism* (Lanham, Md., 1995), pp. 15–28.

Collins, Robert M. "Growth Liberalism in the Sixties: Great Societies at Home and Grand Designs Abroad." In David Farber, ed., *The Sixties* (Chapel Hill, N.C., 1994), pp. 11–44.

Converse, Philip E., Warren G. Miller, Jerrold G. Rusk, and Arthur C. Wolfe. "Continuity and Change in American Politics: The 1968 Election." *American Political Science Review* 63:4 (December 1969): 1083–1105.

Dallek, Robert. "Lyndon Johnson and Vietnam." *Diplomatic History* 20:2 (Spring 1996): 147–162.

DeBenedetti, Charles. "On the Significance of Citizen Peace Activism: America, 1961–1975." *Peace and Change* 9:2 (Summer 1983): 6–20.

———. "Lyndon Johnson and the Antiwar Opposition." In Robert A. Divine, ed., *Vietnam, the Environment, and Science,* vol. 2, *The Johnson Years* (Lawrence, Kans., 1987), pp. 23–53.

Dodd, Lawrence C. "Congress and the Quest for Power." In Lawrence C. Dodd and Bruce I. Oppenheimer, eds., *Congress Reconsidered* (New York, 1977), pp. 269–307.

Dumbrell, John. "Congress and the Antiwar Movement." In John Dumbrell, ed., *Vietnam and the Antiwar Movement* (Aldershot, U.K., 1989), pp. 101–112.

Edsall, Thomas Byrne. "The Changing Shape of Power: A Realignment in Public Policy." In Steve Fraser and Gary Gerstle, eds., *The Rise and Fall of the New Deal Order* (Princeton, N.J., 1989), pp. 269–293.

Elliff, John T. "Congress and the Intelligence Community." In Lawrence C. Dodd and Bruce I. Oppenheimer, eds., *Congress Reconsidered* (New York, 1977), pp. 193–206.

Ferber, Mark F. "The Formation of the Democratic Study Group." In Nelson W. Polsby, ed., *Congressional Behavior* (New York, 1971), pp. 249–269.

Gillon, Steven M. "The Travail of the Democrats: Search for a New Majority." In Peter B. Kovler, ed., *Democrats and the National Idea* (Washington, D.C., 1992), pp. 285–301.

Gould, Lewis L. "Never a Deep Partisan: Lyndon Johnson and the Democratic Party." In Robert A. Divine, ed., *LBJ at Home and Abroad,* vol. 3, *The Johnson Years,* pp. 1–52.

Grasso, Kenneth L. "Catholic Social Thought and the Quest for an American Public Philosophy." In Kenneth L. Grasso et al., eds., *Catholicism, Liberalism, and Communitarianism* (Lanham, Md., 1995), pp. 1–14.

———. "Beyond Liberalism: Human Dignity, the Free Society, and the Second Vatican Council." In Kenneth L. Grasso et al., eds., *Catholicism, Liberalism, and Communitarianism* (Lanham, Md., 1995), pp. 29–58.

Griffith, Robert. "Dwight D. Eisenhower and the Corporate Commonwealth." *American Historical Review* 87:1 (February 1982), pp. 87–122.

Halberstam, David. "McCarthy and the Divided Left." *Harper's magazine,* March 1968, pp. 32–44.

———. "The Man Who Ran Against Lyndon Johnson." *Harper's magazine,* December 1968, pp. 50–66.

Hamby, Alonzo L. "The Liberals, Truman, and FDR as Symbol and Myth." *Journal of American History* 56 (March 1970): 859–867.

———. "The Vital Center, the Fair Deal, and the Quest for a Liberal Political Economy." *American Historical Review* 77 (June 1972): 653–678.

———. "The Mind and Character of Harry S. Truman." In Michael J. Lacey, ed., *The Truman Presidency* (Cambridge, U.K., 1989), pp. 19–53.

Hodgson, Godfrey. "The Establishment." *Foreign Policy* 10 (Spring 1973): 3–40.

Horowitz, David, and Peter Collier. "Who Killed the Spirit of 1968?" *Encounter* (October 1985): 69–73.

Johnson, Robert David. "Congress and the Cold War." *Journal of Cold War Studies* 3:2 (Spring 2001): 76–100.

Katz, Milton S. "Peace Liberals and Vietnam: SANE and the Politics of 'Responsible' Protest." *Peace and Change* 9:2 (Summer 1983): 21–39.

Katznelson, Ira. "Considerations on Social Democracy in the United States." *Comparative Politics* 11 (October 1978): 77–99.

———. "Was the Great Society a Lost Opportunity?" In Steve Fraser and Gary Gerstle, eds., *The Rise and Fall of the New Deal Order* (Princeton, N.J., 1989), pp. 185–212.

Keys, Mary M. "Personal Dignity and the Common Good: A Twentieth-Century Thomistic Dialogue." In Kenneth L. Grasso et al., eds., *Catholicism, Liberalism, and Communitarianism* (Lanham, Md., 1995), pp. 173–196.

Kofmehl, Kenneth. "The Institutionalization of a Voting Bloc." *Western Political Quarterly* 17 (June 1964): 257–258.

Kristol, Irving. "Consensus and Dissent in U.S. Foreign Policy." In Anthony Lake, ed., *The Vietnam Legacy* (New York, 1976), pp. 80–101.

Lacey, Michael J. "The Truman Era in Retrospect." In Michael J. Lacey, ed., *The Truman Presidency* (Cambridge, U.K.), pp. 1–18.

Lewis, R. W. B. "McCarthy and the College Students." In Joseph Frank, ed., *The New Look in Politics: McCarthy's Campaign* (Albuquerque, N.Mex., 1969).

McCarthy, Eugene J. "The Intellectual's Place in American Government." *Texas Quarterly* (Winter 1965): 117–124.

———. "The Christian in Politics." In Patrick Jordan and Paul Baumann, eds., Commonweal *Confronts the Century* (New York, 1999), pp. 63–66.

Mitau, G. Theodore. "The Democratic Farmer-Labor Party Schism of 1948." *Minnesota History* (Spring 1955): 187–194.

Mulder, John M. "Eugene McCarthy and His Theology of Civil Religion." *Dimension: Theology in Church and World* (Fall 1968): 108–125.

Ornstein, Norman J., Robert L. Peabody, and David W. Rohde. "The Changing Senate: From the 1950s to the 1970s." In Lawrence C. Dodd and Bruce I. Oppenheimer, eds., *Congress Reconsidered* (New York, 1977), pp. 7–31.

Page, Benjamin I., and Michael A. Brody. "Party Voting and the Electoral Process: The Vietnam War Issue." *American Political Science Review* 66:3 (September 1972): 979–996.

Peabody, Robert L., Norman J. Ornstein, and David W. Rohde. "The United States Senate as a Presidential Incubator: Many Are Called but Few Are Chosen." *Political Science Quarterly* 91:2 (Summer 1976): 237–258.

Plotke, David M. "Party Reform as Failed Democratic Renewal in the United States, 1968–1972." *Studies in American Political Development* 10:2 (Fall 1996): 223–288.

Polsby, Nelson W. "Strengthening Congress in National Policymaking." In Nelson W. Polsby, ed., *Congressional Behavior* (New York, 1971), pp. 1–23.

———. "Goodbye to the Inner Club." In Nelson W. Polsby, ed., *Congressional Behavior* (New York, 1971), pp. 105–110.

Rae, Nicol C. "Party Factionalism, 1946–1996." In Byron E. Shafer, ed., *Partisan Approaches to Postwar Politics* (New York, 1998), pp. 41–74.

Roche, John P. "The Impact of Dissent on Foreign Policy: Past, Present, and Future." In Anthony Lake, ed., *The Vietnam Legacy* (New York, 1976), pp. 128–138.

Schuman, Howard. "Two Sources of Antiwar Sentiment in America." *American Journal of Sociology* (November 1972): 512–536.

Shafer, Byron E. "'We Are All Southern Democrats Now': The Shape of American Politics in the Very Late Twentieth Century." In Byron E. Shafer, ed., *Present Discontents* (Chatham, N.J., c. 1998), pp. 147–176.

———. "Partisan Elites, 1946–1996." In Byron E. Shafer, ed., *Partisan Approaches to Postwar Politics* (New York, 1998), pp. 75–141.

Sheed, Wilfrid. "Eugene McCarthy: The Politician as Professor." *New American Review* 5 (January 1969): 154–164.

Small, Melvin. "Otto Feinstein, the McCarthy Campaign in Michigan, and Campus Activism During the Cold War." In David L. Anderson, ed., *The Human Tradition in the Vietnam Era* (Wilmington, Del., 2000), pp. 175–194.

Stevens, Arthur G., Arthur H. Miller, and Thomas E. Mann. "Mobilization of Liberal Strength in the House, 1955–1970: The Democratic Study Group." *American Political Science Review* 60:2 (June 1974): 667–681.

Stewart, John G. "Two Strategies of Leadership: Johnson and Mansfield." In Nelson W. Polsby, ed., *Congressional Behavior* (New York, 1971), pp. 61–92.

Strahan, Randall W. "Partisan Officeholders, 1946–1996." In Byron E. Shafer, ed., *Partisan Approaches to Postwar Politics* (New York, 1998), pp. 5–40.

Sundquist, James L. "Congress and the President: Enemies or Partners?" In Lawrence C. Dodd and Bruce I. Oppenheimer, eds., *Congress Reconsidered* (New York, 1977), pp. 222–243.

Tegeder, Vincent. "The Benedictines in Frontier Minnesota." *Minnesota History* 32 (1951): 34–43.

Watkins, Michelle, and Ralph McInerny. "Jacques Maritain and the Rapprochement of Liberalism and Communitarianism." In Kenneth L. Grasso et al., eds., *Catholicism, Liberalism, and Communitarianism* (Lanham, Md., 1995), pp. 151–172.

Wills, Garry. "Memories of a Catholic Boyhood." In Greg Tobin, ed., *Saints and Sinners* (New York, 1999), pp. 228–236.

———. "Waiting for Bobby." *New York Review of Books* (10 February 2000): 18–20.

Wolfe, Christopher. "Subsidiarity: The 'Other' Ground of Limited Government." In Kenneth L. Grasso et al., eds., *Catholicism, Liberalism, and Communitarianism* (Lanham, Md., 1995), pp. 81–96.

C. UNPUBLISHED MATERIALS

Cutbirth, Craig W. "A Strategic Perspective: Robert F. Kennedy's Dissent on the Vietnam War, 1965–1968." Ph.D. dissertation, Bowling Green State University, 1976.

Donaghy, Mary Anderson. "Who Were the People?: An Analysis of Data Obtained from the Grass-Roots Workers in Eugene McCarthy's 1968 Presidential Campaign." M.A. thesis, American University, 1973.

Edie, John A. "The Split in the Minnesota Democratic Farmer-Labor Party, 1946 to 1948." B.A. thesis, Princeton University, 1980.

Haynes, John Earl. "Liberals, Communists, and the Popular Front in Minnesota: The Struggle to Control the Political Direction of the Labor Movement and Organized Liberalism." Ph.D. dissertation, University of Minnesota, 1978.

Hendrickson, Gary Paul. "Minnesota in the McCarthy Period, 1946–1954." Ph.D. dissertation, University of Minnesota, 1981.

Naftalin, Arthur. "A History of the Minnesota Farmer-Labor Party." Ph.D. dissertation, University of Minnesota, 1948.

Palermo, Joseph Anthony. "The Politics of Race and War: Robert Kennedy and the Democratic Party, 1965–1968." Ph.D. dissertation, Cornell University, 1998.

Rosenberg, Michael P. "Congress and the Vietnam War: A Study of the Critics of the War in 1967 and 1968." Ph.D. dissertation, New School for Social Research, New York, 1973.

Sanders, Frederick Clark. "The Rhetorical Strategies of Senator Robert Kennedy and Senator Eugene McCarthy in the 1968 Presidential Primaries." Ph.D. dissertation, University of Oregon, 1973.

Wainstock, Dennis Dean. "The 1968 Presidential Campaign and Election." Ph.D. dissertation, University of West Virginia, 1984.

Zelman, Walter A. "Senate Dissent and the Vietnam War, 1964–1968." Ph.D. dissertation, UCLA, 1971.

D. ONLINE MATERIALS

"St. John's University Hockey Results," at
http://www.gojohnies.com/hockey/hockeyresults.html, last accessed 8 October 2003.

Insight on the News, 20 March 2000, at
http://www.insightmag.com/archive/200002264.shtml, last accessed 23 November 2001.

"Gallup Organization Presidential Job Approval Ratings," at
http://www.ropercenter.uconn.edu/, last accessed 8 October 2003.

"CNN *Cold War:* Interview with Senator Eugene McCarthy," at
http://www.hfni.gsehd.gwu.edu/~nsarchiv/coldwar/interviews/episode-13/mccarthy1
.html, last accessed 23 November 2001.

"1968 and the Presidency: Dumping Johnson—Were Journalists a Catalyst?" Freedom
Forum Discussion, 30 April 1998, at
http://www.freedomforum.org/newseumnews/specialprograms/1968transcript2-1.asp, last
accessed 23 November 2001.

"Where Are My Other Twelve Minutes?", F. E. Peters, undated, at
http://pages. nyu.edu/~fep1/regis2.html, last accessed 8 October 2003.

Brill's Content, August 2000, at http://www.brillscontent.com/2000aug/features/schmidt
_marty2.shtml, last accessed 23 November 2001.

The Progressive Populist, August 1996, at http://www.populist.com/8.96.McCarthy.html, last
accessed 23 November 2001.

A NOTE ON THE TYPE

The text of this book was set in a typeface called Times New Roman, designed by Stanley Morison (1889–1967) for *The Times* (London) and first introduced by that newspaper in 1932.

Among typographers and designers of the twentieth century, Stanley Morison was a strong forming influence as a typographical adviser to the Monotype Corporation, as a director of two distinguished publishing houses, and as a writer of sensibility, erudition, and keen practical sense.

Composed by NK Graphics, Keene, New Hampshire

Printed and bound by Berryville Graphics, Berryville, Virginia

Designed by Iris Weinstein